FRANCE
Trip Planner & Guide

FRANCE
Trip Planner & Guide
Emma Stanford

Passport Books

This first edition published 1994 by
Passport Books,
Trade Imprint of NTC Publishing Group,
4255 West Touhy Avenue,
Lincolnwood (Chicago), Illinois 60646-1975
U.S.A.

914.4
S785

Conceived, edited, designed and produced by
Duncan Petersen Publishing Ltd, 54 Milson Road, London W14 0LB
from a concept by Emma Stanford

Typeset by Duncan Petersen Publishing Ltd;
film output by Reprocolor International, Milan

Originated by Reprocolor International, Milan

Printed by GraphyCems, Navarra

ISBN: 0-8442-9217-6

Library of Congress Catalog Card Number: 93-85445

Editorial director Andrew Duncan
Editor Fiona Duncan
Assistant editors Leonie Glass, Mary Devine,
Nicola Davies and Laura Harper
Art director Mel Petersen
Design assistants Beverley Stewart, Chris Foley
Additional material by Fiona Duncan and Arthur Howcroft
Maps by Chris Foley and Beverley Stewart
Illustrations by Beverley Stewart

Photographic credits
Michael Busselle: pp. 2,7,19,54,67,70,71,82,102,103,111,122,127,130,143,
210, 242, 249, 254, 259, 279, 281, 295, 310; **Yvette Lodge:** pp. 14, 159,
162,166, 170, 175, 179, 294, 331, 334; **John Lloyd:** pp. 22, 27, 35, 38,
51,74, 79, 91, 94, 95, 101, 104, 118, 119, 134, 138,139, 142, 151, 154, 163,
178, 186, 187, 190, 191, 198, 205, 206.

Emma Stanford was born in Malta, the third generation of her family to be born outside their native Britain. Her great-great grandfather founded Edward Stanford Ltd, the largest map and travel bookshop in London – so travel is in her blood. She has journeyed extensively on five continents, but Europe is her base, specifically France. Her first travel assignment was a driving guide to Burgundy, which gave her a love of backroads, Romanesque architecture and good food. Further travels have added much to that list.

She has devised and researched numerous driving tours in France and Europe; contributed to the American Automobile Association's *All-in-One* guides to Europe and written *AAA Paris and the Riviera* as well as several books for the British Tourist Authority. Her recently-published guide, *Exploring Florida*, was selected by the *Washington Post* as its recommended guide 'For Insights'.

The *Versatile Guide* series was developed from Emma Stanford's ideas: she is a believer in friendly, informal advice that combines insight with practical information.

Master contents list

This contents list is for when you need to use the guide in the conventional way: to find out about where you are going, or where you happen to be. The index, pages 344-352, may be just as helpful.

HOWEVER...
There is much more to this guide than the region-by-region approach suggested by the contents list on this page. Turn to page 8 and see also pages 10-11.

Contents

France Overall
- master map

France Overall, pages 30-213, is a traveller's network for taking in the whole country, or large parts of it.

Each 'leg' of the network has a number (ie France Overall: 1); you will also occasionally find it described as a 'National Route', plus the number.

The term National Route does *not* simply mean a line on a map. Each 'route' features a region, and describes many places both on and off the marked route. Think of the National Routes not only as physical trails, but as imaginative ways of connecting main centres and of making travel sense of the whole country.

They are designed to be used in these different ways:

1 *Ignore the marked route entirely*: simply use the alphabetically arranged Gazetteer of Sights & Places of Interest, and the map at the start of each 'route', as a guide to what to see and do in the region, not forgetting the hotel and restaurant recommendations.

2 Follow the marked route by public transport (see the transport box) or by car. You can do sections of the route, or all of it; you can follow it in any direction. Link the routes to travel the length and breadth of France.

Contents

Each route has a section to itself, beginning with an introduction and a simplified map. The page number for each such section is shown on this master map.

Always use the simplified maps in conjunction with detailed maps (suggestions are given on the introductory pages).

On the simplified maps:
RED *marks key sights and centres, not to be missed.*

BLUE *marks important places, certainly worth a visit.*

GREEN *places are for those who aren't in a hurry and want to experience the region in some depth.*

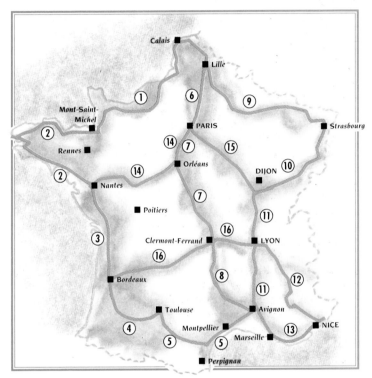

Some practical hints on how to travel red, blue and green are given in the introductory pages and the simplified maps, including key roads and their numbers. Generally, though, there are no absolute rules for going red, blue or green and you are meant to link the places, using a detailed road map, in whatever way suits you best.

Paris has a section of its own, pages 214-233.

The *France Overall* section is ideal for:

■ **Planning**, and undertaking, tours of the whole country, or parts.

■ **Making the journey** to or from your eventual destination as interesting and as rewarding as possible.

■ **Linking** the in-depth explorations of localities provided by the Local Explorations section, pages 234-343.

Contents

The Local Explorations
- master map

The Local Explorations are strategies for exploring all the interesting localities of France. Also described as Local Tours, they complement the National Routes, pages 8-9. **They are designed to be used in these different ways**:

1 *Ignore the marked route entirely:* simply use the alphabetically arranged Gazetteer of Sights & Places of Interest, and the map at the start of each Local Exploration, as a guide to what to see and do in the area, not forgetting the hotel and restaurant recommendations.

2 Use the marked route to make a tour by public transport (see the transport box) or by car. You can do sections of the route, or all of it. (In the introduction it tells you how long you might take to cover everything the quickest way, by car.)

If you are driving, you can generally follow the tour in any direction; usually, the route as marked is an attractive and convenient way to link the places of interest; you may well find other ways to drive it. Always use our map in conjunction with a detailed road map (suggestions are given on each introductory page).

The Local Explorations or Tours, pages 234-343, generally follow each other in a north-south/west-east sequence.

Paris has a section of its own, pages 214-233.

The *Local Explorations* are ideal for:

■ **Planning single-centre holidays**: each Local Exploration encapsulates an area which would make a great holiday. The introductory page to each section is designed to tell you whether the area will suit you: what you can expect; and something of its history, geography, people, customs, food.

■ **Entertaining yourself while you are there**: each section is packed with ideas for things to see and do. The tour, followed in full, can fill several days, and will always make a memorable journey, but most of the sights and places of interest make fascinating day or part-day trips in their own right, not to mention the detours.

■ **Planning multi-centre holidays**. The map on this page shows you at a glance all the interesting localities of France. Combine them at will to experience the different faces of the country; or link them, by means of the national route network described in the France Overall section (pages 30– 213).

Conventions Used in this Guide

A single franc sign – **F** – or several franc signs, such as **FFF**, in a hotel or restaurant entry, denotes a price band. Its object is to give an indication of what you can expect to pay.

Bear in mind that accommodation offered at any one place may well span two or more price bands. Paris has a different set of price bands, see page 216.

Hotels

F	Up to 250 francs
FF	250-450 francs
FFF	More than 450 francs

Prices relate to a double room without breakfast.

Restaurants

F	Up to 120 francs
FF	120-250 francs
FFF	More than 250 francs

Prices are for the set menus, excluding wine and coffee.

⊨ after a heading in **Sights & Places of Interest** means that there is an accommodation suggestion (or suggestions) for that place in **Recommended Hotels**.

✕ after a heading in **Sights & Places of Interest** means that there is a suggestion (or suggestions) for that place in **Recommended Restaurants**.

Hotels and restaurants in this guide are a selection of personal recommendations - not exhaustive lists. They have been chosen to represent interest and quality, or to satisfy specific needs, at every price level.

Opening times, hotels and restaurants
Guidance is given in this guide on the quite wide variations which occur. When no closing times are given, assume that the hotel or restaurant is open all year.

Opening times – museums, galleries, churches and tourist attractions
French national museums and sights are generally closed on Tuesdays except Versailles, the Trianon Palace and the Musée d'Orsay, which close on Mondays. Municipal museums and many regional attractions close on Monday, and often for lunch, noon until 2pm. Small châteaux tend to close from mid October to early March, as do many private or small local museums. Otherwise, museums and attractions are open every day of the year.

But, these are general guidelines only. France is a large, decentralised country: local variations are frequent. This guide therefore notes, for important sights open to the public, the days and months when they are closed. If this information is not given, it is generally because the sight is open all year, or because reliable information is not available. If your enjoyment of a day out is going to depend on gaining entry to a sight, check the precise opening hours with the local Syndicat d'Initiative.

Mileages for routes and tours
Are approximate. In the case of National Routes in the France Overall section, they represent the shortest distances you could expect to travel on the route, almost always the 'red' option.

In the case of Local Tours in the Local Explorations section, they also represent the shortest possible distance you could expect to cover, excluding detours.

Since the routes and tours are designed to be travelled in whole, in part, or indeed not at all, the mileages are given as much for passing interest as for their practical value.

↗ After a place name on a map means that the sight or place of interest is covered in detail in another part of the book. To find out exactly where, look up the place in the **Sights and Places of Interest** gazetteer which follows the map: a cross-reference is given in every case.

Something for Everyone

Getting the most from your guide

Here is a *small* selection of ideas for enjoying France opened up by this guide, aimed at a range of needs and tastes. The list is just a start: the guide offers many, many more ideas for what really matters: suiting *yourself*. You'll find that it takes into account not only your tastes, but how much time you have.

Family holidays
Everywhere, but particularly France Overall: 3 and 16.

Uncomplicated relaxation
Local Explorations: 5.

Scenery, the great outdoors and walking country
France Overall: 4, 8, 12, 14 and 16; Local Explorations: 15.

Châteaux
France Overall: 7 and 14.

Castles
France Overall: 5; Local Explorations: 2 and 14.

Pre-history
France Overall: 3 and 16; Local Explorations: 11 and 17.

Art treasures outside Paris
France Overall: 10, 12 and 13; Local Explorations: 13 amd 14.

Roman France
France Overall: 5 and 11; Local Explorations: 3.

Christmas shopping
France Overall: 9 and 10; Local Explorations: 15.

Wildlife
France Overall: 1 and 4; Local Explorations: 1 and 9.

Cheese
France Overall: 1 and 4; Local Explorations: 1 and 9.

FRANCE:
an Introduction

G o to France and you do more than visit a foreign country. You take part in a way of life, evolved by a people with a genius for living well. From the moment you break into an oven-warm *baguette* in the morning, to the last generous cognac after a five-course dinner, *le style Français* has you in its seductive embrace. This, more than anything else about the country – and there is much else – is what draws Francophiles back time after time: they need to delve a little deeper into the nature of their addiction.

French style is difficult to define, but impossible to miss. It is not just about stripey shirts and berets, food or culture; it is a common appreciation of the good things in life which crosses barriers of class and opinion. The dauntingly chic Parisian office worker with her Chanel shoulder bag has no more money than her counterparts the world over; but she takes added pride in her style. The traditional French café is both the natural preserve of the sophisticated and well-educated as well as the village parlour and unofficial youth club.

Enjoyment of good food and wine is of course a key element of the French way of life. The national passion for *la cuisine* burns throughout the land, from the temples of Bocuse, Robuchon and Meneau to the humblest farm kitchen, and of course in the local market place, perhaps the best place of all to begin a love affair with French cooking. The stalls will be piled high with the freshest local produce – huge beef tomatoes, a dozen different types of salad leaf, peaches and plums, melons and apricots. Don't forget to stop by the *fromagère* with his wares laid out in the shade – fresh goats' cheese wrapped in leaves, heart-shaped Neuchâtel, blue-coated roundels of Saint-Marcellin, nutty Cantal. Then visit the *charcuterie* for salamis, pâtés and carrot salad *en route* to the *boulan-*

gerie for bread, *croissants*, *brioches* and delectable *tartes aux fruits*, reflecting the changing seasons with strawberries, figs and bilberries.

It is a common misapprehension that the French are unfriendly. Not true, unless you mistake for disinterest their respect for your privacy and a certain formality required of *la politesse*. Given a chance, the average French man or woman will open up with enthusiasm after the introductions have been made and the pleasantries exchanged.

Travelling in France is a mixture of major events – grand scenery, inspiring cathedrals, grandiose *châteaux* – and of small pleasures. Often it is the little things that you remember longest: picnicking in a field where seven different types of orchid grow wild; or visiting a small-scale *château* in the Berry where labradors waddle out to meet you and there are family photographs on the piano.

Here are three useful tips for making the most of travels in France:

First, don't visit tourist traps such as *villes perchées* by day when the coachloads are there too. Plan to dine there, or to stay the night when you can see them at their best.

Second, enquire of local hotels or tourist information offices about local events such as festivals, bullfights in the south, Christmas markets in Alsace, or *pardons* in Brittany, which offer a unique opportunity to experience first-hand, even to get involved in, local life and traditions.

Third, do try to visit at least one major restaurant on a trip. Many are expensive, but I still think they are worth every centime, and you can save money by economizing on accommodation – there is more simple, comfortable and relatively cheap accommodation in France, including *chambres d'hôte* or bed-and-breakfast, than any other country in western Europe. Some people forget that it is actually quite easy to eat bad meals and stay in over-priced, poor hotels in France; they are a contradiction of everything that is good about travelling in France, and can spoil the experience. So follow the recommendations in this guide, wisely spend some money from time to time, and you will protect your overall investment in the trip, returning with some life-long memories.

One of the greatest French bargains of all is the countryside, and one of the greatest pleasures is driving the backroads. Do all you can to stray from the *autoroutes*; this book will show you how.

One final piece of advice: accept that you will have to go back, again and again. In European terms, France is a big and tremendously varied country. Getting to know it is a lifetime's work. Thank goodness.

Emma Stanford

BEFORE YOU GO

Climate; when to go, and to which parts

France rarely suffers from extremes of climate. It is cooler in the north, wetter in the west, and greyer in the east. Paris can indeed be delightful in the spring, but it is also hot and humid at the height of summer, and bleak and grey in winter. However, these unremarkable regional and seasonal variations are easily survived with the help of a little educated packing.

Average daily temperatures in Paris range from 37.6°F (3.1°C) in January to 66.2°F (19°C) in July. Nice, on the Côte d'Azur is of course warmer: average daily temperature in January: 41.9°F (5.5°C); in July it is 73.7°F (23.2°C).

The best seasons to visit France are spring or autumn, either side of the main June to August tourist season. In mid-summer, accommodation prices rocket, the roads are jammed and the beaches packed. During winter, November until March, many hotels and some restaurants are closed in summer-oriented holiday areas such as Brittany.

French national holidays are particularly bad days to travel, as are the traditional annual summer holiday weekends at either end of August.

Clothing

Common sense is the only guideline. Nothing beats comfortable footwear whether you are planning to stalk the cultural high spots of Paris or hike in the Pyrenees. Bring (sensible) jewellery if the rue Faubourg Saint-Honoré is your goal.

Seriously, be prepared to wrap up warmly in winter; pack a lightweight raincoat at any time of year; and remember that hotel laundry bills are astronomical. If a meal in a gourmet restaurant is on the agenda, bring something a little dressy. The French are undeniably chic, and it is best to meet them on their own terms.

Documentation

Visas are not required of citizens of the EC, the U.S., Canada and New Zealand provided they have a full passport and plan a business or tourist trip to France lasting no longer than 90 days. Other nationals (including Australians) should apply to the nearest French consulate for a transit visa (three days only), a *carte de séjour* (90 days multiple entry), or a *visa de circulation* (valid for multiple trips of up to 90 days over three years).

Persons over 18 may drive in France on a full overseas driving license. To hire a car you must be 21 or over (or 23 if you do not possess a major credit card) and have been in possession of a full driving licence for at least one year.

Drivers must be able to produce the vehicle registration document and proof of insurance. A policy extension (in the U.K., a 'green card') to make the cover comprehensive while motoring abroad is not obligatory, but without it your insurance is only the legal minimum.

Medical and travel insurance

EC citizens are entitled to health care in other member countries providing they have the reciprocal health care form. But, all medical expenses must be paid for at the time and are reimbursed in part after a long-winded claims procedure. Other nationalities are recommended to purchase (or to arrange as an extension of an existing policy) medical and travel insurance before departure.

Money

Local currency is the French franc (F or FF), divided into 100 centimes. There are 500F, 100F, 50F, and 20F bills, 10F, 5F, 2F and IF coins, plus 50, 20, 10 and 5 centime coins.

Travellers cheques are the best way to guard your money. French franc travellers cheques are useful if you are venturing off the beaten track where the currency exchange rate may not be common knowledge. American Express, Diners Club, MasterCard/Eurocard and Visa/Carte Bleue credit cards are widely accepted – Visa is the most widespread. Apply in advance, and you can be issued with a PIN number which will allow you to use your credit card in French cash dispensers.

Import duty

The regulations follow general EC rules, which were changed in 1993 to allow virtually free movement of goods across EC borders. Instead of the former duty-free allowances, there are now guidelines for individual import and export of such goods as wines, spirits and tobacco. Customs officers still maintain their vigilance, often covertly, against prohibited goods such as drugs and weapons which might assist terrorist activity.

Tourist information outside France
The French Government Tourist Office (also known as Maison de la France) can provide a raft of special interest brochures and useful information. Offices are in most capital cities, including:

Australia c/o UTA, BNP Building (12th Floor), 12 Castlereagh Street, Sydney, NSW 2000.
 Canada 1981 avenue McGill College (Suite 490), Montreal, QUE H3A 2W9; 30 St Patrick Street (Suite 700), Toronto, ONT M5T 3A3.
 Ireland 35 Lower Abbey Street, Dublin 1.
 Netherlands Prinsengracht 670, 1017 KX Amsterdam.
 Germany Westendstrasse 47, Postfach 100-128, D-6000, Frankfurt am Main 1.
 U.K. 178 Piccadilly, London W1V OAL.
 U.S.A. 619 Fifth Avenue (Suite 222), New York, NY 10020-2452; 645 North Michigan Avenue, Chicago, ILL 60611-2836; 9454 Wilshire Boulevard, Beverly Hills, CA 90212-2967; 2305 Cedar Springs Boulevard, Dallas, TX 75201.

Local customs: what to expect and how to behave
McDonalds may have infiltrated the Champs-Elysées, but you can bet that frogs legs and *haute couture* will never be compromised. The French have an intense pride in their cuisine, their *couture* and their culture, which can give an aura of smugness and superiority: but bearing in mind that they have given the world cognac, Chanel and Camus, perhaps they have a point. You won't go far wrong with the French if you give credit where it is due: praise a good meal, compliment a beautiful dress, marvel at a national monument. Once foreigners have gained their confidence, they are usually affability itself. From the moment that your coffee and croissant appear on your first morning in France, you'll be aware that things

are done differently here. (Already, you may have done battle with the draught excluder French hotels provide in lieu of a pillow – the real pillows, large and square rather than oblong, are kept in the wardrobe.) French coffee is strong, black, served in thimbles (except at breakfast, when it comes in a bowl, with or without a handle), and is likely to keep you awake at night. It is the lynchpin of café society, beloved of all French from students to society matrons and accompanies voluble discussions on the most important topics on their minds, which include sport (especially soccer, cycling, tennis), shopping, salacious gossip, cinema, current affairs and philosophy, not necessarily in that order.

Meeting and greeting is an art form in France, and the café is a useful place to observe local ritual. Among friends, the young deliver three or four cheek-smackingly ostentatious kisses at every meeting (frequently extended to never-before-encountered friends of friends); two suffice for their elders. Hand-shaking is *de rigueur* between acquaintances, both on a business and a social level. If you are a visiting head of state, prepare for the presidential embrace. It is polite in a small shop to acknowledge the shopkeeper formally ("*Bonjour madame/monsieur*") and you can include other customers as well ("*messieurs/mesdames*"); the same goes for restaurants or cafés. This form of courtesy is much appreciated and you'll find that it can enhance your status.

Lunch is the main meal of the day in France. Most businesses, tourist attractions and shops close for two hours in the north and up to four or five hours in the south for this event. Plan your day around this; the good news is that this is often the time to find easy (even free) parking in town centres.

If you are doing business in France, patience is more than a help: it is an essential virtue. Be ready for the formalities and elaborate courtesies; prepare some of your own. Also be prepared for frankly expressed reservations about goods or services you are offering, even if your French customer admires what you have to offer and has decided to buy.

Banks and post offices may have a laid-back (but nonetheless efficient) approach, with shirt-sleeved tellers and gossip over the counter, so it pays not to be in a hurry.

GETTING THERE

By air
Paris is the main gateway city for air travellers to France with two international airports: **Roissy-Charles de Gaulle** (23 km NE), and **Orly** (14 km S). There are regular direct or one-stop flights from numerous U.S. centres; most direct flights from Canada are ex-Toronto. The French international airline UTA operates a service between Sydney and Paris. From the U.K., and other European countries, there are also direct flights to several French regional airports such as Bordeaux, Lyon, Nice and Toulouse.

It is worth shopping around for reduced fares such as Apex (booked at least two weeks in advance), and charter deals. There is often a discount for flying mid-week and staying a minimum number of nights. Some long-haul travellers may find it cheaper to fly via low-cost European destinations such as London.

By rail
France's national train service, the SNCF (Société Nationale des Chemin de Fer Français), and other European train networks operate rail links and motor rail services between many European cities. (For details of special deals within France, see Getting Around, page 19.) Boat trains from London's Victoria Station depart regularly throughout the day for Dover, Folkestone and Newhaven to connect with ferry, hovercraft and Seacat crossings, and onward train services.

The Eurotunnel: Travellers between France and Britain will begin using this long-awaited new option in 1994. The subterranean railway link beneath the Channel – 'le Shuttle' – carries cars, motorcyles, coaches and their passengers on a 'loop' between Folkestone and Calais 24 hours a day, every day.

The journey takes 35 minutes from platform to platform or one hour from motorway to motorway. Each shuttle takes 180 cars or 120 cars plus 12 coaches.

Reservations are not needed since the service runs every 15 minutes at peak times. Even during the quietest periods of the night the intention is to offer at least one departure each hour.

You buy tickets from the toll booths on arrival at whichever terminal and take the next available shuttle. Or you can buy your ticket through a travel agent or le Shuttle's customer services department.

The rolling stock are double-decked, taking passengers and cars. The operators describe them as 'modern, air-conditioned, sound-proofed and well-lit'. You 'stay with your car' for the journey, but are allowed to get out and walk around, and you will be able to listen to le Shuttle's radio station and watch the visual display screens to check progress.

Whether these are any comfort to those who are inclined to claustrophobia, or merely anxiety, is another matter. The tunnels, say the operators, are drilled through a layer of impermeable chalk marl.

Access to le Shuttle in Britain is signposted from M20 Junction 11a at Folkestone and in France from the A16 Junction 13 at Calais. Passenger and customs checks are completed before boarding, so you can drive straight off at the other end.

By sea
The shortest Channel crossings between mainland U.K. and northern France are those linking Dover (ferry, hovercraft or Seacat) with Calais/Boulogne; Folkestone (Seacat) with Boulogne; and Ramsgate (ferry) with Dunkerque. The fastest crossing is by hovercraft or Seacat (high-speed catamaran), Calais-Dover in 35 to 40 minutes. There are also ferry services between Newhaven and Dieppe; Portsmouth and Caen/Cherbourg/Le Havre/Saint-Malo; Plymouth and Roscoff; Southampton and Cherbourg; and Poole or Weymouth with Cherbourg. From Eire, there are year-round ferry services between Rosslare and Cherbourg/Le Havre; and summer-only crossings between Cork and Le Havre/Roscoff. Special deals range from discounted three- and five-day breaks to off-season bargains. Make car ferry bookings well in advance for summer holidays.

GETTING AROUND

By car

Most of France's 3,000 km *autoroute* (motorway) network is privately funded and toll booths (*péages*) collect dues at regular intervals. These can be costly on a long journey such as Calais-Menton (1,259 km), where tolls will add up to around 400F. If you do not have the correct change, credit cards are accepted.

Motorways aside, N-roads form the main national route system, though many of the secondary D-roads have been upgraded (some in name alone). These can become congested in summer, especially in the north on roads to the Channel ports. During the French annual holidays, and from mid-July to September 1, even the *autoroutes* can grind to a standstill. The French Ministry of Transport provides maps indicating congested routes and major road works with tips on how to avoid them. Known as *Bison Futé* (wily buffalo), these maps are available free from petrol stations. If you are looking for

• On Paris's left bank, south of Bvd St-Germain.

scenery, roads edged by a green line on maps represent particularly attractive routes.

Petrol (*gas*) is sold by the litre in France. Unleaded petrol is widely available, as is diesel (*gasoil*) but LPG can be difficult to find off the motorways. LPG motorway service stations can provide free LPG location maps.

Car hire is expensive in France, so check out possible fly-drive deals before booking a car through any of the major rental companies such as Avis, Budget and Hertz, all of whom operate in France.

The SNCF offers convenient rail-drive rentals from around 200 destinations in France. For touring holidays of three weeks or more, it is worth investigating leasing options such as Renault's Eurodrive scheme, a purchase/resale plan, which has the additional advantage of being tax-free to non-European citizens.

Regulations: The French drive on the right. Drivers of left-hand drive cars are obliged to have their headlight beams adjusted for driving on the right. Speed limits are posted at 130 kph on toll roads, 110 kph on two-lane highways, 90 kph on lesser roads, and 60 kph or less in built-up areas. Fines for speeding (minimum 1,300F) and drink-driving (2,000-30,000F) are extracted in cash on the spot. The lethal *priorité à droite* rule is being phased out, but still applies in some urban districts: you must give way to drivers coming out of a side turning on the right. Traffic circles are the exception. Seatbelts must be worn in the front and the back of the car and under-IOs may not travel in the front unless strapped into an approved back-facing baby seat.

Taxis: These have illuminated signs on their roofs and can only be picked up from taxi ranks (*stations de taxi*) or summoned by telephone. Check that the taxi has a meter before entering. The pick-up charge is around 11F (more from a railway station), and the rate per kilometre starts at around 3F.

By air

Air Inter is the main domestic carrier serving 30 major business and holiday destinations. Air travel is expensive, though Air Inter does offer discounts for foreign travellers in possession of an international air ticket, and the France Pass for North American visitors. Check with your travel agent.

By bus/coach

There are few long-distance bus routes in France, but local routes operated by the SNCF (French railways) link most notable destinations by-passed by the extensive rail network (see below). SNCF buses leave from the railway station, and major bus stations in large towns are usually located nearby. SNCF bus timetables will be posted at the station, or ask for advice and details of other local services at tourist offices (S.I.).

By rail

The SNCF (Société Nationale des Chemins de Fer Français) operates the most technically advanced train system in the world. Its 3,500 km of track link some 3,000 destinations throughout the country. Services are frequent, punctual and fast: on major routes, high-speed trains (TGV) streak across the country at speeds of up to 300 kph.

If you plan to travel the rail network extensively, the Eurail Pass, available only to non-EC nationals, provides an economic and practical means of unlimited travel throughout France (and indeed continental Europe). Certain age groups are eligible for valuable discounts. Enquire at a main railway station.

European nationals can buy similar unlimited travel passes (in the U.K., the Interail Pass) for railway journeys in Europe but outside their own country, again with discounts for certain age groups. Enquire at a main railway station. The France Vacances Pass, on sale in the U.K., permits four days of unlimited travel during a 15-day period, or nine days within one month. North American visitors can take advantage of the France Railpass, allowing four to nine days of unlimited travel within one month, which also throws in extras such as reduced rates on car hire and museum entry. This is similar to the France Vacances Pass available to Australians and New Zealanders. Senior citizens and families will find special discount cards geared to their needs. For further information, contact:

Australia local branches of National Australia Ltd Travel or Thomas Cook Pty Ltd.
Canada Raileurope Inc, 643 Notre Dame Ouest (Suite 200), Montreal, QUE H3C IHB, tel. (514) 392 1311; 409 Granville Street (Suite 452), Vancouver, BC V6C IT2, tel. (604) 688 6707.
UK/Eire French Railways Ltd, 179 Piccadilly, London WIV OBA, tel. (071) 493 9731.
USA: Raileurope Inc, 226-230 Westchester Avenue, White Plains, NY 10604, tel. (800) TGV RAIL; 100 Wilshire Boulevard, Santa Monica, CA 90401, tel. (213) 451 5150 (also in Chicago, Dallas, Fort Lauderdale, San Francisco).

Important: if you have purchased a ticket or a rail pass in France, it must be validated *before* you board the train for each and every journey. Look for signs *Composer Votre Billet* and the orange ticket-punching machines, usually found at the entrance to the platform.

ESSENTIAL PRACTICAL INFORMATION

Accommodation

French hotels are officially graded from one to four stars on their facilities (not character), and their category is advertised by a blue tin sign with the appropriate number of red stars. There is a wide choice of accommodation styles, and prices are still reasonable by European standards. Local tourist offices (*syndicats d'initiative*, addresses given throughout this guide) can assist with information and bookings.

The French Government Tourist Office (FGTO) can provide accommodation lists and details of organizations such as **Logis de France** with its country-wide network of recommended family-run hotels (mostly in the one- to two-star categories); and **Gîtes de France** which lists 2,500 self-catering properties in rural areas. During the summer season, numerous private houses, from the small to the very grand, open up their spare rooms and post signs offering *Chambres d'Hôte*. Quality varies dramatically (ask to see the room first) and facilities are likely to be simple, but this is often a cheap and friendly way to get bed-and-breakfast.

Camping: The Fédération Français de Camping et Caravanning, 78 rue Rivoli, 75004 Paris, lists more than 11,000 approved campsites in their official guide. The sites are rated from one to four stars and range from out-of-the-way country farms to beach-front tented cities. The FGTO publishes an excellent brochure, *The Camping Traveller in France*, with loads of practical information and details of how to obtain the FFCC guide abroad.

Food, drink and eating out: you will find practical information on these topics on page 29.

Banks and currency exchange

Banks are open Monday to Friday 9am to noon and 2 until 4pm. Some open on Saturday mornings and close on Monday mornings; many close early before bank holidays. *Bureaux de change* keep longer hours and can usually be located at main railway stations. Tourist offices will have details, and some have their own currency exchange facilities.

Breakdowns

If your car does not have hazard lights, a red warning triangle *must* be posted behind (it is sensible to use both). Emergency telephones are posted at 2-km intervals on *autoroutes*. These connect you with rescue services via the traffic police. On other roads, get help from a local garage or call the emergency number provided by your motoring insurance.

Drinking and smoking regulations

Alcohol is served from breakfast until closing in bars and cafés, but drink-driving laws are strictly enforced by breathalizers, on-the-spot fines and worse. It is also worth remembering, despite the tarif posted in every drinking establishment, that you will pay less at the bar, more at a table, and even more on the terrace.

The most recent government anti-smoking campaign is backed up with compulsory non-smoking sections in all restaurants and cafés. Draconian fines are levied on the *patron* and customers who transgress; many small, single dining-room establishments have had to ban smokers altogether.

Electricity

As in most of Europe, French voltage is 220v 50AC; plugs are two-pronged. Take an adaptor for foreign electrical appliances.

Embassies and consulates

Australia 4 rue Jean-Rey, Paris 15e; tel. 40 59 33 00.
Canada 35 avenue Montaigne, Paris 8e; tel. 47 23 0101.
Germany 34 avenue d'Iéna, Paris 16e; tel. 42 99 78 00.
Ireland 12 avenue Foch, Paris 16e; tel. 45 00 89 43.
Netherlands 7-9 rue Eblé, Paris 7e; tel. 43 06 61 88.
U.K. 35 rue du Faubourg Saint-Honoré, Paris 8e; tel. 42 66 91 42; consulate, 16 rue d'Anjou, Paris 8e.
U.S.A. 2 avenue Gabriel, Paris 8e; tel. 42 96 12 02; consulate, 2 rue Saint-Florentin, Paris 8e.

Outside Paris, consular facilities are sparse, though some countries maintain offices in other major cities such as Bordeaux, Lille, Lyon, Marseille and Strasbourg.

Emergencies

For the police, dial 19; ambulance and

fire service, 18. See also Medical matters, below.

Lost property
Foreign visitors should read the instructions which come with their travellers cheques: they explain exactly how to replace them if lost or stolen. Lost travel documents must be reported to the police. Lost or stolen credit cards should of course be reported to the issuing company.

Inform the ticket office about items lost on public transport; property found on the Paris Métro (underground or subway) may end up at the end of the line, where it can be collected. In Paris, lost property is held at the Bureau des Objets Trouvés, 36 rue des Morillons, Paris 15e; tel. 1 48 28 32 36 (open Monday to Friday). Remember to get a

• *The Grande Arche at La Défense, Paris – see page* 29.

statement from the police in order to validate any insurance claim.

Measurements
France operates on the metric system: One litre = 1.7 pints (1 imperial gallon = 4.54 litres; 1 US gallon = 3.73 litres).

One kilogramme (1,000 grams) = 2.2 lbs.

One kilometre (1,000 metres) = 0.62 mile.

Medical matters
Local hospitals are generally well signposted (*Centre Hospitalier*). For non-emergency medical problems, there are chemists or drugstores (*pharma-*

cies) marked by a green cross. After hours they post the name of the nearest 24-hour duty *pharmacie* and doctor on the door; the police can also advise.

Opening hours

Banks: see above, under Banks and currency exchange.

Museums and tourist attractions: see Conventions Used in this Guide, page 12.

Post offices are open Monday to Friday 8am-7pm, Saturday 8am-noon.

Food shops are generally open 7am-6.30 or 7.30pm; some open on Sunday mornings, and most are closed all or for half the day on Monday. Hypermarkets open Monday to Saturday 9am-lpm, though many close Monday morning. Other shops open Monday to Saturday 9 or 10am until 6.30 or 7.30pm; many close all-day or half the day on Monday. Shops in small towns often close for lunch (noon to 2pm). In the south of France, many shops take a siesta between noon or lpm and 3 or 4pm, and stay open later in the evening.

Post and telephone

Post offices (PTT – pey-tey-tey) are marked by a blue and yellow sign. For opening times, see above.

Main post offices will hold mail addressed to individuals on the move until collected in person. The envelope should carry the name of the recipient, the words *Poste restante*, and the name of the place where the main post office is situated. The person collecting the mail pays a small fee (take identification).

Post offices also have *cabines* or booths in which you make telephone calls, paying afterwards. Stamps can also be bought from tobacconists (*tabacs*) and newsagents.

The French telephone system has been simplified to two regions: Paris and its immediate suburbs; and the provinces. All telephone numbers have eight digits. No additional code is required between provincial numbers, or calls within Paris. When calling Paris from the provinces, dial 16, wait for the tone, then dial 1 followed by the eight-digit number. To dial the provinces from Paris, dial 16, wait for the tone, then the eight-digit number.

For international calls, dial 19, wait for the tone, then add the country code, followed by the subscriber's number omitting the initial zero of the area code. To make a collect call (PCV – *pey-sey-vey*) call the international operator on 19 33 11. Public telephones marked with a blue bell can receive incoming calls.

Most public telephones now take phonecards (*télécartes*) which can be bought at post offices, tobacconists (*tabacs*) and newsagents. It is cheaper to call EC countries between 10.30pm to 8am on weekdays, and at weekends after 2pm on Saturday; for cheap rates to the U.S. and Canada, call between noon to 2pm and 8pm to 2am on weekdays, and on Sunday afternoons.

Public holidays

January 1; Easter Day; Easter Monday; Ascension Thursday; Labour Day, May I; VE-Day, May 8; Whit Monday;Bastille Day, July 14; Assumption Day, August 15; All Saints' Day, November 1; Remembrance Day, November 11; Christmas Day.

Time

France is one hour ahead of the U.K., (G.M.T. plus one) and six hours ahead of U.S. Eastern Standard Time. Clocks go forward one hour for daylight saving from the end of March to the end of September.

Tipping

Baggage porters, 5F per item (in addition to usual charge); cinema usherettes, 2F; hairdressers, 10 per cent; taxi drivers, 10-15 per cent; tour guides, 5F per person; waiters (service is generally included, if not) 10 to 15 per cent.

Tourist information

Tourist offices offer a mass of information on local attractions, events and accommodation, and can also help with hotel reservations (usually for a small fee).

In major cities, the *Office de Tourisme* will be well-signposted and probably open seven days a week during the summer season. In smaller towns, local tourist offices are known as *Syndicats d'Initiative* (S.I.), and they may close for the winter as well as on Sundays and Monday mornings.

23

A BRIEF HISTORY OF FRANCE

Pre-history and Ancient

Down in the Périgord region of central western France, caves reveal the artistry of Cro-Magnon man dating from the late Stone Age. The megalithic standing stones of Brittany stand tribute to other early inhabitants of which little is known. It was the Phoenicians who founded the Greek settlement of *Massalia* (Marseille) around 600BC, where the Romans later established *Provincia*, and then gradually moved north to conquer the Celtic tribesmen of the land they called Gaul.

After Julius Caesar defeated the last Gaulish chieftan, Vercingetorix, in 52BC, France remained part of the Roman empire until the 5thC.

The Dark and Middle Ages

Beginning in the 3rdC, the Germanic tribes – Goths, Burgundians and Franks – invaded from the east across the Rhine. The Franks gained supremacy, and their king, Clovis I, converted to Christianity and established his capital in Paris. Two centuries later, Charles Martel turned back the Muslim hoards at Poitiers. His grandson, Charlemagne, was crowned Holy Roman Emperor by the pope in 800, initiating a period of stability and a flowering of the arts and culture.

Lack of a strong heir, feudal rivalries and Viking incursions in the north led to the disintegration of the empire after Charlemagne's death. With the Norman Conquest of England in 1066, English expansion became a constant threat to the French, in which the English were notably assisted by Eleanor of Aquitaine who divorced Louis VII to

KEY DATES

121BC	Romans cross the Alps.
52BC	Julius Caesar defeats Vercingetorix and conquers Gaul.
3rd-5thC AD	Barbarian invasions (Vandals, Visigoths, Franks).
4thC	Gallo-Roman city of Lutèce becomes Paris. Arrival of Christianity.
508	Clovis I, first Christian King of France, settles in Paris. Start of Merovingian period (508-751).
732	Muslim armies defeated by Charles Martel at Poitiers.
751	Start of Carolingian period (751-987).
800	Charlemagne crowned Holy Roman Emperor.
9thC	Norman invasions of France.
987	Hugues Capet elected ruler; start of Capetain dynasty.
1066	Norman invasion of England.
1095	Urban II announces First Crusade at Clairvaux.
1152	Eleanor of Aquitaine marries Henry Plantagenet (future Henry II of England), placing a third of France in English hands.
1180	Philippe II Auguste embarks on 43-year reign.
1209-18	Albigensian Crusades in southern France crush Cathar heretics.
1226	Accession of Louis IX (Saint-Louis); died in 1270 at Tunis during Eighth Crusade.
1253	Founding of the Sorbonne.
1309	Clement V removes papacy from Rome to Avignon.
1328	Philippe IV becomes first Valois king.
1337	Start of Hundred Years War with England.
1356	French king, Jean le Bon, taken prisoner at Poitiers by Edward, the Black Prince.
1415	Henry V of England defeats French at Agincourt.
1429	English routed at Orléans by Jeanne d'Arc (burnt at Rouen 1431).
1453	End of Hundred Years War.
1515	François I, Renaissance connoisseur, introduces finest Italian artists to work on his palace at Fontainebleau.
1562-98	Wars of Religion set Huguenots (Protestants) against Catholics.

marry Henry Plantagenet, bringing a substantial area of France with her.

Philippe II Auguste succeeded in unifying much of France by a series of strategic marriage contracts, conquering Normandy and winning English possessions north of the Loire for the crown. However, a succession crisis contested by Philippe de Valois and Edward III of England developed into the Hundred Years War which lasted until 1453.

Wars of Religion

The emergence of Protestantism clouded the 16thC, dividing the nobility. The Catholic massacre of a Huguenot (French Protestant) congregation in 1562 led to the civil upheaval of the Wars of Religion. Henri IV, a Protestant turned Catholic, eventually stemmed the bloodshed with the Edict of Nantes (1598), which granted Protestants freedom of worship.

Louis XIII (1610-43), and Louis XIV (1643-1715) had the 17thC to themselves. Ably assisted by Cardinal Richelieu, Louis XIII began to restore the principles of an absolutist monarchy by disbanding the Estates General (a feudal parliament made up of the nobility, clergy and bourgeoisie) and consolidated French territory with significant frontier gains from the over-extended Spanish empire. He also built up the economy and extended trade to the colonies. Richelieu and the king died within months of each other, leaving a five year-old heir, Louis XIV. While the queen, Anne of Austria, acted as regent, Cardinal Mazarin continued to implement Richelieu's objectives, and

1594	Henri de Bourbon (Henry of Navarre) converted to Catholicism, and crowned Henri IV at Paris.
1598	Edict of Nantes safeguards Protestants right to worship.
1624	Cardinal Richelieu becomes Prime Minister, represses Protestants and starts Thirty Years War with Hapsburgs.
1643	Accession of Louis XIV, the 'Sun King'; literature, the arts and military architecture (Vauban) flourish.
1659	Treaty of the Pyrenees ends border disputes with Spain (Louis XIV marries Infanta Maria Theresa 1660).
1685	Revocation of Edict of Nantes and suppression of Protestants.
1701-13	War of Spanish Succession (defeated by Duke of Marlborough).
1715	Accession of Louis XV.
1756-63	Seven Years War. France loses her North American colonies.
1769	Napoleon Bonaparte born in Corsica.
1789	Storming of the Bastille.
1792	Declaration of the First Republic.
1793	Louis XVI executed. Robespierre's Reign of Terror.
1804	Napoleon crowned at Notre-Dame. First Empire.
1815	Battle of Waterloo; Napoleon banished to St. Helena.
1830	Charles X loses crown to Louis-Philippe d'Orléans in July Revolution.
1848	Louis-Philippe overthrown by Second Republic.
1852	Napoleon III, Bonaparte's nephew, initiates Second Empire.
1870	Napoleon III deposed. Proclamation of Third Republic.
1889	Paris Exhibition and unveiling of Eiffel Tower.
1900	First Métro (underground or subway) opens.
1914-18	First World War.
1939	Outbreak of Second World War.
1940	Paris bombed; British retreat at Dunkirk.
1944	De Gaulle heads troops of Free French to liberate Paris.
1946	Proclamation of the Fourth Republic.
1954	France inaugurates independent nuclear programme.
1957	EC founded by France, West Germany, Italy, and Benelux.
1958	Creation of French Commonwealth; de Gaulle elected first President of the Fifth Republic.
1981	Socialists take power.
1993	The Right is returned in a landslide election victory.

secure the solid power base that would make France the premier economic and military power of Europe for the latter half of the century. However, the *parlements* (unelected administrative councils) and nobility became increasingly incensed by the gradual disappearance of their privileges and general economic hardships. A series of revolts, known as the *Frondes*, were quickly suppressed, but Louis' famously luxurious lifestyle and fondness for displays of military might further drained resources and support.

The Revolution

The accession of the infant Louis XV heralded another period of regency and attendant squabbles, followed by the disastrous War of the Austrian Succession, and the loss of France's colonies in the Seven Years War. By 1789, with Louis XVI on the throne, the country's finances were in such chaos that the Estates General were recalled. On June 13, the Third Estate (the bourgeoisie) declared itself a National Assembly, and a popular uprising led to the storming of the Bastille in July. During August, feudal obligations and hereditary privilege were abolished, and the Assembly adopted the Declaration of the Rights of Man. As the Revolution gathered momentum, the moderates lost ground. The king was executed in January 1793, and Robespierre emerged as the terrifying guardian of the First Republic. He himself met the fate of many of his victims at the guillotine in 1794.

The Empire

Power passed to a five-man Directorate, which in turn fell to a *coup d'état* led by General Napoleon Bonaparte in 1799. While upholding the principles of the Revolution, Napoleon reorganized the bureaucracy and tax systems, crowned himself Emperor, and set about conquering Europe.

Defeated by the Russian winter (1813), he abdicated, only to return to be beaten by Wellington at Waterloo in 1815. The monarchy was restored in the form of Louis XVIII and Charles X, but lost to Louis Philippe, the 'Citizen King', whose absolutist tendencies encouraged the rise of the Second Republic headed by the elected Louis Napoleon (nephew of the Emperor),

later Napoleon III.

Recent history

Defeat by the Prussians marked the end of Napoleon III's tenure, and the rise of the Third Republic. Dogged by an humiliating peace treaty with Prussia, and political scandals such as the notorious Dreyfuss affair in which a Jewish army captain was framed for treason, France was then savaged by the First World War. Political wrangling coupled with social unrest filled the period between the wars, while the effects of the 1930s depression and the impracticality of the supposedly impregnable Maginot Line defences left the country easy prey to Hitler's military machine.

The First World War veteran Maréchal Pétain signed an armistice with Hitler in the hope of minimizing the damage. His collaborationist government sat at Vichy, and the French facists had a field day rounding up Communists, Jews and other 'dangers to society', while the Resistance fought back. Leader of the Free French forces, General Charles de Gaulle took control of government in 1944, then resigned while the newly declared Fourth Republic dallied with a series of ineffectual coalition governments, got dragged into conflicts in Indochina and Algeria, and became a founder member of the EC in 1957.

De Gaulle was called back to save the day in 1958, and was elected first President of the Fifth Republic in 1959, at the head of his right-wing Gaullist party. Algeria was granted independence in 1962, but the flood of *pieds noirs* refugees (Algerians claiming French nationality) sparked off racial tensions which are still apparent today. Paris, May 1968: the explosive student uprising followed by a general strike finally ousted de Gaulle, and placed Prime Minister Georges Pompidou in power, to be succeeded by another Gaullist, Valéry Giscard d'Estaing. In 1981, François Mitterand's Socialist Party ended the Gaullist reign, but the Socialist celebrations were short-lived. Dogged by scandal and in-fighting between Left and Right, the government lurched through to the economic downturn of the late 1980s to disappear almost without trace in the parliamentary elections of 1993.

The Arts and Architecture

• The controversial Louvre Pyramid, Paris.

Prehistory
The earliest stirrings of art in France seem to have occurred in the Stone Age, some 350 to 100 centuries BC, when Cro-Magnon man introduced the idea of interior decoration with cave paintings such as those found in the Dordogne region. The megalithic stones of Carnac in Brittany, some of which bear traces of abstract carvings, date from the Neolithic period, and were followed by the increasingly sophisticated tools, the weapons and finely-wrought metal jewellery of the Bronze-Age Celts.

Ancient history
The Greeks founded Massalia (Marseille) in the 6thC BC, but the first collective artistic influence arrived from over the Alps with the Romans. In Provence, the amphitheatres of Arles and Nîmes, the magnificent Pont du Gard aqueduct, and remains found at Orange, Vaison-la-Romaine and Saint-Rémy-de-Provence represent some of the finest examples of Roman architecture outside Italy. These classical patterns are evident in the early Christian architecture of the 5th to 10thC, such

as the baptistry of Fréjus cathedral and St John's in Poitiers.

Romanesque
The Capetian dynasty, established in the late 10thC, introduced a degree of stability; from this, and from the power and wealth of the Church, emerged the great ecclesiastical buildings which characterize the Romanesque style: massive pillars, rounded arches and carved capitals, becoming increasingly ornate. There are especially many fine Romanesque churches in Burgundy (Fontenay, Tournus, Vézelay), the Loire (Fontevraud) and Languedoc-Roussillon (Toulouse); regional variations include the Auvergnat style seen at Orcival and Notre-Dame-du-Port in Clermont-Ferrand.

Gothic
The pointed arches and ribbed vaulting of the early Gothic style which first appeared in the mid 12thC (Saint-Denis in Paris) allowed architects to build higher and lighter. Huge areas of stained glass (Chartres and Metz) added to the decoration; the lacy stonework of Flamboyant Gothic flour-

ished in the north from the late 14thC. Notable secular Gothic buildings include the Palais de Justice in Rouen, and the Palais Jacques Coeur in Bourges. Meanwhile, south-western France was being peppered with fortified towns, the *bastides* (see page 204).

Renaissance
Stylistic developments derived from the Italian Renaissance appeared in France at the end of the 15thC, emerging forcefully in the early Loire châteaux such as Chenonceau (1513), Azay-le-Rideau (1518) and Chambord (1519). François I imported Italian artists and craftsmen to transform Fontainebleau, who in turn trained the 'School of Fontainebleau' in the rich and allegorical Mannerist style.

The emergence of a strong and secular court encouraged academic endeavour, notably the works of Montaigne, the poet Pierre de Ronsard and the humanist philosopher, René Descartes.

Classicism
In the 17th-18thC, France was the premier power of Europe, eager to display her wealth and cultural superiority. Le Brun, Le Vau, Claude Perrault and Jules Hardouin Mansart 'Frenchified' Baroque to grandiose effect at Versailles, the Louvre and Les Invalides; Le Nôtre perfected the formal garden; and sumptuous châteaux proliferated in the provinces. Though Claude Lorrain's landscapes and Poussin's classical themes were painted in Italy, the portrait painter Mignard was on the spot to capture the good and the great; and theatrical entertainment was provided by Molière and Racine.

As French society and art soared to ever greater flights of fancy in the 18thC (Marie-Antoinette dressed up as a milk maid, the paintings of Boucher and Fragonard, Rococo decoration), the playwright Voltaire and the philosopher Jean-Jacques Rousseau wrote about their doubts.

Revolution and Romanticism
The consummate republican artist and Napoleonic favourite, Jacques-Louis David, turned away from frivolity and concentrated on powerful historical or classical subjects in the 1780s, giving

them a simple grandeur and purity. This neo-classical influence ran alongside 19thC Romanticism, which also sought to evoke the realities and indeed the heroism of contemporary life and recent history as it affected the artists. In painting, its chief exponents were Géricault and Delacroix; in literature, Balzac, Dumas and Victor Hugo; in music, Berlioz and Chopin.

Realism and Impressionism
The first significant break from the classical tradition came as an off-shoot of Romanticism with Corot's landscapes, and those of Barbizon School artists Millet and Rousseau. Often working in the open air with ready-mixed paints, they strived to achieve a more spontaneous and naturalistic approach than their predecessors. But the new style was far from popular. Public criticism of Socialist painter Courbet's work led him to classify it as 'Realism'; which together with Manet's dramatic use of bold colour and shadow heavily influenced the up-and-coming Impressionists, Monet, Renoir and Pissarro.

The term Impressionism, coined by a disparaging critic at an exhibition in 1874, stuck. As its advocates abandoned form in the pursuit of naturalism, Flaubert and Zola reflected a similar drift in their writing; while Debussy and Ravel explored atmosphere in their music.

Form was still a force to be reckoned with in architecture, however (the neo-Baroque Paris Opéra, Haussman's *grands boulevards*); and the concept of Modernism, new materials and structural skills, inspired the centrepiece of the Paris Exhibition in 1889, the Eiffel Tower.

Twentieth Century
The Fauves ('Wild Beasts') Derain, Matisse and Vlaminck painted the town red (the sky green and the sea orange) at the turn of the century, while Pablo Picasso favoured blue, then explored Cubism with Braque. Between the two world wars, Constructivism, Dadaism, Expressionism and Surrealism excited and confused the art world; literary figures from Hemingway to Beckett flocked to Paris to join Anouilh, Camus and Genet in the cultural crucible of Europe. Meanwhile, Jean-Paul Sartre

formulated the principles of Existentialism; and French cinema, the natural visual extension of Existentialism, flourished with the work of Renoir and Carne, followed, in the 1950s, by Chabrol, Truffaut and Godard.

Almost a century's worth of urban planning has seen the pendulum swing from the first dreary concrete high rises and Le Corbusier's socially admirable but aesthetically disappointing Cité Radieuse to the daring love-it-or-loathe-it Centre Georges Pompidou in Paris. Inner city rejuvenation has led to large-scale restoration projects such as Rouen's half-timbered old town centre, and juxtaposed exciting new buildings with historical monuments as in Nîmes, while Paris has I.M. Pei's glass Pyramide at the Louvre, the spectacular Cité des Sciences et de l'Industrie at La Villette, and Mitterand's bid for immortality, the Grande Arche at La Défense.

Food and wine

Cooking is an art in France, and great chefs can enjoy the star status reserved for screen idols elsewhere. No other country displays such a passionate interest in food, and in the techniques of its culinary champions.

There are three main culinary styles in French cooking: classical, nouvelle and regional. The former, with its complex techniques for rich and varied sauces, delicate soufflés and intricate pâtisseries forms the basis of all other styles. Nouvelle cuisine, developed in the late 1960s and 70s, coincided with the move towards healthier eating and replaced the large portions and creamy sauces of traditional cooking with fresher, lighter combinations designed to maximize texture and flavour; presentation is elegant and stylized. Several nouvelle cuisine dishes have become classics in their own right, including magret de canard (lightly sautéed duck breast served with a reduced wine or fruit sauce). Few restaurants now serve exclusively nouvelle or classical dishes, but a mixture of the two.

The current trend favours wholesome and interesting regional dishes. Today's rising chefs are going back to their roots. Not just parsnips and turnips, but old regional recipes are dug out, dusted off and given a new and tempting look.

Wine is an intrinsic part of French cuisine, and sometimes an essential ingredient. It is of course a huge subject; here are some basic principles:

The chilled white wines of the Loire, (Muscadet, Saumur and Vouvray) make wonderful company for fish and shellfish; so do white Bordeaux, Burgundy or Chablis. A light Beaujolais gets my vote (though a few raised eyebrows) with heartier fish dishes.

Meat and game dishes are typically complemented by the big reds of Bordeaux and Burgundy; but don't ignore sun-baked Côtes du Rhone, and the lesser-known regional wines of the Ardèche, the Dordogne, Languedoc-Roussillon and the Côtes du Ventoux, where standards are being raised with every vintage.

The most delectable golden pudding wines come from Sauternes, southeast of Bordeaux, but there are also Monbazillac from the Dordogne, Beaumes-de-Venise from the Rhone Valley and Prestige d'Automne from the Pyrenean Juraçon region.

Spirits are many and varied, from the grape derivatives cognac, armagnac and fiery marc (distilled from the final pressings of grape pulp) to calvados (apple brandy) and eau de vie which is essentially alcohol flavoured with fruits or herbs.

Eating out

It should come as no surprise that eating out is a national pastime. French restaurants post a copy of the menu outside, which in addition to à la carte choices usually offers different prix fixé menus, and sometimes children's menus. Budget restaurants also serve fairly priced daily specials (plats du jour). Some prix fixé menus offer wine and coffee, all include bread, and most include the service charge (service compris). It is increasingly common not to put water on the table (actively discouraged during summer water shortages), but you can always ask for a carafe d'eau (tap water). Reasonably priced house wines are getting difficult to find, but modest restaurants usually serve vin ordinaire by the quarter- half- or one-litre jug (pichet); in a wine-growing region, check out the vin du pays.

North-Western France

Between Calais and Mont-Saint-Michel
Western Pas de Calais and Normandy

515 km; maps Michelin Nos 236 & 231

The coast of north-western France offers some of the most exciting and picturesque scenery in Europe. Between the sandy beaches of classy Le Touquet, overlooking the Channel, and the popular family holiday centres of Brittany's more sheltered southern coast, you will find the sculpted limestone cliffs of Normandy, the D-Day beaches, resorts both famous and simple, sprawling commercial ports, tiny fishing harbours and the jagged teeth of northern Brittany. Taken in conjunction with France Overall: 2, this section is your key to the north-west shoulder of France from Calais to Nantes, and is the ideal way to discover the best of what the region can offer the visitor.

While France Overall: 2 takes you through Brittany, this leg is essentially concerned with Normandy. The closest coastal region to Paris, Normandy's Channel ports have always been commercially and strategically important. William, Duke of Normandy, set off from here to conquer England, and his heirs spent considerable time and energy coming back. Proximity to Paris was the reason for Normandy's 'discovery' in the 19thC by artists in search of scenery; as was its patronage by fashionable society. The artists headed for Honfleur, Etretat and Rouen; the fashionable for Dieppe, Deauville and Trouville, a pattern still followed in most respects today.

Whereas the Normandy coast is fairly developed, the rural hinterland has remained remarkably *au naturel* (see Local Explorations 6 and 7.) The orchards and half-timbered manor houses of the Auge, the hills and rivers of the Suisse Normande and the rolling forests of the Perche might have been preserved in aspic – which brings me to food.

Normandy is a land literally overflowing with milk and honey – and cheese and cream and apples and calvados – all of which play an important rôle in the gourmet scheme of things. One thing you have to abandon in this region of France is your diet. There is, of course, an abundance of superb fish and shellfish, but a *marmite Dieppoise* or *sauce Normande* will ruin any attempt at calorie control.

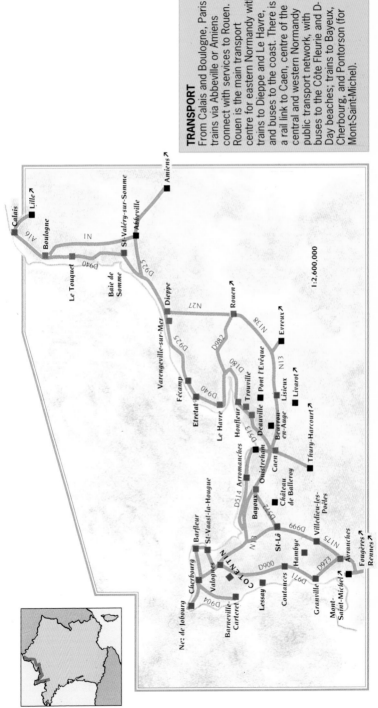

TRANSPORT

From Calais and Boulogne, Paris trains via Abbeville or Amiens connect with services to Rouen. Rouen is the main transport centre for eastern Normandy with trains to Dieppe and Le Havre, and buses to the coast. There is a rail link to Caen, centre of the central and western Normandy public transport network, with buses to the Côte Fleurie and D-Day beaches; trains to Bayeux, Cherbourg, and Pontorson (for Mont-Saint-Michel).

SIGHTS & PLACES OF INTEREST

Note: there are so many green sights in this route that there is not space to list each with an alphabetical heading. However, they are all described in the text below, under headings of associated places. And they are all picked out in **bold** *type. In particular, many green sights on the Cotentin Peninsula are covered under that heading.*

AMIENS
See *France Overall: 6.*

ARROMANCHES-LES-BAINS ⊭
See *D-Day Beaches, page 37, also Recommended Hotels.*

AVRANCHES ⊭ ✕
On the N175, 125 km S of Cherbourg. S.I. rue Général-de-Gaulle. A bustling and attractive town at the bottom of the Cotentin peninsula (see page 36), Avranches has a long and historic association with Mont-Saint-Michel which it overlooks across the bay (see France Overall: 2). In the 8thC, St Aubert, Bishop of Avranches, received two visitations from St Michael commanding him to build a church on the distant rock. When Aubert delayed, the impatient archangel prodded a hole in the abbot's skull, now a treasured relic on display in the Basilique de Saint-Gervais – Saint-Protais.

For a view of the midget Mont-Saint-Michel (midget-sized from this distance) you can head straight for the **Jardin des Plantes**; or walk up to **Square Thomas-à-Becket**, which is also known as *La Plate-Forme*, where a

---

DETOUR – **BALLEROY**
A popular excursion from Bayeux, 17thC **Château de Balleroy** (18 km SW via D572/D13; closed Wed and Nov-Feb) was designed by Mansart with gardens by Le Nôtre. The sumptuous *salon* is hung with Mignard's royal portraits of Louis XIII, Louis XIV and their families; also there is a hot air balloon museum. Nearby, the **Forêt de Cerisy** is a lovely spot for picnicking and walking, and there is an 11thC Norman abbey-church at Cerisy-la-Forêt.

---

grassy plot is chained off to mark the spot where Henry II of England allegedly did public penance in front of the cathedral (now disappeared) for the death of St Thomas at Canterbury.

The **Musée d'Avranches**, beautifully displayed in an annexe of the former episcopal palace, is well-worth a visit for its terrific collections of medieval wood carvings, sculpture, religious art and illuminated manuscripts.

Avranches is a starting point for Local Explorations: 2, covering Rennes and the Border Castles.

BAIE DE SOMME
On the D940, 105 km S of Calais. After a winding 245-km journey from its source near Saint-Quentin, the River Somme finally empties into this broad, sheltered bay where William the Conquerer took refuge from the elements on his way to invade England. A large natural preserve on the northern tip of the estuary surrounds the **Parc Ornothologique de Marquenterre**, a tract of dunes, wetlands and pine woods which offers sanctuary to a spectacular variety of wildfowl.

The fishing villages of **Le Crotoy** and **Saint-Valéry-sur-Somme** face each other across the bay, linked by an attractive steam train ride on the **Chemin de Fer de la Baie de Somme** in summer. Bicycles travel free and the train chugs on to the coast at Cayeux-sur-Mer.

Saint-Valéry is a charming base for exploring the area, a particularly pretty spot with its fishermen's cottages, tree-lined promenade, and 17thC Haute Ville. The S.I. in the Ville Basse has details of local attractions, such as the **Maison de l'Oiseau** bird museum, **Aqualand** water park, boating, and local riding stables.

BARFLEUR
And other green sights marked on the Cotentin Peninsula are covered under Cotentin Peninsula, page 36.

BAYEUX ⊭ ✕
On the N13, 28 km NW of Caen. S.I. 1 rue Cuisiniers (on corner with rue Saint-Martin). Bayeux was the first town to be liberated in 1944, and the fine historic town centre emerged unscathed, which makes visiting its world-famous tapestry all the more enjoyable.

Wrongly attributed to Queen Mathilde in the 18thC, the **Tapisserie** was probably commissioned in England by Odon, Bishop of Bayeux, (also spelt Odo) to decorate the nave of his new cathedral consecrated in 1077. Actually the 'tapestry' is an embroidery of wool on linen, and the 70-m masterpiece is divided into 58 scenes illustrating the background, the preparations for and indeed the Battle of Hastings which culminated in the defeat of King Harold. Audio-visual displays (in French and English) and a blow-by-blow description of events provides a thorough introduction before you experience the real thing, which snakes around a dramatically darkened room in all its glory. The vivid colours are a suprise, and the tale is further enlivened by a delightful border depicting hunting and farming scenes, mythical beasts, animals and birds.

Bishop Odon's **Cathédrale de Notre-Dame** is an arresting medieval edifice with a great Romanesque façade flanked by towers with pointed Gothic spires, a graceful 15thC tower (but an unfortunate 19thC top-knot), and east end supported by an elegant arrangement of buttresses. High windows fill the 12thC nave with light and illuminate beautiful woven and knotted Norman decorative carvings. There is marvellous stained glass, and the triple tiers of arches in the choir are supported on skeins of pillars.

North of the cathedral, the **Musée Baron Gérard** displays fine arts and crafts, ceramics and furniture; on the south side, the **Musée Diocésain d'Art Religieux** parades ecclesiastical treasures including elaborate vestments. The **Musée Mémorial de la Bataille de Normandie** (closed Mon-Fri Nov-Mar), boulevard Fabian-Ware, recounts the events of June 7 to August 2 1944, across the street from the British War Cemetery.

BOULOGNE ⇔ ✕

On the N1, 34 *km* SW *of Calais.* S.I. *quai de la Poste, Ville Basse.* By far the most entertaining Pas de Calais ferry port, Boulogne is also in the running for Europe's largest fishing centre. Not suprisingly, fish feature heavily on the itinerary, be it a weekend spent sampling the local fish restaurants, or a visit to **Nausicaà**, the stunning new national aquarium facing the port.

It is a hearty, but worthwhile climb up to the attractive Ville Haute, its medieval ramparts and cobbled streets preserved like a film set. The main drag, **rue de Lille**, is jam-packed with cafés, restaurants, gift shops, and delicatessens.

Off rue de Lille, the 19thC **Basilique de Notre-Dame** has been squeezed into a gap vacated first by a Roman temple and then a Romanesque cathedral destroyed during the Revolution. Traces of the earlier edifices can be seen in the labyrinthine subterranean crypt. A little further on, rue du Château leads to the **Château-Musée** displaying arts, crafts, ceramics and Napoleonic memorabilia, plus ethnographic objects from Eskimo masks to Egyptian mummies.

For hypermarket shopping, there is a handy **Champion** supermarket on the quay, or head for **Auchan** (N42 east). General shopping is better in the Ville Basse around **rue Thiers**, where **Philippe Olivier** (No.45) deserves a special mention for his gourmet *fromagerie*. And Boulogne's Saturday market, on place Dalton, should not be missed.

If you are heading north for Calais, the D940 makes an attractive alternative to the faster N1, with great views from the cliff-top heights of Cap Gris Nez and Cap Blanc Nez.

CAEN ⇔ ✕

On the N13, 125 *kms* SE *of Cherbourg.* S.I. *place Saint-Pierre.* Capital of Basse Normandie, 15 km inland from the ferry port at Ouistreham, Caen came to prominence in the 11thC as William the Conquerer's Norman headquarters. The otherwise dreary post-war city centre is graced by a suprising collection of fine medieval buildings, several of which were used as civilian shelters during the Allied bombing raids of 1944. This vital information was relayed by the Resistance and the sites were studiously avoided by Allied pilots as they reduced 80 per cent of the town to rubble.

After the Battle of Val-ès-Dunes, when William the Bastard mopped up the Norman nobility and asserted his rights as Duke of Normandy, he married his distant cousin, Mathilda of Flanders, a liaison not approved by the

33

Pope. William was excommunicated. Lanfranc, the renowned Italian scholar and abbot of le Bec, managed to get the decree lifted, and in order to reconcile themselves with the church, the couple each founded an abbey.

William's **Abbaye aux Hommes**, to the west of the town centre, now houses the Hôtel de Ville (open for tours) overlooking colourful gardens. Lanfranc laid the foundation stone of the abbey-church, **Saint-Etienne**, with a superb Romanesque façade which could have come straight from the plains of his native Lombardy. Mathilda's **Abbaye aux Dames**, to the east, has suffered more over the years, but the Romanesque **Eglise de la Trinité**, where the Queen was buried in 1083, remains an impressive edifice.

Around place Saint-Pierre, survivors of the blitz include the 16thC **Hôtel d'Escoville** next to the S.I., and the **Eglise de Saint-Pierre**. Fortunately, the marvellous Renaissance decorations of sinuous figures and foliage, urns and balustrades adorning the east end of the church were untouched when the spire was sent crashing through the nave by a Second World War shell. The restored interior changes character from simple 14thC vaulting to bursts of Flamboyant ribs flowering into pendant keystones above the chancel, and in the finely carved ambulatory chapels.

On a grassy knoll above the church, the citadel ramparts enclose gardens, the **Musée de Normandie**, and recently-refurbished **Musée des Beaux-Arts** (both closed Tues). The latter's impressive collections range from 15thC Flemish and Italian primitives through a notable catalogue of European masters (Rubens, Tintoretto, van Dyck), 19thC Romantics and Impressionists to the present day.

To the north-west of the town centre, Caen's **Mémorial pour la Paix** is a worthy addition to the countless war museums scattered around Normandy. By way of displays and audio-visual presentations, the 'peace memorial' attempts to broaden the picture and introduce a less gung-ho and accusatory style, charting the rise of facism in Germany, collaboration as well as the Resistance during the Occupation, and the D-Day landings from both the German and Allied perspectives.

British visitors bound for the ferry at Ouistreham might like to stock up at the **Leclerc** supermarket, rue Leclerc. For more recherché gourmet treats, don't miss **Hédiard**, cour des Halles.

Caen is the ideal starting point for Local Explorations: 6, The Heart of Normandy.

CALAIS ⇌ ×

On the A26, 292 km N of Paris. S.I. 12 rue Clemenceau. Every year around 10 million British visitors arrive in Calais and most of them disappear over the horizon without so much as a backward glance. In all honesty, they are not missing much, but turn back the clock 700 years, and you find that Calais was the focus of considerable English interest. After the Battle of Crécy in 1346, Edward III laid bloody siege to the city for eight months. Eventually, six local burghers offered themselves bareheaded and barefooted together with the keys to Calais to prevent further slaughter. They were reprieved at the last moment thanks to Queen Philippa, but the English (known as the 'goddons' for their frequent 'god-damns'), remained in control of Calais until 1558. The eventual loss of England's last French possession prompted a despairing Mary Tudor to remark that she would go to the grave with 'Calais' engraved on her heart.

All but rebuilt since the Second World War, the main shopping area is in Calais-Nord, around place d'Armes with its sole pre-War survivor the 13thC **Tour Guet**, and rue Royale. In addition to paintings and sculpture, the **Musée des Beaux-Arts et de la Dentelle**, rue Richelieu, celebrates the city's lace-making industry, introduced from Nottingham in the early 19thC; while across Pont George-V, in Calais-Sud, the fanciful turn-of-the-century Flemish-style **Hôtel de Ville** dwarfs Rodin's superb *Bourgeois de Calais*, and leafy Parc Saint-Pierre, where a German bunker houses wartime relics in the **Musée de la Guerre**.

Calais' big supermarkets, **Continent** and **Mammouth,** are situated out on the main Boulogne road (N1); those in search of wine may find something of interest at **Le Chais,** 40 rue de Strasbourg.

As an alternative to the N1/A1 heading south, you can leave Calais by the

• *Burghers of Calais.*

D940, following signs from the town centre for the **Côte d'Opale**. At first you pass through boring Blériot and **Sangatte** (D940). The latter is the new Eurotunnel terminal. The **information centre** may detain you, otherwise turn right and speed away as fast as you can. The roller-coaster cliff-top road offers marvellous views across the Channel with worthwhile stops at Cap Blanc Nez (for the **Eurotunnel Museum**), and Cap Gris Nez.

CHERBOURG ⊨ ×

On the N13, 125 km NW of Caen. S.I. quai Alexandre-III. Only qualifying for mention by virtue of its status as an incoming ferry port, Cherbourg is best left behind as soon as possible (see the Cotentin Peninsula, page 36).

If you do have time to spare here, you could view the panorama of the town and enormous harbour from the **Fort Roule** with its Second World War museum on the main Valognes road (N13). There is a vast **Auchun** hypermarket off the N13; or plunder the equally huge **Mammouth** or **Continent** supermarkets in town. For wine, try the **Cave du Roy,** rue de la Tour Carrée.

DEAUVILLE ⊨ ×

On the D573, 15 km W of Honfleur.S.I. place de la Mairie. A fashionable resort since the 19thC, Deauville emerged as a ritzy playground, complete with race-track, casinos, a medley of king-size half-timbered seaside 'cottages' and ostentatious hotels lining the flower-packed **boulevard Eugène-Cornuché**. Both Deauville and neighbouring Trouville boast broad sand beaches edged by boardwalks, marinas, casinos and a range of activities such as riding and tennis. Deauville's July-August high season is renowned for racing (steeplechasing and flat), regattas and conspicuous consumption. In September, the town hosts a suprisingly accessible American Film Festival.

On the east bank of the River Toques, **Trouville** (S.I. 32 boulevard Fernand-Moureaux) still operates as a fishing port and town distinct from its resort status, conferred in the 1860s when it was 'discovered' by Napoleon III and his merry men.

The smaller resorts along the so-called **Côte Fleurie**, such as **Cabourg** and **Villiers-sur-Mer** to the west, are pleasant but not exactly bargains. There is a pretty drive east to **Honfleur** (see page 39) on the D513 through rolling, leafy countryside past dozens of small farms offering cider and calvados tastings and sales.

DIEPPE ⚓ ✕

On the D925, 105 km E of Le Havre. S.I. Pont Levis. Flanked by limestone headlands at the eastern end of the Côte d'Albâtre, Dieppe is France's oldest seaside resort and a busy ferry and fishing port. The pebble beach is less of an attraction these days, but the town makes a base for local excursions and is well-endowed with hotels and excellent fish restaurants.

There is always plenty of action in the morning fish market, glittering with a profusion of bream, sole, turbot and scallops. The main shopping street is Grande Rue, south of which the 13th-16thC **Cathédrale de Saint-Jacques** (a popular subject of Pissarro) shows its age, a posse of slathering gargoyles and chapels built by various Dieppois shipping magnates.

Head west through the dark, narrow

COTENTIN PENINSULA

Punching out into the Channel like a clenched fist, the Cotentin peninsula marks the border of Normandy, but mirrors the robust, windswept beauty of Brittany along its western shoreline. Turn west from Cherbourg, on the coastal D45 via tiny **Port Racine**, to the wild, rocky promontary of **La Hague**, and the 120-m cliffs of **Nez de Jobourg**, and you will see what I mean. Mountainous sand dunes sweep south in great arcs to **Barneville-Carteret**, a port and resort anchored in granite behind a jutting headland patrolled by the Sentier des Douaniers footpath. 'Rock-solid' is the first description that springs to mind of **Granville** with its sturdy old stone houses tucked behind ramparts on the cliff-top facing Mont-Saint-Michel bay. This is the place to catch ferries to the Channel Islands, and it is also a popular yachting and holiday centre.

East of Cherbourg, **Barfleur** was once the peninsula's main port. Now its pretty harbour serves as a pleasant yachting and fishing centre. There are terrific views from the Gatteville lighthouse on **Pointe de Barfleur**, where the *White Ship* foundered in 1120 with 300 Anglo-Norman nobles on board including William, heir to the English throne. The young prince's death caused his father, Henry I, never to smile again. South of Barfleur, the D1 passes a lovely 16thC manor, **La Crasvillerie** (picnic spot with a fine view on the

left). **Saint-Vaast-la-Hougue**, known for its oysters, has recently opened a maritime museum on the Ile de Tatihou, an old quarantine station with a Vauban tower 1 km offshore.

Moving inland, the **Val de Saire** is a delight. (You can make an easy three-cornered circuit from the D902 N of Quetthou: take the D26 to le Vast, D25 NE to Valcanville, and return on the D125.) **Valognes** describes itself as the 'Norman Versailles' on account of its mansions, including the 18thC Hôtel de Beaumont (open Jul-Sep); **Lessay** has a beautifully-restored Romanesque abbey-church; and **Coutances** merits a visit for its magnificent cathedral. This perfectly proportioned Gothic *tour de force* has two highly ornamental towers which culminate in a flurry of turrets, from which graceful spires soar on upwards, and there is a fine octagonal lantern tower. In the peaceful, lush Sienne valley, the towering ruins of the 12thC **Abbaye de Hambye** nestle in one of the most serene settings in Cotentin. Due south, **Villedieu-les-Poêles**, a spic-and-span little town with grey stone and white-shuttered houses and a bustling Tuesday market is renowned for the copper and pewter fashioned in its workshops since the 17thC, and for its bell foundry. Its name translates literally as 'God's town of the pots and frying pans'.

You can eat well at Saint-Vaast-la-Hougue and at Hambye: see Recommended Restaurants.

18thC streets or along the promenade to the stalwart 15thC **Château**, perched on the hillside (closed Tues out of season). It houses the **Musée de Dieppe** with local history and crafts exhibits, fine arts including Impressionist paintings and a selection of prints by Normandy-born Cubist artist Georges Braque, which are displayed in rotation, but the *pièce de résistance* is a superb collection of 16th-19thC carved ivories for which the town's craftsmen were justly famed.

There is plenty to see and do around Dieppe, which has public transport connections to **Rouen** (page 41), and **Varengeville** (page 43). Guy de Maupassant, creator of the perfectly-turned short story, was born in the elegant 17th-18thC **Château de Miromesnil** (8 km S via N27; open pm May-Oct; closed Tues) with a lovely walled garden; and keen gardeners should treat themselves to a visit to Frédéric and Catherine Cotelle's gorgeous English-style garden and nursery at **Derchigny-Graincourt** (7 km NE via D925). Shopping: **Olivier**, 18 rue Saint-Jacques, is a tempting town centre delicatessen; and there is a **Mammouth** hypermarket on the N27, or a **Leclerc** at Neuville-les-Dieppe.

ETRETAT ⋈ ✕

On the D940, 28 km N of Le Havre. S.I. place Maurice-Guillard (summer only). A popular small seaside resort, Etretat lies wedged between a pair of much-painted and photographed, but still impressive limestone arches jutting out from the cliffs and into the sea. The town centre has some attractive olde-worlde buildings, such as the rebuilt covered market, **Les Halles**. Above the pebble shore, there are a couple of engaging beached boat-cum-sheds, and paths lead up to the cliffs: the **Falaise d'Aval** to the west, and **Falaise d'Amont** to the east. On top of the latter, the **Musée Nungessor et Coli** commemorates the two early aviators who disappeared on a transatlantic flight in 1927 (closed Mon-Fri out of season).

EVREUX

See Local Explorations: 7.

FECAMP ✕

On the D940, 40 km NE of Le Havre. S.I.

DETOUR – **D-DAY BEACHES**

On the night of June 5-6, 1944, Operation Overlord, the Allied invasion force under the overall command of General Eisenhower, set sail from southern England for the Calvados coast. Convinced by the failure of the 1942 raid on Dieppe that the French channel ports were too well defended, they made for the beaches north and west of Caen. The Americans landed in the western sector at **Utah** (on the Cotentin peninsula) and **Omaha** beaches. British troops went ashore at **Gold**, Canadians at **Juno**, and Anglo-French commandos on the eastern end, **Sword**. A beachhead was established at **Arromanches-les-Bains,** where a Mulberry B artificial port was swiftly assembled to receive 9,000 tons of equipment daily; some four million tons of materials, 500,000 vehicles and more than two million men were put ashore here in the following three months.

The battle for Normandy lasted until late August, at a cost of 100,000 soldiers' lives, many thousands of civilian casualties and some 200,000 buildings destroyed or damaged. Most of the small seaside towns caught in Overlord's initial stages – Courseulles, Arromanches, Tour-en-Bessin – have evolved into lively summer resorts, but the beaches' wartime code names have stuck and in addition to a plethora of municipal and private war museums (the best one is at Caen, see page 33), you can still see the remains of the Mulberry B harbour at Arromanches-les-Bains; the shattered German battery and shell-scarred cliff at **Pointe du Hoc** overlooking Omaha beach; and several dozen poignant and immaculately tended war cemeteries. The main British cemeteries are at **Bayeux, Banneville-la-Campagne** and **Ranville**; the American at **Colleville-Saint-Laurent,** behind Omaha Beach. The largest is the German cemetery at **La Cambe,** where 21,000 soldiers are buried.

• *Etretat.*

rue Alexandre Le Grand. Cod, God and a sticky liqueur are the chief ingredients of Fécamp. It is also a busy summer resort with a pleasant sea-front promenade and marina which has displaced the sadly depleted fishing port.

Fécamp's monastic heritage can be traced back to the 7thC when a monastery was established here to guard a relic of the Precious Blood. By the 11thC, it had become a major pilgrim centre protected by the Dukes of Normandy who founded the **Eglise de la Trinité**. The present Norman Gothic abbey-church dates from the 13thC, and is one of the largest in France, with a bleak unadorned nave, soaring lantern tower and superb chancel decorated with carved Renaissance screens. Pilgrimages still take place on the Tuesday and Thursday after Trinity. From Norman Gothic to nightmarish neo-Gothic, the distinctly theatrical 19thC **Palais Bénédictine** (closed Nov-Easter), rue Alexandre Le Grand, houses a joint museum-cum-PR exercise devoted to the famous local Benedictine liqueur invented by monks in the 15thC. You take in relics from past abbeys and antique alembics before encountering the liqueur itself – adults qualify for a tasting. Two other museums worth a mention are the **Musée des Terre-Neuvas et de la Pêche**, boulevard Albert-1er, which charts the history of the local fishing industry and its exploits on the high seas off Newfoundland; and the **Musée Centre des Arts**, rue Alexandre-Legros, with examples of antique furniture, ceramics and Dieppois ivories displayed in an 18thC *hôtel particulier*.

FOUGERES
See Local Explorations: 2.

LE HAVRE ⊨ ✕
On the A15, 205 km NW of Paris. S.I. place de l'Hôtel-de-Ville. France's second largest port, Le Havre sprawls along the right bank of the Seine estuary behind a forest of cranes and refineries. Founded by François I in 1517, it developed important trade links with

North America during the War of Independence, and later became the major European terminal for the luxury liners of the 1920s-30s. Ferries from England and Ireland still deposit more than a million passengers a year in the port, but few consider staying longer than it takes to raid the giant hypermarkets (**Auchan** at the Centre Commercial Mont Gaillard, and **Mammouth** at Montvilliers).

The post-war city centre, designed by Auguste Perret, is a monument to the dubious charms of concrete. Two notable examples are the elongated **Hôtel de Ville**, juxtaposed by its 17-storey tower; and the **Eglise de Saint-Joséph**, labouring under an 84-m octagonal belfry. The latest architectural talking point, Oscar Niemayer's **Centre Culturel**, lies anchored in a plaza by the Bassin du Commerce like a smoke stack sheered off some gargantuan liner. For a well-illustrated guide to the town's history and urban development, head for the **Musée de l'Ancien Havre**, 1 rue Jerôme-Bellarmato, in the Saint-François district (closed Mon-Tues).

One excellent reason to delay your departure from Le Havre is the **Musée des Beaux-Arts André-Malraux** (closed Tues), at the port entrance on place Guynemer. The metal and glass construction provides a spacious and well-lit environment for exceptional collections of 19th-20thC French paintings from local boys Eugène Boudin and Raoul Dufy, Impressionists including Monet, Pissarro, Renoir and Sisley, and modern abstract artists such as Dubuffet and Lurçat.

HONFLEUR 🚤 ✕
On the D513, 15 km NE of Deauville. S.I. place Boudin. A picture-postcard Norman port in the Seine estuary, Honfleur gathers its skirts around the **Vieux Bassin**, the historic port where Samuel Champlain set sail to found Quebec in 1608. The entrance to the basin is still guarded by the twin-turreted remnants of **La Lieutenance**, the former governor's residence, while a delightful collection of tall and pencil-thin buildings faced in brick and grey slate cast wobbly reflections over the water from **quai Sainte-Catherine**. Opposite, on quai Saint-Etienne, two small museums, the **Musée de la Marine** and

Musée du Vieux Honfleur display nautical memorabilia and local history (closed Mon-Fri out of season).

Edged in by narrow streets bulging with galleries, crisp linen-clad restaurants and window boxes bursting with rambling geraniums, the wooden **Eglise de Sainte-Catherine** was built by local shipwrights after the Hundred Years War. Supported on stone piers, the wooden building is cloaked in chestnut wood shingles with delicate carved angels decorating the porch, its twin naves are supported on wooden posts. The separate belfry sports a clock tower above its square half-timbered base. Despite Samuel Champlain's exploits in the New World, the town's chief claim to fame lies in its 19thC artistic connections. It was the birthplace of Eugène Boudin, a forerunner of the Impressionist movement, who tutored the young Monet, and was visited by the likes of Renoir and Cézanne. Dufy, Corot and Courbet also spent time here, and several of the fruits of their labours are displayed in the excellent **Musée Eugène Boudin** (closed Tues).

In the good old days, penniless artists gathered at Mère Toutain's **Ferme Saint-Siméon**, now a gorgeous luxury hotel, where you can stay in Corot's bay-windowed studio (see Recommended Hotels). Transformed from cheap artists' haunt to popular resort, Honfleur's many restaurants offer few bargains. A pleasant alternative is to pick up picnic materials from local shops and perch on the harbour wall or take refuge from the crowds in the public gardens along from quai des Passengers.

LILLE
See France Overall: 9.

LISIEUX 🚤 ✕
On the N13, 80 km W of Rouen. S.I. 11 rue d'Alençon. Commercial centre of the Auge, Lisieux is somewhat short on charm for which this region is renowned. However, this is of little consequence to the town's chief stock-in-trade, the steady stream of pilgrims to the irredeemably tasteless neo-Byzantine **Basilique de Sainte-Thérèse**, erected in memory of St Theresa of Lisieux. Born Thérèse Martin at Alençon in 1873, the deeply pious

young girl petitioned the pope to join a convent aged 15, and then went on to die of tuberculosis at only 24, having completed her spiritual memoires, *History of a Soul*.

St Theresa herself was fortunate enough to worship in the fine **Cathédrale de Saint-Pierre**, founded in 1170, with a splendid Flamboyant chapel commissioned by Pierre Cauchon, the bishop of Lisieux who stage-managed Joan of Arc's trial for the English. Nearby, the **Palais de Justice** is housed in the former bishop's palace overlooking pleasant public gardens. Lisieux has a couple of small museums, and you can make a tour of the various St Theresa sites including the Martin family home, **Les Buissonnets**.

Rather more entertaining, the S.I. provides maps to guide you around the cheese, cider and calvados producers of the **Vallée de la Vie**, stretching south of town towards Livarot (see Local Explorations: 6), Vimoutiers (see Local Explorations: 6) and Gacé. En route to Caen, **Beuvron-en-Auge** (28 km W via N13/D49) is one of the most picturesque Auge villages, full of delightful half-timbered buildings, plus a good restaurant (see Recommended Restaurants).

LIVAROT
See Local Explorations: 6.

MONT-SAINT-MICHEL
See France Overall: 2.

RECOMMENDED HOTELS

ARROMANCHES-LES-BAINS
La Marine, F-FF; *quai du Canada; tel. 31 22 34 19; credit cards V; closed mid-Nov to Mar.*

Pleasant modern hotel with simple sunny rooms, and a seafood restaurant on the promenade.

AVRANCHES
Croix d'Or, F-FF; *83 rue de la Constitution; tel. 33 58 04 88; credit cards V; closed mid-Nov to mid-Mar.*

A 300-year-old Norman coaching inn with rooms in a broad price range. Pretty garden, and a restaurant serving regional dishes.

Auberge de la Sélune, F-FF; *2 rue Saint-Germain, Ducey (10 km SE via D78); tel. 33 48 53 62; credit cards DC, MC, V; closed Mon Oct-Feb, and mid-Jan to mid-Feb.*

Plain but comfortable village hotel with a pretty riverside garden (salmon fishing by arrangement). Delicious home cooking.

BARNEVILLE-CARTERET
Les Iles, F-FF; *9 boulevard Maritime; tel. 33 04 90 76; credit cards AE, V; closed Mon off season, mid-Jan to mid-Feb.*

Beach-front family hotel and seafood restaurant (half-board only in season).

BAYEUX
Hôtel d'Argouges, FF; *21 rue Saint-Patrice; tel. 31 92 88 86; credit cards AE, DC, MC, V; open year round.*

Elegant 18thC *hôtel particulier* and annexe with a warm welcome, in easy walking distance of the sights.

Reine Mathilde, F-FF; *23 rue Larcher; tel. 31 92 08 13; credit cards AE, V; closed Sun mid-Nov to mid-Mar, and mid-Dec to Feb.*

Pleasant, central small hotel with modern rooms in an old house. Café-restaurant open in summer.

BOULOGNE
Alexandra, F; *93 rue Thiers; tel. 21 30 52 22; credit cards V; open year round.*

Central, old-fashioned and a bargain. The S.I. is helpful with other budget recommendations.

Métropole, FF; *51 rue Thiers; tel. 21 31 54 30; credit cards AE, V; closed mid-Dec to early Jan.*

Pleasant central hotel with spacious rooms and a small garden.

CAEN
Hôtel Les Cordeliers, F; *4 rue Cordeliers; tel. 31 86 37 15; credit cards V; open year round.*

A 17thC building with a garden tucked away on a quiet street off rue Gemare. Simple rooms, and bar.

Le Relais des Gourmets, FF; *15 rue Geôle; tel. 31 86 06 01; credit cards AE, DC, V; open year round.*

The 32 attractive and sound-

RENNES
See Local Explorations: 2.

ROUEN
A 'red' stop on this National Route, but covered under Local Explorations: 7.

SAINT-LO
On the D972, 78 km S of Cherbourg. S.I. 2 rue Havin. Named the 'Capital of Ruins' after the Battle of Normandy, Saint-Lô has risen again around a handful of relics. One of the most moving is the creeper-clad portal of the old prison on **place de Gaulle**, left as a monument to deportees and members of the Resistance, also the soldiers and unprotected prisoners who died in the battle of July 1944.

Just below place de Gaulle, the badly damaged **Eglise de Notre-Dame** (with a shell case still embedded in its wall) has been simply and strikingly repaired with a sheer face of sea-green slate bricks inset with modern bronze doors. Inside, a small collection of carved masonry rescued from the wreckage hangs next to photographs of the devastation; and the modern stained glass includes Max Ingrand's *St Thomas à Becket* at the top of the right aisle.

On place Champ du Mars, the **Musée des Beaux-Arts** (closed Tues) has more to offer than the sterile, white-tiled *ensemble culturel* might lead you to believe. There are some terrific 19thC paintings by the likes of Boudin, Corot and Millet, plus Léger and a Jean Lurçat

---

proofed rooms are the best in town.

CALAIS
Meurice, FF; *5 rue Edmond-Roche; tel. 21 34 57 03; credit cards AE, DC, V; open year round.*
Quiet, modern hotel with classy restaurant, highly rated by locals.

Hotel Windsor, F; *2 rue Commandant-Bonningue; tel. 21 34 59 40; credit cards AE, DC, V; open year round.*
In the direction of the port from place d'Armes. Simple, comfy and well-priced rooms. Call ahead.

CHERBOURG
Louvre, F-FF; *2 rue Henri-Dunant; tel. 33 53 02 28; credit cards AE, V; closed Christmas and New Year.*
Traditional town-centre hotel with spacious, modern rooms, private garage and friendly staff.

Moderna, F; *28 rue de la Marine; tel. 33 43 05 30; credit cards AE, V; open year round.*
Central family hotel with 25 bright, modern rooms close to the port.

COUTANCES
Verte Campagne, F; *Hameau Chevalier, Trelly (12 km S via D7/349/D539); tel. 33 47 65 33; credit cards V; closed two weeks Dec, two weeks Feb.*
Lovely old Norman farmhouse, creeper-clad, cosy and inviting. Very plain bedrooms, but a simple country inn of great character.

DEAUVILLE
Hôtel du Golf, FF-FFF; *Mont Canisy (3 km S via D278); tel. 31 88 19 01; credit cards AE, DC, MC, V; open year round.*
Deauville's only stylish option, in the **FF** category, perched above town with views of the coast. Luxurious rooms, golf, tennis, pool and elegant dining in *La Pommerie*.
If money is no object, **Le Royal**, boulevard Eugène-Cornuché *(tel. 31 98 66 33)*, and **Le Normandy**, 38 rue Jean-Mermoz *(tel. 31 98 66 22)* are the super-deluxe classics.

DIEPPE
Les Arcades, F; *1-3 arcades de la Bourse; tel. 35 84 14 12; credit cards V; closed Christmas and New Year.*
Godsend for weary ferry passengers, opposite the port. Cheap, clean rooms; simple restaurant. Call ahead.

Auberge du Clos Normande, FF; *22 rue Henri-IV, Martin-Eglise (7 km SE via D1); tel. 35 82 71 01; credit cards AE, DC, V; closed Mon-Tues, two weeks Apr, four weeks Nov-Dec.*
Peace and quiet in a delightful small hotel-restaurant with gardens by the river. Generous *cuisine Normande* (plenty of fish) in the beamed dining room of the 15thC house.

ETRETAT
Le Donjon, FFF; *chemin de Saint-Clair; tel. 35 27 08 23; credit cards AE, DC, V; open year round.*
Cliff-top, mini-château ideal for a ➡

tapestry from the 20thC.

Horsy types should get a kick out of the **Haras de Saint-Lô**, rue Maréchal-Juin (open mid-Jul to mid-Feb). This national stud farm is one of the largest breeding centres in France, home to more than 120 stallions. There is a free show and carriage parade on Thursdays in August.

SAINT-VALERY-SUR-SOMME
See Baie de Somme, page 32.

THURY-HARCOURT
See Local Explorations: 6.

LE TOUQUET ⌫ ✕
On the N39, 63 km SW of Calais. S.I.

Palais de l'Europe. Le Touquet-Paris-Plage (to give it its full title) sprang from the grand 19thC tradition of Englishmen abroad 'discovering' beaches the French had previously overlooked (through lack of interest it must be said) – Lord Brougham at Cannes, for instance, and in this case Yorkshire businessman John Whitley. The 'Paris-Plage' was a splendid advertising wheeze (Le Touquet is more than 200 km from the capital), enticing the great and the good to disport themselves in its fashionable hotels and casinos and on the magnificent beach. Satisfied customers included Sarah Bernhardt, Louis Pasteur, and the future Edward VII; it was still all the rage between the

➡ romantic break. Individually-decorated rooms, candle-lit dining room, and pool terrace far above the crowds.

Normandie, F-FF; place Foch; tel. 35 27 06 99; credit cards AE, V; open year round.

Refurbished town-centre hotel with popular modern-rustic dining room (closed Wed lunch-Thur Oct-Easter).

FECAMP and HAMBYE
See Recommended Restaurants.

LE HAVRE
Hôtel Foch, F-FF; 4 rue Caligny; tel. 35 42 50 69; credit cards AE, DC, V; open year round.

Quiet, central hotel with spruce and comfy rooms near the marina.

Hôtel Parisien, F-FF; 1 cours de la République; tel. 35 25 23 83; credit cards AE, V; open year round.

Handy station hotel with basic but spotless rooms.

Also the larger **Astoria**, 13 cours de la République; (tel. 35 25 00 03), which has a restaurant.

HONFLEUR
Le Belvédère, F-FF; 30 rue Emile-Renouf; tel. 31 89 08 13; credit cards V; closed mid-Nov to mid-Dec, three weeks Jan.

Sprawling, yet comfortable house above the town with a good restaurant (closed Sun dinner-Mon Oct-Apr). Pretty gardens; peace and quiet.

Hôtel du Dauphin, F-FF; 10 place Pierre-Berthelot; tel. 31 89 15 53; credit cards DC, V; closed Jan.

Small hotel, neat as a pin and recently redecorated, a couple of steps away from Sainte-Catherine.
Ferme Saint Siméon; FFF; rue Aldolphe-Marais; tel. 31 89 23 61; credit cards AE, DC, MC, V; open year round.

Top-notch Relais et Châteaux establishment with all the necessary accoutrements including leisure centre, indoor pool and luxurious restaurant.

LISIEUX
Coupe d'Or, F-FF; 49 rue Pont-Mortain; tel. 31 31 16 84; credit cards AE, DC, MC, V; open year round.

Conveniently central old-fashioned hotel-restaurant. Popular dining room with a wide variety of menus.

SAINT-VAAST-LA-HOUGUE
Hôtel France et Fuchias, F-FF; rue Maréchal-Foch; tel. 33 54 42 26; credit cards DC, V; closed Jan to mid-Feb.

An old favourite within easy striking distance of Cherbourg. Peaceful, old-fashioned rooms in main house, more sophisticated ones in the annexe. Appealing conservatory dining room.

SAINT-VALERY-SUR-SOMME
Hôtel du Port et des Bains, F; 1 quai Blavet; tel. 22 60 80 09; credit cards V; closed Nov.

Picturesque quay-side inn with 14 simple rooms. The rustic dining room is a local favourite.

wars when P.G. Wodehouse lived here.

After a post-war slump, Le Touquet is back on form. Luxurious mansions hidden in the woods give way to a chic and bustling town centre, its narrow streets crammed with smart little boutiques, galleries and perfumeries, not to mention the celebrated fishmonger-cum-restaurant, **Chez Pérard**, 67 rue de Metz, which sells jars of its own-brand fish soup. There are gorgeous flowers, grand hotels, and the uproariously kitsch Hôtel de Ville, jewel in the crown of a wondrously bizarre collection of seaside architectural follies running the gamut from full-blown Gothic and Scottish Baronial to half-timbered rustic mansions and Swiss chalets.

LE TOUQUET
Château de Montreuil, FFF; *chaussée Capuchins, Montreuil (18 km E via N39); tel. 21 81 53 04; credit cards* MC, V; *closed mid-Dec to late Jan.*

Gorgeous 1930s country house set in peaceful English gardens. Each luxurious room has its own character. Christian Germain's cuisine has a Michelin star and numerous fans.

Novotel, FF-FFF; *La Plage; tel.* 21 09 85 00; *credit cards* AE, DC, MC, V; *closed Jan.*

Sea-front spa hotel at the southern end of the beach. Rooms are large, bright and well-equipped with sea views; restaurant, pool and sauna.

Westminster, FFF; *avenue Verger; tel.* 21 05 48 48; *credit cards* AE, DC, MC, V; *closed Jan to mid-Feb.*

The last of Le Touquet's hey-day hotels, elegantly overhauled and luxuriously appointed.

In the same price bracket, the smaller, but very swish Norman-style **Le Manoir** *(tel. 21 05 20 22)*, has its own golf course in a secluded woodland setting.

VARENGEVILLE-SUR-MER
La Terrasse, F-FF; *Vasterival (3 km NW on D75); tel.* 35 85 12 54; *credit cards* V; *closed Oct to mid-Mar.*

Turn-of-the-century house edged by pines and perched above the shore. 25 rooms (half-board only), fish specialties in the restaurant, and a tennis court.

Le Touquet is looking very sporty in the 1990s with tennis, riding, sailing, clay pigeon shooting and two-and-a-half golf courses near by. The vast sand beach (over 1 km wide at low tide) is a popular venue for land-yachting, and if the trek to the water's edge seems too far, there is the **Aqualud** pool complex on the promenade. If you owe the kids a treat, head for the **Bagatelle** amusement park at Merlimont (12 km S) for 26 acres of roundabouts, rides and fast food.

TROUVILLE
See under Deauville, page 35.

VARENGEVILLE-SUR-MER ⚐
On the D75, 10 km W of Dieppe. When Guillaume Mallet set to work on his country estate in 1898, he had some novel ideas. **Le Bois des Moutiers** was one of British architect Edwin Lutyens' first commissions, a stylish Arts and Crafts Movement manor, unique in France, and full of delightful eccentricities. But Mallet's real *tour de force* was the garden. Lutyens and Gertrude Jekyll collaborated on the walled gardens surrounding the house, which feature massed herbaceous borders divided by sculpted yew, glorious scented roses, clematis, lilies and cataracts of white wisteria. The lawn slopes down towards the sea and a woodland treasury of dramatic rhododendrons, azaleas, iris-edged streams and bosky glades carpeted with ferns (open mid-Mar to mid-Nov; house Jul-Aug only).

Just down the road is the churchyard where Georges Braque is buried beneath a rather ordinary mosaic affair. The interior of the little **Chapelle Sainte-Marguerite** boasts some luminous Braque stained glass, a couple of good memorials, and 16thC carved pillars decorated with a seasick mariner, pert mermaid, scallops and other nautical devices.

Dieppe's most famous 16thC shipowner, Jean d'Ango, built a country retreat at Varengeville, and the courtyard of **Maison d'Ango** is worth a detour. Part-palace, part-manor, part-barn, it encloses a spendidly ornate brick-patterned dovecote.

RECOMMENDED RESTAURANTS

AVRANCHES
Le Commerce, F; 5 *rue Général-de-Gaulle; tel.* 33 58 07 66; *cards* DC, V.

Welcoming dining room, steaming bowls of garlicky stuffed mussels and other regional dishes.

See also Recommended Hotels.

BAYEUX
Lion d'Or, FF-FFF; 71 *rue Saint-Jean; tel.* 31 92 06 90; *credit cards* AE, DC, MC, V; *closed mid-Dec to mid-Jan.*

Michelin-starred restaurant in Bayeux's smartest hotel. Faultless classical cuisine, fresh lobster.

La Rapière, F-FF; *off* 53 *rue Saint-Jean; tel.* 31 92 94 79; *closed Tues dinner-Wed off season.*

Popular little beamed restaurant, value-for-money menus – great fish soup, oysters, trout, veal *Normande* (with cream and apples).

BEUVRON-EN-AUGE
Le Pavé d'Auge, FF; *place du Village; tel.* 31 79 26 71; *credit cards* V; *closed Mon (except lunch Mar-Nov)-Tues, three weeks Jan, end Nov to mid-Dec.*

This bastion of Normandy cuisine is now in the young and capable hands of the Bansards. His simmered prawns and mussels in cider and *poulet Vallée d'Auge* are classics, and she is a superb *patissière.*

BOULOGNE
La Matelote, FF-FFF; 80 *boulevard Sainte-Beuve; tel.* 21 30 17 97; *credit cards* V; *closed Sun dinner, Christmas to mid-Jan.*

The fish restaurant in Boulogne with a reputation for light, innovative cuisine.

CAEN
Alcide, F; 1 *place Courtonne; tel.* 31 44 18 06; *credit cards* V; *closed, Wed dinner and Sat, except in Aug, Jul, two weeks Dec.*

Old-established bistro serving traditional dishes or just stick to the ever-delicious *steak frites.*

La Bourride, FFF; 15-17 *rue du Vaugueux; tel.* 31 93 50 76; *credit cards* AE, DC, MC, V; *closed Sun-Mon, three weeks Jan, two weeks Aug-Sep.*

Chef Michel Bruneau is one of the most talented and individual exponents of *cuisine Normande* in his historic beamed inn below the castle.

CALAIS
Le Channel, F-FF; 3 *boulevard de la Résistance; tel.* 21 34 42 30; *credit cards* AE, DC, MC, V; *closed Sun dinner, Tues, two weeks Jun, Christmas to mid-Jan.*

Old pre-ferry favourite facing the harbour in Calais-Nord. Extremely good value weekday (**F**) menu.

See also Recommended Hotels.

CHERBOURG
L'Ancre Dorée, F-FF; 27 *rue de l'Abbaye; tel.* 33 93 98 38; *credit cards* AE, DC, V; *closed Sat lunch, Mon.*

To the north of the city centre, this is a seafood and shellfish heaven.

Le Vauban, F-FF; 22 *quai de Cligny; tel.* 33 44 28 45; *credit cards* V; *closed Thur Oct-Apr.*

Family-orientated downstairs dining room (smarter upstairs), opposite the Customs House.

DEAUVILLE
Le Spinnaker, FF-FFF; 52 *rue Mirabeau; tel.* 31 88 24 40; *credit cards* AE, V; *closed Wed, Thur off season, Jan to mid-Feb.*

Pascal Angenard's customers happily squeeze into this little dining room to sample his carefully constructed cuisine. Delicious lobster roasted with mature cider vinegar.

DIEPPE
Marmite Dieppoise, F-FF; 8 *rue Saint-Jean; tel.* 35 84 24 26; *credit cards* V; *closed Sun dinner-Mon, Thur dinner off season, last two weeks Jun, Christmas to New Year.*

Named for the local speciality, this is the place to sample Dieppe's delicious, creamy fish soup flavoured with turbot, sole, mussels.

Les Tourelles, F; 43 *rue du Commandant-Fayolle; tel.* 35 84 15 88; *closed Wed, Tues dinner off season.*

Friendly but basic restaurant by the casino serving traditional fish soup,

salmon steaks and the rest.
See also Recommended Hotels.

ETRETAT
Le Galion, FF; *boulevard René-Coty; tel. 35 29 48 74; credit cards* AE, MC, V; *closed Thur-Fri lunch off season, mid-Jan to mid-Feb, two weeks Dec.*

Attractive beamed dining room in an historic building. Mainly fish menu.

FECAMP
Auberge de la Rouge, F-FF; *Saint-Leonard (2 km S via D925); tel. 35 28 07 59; credit cards* AE, DC, MC, V; *closed Sun-dinner, Mon, three weeks Feb.*

Pretty country-style surroundings and tables in the garden. Short but eclectic menu (**F** menu weekdays).

Also eight pleasant, comfortable and well-equipped rooms.

Le Maritime, F-FF; *2 place Nicolas-Selles; tel. 35 28 21 71; credit cards* V; *closed Tues Oct-Mar.*

Large restaurant overlooking the port. Menu designed to suit all tastes plus tasty fish dishes such as perch flamed with pernod.

HAMBYE
Auberge de l'Abbaye, F-FF; *2 km S of abbey via D51; credit cards* AE, V; *closed Sun dinner-Mon, two weeks Feb, three weeks Sep-Oct.*

Good home cooking; friendly; well-chosen country wines.

Also **Les Chevaliers**, *(tel. 33 90 42 09)*, equally good.

LE HAVRE
Lescalle, F-FF; *39 place de l'Hôtel de Ville; tel. 35 43 07 93; credit cards* AE, V; *closed Sun dinner-Mon, Aug.*

High-ceilinged, plant-filled and busy dining room with terrace. Varied menu, from garlicky snails and seafood dishes to veal.

La Petite Auberge, FF; *32 rue Sainte-Adresse; tel. 35 46 27 32; credit cards* AE, V; *closed Sun dinner-Mon, one week Mar, three weeks Aug.*

Pint-sized Norman restaurant which is worth seeking out. Fresh local ingredients are used to advantage. Excellent set-price menus (**F** on weekdays).

HONFLEUR
L'Assiette Gourmande, FF-FFF; *8 place Sainte-Catherine; tel. 31 89 24 88; credit cards* AE, DC, MC, V; *closed Sun dinner, Tues, mid-Nov to mid-Dec.*

Brick and timber augmented by a terrace. Gerard Bonnefoy's inspired cuisine marries the best fresh ingredients in unusual combinations.

Au Gars Normande, F-FF; *8 quai des Passengers; tel. 31 89 05 28; closed Sun dinner, Mon off season.*

Seafood specialities in a popular spot facing the harbour. Mussels, scallops, skate in a cream sauce, and tiny shrimps (*crevettes grises*), most common in the autumn.

LISIEUX, SAINT-VAAST-LA-HOUGUE and SAINT-VALERY-SUR-SOMME
See Recommended Hotels.

LE TOUQUET
Café des Arts, FF; *110 rue de Paris; tel. 21 05 21 55; credit cards* AE, DC, MC, V; *closed Mon, Tues off season, Christmas to New Year.*

Attractive 1930s split-level dining room in the town centre. Tempting, light cuisine.

Aux Pêcheurs d'Etaples, F-FF; *quai de la Canche, Etaples (5 km E via N39); tel. 21 94 06 90; credit cards* V; *closed Jan.*

Family-friendly, bright modern eaterie owned by the local fishing co-operative: crabs, prawns, oysters, eel, sole, trout and monkfish.

TROUVILLE
La Petite Auberge, F-FF; *7 rue Carnot; tel. 31 88 11 07; credit cards* AE, V; *closed Wed off season, Tues dinner Sep-June, three weeks Jan, one week June, two weeks Dec.*

In a side street off place du Maréchal-Foch, this friendly and popular little dining room serves a varied menu. Book ahead in season.

Les Vapeurs, FF; *160 boulevard Fernand-Moureaux; tel. 31 88 15 24; credit cards* V; *closed Tues dinner-Wed off season, four weeks Jan-Feb.*

Bustling brasserie-style fish restaurant. Open until late.

North-Western France

Between Mont-Saint-Michel and Nantes
Brittany

570 km; map Michelin No. 230

Rugged cliffs and jagged inlets, sandy beaches and muddy estuaries, Brittany is edged by some 1,800 km of coastline, and its moods are as varied as the scenery, swinging from menacing to invigorating, sunnily inviting to misty and dank, as if by magic. That same sense of sorcery in the air permeates the tapestry of Celtic history and legend which weaves around the *Armor* and the *Argoat*, the ancient Breton words for the 'Country of the Sea' and the 'Country of the Woods'.

The Bretons are a race apart. Both their language and culture have more in common with other Celtic peoples – Irish, Welsh and Cornish – than with France, a fact celebrated in frequent Celtic festivals (Quimper in July, and Lorient in August are the biggest). Religion also plays an important role in Breton life with a host of unofficial local saints adopted from the ranks of early Christian missionaries from Britain, and a multitude of annual processions known as *pardons*.

Most visitors to Brittany head straight for the seaside, north to the Côte d'Emeraude around Saint-Malo, and the Côte de Granit Rose (see Local Explorations: 1), or south to the Golfe de Morbihan and Côte d'Amour. These family resorts are generally full to bursting at the height of the July-August season (when most hotels enforce obligatory half-board terms), and firmly shuttered from October to May – worth remembering if you visit out of season. But don't miss out on the salty little fishing communities of Finistère in the west, clinging to wind-swept headlands like the shellfish for which Brittany is justly famed. Also venture into the Breton *Argoat*: the inland hills and forests of the Parc Naturel Régional d'Amorique in the west, or the eastern borderland fortresses and ancient *Brocéliande* near Rennes, setting for Arthurian legend (see Local Explorations: 2).

Red route followers will find that the main N176 and N12 parallel the north coast: the N165 does the same job in the south and west. These roads are the basis of the blue and green routes, but there are more opportunities to dive off to the coast, or take in some *Argoat*. One way of seeing this is to drive the useful corner-cutter between Morlaix and Pleyben (for Quimper): the minor but attractive D769/D14 via Huelgoat.

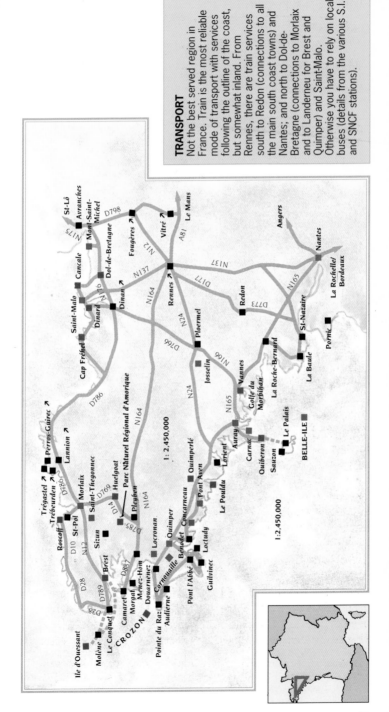

SIGHTS & PLACES OF INTEREST

AURAY 🚢 ✕

On the N165, 17 km W of Vannes. S.I. rue du Lait. The town centre, above the right bank of the River Loch, gathers around the triangular place de la République, in front of the 18thC Hôtel de Ville. Behind it there is a covered

---

PARC NATUREL REGIONAL D'AMORIQUE

The national park, created in 1969, protects a broad swathe of sparsely populated hinterland curving south and west from its eastern border north of Huelgoat along the spine of the Monts d'Arrée to the Crozon peninsula and offshore to incorporate the islands of Molène and Ouessant (see page 49). It is a wild region of desolate gorse-edged uplands and dense green woodlands shot through with streams, lakes, and rivers littered with huge moss-backed boulders. The highest 'mountain', **Roc'h Trévezel** (12 km north-west of Huelgoat, off the D785) rises to a mere 384 m, but Trévezel's peaked crown jutting out of a windswept moorland plateau is impressively rugged and gives magnificent views north to the coast, and south past the Montagne Saint-Michel to the Montagnes Noires.

This is prime rambling country, and one of the few areas where backwoods camping is permitted. The park headquarters at **Menez-Meur** (off the D342, 10 km S of Sizun, open daily June to September only) is well-supplied with information, as well as local wildlife on show in its animal reserve. Accommodation and tourist facilities within the park are somewhat basic and in short supply; the lake-side town of **Huelgoat** is the best bet for supplies and hotels, but bursting with backpackers in summer, so book ahead.

For further information, contact the Domaine de Menez-Meur, tel. 98 21 90 69/98 68 81 71; or the Huelgoat S.I., 14 place Aristide Briand, tel. 98 99 71 24. Both are closed in winter.

---

market, the S.I. and 17thC Eglise de Saint-Gildas. However, the town's pride and joy lies on the opposite bank of the Loch in the overwhelmingly picturesque **Quartier Saint-Goustan**.

Leave the car in the upper town if you can, and make the steep descent to the waterfront on foot. Across the little bridge, **Quai Benjamin-Franklin** once bustled with stevedores and strange foreign cargoes. Now it just bustles with strange foreigners. Benjamin Franklin disembarked here in 1776 to parlay with the French king and drum up support for the American War of Independence; the house where he stayed (No. 8) is now a café-restaurant. Behind the waterfront, narrow cobbled streets lined with 15th-16thC houses clamber up to the church. There are views from the path along the opposite bank; or you can take a boat trip to Belle-Ile (see below).

One of the most famous Breton *pardons* takes place at **Sainte-Anne-d'Auray** (6 km north-west via D7) on July 26.

Nearby, the **Monument aux Morts** honours the 250,000 Breton dead of the First World War.

BELLE-ILE 🚢 ✕

Daily car ferries from Quiberon. S.I. Gare maritime. Nicolas Fouquet, Louis XIV's ambitious superintendant of finances, once owned this beautiful island a 45-minute boat trip from Quiberon. Having incurred the wrath of his master, the importunate Fouquet was snatched by d'Artagnan (of Musketeers fame), and sentenced to life imprisonment before he could take refuge behind the massive star-shaped ramparts of the fortress overlooking the port.

Le Palais is the main town, and you shouldn't miss a free stroll around the fortified **Citadelle**. A prison until 1961, it now houses a local history museum. During the 19thC, the island was a favoured retreat of artists and literati from Monet to Sarah Bernhardt, who has a fort named after her at Pointe des Poulains. To get to grips with the scenery, there are bikes and mopeds for hire at the port, and a footpath picks its way around Belle-Ile's north-western **Côte Sauvage**. The heart of the island is farmland with clusters of little whitewashed cottages, and the protected east coast offers a couple of fine beaches.

If you are staying on the island, the friendly little port of **Sauzon** is an alternative to le Palais, but a word of warning: at the height of the summer season Belle-Ile's population quadruples in size and accommodation is scarce; off-season most hotels and restaurants are closed.

BENODET ⇔ ×
See Concarneau, page 50 and Quimper, page 55.

BREST ⇔ ×
On the N12/N165, 60 km W of Morlaix. S.I. 1 place Liberté. A key maritime centre from its earliest days, present-day Brest is the home base of the French Atlantic Fleet. The city was pulverized by the Allies during the Second World War, and its charmless reconstruction is a drawback from the visitor's point of view.

However, the natural harbour setting of the Rade de Brest is still very fine, protected from the south by the out-flung arm of the Crozon peninsula. For a stimulating view, head for the 15th-18thC **Château** (closed Tues) on the left bank of the River Penfeld where it runs into the bay. In addition to views, the castle houses the **Musée Maritime**; **Oceanopolis**, by the Port de Plaisance du Moulin Blanc (closed Mon off season), plumbs the depths with around 2,600 square metres of

exhibits, aquariums and a model ship navigation basin; also a handy on-site restaurant.

CANCALE
On the D201/D355, 14 km E of Saint-Malo. If you have a yen for oysters,

---

DETOUR – ILE D'OUESSANT
The English translation of Ouessant is 'Ushant' – as anyone will know who has listened to the inimitable tones of the BBC shipping forecast. The island is served by a daily boat service from Brest. (There is a shorter hour-long crossing from Le Conquet.) Crowned by a radar tower, the 7 km-long island is an annexe of the Parc Naturel Régional d'Amorique, with a small town, free-ranging sheep, and an impressively rocky and wind-swept north-western shoreline. Here the **Phare de Créac'h** marks the southern entrance to the Channel with a lighthouse museum at its base. There are footpaths along the cliffs which make vertiginous roosts for seabirds; above the port, the **Phare du Stiff** began life as a Vauban watchtower in the 17thC. To get about, bicycles can be hired from the port, and in the town of Lampaul (4 km W by bus).

DETOUR – CROZON PENINSULA
Between the Rade de Brest and Baie de Douarnenez, this jagged peninsula grabs at the sea like a paw with four claws. Daily ferries from Brest dock at Le Fret; arriving by car, your first stop should be the summit of **Menez-Hom** (330 m) which gives spectacular views across the cliffs and bays, and back to the Montagnes Noires (of which this is the western extent) and the Monts d'Arrée.

Crozon, the main town, is of little interest; but the yachting centre and resort of **Morgat** (3 km south-west) is a more enticing prospect with a fishing port, curving sandy beach, and summer-season boat trips to colourful grottos eroded from the

cliffs. (For a short break, try the **Hôtel La Ville d'Ys, F-FF**; *tel. 98 27 06 49; closed Nov-Easter*, with a marvellous location on quai Kador.)

The D887 heads south-west from Morgat for the Cap de la Chèvre, and Plage de la Palud, which is great for blustery walks (but strong waves make swimming inadvisable). On the north coast of the west-pointing claw, **Camaret** makes a pleasant base with a handful of hotels near the port where fishermen land spiny lobsters, plus a maritime museum in the small-scale Vauban fortress. (Two useful hotels on the quayside are the **Styvel, F**; *tel. 98 27 92 74; open year round*; and the **Vauban, F**; *tel. 98 27 91 36; closed Dec-Jan*.)

there are few better places to satisfy your craving. Since Roman times, Cancale's slithery crustaceans have been deemed fit for emperors and kings: daily consignments rattled their way to Versailles – and Napoleon paved the retreat from Moscow with their shells. Seafood restaurants line the front, and there are views of the oyster beds (*parc à huitres*) from the Sentier des Douaniers footpath to **Pointe du Hock**, facing Mont-Saint-Michel.

Between Cancale and Saint-Malo, the D201 wiggles prettily along the cliffs passing a spectacular viewpoint at **Pointe du Grouin**. If the mist is lying on the water, the Mount appears to float above the horizon like a mirage. If you are in more of a hurry, cut across the peninsula on the D355.

CAP FREHEL
On the D16/D34A, 37 km W of Dinard.
Most impressive in spring, when the red granite is covered with beautiful wild flowers, this dramatic wave-lashed headland is ideal for clearing the head. In fine weather you can sometimes spot Jersey; but you may equally be wrapped in a dense sea fog, seeing nothing and hearing only the sound of wind and waves and the ominous hooting of fog horns. Park at the lighthouse (visits in season), and stroll around the cape. There is a handy café.

CARNAC ⚓ ✕
On the D119/D781, 14 km S of Auray. S.I. avenue Druides; place de l'Eglise (in season). Celebrated for its oysters and its menhirs, Carnac has also developed a pleasant seaside resort annexe, **Carnac-Plage**, which stretches along several miles of sandy beach. Carnac's mysterious menhirs constitute one of the most important prehistoric sites in Europe, but their origins remain uncertain. Believed to be the work of a little-known pre-Gaulish people sometime between 3500-1800BC, the bizarre spectacle numbers around 4,000 standing stones arranged in parallel lines along the D196 north of town. Some groups of stones have been corralled in unsightly plastic fencing and provided with football stadium-type viewing platforms (which many locals reckon is a short step away from creating some ghastly themed 'Menhirland'); and there is a multi-media

menhir 'spectacular', **Archéoscope de Carnac** (continuous shows daily in season) by the Alignements du Ménec. However, it is still possible to savour, at least partially, the atmosphere by roaming around other groups planted amidst ferns and gorse. Several riding stables near the **Alignements de Kermario** offer horse-back tours. The **Musée de Préhistoire**, 10 place de la Chapelle (in Carnac-Ville), displays literally thousands of finds from sites around Carnac. The presentation is somewhat dry: miniscule shards of pottery are not really evocative, even for the most imaginative layman. However, mention is made of the local legend that the stones were petrified Roman soldiers. Some 19thC archaeologists misinterpreted this fanciful tale, concluding that the stones (some weighing up to 350 tons) had been used by Roman soldiers to stop their tents blowing away.

CONCARNEAU ⚓ ✕
Off the D783, 24 km SE of Quimper. S.I. quai d'Aiguillon. France's third largest fishing port has landed itself a new source of revenue – tourism. In addition to mackerel, sardines, anchovies and tuna, Concarneau hauls in an enthusiastic crowd of summer visitors and offers a year-round attraction in its **Ville Close**. This old granite-walled citadel built on a rocky outcrop in the bay, and tethered to the shore by a causeway, has been fortified for almost 1,000 years. You can patrol Vauban's 17thC **ramparts** (Easter to Oct), with views across the port and a jumble of roof tops; then wander into the well-preserved grid of streets.

On the main drag, the **Musée de la Pêche** gives an insight into the fishing industry by way of an admirable collection of nautical paraphernalia, model ships and tours of a trawler tied up alongside the dock. Meanwhile, back on the street, every imaginable Breton souvenir from pottery and striped sailor jerseys to plastic nets containing chocolate sardines pops up among the galleries and *crêperies*.

DINAN
See Local Explorations: 2.

DINARD ⚓ ✕
Off the D168, 11 km W of Saint-Malo.

Across the Rance estuary from Saint-Malo, Dinard has a certain faded charm with its sandy beaches, expensive hotels and grand villas, relics of its turn-of-the-century heyday, but there is little to detain you beyond a stroll along the seafront **Promenade Clair de Lune**. The beaches make a pleasant change if you are based in Saint-Malo, and regular ferry services make the ten-minute crossing.

DOL-DE-BRETAGNE ⊯ ×
On the N176, 28 *km* SE *of Saint-Malo.* Crowned by a majestic 13thC cathedral, Dol is the capital of the marshland region known as the **Marais de Dol**. Near the cathedral, broad Grande-Rue-des-Stuarts and rue Le-Jamptel boast a cache of medieval and Renaissance buildings.

DOUARNENEZ ⊯ ×
See Quimper, page 55.

FOUGERES
See Local Explorations: 2.

HUELGOAT ⊯ ×
See Parc Naturel Régional d'Amorique, page 48.

JOSSELIN ⊯ ×
On the N24/D4, 50 *km* NE *of Vannes.*

• *Mont-Saint-Michel.*

The best way to approach Josselin is from the south on the D4. As you cross the River Oust, there is a superb view of the **Château de Josselin** rising sheer from the water's edge, its slate-tiled conical towers glinting in the sun. Built by Jean II de Rohan in the 15thC, on a site dating back to 1,000 AD, the castle is a shadow of its former self, but the courtyard façade (now over-looking gardens) is a beauty, richly carved and ornamented with pinnacles, gables and balustrades. The de Rohan family still own the castle, which is open to the public together with a delightful doll collection, the **Musée des Poupées** (open daily Jun-Sep; reduced hours Wed and weekends off season; closed Nov-Feb).

The town itself is worth exploring for its fine old half-timbered and slate-roofed houses in the neighbourhood of the basilica. Founded in the 11thC, the **Basilique de Notre-Dame-du-Roncier** marks the spot where a 9thC peasant discovered a miraculous statue of the Virgin in the brambles (*roncier*). A famous annual *pardon* is celebrated here on September 8.

LANNION
See Local Explorations: 1.

LOCRONON

O*n the* D63, 17*km* N *of Quimper*. This picturesque old sail-making centre clusters around a well preserved Renaissance church square edged by granite houses. If it looks like a film set, that's because film crews and tourism have come to the rescue since the French Navy abandoned sail power. With a few cosmetic changes, Roman Polanski substituted Locronon for an English West Country village for one of his films. Today, the former sail workshops bulge with Breton crafts.

The focal point of the square, the **Eglise de Saint-Ronan** is named for a 5thC Irish monk, whose tomb lies in the adjacent chapel; scenes from his life appear on the pulpit.

MONT-SAINT-MICHEL ✉ ✕

O*n the* D976, 9 *km* N *of Pontorson*/52 *km* W *of Saint-Malo*. One of the most photographed vistas in France, this extraordinary monument really can take your breath away. The ethereal beauty of the vast abbey, apparently moulded to fit its rocky base and cast adrift on the broad sandy bay, can always amaze, whether reflected on calm, glassy water in the early morning sun, as a silhouette at sunset, or even with a background of grey clouds.

The Mont is, of course, not adrift, though plenty of pilgrims lost their footing and their lives in the quicksands before the present causeway was built out to the firmly anchored rock. From the fortified King's Gate, you have to run the gauntlet of Grande Rue, a truly ghastly scrum of tacky souvenir shops and trippers which eases somewhat as you near the **abbatial complex** (guided tours only, daily in French; English

DETOUR – CORNOUAILLE

The ancient kingdom of Cornouaille once stretched far north and east of its capital, Quimper (see page 55), but only the south-western corner of Finistère, a region still deeply rooted in tradition, continues to bear the original Celtic name given it by early Cornish settlers.

Fishing remains the chief local industry (the treacherous seas proving inhospitable to tourists), and heading 10 km west from Locronon (see above) or 23 km north-west from Quimper (see page 55), the first town you reach is **Douarnenez**, a busy fishing port boldly styled the 'European Capital of Maritime Heritage'. This is on account of its lively **Port-Musée**, laid out along the quays of the Port-Rhu, where in addition to the newly-opened **Musée du Bateau**, you can explore a tug and sail boats tied up to the quay, take a boat trip, visit the boatyards and ogle an aquarium.

Further west, overlooking the wide Baie de Douarnenez, the **Réserve Ornithologique du Cap Sizun** (open March to September) is a favoured nesting spot for seabirds; and the road continues on to **Pointe du Van**, which flanks the grimly-named Baie des Trépassés (Bay of the Dead) opposite **Pointe du Raz**, the most westerly tip of France.

Guides lead treks out along the narrow headland; sensible footwear is a must.

At the foot of a wooded hill on the Goyen, **Audierne** has a sheltered port specializing in crayfish, lobsters, and summer-season boat trips to the **Ile de Sein**, an hour away. At the southern end of the Baie d'Audierne, **Saint-Guénolé** clings to the Penmarch peninsula, and another clutch of salty little fishing villages such as **Kérity**, **Guilvinec**, and **Lesconil** follow the coast around to picturesque **Loctudy** with a Romanesque church hidden behind an 18thC façade, and boat trips up the Odet to Quimper.

Off the D2, 2 km north of Loctudy, **Château de Kerazan** (open pm, May to mid-Sept) was donated to the Institut de France by the Astor family. The manor house, dating from the 16thC, now houses a splendid art collection including many Breton scenes by Auguste Goy and Maurice Denis. For a vision of old Brittany, head 4 km north to the capital of the Pays Bigouden region, **Pont-l'Abbé** (20 km south-west of Quimper), where the two summer-season museums of regional customs and costume are often trumped by the sight of local people out shopping in traditional dress.

tours in season). Spurred into action by several visitations from St Michael, St Aubert, an 8thC Bishop of Avranches, built a chapel on the *mont*, later augmented by a Carolingian abbey, which in turn became the crypt for the subsequent Romanesque abbey. Between 1211 and 1228, a series of superb Gothic buildings were added to the north, known simply as **Le Merveille**, and to the south; the abbey chancel was rebuilt in Flamboyant style during the 15thC, and a new crypt added. The hour-long tour covers much ground, and the guides provide plenty of historical detail.

MORLAIX ➡ ✕
On the N12/D786, 60 *km E of Brest. S.I. place des Otages.* Set in a plunging forested valley on the Dossen estuary, sleepy Morlaix is dominated by an imposing railway viaduct which strides blithely through the town centre, its two tiers of arches raised 58 m above the waterfront. There has been a settlement here since Roman times, and it was an important trading port during the 16th-18thC.

Down on the front, Morlaix's modest tobacco industry still occupies a collection of rather distinguished 18thC buildings (visits on Wed), and the steep streets beneath the viaduct make a pleasant stroll. The **Eglise de Saint-Mélaine** has Renaissance frescoes in the south porch, a painted ceiling edged with carvings, and monsters munching on the roof beams. The infant Mary, Queen of Scots, *en route* from Roscoff to Paris, once took shelter in the former Dominican convent church which now houses the **Musée des Jacobins**, place des Jacobins (closed Tues except Jul and Aug). Collections of archaeological finds, medieval statuary and Breton furniture are joined by a selection of 17th-19thC paintings, including a lovely rain-washed *Belle-Ile-en-Mer* by Monet. A short walk away, the rather forlorn **Maison de la Duchesse Anne** overlooks square Allende. Anne de Bretagne stayed here on a tour of her dominions in 1505, and behind the 16thC corbelled façade, the courtyard is embellished by a spiral staircase.

Brittany's Parish Closes make a popular outing from Morlaix (see page 55); and the D786 runs north-east from

Morlaix to Lannion which is on the route of Local Explorations: 2.

NANTES ➡ ✕
On the N165, 230 *km SE of Quimper. S.I. place du Commerce.* Brittany's largest city, though now technically part of the Pays de la Loire, Nantes lies 50 km inland from the sea. In 939, it became capital of the Duchy of Brittany, and during the Middle Ages shared the title by turns with its great rival Rennes (see page 243). A considerable face-lift is currently underway in the city centre around **place des 50 Otages**, and the city council must be congratulated on their efficient, ecologically-sound tram system.

Despite severe wartime damage, Nantes has preserved pockets of its 18thC character, and the monumental **Château des Ducs**. The present edifice was founded by Duke François II in the 15thC, when jousting tournaments were held in the vast courtyard and the infamous Bluebeard (Gilles de Rais) was a captive in the dungeons. The buildings house three museums (all open daily Jun-Sep, closed Tues Oct-May): the **Musée d'Art Populaire Breton**, with its costumes and crafts; the **Musée des Salorges**, which traces the city's trading history; and the **Musée des Arts Décoratifs**, contemporary textiles in this case, which is also used for temporary exhibitions.

A short distance away, the **Cathédrale de Saint-Pierre-et-Saint-Paul** should have disappeared years ago. Plagued with dreadful accidents, the most recent a fire in 1972, its austere façade (the canopied niches of the Flamboyant portal swept clear of statues) looks rather forlorn. Inside, cleaning operations have revealed a soaring, light-filled and elegant building with restrained decorations which heighten the dramatic effect of Michel Colombe's tomb for François II and Marguerite de Foix. Commissioned by Anne of Brittany, the couple's daughter, the marble tomb in the south transcept is one of the finest Breton masterpieces of the Renaissance period. A free bonus is the cathedral treasure, on display in the crypt, and a history of the cathedral site from its 6thC Gallo-Roman origins.

Carvings rescued from the cathedral are on display in the **Musée Dobrée**

• *The Parish Close of Guimiliau, where the calvary can claim to be the most magnificent in Brittany.*

place Jean V, (closed Tues) together with the diverse collections amassed by 19thC shipowner Thomas Dobrée, and those of the Musée Départemental de Loire-Atlantique, which extends to the **Musée Archéologique**, and 15thC **Manoir de la Touche**. Other museums include the **Musée Jules-Verne**, 3 rue de l'Hermitage (closed Tues), in the crumbling 18thC Ile de Feydeau district, which commemorates the popular science fiction novelist born in Nantes.

There is good shopping in Nantes, and smart rue Crébillon gives access to the 19thC Passage Pommeraye, a glass-roofed Victorian shopping mall on three levels. A handful of parks and gardens provide an escape from the bustle, including **Grand Blottereau** with its exotic greenhouses (open weekends). The helpful S.I. has details of boat trips on the Erdre and Sèvre, visits to Le Corbusier's *Cité Radieuse* across the Loire, and summer season guided walks.

PERROS-GUIREC
See Local Explorations: 1.

54

PONT-AVEN
On the D783, 14 km E of Concarneau. A pleasant small town on the River Aven which once prospered as a mill town. An old water mill still sits by the bustling port, but it is Pont-Aven's artistic connections which fuel its flourishing tourist industry and furnish the streets with dozens of art galleries.

When Paul Gauguin packed in his job as a stockbroker and moved here in 1886, the town was already a popular artists' community. Though styled the leader of the Pont-Aven School, Gauguin was much influenced by another Pont-Aven artist, Emile Bernard, with whom he abandoned Impressionism for the brilliant colours and powerful forms of Synthetism.

A gentle stroll upstream to the riverside gardens of **Bois d'Amour** passes several inspirational views; and further uphill, the Breton-style **Chapelle de Trémalo** contains the 16thC statue on which Gauguin modelled his *Yellow Christ.*

QUIBERON 🛏 ✕
On the D768, 15 km S of Carnac. S.I. *7 rue de Verdun.* At the tip of the Quiberon peninsula, this popular summer resort boasts a sandy beach and small harbour, **Port-Maria,** where ferry ser-

vices set out for Belle-Ile (see page 48), and the smaller islands of **Hoëdic** and **Houat**. The latter has particularly good beaches. Stick to the sheltered east coast of the Quiberon peninsula if you want to swim; the west coast, known as the **Côte Sauvage**, is for scenery and blustery walks.

QUIMPER 🚗 ×

Off the N165, *72k m S of Brest/230 km NW of Nantes* S.I. *7 rue Deese (off place de la Résistance).* At the confluence (*kem-per*) of the rivers Odet and Steir, Quimper is the oldest Breton city, founded by Gradlon, King of Cornouaille (see page 52), in the 6thC. So the legend goes, Gradlon once lived in the beautiful city of Ys in the Baie de **Douarnenez**. (It is said that the name Paris is derived from *Par-Ys*, 'like Ys'.) The city was protected from the sea by a dyke to which the king had the only key, made of gold. His daughter Dahut stole the key for her lover, the Devil, who promptly opened the floodgates and Ys was drowned. As Gradlon fled for dry land on his trusty steed, his daughter in tow, a heavenly voice commanded him to cast the devilish Dahut into the sea, which he did. She became a siren, while he went on to found Quimper, well inland you may note.

The heart of town radiates from the Gothic **Cathédrale de Saint-Corentin**, topped by two steeples. Despite being added in the 19thC, the steeples have blended in remarkably well; between them a diminutive Gradlon advances on the city *sans* Dahut. The interior, huge and high, has some fine 15thC glass in the nave, and the choir leads off at an angle, necessitated when the architect discovered an obstacle in his path. Housed in the former episcopal palace next door, the **Musée Breton** (closed Mon Jun-Sep; Mon-Tues Oct-May) is looking very smart – all glass, granite and bleached wood. Cleverly laid-out with caches of spearheads and Roman *sesterces* (coins), spot-lit medieval carvings, fur-

---

BRITTANY'S PARISH CLOSES

A uniquely Breton phenomenon dating from the 16th-17thC, the Parish Closes (*enclos paroissiaux*) contain some of the finest, and certainly most ornate, examples of local architecture and sculpture. Calvaries, the stone crosses decorated with carved figures representing scenes from the Crucifixion and Passion of Christ, are found in many Breton churchyards, but those of the Close complexes are immeasurably grander and form just one element of a group which may include a triumphal arch (representing the victorious ascent to heaven), and an ossuary, or charnel house, where the bones of exhumed bodies were placed to make room in the cramped graveyards for further burials.

Morlaix is the closest town to the three most interesting of the parish closes and buses from there serve all three villages. The Parish Close of **Saint-Thégonnec** (off N12, 13 km south-west of Morlaix) exhibits all three of the traditional elements, starting with a triumphal arch festooned with pinnacles, orbs and carved niches. To the left, the 17thC ossuary sits on top of a small crypt containing a carved and painted rendering of the Holy Sepulchre; the superb calvary across the yard dates from 1610. Behind the severe granite exterior of the church, the east end of the building is cloaked from floor to ceiling with lavishly painted and gilded wood carvings of well-fed cherubs, flocks of angels and legions of saints; and the pulpit is a work of art.

The richness of Saint-Thégonnec's decoration was in no small measure due to intense rivalry with the neighbouring village of **Guimiliau** (7 km south-west). Guimiliau's calvary is the acknowledged *grand fromage* of Breton calvaries with more than 200 figures carved 1581-88.

Last but not least of this trinity of neighbouring closes, **Lampaul-Guimiliau** (3.5 km north-west) has perhaps the simplest close complex, but its church has a marvellous baldaquin canopy over the font, carved altar pieces and a Crucifixion balanced on a beam over the nave. Other Parish Closes in the region include La Roche, La Martyre, Ploudiry and Pleyben.

---

niture and Breton costumes are effectively displayed alongside contemporary paintings, sculpture and even advertising posters extolling the delights of rural Brittany circa 1900.

The **Musée des Beaux-Arts**, 4 place Saint-Corentin (closed Tues), features a notable collection of drawings, plus Pont-Aven School and Breton scenes from the lines of Corot, Serusier and Max Jacob.

The cobbled streets of Vieux Quimper, to the west of the cathedral, are lined with shops, cafés and *crêperies*. Quimper pottery (*faïence*) is everywhere – you can learn its history at the **Musée de la Faïence**, 14 rue Bousquet, and visit the workshops of **H.B. Henriot**, rue Haute in the Locmaria district nearby.

From Quimper, there are daily boat trips down the Odet to the beach resort of **Bénodet** at the mouth of the river (schedules, tel. 98 57 00 58, or ask at the S.I.).

QUIMPERLE
Off the N165, 17 km E of Pont-Aven. Somewhat off the tourist trail, Quimperlé marks the spot where the Rivers Ellé and Isole unite to form the Laïta for the final short stretch to the sea. The Old Town is cradled in a loop between the rivers, a muddle of medieval streets and Renaissance houses crowded around the 12thC **Eglise de Sainte-Croix**, which was modelled on Jerusalem's Holy Sepulchre. Its Romanesque apse is original, and there are fine capitals in the crypt, but much else has had to be rebuilt.

RENNES
See Local Explorations: 2.

ROCHE-BERNARD, LA ⊭ ✕
See Cruising on the River Vilaine, page 57.

ROSCOFF ⊭ ✕
On the D58, 26 km NW of Morlaix. S.I. 46 rue Gambetta. A fishing centre and ferry port (services from Plymouth and Cork), Roscoff's old stone houses, bulging window boxes and picturesque harbour contribute to its reputation as a popular if small-scale summer resort-cum-hydrotherapy centre.

Rue Gambetta acts as the main drag leading to the 16thC **Eglise de Notre-Dame-de-Kroaz-Baz** with its flamboy-

DETOUR – LE POULDU
There is a pretty drive south of Quimperlé, along the D49 as it cuts through the oaks and beechwoods of the **Forêt de Carnoët** to the little port of le Pouldu, at the mouth of the Laïta. Gauguin moved here from Pont-Aven, and there is a monument to him by the Chapelle de Notre-Dame-de-la-Paix.

ant belfry sculpted with ships and bristling cannons. The principal beaches lie to the west of town; or there is the **Ile de Batz**, a 15-minute boat trip across the bay with its fine white sand beaches, seaweed industry, small town, youth hostel and camping for escapists.

SAINT-MALO ⊭ ✕
On the D168, 28 km NW of Dol-de-Bretagne 169 km N of Rennes. S.I. esplanade Saint-Vincent. Distinct from the French, and even the Bretons, the native inhabitants of Saint-Malo are *Malouins*. Their corsair-adventurer forefathers roamed far and wide from this granite-walled island citadel: Jacques Cartier landed in Canada in 1534; Malouin settlers named the *Malvinas* or Falkland Islands off Argentina; and during the 17th-18thC, Duguay-Trouin and Surcouf legitimately terrorized Channel shipping on the authority of the French king.

Bordered by the sprawling modern city, and flanked by the resorts of Saint-Servan and Paramé, the ancient citadel or **Ville Close** (follow signs for *intra muros*) is one of the most popular tourist sites in Brittany. More than 80 per cent of its buildings and ramparts were destroyed during the Second World War, but painstaking reconstruction has restored the shadowy warren of cobbled streets complete with their 16th-18thC houses. The press of human traffic at the height of the summer season can become unpleasantly claustrophobic, but the **ramparts** provide a breather with a bird's eye view of the roof-tops to one side, and the Channel to the other.

There is access to the ramparts from the Porte Saint-Vincent, near the Château which houses the **Musée de la Ville** (closed Tues off season) in the

Great Keep. Steps wind up past displays detailing local history from slave trading and seafaring to piracy and the Nazi occupation. From the watchtower, there is a superb 360-degree panorama, and you can see the **Ile du Grand Bé** just offshore, where the 19thC writer Chateaubriand is buried. A stroll across the causeway to the island is a favourite outing, but check the tides or you may get stranded out there.

In the heart of the Ville Close, the 11th-18thC **Cathédrale de Saint-Vincent** boasts some fine stained glass and Jacques Cartier's tomb. Beyond the ramparts, you can walk north along the beach to **Paramé**; or head south to **Saint-Servan,** where the 14thC Tour Solidor guards the Rance estuary and sells tickets to a sail ship museum.

Across the estuary, the 19thC resort of **Dinard** flaunts a handful of grand old hotels (see page 50). It can be reached by road via the world's largest tidal barrier, or there are frequent boat services. Boats also depart for trips up the Rance to the fortified town of **Dinan**, described in Local Explorations: 2.

SAINT-THEGONNEC ✕

See Brittany's Parish Closes, page 55.

TREBEURDEN, TREGASTEL AND TREGUIER

See Local Explorations: 1.

CRUISING ON THE RIVER VILAINE

The road between Vannes and Nantes passes the little town of La Roche-Bernard at the head of the Vilaine estuary. This is a lovely river, winding between meadows to the sea. If you want a short canal cruise, without the rigours of locks, but with plenty of peace and quiet, the Vilaine south of Redon is ideal. Not all cruiser hirers operate on the seaward stretch: two which do are Hoseasons and Locaboat Plaisance (see page 196) or contact the Comité Régional de Tourisme, 746 rue de Paris, 35069 Rennes cedex; tel. 99 28 43 30, and ask for their brochure *Tourisme fluvial en Bretagne.*

DETOUR – **SAINT-POL-DE-LEON**

Just south of Roscoff through the artichoke fields (6 km via D769), the unassuming town of Saint-Pol-de-Léon harbours two notable examples of Breton ecclesiastical architecture. Built between the 13th-16thC from local stone, the former **Cathédrale de Saint-Paul** is a remarkably harmonious and elegant building, its façade flanked by towers and the interior decorated with fine stained glass and 16thC choir stalls.

A short walk downhill, the 14th-15thC **Chapelle de Kreisker** boasts the original Breton Kreisker-style spired belfry widely copied thoughout the region. This Gothic extravaganza is 75 m high, with views across the countryside to the coast and south to the Monts d'Arrée.

VANNES ✕

On the N165, 110 km NW of Nantes. S.I. rue Thiers (near the port). A bustling city on the **Golfe de Morbihan**, Vannes takes its name from the ancient Celtic *Veneti* people, who held out against the Romans after most of the rest of Gaul had been conquered. The Breton hero Nominoë established the first capital of the united Breton kingdom here in the 9thC, and the Act of Union annexing Brittany to the French crown was signed in the ancient covered marketplace, La Cohue, in 1532.

The liveliest corner of town is **Vieux Vannes**, clambering up the hillside behind the port. Encircled by listing, half-timbered buildings, the **Cathédrale de Saint-Pierre** dates back to the 13thC. Though **La Cohue** (opposite the cathedral) prefers not to call itself a museum, it does house Vannes' fine arts collection, space for temporary exhibitions and displays covering the history, wildlife and industries of the Golfe de Morbihan. For something more colourful, the **Aquarium de Vannes**, at Parc du Golfe (5 km S of the town centre), presents 600-plus species of marine life. Boat trips from the **gare maritime** nearby set sail around the Gulf.

VITRE

See Local Explorations: 2.

RECOMMENDED HOTELS

AURAY
Hôtel du Loch, FF; *La Petite Forêt; tel. 97 56 48 33; credit cards* V; *closed Christmas to New Year.*
Comfortable, modern hotel with a garden, and excellent restaurant, **La Sterne** (closed Sun dinner Nov-Mar).

BELLE-ILE
Hôtel-Village La Désirade, FF-FFF; *at Le Petit Cosquet; tel. 97 31 70 70; credit cards* AE, DC, V; *closed Jan-Feb.*
Exclusive little 'village' with modern cottages around the pool terrace. Owner Marcel Multon has his own local restaurant **La Forge** (**FF**; *tel.* 97 31 51 76; *closed Wed off season*).

Le Phare, F; (*half-board in season*); *quai Querveur, at Sauzon; tel.* 97 31 60 36; *closed* Oct-Apr.
Basic rooms, a magnificent setting by the lighthouse, and a good little waterfront restaurant.

BENODET
Gwel Kaër, FF-FFF; (*half-board in season*); *avenue de la Plage; tel.* 98 57 04 38; *credit cards* V; *closed Sun pm-Mon off season, mid-Dec to Feb 1.*
Attractive small hotel-restaurant with a terrace and bar bordering the beach. Fresh sunny rooms, most with private terrace or balcony.

BREST
Pointe Sainte-Barbe, F-FF; (*half-board in season*); *at Le Conquet* (24 *km* W *via D789); tel.* 98 89 00 26; *credit cards* AE, DC, MC, V; *closed Nov to mid-Dec.*
Pleasant family-style seaside hotel on the headland with sea views; steps to the beach; and a restaurant serving fresh seafood.

CANCALE
See Recommended Restaurants.

CARNAC
Le Bateau Ivre, FF-FFF; (*half-board in season); 71 boulevard de la Plage; tel.* 97 52 19 55; *credit cards* AE, DC, V; *closed Jan to mid-Feb.*
Prices are higher on the beach, but this small hotel is one of the better deals. 21 rooms with kitchenettes and terraces; pool; restaurant.

Lann-Roz, FF; 36 *rue de la Poste; tel.* 97 52 10 48; *credit cards* AE, DC, V; *closed Wed off season, and Jan.*
Super little *logis* with 13 small, quiet rooms, plus six-bed garden annexe. Good food and popular.
Also the similar, but cheaper, **Râtelier**; (4 *chemin Douët; tel.* 97 52 05 04), which offers rooms and a restaurant in an old Breton farmhouse.

CONCARNEAU
L'Océan, FF; *plage des Sables-Blancs; tel.* 98 50 53 50; *credit cards* AE, DC, MC, V; *open year round.*
Some 70 rooms including duplex family apartments across from the beach. Pool, and restaurant.
Also the small, modern and neat **Ty, Chupen Gwenn** (**FF**; *tel.* 98 97 01 43), nearby.

DINARD
La Reine Hortense, FFF; 19 *rue de la Malouine; tel.* 99 46 54 31; *credit cards* AE, DC, MC, V; *closed mid-Nov to mid-Mar.*
Elegant turn-of-the-century villa facing the beach. Rooms with sea views; spendid *salon*; garden terrace.
If you fancy a real *palais-hotel* in this price bracket, head for the town-centre **Grand Hôtel** (*tel.* 99 46 10 28).
See also Recommended Restaurants.

DOL-DE-BRETAGNE
See Recommended Restaurants.

DOUARNENEZ
Auberge de Kerveoc'h, F-FF; *route de Quimper* (5 *km* SE *via D765); tel.* 98 92 07 58; *credit cards* V; *closed early Oct-Easter.*
Lovely old farmhouse set in a large garden with 14 individually decorated rooms. Rustic dining room; reservations advisable.

HUELGOAT
Hôtel du Lac, F; *rue du Général-de-Gaulle; tel.* 98 99 71 14; *credit cards* V; *closed Nov-Dec.*
Basic rooms and a cheap and cheerful restaurant opposite the lake.
Another option is **An Triskell**, on

route Pleyben (**F**; *tel. 98 99 71 85*), with
ten rooms and a garden.

Auberge de Meilh-Skiriou, F; *route
du Faou, at Brasparts (21 km SW via
D14/D21; tel. 98 81 12 29; closed Mon-
Tues lunch off -season, Nov to mid-Feb.*
   Simple rooms in an old Breton farm-
house. Home cooking in the restau-
rant; kid's games in the garden.
   See also Recommended Restaurants.

JOSSELIN
Hôtel du Château, F-FF; *rue du
Général-de-Gaulle; tel. 97 22 20 11; credit
cards AE, DC, V; closed Feb, and one week
Christmas*
   Comfortable *logis* in a marvellous
position on the riverbank. Good tradi-
tional restaurant with a sunny terrace.
   See also Recommended Restaurants.

MONT-SAINT-MICHEL
See Recommended Restaurants.

MORLAIX
L'Europe, F-FF; *1 rue d'Aiguillon; tel.
98 62 11 99; credit cards AE, DC, V; open
year round.*
   Town-centre hotel with modernized
rooms and a pleasant terraced
brasserie. The Victorian dining room
features Breton specialities.

NANTES
L'Hôtel, FF; *6 rue Henri -IV; tel. 40 29
30 31; credit cards AE, DC, MC, V; open
year round.*
   A highly recommended central
address facing the château. Garden-
facing rooms are quietest. No restaurant, but delicious breakfasts.

Hôtel Cholet, F; *10 rue Gresset; tel. 40
73 31 04; credit cards V; open year round.*
   Bargain find in the city centre near
place Graslin. Friendly, scrupulously
clean and soundproofed.

QUIBERON
Gulf Stream, FFF; *17 boulevard Cha-
nard; tel. 97 50 16 96; credit cards AE, V;
closed mid-Nov to early Feb.*
   Delightful hotel converted from two
old houses facing Grand Plage. Pretty
rooms furnished with antiques. Shady
garden for postcard duty.

QUIMPER
Hôtel Gradlon, FF; *30 rue de Brest; tel.
98 95 04 39; credit cards AE, DC, MC, V;
closed 2 weeks at New Year.*
   An easy stroll from the centre. Quiet
rooms ranged around a pretty inner
courtyard. No restaurant.

LA ROCHE-BERNARD
Auberge des Deux Magots, FF; *1
place du Bouffay; tel. 99 90 60 75; cards V;
closed Sun dinner (off season), Mon, mid-
Dec to mid-Jan, 1 week Jun, 1 week Oct.*
   A handy overnight stop between
Nantes and Vannes. Comfy rooms,
and first-class regional cuisine.
   See also Recommended Restaurants.

ROSCOFF
Bellevue, FF; *rue Jeanne d'Arc; tel. 98
61 23 38; credit cards V; closed mid-Nov to
mid-Dec, mid-Jan to mid-Mar.*
   Pleasant modern hotel at the eastern end of the harbour with 18 small
rooms, and a sea-front restaurant.
   Distinctly grander, the **Brittany** (**FF-
FFF** *tel. 98 69 70 78*), occupies a reconstructed 17thC manor house.
   See also Recommended Restaurants.

SAINT-MALO
La Cité, FF-FFF; *26 rue Sainte-Barbet;
tel. 99 40 55 40; credit cards AE, V; open
year round.*
   A smart, new and extremely comfortable hotel in the Ville Close. Big
rooms and helpful staff.

La Korrigane, FF-FFF; *39 rue le
Pomellec, St-Servan; tel. 99 81 65 85;
credit cards AE, DC, MC, V; closed mid-
Nov to mid-Mar.*
   Elegant turn-of-the-century mansion.
Bedrooms are small, but very pretty.
No restaurant, no licence.

SAINT-THEGONNEC
See Recommended Restaurants.

VANNES
Hôtel Mascotte, FF; *avenue Jean
Monet; tel. 97 47 59 60; credit cards AE,
V; open year round.*
   Near the Palais des Congrès, it is
spotless, modern and convenient.
   For an Old Town money saver, try
the **Hôtel des Remparts** (**F**; *tel. 97 54
11 90*).

RECOMMENDED RESTAURANTS

AURAY

La Closerie de Kerdrain, FF-FF; 14 *rue Louis-Billet; tel.* 97 56 61 27; *credit cards* AE, DC, MC, V; *closed Tues off -season, Jan to early Feb.*

Gorgeous surroundings in a Renaissance town house. Elegant and original cooking: well-chosen Loire wines.

L'Eglantine, F; *place Saint-Saveur; tel.* 97 56 46 55; *credit cards* V; *closed Wed (except Jul-Aug)*

Up the hill in the Saint-Goustan quarter, this pleasant spot makes a feature of generous home cooking.

See also Recommended Hotels.

BELLE-ILE

Le Contre-Quai, FF; *rue Saint-Nicolas, at Sauzon; tel.* 97 31 60 60; *credit cards* V; *closed Sun dinner, Mon (except Jul-Aug), Nov to mid-Apr.*

Cosy dining room in old fisherman's cottage. Tempting seafood menus.

BENODET

Ferme du Letty, FF-FFF; *at Letty (2 km SE via D44); tel.* 98 57 01 27; *credit cards* AE, DC, V; *closed Wed (except Jul-Aug)-Thur lunch, mid-Oct to Mar 1.*

Take one Breton farmhouse, convert with care, add scenery and invite Jean-Marie Guilbaut to season with his elegant and delicious cuisine.

BREST

L'Espérance, F; 6 *place de la Libération; tel.* 98 44 25 29; *closed Sun dinner-Mon.*

L'Espérance does a useful line in no-nonsense *bretois* cooking.

Off rue de Siam, the **Crêperie des Fontaines, (F**; 44 *rue Jean-Macé; closed Sat lunch and Sun)*, serves up a variety of *crêpes* and piles the salads high.

CANCALE

Le Cancalais, F-FF; *quai Gambetta; tel.* 99 89 61 93; *credit cards* V; *closed mid-Dec to mid-Jan.*

Best of the bunch on the harbour with a terrace and hotel attached (**F**). Humungous seafood platters.

CARNAC

Auberge de Kerank, FF; *route de Quiberon, at Plouharnel (4 km W via D781/D768); tel.* 97 52 10 48; *credit cards* V; *closed Sun dinner-Mon off season, four weeks Nov-Dec, Jan to mid-Feb.*

Lovely old fisherman's cottage by the sea. Fresh and unfussy fish dishes as well as regional favourites.

See also Recommended Hotels.

CONCARNEAU

Le Gallion, FF-FFF; 15 *rue Saint-Guénolé; tel.* 98 97 30 16; *credit cards* AE, DC, MC, V; *closed Sun dinner-Mon off season, mid-Jan to early Mar, two weeks Nov.*

Chic-rustique dining room in the Ville Close. Henri Goanac'h could have earned his Michelin star for his flavourful *cotriade* (fish soup-cum-stew) alone. Try the *bourdaloue*, an apple and almond Breton pudding.

DINARD

Altaïr, F-FF; 18 *boulevard Féart; tel.* 99 46 13 55; *cards* AE, DC, MC, V; *closed Sun dinner-Mon, mid-Nov to mid-Dec.*

Generous seafood platters, and a knock-out pear *gratin* with praline ice cream; cosy dining room; terrace.

DOL-DE-BRETAGNE

La Bresche Arthur, FF; 36 *boulevard Deminiac; tel.* 99 48 01 44; *credit cards* V; *closed Sun dinner-Mon off season, three weeks Jan, three weeks Nov.*

Attractive dining room and terrace; market-fresh dishes.

The Bresche also has 24 pleasant rooms. Alternatively, the **Hôtel de Bretagne** (**F**; 17 *place Châteaubriand; tel.* 99 48 02 03) is a welcoming *logis*.

DOUARNENEZ

Hostellerie des Arcades, F-FF; 67 *rue du Commandant-Fernand; tel.* 98 74 00 64; *credit cards* V; *closed Sun dinner.*

On the west bank of the Port-Rhu, this is something of a local favourite. Rustic surroundings and traditional menu. *See also* Recommended Hotels.

HUELGOAT

Auberge de la Truite, F-FF; *at Loc-maria-Berrien-Gare (7 km SE via D769); tel.* 98 99 73 05; *credit cards* V; *closed Sun dinner, Mon off season, Jan to mid-Apr.*

Real *cuisine du terroir* and generous portion control. Traditional Breton interior; wine list. Five quiet rooms (**F**).

JOSSELIN
Les Frères Blot, F-FF; *Hôtel du Commerce, 9 rue Glatinier; tel. 97 22 22 08; credit cards AE, V.*

A welcoming spot with fine views over the Oust valley, and good regional cooking from the Blot brothers.

MONT-SAINT-MICHEL
Le Mouton Blanc, F-FF; *Grande Rue; tel. 33 60 14 08; credit cards V; closed Wed off season, end-Nov to early Feb.*

Some of the most competitive prices on the *mont*. The main dining-room is housed in a Renaissance historic monument; regional specialities. Also 26 small rooms.

MORLAIX
Patrick Jeffroy, FF-FFF; *at Plounérin (22 km E, off N12); tel. 96 38 61 80; credit cards V; closed Sun dinner-Mon off season, two weeks Feb, two weeks Oct.*

A gourmet detour which also offers three small but pretty rooms (**FF**). The talented M. Jeffroy does amazing things with fish, including, a distinctly exotic turbot with spices and mango.

NANTES
Auberge du Château, FF; *5 place de la Duchesse Anne; tel. 40 74 05 51; credit cards V; closed Sun-Mon, New Year, and three weeks Aug.*

Intimate little restaurant with a log fire, skilful cuisine, good-value menus and excellent Loire wines.

Le Cigale, F-FF; *4 place Graslin; tel. 40 69 76 41; credit cards V.*

Turn-of-the-century brasserie with a pavement terrace. For a quick bite, try the *formule rapide*.

QUIBERON
Le Relax, F-FF; *27, boulevard Castero; tel. 97 50 12 84; credit cards DC, V; closed Sun dinner, Mon off season, Jan to mid-Feb, Nov-Dec.*

Great seafood and a terrace overlooking the Plage de Kermorvan.

QUIMPER
L'Ambroisie, F-FF; *rue Elie-Fréron; tel. 98 95 00 02; credit cards AE, DC, MC, V; closed Sun dinner off season.*

Intimate and attractive setting for seasonally inspired cooking. Gou-

jonettes of sole with asparagus, and a scrumptious raspberry *feuilleté*.

QUIMPERLE
Bistro de la Tour, F-FF; *2, rue Dom Morice; tel. 98 39 29 58; cards AE, V; closed Sat lunch, Sun dinner off season, Mon.*

A favourite haunt near Sainte-Croix. Select a table amongst the bric-à-brac, check out the seafood dish of the day, or settle for duck or wild salmon with a lime *confit*.

LA ROCHE-BERNARD
Auberge Bretonne, FF-FFF; *2 place du Guesclin; tel. 99 90 60 28; credit cards MC, V; closed mid-Nov-to mid-Dec.*

A gastronomic treat (two Michelin stars) with rooms. Jaques Thorel's cooking is based on local tradition, with light and imaginative touches.

See also Recommended Hotels.

ROSCOFF
Chardons Bleus, F-FF; *4, rue Amiral-Réveillère; tel. 98 69 72 03; credit cards V; closed Thur (except Jul-Aug), and Dec-Feb.*

Relaxed restaurant offering fairly priced menus with plenty of choice. Also ten rooms (**F-FF**).

SAINT-MALO
Chez Chantal, F; *2 place aux Herbes; tel. 99 40 93 97; credit cards V.*

Friendly *crêperie* in the Ville Close. Generous seafood *galettes* oozing prawns, scallops and flaked fish.

Les Ecluses, F-FF; *gare maritime de la Bourse; tel. 99 56 81 00; credit cards V; closed Sun dinner-Mon, except Jul-Aug.*

Conservatory-style dining room in the port.

SAINT-THEGONNEC
Auberge Saint-Thégonnec, F-FF; *tel. 98 79 61 18; credit cards AE, DC, V; closed Sun dinner-Mon off season, mid-Dec to mid-Jan.*

A welcoming *logis* opposite the church with a pretty dining-room.

VANNES
Le Brick, F; *25, rue Ferdinand-le-Dressay; tel. 97 47 31 18; credit cards AE, V; closed Sun-Mon.*

A popular bar-restaurant.

Between Nantes and Bordeaux
Vendée and Charente-Maritime

325 km; map Michelin Nos 232 and 233

S andy beaches and misty marshes, brash resorts and historic ports, this mid-section of the Atlantic coast is something of a lucky dip with a prize for everyone. Families armed with buckets and spades flock to the safe, sunny seashore (happy campers to Royan and the islands, less rugged types to the apartment blocks of Sables d'Olonne); others track down Roman relics at Saintes or the Romanesque churches at Aulnay and Talmont; and, of course, wine enthusiasts follow their noses to Bordeaux (see Bordeaux wines, page 66). Though local fishermen do still fish, and the green-tinged *huîtres* from Marenne and Oléron account for more than half the country's total oyster harvest, tourism reaps the biggest rewards. During the height of the summer season prices rocket to almost double their low season rates, accommodation is booked up months in advance, and unless you are a lemming with advance reservations, August is best avoided.

In spring and autumn the region is at its best. There is room to stroll around the lovely 17th-18thC streets of La Rochelle, relax over a long seafood lunch, or catch a boat to tiny Ile d'Aix where the bicycle, not the motor car, reigns. Stop to explore the watery charms of the Marais Poitevin national park covered in Local Explorations: 3; and head inland on the same tour to historic Poitiers; or follow the River Charente to Colbert's safe port at Rochefort, sleepy Saintes, and the brandy town of Cognac. And leave plenty of time to savour Bordeaux.

The main road between Nantes and Bordeaux is the N137, which touches on all the major towns mentioned in this section. Red route followers in a real hurry will follow this route, with the option of hopping on to the A10 autoroute. However, there is a difficult decision to be made over the Ile de Noirmoutier, one of the lovely islands off this stretch of the coast which deserves its red designation. For blue and green travellers at least one of the islands is a must, and there are roads that parallel most of the coast which I would encourage you to follow – except in the summer season.

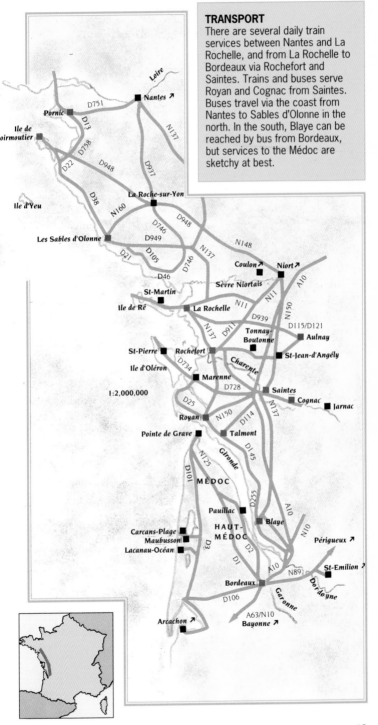

TRANSPORT
There are several daily train services between Nantes and La Rochelle, and from La Rochelle to Bordeaux via Rochefort and Saintes. Trains and buses serve Royan and Cognac from Saintes. Buses travel via the coast from Nantes to Sables d'Olonne in the north. In the south, Blaye can be reached by bus from Bordeaux, but services to the Médoc are sketchy at best.

1:2,000,000

SIGHTS & PLACES OF INTEREST

AULNAY

On the D950, 18 km NE of Saint-Jean-d'Angély. A former pilgrim staging-post, the **Eglise de Saint-Pierre** stands at the edge of the village shaded by cypress trees and adorned with remarkable carvings. The central portal is flanked by scenes representing Christ in Majesty and the Crucifixion of St Peter; then follow round to the south doorway with its hooped bands of closely packed figures, mythical birds and beasts overlooked by a frieze of grotesques. The capitals of the nave are equally splendid with the renowned annotated small-eared elephants by the south transcept (a Latin inscription reads 'These are elephants' for the edification of bemused medieval peasants), and there is a beautifully decorated window in the apse.

ARCACHON

See France Overall: 4.

BAYONNE

See France Overall: 4.

BLAYE 🏨

On the D669, 48 km N of Bordeaux. S.I. allées Marines. Encircled by vineyards on the east bank of the Gironde, sleepy Blaye crouches behind its vast, overgrown **Citadelle**. The site has been fortified since Roman times, but the present fortifications are the work of Maréchal Vauban, Louis XIV's celebrated military architect. Together with the ruined Fort Médoc on the west bank

RECOMMENDED HOTELS

BLAYE
Château La Grange de Luppé, F; 1.5 km N on D255; tel. 57 42 80 20; credit cards AE, DC, V; open year round.
Endearing small château surrounded by large private grounds. Twelve simple rooms.

La Citadelle, F-FF; place d'Armes; tel. 57 42 17 10; credit cards AE, DC, V; open year round.
Rooms are disappointingly modern, but there are fine views of the estuary from the pool-side terrace-bar.

BORDEAUX
Hôtel de la Presse, F-FF; 6-8 rue Porte-Dijeaux; tel. 56 48 53 88; credit cards AE, DC, V; open year round.
Small, central and value for money. Quieter rooms overlook the courtyard.

Normandie, FF; 7 cours XXX-Juillet; tel. 56 52 16 80; credit cards AE, DC, MC, V; open year round.
Plain, comfortable modern rooms in a well-placed 18thC corner block.

Sainte-Catherine, FF-FFF; 27 rue Parlement-Sainte-Catherine; tel. 56 81 95 12; credit cards AE, DC, MC, V; open year round.
Richly decorated and spacious rooms in a splendidly restored 18thC mansion.

NOIRMOUTIER-EN-L'ILE
Les Douves, F-FF; 11 rue des Douves; tel. 51 39 02 72; credit cards AE, DC, V; closed mid-Dec to early Feb.
Pleasant logis with rooms around a courtyard pool terrace; good restaurant.
See also Recommended Restaurants.

OLERON, SAINT-PIERRE-D'
Motel Ile de Lumière, FF-FFF; avenue des Pins, La Cotinière, 3 km SW of Saint-Pierre on D274; tel. 46 47 10 80; credit cards V; closed Nov-Mar.
Up-market family motel by the sea with pool, tennis and gardens. No restaurant.
See also Recommended Restaurants.

RE, ILE DE
Le Martray, F; at Le Martray, 3 km E of Ars-en-Ré on D735; tel. 46 29 40 04; credit cards AE, DC, V; closed Nov-Apr.
A maison typique facing the beach. Pleasant terrace and good dining room. Half board in season.

ROCHEFORT
Hôtel des Vermandois, F-FF; 33 rue Emile-Combes; tel. 46 87 09 87; credit cards V; closed Christmas to New Year.
Eleven great value rooms which are squeezed into a pleasantly-renovated 18thC house.

and Fort Pâté in mid-stream, it was designed to protect Bordeaux from the British fleet.

Inside the citadel, which measures almost 1 km long and 0.5 km across, there is a clutch of apricot-coloured cottages laced with climbing roses, craft shops and tea rooms which cater for trippers in season.

There are cheaper hotels in town; and several daily ferries across to Lamarque on the Médoc peninsula (details from the S.I.).

BORDEAUX ⇌ ✕
On the A10/A63, 325 km S of Nantes/185 km N of Bayonne. S.I. 12 cours du XXX-Juillet. Although Bordeaux, is France's eighth largest city, it is pleasantly relaxed and oddly provincial despite the obvious trappings of its wealth.

CYCLING ALONG THE GIRONDE
This is easy bicycling country, and there is a very pleasant stretch between Royan and Blaye (D25/D145), which dawdles along the Gironde estuary and somewhat inland. There are regular ferry services across to the Médoc peninsula from both Royan and Blaye making a neat two-day circuit.

This is a city built on wine, 'dedicated to the worship of Bacchus in the most discreet form' according to Henry James. One in six *Bordelais* works in the wine industry.

The region was put on the map by the Romans, and the wines of *Burdi-*

Le Prieuré, FF; *at Tonnay-Boutonne, 21 km E of Rochefort on D739; tel. 46 33 20 18; credit cards V; closed Dec-Feb.*

Attractive white-shuttered Charentais building, previously the private home of the hotel's owners. Friendly atmosphere; bedrooms recently upgraded – and the mooted pool should be built by now.

ROCHELLE, LA
France-Angleterre et Champlain, FF; *20 rue Rambaud; tel. 46 41 34 66; credit cards AE, DC, MC, V; open year round.*

Lovely old townhouse with big, well-equipped rooms and a pretty garden.

Hôtel François-ler, F-FF; *15 rue Bazoges; tel. 46 41 28 46; credit cards AE, DC, MC, V; open year round.*

Excellent, peaceful and central hotel in a renovated *hôtel-particulier*. Spacious rooms, interior courtyard and bar.

BED-AND-BREAKFAST
33 Rue Thiers, FF; *33 rue Thiers; tel. 46 41 61 62 23; credit cards none; open year round.*

18thC town house owned and run by French/American cookery writer Maybelle Iribe. Individually decorated rooms with an eclectic mix of furniture. Wonderful breakfasts; dinner also served.

ROYAN
Family Golf Hôtel, FF; *28 boulevard Garnier; tel. 46 05 14 66; credit cards V; closed Oct to Easter.*

Refurbished sea-front hotel with views across the estuary.

SABLES D'OLONNE
Atlantic Hôtel, FF-FFF; *5 promenade Godet; tel. 51 95 37 71; credit cards AE, DC, MC, V; closed Thur Oct-Apr, and mid-Nov to mid-Dec.*

Family hotel on the beach with small, but airy rooms; a range of facilities and indoor/outdoor pool. Half-board in season.

SAINTES
Relais du Bois Saint-Georges, FF-FFF; *rue Royan (1.5 km W on D137); tel. 46 93 50 99; credit cards V; open year round.*

Set in a park on the western edge of town. Peaceful and elegant; attractive well-equipped rooms, and a very pleasant restaurant.

See also Recommended Restaurants.

YEU, ILE D'
La Côte Sauvage, F; *at Port de la Meule; tel. 51 58 35 83; credit cards V; closed Sep to Easter.*

Ten simple rooms around a courtyard with trailing vines and wooden shutters. Straightforward home cooking. Half board only.

gala were favoured above all others by successive emperors. Charlemagne created the city capital of the Duchy of Aquitaine in 788; later Eleanor of Aquitaine handed it to England on her marriage to Henry Plantagenet (later Henry II of England) in 1153. The English remained in control for 300 years and developed an exceptional fondness for Bordeaux wines, a taste which contributed handsomely to the city's fortunes for centuries to come.

The 18thC was a boom time in Bordeaux, its *Age d'Or*. Aubert, Marquis de Tourny, the *intendant* (govenor), set about creating an elegant city centre worthy of such an illustrious bastion of the wine trade and in doing so demolished most of the medieval town. There are no promenades along the banks of the chocolate-brown Gironde, its business-like wharves separated from the city centre by a six-lane highway. But the heart of Bordeaux is immensely walkable with tree-lined boulevards, leafy parks and squares, sidewalk cafés and a maze of side streets.

The centrepiece of the 18thC town is **place de la Comédie**, where Victor Louis' 1780 **Grand Théâtre** sports its elegant colonnade and classical statues. To the south, between rue Sainte-Catherine and the river, **quartier Saint-Pierre** was the fashionable haunt of Bordeaux's wealthy merchants with many fine mansions around place du Parlement and place Saint-Pierre. Cours du XXX-Juillet leads north to the

BORDEAUX WINES – AND TOURING THE CHATEAUX

Bordeaux is a Mecca for vinophiles, and its finest wines are unrivalled – in quality, in price, and in complex, subtle, delicious flavours. Bordeaux the wine-producing region is actually a galaxy of regions, sub-regions and estates: to know them all is a lifetime's study for the enthusiast, usually never completed.

Among the most famous major regions within Bordeaux are Médoc, Graves, Saint-Emilion and Pomerol. The Médoc can perhaps be described as the Bordeaux heartland: it spreads south along the Gironde from the tip of the Médoc peninsula nearly to the city itself. The poor gravelly soil, with excellent drainage into the river, is useless for most types of farming, but ideal for vines.

The earliest records of vine cultivation in the region date from Roman times, and the introduction of a grape variety known as *Vitis biturica*, probably the ancestor of cabernet sauvignon. Cabernet grapes, with the judicious addition of merlot, still form the basis of the Bordeaux reds. Bordeaux's white wines, generally grown south and east of the Garonne, are made from the semillon and sauvignon blanc grape varieties.

In addition to the French AOC (*appellation d'origine contrôlée*) regulations, which ensure the right grapes are harvested in the right place at the right time, Bordeaux's wine growers aspire to a grading under the official *Grands Crus* classification system introduced in 1855. Growers were graded according to the price their wines had fetched over the previous hundred years, and top performers were awarded the right to label their wines Grand Premier Cru. At the top of the league, which to most wine enthusiasts' amazement has hardly been revised since 1855, are the four Haut-Médoc châteaux of Latour, Lafite, Margaux and Mouton-Rothschild (added in 1973); Château Haut-Brion from the Graves; and Château d'Yquem from Sauternes. There are four lesser *cru* (growth) classifications with several bewildering sub-divisions; and of course the fact that each year's vintage can be of differing quality adds a further degree of confusion for the amateur.

Visiting Haut-Médoc's great châteaux is no happy-go-lucky affair, and plans should be laid well in advance. Though the vineyards of the Médoc were among the last to be planted in the 17thC (this used to be bandit country), most of its châteaux have since risen to such dizzy heights of complacency that only serious wine types are admitted by appointment. One way round this is to join one of the Bordeaux S.I.'s guided tours (Jun to mid-Oct except Wed and Sat), though these do not

shady expanses of the **Esplanade des Quinconces** and the grandiose late-19thC **Monument des Girondins** which commemorates Bordeaux's liberal deputies executed during Robespierre's Reign of Terror. Streets radiate from here north to the botanical gardens and natural history museum in the **Jardin Public**; and west to place de Tourny where a statue of the urban-planning Marquis surveys his handiwork.

Bordeaux's smartest shopping street, **cours de l'Intendance**, runs from place de la Comédie to **place Gambetta**. Around the square, cafés spill out from beneath arcaded Louis XV-style buildings and overlook the central garden through a stream of

traffic. This is where the Revolutionary guillotine was set up, and where city centre buses now stop. A ten-minute walk north-west, the **Eglise de Saint-Seurin** was a minor pilgrimage stop; Charlemagne is said to have deposited Paladin Roland's legendary *oliphat* (horn) here. Though the horn is long gone, there is a superb 13thC carved portal.

Antique sellers ply their wares along rue Bouffard south from Porte Dijeaux

include either châteaux Margaux (tel. 56 88 70 28), or Mouton-Rothschild (tel. 56 59 22 22). For more detailed information about wine-making and châteaux visits throughout the region, contact the helpful **Maison du Vin**, cours XXX-Juillet, 33000 Bordeaux (tel. 56 52 82 82).

If you are content to look but not enter, the D2 heads north from Bordeaux into big vine country. Take a picnic – restaurants are few and far between. A fun option is to return part of the way down the east bank of the Gironde through the vineyards of Blaye and Bourg, which was the original cradle of Bordeaux's wine trade. A short ferry ride connects Lamarque to **Blaye** (page 64), then take the D669.

Some 25 km north of Bordeaux on the D2, **Château Prieuré Lichine** at Cantenac offers free guided tours year-round. The main buildings occupy a 16thC Benedictine monastery. **Margaux** is a pretty village with more than its share of gracious houses, a Maison du Vin where you can buy but not taste and glimpses of the chapel and roof-tops of the magnificent Empire-style Château Margaux. There is also an extremely sumptuous Relais et Châteaux hotel, the **Relais de Margaux (FFF**; *tel. 56 88 38 31)*, set in a secluded 35-acre estate which stretches down to the Gironde.

At Lamarque, you can make a quick detour to the ferry (*bac*) and

• Médoc *harvest.*

check the timetable for later in the day. Next up is **Château Beychevelle**, a delightful pocket-size mansion built in 1757, just inside the *commune* (wine region) of Saint-Julien. Its reputation is superb. **Pauillac**, despite its top-heavy cluster of *Grands Premiers Crus* (Lafite, Latour and Mouton-Rothschild) is a scrubby little place with an oil refinery on the front. I prefer to feast my eyes on **Château Lafite-Rothschild** further along the D2. Just up the hill, after the splendid façade of **Château Cos d'Estournel** (one of Sainte-Estèphe's finest *cru classé*), take the little D2E for **Sainte-Estèphe** and its summer season Maison du Vin (a Cru Bourgeois Supérieur from Château de Pez is a worthwhile buy here).

to the **Musée des Arts Décoratifs**. The museum's collections of porcelain, glass and furniture are displayed in the Hôtel de Lalande, an 18thC townhouse. Nearby, the **Centre Nationale Jean Moulin**, place Jean-Moulin, named for the famous French Resistance leader, turns its attentions to life under the Nazi occupation.

The heavily buttressed **Cathédrale de Saint-André** stands apart from its 15thC belfry on place Pey-Berland. Almost as big as Notre-Dame in Paris, but rather less exciting, the 11th-13thC ribbed nave flowers into a fine Rayonnant Gothic choir. (Rayonnant describes the transitional phase between early Gothic and Flamboyant Gothic.) Behind the Hôtel de Ville, the **Musée des Beaux-Arts** overlooks the gardens off cours d'Albret (closed Tues). It is small and well-proportioned and includes a Breughel, a Rubens, a Matisse and a summery Renoir of plump strawberries; also works by *Bordelais* artist Albert Marquet, and Médoc landscapes from Odilon Redon.

Not to be missed is the **Musée d'Aquitaine**, 20 cours Pasteur, for a fascinating overview of Bordeaux and the region. Together with artefacts from Roman *Burdigala* and de Tourny's original street plans, there are displays of local costume and crafts, oyster cultivation and the strange life of the Landais shepherds who herd their flocks across the marshes balanced on stilts. Cours Pasteur runs on to the **Porte d'Aquitaine**, the ancient city gate, and there is a rather seedy district of run-down houses and narrow streets heading east to the river and the **Tour Saint-Michel**, a 109 m-high hexagonal tower detached from its tatty 15thC church. The shopping on **rue Sainte-Catherine** picks up as you head back to place de la Comédie, though for picnic provisions the new **Marché Couvert**, off allées de Tourny near Notre-Dame church, is the best bet.

For wine, make straight for the **Vinothèque de Bordeaux**, 8 cours de XXX-Juillet, which stocks more than 200 labels from the Bordeaux growing areas. For more information and details of wine tours, pop over the road to the helpful **Maison du Vin de Bordeaux**, 3 cours du XXX-Juillet (tel. 56 52 82 82; closed Sun).

COGNAC ✕

On the N141, 27 km E of Saintes. S.I. 19 place Jean-Monnet. A prosperous town on the River Charente, Cognac literally exudes brandy. In the town centre, three major producers offer free tours of their *chais* (warehouses). **Martell,** place Martell, is the oldest, (closed Sat-Sun except Sat Jul-Aug); while **Hennessy**, founded by an Irishman when he retired from the French army in the 1760s, resides on quai des Flamands (closed Sat, Sun except Sat Jun-Sep). The advantage of the **Otard** tour is a chance to see over the remains of the 13thC Château de Cognac, where François I was born in 1494 (closed Sat-Sun Oct-Mar).

The S.I. has details of summer season boat trips up the Charente to **Jarnac** (15 km E); and there is plenty of space for car-weary kids to run around, or have a picnic by the river and a swim in the **Parc François-1er**.

COULON
See page 24.

NANTES
See France Overall: 2.

NOIRMOUTIER, ILE DE 🛏 ✕
Toll bridge at Fromentine, off D22 43 km S of Pornic; D948 causeway; ferries from Pornic. The most satisfactory means of getting to this 22 km-long island is definitely the **Passage du Gois**. This causeway by-passes the expensive toll bridge but is only accessible for three hours either side of low tide.

Each summer, peaceful Noirmoutier undergoes a startling metamorphosis into popular holiday resort. Beyond the salt pans, its modest dunes unfurl along the west coast fringed with samphire, while the north-eastern coast rears up into a couple of headlands above rocky bays. There is mimosa in mid-winter and potatoes in the autumn. A monastery was founded here in the 5thC, and the main town, **Noirmoutier-en-l'Ile**, has a church with an 11thC crypt, also a 12thC **Château-Musée**, and well-stocked Tuesday and Friday market.

From April to October there are boat services from Noirmoutier (75 minutes) to the half-pint-sized **Ile d'Yeu** (services from mainland Fromentine year-round). On Yeu old-fashioned sit-up-and-beg bicycles can be hired from the quayside at **Port-Joinville** for the 3-km cycle ride across the tiny island to **le Vieux Château** which juts out from the ragged granite cliffs of the Côte Sauvage. The spick-and-span village of **Port de la Meule** prefaces the beaches of **L'Anse des Vieilles**.

NIORT
See Local Explorations: 3.

OLERON, ILE D' ⊭ ×
Toll bridge 6 km W of Marennes, 30 km S of Rochefort. Between Royan and Rochefort, France's second largest island (after Corsica) is celebrated for its oysters and miles of sandy beaches. The first sizeable town over the bridge is **Le Château** (S.I. place de la République), with an old fortress once owned by the Dukes of Aquitaine and remodelled by Vauban. Along the east coast, a patchwork of marshland and glittering pools edge more oyster parks, and there are numerous small hamlets and fishing villages reaching north to the main town of **Saint-Pierre** (S.I. place Gambetta). The best beaches are in the north-east, such as sheltered **Boyardville**, which also has a pretty port. Bird lovers should make for the **Marais aux Oiseaux**, a bird reserve-cum-breeding and rescue centre (off the D126 W of Saint-Pierre).

PERIGUEUX
See France Overall: 16.

PORNIC ×
On the D751, 50 km W of Nantes. .A popular summer weekend escape for the *Nantais*, this pretty little fishing port is a useful starting point for a run down the coast. The harbour is guarded by one of Gilles de Rais's (aka Bluebeard) castles, this one dating from the 14thC. Foot passengers can catch summer season ferry services from here across to the **Ile de Noirmoutier** (see page 68). For beaches, head west to the Plage Mombeau and Plage des Sablons en route to Sainte-Marie-sur-Mer (3 km W).

RE, ILE DE ⊭ ×
See La Rochelle, right.

ROCHEFORT ⊭ ×
On the N137, *32 km S of La Rochelle.* S.I. *avenue Sadi-Carnot.* On the River Charente, 15 km inland from the sea, Rochefort was commissioned as a safe port and arsenal by Louis XIV's Minister for the Navy, Colbert. The town was built from scratch between 1665-72, and its military bearing is immediately obvious in the neat grid of streets and sturdy architecture. The most unusual edifice is the **Corderie Royale**, rue Toufaire, the longest building in France at 374 m, former site of the royal ropeworks. At one end the **Centre International de la Mer** houses rope-making and maritime displays, and the surrounding gardens abound with foreign species brought back by sailors. A short walk away, the **Musée de la Marine**, place de la Gallossinnière (closed Tues), bulges at the seams with figureheads, sextants and assorted nautical odds and ends.

On a rather different tack, 19thC novelist 'Pierre Loti' sailed the Seven Seas as a career naval officer named Julien Viaud before settling down in Rochefort. His travels provided suitably exotic backgrounds for a series of romantic novels and also furnished the **Maison de Pierre Loti**, 141 rue Pierre Loti (closed Sun am, Mon am, and Tues in winter), in bizarre style complete with mosque, sumptuous banqueting hall and Turkish den where 'Loti' would fuel his imagination with the help of a hookah.

ROCHELLE, LA ⊭ ×
On the N11/N137, *140 km S of Nantes/182km N of Bordeaux.* S.I. *place du Petite Sirène.* A seaside resort with character and charm, La Rochelle offers its delightfully-preserved Old Town centre together with an entertaining combination of beaches and boat trips plus a half-dozen or so museums and attractions including free municipal bike hire. Not surprisingly, it is very popular, and accommodation is booked up several months in advance for the summer season.

One of the jewels in the crown of Eleanor of Aquitaine's dowry, the sheltered port was granted an independent charter in 1199, and flourished during the medieval period. With the arrival of Protestantism in the 16thC, it became a Huguenot stronghold and later a thorn in the side of Richelieu. He blockaded the harbour in 1627, and brought

• *Ile d'Oléron oyster boats.*

the town to its knees with a 15-month siege: just 5,000 of the original 28,000 inhabitants survived. Trade with the New World – Canada, America and the West Indies – revived La Rochelle's fortunes. Shipowners and merchants rebuilt the town, often using granite ballast to construct their splendid residences.

The town centre is compact and easy to explore. Its medieval walls were largely demolished by Richelieu, but an 18thC archway, the **Porte de la Grosse-Horloge**, marks the entrance to the Old Town off quai du Pierre. Head south down cours des Dames for **Tour de la Chaine**, a 14thC watch tower at the narrow entrance to the harbour basin. A hefty chain used to be towed across to its twin, **Tour Saint-Nicolas**, to close the inner harbour at night. The elevated old sea wall, rue sur les Murs, leads to a third tower, **Tour de la Lanterne**, once a primitive lighthouse with a fire burning inside. La Rochelle's beach suburb lies to the west.

The grid of streets north of the Grosse- Horloge are packed with splen-

did medieval buildings, Renaissance mansions and 17th-18thC town houses. Arcaded **rue du Palais** is the main shopping street, off which rue Dupaty leads east to the **Hôtel de Ville** with a wonderful Renaissance courtyard. Rue des Augustins features the two-storey loggia and turrets of the **Maison Henri II**; and rue Fleuriau is home to the fascinating **Musée du Nouveau Monde** (closed Tues), its displays of prints, maps and assorted Americana laid out in the former home of a wealthy merchant family. The 18thC **Cathédrale** is of slight interest, but there are two more museums in its vicinity: the **Musée des Beaux-Arts**, rue Gargoulleau, with an important portrait of Martin Luther by Cranach the Elder (closed Sun am, Tues); and the **Musée d'Orbigny-Bernon**, 2 rue Saint-Côme (closed Sun am, Tues), which focuses on regional history and traditions, plus a notable ceramics section. (Joint-entry museum tickets available.)

Back down on the front, the **Musée Maritime** offers a 76-m frigate for inspection in the Bassin des Chalutiers; and there is a hi-tech **Aquarium** at the Port des Minimes. A children's favourite is the **Musée des Automates**, rue de la Desirée, with an entrancing crowd of mechanical puppets; also the neighbouring **Musée des Modèles Réduits** (joint tickets), featuring scale models of boats, trains, planes and more.

Reached by a causeway (toll) or bus-boat connection from the mainland, the **Ile de Ré** is shaped like a prawn, its body surrounded by superb beaches and its saltmarsh tail hooked around oyster beds. **Sablonceaux** is a popular spot just over the causeway with beaches, restaurants, bicycle and moped hire. Moving north, Ré bears an uncanny resemblance to a Greek island with its whitewashed buildings, vines, fishing boats and feathery fields of asparagus. **Saint-Martin**, the capital, has a fortified harbour guarded by one of Maréchal Vauban's many citadels. This one served as a prison and transit point for criminals condemned to hard labour in the colonies. The S.I. is on avenue Victor-Boutailier, and nearby the **Musée Naval et E-Cognacq** presents maritime history and local crafts displays in the 15th-17thC Hôtel Clerjotte (closed Mon, Tues in winter).

Another day trip is the **Ile d'Aix**, a real island only accessible by boat. Just 2 km long, it mixes beach and marsh, pines, oaks, charming cottage gardens and the town of **Le Bourg**, where Napoleon spent his last days on French soil before exile to St Helena. The **Musée Napoléon** is stuffed with the Emperor's clothes and memorabilia; and there is a **Musée Africain** where the stuffing is largely wildlife and weaponry. Summer season ferries depart from La Rochelle and the Ile d'Oléron; in service year-round, the shortest crossing is from Pointe de la Fumée, near Fouras (30 km S of La Rochelle).

ROYAN ☕ ✕
On the D733, 40 km S of Rochefort. S.I. *place de la Poste.* A popular family resort with lovely beaches, camp sites in the pine forests and a daily market in the covered *halles* on boulevard Aristide-Briand. The town is no beauty, rebuilt in functional concrete after the Second World War, but café-bars and restaurants are in plentiful supply, their striped awnings and plant tubs providing a dash of colour.

In addition to various summer sea-

• *The toll bridge linking Ile d'Oléron with the mainland.*

son boat trips, regular year-round ferry services make the 20-minute crossing to Pointe de Grave on the tip of the Médoc peninsula for easy access to the Côte d'Argent resorts of Soulac, Carcans-Plage, Maubuisson and Lacaneau-Océan. At Palmyre (10 km NW via the D25), the **Parc Zoologique** is France's second largest zoo with big cats and other exotica roaming around the Fôret de la Coubre.

SABLES D'OLONNE, LES ☕ ✕
On the N160, 95 km S of Nantes. Sand, sun, surf and *baguettes* in a 'Miami meets Torremolinos and attacks a French fishing port' scenario. Great beaches backed by high-rise apartments ensure a hectic family-orientated two-and-a-half month summer season. There is an unlikely cultural diversion in the fine modern art collection on show in the **Musée de l'Abbaye Sainte-Croix**. Of wider appeal, the **Musée Automobile de Vendée**, route de Talmont (8 km E), features working models from the 1880s to 1960s (closed Nov to Apr).

71

SAINT-EMILION
See France Overall: 16.

SAINTES 🛏 ✕
*On the N137/A10, 115 km N of Bordeaux.
S.I. 52 cours National.* An attractive market town on both banks of the River Charente, Saintes was the regional capital of the Saintoge in Roman times. During the 11thC, it developed into an important religious centre and pilgrim stop on the Route Saint-Jacques to Santiago de Compostela.

On the right bank of the river, the leafy main street, **cours National**, boasts a number of fine 19thC buildings including the pretty Théâtre. Pedestrianized rue Alsace-Lorraine leads into the Old Town, where the **Musée des Beaux-Arts**, rue Victor-Hugo (closed Tues), displays its unusual collection of Sèvres china in the **Annexe Echevinge**, and the **Cathédrale de Saint-Pierre** crumbles per-

---

> **RIVER TRIP TO COGNAC**
> A pleasant excursion from Saintes is by river to the brandy town of **Cognac** (see page 68). The S.I. has details of summer season boat trips up the Charente to Cognac and on to Jarnac.

---

ceptibly into a quiet square at the bottom of the street. A bit of a hike to the west, across cours Reverseaux, the pilgrim church of **Saint-Eutrope** is in far better shape. It is built on top of an ancient crypt, a short walk from the Roman **Arènes**. Back down in a quiet street near quai de Verdun, the regional furniture, costumes and knick-knacks of the **Musée Dupuy-Mestreau**, 6 rue Monconseil, are laid out in an elegant 18thC town house once owned by the Marquis de Monconseil (closed Mon).

RECOMMENDED RESTAURANTS

BORDEAUX
Les Noilles, F-FF; *12 allées de Tourny; tel. 56 81 94 45; credit cards* V.
Old-fashioned *brasserie* serving local classics such as oysters with spicy sausage.

Les Plaisirs d'Ausone, FF; *10 rue d'Ausone; tel. 56 79 30 30; credit cards* AE, V; *closed Sat lunch, Sun-Mon lunch, three weeks Aug.*
Cool, vaulted dining room, imaginative cooking and excellent fresh ingredients. The set menus are well-conceived and fairly priced.

Le Vieux Bordeaux, FF; *27 rue Buhan; tel. 56 52 94 36; credit cards* AE, DC, V; *closed Sat lunch, Sun, two weeks Feb, three weeks Aug.*
A local favourite maintaining remarkably low prices despite its Michelin star. Sunny dining room and terrace; delicious pink duck with foie gras and peaches.

COGNAC
Le Coq d'Or, F-FF; *33 place François-Ier; tel. 45 82 02 56; credit cards* AE, DC, MC, V; *closed Sun, and Fri dinner in winter.*

Busy lunch-time spot with 1960s decoration but traditional food and service. Sample the chicken cooked with local *pineau*.

NOIRMOUTIER-EN-L'ILE
Fleur de Sel, FF; *rue des Saulniers; tel. 51 39 21 59; credit cards* V; *closed Nov-Apr.*
Pretty dining room with tables in the garden serving the best seafood on the island.
Also 35 comfortable modern rooms facing the lawn (**FF-FFF**) and a pool.

OLERON, ILE D'
Les Bains, F-FF; *at Boyardville; tel. 46 47 01 02; credit cards* AE, V; *closed Oct-May.*
Scrumptious regional seafood specials – fish terrine, sea perch with oysters – outdoor tables overlook the port.
Also 11 simple (**F-FF**) rooms.

PORNIC
Beau Rivage, F-FF; *plage de la Birochère; tel. 40 82 03 08; credit cards* AE, DC, MC, V; *closed Mon, Thur dinner in winter, Jan.*
Copious and classic seafood dishes, such as a shellfish fricassée plus a huge sunny verandah.

Follow the quays round to the foot-bridge by the covered market. You can pick up picnic ingredients here and head for the **Jardin Public** across the Charente. On the opposite bank, the **Arc de Germanicus** marks the position of the old Roman bridge, near the **Musée Archéologique** (closed Tues, and Nov-Mar). This is a treasure trove of statues and carvings propped on mismatched plinths; more delicate exhibits such as glass and fishing tackle discovered beneath the 4thC city ramparts reside in a nearby hut. Off rue de l'Arc de Triomphe, the entrance to the **Abbaye aux Dames** is on place Saint-Pallais (named for the little Romanesque church just inside the walls). The abbey's marvellous portal is a riot of angelic and fantastical imagery in high contrast to the simple interior with its single nave, domed transcept and tunnel-shaped sacristy, once a 15thC chapel.

TALMONT

On the D25, 16 km SE of Royan. A tiny village of low whitewashed cottages and 3-m high hollyhocks on the Gironde estuary, Talmont has a lovely Romanesque church in the **Eglise de Sainte-Rade-gone**. It was built 1140-70 by Benedictine monks, and despite its fortress-like appearance boasts a fine flowering of neat blind arches, heraldic symbols and gargoyle decorations. As befits a mariners' church, there are ferocious-looking sea beasts fighting it out by the porch (beneath marvellous acrobats) and some endearing bug-eyed fish posted around the feet of the pillars inside. Then stroll down through the narrow streets to the water's edge for a look at the wooden fishing huts perched on stilts and hung with gaping nets.

YEU, ILE D' 🏠

See Noirmoutier and Ile de Ré, pages 68 and 69.

RE, ILE DE
La Salicorne, F-FF; *16 rue de l'Olivette, at Couarde-sur-Mer; tel. 46 29 82 37; credit cards V; closed Nov -Easter.*

Well worth seeking out for Luc Dumont's super-fresh, bargain-priced seafood menus and classic dishes. Good wines and terrace.

Also five very simple (**F**) rooms.

ROCHEFORT
Le Tourne-Blanche, F-FF; *56 avenue Charles-de-Gaulle; tel. 46 99 20 19; credit cards AE, V; closed Sun dinner-Mon, one week Jan, two weeks Jul.*

Local favourite serving fresh, well priced dishes such as *moules à la charentaise.*

ROCHELLE, LA
Bistro de l'Entract, FF; *22 rue Saint-Jean-du-Pérot; tel. 46 50 62 60; credit cards V; closed Sun.*

Near the Tour de la Chaine, M. Coutanceau's (see below) side-show dishes up simplified versions of his spectacular cuisine.

Richard Coutanceau, FF-FFF; *plage de la Concurrence; tel. 46 41 48 19; credit cards AE, DC, V; closed Sun, and Mon in winter.*

Elegant decoration, bay views and a gastronomic *tour de force* at work.

Bass *carpaccio* with green peppercorns, lightly curried turbot with winkles, duckling, lobster. Excellent service; two Michelin stars; book ahead.

ROYAN
Le Chalet, F-FF; *6 boulevard de la Grandière; tel. 46 05 05 90; credit cards AE, V; closed Wed in winter, and Feb.*

Attractive surroundings and light, classical cooking with the emphasis on seafood.

SABLES D'OLONNE
Le Navarin, F-FF; *18 place Navarin; tel. 51 21 11 61; credit cards V; closed Sun dinner-Mon in winter, two weeks Oct.*

Views over the port and classical cuisine created from market-fresh produce.

SAINTES
Hôtel Commerce-Mancini, F-FF; *rue Messageries; tel. 46 93 06 61; credit cards AE, DC, MC, V; closed Sat lunch and Sun in winter.*

Old-fashioned hotel dining room serving reliable classic cuisine. Also 35 plain rooms year round.

For something lighter and less formal, try **Le Jardin du Rempart, F**; *36 rue du Rempart (tel. 46 93 37 66).*

<u>South-Western France</u>
Between Bordeaux and Toulouse
The South-West Coast and the Pyrenees–Aquitaine

710 km; maps Michelin Nos 234 and 235

A magnificent journey which, taken in conjunction with France Overall: 5, Between Toulouse and Avignon, blazes a trail from Bordeaux through the Pyrenees to the Mediterranean coast and arrives in Provence – or vice versa. Whichever way you approach it, the scenery is magnificent, and everyone from hikers and history buffs to sunseekers and gourmets will find plenty to grab their attention.

Between Bordeaux and Toulouse, the fastest road is the A62. This route gives access to the gentle countryside of Gascony to the south (see Detour – Gascony, page 83) and to the valley of the Lot to its north (see Local Explorations: 4), but it would deny you the chance to travel through the splendid Pyrenees, which it entirely by-passes. Instead, my chosen route makes a dog-leg: leaving Bordeaux (see France Overall: 3) it skims through the pine forests of the Landes on the A63/N10, parallel to some of Europe's finest beaches along the Côte d'Argent. At Bayonne (the starting point for Local Explorations: 5) it enters Basque country. Between Bayonne and Pau, red routers in a tearing hurry can use the A64, but everyone else should follow the disjointed sections of the D918, which makes the best route through the west and central Pyrenees. Even racing red routers should use the mountain roads between Pau and Saint-Gaudens, avoiding boring Tarbes and catching some Pyrenean scenery. Between Saint-Gaudens and Toulouse they can use the fast N117 whilst dawdling blue and green route followers can wend their way via Bagnères-de-Luchon and Saint-Bertrand-de-Commignes to (or from) Foix – and can use the N20 for a quick sprint between Foix and Toulouse. Do not attempt to rush this Pyrenean route, for you will need plenty of time to ogle the scenery and tackle the winding roads in safety.

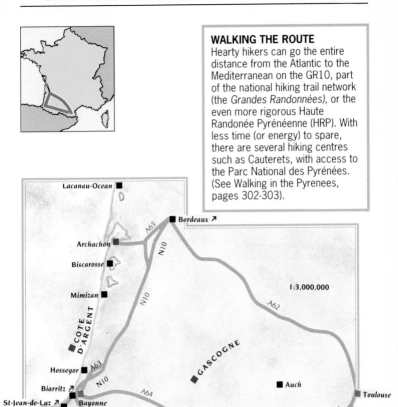

WALKING THE ROUTE

Hearty hikers can go the entire distance from the Atlantic to the Mediterranean on the GR10, part of the national hiking trail network (the *Grandes Randonnées)*, or the even more rigorous Haute Randonée Pyrénéenne (HRP). With less time (or energy) to spare, there are several hiking centres such as Cauterets, with access to the Parc National des Pyrénées. (See Walking in the Pyrenees, pages 302-303).

TRANSPORT

There are flights and fast TGV train services between Paris and both Bordeaux (3 hours) and Toulouse (5 hours 10 minutes); services also link the two. From Bordeaux, frequent trains serve Bayonne (train and bus connections to the Basque Coast and Saint-Jean-Pied-de-Port). Bayonne-Toulouse trains stop at Pau (connections to Oloron-Sainte-Marie), Lourdes and Saint-Gaudens. Lourdes is the best place to pick up bus connections to Bagnères-de-Bigorre, Cauterets, and Luz-Saint-Sauveur (for Gavarnie).

SIGHTS & PLACES OF INTEREST

ARCACHON

On the N250, 64 km SW of Bordeaux. Famed for its oysterbeds, Arcachon has been a favourite weekend retreat for the *Bordelais* since trains started running in the mid 19thC. (Frequent daily services from Bordeaux take 40 minutes.) Local marine life is on display at an aquarium on avenue de Gaulle, but the main attraction is the beach and magnificent 114 m-high **Dune du Pilat** (10 km via D218), Europe's largest sand dune. (Buses and bike hire from the railway station.) Birdwatchers can while away several hours at the **Parc Ornithologique du Teich** (14 km via D610). This wetlands preserve is a great place to spot herons, storks and wildfowl: there are several hides and a ranger station.

BAGNERES-DE-BIGORRE

On the D935, 22 km SE of Lourdes. Once visited by luminaries including Georges Sand and Tennyson, this quiet, leafy spa town makes a pleasant pit stop before or after the switchback drive over Col du Tourmalet. There are several café-bars on central place aux Thermes, opposite the little Musée Salies, and you can stretch your legs in the Parc Thermal de Salut.

BAGNERES-DE-LUCHON

On the D125, 47 km S of Saint-Gaudens. S.I. *18 allées d'Etigny.* A fashionable Central Pyrenean spa town which makes a base for several excursions. The bustling main street, allées d'Etigny, is well-supplied with shops, cafés and eateries, and you can pop in to take a cure in the *station thermal*, fed by 80 mountain springs. The S.I. provides details of several popular walking trails along the Spanish border. One of the best starts from **Lac d'Oô** (14 km SW via D618/D76); also, the Vallée du Lys (32 km S via D125/D46). A rack railway hauls up to Superbagnères (1,800 m), and there is skiing in winter.

BAYONNE ⌨ ✕

On A63/N10, 7 km E of Biarritz. S.I. *place de la Liberté.* For visitors heading south, this is the first real contact with Basque country. Some 5 km inland from the Golfe de Gascogne, Bayonne is the capital of the Pays Basques clustered around the confluence of the Rivers Ardour and Nive, with a deep-water port and attractive small-town atmosphere.

Bayonne's history begins with the Roman settlement of Lapurdam. In the 12thC, the city transferred to English hands under the terms of Eleanor of Aquitaine's dowry on her marriage to Henry II, and prospered under English rule, developing into a successful centre of the wine trade. Harshly treated when the French regained control in 1451, the city's fortunes rose again in the 18thC on the strength of its locally-produced bayonets. Today, aircraft parts and concrete are the main local industries.

The narrow, shady streets of the town centre are pleasantly tourist-free. On the west bank of the Nive, **Grand Bayonne** is the central shopping area leading up to the **Cathédrale de Sainte-Marie.** Built in the 13th-16thC in the northern-Gothic style (the twin towers that rise above the town were not completed until the 19thC), the well-worn building has some lovely 16thC glass, French and English coats-of-arms in the nave, and a peaceful grassy cloister.

Cross the Nive by one of the connecting bridges to **Petit Bayonne** for the museum and restaurant quarter with its tall, Basque-style half-timbered façades and picturesque frontispiece of arcaded houses on the quayside. The **Musée Basque,** rue Marengo, makes a fascinating introduction to local crafts and folklore (currently closed for renovations). For an unexpected treat, stop off at the **Musée Bonnat,** rue Jacques-Lafitte (closed Tues), built around native 19thC society artist Léon Bonnat's fine personal collection. Bonnat had a say in designing the interior, and you start at the top with some marvellous Italian Primitives and Renaissance works, Rubens sketches, and a smooth Spanish *Baigneuse* by Ingres. Among the bronzes and Géricault's equine studies, look out for Bonnat's *Self-Portrait,* and his carefully observed portraits on the ground floor.

Midweek and Saturday markets take place on the quays. To sample a *pelota* game, head for the Trinquet Saint-

André on Thursdays (4 pm). There are bullfights in August and September; and a jazz festival in July.

See also Local Explorations: 5.

BIARRITZ
See Local Explorations: 5.

BORDEAUX
See France Overall: 3.

CAMBO-LES-BAINS
See Local Explorations: 5.

CAUTERETS ⇥ ✕
On the D920, 20 km S of Lourdes. S.I. place Clemenceau. Daily bus service from Lourdes. Cauterets is one of the main Pyrenean walking, mountaineering and winter-sports centres, squeezed into a spectacular wooded valley, on the edge of the **Parc National des Pyrénées Occidentales**. Though the town still attracts devotees to its spa facilities, most visitors use the town as a base for exploring the mountains.

First stop for would-be hikers, the Maison du Parc, on place de la Gare, offers general information about the national park, a small museum and seasonal film shows. The Maison de la Montagne, place Clemenceau, supplies more detailed information about trails, weather conditions, climbing lessons and guided walks in summer, plus advice on routes, maps and where to hire gear from mountain bikes to boots and skis. The GR10 runs just south of town, and there are numerous short- and medium-distance hikes in the vicinity. (See **Walking in the Pyrenees,** pages 302-303.)

COTE D'ARGENT
Between Soulac-sur-mer and Biarritz. The 'Silver Coast' unfurls along the Atlantic seaboard in a magnificent swathe of white sand stretching some 200 km

---

BEACHES, BOAT TRIPS AND BIKES
Some of the best beaches along the Côte d'Argent (which is really one long, arrow-straight strip of sand) are away from the unprepossessing resorts, just broad unspoilt expanses of fine white sand backed by dunes. South of Mimizan, the D652 gives access to uncrowded beaches from the villages of **Lit-et-Mixe, Saint-Girons, Moliets** and **Messanges**.

The anonymous pine lands of the Forêt des Landes marches right up to the coast. As a complement to the beaches and sea-bathing (which can be hazardous – pay attention to warnings), a series of tranquil lakes are strung along the fringes of the forest. They are excellent for families, with sandy beaches and facilities for fishing, sailing, windsurfing and water-skiing. Two of the most pleasant are **Etang de Cazaux et de Sanguinet** and **Etang de Biscarosse et de Parentis** immediately to the north and south of **Biscarosse**. Prettiest of all is the reed-fringed **Etang de Soustons.** The little rivers which lead from these lakes to the sea a few kilometres away are known as *courants.* Just south of Saint-Girons, still on the D652, the Etang de Léon

(fishing and windsurfing) is linked to the sea by a ravishingly pretty *courant.* You can take a delightful boat trip (in a flat-bottomed punt) along this **Courant d'Huchet** which winds, carpeted by waterlillies, between over-hanging willows, alders, hibiscus and tamarisk. Trips last between 1 and 4 hours, depending on how far you go. Enquire at the Bureau des Bataliers, tel. 58 48 75 39.

You could stay the night at the simple, and peaceful **Hôtel du Lac, F** at Léon *(tel. 58 48 73 11);* or, more up-market, 20 km S at **La Bergerie, FF** *(avenue du Lac; tel. 58 41 11 43),* a civilized Landais house with a good dining room. Alternatively, stay at **Les Huitrières du Lac, F** *(1187 avenue du Touring Club, Hossegor; tel. 58 43 51 48)* just to indulge in the inexpensive seafood served in the restaurant with a lovely lake-side position.

The flat countryside of the Landes makes cycling attractive and there are cycleways along the coast and in the forest. Contact Comité departmental de Cyclotourisme, 12 rue Gabriel-Fauré, Saint-Paul-les-Dax; tel. 58 74 27 52 for a list of itineraries.

between the mouth of the Gironde and Biarritz. Edged by pine forest, the dunes march up to 5 km inland interspersed by two-bit towns packed to the gills with bronzed youth in summer, then shut up and virtually deserted from September to May.

Surfing is the name of the game here with world-class events held at **Lacanau-Océan** and **Hossegor** in mid to late August. **Soulac** (to the north of Lacanau), **Biscarrosse** and **Mimizan** are also popular. Swimmers should beware strong currents.

FOIX

On the N20, 84 km S of Toulouse. A Cathar stronghold which survived four sieges by Simon de Montfort, Foix spreads out along the Ariège valley beneath the towers of its 11thC fortress. The three towers, one of which houses a small local history and crafts museum, are all that remains of a great **Château** where the distinguished Counts of Foix and Viscounts of Béarn once held court; the views across the valley to the snow-capped mountains are superb. Below, the Gothic **Eglise de Saint-Volusien** has a fortified choir with fine 15thC stalls, and the attractive Old Town streets are lined with 16th-17thC buildings.

GAVARNIE, CIRQUE DE

See Luz-Saint-Saveur, this page.

HENDAYE

See Local Explorations: 5.

LOURDES

On the D937 and N21, 43 km SE of Pau. S.I. place du Champ-Commun. Each year around five million Catholic pilgrims

---

BOAT TRIP AND WATERSPORTS AT FOIX

Children particularly will enjoy a boat trip (daily Easter-Sept; Sun Oct-Easter) on Europe's largest underground river, **Labouiche**, 6 km north-west of Foix. Proficient canoeists can try their luck on the gushing Arriège: canoe hire from Foyer Léo Lagrange, tel. 61 65 44 19. There is gentler canoeing, plus fishing and waterskiing on **Lac de Labarre**, just north of Foix.

---

flock to the site on the banks of the Gave de Pau where 14 year-old miller's daughter Bernadette Soubirous witnessed 18 separate visions of the Virgin Mary in 1858. Many are invalids in search of a cure.

It is hard to remain objective about the rampant commercialism that spills out of the shop fronts leading to the 'Cité Réligieuse' – Virgin Mary bedside lamps in baby blue and white, statuary and confectionary all emblazoned with an inscription from Lourdes – or the patient queues of pilgrims winding along the river bank waiting to fill plastic cartons with water from the dank **Grotte de Massabielle** amidst a collection of rusting crutches. The mock-Byzantine **Basilique du Rosaire** is a model of l9thC bad taste; above it the **Basilique Supérieur** at least displays some touching votive offerings; while beneath the gardens, the **Basilique Saint-Pie X** has all the spirituality of a concrete bunker, which is exactly what it is.

Non-pilgrims will find refuge in the **Château-Fort et Musée Pyrénéen** (open Apr-Oct) which physically if not spiritually dominates the town perched on a rocky crag. A former feudal stronghold and prison, the castle contains a terrific museum of local crafts, archaeological and geological finds, stuffed examples of local wildlife, 18thC ceramics, and a room devoted to Pyrenean mountaineers.

LUZ-SAINT-SAVEUR ⛳

On the D921/D918, 31 km S of Lourdes. S.I. place du 8-mai. A minor ski resort close to Lourdes (via N21/D921; daily bus service), Luz guards the only approach to the spectacular Cirque de Gavarnie. While in Luz, you can pick up hiking information from the S.I., and stop off for a look at the **Eglise de Saint-André,** built in the 12thC and fortified by the Knights of St John two centuries later. The squat, sturdy complex is encircled by crenellated ramparts, there are carved escutcheons around the roof of the circular *donjon*, and a carved porch.

Gavarnie is a further 20 km S (daily bus service) via the aptly-named stony wilds of the Chaos de Coumély. You can also walk it on GR10. Mules and donkeys ply the trail up to the **Cirque de Gavarnie** (a 2-hour round trip), but

it is a pleasant walk through beech woods. Glacial erosion swept out the magnificent natural amphitheatre measuring 3 km across, with walls that rise in three distinct tiers to a height of more than 1,600 m, backed to the east by 3,000-m peaks. A vertical breach, the *Brèche de Roland*, slashes 100 m into the wall, said to have been carved by Durandal, the magic sword of Paladin Roland, one of Charlemagne's 12 legendary knights. To the left, Europe's highest waterfall, the Grande Cascade, plunges 442 m down to a fast-flowing river.

Try to avoid weekends and time your visit for the early morning or late afternoon in order to miss the over-burdened mule trains.

• *Luz-Saint-Sauveur.*

Alternatively, take the left-hand fork out of Gèdre (D922) to the impressive, but less popular Cirque de Troumouse. In Gavarnie you can eat very well in the delightfully decorated **La Ruade, F**, (tel. 62 92 48 49).

OLORON-SAINTE-MARIE

On the N134/D936, 35 *km* SW *of Pau.* To be honest, Oloron is rather a grim little town, but that could be blamed on a rainy day. It does, however, boast two notable churches. The delights of the **Eglise de Sainte-Croix** are something of a closed book to amateurs, but the oldest Romanesque church in the Béarn region sports an unusual 13thC dome with an eight-pointed star picked out in brickwork by Spanish artisans echoing the Grand Mosque at Cordoba. This, apparently, will enchant architectural and ecclesiastical historians. Otherwise, the interior restoration work can be described as crude at best.

The highlight of the former cathedral, **Sainte-Marie**, is a truly wonderful portal commissioned by Count Gaston IV, a veteran of the First Crusade, and carved from Pyrenean marble. Beneath a Descent from the Cross, the 24 Elders of the Apocalypse strum serenely on stringed instruments and wave the odd rattle, while Man bustles about his seasonal calender of fattening geese and slaughtering pigs. The noble count and his steed put in an heroic appearance trampling careless Saracens; while those that escape are chained to the central pillar.

PAU ⇔ ✕
On the A64/N117, 107 km E of Bayonne, 192 km W of Toulouse. S.I. place Royale. A

Gallo-Roman town which became the medieval seat of the Lords of Béarn, Pau was the birthplace of Henri IV. Bought up a Protestant, Henri proved a consummate politician, converting to Catholicism to enable his accession with the famous quip "Paris is worth a mass". He then pacified the Protestant *Béarnais* by assuring them that France was being added to Béarn rather than vice versa. Béarn was not annexed to France until Louis XIII's reign.

Pau has an unusual English connection started by soldiers from Wellington's army. After the defeat of the French at Orthez in 1814, many opted to stay on. Later, the bracing yet sheltered climate was endorsed by one Doctor Alexander Taylor, and a steady stream of invalid British journeyed south to take the air. To mitigate the boredom, they introduced the natives to croquet, golf, cricket and fox hunting. After Queen Victoria opted for Biarritz in 1889, the fashion declined.

A stroll along the **Boulevard des**

Pyrénées not only bears out the wisdom of Doctor Taylor's theory, but affords the most stupendous view over the Gave de Pau to the mountains. An orientation table identifies all the peaks gathered around the massive Pic du Midi du Bigorre, including the great Pyrenean mountain, Vignemale (3,298m).

The main sight in town is the **Château de Pau**, rue du Château, heavily restored in the 19thC. A red-brick keep, built by Gaston Fébus around 1370, survives in marked contrast to the ornate Renaissance courtyard with its much-repeated H and M motif representing Henri d'Albret and Marguerite d'Angoulême (sister of François I of France), Henri IV's grandparents. Guided tours trail through the grandiose 19thC apartments decorated with some fine tapestries and period furniture; also what is believed to be Henri IV's cradle, a giant tortoise shell (for longevity), is now on show festooned with standards and an elaborate helmet. The kitchens feature some rather engaging carvings of boars, cows, deer and other roasts on the hoof. Across the courtyard, the **Musée Béarnais** provides an overview of local culture, crafts and natural history and archaeology.

Military buffs might fancy a quick pilgrimage to the **Musée Bernadotte,** rue Tran (closed Mon, Jan), birthplace of one of Napoleon's finest commanders. Jean-Baptiste Bernadotte (1763-1844) later became the King of Sweden. The ugly modern **Musée des Beaux-Arts,** rue Mathieu-Lalanne (closed Tues), is worth a stop for its collection of fine Pyrenean scenes and works by Rubens, El Greco and Dégas amongst others.

PIC DU MIDI DE BIGORRE

Off the D918, 35 km S of Bagnères-de-Bigorre. At the top of the Col du Tourmalet (2,114 m), the highest mountain pass in the Pyrenees, a 5-km toll road (Jun-Sep) winds on up to the desolate peak

cious; convenient for Château and Old Town.

SAINT-JEAN-PIED-DE-PORT
Arcé, F-FF; *Saint-Etienne-de-Baïgorry; (10 km W of Saint-Jean-Pied-de-Port via D15) tel. 59 37 40 14; credit cards* MC, V; *closed mid-Nov to mid-Mar.*

Family-run since 1864, enlarged, modernized, but still delightful, with a lovely riverside setting. Excellent regional food on the terrace, overhung by chestnut trees. Some rooms are large, and some have terraces or balconies.

See also Recommended Restaurants.

TOULOUSE
Altéa Wilson, FF; *7 rue Labéda; tel. 61 21 21 75; credit cards* AE, DC, MC, V; *open year round.*

Central, and recently refurbished. Family deals and piano bar; private parking. Cheaper sister hotel, **Altéa Matabiau** (tel. 61 62 84 93), by the station.

Clocher de Rodez, F; *14-15 place Jeanne d'Arc; tel. 61 62 42 92; credit cards* AE, DC, V; *open year round.*

Just across the inner city ring road, this comfortable old hotel has 46 rooms, parking, a restaurant and bar.

Grand Balcon, F; *8 rue Romiguières; tel. 61 21 48 08; no credit cards; closed Christmas, and three weeks Aug.*

Right on corner of place du Capitole, Saint-Exupéry slept here in between mail runs to Africa in the 1920s. Rooms for up to four people; very friendly.

Grand Hôtel de l'Opéra, FFF; *place du Capitole; tel. 61 21 82 66; credit cards* AE, DC, MC, V; *open year round.*

Lovely hotel which boasts a pool and garden right in the city centre. Sound-proofed rooms, air conditioning, excellent facilities, and helpful staff. Local gourmet haunt (see Recommended Restaurants).

Royale, FF; *6 rue Labéda; tel. 61 22 38 70; credit cards* AE, DC, MC, V; *open year round.*

Charming, prettily redecorated town house off place Wilson. The rooms are grouped around a peaceful atrium adorned with Arab tiles and iron grilles.

of the Pic (2,865 m). Crowned by an observatory established in 1882, and a television mast, the views are indeed breathtaking.

SAINT-BERTRAND-DE-COMMIGNES

Off the N125, 17 km SW of Saint-Gaudens. Turn off the N125 at Valcabrère, and the road to Saint-Bertrand traverses the site of an ancient Roman settlement once occupied by a population of 60,000. It was laid waste in the 5thC, and a later village on the wooded hillside fared no better, but its ruins were chosen by Bishop Bertrand of Commignes as the site of a great cathedral founded in 1120.

A man-made highlight of the Pyrenees, the pale, weathered façade of the **Cathédrale de Sainte-Marie-de-Commignes** sits above an attractive village square edged by a clutch of 15th-16thC houses. To the left of the stout, aisle-less nave an ornate 16thC organ loft is reached by a spiral staircase alongside the pulpit. In the superb High Renaissance choir, the 66 carved choir stalls are worth lengthy investigation. Each stall is an individual masterpiece: hounds, monkeys, cherubs, slathering grotesques and human frail-

• *Cloister, Saint-Bertrand-de-Commignes.*

ties from envy and avarice to lust clamber around the misericordes and arm rests; canopies are inset with stars and backed by relief portraits of saints. Behind the altar, St Bertrand's shrine is decorated with scenes from his life dating from the 15thC.

Then take a turn around the cloister overlooking the valley and admire the capitals to the distant chime of goat bells drifting up from the pastures.

SAINT-JEAN-DE-LUZ
See Local Explorations:5.

SAINT-JEAN-PIED-DE-PORT ✉ ✕
On D918/D933, 53 km SE of Bayonne. S.I. place Charles-de-Gaulle. Ancient capital of Basse Navarre, this picturesque village is named for its site at the 'foot of the pass' (*pied de port*) which crosses the Col de Roncevaux into Spain. Roncevaux, now on the Spanish side of the border, is notorious in French folklore for being the scene of Paladin Roland's demise. One of Emperor Charlemagne's trusted knights, Roland was ambushed by Basques as he returned from battling with the Moors. At a later date, the Basque assassins

were transformed into wily Saracens for greater dramatic effect in the epic poem *Le Chanson de Roland.*

During the Middle Ages, Saint-Jean was an important pilgrim staging post on the Route Saint-Jacques to Santiago de Compostela. The main pilgrim routes across France from Paris, Vézelay and Le Puy joined up here before tackling the mountains. Behind red sandstone walls, the Haute Ville is a single cobbled street, **rue de la Citadelle,** leading down from the Porte Saint-Jacques to the Porte d'Espagne by the River Nive. Above the 16th-18thC shuttered houses, a 17thC Vauban fortress dominates the scene.

There are plenty of walking and hiking opportunites around the town. The S.I. has free maps and details of itineraries from a gentle one-hour stroll to serious hikes up towards the Spanish border. The coast-to-coast walking path (GR10) and pilgrim route (GR65) strike up past traditional Basque farmhouses to the summer pastures. Sheep cling to the perpendicular slopes, and the ewes' milk is used to make *brébis,* the most common Pyrenean cheese, available in several strengths from creamy to tongue-withering. Another favourite spot is the beechwoods of the **Forêt d'Iraty** (25 km SE via the D18) which spans the Spanish border.

Packed with tourists (and a sprinkling of pilgrims) in summer, it is advisable to book accommodation in Saint-Jean in advance. Foodies should make a gourmet pilgrimage to Firmin Arrambide's Les Pyrénées (see under Recommended Restaurants).

TOULOUSE ⌖ ✕

On A61/A62/N117 *245 km SW of Bordeaux,* 401 *km E of Marseille. S.I. Donjon du Capitole, rue Lafayette.* An outpost of the Visigoths, and later the Franks, Toulouse enjoyed an independent and prosperous passage through the Middle Ages under the rule of the Frankish Counts of Toulouse (who christened a bewildering number of their sons Raymond).

Independence came to an abrupt end with the arrival of Simon de Montfort and his merciless men during the Albigensian crusades: Languedoc and Toulouse passed to the French crown in 1271. Government, however, remained liberal, controlled by the city

fathers, or *capitouls,* and the woad (blue dye) business introduced a new-found prosperity enabling several successful merchants to construct magnificent *hôtels particuliers* during the 16th-17thC.

Aeronautics is the city's present stock in trade. Author of *The Little Prince,* Antoine de Saint-Exupéry, and other pioneer aviators operated a mail service to Africa from Toulouse in the 1920s; today, Aerospatiale builds airbuses and rocket parts for satellite launchers. Toulouse is also a market for wine, cereals and fruit harvested on the rich Garonne plain, and its university is one of the largest in the country. Known as the 'ville rose' for its rosy red-brick buildings, Toulouse deserves to be savoured. A good place to start is the main square, **place du Capitoule,** where cafés jostle for space beneath cool arcades facing the 18thC façade of the Hôtel de Ville. Overflowing with booksellers and antiques dealers, rue du Taur leads to the **Basilique Saint-Sernin,** the largest Romanesque church in France and a superb example of Midi architecture. Dedicated to Saint-Saturnin, the first bishop of Toulouse, this colossal pilgrim church is crowned by an elegant octagonal belfry which rises in five tiers

---

DETOUR – GASCONY
To the north of the Pyrenean route, between Bordeaux and Toulouse, and bordered to the north by the River Garonne, lies the peaceful region of Gascony. At its heart is the cathedral city of **Auch,** but **Condom,** (44km NW via D930), makes a lovely base. Here, the **Hôtel des Trois Lys,** FF, 38 *rue Gambetta; tel.* 62 28 33 33 is deliciously smart and small, with an inviting pool (no restaurant); **Logis des Cordeliers, F-FF,** *rue des Cordeliers; tel.* 62 28 03 68 is less expensive, also with a pool and a separate restaurant set in a restored 14thC chapel. From Condom, you can visit the pretty *bastide* towns of **Fourcès, Montréal** and **Plaisance;** the village of **Laressingle,** and the churches of **Flaran** and **La Romieu,** all set in lush countryside.

---

pierced by rounded Romanesque and pointed Gothic arches. Below, the exquisite 12thC carvings of the Porte Miégeville illustrate biblical tales. The interior exudes an extraordinary aura of strength and simplicity. Double aisles supported on pink brick and dove-grey piers flank the soaring nave with its arched galleries. It is worth the fee to gain access to the ambulatory for the marvellous capitals in the transcept, the llthC marble reliefs near the entrance to the crypt, and the 16thC choirstalls.

Across place Saint-Sernin, a former 16thC college building has been transformed into the **Musée Saint-Raymond,** which houses the city's archaeological collections. Roman sculpture, glass and pottery are displayed alongside ceremonial and religious artefacts and a significant coin collection (closed Tues).

Toulouse delights in another ecclesiastical treasure in the **Couvent des Jacobins,** off rue Lakanal (closed Sun am). Founded in 1230 by the Dominicans, whose namesake preached against the Cathars in Saint-Sernin, it presents a daunting precipice of red brick towering above the Parvis des Jacobins. The suprise is the sparsely elegant interior, a simple double nave divided by seven delicate pillars which flower into vaulted ribs. The last pillar pushes out an exuberant flourish of 22 polychrome branches like a mighty palm tree. An Italianate cloister encloses a neat pattern of miniature box hedges and has a lovely view of the octagonal belfry.

A roundabout route to the next 'must see' could take in two of the finest Renaissance *hôtels particuliers*, the **Hôtel de Bernuy,** rue Gambetta (now a high school), and the **Hôtel**

RECOMMENDED RESTAURANTS

BAYONNE
Au Bon Vieux Temps, FF; 24 *rue des Cordeliers; tel. 59 59 78 94; credit cards MC, V; closed Sun dinner, Mon in winter, and mid-Feb to mid-Mar.*
Cosy little dining room in Petit Bayonne. Behind lace curtains, savour a steaming *marmite* of rock fish, duck roasted with raspberry vinegar and generous desserts.

Chez Jacques, F; 17 *quai Jauréguiberry; tel. 59 25 66 33; credit cards, none; closed evenings.*
A great lunchtime seafood spot with outdoor tables by the riverside.

CAUTERETS and LUZ-SAINT-SAVEUR
See *Recommended Hotels, above.*

PAU
Pyrénées, F; *place Royale; tel. 59 27 07 75; credit cards AE, DC, V; closed Sun, and three weeks in Aug.*
Local favourite with bar and outdoor dining. Friendly atmosphere, wine by the carafe and hearty local cuisine.

Table d'Hôte, FF; 1 *rue du Hédas via Pastage Parentry, a flight of steps at 25 rue des Cordeliers); tel. 59 27 56 06; credit card V; closed Sun-Mon lunch.*
Atmospheric dining-room featuring bare brick walls and low lighting beneath rue des Cordeliers. Fishy specials (mouth-watering warm salmon salad), game dishes in season, and local wines – try a Juraçon from just south of town.

SAINT-JEAN-PIED-DE-PORT
Etche-Ona, F; *closed Fri (except school hols), and Nov to mid-Dec.*
Good Basque-style restaurant serving tasty local cuisine with *nouvelle* touches – plenty of red peppers and grilled fish. Also five rooms; simple, spotless and good value.

Pyréneés, FF-FFF; 19 *place Charles-de-Gaulle; tel. 59 37 01 01; credit cards AE,DC, V; closed Mon dinner Nov-Mar, Tues mid-Sep to end Jun, mid-Nov to mid-Dec, three weeks Jan.*
Firmin Arrambide's elegant dining room is a Pyrenean shrine for pilgrim gastronomes. Concentrating on the finest local produce and seafood, the delectable menu introduces such treats as a lobster consommé flavoured with coriander, stuffed lamb's fillet, partridge served with mushroom ravioli, duck breast with spices and Arrambide's exquisite Ardour salmon lightly grilled with

d'Assézat, rue de Metz. Further east on rue de Metz, the **Musée des Augustins** contains a treasury of superb Romanesque sculpture rescued from former churches and religious foundations such as the 12thC Prieuré de la Daurade. Strikingly displayed on modern plinths, intricately carved scenes of monsters and merchants, storm-tossed galleys, beasts and the beatified provide hours of entertainment. There are stone sarcophagi (some dating back to Roman times) decorated with coats-of-arms, swags of vine and carved figures on display in the sacristy; a van Dyck and a Vannuci in the church; and a so-so fine art collection with a couple of lovely, sketchy works by Toulouse-Lautrec in the l9thC section. Closed Sun am, Tues.

Other Toulousian museums include the broad-ranging applied arts and crafts collections of the **Musée Paul-Dupuy**, 13 rue de la Pleau, and the somewhat turgid **Musée du Vieux-Toulouse**, 7 rue du May.

Take a break at a café in **place Wilson** or **place Saint-Georges** for a ring-side view of the action in the chic shopping district; department stores line rue d'Alsace-Lorraine. For picnic ingredients, explore the delights of the vast **Marché Couvert,** by Parking Victor-Hugo: stall after stall groaning with fresh fruit, glossy vegetables, cheeses, *charcuterie*, fresh bread and lots more.

Driving in Toulouse is to be avoided. The town centre is a nightmare of narrow one-way streets, pedestrian thoroughfares and inadequate parking. It is best to leave cars in the Parking Jean-Jaurès, between the rail station and inner city ring boulevard.

See France Overall: 5 and Local Explorations: 10 and 11.

béarnaise – heavenly.

If you cannot bear to leave, there are 18 lovely rooms in this 17thC town house. Relais et Châteaux luxury, garden and pool.

TOULOUSE
Auberge Louis XIII, F; 1 *bis rue Tripière; credit cards, none; closed weekends, all Aug.*

Popular budget restaurant dishing up groaning platters to students. You can go slightly more up-market next door at **Place du May**, 4 rue du May (still F).

Brasserie des Beaux-Arts, FF; 1 *quai de la Daurade; tel. 61 21 12 12; credit cards AE, DC, V; open daily until one am.*

Bustling, ever-popular art nouveau-style dining room lined with mirrors and brass. Good brasserie menu (salmon with sorrel, chicken fricassée), value-for-money lunches, house wine by the carafe.

Chez Emile, FF; 13 *place Saint-Georges; tel. 61 21 05 56; credit cards AE, DC, MC, V; closed Sun-Mon, Christmas to New Year.*

Split-level dining with seafood menu served on the ground floor, and rather cheaper regional specials on the first level. Attractive surroundings, outdoor dining and special menu in summer.

Jardins de l'Opéra, FFF; 1 *place du Capitole; tel. 61 23 07 76; credit cards AE, DC, MC, V; closed Sun, public holidays, one week early Jan, and three weeks Aug.*

In the courtyard of the red-brick Grand Hôtel de l'Opéra, this theatrically-elegant dining room is a magnificent back-drop for Dominique Toulousy's inspired cuisine. Hearty regional dishes, such as pigeon stuffed with young cabbage and *foie gras*, or *cassoulet* are reinvented to literally melt in the mouth. The lightness of touch is also translated into delicate modern combinations, demonstrated to perfection in the *foie gras* ravioli with truffle juice. Desserts are fresh but wildly refined and totally delicious. Book a table on the poolside terrace in summer.

Tartina de Burgos, F; 27 *avenue de la Garonette; credit cards none; closed Sun-Mon.*

Relaxed Spanish joint down towards the Garonne. Fill up on *paella*, or snack at the tapas bar, and drink copious quantities of plonk in convivial company.

Between Toulouse and Avignon
Languedoc-Roussillon

335 km; maps Michelin Nos 235 and 240

Historically and culturally, the south-west has developed at several removes from the rest of the country. During the Middle Ages, the Pyrenean foothills were dotted with a number of independent provinces, such as Béarn and Foix, satellites of the ancient kingdom of Navarre. North of Foix, the counts of Toulouse presided over their extensive domaines in Languedoc, stretching east to the Rhône, and south to Roussillon, the Catalan region at the eastern extent of the Pyrenees. The Toulousian court was renowned for its liberality and civilizing influence; indeed Languedoc took its name from the language of the troubadours, *langue d'Oc* or Occitan, a fusion of Latin and French distinct from the northern *langue d'Oil*.

The countryside around Toulouse is scattered with Cathar strongholds, towns and villages fortified by a fundamental Christian sect which rebelled against church corruption and materialism, much to papal disgust. They became the target of the bloody 13thC Albigensian crusades, a popular cause with the French crown, which was then able to gain a foothold in the south, annexe the independent principalities and suppress the traditional *langue d'Oc*. North of Toulouse, Local Explorations: 10 explores the Albigeois region in depth. To the east, distinctly Mediterranean Roussillon, and its capital, Perpignan, remain strongly Catalan in character, and are featured in Local Explorations: 11.

Inland from the Mediterranean coast, between Narbonne and Avignon, there are numerous traces of the Roman period: Nîmes' vast arena and elegant temple, the impressive Pont du Gard aqueduct, even the name Provence is derived from the Roman *Provincia*.

Between Toulouse and Avignon (both of which merit several days' stay), I am inclined to jump on the autoroute (A61/A9), making strategic breaks along the way for fairytale Carcassonne, for Local Explorations: 11; for Sète in the oyster season or for Nîmes, depending on how much time you have to spare. The lesser roads follow much the same route as the A61 across the broad stony plain to the coast, so the views are not spectacularly different, and along the coast the A9 allows you to avoid the slow non-*autoroute* traffic between the towns. Combine this route with France Overall: 4 for a magnificent journey which will take you from Provence and the Mediterranean coast, through the Pyrenees to the beaches of the Côte d'Argent – or vice versa.

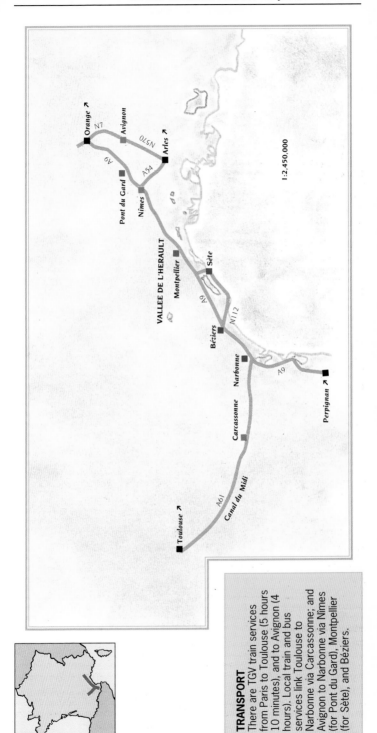

1:2,450,000

VALLÉE DE L'HERAULT

Orange
Avignon
Arles
Pont du Gard
Nîmes
Montpellier
Sète
Béziers
Narbonne
Carcassonne
Perpignan
Toulouse

N7
N570
A9
A54
A9
N112
A9
A61
Canal du Midi

TRANSPORT
There are TGV train services from Paris to Toulouse (5 hours 10 minutes), and to Avignon (4 hours). Local train and bus services link Toulouse to Narbonne via Carcassonne; and Avignon to Narbonne via Nîmes (for Pont du Gard), Montpellier (for Sète), and Béziers.

SIGHTS & PLACES OF INTEREST

ROUTE DE PIEMONT

If you want to cross Languedoc-Roussillon, but are more interested in the beautiful, sometimes savage scenery of the region than in the historic towns which my route encompasses, then consider following the Route de Piémont. It runs from Perpignan in the south to the Alès or Mende in the north, taking in the Corbières mountains, the Aude gorges, the Montagne Noir, the Minervois and Espinouse hills, garrigue country, the Tarn River, the Cevennes, the Aubrac and Margaride hills.

Contact the Languedoc-Roussillon Tourist Board, 27 rue de l'Aiguillerie, 3400 Montpellier; tel. 67 22 31 00 and ask for their map of the route.

ARLES

*See Local Explorations:*16.

AVIGNON ⇌ ✕

On the A7/N7/N570, 95 km NE of Montpellier, 82 km N of Aix-en-Provence. S.I. 41 *cours Jean-Jaurès.* Tucked in a kink of the Rhône, and surrounded by vineyards, Avignon awaits its annual summer invasion of the cultural classes cloaked in medieval walls and reflected glory. The Romans established a settlement here (Avenio) which prospered in the 12thC when a local shepherd lad (later Saint Bénézet) set about building a bridge across the Rhône with the help of a sturdy angel. The result has been immortalized as the *pont d'Avignon* of the famous song. In 1309, Pope Clément V transferred his court to Avignon from Rome hoping to escape endemic corruption and armed struggles, but the vice came too, and Petrarch reported the city 'a sewer where all the filth of the universe has gathered'. Avignon remained a papal state after the resident popes departed (1377) until the French annexed the city in 1789.

The town centre remains enclosed by anti-Pope Benedict XIII's 14thC walls – unless you are staying in town it is wise to park outside on the Rhône side of town. At the heart of the Old Town, **place de l'Horloge** is the place to watch the world go by from a café table. Check out the passing parade of street entertainers and the l9thC mechanical figures stepping around the Hôtel de Ville's clock tower.

The main sights lie to the north around the cobbled expanses of place du Palais. One of Europe's most monumental medieval edifices, the **Palais des Papes** is in fact two palaces for the price of one. Arranged around a central courtyard, the **Vieux-Palais** reflects the Cistercian simplicity of Benedict XII, a former monk, while the **Palais-Neuf** bears the flamboyant hallmarks of an entirely different character, the luxury-loving Clément VI. Much of the original decoration has been stripped; soldiers billeted in the palace during the l9thC vandalized the site and hacked away frescoes to sell. However, there are traces of its former grandeur in Matteo Giovanetti's frescoes in the chapels and Grande Audience, Gobelins tapestries in the Consistoire, and Clément VI's beautifully-restored suite in the Palais-Neuf which graphically illustrates how a broad-minded Prince of the Church could appreciate more earthy pursuits.

While its exterior is rendered somewhat ridiculous by the addition of a l9thC topknot featuring a weeping Virgin, candles throw little light on the interior of the **Cathédrale de Notre-Dame-des-Doms.** Persevere in the gloom and you will find a couple of papal tombs, a 12thC white marble papal throne and stained glass which comes to life on a sunny day. Behind the cathedral, a path leads up to the **Jardin de Rocher** with views over the town and across the Rhône to **Villeneuve-lès-Avignon**, founded by Philippe le Bel. The French king also built the landmark 13thC tower to keep an eye on papal antics on the opposite bank.

At the top of the square, the excellent if somewhat overpowering **Musée du Petit-Palais** fills a former 14th-15thC episcopal palace to bursting with some 300 medieval Italian masterpieces, plus sculpture, carvings and works from the 14thC School of Avignon, displayed in restored and individually decorated galleries.

For a more eclectic selection of artworks, do not miss the **Musée Calvet**, 65 rue Joseph-Vernet, housed in the faded charm of the 18thC Hôtel de Villeneuve-Martignan (closed Tues). Amidst moulded ceilings and panelled walls, there is an Egyptian mummy, Roman pottery, crowded Breughal scenes (*La Kermesse*), Vernet seascapes, a tortured Soutine and delightful Utrillo amongst others. In 1782, the Montgolfier brothers tested their hot air balloon in the courtyard, now home to a couple of peacocks.

Take a stroll around the **Quartier de la Banasterie** (basket weaving) for a taste of 17th-18thC architecture, stopping for a look at the Renaissance **Eglise de Saint-Pierre**, place Saint-Pierre, with its marvellous carved door featuring an Annunciation, St Jerôme walking his lion and more. The southern end of **rue des Teinturiers** is a picturesque spot where the cobbled street divides a huddle of artisans' cottages from waterwheels on the narrow canal. The much sung-about **Pont Saint-Bénézet** juts out into the Rhône from the northern section of the city walls. Just four of its original 22 arches remain. Too narrow to dance on, revellers probably partied on the island of La Barthelasse, *sous* (under) rather than *sur* the bridge.

The annual **Festival d'Avignon** (mid-July to mid-August) winds the town up to fever pitch. Accommodation is in short supply as arts enthusiasts descend for a kaleidescope of theatre, film and dance with music and a lively fringe scene ('le off') thrown in for good measure. For information, contact the Bureau du Festival, 8bis rue de Mons, tel. 90 82 67 08.

To explore the Camargue, see Local Explorations: 16.

BEZIERS ⊨

On the N113, *65 km SW of* Montpellier. S.I. 27 *rue du 4* Septembre. Despite wine, rugby and a bloody history, Béziers is somewhat short on attractions. Reached by a network of steep, medieval streets, the **Cathédrale de Saint-Nazaire** replaced an earlier edifice destroyed during the sack of Béziers in 1209. During the Albigensian crusades, Simon de Montfort's troops destroyed the city and slaughtered its people after they gave refuge to a handful of Cathars. In nearby place

de la Révolution, the **Musée des Beaux-Arts** (closed Sun am, Mon) offers a collection of Greek vases plus paintings including works by Goya, Delacroix and Dufy.

Near the rail station, the **Musée du Vieux Bitterois** (meaning inhabitant of Béziers), avenue de la Marne, does an eclectic line in local nicknacks from costumes and crafts to relics rescued from the ships' graveyard around Cap d'Agde (closed Mon).

Take a stroll in the attractive **Plateau des Poètes** with its leafy paths and literary busts; or sample café society on plane-tree dappled **allée Paul-Riquet**. Riquet was the local visionary responsible for building the Canal du Midi (see below). The local S.I. has information on canal trips which cruise slowly past the serried ranks of vineyards.

CARCASSONNE ⊨

On the A61/N113, *93 km SE of Toulouse.* S.I. 15 *boulevard* Camille-Pelletan (Ville Basse). Described by Henry James as "an enormous toy", the *Cité* of Carcassonne is Europe's largest and most carefully preserved medieval fortress. It could have been dreamed up by Dis-

---

CANAL DU MIDI

One of Europe's oldest canals, dating from the time of Louis XIV the Canal du Midi links the Bay of Biscay with the Mediterranean. It stretches from Bordeaux to Agde, from where the Canal du Rhône à Sète carries on to Beaucaire via Aigues Mortes. Between Toulouse and Sète, therefore, you could complete this National Route by boat with fabulous scenery along the way. Spring and autumn are the best seasons for cruises on the Canal du Midi: it gets very crowded with pleasure craft in summer; temperatures soar; and you can't jump into the dirty canal to cool off. For details of cruiser hirers, see page 196, or contact the Languedoc-Roussillon Tourist Board, 27 rue de l'Aiguillerie, 3400 Montpellier; tel. 67 22 81 00 and ask for their brochure on canal cruises, *Tourisme Fluvial*. Day trips are also available.

ney, but in fact owes its origins to the Romans, Visigoths and Saracens who laid the foundations for the massive double-walled fortifications, crenEllated ramparts and romantic profusion of grey-tipped conical towers. Simon de Montfort captured the stronghold in 1209, masterminding his vicious suppression of the Cathar heretics from the Château-Comtal – a fortress within a fortress – which was further strengthened by Saint-Louis.

Stripped of its strategic importance by the Treaty of the Pyrenees (1659), La Cité was gradually abandoned, while the Ville Basse, a 12thC *bastide* on the plain, developed into a prosperous market town. Irrepressible 19thC architect and restorer, Viollet-le-Duc set to work on the site in 1855, and his all-too-perfect restoration has been the subject of hot debate amongst purists. However, without his attentions little would remain now, and although La Cité is a tourist trap, it should be seen. Entrance to **La Cité** is free (except for the Château), and maps and information are available from an S.I. outpost in the Porte Narbonnais during summer. Narrow streets lead up to the **Château-Comtal**, reached by a bridge across the moat. There are guided tours, a couple of small exhibits, and wooden walkways around

the battlements. Then head for the **Basilique de Saint-Nazaire**, its roofline edged by fearsome gargoyles. The Romanesque nave with great rounded pillars and simple capitals ends in a lovely Gothic choir and beautiful stained glass. Behind the church, there is an entrance to **Les Lices**, the area between the twin battlements, where a re-creation of its medieval appearance includes giant catapults and workshops. A pleasant alternative to the usual tourist tat hawked on the main drag, the craft shops on **rue du Plo** sell pottery and jewellery as well as local produce such as honey and dried herbs.

Carcassonne is a useful starting point for both Local Explorations: 10 and Local Explorations: 11.

MONTPELLIER ⊯ ✕

On the A9/N113, 51 km W of Nîmes. S.I. allée du Tourisme (off place de la Comédie). A flourishing trading post and centre of learning since the 10thC, Montpellier was temporarily flattened for its Protestant sympathies during the Wars of Religion, then rose again in a welter of imposingly severe 17th-18thC *hôtels particuliers*. Around 100 of these sur-

• *Opposite: Béziers.*

DETOUR – **VALLEE DE L'HERAULT**

As an antidote to the rigours of the large bustling towns which are strung out along this route, take time out to follow Local Explorations: 10 or 11, or, if time is short, side step from **Montpellier** into the strange and rugged foothills of the Massif Central. From Montpellier take the D986 to **Saint-Martin-de-Londres**, worth investigating for its typical Languedocian Romanesque priory church entirely surrounded by ancient houses. Leave by the D212, then turn left onto the D4 which traverses wild and denuded Garrigues country before descending to the chalk-walled **Gorges de l'Hérault** and the picturesque village of **Saint-Guilhem-le-Désert**. squeezed into a narrow side gorge. The charming village square faces an important Romanesque abbey church

with a notable apse and the remains of a cloister, the rest of which has since 1914 been a star attraction of the Cloisters museum in New York. Walk up the Gorges du Verdus to the **Cirque de l'Infernet**, known as the 'end of the world'. Back in the village, you might lunch at the **Hôtel Fouzès, F** (with fine views). Continue south on the D4 to the **grotte de la Clamouse**, full of extraordinary stone pillars and other rock formations and the subject of a tragic legend. Over the adjacent Pont du Diable (views of the gorges), take the D27 via Aniane to the N109 for Montpellier.

Anyone looking for swimming, beaches and watersports should head west on the N109 to **Lac du Salagou**, a vast man-made lake given character by the purple fingers of surrounding hills which stretch into the water.

vive in the Old Town, also known as Lou Clapas (the rubble), though somewhat inaccurately after a recent rash of gentrification. Several now house public offices, such as the **Hôtel de Saint-Côme** (Chamber of Commerce), on Grand Rue Jean-Moulin (close to the home of the Second World War Resistance hero), and the **Hôtel de Ganges** (prefecture), off rue Foch.

Place de la Comédie is the bustling marble-flagged heart of things. Nicknamed 'L'Oeuf' (the egg), it is topped by the **Opéra**, a decorative flourish of l9thC exuberance, and tails off into broad tree-lined Esplanade Charles-de-Gaulle, off which the **Musée Fabre** is top attraction (closed Mon). François Xavier Fabre (1766-1837) was an enthusiastic if only moderately talented pupil of David. However, he and his *amoureuse* the Countess of Albany (widow of the Young Pretender) amassed an extensive collection of 17th-l9thC paintings including three Rubens, some attractive Vernet seascapes, Houdon marbles and a fine selection of Dutch and Flemish works.

Rue Foch carves a triumphal path through the Old Town to the **Promenade du Peyrou**, a pleasant place to take the air, admire a very distant view of the Cévennes and an 18thC aqueduct modelled on the Pont du Gard which once provided water for the fountains. To the north lies the Faculté de Médécine, where Rabelais was a student, and which includes a notable collection of French and Italian drawings in the **Musée Atger**. Further down the hill, the **Jardin des Plantes** is France's oldest botanical garden, founded so medical students could experiment with herbs. Sadly, it is not looking too healthy these days.

On the cultural front, there is always something on the go in town, particularly during summer when music, theatre and dance festivals overlap from mid-June through July; new films get a showing in the latter part of September.

For an easy excursion into the southern Massif Central from Montpellier, see page 90.

NARBONNE ⚓ ✕

On the N113 60 km W of Carcassonne. S.I. place Salengro. Dwarfed by the grandiose bulk of its Gothic cathedral, Narbonne was the first Roman colony in Gaul, Narbo Martius. A major trading and ecclesiastical centre in the Middle Ages, the town was diminished by war and pestilence, then lost direct access to the sea when the River Aude changed course. Today, Narbonne is a market for Corbières wines, and restoration around the Canal de la Robine (an offshoot of the Canal du Midi) makes for pleasant walks along the banks past painted barges and a flower market on cours de la République.

RECOMMENDED HOTELS

AVIGNON

Hôtel d'Europe, FFF; 12 *place Crillon; tel.* 90 82 66 92; *credit cards* AE, DC, MC, V; *open year round.*

A 16thC mansion just inside the city walls, this is one of the best hotels in Provence. Napoleon stayed here and would still feel at home amongst the tapestries, antiques and period furnishings. The lovely suites and bedrooms are complemented by faultless service and a distinguished restaurant (see Recommended Restaurants).

La Ferme, FF; *chemin des Bois,* Ile de la Barthelasse; *tel.* 90 82 57 53; *credit cards* MC, V; *closed* Jan.

Follow signs from Pont Daladier to this 16thC farmhouse on an island in the Rhône. Choice of accommodation in rooms and modern apartments or twee gypsy caravans. Quiet, sunny garden, restaurant, pool, tennis.

Hôtel de Mons, F; 5 *rue Mons; tel.* 90 82 57 16; *credit cards* AE, DC, V; *closed mid-Dec to mid-Jan.*

Wacky little hotel stuffed into a converted 13thC chapel just off place de l'Horloge. Limited space, but plenty of character.

Primotel Horloge, FF; *place de* l'Horloge; *tel.* 90 86 88 61; *credit cards* AE, DC, MC, V; *open year round.*

Very pleasant modern hotel snuck in between historic buildings beside the busy main square. Remarkable soundproofing in the 70 rooms, and tasteful 'period' decoration.

Pope Clément IV sent a foundation stone from Rome, and work began on the **Cathédrale de Saint-Just** in 1272. It stopped well short of the original plans when the city walls got in the way. Without a nave, the soaring choir is one of the tallest in France, pierced by a twin tier of superb 14thC stained glass windows. Stroll around to the Gothic cloister for a picturesque view of the roofs, a cat's cradle of turrets, arches and fearsome gargoyles picked out against the sky. From a terrace on the right, you can see the *donjons* and solidly buttressed walls of the fortified **Palais des Archevêques** (closed Mon Oct-May). Inspired by the Palais des Papes in Avignon, it now houses, around the inner courtyard, an excellent archaeological museum (paleolithic tools, beautiful Roman mosaics), and opposite, a fine arts collection displayed in the restored archbishop's apartments.

North of the cathedral complex, a snippet of Narbo Martius, part of a

BEZIERS
Le Castelet, F-FF; *route de Narbonne (4 km SW via N113); tel.* 67 28 82 60; *credit cards* AE, DC, MC, V; *open year round.*

A little way out of the town centre, the rooms here are quiet and comfortable. Rather stuffy but very acceptable and well-priced restaurant – you can escape to tables on the pool terrace in summer.

CARCASSONNE
Le Donjon, FF; *2 rue du Comte-Roger; tel.* 68 71 08 80; *credit cards* AE, DC, MC, V; *open year round; restaurant Mon-Sat dinner only.*

Attractive hotel-restaurant in an historic building at the heart of La Cité. Rooms are small but pleasant, there is a pretty courtyard garden, and tempting regional cuisine in the dining room.

MONTPELLIER
Grand Hotel du Midi, FF; *22 boulevard Victor-Hugo; tel.* 67 92 69 61; *credit cards* AE, DC, MC, V; *open year round.*

A smartly refurbished l9thC hotel with 47 spacious rooms. Handy location just off place de la Comédie; piano bar.

Le Palais, F; *3 rue Palais; tel.* 67 60 47 38; *credit cards* MC, V; *open year round.*

Hotel with 26 cheap and cheerful rooms in the Old Town, a short step from rue Foch.

Bed-and-Breakfast
Résidence Serenis; F; *chemin de Bouisson, Saint-Georges d'Orques (6 km W via N109/D27E); tel.* 67 75 07 67; *open year round.*

Sympathetic but functional modern guest wing attached to the home of M. and Mme. Gay. The building includes a well-equipped kitchen for guests' use, and there is a pretty courtyard with tables and chairs and a barbecue under an apricot tree.

NARBONNE
La Résidence, FF; *6 rue ler Mai; tel.* 68 32 19 41; *credit cards* V; *closed Jan.*

Welcoming, central townhouse hotel with 26 attractive rooms, and a series of pretty little *salons* off the hallway.

NIMES
Majestic, F; *10 rue Pradier; tel.* 66 29 24 14; *credit cards* MC, V; *open year round.*

A short walk from the town centre; clean, light rooms with shower/WC.

Relais du Moulin, FF; *avenue Paul-Mendes-France (4 km SE via N113); tel.* 66 84 30 20; *credit cards* AE, MC, V; *closed Sun-Mon, Nov.*

Elegant converted mill with bedrooms decorated *à la Provençale.* Gardens and terraces for a spot of quiet postcard writing. Good restaurant (half-board).

See also Recommended Restaurants.

SETE
Le Grand, F-FF; *17 quai Maréchal de Lattre-de-Tassigny; tel.* 67 74 71 77; *credit cards* AE, DC, MC, V; *closed Christmas to New Year.*

Bargain rates, central canal-side location with lovely views, and 47 very pleasant and comfortable rooms.

Roman **Horreum**, has been excavated to reveal two rows of stalls where grain and other foodstuffs were stored.

Local Explorations: 11 can be reached convieniently from Narbonne.

NIMES 🛏 ✕

On the N113, 51 km NE of Montpellier. S.I. 6 rue Auguste. Named for the water sprite *Nemausus*, Nîmes has been hailed the 'Rome of France'. There are seven hills and a sprinkling of Roman ruins, but the town is not content to sit on its laurels and is investing in the future with dramatic new building projects such as Norman Foster's arts and archive complex on place de la Maison Carré, right opposite one of the best-preserved Roman temples in existence.

Nîmes is no stranger to controversy. A Protestant stronghold, it suffered at the hands of Simon de Montfort's crusaders, and emerged in tatters from the Wars of Religon. Textiles

• Opposite: Cathédral de Saint-Just, Narbonne.

• Narbonne.

secured its fortunes in the 18thC with cloth *de Nîmes*, better known the world over as denim.

Starting from the S.I., the **Maison Carré** will be your first stop. Set in a rectangular basket of pillars, the elegant proportions of this former Roman temple inspired Arthur Young to declare it 'one perfect whole of symmetry and grace'. Erected during the late IstC, it may have been dedicated to Emperor Augustus' heirs Caius and Lucius, and reflects a harmonious Greek influence in its restrained simplicity, Corinthian capitals and frieze.

Boulevard Victor-Hugo leads down to Nîmes' 50AD amphitheatre, **Les Arènes**, the surprising pivot of a major traffic intersection. It is a colossal edifice ringed by 34 tiers of seats, sufficent for a capacity audience of 20,000 armchair gladiators, and reached by an amazingly complex network of corridors and steps. During the Barbarian invasions, the townspeople sheltered here, and right up until the l9thC it housed a ragbag collection of squatters and itinerants. Concerts and bull-fights draw the crowds today with recourse to an inflatable roof should the weather prove inclement.

Behind the amphitheatre, **place du Marché** is enlivened by a jaunty modern fountain complete with the town's coat-of-arms, the chained crocodile – a cheeky allusion to Augustus' defeat of Anthony and Cleopatra in Egypt. **Place aux Herbes** is another attractive spot by the severely knocked-about cathedral. In the nearby bishop's palace, the **Musée du Vieux-Nîmes** offers displays of local historical and cultural interest, costumes and furniture. The **Musée Archéologique**, 13 boulevard Amiral-Courbet, records the Gallo-Roman period with the help of artworks, utensils and coins. There is also a rather unexciting **Musée des Beaux-Arts**, rue de la Cité-Foulc (south of Les Arènes), though it does host contemporary exhibitions. (All closed Sun in winter.)

A wander down the tree-lined canal on Quai de la Fontaine will bring you to the **Jardin de la Fontaine**. Laid out in the 18thC around the Nemausus spring, these lovely formal gardens planted with chestnut trees and statuary lead up wooded Mont Cavalier to the Roman **Tour Magne** which affords terrific views over the town.

Nîmes' **bullfighting** season runs from May through September with another important *corrida* in February. If you do not fancy the full blood-and-glory affairs, look out for the bloodless (generally, and rarely the bull's) *courses de la concarde*. This traditional Provençal version sees agile young daredevils attempting to snatch a rosette off the bull's head armed with just a metal *razeteur*.

ORANGE
See France Overall: 11.

PERPIGNAN
See Local Explorations: 11.

PONT DU GARD
On the D981, off N86/A9, 23 km E of Nîmes. Around 19AD the Romans embarked on an ambitious scheme to transport fresh water from the source of the River Eure at Uzès down to Nîmes. A 50-km aqueduct did the trick,

and the magnificent triple tier of arches spanning the rock-strewn River Gard, near Remoulins, stands as an impressive monument to their skill.

There are buses from Avignon and Nîmes, plus day trippers aplenty during summer.

SETE ⇥ ✕
On the N112, 35 km S of Montpellier. On my last visit an enterprising road-side oyster stall marked the Sète exit off the

RECOMMENDED RESTAURANTS

AVIGNON
Café des Artistes, FF-F; *place Crillon, tel.* 90 82 63 16; *credit cards* AE, DC, MC, V.

Glassed-in café-restaurant with a terrace in this lovely square. Irresistable nibbles served with aperitifs, fresh ravioli with Provençal herbs, garlicky rabbit with fried field mushrooms, citrus terrine, or a simple omelette and salad.

Le Petit Bedon, FF; 70 *rue Joséph-Vernet; tel.* 90 82 33 98; *credit cards* AE, DC, MC, V; *closed Sun, and last two weeks* Jun.

Rated the best meal under 250F in the city by other chefs and numerous locals alike. Robust Provençal cuisine with plenty of fish dishes. Bargain lunch menu.

Tache d'Encre, F; 22 *rue des Teinturiers; tel.* 90 85 46 03; *credit cards* V.

Music over matter. Actually, the basic menus are OK, but the real draw is the entertainment. Live music from jazz to rock to salsa Fri-Sat and some week nights.

La Vieille Fontaine, FFF; 12 *place Crillon; tel.* 90 82 66 92; *credit cards* AE, DC, MC, V; *closed Sat lunch, Sun, and one week mid-Aug.*

A sort of Provençal rustic elegance replete with oak beams, chandeliers and armchair seating lends a relaxing ambience to Avignon's venerable Vieille Fontaine in the Hôtel d'Europe (see Recommended Hotels). The menu is admirably tailored to the mood with a distinctly regional flavour to the thundering La Languedocienne (A9) autoroute.On the seaward side of the Bassin de Thau, Sète harvests oysters and mussels, and stages historic water jousting tournaments, the *joutes nautiques*, in summer. It is a bustling fishing port in the lee of Mont Saint-Clair, with a host of fish restaurants, a sailor's cemetery where the poet Paul Valéry is buried, and the **Musée Valéry**, rue Denoyer, containing memorabilia of the local poet and a small but interesting

collection of modern paintings. At the southern end of the Bassin de Thau (20 km), **Agde** was founded by the Greeks and built of black volcanic rock from Mont Saint-Loup. **Cap d'Agde** plays host to one of France's largest naturist colonies, and a museum of antiquities, many recovered from the 'ships' graveyard' offshore.

TOULOUSE
See France Overall: 4.

richly coloured lobster soup laced with red peppers, salmon with oysters and local truffles, pigeon risotto and market-fresh vegetables. The wine list may require a helping hand – a good excuse to consult the wisdom of maitre d'-cum-sommelier Jacques Napais; and there are lamp-lit tables in the cobbled fountain courtyard in summer.

MONTPELLIER
Le Louvre, FF-F; 2 *rue de la Vieille; tel.* 67 60 59 37; *credit cards* DC, MC, V; *closed* Sun-Mon (*open for dinner in summer*), *Sat lunch in summer, May, and 2 weeks in* Nov.

Ideally placed close to the main markets, this relaxed local bistro takes its pick of the finest seasonal produce.

Le Vieil Ecu, F; *place de la Chapelle Neuve; credit cards* V; *closed for lunch* Sun-Mon.

Dine in a 16thC chapel or on its terrace facing one of the most delightful squares in town. Fixed price menu, value-for-money *plats du jour*, and generous helpings.

I have also been recommended **Le Ménestrel, F**, (*place de la Préfecture; tel.* 67 60 62 51), set in a 13thC grain hall. Michelin give it a red R.

NARBONNE
L'Alsace, FF-F; 2 *avenue* Pierre-Sémard; *tel.* 68 65 10 24; *credit cards* AE, DC, MC, V; *closed* Mon dinner-Tues, *and mid-Nov to mid-Dec.*

Seafood literally spills out of the door here in a guard of honour of massed crustaceans. Sample *bourride*, a meaty traditional fish stew, or dig into intimidating platters of *fruits de mer*.

NIMES
L'Enclos de la Fontaine, FFF; *quai de la Fontaine; tel.* 66 21 90 30; *credit cards* AE, DC, MC, V; *closed* Sat lunch.

Half-way down the quay, in the extremely smart Imperator Concorde hotel, this chic, light and airy dining room extends into a ravishing garden patio in summer. Classically trained cuisine tempered with modern combinations and regional influences results in delicate shrimps and scallops flavoured with fresh orange, sea bass in a light lime sauce, tastily balanced beef olives, beautifully-presented desserts.

Should you feel like staying on, there are 65 luxurious rooms upstairs.

Le Magister, FF; 5 *rue Nationale; tel.* 66 75 11 00; *credit cards* AE, DC, MC, V; *closed* Sat lunch, Sun, two weeks Aug.

Very good value menus and considerable comfort in an old butcher's shop. Regionally-inspired cuisine organized around the very best local market produce.

Les Persiennes, F; 5 *place de l'Oratoire; credit cards* V; *closed* Sun-Mon.

Home cooking in attractive surroundings. Recommended is a raid on the well-stocked, fixed-price and unlimited quantity *hors d'oeuvre* bar.

SETE
La Racasse, F; 27 *quai du Général-Durand; tel.* 67 74 38 46; *credit cards* AE, DC, V; *closed* Tues, *and* Jan.

Bustling quay-side seafood spot with great value menus and plenty of atmosphere. Gorge yourself on stuffed mussels, scallops, squid, monkfish stew, turbot, tuna, et al.

Between Calais and Paris
Inland Pas de Calais, the Somme and Oise
295 km; maps Michelin Nos 236 and 237

Sugar beet, spreading farmland and battlefields seem to be the main constituents of the countryside south from Calais towards Paris. The region is by-passed to the east by the main Paris-to-the-coast corridor, the A26/A1, and few visitors get around to stopping off at the two highlights of the region, France's tallest cathedrals at Amiens and Beauvais. Perhaps understandably: the towns have until recently offered little else in the way of tourist-friendly diversions, and both suffered from sadly unimaginative rebuilding after the Second World War.

Amiens has fared better: the purity of its great Gothic cathedral is unmatched, the old canal-side artisans' quarter of Saint-Leu has been attractively restored, there is plenty to admire in the Musée de Picardie, and summer season boat trips explore a watery maze of miniature market gardens on the edge of town.

Besides its cathedral, Beauvais has the national tapestry gallery: not to everyone's taste, but the gallery's themed exhibitions provide a rare chance to view masterpieces of this under-rated art form as well as demonstrating its versatility.

In the north of the region, Saint-Omer makes a convenient break an hour's drive from Calais; while Amiens, mid-way between Calais and Paris, is well situated for making a longer pause, perhaps staying the night. East of Amiens lie the First World War battlefields of the Somme, scattered with memorials to the dead and beautifully-tended cemeteries (see Circuit de Souvenir, page 104). Head north-west, and you come across one of the prettiest corners of the region, the Vallée de la Canche around Hesdin, where the French and the English fought two key battles during the Hundred Years War: Crécy and Agincourt.

Blue route followers, and red routers who decide to forsake the *autoroute,* will find the main roads fairly fast. The N43 heads south-east of Calais via Saint-Omer to Béthune for the D916/N25 to Amiens; the N1 links Amiens and Paris via Beauvais. For green route travellers with more time to spare, the D928/N1 between Saint-Omer and Amiens is a more pleasant drive, passing through Hesdin and Le Boile in the Authie Valley (see Saint-Omer, page 103.)

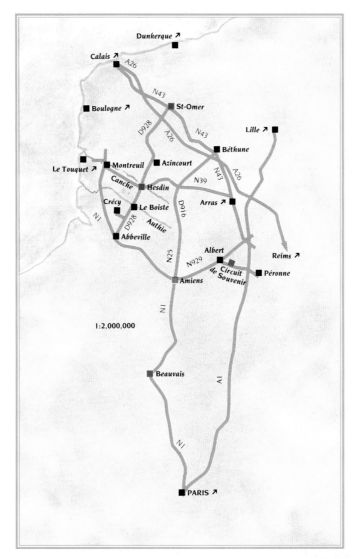

TRANSPORT
There are frequent daily train services between Calais and Paris via Amiens; and between Paris and Beauvais. Between Amiens and Beauvais buses provide the best link. For the Somme, buses and trains from Amiens serve Albert and Arras (see France Overall: 9). Local services to Hesdin are very sketchy and do not cover the battlefield sites.

SIGHTS & PLACES OF INTEREST

AMIENS ⊯ ✕

On the N25/N1, 145 km S of Calais/150 km N of Paris. S.I. 1 rue Jean-Catelas. The capital of Picardy, Amiens is placed with uncanny precision almost exactly mid-way between Calais and Paris. That is not a particularly good reason to stop here; the cathedral is.

For a town that was severely knocked about during both World Wars, Amiens was extraordinarily lucky to hang on to the **Cathédrale de Notre-Dame**. Twice the size of Notre-Dame in Paris, it is one of France's Gothic masterpieces, and took less than a century to build. The great west portal is decorated with more than 3,000 statues, while the soaring nave restrains itself to a frieze lining the clerestory like a sculpted window box. There are splendid 13thC tombs, groups of carved figures depicting tales from the life of St Firmin, Amiens' first bishop, and guided tours of the ornate 16thC choir stalls adorned with some 4,000 figures.

North of the cathedral, the old canal-side weavers' and dyers' district, **quartier Leu**, has been gentrified within an inch of its life. Craftsmen, antique dealers, artists and yuppies have moved into the Flemish-style buildings and waterfront apartments attracting a complement of bistros and sidewalk cafés. **Quai Belu** is a good place to hang out and watch the world go by.

Other diversions include the excellent **Musée Picardie**, 48 rue de la République (closed Mon), its 15th-20thC fine arts, archaeological and medieval displays enhanced by a new-look layout; and the graciously appointed 18thC **Hôtel de Berny**, 36 rue Victor-Hugo (closed Mon), furnished with all manner of glittering Louis XV and Louis XVI pieces from furniture to fans. A leisurely excursion for a sunny day is a trip around the *hortillonages*, Amiens' island market gardens. Flat-bottomed boats putter around the canals edged by massed marsh buttercups, willows, rows of parsley, lettuces, shallots, orchards and flower-filled gardens (Apr-Oct pm). Boat loads of produce wind up at the colourful Saturday morning **Marché sur l'Eau**, which is held on place Parmentier.

ARRAS

See France Overall: 9.

AZINCOURT

See Hesdin, page 102.

BEAUVAIS ✕

On the N1, 76 km N of Paris. S.I. rue Beauregard. Beauvais' famous **Cathédrale de Saint-Pierre**, a blackened hulk crouched to one side of the post-war town centre, looks somewhat ominous: no competition for the classic Gothic beauty of Amiens. In 1225, the Bishop of Beauvais drummed up sufficient support for his pet project to set about building the biggest, tallest cathedral in Christendom. By 1263, the massive choir was completed, only to collapse in 1272. It was repaired and fell again in 1284. Buttresses were built, the transcept tacked on, and then the temptation to add a spire despite the lack of a supporting nave spelled disaster yet again. Further construction was halted after the steeple toppled in 1573, and St Peter's was never completed.

The building looks distinctly unbalanced and grim from the outside, but it improves at the main door, its Renaissance panels heaving with carvings. The interior is neck-crickingly high, and the ambulatory chapels gleam with marvellous stained glass, some of which dates from the 13thC. You can't miss the **astronomical clocks**, the original a picture of restraint beside the 19thC version with

---

SAINT-OMER TO AMIENS
Green route followers travelling between Saint-Omer and Amiens may prefer to use the D928/N1 rather than the more direct D916/N25. It passes through Hesdin (see page 102) in the pretty Vallée de la Canche, and through **Le Boiste**, a traditional basket-weaving centre, in the equally pretty Vallée de l'Authie. If you have time, take a picnic and follow the river 15 km westwards to the former cistercian **Abbaye de Valloires** (open Mar-Oct). South of the Authie Valley is Crécy, where a good lunch can be had (see also Hesdin).

RECOMMENDED HOTELS

AMIENS
Le Prieuré, F-FF; 17 *rue Porion; tel.*
22 92 27 67; credit cards AE, DC, MC,
V; *open year round.*

Pretty hotel with cobbled courtyard
and another enclosed one, full of
greenery. Rooms vary, some very
small, all with character. Family run –
reports of muddled management in
the past.

SAINT-OMER
Hostellerie des Trois Mousque-
taires, F-FF; *Château du Fort de la*
Redoute, Aire-sur-la-Lys (14 km S N43);
tel. 21 39 01 11; *credit cards* AE, DC,
MC, V; *closed Sun dinner-Mon off season,*
mid-Dec to mid-Jan.

A fanciful 19thC brick-and-timber
house with a modern extension. Pretty rooms and copious menus. Play
area and seating in the garden, where
a *blockhaus* built for Field-Marshal
Rommel now houses the vegetable
store.

RECOMMENDED RESTAURANTS

AMIENS
Auberge du Vert-Galant, F; 57
chemin de Halage; tel. 22 91 31 66;
credit cards V; *closed Wed dinner.*

Café on towpath near the *hortillon-*
nages (see page 100) offering local
specials such as *ficelle picarde* (a
ham, cheese and mushroom *crêpe*)
and fresh water fish dishes.

La Bonne Auberge, F-FF; 69 *route*
Nationale, Dury-lés-Amiens (5 km S on
N1); credit cards AE, V; *closed Sun din-*
ner-Mon, mid-Sep to mid-Oct.

If you want to avoid Amiens but
need a pit-stop in the region, this is
an excellent choice. Raoul Beaus-
sire's cooking is from the old school,
genuine and reliable. There are some
bargain fixed-price menus and the
service is friendly.

Down the road at No.78, **L'Auber-**
gade (tel. 2289 5141) has a Michelin star and classic cooking.

• *Pierrefonds.*

La Couronne, F-FFF; 64 *rue Saint-*
Leu; tel. 22 91 88 57; *credit cards* V;
closed Sat, Sun dinner, mid-Jul to mid-
Aug.

A favourite Amiens restaurant, popular with businessmen at lunchtime,
recently enlarged. Good classic cooking with a low-price weekday menu,
and rather more expensive à la carte
choices.

La Soupe à Cailloux, F-FF; 16 *rue*
des Bondes; tel. 21 91 92 70; *credit cards*
AE, V; *closed Mon, two weeks Jan.*

Attractive spot with a sprinkling of
pale wood tables in the quartier Saint-
Leu. Good, fresh regional dishes such
as chicken with a creamy sauce made
from local *maroilles* cheese.

BEAUVAIS
Le Marignan, F-FF; 1 *rue Malherbe;*
tel. 44 48 15 15; *credit cards* AE, V; *closed*
Sun dinner-Mon, one week Feb, one week
Aug.

Popular, value-for-money ground
floor brasserie offering plenty of variety. More expensive classic cuisine in
the restaurant upstairs.

SAINT-OMER
Belle Epoque, F-FF; 3 *place Painlevé;*
tel. 21 38 22 93; *credit cards* V; *closed*
Wed.

Best of the bunch near the main
square; Flemish specialities.

• *Longpont, Oise.*

its scores of dials and enamelled faces ranging from the size of a dinner plate to a thumbnail.

A famous tapestry centre, Beauvais is a natural site for the **Galerie Nationale de la Tapisserie** (closed Mon) housed in an ugly, concrete building to the east of the cathedral. The exhibits change regularly and there is an element of pot-luck, but you can always be assured of both antique and modern pieces in some form. To the west, a gateway flanked by towers topped with witches' hats leads to the **Musée Départemental de l'Oise**, which harbours assorted local history and fine arts displays (closed Mon). For more dazzling stained glass, turn south for the **Eglise de Saint-Etienne**, rue Malherbe, and its rose window depicting the Wheel of Fortune.

BOULOGNE
See France Overall: 1.

CALAIS
See France Overall: 1.

CRECY
See Hesdin, below.

DUNKERQUE
See France Overall: 9.

HESDIN
On the D928, 85 km SW of Saint-

Omer.Straddling the river in the Vallée de la Canche, Hesdin is flanked by two major medieval battlefields. The town itself merits a stop for its cobbled main square, 16thC Hôtel de Ville, pretty houses and walks along the attractive river valley.

The opening shots – or rather arrows – of the Anglo-French Hundred Years War were let off at **Crécy** (20 km SW via D928/D938) on August 26, 1345. Under the command of Edward III, the English archers carried the day, armed for the first time with longbows. King Edward watched the battle from a windmill, replaced these days by a viewing platform on the D111 from Crécy-en Ponthieu to Wadicourt. Blind King John of Bohemia died in the battle roped to his horse and was buried by Edward. The 16-year-old Prince of Wales (the Black Prince), who performed gallantly on the day, was rewarded with permission to adopt King John's crest of three ostrich plumes, which remain the badge of the Prince of Wales to this day.

If it is lunchtime while you are at Crécy, look no further than the **Auberge le Caron, F;** *Crécy-en-Ponthieu; tel 22 23 51 14.* The *auberge* offers a sound-value three-course lunch and has six basic rooms.

To the north, **Azincourt** (15 km via D928/D71) was the site of the Battle of Agincourt on October 25, 1415. Henry V of England, 1,000 men-at-arms and 6,000 archers lined up behind a pallisade of pointed stakes facing a French army of 25,000. The battle was swift, bloody and muddy. The French cavalry, unable to charge through the pallisade, got stuck in the mud and were cut down by a hail of arrows. It was said with some justice that 'the flower of French chivalry was destroyed in a single day.'

LILLE
See France Overall: 9.

> **WALKING IN THE HESDIN AREA**
> The Vallée de l'Authie is pleasant walking country. Follow the GR123 from Wadicourt across the Authie to the River Canche, and the GR121 along the Canche from Beaurainville via Hesdin to Trévent.

• *Sleepy St-Jean-aux-Bois, Oise.*

PARIS
See pages 214-233.

REIMS
See France Overall: 9.

SAINT-OMER ⋈ ✕
On the N43, 45 *km* SE *of Calais. S.I. boulevard Pierre-Guillain.* If you are heading back to the coast with time to spare, Saint-Omer makes a pleasant break about an hour from the ferry ports. The town is an ancient crossroads between Flanders and Artois, with a bustling Saturday market held on central place du Maréchal Foch, in front of the Hôtel de Ville. A couple of narrow pedestrianized streets lead off the main square towards the 13th-16thC basilica: one street has a smart line in boutiques and food stores, the other tends towards café-restaurants and lawn mower repair shops.

Take a turn around the outside of the Gothic **Basilique de Notre-Dame** with its full complement of moss-tipped flying buttresses and hundreds of carved heads decorating the east end. The interior also has its share of statuary, and blue-green glass casts a submarine glow around the ambulatory. The Chapelle de Notre-Dame is stuffed with heart-shaped votive offerings.

On rue Carnot, the 17thC **Musée-Hôtel Sandelin** (closed Mon-Tues) displays fine arts, porcelain and furniture, plus the 12thC *Pied de Croix de Bertin*, a finely-wrought gold and enamel church treasure. The **Musée Henri Dupuis** (closed Tues) boasts a superb 18thC Flemish kitchen decorated with gorgeous tiles in addition to natural history exhibits.

Stretch your legs amongst the topiary in the **Jardin Public** (opposite the S.I.); or you can take to the **watergangs**, a network of little canals carved through the Audomarois marsh. Boats can be hired from points along route de Clairmarais (the D209, east of the railway station); or take the one-hour and 45 minute guided tour with Captain Beese, 4 rue de Longueville (tel. 21 98 66 74).

LE TOUQUET
See France Overall: I.

• *First World War Armistice Clearing, Compiègne.*

CIRCUIT DU SOUVENIR

55 km; Michelin regional map No. 52.
The Circuit du Souvenir is a signposted tour of First World War battlefields in the area of the Somme. One million men were killed or wounded in the 1916 Battle of Somme, and each village has its own immaculate cemetery or poignant monument. This itinerary starts at Péronne and follows the *circuit* in an anti-clockwise direction.

The passage of time has made this pilgrimage no less popular; in fact there is probably more interest in touring the battlefields now than ever before.

The museum at Péronne, **L'Historial de la Grande Guerre**, place du Château (closed Dec to mid-Feb), traces the effects of the war on both the combatants and the civilians back home; and the social revolution it provoked. (The **Hostellerie des Ramparts**, 22 rue Beaubois, could be useful for lunch.)

The village of **Bouchavesnes** added **Bergen** to its name in honour of a wealthy Norwegian benefactor who helped this devastated town and donated the statue of Maréchal Foch. Just before **Rancourt** are three cemeteries, German, British and the largest French cemetery on the Somme.

After Combles comes **Guillemont**, where Raymond Asquith, son of the then British Prime Minister, and one of the brightest stars of his generation, is buried at Guillemont Road Cemetery with more than 2,000 others. Just before **Longueval**, is the South African memorial and Museum at Delville Wood (closed Mon). The original wood was blasted to pieces during five days of hell in July 1916 when more than 2,000 out of 3,000 South African soldiers were killed. The impressive memorial is surrounded by an oak wood sown from South African acorns. Attractive woodland paths mark the progress of the battle and the only hint of the past horrors are the occasional overgrown trench or rusty piece of ammunition.

Before **Martinpuich** on the edge of the Bois des Fourceaux a touching Scottish memorial, in the form of a cairn of 192 stones, commemorates the 192 Highlanders who died here.

Turn left on to the D929 and make for **Pozières**. Strategically placed on the Albert to Bapaume Road, the village had been completely destroyed by August 1916. Amongst the memorials, notice the one dedicated to the British Tank Corps: tanks first went into action from here.

After Pozières, leave the main road, turning right on the D73 for **Thiepval**. This was the site of a long and bloody siege where on one day 20,000 British soldiers were killed, and 38,000 were wounded. The magnificent Memorial to the Missing can be seen for miles around. Designed by Sir Edwin Lutyens, it is a huge and terrible reminder of the 73,412 men who have no known graves and whose names are engraved on 16 pillars supporting the massive archway. The fairytale tower of the 36th Ulster Division Memorial lies beyond Thiepval. It is a replica of a tower on the Marquis of Dufferin and Ava's estate near Belfast where the division first trained. After ploughing, the lines of the old German trenches are clearly visible in the surrounding fields.

Nowhere are the realities of war so easily imagined as at the Newfoundland Memorial Park near **Beaumont-Hamel.** Here a whole Canadian Regi-

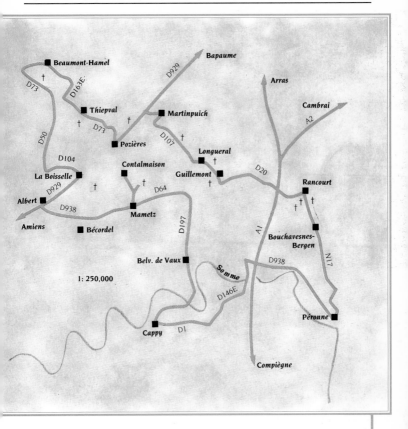

ment was all but wiped out. A huge Caribou watches over the No Man's Land, with its well-preserved trenches, wisps of barbed wire and one surviving petrified tree – the `Danger Tree'. Beyond No Man's Land, behind what were German lines, lie two secluded cemeteries.

Back on the D929, **La Boisselle** is the site of the largest crater on the Western Front, caused by more than 27,000 lbs of explosives. Known as the Lochnagar Crater, it has been bought and preserved by an Englishman.

Albert is an industrial town, totally rebuilt after the war. The Vierge Dorée (Golden Virgin) on top of the basilica was shelled in 1915 and hung precariously from the dome for three years – a famous landmark until the tower was destroyed. In the tunnels beneath the basilica a wartime trench system containing contemporary artefacts and equipment has been recreated for visitors (closed Nov-Apr).

Just off the road to Bécordel is the Dartmoor Cemetery containing the graves, amongst others, of the oldest soldier, at 67, to be killed on the Somme; the recipient of a Victoria Cross; and a father and son who were killed on the same day serving in the same regiment.

At **Mametz**, turn left for Cantalmaison: off the road to the right a track, chemin des Gallois, leads to the 38th Welsh Division Memorial topped by an unexpectedly dramatic red dragon. The road from Marincourt to Eclusier passes the **Belvedère de Vaux** on a wide bend in the River Somme: there are lovely views of the river with its many little green islands. At the **Cappy** station, east of Eclusier, there is a stretch of narrow gauge railway line identical to that which supplied the battlefields. Tourist trains run Sun pm May-Sep; Sat, Sun, Wed mid-Jul to end Aug.

<u>Central France</u>

Between Paris and Clermont-Ferrand
Berry and the Auvergne - Northern Massif Central

445 km; maps Michelin Nos 237, 238 and 239

The Massif Central, the vast granite plateau at the centre of France, is sometimes referred to as *la France profonde*. It is the heartland of France, isolated and rugged, steeped in tradition, and long ignored by both politicians and tourists alike. On the plus side it is for the most part industry-free, but this is reflected in its status as one of the poorest areas of the country. Times are changing, however, and the growth of cities such as Lyon and Clermont-Ferrand, which has depopulated many of the tiny villages, has also improved communications links.

Today, more and more people want to experience 'the real France', and tourism is a growth industry; however, the locals take a cautious attitude to visitors. They have had the sense to preserve tracts of the most beautiful and inaccessible landscapes in the form of national parks, notably the marvellous Parc Naturel Régional des Volcans d'Auvergne, which lies in a region of extinct volcanoes west of Clermont-Ferrand covered in Local Explorations: 9.

This section covers the northern section of the Massif Central, and incorporates the old province of Berry, one of the richest and most important regions of France during the Middle Ages. Bourges is its historic capital with a fine cathedral and streets of Renaissance mansions. To the north, Orléans was the capital of the country under the old royal dynasty of Capet, and scene of Joan of Arc's victory over the English, the turning point in the Anglo-French Hundred Years War. Numerous small châteaux, many of which are still privately-owned and inhabited, dot the countryside along the Route Jacques Coeur (page 110), and make a pleasant change from the echoing glories of the Loire Valley.

Between Paris and Clermont-Ferrand, the A10 and A71 *autoroutes* cut a swift path via Orléans and Bourges. Main roads, such as the N20/N144/N9 parallel the *autoroute* for blue route followers, but it is more fun to zig-zag about, taking in part of the Route Jacques Coeur around Bourges, and the spa town of Vichy. The ideal green route would be a combination of gentle meander along the Loire between Orléans and Gien, and either the Route Jacques Coeur or a sortie into the watery Sologne region via Souvigny-sur-Sologne and Romarantin-Lanthenay. The Sologne was the childhood home and inspiration of novelist Alain Fournier; and there is another literary association at Nohant, where George Sand kept her country retreat.

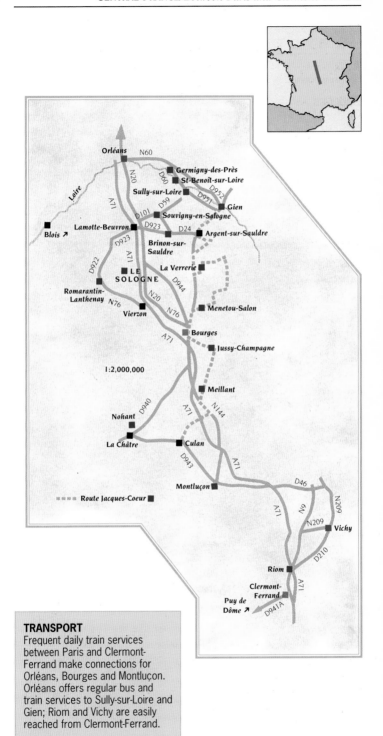

Route Jacques-Coeur ▪

1:2,000,000

TRANSPORT
Frequent daily train services
between Paris and Clermont-
Ferrand make connections for
Orléans, Bourges and Montluçon.
Orléans offers regular bus and
train services to Sully-sur-Loire and
Gien; Riom and Vichy are easily
reached from Clermont-Ferrand.

SIGHTS & PLACES OF INTEREST

BLOIS
See France Overall: 14.

BOURGES ⋈ ✕
Off the A71, 120km S of Orléans. S.I. 21 rue Victor-Hugo. The province of Berry lies at the heart of France, and Bourges is its chief town. A substantial settlement by the time the Romans arrived to sack it, Bourges later rose to prominence in the 14thC under the guidance of Jean de Berry, whose elegant and cultured court rivalled that of the dukes of Burgundy at Dijon. It positively flourished during the 15thC, as did Jacques Coeur, a local goldsmith-turned-merchant moneybags, and Minister of Finance to Charles VII. The local tourist board has alighted upon the symbolic Coeur (heart) as a device for promoting the region, and devised the Route Jacques Coeur for which Bourges is a starting point.

Chief among the town's treasures is the **Cathédrale de Saint-Etienne**.

Being somewhat off the beaten track, its glories are rarely swamped by coach parties, so there is plenty of room to stroll around and admire the elegant flying buttresses and superb west façade adorned with scenes from the Last Judgement. The interior is dramatically high and powerfully plain, inset with stained glass. The best of this (quite the equal to Chartres) is in the choir. Cleaned and restored to extraordinary brilliance it dates from the 13thC. Guided tours visit the crypt containing Jean de Berry's tomb; Burgundian snails with little faces grin from the curly cabbage leaves carved around the doorway.

The Old Town stretches downhill north of the cathedral in a muddle of cobblestone streets. On rue Moyenne, stop off at the **PTT** for a quick inspection of its carved figures wearing 16thC headgear and fashionable long-toed slippers. Then cut across to the **Palais Jacques-Coeur** and a further riot of exuberant carvings including blind windows with stone onlookers. Regular tours explore this gem of

RECOMMENDED HOTELS

BOURGES
Angleterre, FF; *1 place des Quatre-Piliers; tel.* 48 24 68 51; *credit cards* AE, DC, MC, V; *open year round.*
Attractive small hotel in a refurbished town house close to the Palais Jacques-Coeur.

Les Tilleuls, F; *7 place de la Pyrotechnie; tel.* 48 20 49 04; *credit cards* AE, DC, MC, V; *open year round.*
A notable bargain, just south of the town centre. Fresh and attractive modern or traditional style rooms, restaurant, sunny garden with a climbing frame and bike hire.

BRINON-SUR-SAULDRE
Auberge de la Solognote, FF; *tel.* 48 58 50 29; *credit cards* V; *closed four weeks Feb-Mar, ten days May-June.*
Peace and quiet, lovely rooms, breakfast in the courtyard and the charming Girards on hand to advise. Great base for exploring the Sologne, and working up an appetite for M. Girard's delicious Michelin-starred cui-

sine. Winter menus feature plenty of Sologne game.

CLERMONT-FERRAND
Dav'Hôtel Jaude, F-FF; *10 rue Minimes; tel.* 73 93 31 49; *credit cards* AE, MC, V; *open year round.*
In a quiet alley off place Jaude. Recently renovated. Charming welcome, big breakfasts.

Hôtel Gallieni, F-FF; *51 rue Bonnabaud; tel.* 73 93 59 69; *credit cards* AE, DC, MC, V; *open year round.*
Bland but comfortable businessmen's choice, a short walk from place Jaude; as is its smarter neighbour the **Altéa Gergovie, FF-FFF**, 82 boulevard Gergovia (tel. 73 34 46 46).

GIEN
Le Rivage, FF-FFF; *1 quai Nice; tel.* 38 67 20 53; *credit cards* AE, DC, MC, V; *open year round (restaurant closed three weeks Feb-Mar).*
An elegant and relaxing mixture of antique and modern furnishings, thoughtfully equipped rooms, and a Michelin-starred restaurant.

15thC domestic architecture, largely unfurnished but crammed with curios and innovations such as the indoor privys. Bourges has restored several fine Renaissance mansions to house its museums (joint entry tickets; closed Tues): the **Musée du Berry**, rue des Arènes, displays local history exhibits in the Hôtel Cujas; the **Musée Estève**, 13 rue Edouard-Branly, houses modern arts; and the sumptuous **Hôtel Lallement**, 6 rue Bourbonnoux, has been furnished in rich 17th-18thC style, just off **rue Coursarlon** with its shops and half-timbered medieval buildings leading down to **place Gordaine**.

CLERMONT-FERRAND ⇄ ✕

On the A71/N9, 195 km S of Bourges.
S.I. *69 boulevard Gergovia.* Nicknamed the *ville noire* for the black volcanic rock with which much of it is built, Clermont-Ferrand was once two towns. Urban II launched the First Crusade from the church town of Clermont in 1095; the dukes of Auvergne founded Montferrand, its secular rival, in the 12thC.

The two had merged by the time Charles Macintosh's niece arrived on the scene in the early 19thC. Madame Daubrée had learned a trick or two from her raincoat-inventing uncle and made bouncy rubber balls to amuse her offspring. Her husband took the idea a step further and founded a rubber business which later grew into the giant Michelin tyre company still based here.

Under siege from its smoggy industrial outskirts, Clermont is a surprisingly pleasant place, and a natural base for expeditions into the bizarrely beautiful volcanic hinterland. The centre of town is **place Jaude** edged by shops and cafés and surveyed by a statue of the Gaullish chieftan Vercingetorix, who allegedly defeated Julius Caesar at nearby Gergovie. The Old Town lies to the north, around **place Saint-Pierre** with a lively Tuesday to Saturday market, and rue des Gras, home of the **Musée Ranquet**. an eclectic small museum.

At the top of the street, the **Cathédrale de Notre-Dame** bears its mas-

---

LAMOTTE-BEUVRON
Moulin de Villiers, F-FF; *Nouan-le-Fuziliers, 7 km S of Lamotte-Beuvron via D44; tel. 54 88 72 27; credit cards* MC, V; *closed Jan to mid-Mar, two weeks Sep.*

A brick-and-timber converted mill, simple and secluded. Fishing in the little lake, walking in the private park. Excellent home cooking.

ORLEANS
Hôtel d'Arc, FF; *37 rue de la République; tel. 38 53 10 94; credit cards* AE, DC, MC, V; *open year round.*

Traditional town-centre hotel with comfortable modern rooms and helpful staff.

Jackotel, F-FF; *18 cloître Saint-Aignan; tel. 38 54 48 48; credit cards* V; *open year round.*

Peaceful, modern hotel set in a courtyard off a church square south of rue de Bourgogne.

SOUVIGNY-EN-SOLOGNE
Auberge de la Croix Blanche, F-FF; *rue Eugène-Labiche; tel. 54 88 40 08; credit cards* V; *closed mid-Jan to Mar; restaurant closed Tues dinner-Wed.*

Set centre-stage in a typically peaceful and pretty Solognote village, a brick-and-timber building with all the attributes of an old-fashioned French *auberge*. Some rooms are in a pleasant annexe down the road – but not so good if you want to leave the children asleep while you dine.

In the same village, the **Perdrix Rouge, F-FF** , *tel.* 54 88 41 05, has a Michelin red R for good value, and a lovely garden.

VICHY
Hotel de Grignan, F-FF; *7 place Sévigné; tel.* 70 32 08 11; *credit cards* AE, DC, MC, V; *closed mid-Oct to mid-Nov.*

One of Vichy's largest hotels completely renovated from top to bottom. Comfortable rooms; value-for-money restaurant.

Hotel Regina, FF-FFF; *4 avenue Thermale; tel.* 70 98 20 95; *credit cards* AE, V; *closed mid-Oct to mid-Apr.*

Grand old spa hotel with well-equipped rooms, a garden and a restaurant.

See also Recommended Restaurants.

sive Gothic bulk lightly, supported on
astonishingly slender volcanic rock pillars – similar to the granite construc-
tions found in northern France. Built
more than a century earlier, the
Basilique de Notre-Dame-du-Port,
off rue du Port, is more typical of the
region. Ignore the dreadful belfry, and
the mottled yellow-grey stone church
is pure Auvergnat Romanesque, its
interior decorated with marvellous
carved capitals: crusaders in chain-
mail, priests in voluminous robes, Eve
in an Eden full of pineapples. A short
walk away on place de la Poterne, the
Fontaine d'Amboise is an indulgent
profusion of Renaissance carving.

South of the city centre, the **Jardin
Lecoq** provides a lush green breathing
space across the street from the
archaeological and natural history
museums, the **Museé Bargoin** and
Museé Lecoq. The sedate spa suburb
of **Royat** lies out to the west of town.

For maps and guides to the **Parc
Naturel Régional des Volcans
d'Auvergne**, there is a good bookshop opposite the S.I., and also the
CHAMINA office at 2 rue Saint-Pierre-le-
Vénérable (tel. 73 92 81 44) for hiking
and climbing information.

The highspots of the Auvergne are
covered in Local Explorations: 9.

GIEN ♿

And other places marked along the
Route Jacques Coeur, see **La Route
Jacques Coeur**, below.

MONTLUCON

On the N144, *100 km S of Bourges.* S.I.

avenue Max-Dormoy. Montluçon gathers
pleasantly around its elevated old town
and 15thC château. On place Piquant,
the distinctly home-spun **Maison
'Vieux Montluçon'** offers a selection
of dusty Gallo-Roman remains, lace
bonnets and antique photographs of
old codgers with 3 m-long beards.

Grande Rue leads up to pretty place
de Notre-Dame and its welcoming
cafés, above which the **Château-
Musée des Ducs de Bourgogne**
looks out over town to the distant
mountains. In addition to regional history and crafts displays, the château
also houses a splendid collection of
traditional hurdy-gurdies all lovingly
carved and ornamented; (closed Tues).

NOHANT

On the D943,35 *km* NW *of Culan.*Cars
have to park across the main road
from this perfectly preserved little hamlet, beloved home for more than 40
years of novelist George Sand
(Baroness Dudevant). Weathered stone
cottages with beautiful gardens, an
auberge and tiny church surround the
green, and the 17thC **Château
George-Sand** contains mementoes
and Sand's tomb in the courtyard
(closed mid-Oct to March). Here the
baroness took refuge to write and
entertain Chopin, Balzac, Flaubert and
the painter Delacroix.

Nearby **La Châtre** has a George
Sand museum and a few hotels.

ORLEANS ♿ ✕

On the A71/N20, *130 km S of Paris.* S.I.
place Albert-1er. One of the great cities

LA ROUTE JACQUES COEUR ♿ ✕
Though nowhere near as impressive
as their counterparts along the Loire
Valley, these small châteaux (many of
them more akin to overgrown manor
houses) have that elusive ingredient
known as charm. At the last count, 17
local sites appeared on this tourist
route which starts on the north bank
of the Loire near Gien and reaches
south to Culan. At **Gien**, 68 km south-
east of Orléans, the 15thC château
houses a hunting museum (open Mar-
Dec). Other highlights along the way
include: pretty lake-side **Château de
la Verrerie** with frescoes in the

16thC chapel and an elegant
Renaissance gallery (20 km south-
east of Argent-sur-Saulare; open Mar-
Dec); **Château Menetou-Salon**, (20
km north of Bourges on the D11;
open Easter-Nov), which also has a
car museum; 17thC **Château Jussy-
Champagne**, (22 km south-east on
the D15; open mid-Mar to mid-Nov),
with its formal gardens; and the richly
ornamented Gothic-Renaissance
Château Meillant, (40 km south, on
the D37; open Feb to mid-Dec). The
S.I. in Bourges can provide maps of
the Route Jaques-Coeur with
descriptions in several languages and
information about bike rentals.

• *Cloud-capped: Puy-de-Dôme, Auvergne.*

of medieval France, but badly bombed in the Second World War, Orléans rather rests on its laurels. It has become a sort of Joan of Arc urban theme park littered with shops, streets and dozens of statues commemorating the 'Maid of Orleans' who liberated the city from the English in 1429.

An equestrian statue of Joan commands the huge main square, place du Martroi, and the **Maison Jeanne d'Arc**, 3 place du Général-de-Gaulle (closed Mon), lies a short walk away. The Maid stayed here after her victory, and there are models, costumes and audio-visual displays detailing the siege of the city. Rue Jeanne d'Arc runs straight as an arrow into the **Cathédrale de Sainte-Croix**, crowned by twin coronets of lacy stonework. Stained glass windows recall the legend of the Maid with the English cast not only as villains but warty monsters to boot, and Charles VII looks indescribably daft in red slippers.

Beside the cathedral, the **Musée des Beaux-Arts** offers 17th-19thC portraits and an impressive modern collection (Monet, Dufy, Picasso, Miró). Across the street, the Hôtel de Ville is housed in the handsome 16thC brick and stone **Hôtel Groslot**, which opens its beautifully-furnished public rooms (closed Sun).

A favourite corner of Orléans is the **Musée Archéologique et Historique**, in the Hôtel Cabu, off rue Charles-Sanglier (closed Tues.) Its rare Gallo-Roman bronzes – a prancing horse, ruff-backed boar, tiny dancers and ball players – are a delight; there

DETOUR – **UPSTREAM FROM ORLEANS**

There are several diversions on the banks of the Loire above Orléans. First up is the little church at **Germigny-des-Prés** (29 km east, off the D60). Dating from the time of Charlemagne (9thC, except 11thC nave) it contains a wonderful 9thC Byzantine mosaic in the east apse which was uncovered in 1840. Glowing with colour, the glass mosaic depicts the Ark of the Covenant.

A little further on is the Romanesque abbey church at **Saint-Benoit-sur-Loire** (35 km south-east, via D60) with a covered porch laid out in three aisles of arches carved with capitals. The **Château de Sully**, at **Sully-sur-Loire** (40 km south-east, on the D951) dips its feet into the river beneath a imposing array of machiolations, arrow slits and pointed towers. Tours include the portrait-lined Salle des Tableaux and magnificent Grand Salon (open Mar-Nov).

are old stone shop signs, furniture and an enormous collection of 18th-19thC engravings attached to religious, political and downright scandalous broadsheets, once a thriving local industry.

Orléans celebrates the ubiquitous Joan with a rumbustious festival on May 7-8. There is a **jazz festival** in the first week of July. For cheap eats, check out the cafés and ethnic restaurants on rue de Bourgogne; picnic ingredients can be gathered in the covered market on place du Châtelet.

PUY DE DOME
See Local Explorations: 9.

RIOM ×
On the N9, 15km N of Clermont-Ferrand. S.I. 16 rue du Commerce. A quietly prosperous town of modest proportions and discreet charm, Riom was once the capital of the dukes of Auvergne. They ruled from a grand palace built by Jean de Berry in the 14thC, but only the **Sainte Chapelle** (closed Sun) remains (worth a visit for its lovely stained glass). Vieux Riom dates from the 16th-17thC commercial boom. Its broad streets are lined with fine Renaissance buildings constructed from local volcanic stone and decorated with carvings.

The S.I. provides a free walking map which includes the **Musée Mandet**, 4 rue de l'Hôtel de Ville (closed Tues), housing archaeological finds and a so-so collection of paintings.

A must is the **Eglise de Notre-Dame-du-Marthuret**, rue du Commerce, which is not much to look at, but contains an enchanting 14thC statue of a Madonna and Child known as *La Vierge a l'Oiseau* – a tiny bird sits in the Child's outstretched hand.

ROMARANTIN-LANTHENAY
And other places marked green in the Sologne area – **Souvigny-en-Sologne** (⊨ ×) and **Brinon-sur Sauldre** – see Le Sologne, below.

LE SOLOGNE ⊨ ×
Anyone who has fallen under the spell of Alain Fournier's mysterious and evocative novel *Le Grand Meulnes* will want to visit the Sologne, his childhood home and setting for the book. A large

---

RECOMMENDED RESTAURANTS

BOURGES
Couscousserie Chez Malik, F; 40 *rue Bourbonnoux; tel. 48 24 59 85; credit cards* V; *closed Mon, and Aug.*

Downtown Bourges on a Sunday night is virtually a restaurant-free zone. Thank heavens for Madame Malik and her excellent couscous.

Le Jardin Gourmand, F-FF; 15*bis avenue Ernest-Renan (towards Nevers); tel. 48 21 35 91; credit cards* AE, V; *closed Sun dinner-Mon, one week mid-Jul, mid-Dec to mid-Jan.*

Attractive spot a little way out of the town centre. Natural wood, fresh flowers, light modern cooking and charming service.

CLERMONT-FERRAND
Le 1513, F; 3 *rue des Chaussetiers; tel. 73 92 37 46; credit cards* AE, MC, V.

An historic building transformed into a popular *crêperie*. Open from lunch until late; huge choice of pancakes and salads.

Le Green, F-FF; 10 *rue Saint-Adjutor; tel. 73 36 47 78; credit cards* V; *daily.*

Tiled floors, natural wood and sunlight; Auvergnat, seafood and low-cal menus. The four-course Auvergnat (**F**) is terrific; plus decent local wines in earthernware *pichets*.

Jean-Yves Bath, FF-FFF; *place du Marché Saint-Pierre (upper floor); tel. 73 31 23 23; credit cards* V; *closed Sun-Mon lunch, three weeks Feb, one week Aug, two weeks Oct-Nov.*

The modern decoration is somewhat uncompromising and several of M. Bath's creations test the outer limits of gourmet experimentation. However, he is on safe ground with a lobster *cassoulet* and dishes with a regional twist such as ravioli stuffed with Cantal cheese and served in a herb-flavoured meat juice.

Simpler Bath dishes can be enjoyed for half the price in the ground floor bistro, **Le Clos Saint-Pierre**, *tel. 73 31 23 22.*

GIEN
See Recommended Hotels.

infertile area of ponds, streams and woods, dotted with pretty villages and low brick-and-timber buildings, the Sologne has a strange, misty and moody quality. Nowadays it is prized for shooting and fishing. **Sauvigny-en-Sologne** and **Brinon-sur-Sauldre** are peaceful and attractive Solognote villages, both with typical galleried churches; nearby, 13 km north-east of Brinon-sur-Sauldre, the **Etang de Puits** offers watersports. West of the A71 *autoroute* at Lamotte-Beuvron, the D922 is a signposted tourist route through the region, to the main town of **Romarantin-Lanthenay**, with a preponderance of fine old brick-and-timber buildings and an interesting **Musée de Sologne** (closed Tues); also the renowned restaurant **Grand Hôtel du Lion d'Or, FFF** 69 rue Clemenceau tel. 54 76 00 28; plus 13 luxury rooms.

VICHY ⌑ ✕

On the N209, 54 km NE of Clermont-Fer-rand. S.I. 19 rue du Parc. A stylish pre-War spa packed with hotels, Vichy was eminently suited for the role of HQ to Maréchal Petain's puppet government when it abandoned Paris to the Germans in 1940. Since then the unfortunate spa has been trying to wash its hands of the affair. The stigma remains however, as do hotels such as the Thermale, which housed the defence ministry. The department of justice occupied the Carlton; the Gestapo took over the Portugal; and Parliament met in the opera house.

For all that, Vichy is a pleasant if somewhat geriatric town. *Curistes* stroll in the central **Parc des Sources** in between trips to the various springs – some you bathe in, some you drink, and they all reek of sulphur.

The least noxious is the Celestin, and there are five more major springs dotted around town. Vichy boasts excellent sporting facilities from golf and tennis to kayaking on the Allier and watersports on the lake. Enquire at the S.I. for details of the one-week *passeport sportif*. More gentle exercise opportunities are afforded by the paths and riverside walks in the English-style **Parc de l'Allier** laid out for Napoléon III.

MONTLUCON
Le Grenier à Sel, FF-FFF; *8, rue Sainte-Anne; tel. 70 05 53 79; credit cards AE, DC, V; closed Sun dinner-Mon.*

Delightful town centre restaurant (Michelin star) with a warm welcome and garden dining in fine weather.

Also four rooms, **FFF**.

ORLEANS
Les Antiquaires, FF-FFF; *2 rue au Lin; tel. 38 53 52 35; credit cards AE, DC, V; closed Sun-Mon, three weeks Apr-May, two weeks Christmas.*

Well-earned Michelin star for Michel Pipet's stylish seasonal repertoire: red mullet baked with a herb *pistou*, veal kidneys with horseradish.

La Chancellerie, F-FF; *27 place du Martroi; tel. 38 53 57 54; credit cards AE, V; closed Sun.*

Terraced brasserie on the main square run by a wine lover. Terrific choice of wines by the bottle or glass; long and varied menu.

RIOM
Les Petits Ventres, F-FF; *6 rue Anne-Dubourg; tel. 73 38 21 65; credit cards AE, V; closed Sat lunch, Sun dinner (except Jul-Aug), Mon, two weeks Aug-Sept, one week Nov.*

Two dining rooms – one cosy, one sunny – and a menu for all seasons. Homemade duck paté, farm-fresh chicken with mushrooms, and traditional Auvergnat dishes.

VICHY
Brasserie du Casino, F-FF; *4 rue du Casino; tel. 70 98 23 06; credit cards AE, V; closed Wed-Thur lunch, and Nov.*

An authentic 1920s brasserie – all gleaming wood and polished brass. Extensive menu, tables on the terrace and evening piano bar.

La Colombière, F-FF; *at Abrest, 5 km S via D906; tel. 70 98 69 15; credit cards AE, DC, MC, V; closed Sun dinner off season, Mon except lunch in season, mid-Jan to mid-Feb.*

A converted dovecote set in shady gardens by the banks of the Allier. Very good value light but traditional cooking and charming service, plus four quiet and simple rooms.

Between Clermont-Ferrand and Avignon
The Southern Massif

385 km; maps Michelin Nos 239 and 240

Twenty years ago, a tourist in the Southern Massif was about as common as a blizzard in June. Traditionally poor and sparsely populated, the region is both rugged and isolated, visited by arctic winters in the northern uplands and scorching summers in the southern hills. Its magnificent scenery, by turns dramatic and desolate, is the chief attraction.

The best way to appreciate the terrain is to spend a couple of days in the Parc National des Cévennes. The second largest national park in France casts its boundaries around two contrasting geological features, the weatherbeaten limestone plateaux of the Grands Causses and the lonely ridges of the Cévennes hills descending in choppy waves at the southern extreme of the Massif Central. The *causses* are bracing walking country topped by hamlets and fortified farmhouses. Between the Causse Méjean and Causse Sauveterre, the River Tarn has carved out one of the most spectacular gorges in France, while underground rivers and rainfall have created great caverns filled with stalagmites.

Further hiking opportunities abound to the north around Saint-Flour and the Plomb de Cantal, an outpost of the volcanic Auvergne (the highspots of which are covered in Local Explorations: 9).

One of the Cévenne's most spectacular drives is the corniche des Cévennes, a winding mountain road built for Louis XIV's troops in the early 18thC. In 1685, when the Revocation of the Edict of Nantes sent Huguenots into hiding, many took refuge in the Cévennes and waged a guerrilla war against the king's army until the Camisard ('white shirt') uprising was brutally crushed in 1704.

The focus of this section remains, however, the Parc National des Cévennes. (Details, page 117.) To approach it from the north, there are two options: the fast N9 to Millau, or the (preferable) N9/N102 blue route to Le Puy with a green detour on the D588/D906 up into the Livradois from Brioude. The N88 then dog-legs to Mende and picks up the N106 for Florac. From Avignon, to the south-east, the D981 climbs the *garrigue* to Uzès, then the D982 cuts across to Anduze, Saint-Jean-du-Gard and the Corniche des Cévennes.

TRANSPORT
Patience is a prerequisite for exploring the region without a car. Paris-Nîmes train services travel via Clermont east to Le Puy and Le Monastier for connections to Mende and Millau. Alternatively, Clermont–Aurillac trains stop at Neussargues-Moissac for connections to Saint-Flour, Mende and Millau. Daily buses serve most towns and villages in the national park, and run from Florac down to Alès for Anduze, Uzès and Avignon.

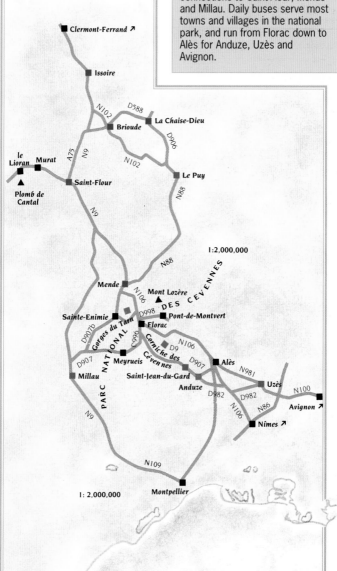

1:2,000,000

115

SIGHTS & PLACES OF INTEREST

ANDUZE ♨ ×

On the D907, 60 km W of Avignon. S.I. plan de Brie. Anduze, the eastern 'Gateway to the Cévennes' on the Gardon d'Anduze, makes a useful base for excursions into the Parc National des Cévennes. It is an attractive small town with winding streets and an old clock tower, the sole remnant of the original château and fortifications demolished on Richelieu's orders in 1629. Pottery is made here.

The Camisard hero Roland was born in the hamlet of **le Mas Soubeyran** (7 km NW via the D50) in 1680. His birthplace is now a pilgrimage for Protestants, several thousand of whom gather here each September to commemorate the suffering of their forebears. Roland's house, with the hidey-hole where our hero concealed himself during raids by the king's troops, forms part of the **Musée du Désert** (closed-Nov-Mar). Among displays which recall the 'wilderness' years of French Protestantism are ingenious folding altars, bibles and scores of documents. Just up the road from the museum, a throng of stalagmites ranged about the cool limestone cavern of the **Grotte de Trabuc** has earned itself the nickname the Hundred Thousand Soldiers (closed mid-Oct to mid-Mar).

From May to September (for schedules, tel. 66 85 19 06), a steam train puffs through the hills to Saint-Jean-du-Gard with a stop at the **Bambuseraie de Prafrance** (2 km N via the D129). More than 60 varieties of bamboo rustle dryly in the breeze and additional shade is provided by an arboretum planted with sequoias, oaks and scented magnolias (closed Nov-Mar).

AVIGNON

See France Overall: 5.

BRIOUDE

On the N102, 60 km NW of Le Puy. Sleepy Brioude has two claims to fame: its spring salmon, and the basalt and sandstone **Basilique de Saint-Julien**. One of the last Romanesque churches built in the Auvergne, its fat pillars wear traces of frescoes beneath carved capitals, and there are 13th-14thC frescoes in an upper chapel.

For a glimpse of the famous salmon swimming up the Allier, try the bridge at Vieille-Brioude (4 km S), or the one east of town on the road to la Chaise-Dieu (D588).

CHAISE-DIEU, LA

On the D906/D499, 40 km NW of Le Puy.S.I. place de la Mairie. Perched on a plateau in the Livradois, this hill village, 'Seat of God', grew up around an 11thC abbey. Despite its isolated position, the abbey flourished and once rivalled Cluny for wealth and influence. When one of its graduates, Clement VI, was elected pope in 1342, he rewarded his *alma mater* with a splendid abbey church, and chose to be buried here.

The **Eglise de Saint-Robert** is famous for its 15thC *danse macabre* frescoes in the choir (closed Tues in winter). The skeletal figure of Death weaves his way through all walks of life from well-dressed nobles and portly clerics to craftsmen, beneath which the legend reads *'This is you'*. Above the elaborately carved choir stalls, superb 15thC Flemish tapestries depict biblical scenes; and there is a fine Gothic cloister.

On place de l'Echo, check out the accoustics in the **Salle de l'Echo**, where priests would hear the confessions of the sick at a safe distance. Two people standing at opposite corners of this room, facing the wall, can hold audible whispered conversations.

CLERMONT-FERRAND

See France Overall: 7.

CORNICHE DES CEVENNES

See Parc National des Cévennes, page 117.

GORGES DU TARN

See Parc National des Cévennes, page 117.

ISSOIRE

On the N9, 38 km S of Clermont-Ferrand.S.I. Hôtel de Ville. A Protestant stronghold all but razed to the ground during the Wars of Religion, Issoire now conceals its one remaining (and redeeming) feature behind a dreary sprawl of factory suburbs. The handsomely-proportioned 12thC **Eglise de Saint-Austremoine** is one of the finest Romanesque buildings in the Auvergne, its interior still bizarrely impressive despite the addition of garish 19thC decoration. The sturdy simplicity of the crypt is a relief. Take time to inspect the sculpted capitals, a 15thC mural of the *Last Judgement* in the narthex, and the zodiacal symbols adorning the outside walls of the chapels by the car park.

MENDE ⊨ ×
On the N106/N88, 95 km SW of Le Puy. S.I. 14 boulevard Henri-Bourrillon. Nestled in the Lot Valley on the northern edge of the Parc National des Cévennes, the pint-sized capital of Lozère radiates from a higgledy-piggledy medieval town centre which can be crossed on foot in five minutes flat. The narrow cobbled streets, arches and twisting alleys crowd around the jaundiced yellow stone flanks of the **Cathédrale de Notre-Dame**, rebuilt after the 16thC Wars of Religion. The cathedral is a showcase for a comprehensive selection of stained glass through the ages, Aubusson tapestries hung in the chancel, 17thC carved choirstalls, and a typically Auvergnat

---

PARC NATIONAL DES CEVENNES
Designated in 1970, the national park extends south and east of Mende (see above) across a broad swathe of rugged highlands. For the most part it falls within Lozère, the least populated *département* in France, a one-time refuge for Camisards and war-time Resistance fighters, where Robert Louis Stevenson marvelled at the primitive beauty of the hills '*as rude as when God made them at first*'.

Mont Lozère rises in the east, a great granite leviathan 1,699 m high and source of the River Tarn. This is prime walking country with wide stretches of undulating, high grasslands, doughty sheep and scattered stone farm buildings set four-square against the freezing winters. The GR68 makes an energetic hiking tour of Mont Lozère, or there are less strenuous discovery paths from the Mas Camargues and Mas de la Barque with guided walks operating during July and August. The **Ecomusée** at Pont-de-Monvert is a helpful introduction to the region with maps, information sheets and exhibits, also a *gîte* for hikers (open May-Sep and in the spring holidays).

The park headquarters (closed Sat-Sun in winter) are in **Florac**, a relaxed little one-horse town at the northern end of the Corniche des Cévennes. Florac makes a convenient starting point for a circular tour of the dramatic **Gorges du Tarn** and the **Gorges de la Jonte**, deep craggy ravines carved out of the *causses* and followed by twisting, cliff-hanging roads which leave you with a heightened respect for dynamite and navvies. Along the way, there are several delightful villages such as perpendicular **Sainte-Enimie** on the Tarn, with its slippery cobbled alleys and medieval houses, and **Meyrueis** on the Jonte (both useful stopovers for exploring the region). **Millau** is another popular base with good public transport connections (see page 118). Helpful S.I.s are bursting with information and details of campsites, mountain bike rental depots (several offer to haul you up the *causses* so you can pedal down with ease), pony trekking, canoeing, and local excursions. Near Meyrueis, there are two famous cave complexes complete with bizarre limestone rock formations: **Aven Armand** (11 km NW off the D986; open Apr-Oct), and the **Grotte de Dargilan** (8 km W on the D139; open Easter-Oct), also known as the 'Pink Cave'.

South of Florac, **Mont Aigoual** (1,565 m) is a favourite with walkers, its forests and high pastures encircled by the GR66. There are several well-signposted walking trails that take you scrambling across the desolate sun-baked heights of the **Causse Méjean** (between the Tarn and the Jonte), while the long-distance footpaths, the GR6 Rhône-Cévennes and GR7 Vosges-Pyrénées, traverse the region and cross each other just south of Florac. The GR67 follows the dusty heather-covered ridges of the Cévennes down to Camisard country and the terraced Gardon valleys planted with vines, mulberry trees and spreading sweet chestnuts.

• *Millau.*

Black Virgin. Just off place du Beurre, the **Musée Ignon-Fabre** (closed Sun) houses local history exhibits. A short walk north of the centre, via the quaintly named rue Chou-Vert ('green cabbage street'), the **Pont Notre-Dame** has borne traffic across the Lot since the 13thC.

MILLAU 🏨 ✕
On the N9, 77km SW of Florac. S.I. 1 avenue Alfred-Merle. A lively and attractive market town on the Tarn, Millau's stock in trade is leather and glovemaking. A score of small factories (signposted off the ring boulevard) wel-

> ### FISHING IN THE AUVERGNE
> Paradise for the keen fisherman, the Auvergne boasts a great variety of waters - rivers, lakes, volcanic crater lakes and reservoirs – that are home to an even greater variety of fish – salmon, trout, grayling, carp, pike and bream amongst others. Game and coarse fishing are both to be had. For more information contact the Comité Régional du Tourisme, 43 avenue Julien, B.P. 395, 63011 Clermont-Ferrand cedex (tel. 73 93 04 03).

come visitors. The medieval town centre is a warren of narrow, shop-filled streets huddled around a 14thC belfry and pretty place du Maréchal-Foch. Two enormous plane trees shade the little square with its fountain centrepiece and row of arcaded buildings. In one corner the 12thC façade of the **Eglise de Notre-Dame-de-l'Espinasse** is topped by an octagonal tower; in another you can get to grips with the glovemaker's art at the **Musée de Millau**, housed in the 18thC Hôtel de Pegayrolles, together with exhibits detailing the prehistory of the Causses, collections of Gallo-Roman pottery and antique dolls (closed Sun in winter).

NIMES
See France Overall: 5.

PUY (-EN-VELAY), LE 🏨 ✕
On the N102, 130 km SE of Clermont-Ferrand. S.I. place du Breuil. An historic pilgrim rendezvous on the Route Saint-Jacques to Santiago de Compostela, Le Puy unfurls across a fertile valley interrupted by a clutch of irregular volcanic outcrops called *puys.* Not to be outdone by the wonders of nature, the locals have topped these heights with creations of their own, such as the Romanesque chapel of **Saint-Michel-d'Aiguilhe**, to the north of town. Perched on the 80 m-high Rocher d'Aiguilhe, it is a stiff 268-step climb, but the chapel, with its carved portal, mosaics, murals and cunning architecture, is worth the effort, as are the views.

Le Puy's old town scales two lesser *puys* in a cat's cradle of narrow contour-hugging streets bisected by perpendicular rue des Tables. A monumental flight of steps takes over where the street ends, leading into the cavernous maw of the **Cathédrale de Notre-Dame** beneath a Byzantine arrangement of striped stonework. The Romanesque church is a show-stopper, by turns ornate and severe. Wrapped in the volcanic stone gloom there are capitals and frescoes, a Black Virgin behind a cloud of censers, and ecclesiastical treasures on display in the sacristy. Take a turn around the beautiful cloister and the quiet lanes behind the cathedral, then muster up the strength for an assault on the **Rocher Corneille**, another *puy,* which

• *Tarn Gorge.*

supports a towering 19thC statue of Notre-Dame-de-France, struck in gunmetal captured during the Crimean War.

SAINT-FLOUR ⊨ ✕

On the N9/N106, 115 km S of Clermont-Ferrand. S.I. 2 place d'Armes. The old capital of Haute Auvergne, Saint-Flour is a pleasant town and handy base for exploring the Cantal mountains to the west. All roads seem to lead uphill to the market square, place d'Armes, and plain, fortress-like façade of the 14thC Gothic **Cathédrale de Saint-Pierre**. There are sweeping views from a terrace behind the cathedral, and two museums on the square. Local crafts, costume and customs are displayed in the **Musée de la Haute Auvergne**; anything else from furniture to *faïence* finds itself quartered in the **Musée Drouet** (both closed Sun in winter).

The **Cantal mountains** once formed part of an enormous extinct volcano, a serious match for Mount Etna in its day. Three impressive peaks remain, rooted in deep valleys and cloaked in grassy meadows. Saint-Flour is balanced on a tongue of basaltic lava rock which extends west towards the 1,855 m-high **Plomb de Cantal**, about 30 km as the crow flies by the GR4 hiking route; or 40 km by road via Murat to **le Lioran**, the Cantal's main winter ski station, where the S.I. dispenses hiking and skiing information.

119

SAINT-JEAN-DU-GARD ⊯

On the D260/D907, 53 km SE of Florac.
S.I. place Rabaut-Saint-Etienne. This
delightful Cévenole village at the southern end of the Corniche des Cévennes
was the final destination of Robert
Louis Stevenson on his *Travels with a
Donkey*, a published account of his
190-km hike across the Cévennes. A
small museum, the **Musée des Vallées Cévenoles** (95 Grand'Rue) provides a gentle introduction to local
history and traditional industries from
the cultivation of silk worms to sweet
chestnuts (open May-Sep Tues-Sat,
Sun pm). During the season, a steam
train runs south through fine scenery
to Anduze (see page 116).

UZES ⊯

*On the D981, 40 km NW of Avignon. S.I.
avenue de la Libération.* In the dusty,
scrub-covered hills of the *garrigue*,
Uzès announces itself with a flourish of
medieval towers. The focal point of this
attractive old town is place de la
République (locals call it the **place aux
Herbes**) with its arcaded buildings and
colourful Saturday morning market laid
out under the trees.

Two of the most imposing towers,
including the original 11thC watchtower, are attached to the **Duché d'Uzès**,
a feudal castle founded (and still inhabited) by the Crussol d'Uzès family. An
homogenous pile of Renaissance and
classical additions houses appart-
ments furnished in Louis XIII-XV styles
with paintings and tapestries; there is
also a 15thC Gothic chapel, a waxworks exhibit and panoramic views
from the Tour Bermonde (closed Mon
Sep-May). Across place du Duché, the
18thC Hôtel de Ville hosts summer season concerts in the courtyard.

Head east on rue Boucairie for the
17th-19thC **Cathédrale de Saint-
Théodorit**, rebuilt after the Revolution.
Its elegant Italianate campanile, the
12thC **Tour Fenestrelle**, was part of
the original edifice. From **place Jean-
Racine** there are views south to the
Alzon Valley. The River Eure rises nearby, tapped by Roman engineers in 19
AD to provide Nîmes with fresh water.
An impressive section of their 50 km-
long aquaduct, the **Pont du Gard**, still
stands 16 km south of town on the Avignon road (see page 96).

RECOMMENDED HOTELS

ANDUZE
La Regalière, F; *route de Saint-Jean-du-
Gard; tel.* 66 61 81 93; *credit cards* AE, V;
closed Jan to mid-Mar.
  Peaceful *logis* in large grounds with
a pleasant terraced restaurant serving
Cévenole dishes (closed Wed lunch dur-
ing winter).

FLORAC
Grand Hôtel Parc, F-FF; 47 *avenue*
Jean-Monestier; *tel.* 66 45 03 05; *credit
cards* AE, DC, MC, V; *closed mid-Dec to
Mar.*
  Friendly and comfortable family hotel
set back from the main street with a
walled garden and swimming pool.
Sound traditional cooking.

MENDE
Hôtel de France, F; 9 *boulevard* Lucien-
Arnault; *tel.* 66 65 00 04; *credit cards* V;
closed mid-Dec to mid-Jan.
  Welcoming *logis* with 28 simple bedrooms and good-value half-board deals
for stays of three days or more. The
restaurant is a local favourite serving
regional dishes such as a generous
salade quercynoise with smoked duck
breast and nuts, and poached fresh
trout.
  Another option is the bland Best
Western **Lion d'Or (FF)**, 12 boulevard
Britexte, tel. 66 49 16 46, which
redeems itself somewhat with an outdoor pool and garden.

MEYRUEIS
Château d'Ayres, F-FF; 1.5 *km E via*
D57; *tel.* 66 45 60 10, *credit cards* AE, DC,
MC, V; *closed Nov-Apr.*
  Lovely old stone château with creeper-clad walls and white shutters. A family enterprise with 24 spacious bedrooms, a comfy antique-filled salon and
restaurant. Pool and tennis court; pony
trekking by arrangement. A great base.

Family Hôtel, F; *rue de la Barrière; tel.*
66 45 60 02; *credit cards* AE, MC, V; *closed
mid-Nov to mid-Apr.*
  Family-style *logis* in a big old house
in the heart of the village; garden and
swimming pool at the back. Friendly
welcome in the restaurant.

MILLAU

Château de Creissels, FF; *route de Saint-Affrique, at Creissels (D992 2 km W of the Pont Lerouge); tel. 65 60 16 59; credit cards AE, DC, V; closed Jan to mid-Mar.*

Simple, fairly-priced rooms in a rambling, much-added-to château. Innovative menus served in the vaulted dining room. Shady garden.

PUY, LE

Dyke Hôtel, F; *37 boulevard Maréchal-Fayolle; tel. 71 09 05 30; credit cards V; open year round.*

Simple, comfortable rooms recently refurbished in bleached wood and colourful fabrics.

SAINT-FLOUR

L'Europe, F-FF; *12 cours des Ternes; tel. 71 60 03 64; credit cards V; open year round.*

Convenient overnight stop at the entrance to the Old Town. Room prices vary according to the view (town or valley). There is a value-for-money restaurant with huge picture windows; locals frequent the bar.

SAINT-JEAN-DU-GARD

L'Oronge, F; *103 Grand'Rue; tel. 66 85 30 34; credit cards AE, DC, V; closed Sun dinner-Mon winter, Jan-Mar.*

Venerable 17thC posthouse. The simple rooms have hefty beams and bare stonework, and the dining room serves copious home cooking.

SAINTE-ENIMIE

Château de la Caze, FFF; *at La Malène (5 km W via D907b); tel. 66 48 51 01; credit cards AE, DC, MC, V; closed Nov-May.*

Romantic 15thC château, complete with turrets, beside the Tarn. Gorgeous antiques, enormous fireplaces, four-posters and every comfort. Lovely dining room serving Lozèrien cuisine.

UZES

Hôtel d'Entraigues, FF; *8 rue de la Calade; tel. 66 22 32 68; credit cards AE, DC, MC, V; open year round.*

Charming central hotel in a 15thC building near the cathedral. Elegant comfortable rooms, and the delicious **Jardins de Castille** restaurant with a roof-top terrace.

RECOMMENDED RESTAURANTS

ANDUZE

Auberge du Fer à Cheval, F; *at Mialet (10 km N via D129/D50); tel. 66 85 02 80; credit cards V; closed Sun dinner-Mon, Tues-Fri Oct-Nov, Dec to mid-Mar.*

Rustic charm and real value-for-money menus in an old Cévenole house convenient for le Mas Soubeyran.

FLORAC

See Recommended Hotels.

MENDE

See Recommended Hotels.

MILLAU

La Marmite du Pêcheur, F-FF; *14 boulevard Capelle; tel. 65 61 20 44; credit cards AE, DC, MC, V; closed Wed, Feb.*

Stone arches span a narrow downstairs dining area (more room upstairs). The house speciality is a *marmite* of monkfish and mussels in fragrant saffron-scented stock.

Auberge Occitane, F; *15 rue Peyrollerie; credit cards AE, MC, V; closed Sun-Mon, Mar.*

Cosy hearth-side setting in an historic building. Regional menus include *salade aveyronnaise* with roquefort and nuts, pork with juniper, trout and numerous lamb dishes.

PUY, LE

L'Ecu d'Or, F-FF; *59-61 rue Pannessac; tel. 71 02 19 36; credit cards AE, DC, MC, V; closed Sun.*

Cheerful vaulted dining room with murals in a medieval building. Regional cooking and delicious fish dishes such as smoked trout mousseline.

SAINT-FLOUR

Chez Geneviève, F; *25 rue des Lacs; tel. 71 60 17 97; credit cards MC, V; closed Sun.*

Homely little restaurant with a great value *plat du jour* daily, as well as dishes such as lamb with herbs, or veal escalope in cider.

UZES

See Recommended Hotels.

<u>North-Eastern France</u>

Between Calais and Strasbourg
The North-East

453 km; maps Michelin Nos 236, 241 and 242

G iven the choice, few holidaymakers devote as much as a day of their precious vacations to this corner of France. The northern Europeans, particularly the Dutch and British, tend to stream southwards without a sideways glance.

North-eastern France, however, has many faces and not a few pleasant surprises. Lille, for instance, surrounded by the furnaces and coal fields of the northern industrial belt, has an historic almshouse, testament to the city's wealth and importance dating back to the Middle Ages. The market town of Arras, once famous for its tapestries, boasts a heart of splendid Flemish-style buildings. And Laon's cathedral is a beauty. Beyond the towns, mile after mile of beet and wheat carpet the plains, interspersed with neat, carefully-tended cemeteries and sombre memorials to the dead of the two world wars.

On the south-eastern horizon, Champagne is still rather flat in terms of the view, but the champagne town of Reims bubbles along with its superb cathedral. Further east, Lorraine is better known for its quiche than for the art cities of Metz and Nancy, both of which merit a stopover; and just over the wooded slopes of the Vosges, the Euro-capital of Strasbourg (France Overall: 10) is juxtaposed with the picture-book villages described in Local Explorations: 12. Turn south (France Overall: 10), and eventually you reach Dijon, the gateway to Burgundy.

No stop on this route is more than a couple of kilometres off the *autoroute,* which makes things easy for red route followers. Between Nancy and Strasbourg, a slow but attractive option off the N4 is the D992/D392 to (or from) Schirmeck, then cut through via the D130/D426 to (or from) Barr or Obernai described in Local Explorations: 12.

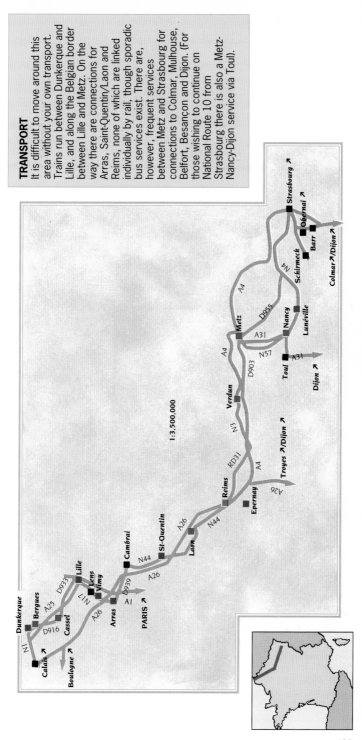

1:3,500,000

SIGHTS & PLACES OF INTEREST

ARRAS 🚗 ✕

Off the A1/A26, 51 km S of Lille. S.I. Hôtel de Ville, place des Héros. Named for its famous tapestries (from the Italian *arazzi*), the market town of Arras is arranged around two splendid squares lined with arcaded and gabled 17th-18thC Flemish town houses.

The larger of the two, **Grand' Place**, is linked by a short street to **place des Héros** and the 15thC **Hôtel de Ville**, a thoroughly Flamboyant affair, its steep slate roof pierced with mini dormers and topped by a belfry from which a carillon strikes the quarters. You can climb the belfry for a bird's-eye view, and enquire at the S.I.

about guided tours beneath the city centre around a network of historic underground passages used as shelters during the First World War. To the north, the stately 18thC former Benedictine Abbaye de Saint-Vaast houses several Arras tapestries in the **Musée des Beaux-Arts**, place de la Madeleine.

Down in the Basse Ville, Sir Edwin Lutyens's **Mémorial Britannique** commemorates 36,000 missing soldiers from the First World War. A short walk away, across boulevard Charles-de-Gaulle at the foot of the Vauban citadel, the **Mur des Fusilles** is a Second World War monument to 200 Resistance fighters, mostly miners, executed by firing squad in 1942.

See also Vimy Ridge, page 132.

RECOMMENDED HOTELS

ARRAS
Ostel des 3 Lupars, FF; *47 Grand' Place; tel. 21 07 41 41; credit cards* AE, DC, V; *open year round.*

Friendly hotel in a 17thC house at the bottom of the square. Well-equipped rooms with a sprinkling of beams; sauna.

DUNKERQUE
Hirondelle, F-FF; *46 avenue Faidherbe, at Malo-les-Bains* (1.5 km NE); *tel. 28 63 39 15; credit cards* V; *open year round.*

Simple modern rooms and a reasonable restaurant five minutes' walk from the sea front.

LAON
L'Angleterre, F-FF; *10 boulevard de Lyon; tel. 23 23 04 62; credit cards* AE, DC, MC, V; *open year round.*

Traditional hotel-restaurant in the Ville Basse. Some comfy refurbished rooms, others somewhat worn, but cheap and clean (front rooms are noisy).

See also Recommended Restaurants.

LILLE
Royal Hôtel, FF; *2 boulevard Carnot; tel. 20 51 05 11; credit cards* AE, DC, V; *open year round.*

Big old city centre hotel with simply furnished refurbished rooms; helpful staff add a personal touch.

LUNEVILLE
Hôtel des Pages, F-FF; *rue Chanzy; tel. 83 74 11 42 credit cards* V; *open year round.*

Just over the bridge from the château; ultra modern but comfortable; restaurant.

METZ
Grand Hôtel de Metz, F-FF; *3 rue des Clercs; tel. 87 36 16 33; credit cards* V; *open year round.*

Amazing value two minutes from the cathedral. Well-equipped, attractively refurbished rooms; private parking available.

Hôtel du Théatre, FF; *Port Saint-Marcel (behind 7 rue du Pont Saint-Marcel); tel. 87 31 10 10; credit cards* AE, DC, MC, V; *open year round.*

Convenient and pleasant little hotel-restaurant complex. Comfy, modern rooms with marble bathrooms; friendly young staff; sauna, pool, and free parking.

NANCY
Crystal Hôtel, F-FF; *5 rue Chanzy; tel. 83 35 41 55; credit cards* AE, DC, MC, V; *open year round.*

Off rue Stanislas, and more attractive inside than out. Modern rooms in pastel shades; close to restaurants.

Hôtel-Restaurant Choley, F; *28 rue Gustave-Simon; tel. 83 32 31 98; credit cards* V; *open year round.*

BARR
See Local Explorations: 12.

BERGUES
On the D916, 9 km SE of Dunkerque. En route between Dunkerque and Lille, the flat plain of French Flanders is punctuated by two very pretty towns worth pausing in, Bergues and Cassel. Bergues sits snugly behind its powerful brick fortifications, a town of neat lanes and a network of canals also part of Vauban's defence system. In the town centre, there is a fine **belfry**, and the **Musée Municipal** (closed Fri) which contains Georges de la Tour's lovely *Joueur de Vieille*.

On an isolated knoll rising from the farmland (Mont Cassel, 174 m), perches **Cassel**, a delightful place of narrow streets and steps and a cobbled *place* lined with fine buildings, including the **Hôtel de la Noble Cour**, now the local museum.

BOULOGNE
See France Overall: 1.

CALAIS
See France Overall: 1.

CASSEL
See Bergues, this page.

COLMAR
See France Overall: 10.

DUNKERQUE 🛏 ✕
On the N1, 42 km E of Calais (15 km W of the ferry terminal; free bus service). S.I. Le

---

An 18thC house opened as a hotel in 1875. Basic and quiet; good restaurant (**F-FF** menus); conveniently situated.

Grand-Hôtel de la Reine, FFF; 2 *place Stanislas; tel.* 83 35 03 01; *credit cards* AE, DC, MC, V; *open year round.*

Gorgeous Relais et Châteaux hotel in an elegant 18thC *palais*; listed staircase and public rooms; bedrooms decorated in Louis XV style; superb service; fine restaurant.

REIMS
Le Bon Moine, F; 14 *rue des Capuchins; tel.* 26 47 33 64; *credit cards* MC, V; *closed Sun (except Jul-Aug), Christmas and New Year.*

Spotless and central (opposite Parking Cathédrale) with a jolly bar and value-for-money regional restaurant popular with the locals.

Château des Crayères, FFF; 64 *boulevard Henri-Vasnier; tel.* 26 82 80 80; *credit cards* AE, DC, MC, V; *closed Christmas to mid-Jan.*

An exquisite turn-of-the-century château-hotel. Marble columns, a swooping staircase; panelling and tapestries; sumptuous rooms overlook the park; and Gerard Boyer's legendary cuisine earns the full three Michelin stars.

Hôtel Crystal, F-FF; 86 *place Drouet d'Erlon; tel.* 26 88 44 44; *credit cards* AE,

V; *open year round.*

Down a passage with a leafy courtyard; stuffy furniture; but a smiling welcome.

The **Continental, FF**, 93 *place Drouet d'Erlon; tel.* 26. 40 39 35, is smarter and occupies a fine old building.

Cheval Blanc, FF; Sept-Saulx - (23 *km south east of Reims via N44/D37); tel.* 26 03 90 27; *credit cards* AE, DC, V; *closed mid-Jan to mid-Feb.*

A good choice between Reims and Verdun/Metz. Traditional village centre coaching inn with rustic bedrooms in an annexe.

SAINT-QUENTIN
France et Angleterre, F; 28 *rue Emile-Zola; tel.* 23 62 13 10; *credit cards* AE, V; *open year round.*

Central hotel with comfy modernized rooms; those at the rear are quieter. Breakfast only.

See also Recommended Restaurants.

VERDUN
Le Saint-Paul, F; 12 *place Saint-Paul; tel.* 29 86 02 16; *credit cards* DC, V; *closed Dec.*

Friendly small hotel, something of an unofficial 'battlefields club' in season; good regional restaurant.

Beffroi, rue Clemenceau. An ugly and largely post-war industrial port, Dunkerque is generally avoided by passengers passing through to or from the U.K. Faced with a couple of hours in town, the best shopping is around rue Clemenceau, though the hypermarkets are out on the N1 toward the ferry port.

The **Musée des Beaux-Arts**, place du Général-de-Gaulle (closed Tues), adds natural history and a section covering the May-June 1940 retreat from Dunkirk to its fine arts collections. Modern art enthusiasts should investigate the **Musée d'Art Contemporain** (closed Tues), a 15- to 20-minute walk north on avenue des Bains. It has a suprisingly enjoyable array of post-war work by Appel, Vasérely and others; and you can wander around the sculpture garden.

DIJON
See France Overall: 10.

EPERNAY
See page 130.

LAON 🛏 ✕
On the N44, 58 km NW of Reims. S.I. place de la Cathédrale. Laon's historic Ville Haute seems a complete mystery when you are in the modern Ville Basse – especially if it is shrouded in a veil of mist. You can get to the Ville Haute from the Poma 2000 station in the Ville Basse: the Poma, a tiny electric train, scales the cliff to the heart of the Old Town, where footsteps echo in the narrow streets of 17th-18thC houses.

The views from the ramparts which still enclose old Laon are best appreciated on a clear day, but the major sight in town, the **Cathédrale de Notre-Dame**, is just as spectacular wreathed in fog. It sports seven towers, two of which heave the monumental façade skyward above the heavily carved triple portal and arcades, later copied at Reims and Chartres. A rhino and a hippo guard the main door, also human figures and gargoyles; even lofty silhouettes of horned cattle said to resemble the beasts that hauled the stone up from the plain. The interior of this Gothic marvel is no disappointment either, its white stone lit by a stunning rose window and narrow lancets in vivid blues and reds.

Behind the cathedral, the 17thC **episcopal palace** is arranged around a spacious courtyard, and there is access to the northern rampart walk. Stroll south, and the **Musée de Laon**, 32 rue Georges-Ermant, displays an extensive collection of Greek vases, Gallo-Roman and Merovingian finds, plus an octagonal 12thC Chapelle des Templiers in the garden. Three 13thC gateways breach the southern ramparts; near the westerly Porte de Soissons, the early-Gothic **Eglise de Saint-Martin** provides the focus of the Le Bourg quarter.

LILLE 🛏 ✕
On the A25, 76 km SE of Dunkerque. S.I. place Rihour. The common perception of Lille as a grim, grey industrial city besieged by smokestacks and slag heaps is only half true. A prosperous trading centre since the 14thC, and part-time residence of the Burgundian dukes (Philip the Good built the Palais de Rihour which houses the S.I.), Vieux Lille has plenty to show for its affluent past, and one of the richest art museums outside Paris.

Lille was the birthplace of Général de Gaulle, so it is no suprise that the central square has been renamed for him, though it's often still referred to as **Grand' Place**. It is home to the 17thC **Ancienne Bourse**, a splendid Flemish baroque extravaganza which now hosts a tame flea and flower market in its arcaded courtyard. Grandly appointed it may be, but it does not equal the riotously ornate turn-of-the-century **Opéra** and **Nouvelle Bourse**, place du Théâtre, the latter reeling under a ridiculous belfry.

To the north, the cobbled streets of Vieux Lille have a distinctly Flemish air. There are plenty of Frenchified *hôtels-particuliers* too, a 19thC cathedral, and the historic **Hospice Comtesse**, rue de la Monnaie, founded by Jeanne de Flandre in 1237. Rebuilt after a fire in the 15thC, the Salle des Malades has the coats-of-arms of its various benefactors painted on the ceiling and niches where sick beds once lined the long room. A museum in the old nuns's quarters displays antique furniture, paintings, china, and some beautiful tiles in the kitchens (closed Tues).

Charles de Gaulle was born in a quiet street a further ten-minute walk north

of here. The house has been turned into a small **museum** plastered with photographs and news cuttings around the black Citroen which carried the president through an assassination attempt in 1962. To the west is Vauban's massive **Citadelle** - 60 million bricks in a multi-pointed star still occupied by the French army (guided tours on Sun), and bordered by the Bois de Boulogne where 700 trees have been planted in memory of Second World War deportees.

South of place Rihour, rue Neuve and rue de Béthune constitute Lille's main shopping district, and lead towards place de la République and the **Musée des Beaux-Arts** (closed Tues). Flemish painters from the 15th-17thC are particularly well-represented (Bouts, Rubens, van Dyck); Rodin and the Impressionists (Monet, Renoir, Sisley) come courtesy of the Masson legacy; and treasures of the ground floor antiquities section include sculpture, ceramics and tapestries. For modern art, venture out to the eastern suburb of Villeneuve-d'Ascq and the **Musée d'Art Moderne** (closed Tues) where jaunty Calder mobiles decorate the lawn. The permanent collection includes works by Braque, Modigliani and Picasso, and there are interesting temporary exhibitions.

• *Small town near Metz, Moselle region.*

LUNEVILLE

On the N4, 30 km SW of Nancy. S.I. Le Château. Spread around its château, a mini-Versailles built for Duke Leopold I between 1703-20, Lunéville lies on the banks of the Meuthe. **Château de Lunéville** was a favourite country retreat of the ex-king of Poland, Stanislaus Leszczynski, who built a pottery works nearby for which the town became famous. For a time it hosted gatherings of the good and the great, and a grand time was had by all until Stanislaus died by falling into his own fireplace. The rambling structure is put to more prosaic use these days, with fire trucks housed in one wing; offices and the S.I. in the other.

The **Musée de Lunéville** (closed Tues) is housed here too, with a small collection of 18th-20thC local ceramics, glass from neighbouring Baccarat, and paintings which are fun rather than impressive, including portraits of the portly Stanislaus, his various châteaux and court flunkies. The formal riverside gardens, the **Parc des Bosquets**, have been revived.

A godsend for cycle and motorcycle enthusiasts with château-fatigue, M. Chapleur proudly presents his amazing **Musée de la Moto et du Vélo** (closed

Mon), across from the S.I. The entrance, with a bike pedal for a door-handle, gives on to three closely packed floors of pre-1940 two-wheeled transport comprising some 200 cosseted exhibits plus a mass of engines, lamps, badges and posters.

METZ ⇌ ✕

On the A31, 53 km N of Nancy. S.I. place d'Armes (also Gare-SNCF). Strategically sited at the confluence of the Rivers Moselle and Seille, Metz was a Roman settlement and later flourished as an independent city-state during the Middle Ages. Annexed by France in 1552, it was transformed into a border stronghold, and the city centre, which is peppered with monumental buildings in mustard-yellow Jaumont stone, also owes much to 18th-19thC urban planning.

Driving around Metz's one-way streets is frustrating, so make for Parking Cathédrale. The enormous pinnacled and ornamented **Cathédrale de Saint-Etienne** is a showcase for a dazzling array of 13th-20thC stained glass. From the aisles to the roof of the nave (the third tallest in France after Amiens and Beauvais), three tiers of windows filter a kaleidoscope of coloured light. The left transcept is virtually a wall of glass ensconced in slender Flamboyant Gothic frames, with Chagall's lemony-yellow *Earthly Paradise* to one side; the show continues around the choir and ambulatory chapels.

Nearby, the **Musées de Metz**, 2 rue du Haut-Poiriers (closed Tues), are housed under one roof in a maze of interconnecting rooms to which there is no map. Leave plenty of time and energy to explore here, for as well as getting hopelessly lost, there is an enormous amount to see. Journey through Roman Metz via pottery, sarcophagi and the odd chariot brakeshoe before being hijacked by architecture (superb Merovingian sculpture from the 7th-10thC Eglise de Saint-Pierre-aux-Nonnains). The Renaissance section is equally fascinating, but the Beaux-Arts section is missable with its hefty Flemish collections; as is the small and rather moth-eaten military corner.

Wander down to the river for a view of the bridges from Pont des Roches, with the grand 18thC yellow stone

Théâtre stretched along the opposite bank. The main shopping centre leads west of place d'Armes in a grid of pedestrianized streets which runs downhill to **place Saint-Louis** lined with arcaded shops. Keep heading west for the handsome **Palais de Justice** on place de la République, and the **Esplanade** gardens near the ancient Eglise de Saint-Pierre-aux-Nonnains, parts of which date from the 4thC. The imposing 19thC railway station lies south of the centre in the Prussian-built Neustadt.

The S.I. provides a handy map of quayside walks around town. The tree-lined river banks are decked with flowers, as are the bridges, and there are lovely views as you stroll along the Moselle from Quai du Rimport to Quai des Régates (about 1 km); or you could hire a bicycle from the station and pedal down the Canal de Jouy, past the anglers, to the **Jardin Botanique** at Montigny-les-Metz (about 3 km round trip).

NANCY ⇌ ✕

On the A31, 53 km S of Metz. S.I. 14 place Stanislas. The capital of Lorraine, Nancy's main attraction lies in its charm as an open-air showcase for two great periods of architecture and decorative arts.

The first is credited to Stanislas Leszczynski, the ex-king of Poland and father-in-law of Louis XV, who created the elegant 18thC New Town in honour of Louis - and because he thoroughly enjoyed building, along with wine, women and song. The second is the Art Nouveau period, which saw the rise of the influential Ecole de Nancy.

To start, make for **place Stanislas**, the centrepiece of the 18thC `New Town' designed by Emmanuel Héré. The **Hôtel de Ville** lines the entire west side of the *place*, with two square buildings apiece to the north and south, including the Théâtre and Musée des Beaux-Arts. To the east, two one-storey blocks flank rue Héré and a triumphal arch, while all around fancy balustrades conceal the roofs and playful stone cherubs threaten to tip monumental urns on to the heads of passers-by. At each corner, Jean Lamour's magnificent gates tilt gilded decorations at the sunlight, backdrops in the eastern corners for Barthelémy

Guibal's *Neptune* and *Amphitrite* fountains. On the cobbled square, a statue of the stocky Stanislaus points helpfully to the S.I.

First stop is the **Musée des Beaux-Arts** (closed Mon am, Tues; joint tickets with the Musée de l'École de Nancy, see below), which includes a fine 19th-20thC section with works by Dufy, Matisse, Modigliani and Utrillo; also Daum glass from the renowned local *verrerie*. The **Daum** factory, at rue des Cristalleries, has its own museum-cum-gallery (closed Sun), and gives weekday morning glass-blowing demonstrations.

Between place Stanislas and the Old Town, **place de la Carrière** is another impressive piece of 18thC town planning leading to **Grande Rue** and the Old Town. The Palais Ducal, 64 Grande Rue, houses the excellent **Musée Historique Lorrain** (closed Tues) with archaeological finds, medieval sculpture, paintings and pottery. The adjacent **Musée des Arts et Traditions Populaire** (closed Mon) displays crafts treasures in a series of reconstructed 19thC interiors laid out in the former Couvent des Cordeliers. The convent's Chapelle Ducale was the traditional burial place of the Dukes of Lorraine, whose tombs are works of art in their own right. A joint ticket to the two museums also covers entry to the 14th-15thC fortified city gate, **Porte de la Craffe**, which is at the end of the street.

Nancy's legacy of artistic endeavour and skilled craftsmen made it a natural rallying point for the turn-of-the-century Art Nouveau movement. The master glassmaker and ceramicist Emile Gallé founded the Ecole de Nancy with the help of fellow *verrier* Antonin Daum, and the cabinetmaker Louis Majorelle; meanwhile a handful of architects enlivened the town with masterpieces including the **Chamber of Commerce**, 40 rue Henri-Poincaré; the superb **Café Excelsior** , 3 rue Mazagran; and Majorelle's outstanding house at 1 rue Louis-Majorelle (Art Nouveau walking maps from the S.I.).

A splendid collection of Art Noveau arts and crafts can be found at the **Musée de l'Ecole de Nancy**, 36 rue du Sergent-Blandan (closed Tues), in a house built for a major patron, Eugène Corbin. Accompanied by a heady whiff of polish, the sculpted, curvelinear lines of a wooden desk take on the appearance of a ship's prow tailor-made for a captain of industry; a cow-parsley motif is transformed into an elegant radiator cover; and Gallé's *Aube et Crépuscule* (dawn and dusk) bed becomes a magic carpet with its curtain-winged moth and shimmering butterfly head- and tailboards. This is a real treat, even for those who aren't Art Nouveau fans.

OBERNAI

See Local Explorations: 12.

PARIS

See pages 214-233.

REIMS ⊯ ✕

On the A26, 203 km SE of Lille. S.I. square du Trésor. Capital of one of the most famous wine-growing regions in the world, Reims has Roman origins. Clovis, the first King of the Franks, and subsequent scourge of the Moors, was baptised here in 496, and the significance of this act was not lost on future kings of France, 26 of whom elected to be crowned in the city.

The coronations took place in the **Cathédrale de Notre-Dame**, founded in 1211, but not completed for almost 300 years. One of the finest

---

DETOUR – **EPERNAY**

The town that Champagne built, Epernay prospers beside the Marne south of Reims (26 km via the N51). On avenue de Champagne, the **Hôtel de Ville** occupies a house built for the Moët family, and across the street **Moët et Chandon**, 20 avenue de Champagne (open daily Oct-Apr, Sat- Sun only Nov-Mar), offer electric train tours of their *caves* (some 30 km of tunnels), plus tastings and Napoleonic memorabilia (the Emperor forgot his hat after a visit).

Several other champagne houses entertain visitors; and if you want to stay over, try the convenient and comfortable hotel-restaurant **Les Berceaux, FF**; *13 rue des Berceaux; tel.* 26 55 28 84; *credit cards* AE, DC, MC, V; *open year round.*

• *Champagne country.*

Gothic cathedrals in the land, its stunning west front though badly scarred is simply covered in 13thC carvings - look for the *Smiling Angel* and friends decorating the north (left) portal. There is a further surfeit of statuary decorating the interior wall, and richly carved friezes encircle the pillars in the soaring but otherwise simple nave. The 13thC stained glass is glorious in the sunlight, also the Chagall windows in the ambulatory with their luminous deep blues and purples cut with green and red. The **Palais de Tau**, an elegant 17thC former bishop's palace, houses the cathedral treasury's tapestries, jewellery and more sculpture.

A short walk from the cathedral, the **Musée Saint-Denis** 8 rue Chanzy (closed Tues), presents a comprehensive selection of European art from the Renaissance to the present-day. Of particular interest are the Dutch and Flemish School portraits, some 30 Corots, minor works by Monet, Renoir, Pissarro, and Fauve artists Dufy and Matisse;

also Foujita, who marked his conversion to Catholicism by decorating a **chapel** at 33 rue du Champ de Mars (closed Wed). The city centre was largely destroyed during the First World War, and has been rebuilt around a handful of surviving edifices. The main shopping area is sandwiched between rue Libergier and the inner ring boulevards, bisected by **place Drouet d'Erlon** (actually a street), the entertainment district with restaurants, cafés, cinemas and shopping malls squeezed in amongst the hotels.

To the east, behind a sunken 3rdC Gallo-Roman **cryptoporticus** on place Forum, the yellow sandstone turrets and half-timbered gables of the **Hôtel le Vergeur** (closed Mon) mark a treasure house of local history furnished with antiques, plus remarkable sets of Dürer engravings (guided tours only; patience of Job an advantage). Follow rue Colbert north for a look at the splendid 17thC **Hôtel de Ville** with an equestrian statue of Louis XIII decorating a pediment; then rue de Mars leads to another Roman relic, the triple-arched **Porte de Mars**. Across the boulevards, the **Salle de la Reddition**, 12 rue Franklin-Roosevelt, was General Eisenhower's headquarters from the early spring of 1945, and the German surrender was signed here that May.

Overshadowed by the famous cathedral, the **Basilique de Saint-Remi** (a 15-minute walk south on rue Simon), is sadly neglected by visitors. Named for the young bishop who baptised Clovis, it predates Notre-Dame by 200 years, and although much-altered the immense Romanesque nave and early Gothic choir are a remarkable sight. The **Musée Saint-Remi**, in the old abbey buildings, houses pre-Renaissance items including archaeological relics, tapestries and armour.

Another reason to venture south is champagne. Since Dom Perignon introduced bubbles to Champagne's flat wines with a second fermentation in the 17thC, Reims has been a major trading centre, and several big-name **champagne houses** open their doors to visitors. Both **Tattinger**, 1 place Saint-Niçaise, and **Piper-Heidseick**, 51 boulevard Henri-Vasnier, extract a small charge; **Pommery**, 5 place du Général-Gouraud, opens by appointment only (tel. 26 61 62 55). A five-minute walk from the Porte de Mars, **Mumm**, 34 rue Champ du Mars, is open daily for free.

Although it is even more off the beaten track, vintage car buffs should not miss the **Centre du l'Automobile Française**, 84 avenue Georges-Clemenceau (1 km E of the cathedral; open Mar-Nov daily, Dec-Feb Sat-Sun). Amassed by designer Philippe Charbonneaux, 150 lovingly conditioned cars share the billing with 2,000 antique and modern models and toys.

SAINT-QUENTIN ⚓ ✕

On the N44, *45 km* NW *of Laon.* S.I. *place de l'*Hôtel *de Ville.* Elevated above the plain and the Somme (which rises some 10 km to the north-east), Saint-Quentin spreads its industrial outskirts around a pleasant town centre. Philip II of Spain laid siege to the town in 1557, and captured the Constable of France, Montmorency, but left the **Basilique** standing; First World War German troops had other ideas and mined the entire edifice, but ran out of time before setting the charges. Its Gothic bulk, much-restored, looms large, and there is an unusual tiled pattern like a maze in the nave which the faithful were expected to follow on their knees.

The **Musée Antoine Lécuyer**, rue Lécuyer (closed Mon), merits a visit for its 78 portraits of 18thC bigwigs by local-born artist Maurice Quentin de la Tour; while the **Musée Entomologique**, rue des Cannoniers (closed Sun), spotlights the insect world in most of its weird, wonderful and stomach-churning forms. This is one of the finest collections in the world consisting of more than one million poison-tipped and velvet-winged exhibits.

STRASBOURG

See France Overall: 10.

VERDUN ⚓ ✕

On the N3, *65 km* W *of Metz.* S.I. *place de la* Nation *(right bank of the* Meuse*).* Inescapably associated with the carnage of the First World War, Verdun sits beside the Meuse on a site first fortified by the ancient Gauls. Vauban had a hand in its defences, and by the turn of the century the town was ringed by 38 forts and earthworks. During the initial stages of the First World War, the main battle arena was concentrated further north, but a German decision to outflank the French trenches required the storming of Verdun. The battle commenced on February 21, 1916, and continued until August 20, 1917. German High Command's decision to end the deadlock on the Western Front and 'bleed the French army to death' had failed, at a cost of almost one million lives.

The actual town is lively and pleasant in the sunshine. A steep climb from the river in the old quarter, the **Cathédrale de Notre-Dame** has survived, as has the elegant 18thC bishop's palace, its decorative carvings spruced up and roof urns newly gilded. Nearby, the **Musée de la Princerie**, rue de la Belle Vierge (closed Tues; Oct-Mar), houses its collections in some splendour; the antique confectioner's utensils were used to make *dragées*, the town's speciality sugared almonds.

However, most visitors are here to tour the battlefields, and come to Verdun to visit Vauban's **Citadelle Souterrain** (closed Jan), rue du Ru, a 4-km tunnel complex where thousands of soldiers found shelter during the fighting, and which has been turned into a war museum. Also, Rodin's powerful **Monument de la Défense**, on avenue Alsace-Lorraine (D903).

Verdun's S.I. offers summer season guided tours and a good selection of French and foreign language guides to the **battlefields** (10 km N of town on the D913). The main stops are the forts of **Douaumont** and **Vaux,** and the **Musée-Memorial de la Bataille de Verdun** at Fleury. Not to be missed, and impossible to forget, **Fort de Douaumont** commands the ridge, and should have been the strongest link in the defence system. Its hopelessly inadequate complement of French territorials was overrun by German troops within days, and the Germans then held the fort for eight agonizing months, some 3,000 soldiers crammed into the dank, rat-infested subterranean passages which drip with stalactites; the vents were blocked for fear of gas attacks. The French re-offensive of October 1916 was spearheaded by Moroccan troops, who were mercilessly sacrificed by

General Magnin (later the hero of the hour). Their gravestones face Mecca amongst the field of crosses in the **Cimetière Nationale** where 15,000 men are buried. More sobering still is the **Ossuaire de Douaumont**, which contains the remains of 130,000 unknown soldiers, its vaults crammed with the names of the missing, and described by the president of the ossuary committee in 1932 as the 'rampart against forgetfulness'.

VIMY RIDGE
On the D55, 8 km NE of Arras. It is almost 80 years since the battle for `Hill 145' (the highest point of the 22-km ridge) was won by the Canadian Corps on April 9-10, 1917. The Germans had held the ridge since 1914, and some 200,000 Canadian, British, French and German soldiers are buried on its slopes. After the flat, featureless landscape of the northern plains, Vimy still has the power to shock and to

RECOMMENDED RESTAURANTS

ARRAS
La Rapière, F; *44 Grand'Place; tel. 21 55 09 92; credit cards AE, DC, V; closed Sun dinner.*
Simple, small dining room and sound value with fluffy omelettes and a choice of local dishes such as braised chicory, sweetbreads in beer, also châteaubriand with Roquefort.

BERGUES
Cornet d'Or, FF; *26 rue Espagnole; tel. 28 68 66 27; credit cards AE, V; closed Sun dinner-Mon, mid-Jun to mid-Jul.*
Michelin-starred cuisine in somewhat formal surroundings: rabbit *compôte*, partridge *pot-au-feu*, good local cheeses.

DUNKERQUE
Métropole, F-FF; *28 rue Thiers; tel. 28 66 85 01; credit cards AE, V; closed mid-Dec to mid-Jan.*
Traditional town centre hotel dining room, recently redecorated, with good value *menu d'affaires* for local businessmen (wine included).
Recommended for seafood: **Restaurant l'Iguane, F**; *14 Digue des Allies; tel. 28 63 67 26.*

LAON
La Bannière de France, F-FFF; *11 rue Franklin-Roosevelt; tel. 23 23 21 44; credit cards AE, DC, MC, V; closed mid-Dec to mid-Jan.*
A 17thC coaching inn in the Ville Haute, the Bannière's broad price band reflects its desire to please. Classic dishes and more innovative creations do just that.
Also 18 spacious and flowery rooms (**F-FF**).

LILLE
La Houblonnière, F-FF; *42 place du Général-de-Gaulle; tel. 20 74 54 34; credit cards V; open daily.*
Fairly priced local specialities served in the rustic dining room or on the terrace. *Houblonnière* means hopfield, so check out the extensive beer list.

L'Huîtrière, FFF; *3 rue des Chats - Bossus; tel. 20 55 43 41; credit cards AE, DC, V; closed Sun dinner, mid-Jul to Sep.*
Walk through a wonderful fishmonger's decorated with its original ceramic tiles into a formal, red-plush and wood-panelled dining room to feast off truly fresh fish and shellfish.

Aux Moules, F; *34 rue de Béthune; tel. 20 57 12 46; open daily.*
Mussels are a *Lillois* favourite, and this is the place to find them in numerous guises. Other regional dishes and boutique beers crop up on the menu.

METZ
La Chaudée, F; *5 rue de l'Abreuvoir - by a car park off place Saint-Louis; tel. 87 76 91 49; credit cards V; closed Mon.*
Traditional Lorraine specialities at bargain prices – quiche, tongue cooked in Moselle wine, and *spätzle* with gruyère, bacon, mushrooms and croutons. Relaxed and friendly.

Restaurant de Pont Saint-Marcel, F-FF; *1 rue du Pont Saint-Marcel; tel. 87 30 12 29; closed Sun dinner-Mon.*
Simple waterfront dining room with a tiny summer terrace overlooking the Moselle. Generous regional cooking and walls decorated with murals.
Also **Bistro du Port, FF**, Port Saint-Marcel: all bright, zappy colours, hip waiters, and a modern fish-based menu.

move. It remains unnaturally quiet, and nothing but pines will grow in the thin, chaotically pock-marked soil, where deep craters 'though carpeted in grass' will not disappear for generations, if ever. Sandbagged trenches wind through the hillocks, the front line trenches a clothesline apart, and here and there gun emplacements lie abandoned in the thick red mud.

The land around Vimy is owned by the Canadians in perpetuity. From April to mid-November guided tours visit the trenches and tunnel complex, and an information centre is manned year-round near the soaring limestone **Vimy Memorial** overlooking the Douai Plain. Back on the D937, at la Targette, the **Musée Militaire de la Targette** contains 2,500 First World War *objets de guerre* from Kaiser Bill helmets and uniforms to tobacco tins.

NANCY
L'Entr'act, F; 123 *Grande Rue; tel. 83 36 62 71; credit cards* V; *closed Sun.*

Black-and-white film star snaps on the walls and a light trad-modern menu featuring a snail *soupière au Riesling,* stuffed cabbage with haddock, pasta with smoked salmon.

Rue des Maréchaux
This restaurant alley off Grande Rue caters for all tastes from pizza and Chinese take-aways to fish and Lyonnais specials. This, however, is the undisputed pick of the bunch:

La Gentilhommière, FF; 29 *rue des Maréchaux; tel. 83 32 26 44; credit cards* V; *closed Sat lunch-Sun, two weeks Feb, three weeks Aug.*

Terracotta tiles and checkered fabrics, earthy but elegant like the food. Mussels and scallops on a bed of leeks, nourishing *pot au feu 'de nos grand-meres',* puddings for seasoned chocoholics, sorbets and seasonal fruit creations.

REIMS
Continental, F-FF; 95 *place Drouet d'Erlon; tel. 26 47 01 47; credit cards* AE, DC, MC, V; *closed Sun dinner-Mon, two weeks Feb.*

Pink and gold ceiling, smart napery and attentive service. Traditional grills, sole, duck with blackcurrants, and other good-value *plats* and omelettes.

Le Florence, FF-FFF; 43 *boulevard Foch; tel. 26 47 12 70; credit cards* AE, DC, MC, V; *closed Sun, three weeks Aug.*

Elegant establishment with a very pretty summer terrace. The food shines year round – oyster and prawn consommé with thyme, veal sweetbreads and snails in a *jus* of truffles; lobster in champagne. Michelin star.

Au Petit Comptoir, F-FF; 17 *rue de Mars; tel. 26 40 58 58; credit cards* V; *closed Sun, two weeks Aug, Christmas to mid-Jan.*

Delightful turn-of-the-century bistro. Enjoy pâté with a quince *cômpote,* salmon poached with chicory, and a super-rich *crème de marrons* with chocolate sauce.

SAINT-QUENTIN
Le Château, FF-FFF; *at Neuville-Saint-Amand (3 km SE via rue Général-Leclerc and D12); tel. 23 68 41 82; credit cards* AE, DC, V; *closed Sat, Sun dinner, three weeks Aug, Christmas to New Year.*

One of the best restaurants in the region, and a lovely setting. M. Meiresonne has earned a Michelin star for his fresh classical dishes such as duck breast with cider, grilled salmon with fennel butter, veal sweetbreads with mushrooms.

Also six pleasant **FF** rooms.

Le Pichet, F-FF; 6 *boulevard Gambetta; tel. 23 62 03 67; credit cards* V.

Chalet-style bistro with a range of no-frills dishes – snails, scallops, salmon steaks and a good duck with calvados.

The **FF** menu at the Michelin-starred restaurant **Président**, in the Grand Hôtel, 6 *rue Dachery; tel. 23 62 69 77)* is said to be excellent value and delicious.

VERDUN
See Recommended Hotels.

<u>Eastern France</u>

Between Strasbourg and Dijon
Alsace and Franche-Comté

331 km; maps Michelin Nos 242 and 243

Planted between the crumpled Vosges mountains and the Rhine lies the Euro-capital of Strasbourg, a crossroads city of Europe, and junction with the unglamorous but under-estimated route to the Channel via Metz and Reims (France Overall: 9). Strasbourg is also the capital of Alsace, least French of all the provinces of France, and Franco-German bone of contention for many years. The countryside is densely populated by villages of orderly, half-timbered houses, with an embarrassment of inns and restaurants in which to sample the characteristic local cooking with much more to it than beer and *choucroute*.

Due south of Strasbourg, Colmar is a charming place, full of interest, including the most visited museum outside Paris. Industrial Mulhouse also harbours a clutch of terrific museums, while the southerly portion of this route incorporates the capital of the ancient Dukes of Burgundy at Dijon, and the historic province of Franche-Comté. As the name – Free Country – suggests, the latter is a traditionally independent region comprising the peaceful green valleys of the Saône and Doubs, the whaleback folds of the Jura mountains bordering Switzerland, and the fortified towns of Belfort and Besançon.

The route is a dogleg obviously marked out by *autoroutes*, but between Strasbourg and Thann (for Belfort) even red routers should try to take in Local Explorations: 12. For blue and green route followers, the less well-known face of Franche-Comté is explored in Local Explorations: 14, which is a far preferable alternative to the N83 truck route between Belfort/Besançon and Dijon. There is another chance to get off the beaten track with Local Explorations: 13, easily accessible from Dijon.

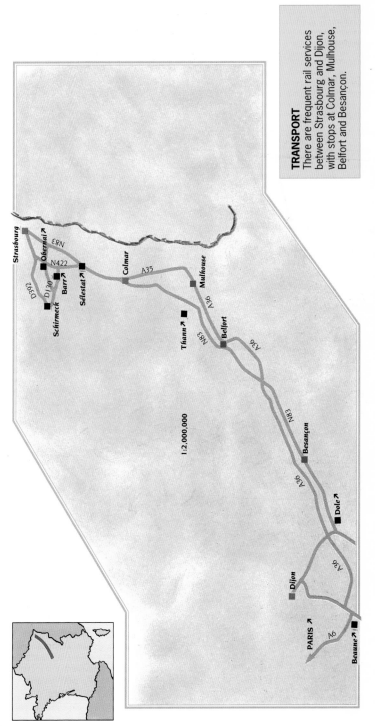

SIGHTS & PLACES OF INTEREST

BARR

See Local Explorations: 12.

BEAUNE

See France Overall: 11.

BELFORT 🚇 ✕

On the N83/A36, 98 km NE of Besançon. S.I. place de la Commune. Guarding the gap between France's natural eastern defences, the Jura and Vosges mountains, Belfort has a long history of military derring-do, a Vauban fortress and the famous Lion de Belfort monument to prove it. The Old Town lies on the east bank of the River Savoureuse, dominated by the vast red sandstone **Château** which crouches on a site fortified since the 13thC. From the car park a path leads down to a covered passage and entrance to the **Lion de Belfort** viewing platform.

Carved from local stone by Frederic Bartholdi (who also gave New York the Statue of Liberty), the 22-m lion commemorates the exploits of Colonel Denfert-Rochereau and his 16,000 French troops who held a German army numbering 40,000 at bay for over a hundred days during the Franco-Prussian War (1870-71). For more local and military history, head for the **Château-Musée**.

DETOUR – **RONCHAMP**
In complete contrast to Vauban's demonstration of military might (see Belfort, this page), there is a rare example of inspired 20thC ecclesiastical architecture in Le Corbusier's **Chapelle de Notre-Dame-du-Haut**, at Ronchamp (21 km NW of Belfort via the N19). Perched above the town on a wooded hill, its concrete curves are arranged around flat white walls pierced with unmatching windows like a ticker-tape code. The spartan interior is lit by shafts of primary reds, blues and yellows filtered through glass.

In the same direction, but via the more northerly D13, lies the Etang de Malsancy for swimming and watersports.

From Belfort you can link with Local Explorations: 12 for further discovery of Alsace.

BESANCON 🚇 ✕

On the N83/A36, 82 km E of Dijon. S.I. place de la 1re Armée Française (across Pont de la République). An important town since Roman times, one-time centre of the watch-making industry, and capital of Franche-Comté, Besançon lies in a river valley fringed by hills on the edge of the Jura. The pleasant old town centre, la Boucle, lies in a loop of the Doubs overlooked by yet another Vauban citadel.

At the northern edge of the old town, facing place de la Révolution, the excellent **Musée des Beaux-Arts et d'Archéologie** (closed Tues) runs the gamut from Egyptology to Picasso. The main street, **Grande Rue**, bisects the old town along the path of the original Roman road, and crosses central place du Huit-Septembre. This cobbled square is flanked by a baroque church, and the 16thC **Hôtel de Ville** faced in broad bands of yellow and grey stone. Just behind it is the ornate and slightly older **Palais de Justice**. Further down Grande Rue, the new **Musée du Temps** (closed Tues) is amassing its collections of antique and gloriously decorative timepieces in the **Palais Granvelle**, a Renaissance mansion with a fine arcaded courtyard built by one of Besançon's leading families. The writer Victor Hugo was born nearby, as were cinematography pioneers, the Lumière brothers.

At the top of the street, beyond a little square littered with a handful of Roman remains, the **Porte Noire**, a triumphal arch dating from the 2ndC AD leads to the **Cathédrale de Saint-Jean**, from which it is a steep 15-minute hike up to the **Citadelle** and its four well-worth-the-climb museums (all closed Tues).

The **Musée Agraire** illustrates traditional farming methods. Regional crafts are displayed in the **Musée de Folklore Comtois**. The **Musée de la Résistance et de la Déportation** takes an unsentimental and laudably unsensational look at the Nazi occupation; and the favourite with children is the **Musée d'Histoire Naturelle** complete with aquarium, an insectarium and a zoo park.

RECOMMENDED HOTELS

BELFORT
Le Saint-Christophe, F; *place d'Armes; tel. 84 28 02 14; credit cards* V; *closed Christmas to New Year.*
Convenient *logis* below the château with simple but spacious rooms; restaurant.

BESANCON
Hôtel du Nord, F-FF; *8-10 rue Moncey; tel. 81 81 34 56; credit cards* AE, DC, MC, V; *open year round.*
Town centre hotel between Grande Rue and rue des Granges. Smart new foyer, 44 recently refurbished rooms; parking.

Hôtel de Paris, F-FF; *33 rue des Granges; tel. 81 81 36 56; credit cards* AE, DC, MC, V; *open year round.*
Plain, but quiet rooms overlook an interior courtyard where breakfast is served in summer. Cheery young staff.

COLMAR
Hôtel Rapp, FF; *1-5 rue Weinemer (off rue Bethe-Molly); tel. 89 41 62 10; credit cards* AE, DC, V; *open year round.*
Unusually warm welcome from a modern and functional hotel. Pool; restaurant (**F-FF**) serving Alsacien specialities.

Hôtel Saint-Martin, FF-FFF; *38 Grand' Rue; tel. 89 24 11 51; credit cards* AE, MC, V; *closed Jan, open at weekends only Dec and Feb.*
Super old coaching house just south of St Martin's. Traditional furnishings and up-to-date comforts; breakfast only.

Auberge d'Art Zenheim, F-FF; *30 du Sponeck, at Art Zenheim (15 km north-east via D111); tel. 89 71 60 51; credit cards* MC, V; *closed Mon dinner-Tues, mid-Feb to mid-Mar.*
Delightful auberge with ten pretty rustic rooms, and a popular beamed restaurant (FF) serving Alsacien and traditional cooking. Summer terrace.

DIJON
Les Alleés, F; *27 cours du Général-de-Gaulle; tel. 80 66 57 50; credit cards* AE, V; *open year round.*
South of the city centre but walkable from there, this simple but pleasant modern hotel has its own garden.

Hôtel Wilson, FF; *place Wilson; tel. 80 66 82 50; credit cards* V; *open year round.*
Small, comfortable hotel in a 17thC coaching inn close to all the sights. Rooms are individually decorated and the hotel's restaurant, **Thiber**, has a Michelin star.

Parc de la Colombière, FF; *49 cours du Parc (2 km S of the centre via D996); tel. 80 65 18 41; open year round.*
At the lower end of the FF price range, the Parc's modern rooms overlook its namesake; and there is a good restaurant (closed mid-Nov to mid Mar).
See also Recommended Restaurants.

MULHOUSE
Bourse, FF; *14 rue Bourse; tel. 89 56 18 44; credit cards* AE, DC, MC, V; *closed Christmas to New Year.*
Fine town centre hotel with pleasant refurbished rooms. No restaurant.

Hôtel de Bâle, F-FF; *19 passage Central; tel. 89 46 19 87; credit cards* V; *open year round.*
Central, cheap and comfy with modern rooms.

STRASBOURG
Au Cerf d'Or, FF; *6 place de l'Hôpital (across Pont Saint-Nicolas, and first right); tel. 88 36 20 05; credit cards* DC, MC, V; *open year round.*
No beauty, but reasonably-priced and convenient. Rooms in 16thC building with bar (quiet local haunt) and dining room, plus brand new annexe with pool.

L'Europe, FF-FFF; *38 rue des Fosses des Tanneurs; tel. 88 32 11 94; credit cards* V; *open year round.*
Some rooms in an old building (Voltaire and Goethe stayed here), some in the new, but all comfortable and attractive.
See also Recommended Restaurants.

• *Colmar.*

From Besançon you have easy access to Local Explorations: 14.

COLMAR ⇔ ✕

On the N83, 70 km S of Strasbourg. S.I. 4 rue des Unterlinden. The lively capital of Haut-Rhin, Colmar sprawls across the plain around a toy-town centre of picture-book winding streets and pastel-painted half-timbered houses. Its tourist credentials are augmented by a helpful S.I. with plentiful information about the region, its public transport and outdoor pursuits.

Across from the S.I., the broad-ranging and hugely popular **Musée d'Unterlinden** (closed Tues) is laid out in a former Dominican convent, where a 13thC chapel houses the *Issenheim Altarpiece*. Intended as a single unit, it is now displayed in three sections: the first two are masterpieces painted by Mathias Grünewald at the end of the Gothic period (about 1512-16) with a glimmer of the developing Renaissance style; the third contains rather earlier sculptures (c. 1490) by Nicholas de Haguenau. The central retable depicts a tortured Crucifixion, the Christ -figure stretched on the cross with splayed upturned hands, flanked by Saint John with the Virgin and Mary Magdalene, and John the Baptist. Below there is a scene from the Entombment, while Saint Sebastian and Saint Anthony

appear on the hinged wings. Close by, the old **Eglise des Dominicans** charges a somewhat extortionate fee for its 14thC stained glass and another precious altarpiece, Martin Schongauer's lovely *Vierge au buisson de roses*.

Stroll down rue des Têtes to see the **Maison des Têtes**, its Renaissance façade decorated with numerous carved heads. On rue des Marchands, the birthplace of 19thC sculptor Frederic Bartholdi has been turned into a small **museum** with sketches of his most famous *oeuvre*, the Statue of Liberty (closed Mon-Fri Nov-Mar).

On place de la Cathédrale, the 13th-14thC **Collégiale de Saint-Martin** is commonly described as 'the cathedral'. Inside there is some beautiful glass, and vaulted passages with floral keystones lead to the ambulatory chapels decorated with carvings and gilded retables.

Leave the square at the southern end, past the 16thC **Maison Pfister** with its painted façade, and there are more fine houses on Grande Rue. Down by the River Lauch, **quai de la Poissonerie** flaunts a row of unbelievably cute fishermen's cottages (several of which harbour fish restaurants) in the **Petite Venise** a popular tourist haunt.

• *Opposite: Colmar.*

DIJON 🛏 ✕

On the A31, 82 km W of Besançon; off the A6, 312 km SE of Paris. S.I. place Darcy.
A former Roman stronghold on the ancient military and trade routes between Lyon and Mainz, Dijon was chosen as the capital of the Duchy of Burgundy in the 10thC. During the 13th-14thC, the city flourished under the colourful rule of its wealthy and powerful Valois dukes who built Dijon into a renowned cultural and commercial centre capable of sustaining its importance even after the duchy was annexed by the crown in 1476.

A major road and rail junction, Dijon is also a prosperous industrial centre, but its character is typically relaxed and Burgundian. No matter how you rush at it, this city will slow you down – encourage you to linger on its elegant streets, in its museums, to touch the lucky owl outside the Gothic church of Notre-Dame, and to savour its gastronomic treats.

The city centre's maze of one-way streets and pedestrian thoroughfares is a strong argument for taking in the sights on foot. Start on place Darcy (a short walk from the station), and head for **rue de la Liberté**, the main shopping street, straddled by an 18thC triumphal arch, **Porte Guillaume**. Two-thirds of the way up, **place Rude** is a lovely old square with a clutch of popular cafés circling a fountain. The bronze statue of a *vigneron* trampling grapes is by the Bugundian artist François Rude. There are some fine medieval and Renaissance mansions in **rue des Forges**; then make a detour for the beautiful 13thC **Eglise de Notre-Dame** with its gargoyles, glass, famous Black Virgin, and Jacquemart clock. The lucky *chouette* (owl) is on the north wall in rue Chouette.

To the south, the grandiose **Palais des Ducs** is the historic power centre of Burgundy. Much altered in the 17thC, you can walk through the palace courtyards to place de la Libération, stop off to visit the Salle des Etats, and climb the 15thC Tour Philippe le Bon for a panoramic view across town and beyond. The **Musée des Beaux-Arts** (closed Tues), in the East Wing, houses one of the finest regional art collections in the country, graced by masterpieces from every great school and age of European art.

You can also see the vast palace kitchens on the ground floor, and the superb Salle des Gardes with the tombs of Philippe le Hardi and Jean sans Peur, which were moved here from the Chartreuse de Champmol.

Off the sweeping crescent of Hardouin-Mansard's **place de la Libération**, the **Musée Magnin**, 4 rue des Bons-Enfants (closed Sat), is a 17thC *hôtel-particulier* with original furnishings and a fine collection of 16th-19thC paintings. Further south, the 16thC **Palais de Justice** is the former Burgundian parliament ranged behind a splendid Renaissance façade. The **Musée de la Vie Bourguignonne**, 17 rue Sainte-Anne, turns the clock back with costume displays, rural crafts and viniculture; and there is a museum of church art, the **Musée d'Art Sacre**, next door (closed Tues).

CRUISING THE SAONE

One of the most peaceful, attractive and least populated stretches of inland water you can cruise in France is the River Saône as it wends away from Burgundy into the wooded hills and lush pastures of the lower Vosges. A week-long one-way cruise from Dijon will take you first on the attractive Canal de Bourgogne as far as Saint-Jean-de-Losne, where you connect with the Saône. It progresses at first majestically, and then idyllically past pretty villages and mellow châteaux as far as Corre or thereabouts (depending on which firm you hire from). The advantage of the river over the canal is that you can tie up anywhere, you can jump in to cool off, and though there are plenty of locks, there are long stretches without. Bikes can be hired with the boat and enable you to explore the countryside or to ride alongside on the towpath: a wonderful extra dimension for adults and children, for the towpaths and surrounding country lanes are virtually empty of traffic. See Canal Cruising in Burgundy, page 196, for information about cruiser hirers.

To the west, the 13th-14thC **Cathédrale de Saint-Bénigne** sports a roof coloured by traditional glazed tiles and a rare 10thC rotunda in the crypt. Nearby, the **Musée Archéologique** displays Gallo-Roman finds and medieval art in part of the original abbey building. One of the best exhibits here is Flemish sculptor Claus Sluter's *Head of Christ*, taken from the **Chartreuse de Champmol**, avenue Albert-1er (2 km W). Founded as an abbey and ducal burial place by Philippe le Hardi in 1383, the Chartreuse is now a mental institution and most of its treasures (such as the tombs in the Salle des Gardes) have been redistributed around local museums. However, visitors can still gain access to Sluter's *Puits de Moïse* (Well of Moses) with its superb Old Testament figures, and the carved chapel portal (inside the main door). On the way back into town, the 19thC botanical gardens occupy part of the **Jardin d'Arquebuse**, near the station.

On the food trail, there is no better place to start than Dijon's main covered market, the **Halles Centrales**, rue Claude Ramey (Tues, Fri, and Sat). Put together a gourmet picnic with local cheeses from Epoisses, Saint-Florentin and Semur-en-Auxois, *jambon persillé* (ham and parsley in white wine aspic), and *tarte bourguignon* (meat and mushroom pie). **Grey-Poupon**, 32 rue de la Liberté, is *the* mustard shop in town (established 1777); **Mulot et Petitjean**, 13 rue Boussuet, do a fine line in *creme de cassis, cassissines* (little blackcurrant sweets), and *pains d'épices* (spiced honey cakes); for snails, track down **L'Escargot de Bourgogne**, 14 rue Bannelier.

DOLE

See *Local Explorations*: 14.

MULHOUSE 🏨 ✕

On the A36, 43 km S of Colmar. S.I. 9 avenue Maréchal-Foch. After the toy-town charms of the Alsace Wine Route (see Local Explorations: 12), this sprawling industrial metropolis makes a bizarre contrast and may seem best avoided. However, Mulhouse is a repository for half-a-dozen good to great museums well worth a detour.

The two nationally important museums are out in the suburbs. To the

---

DIJON COOKERY DAY

Whilst in Dijon, amateur gourmets can book a day out with Jean-Pierre Billoux, Michelin-starred chef of the Hôtel la Cloche (see Recommended Restaurants). After a morning session in the market, watch Billoux at work and taste the results. Details from **Bourgogne Tour Incoming**, 14 rue du Châpeau-Rouge, 21000 Dijon; tel. 80 30 49 49.

---

north, the **Musée National de l'Automobile**, avenue de Colmar, chronicles the history of the motor car through more than 500 vehicles from a 1878 steam-driven Jacquot to the Porsches and Ferraris of the 1960s. Most of the exhibits were amassed by industrial heavyweights, the Schlumpf brothers, including the largest collection of Bugattis (129) in the world. To the west, you will find the **Musée Français du Chemin de Fer**, at Dornach. Elegant French rolling stock such as a sumptuous roving drawing-room built for Napoleon III's ADC; several steam locomotives including the gleaming Art Deco-style *Président de la République*; signal boxes and railroad memorabilia are displayed in a disused station. The adjacent **Musée du Sapeur-Pompier** features terrific firemen's helmets, engines and firefighting equipment dating back to pre-Revolutionary days.

In the city centre, the gabled and gilded 16thC Hôtel de Ville houses the **Musée Historique**, 4 rue des Archives. The **Musée des Beaux-Arts**, 4 place Guillaume-Tell, has some fine Flemish works; but best of all is the **Musée de l'Impression sur Etoffes**, 3 rue des Bonnes-Gens (closed Tues in winter), with its stunning collections of fabrics and printed textiles from around the world. In a related field, the **Musée du Papier-Peint**, rue Zuber, in the suburb of Rixheim (6 km E via route de Mulhouse) plunders the archives of wallpaper manufacturers Zuber & Co. (which date from 1791) to dramatic effect.

Children might appreciate a romp around the **Parc Zoologique et Botanique** (S via boulevard Léon-Gambetta) with more than 1,000 animals

• *Cêp* (boletus) *mushrooms.*

from cheetahs to zebras. Another outdoor attraction is the **Ecomusée de Haut-Alsace**, at Ungersheim (12 km N via D430/D44), with 30-plus reconstructed 15th-19thC traditional Alsacien buildings.

See also Local Explorations: 12.

OBERNAI
See Local Explorations: 12.

PARIS
See pages 214-233.

SELESTAT
See Local Explorations: 12.

STRASBOURG ⇌ ✕
On the A4/N83, 161 *km* SE *of Metz/*112 *km* N *of Mulhouse.* S.I. *place de la Cathédrale.* First German, and then French (with the odd Prussian incursion), Strasbourg is the capital of Alsace,

• *Place d'Arcy, Dijon.*

and a seat of the European Parliament with its attendant court and councils. The city was built at one of the major 'crossroads' of Europe (from which it derives its name), and between its historic heart and modern satellites offers an enduring tradition of commercial prosperity and humanist ideals.

Johann Gutenburg invented moveable type here in the 15thC, the university was founded in the 16thC, and the Reformation was preached from the city's pulpits. Surprisingly, perhaps, Strasbourg rather than Marseille is the home of the *Marseillaise*, composed by Roget de l'Isle in 1712, and first performed in place Broglie as the *Chant de Guerre de l'Armée du Rhin*.

The Old Town is conveniently encapsulated on an island in the River III. At its heart is the magnificent Gothic **Cathédrale de Notre-Dame**, a cloudspearing, pink-brown monster festooned with carvings, a forest of pinna-

143

cles and a 142-m spire with a viewing platform. Inside, the stained glass is sensational, with colours so rich and patterns so dense that the interior is almost pitch black. In the south transcept the *Pilier des Anges* is adorned with 13thC carvings; and an astronomical clock goes through its paces at 12.30 pm daily. A franc in the light meter by the pulpit reveals a virtuoso masterpiece of stone carving reminiscent of petrified lace.

South of the cathedral, Strasbourg's main museums (all closed Tues) are conveniently grouped together starting with the **Musée de l'Oeuvre Notre-Dame**, 3 place du Château, which displays sculpture rescued from the cathedral façade, stained glass and medieval and Renaissance art. Next door, the swanky apartments of the 18thC Palais Rohan, built for the powerful prince-bishops of the Rohan family, house three museums with room to

RECOMMENDED RESTAURANTS

BELFORT
Pot au Feu, FF; 27 *bis Grande'rue; tel. 84 28 57 84; credit cards V; closed Sun, Mon, one week Jan, two weeks Aug.*
   Home cooking with an elegant edge and a special way with traditional *pots au feu* of various kinds (the original one-pot cooking). Near Porte de Brisach.

BESANCON
Mungo Park, FF-FFF; 11 *rue Jean-Petit; tel. 81 81 28 01; credit cards V; closed Sat lunch, Sun, two weeks Feb, two weeks Aug.*
   Elegant and innovative modern restaurant – herb ravioli infused with coriander, fennel and artichoke, pigeon breast in ginger-flavoured cream sauce, hot soufflés.

Poker d'As, F-FF; 14 *square Saint-Amour; tel. 81 81 42 49; credit cards AE, DC, MC, V; closed Sun dinner-Mon, three weeks Jul, Christmas to New Year.*
   Cosy dining room with copper pans and plenty of wood. Favourite dishes include pheasant with marsala, thyme-flavoured *moules*, guanaja *gâteau* (solid chocolate) or a refreshing clementine sorbet.

COLMAR
Les Tanneurs Winstub, F-FF; 12 *rue des Tanneurs; tel. 89 23 72 12; credit cards AE, DC, V; closed mid-Dec to mid-Jan.*
   A veritable *maison alsacienne* with darkened interior and palid pot plants. Home-cooked quiche, *choucroute* salad with smoked duck, trout in a Riesling sauce.

Maison des Têtes, FF-FFF; 19 *rue des Têtes; tel. 89 24 43 43; credit cards AE, DC, MC, V; closed Sun dinner-Mon, two weeks Jul.*
   Wood-panelling and heaps of atmosphere. Mixed regional and classical menu from venison *mit spätzle* to veal *piccata*, and a delicious apple and pear *clafoutis*.

DIJON
Au Bec Fin, F; 47 *rue Jeannin; tel. 80 66 14 77; credit cards V; closed Sat lunch and Sun.*
   Plenty to tempt the palate from duck or grouper with tomato sauce to a spicy pork casserole. Summer terrace.

Jean-Pierre Billoux, FF-FFF; Hôtel *la Cloche, 14 place Darcy; tel. 80 30 11 00; credit cards AE, V; closed Sun dinner-Mon, two weeks Feb, two weeks Aug.*
   A suitably elegant setting for chef Billoux's fresh and beautifully balanced cuisine. Classic dishes are re-invented by the use of subtle additions such as a hint of curry in the lobster, a *millefeuille* of turnips and potatoes with *foie gras de canard*. Superb wine list; serious prices.
   The Relais et Châteaux hotel (**FFF**) has 76 rooms equipped with every comfort.

Le Rallye, F-FF; 39 *rue Chabot-Charny; tel. 80 67 11 55; credit cards AE, DC, MC, V; closed Sun, three weeks Feb-Mar, three weeks Jul-Aug.*
   Relaxed atmosphere and consistently good value light, traditional cooking – smoked goose breast with a lentil salad, calf's liver with honey and lemon.

spare: the **Musée Archéologique**, one of the richest in France; the **Musée des Beaux-Arts**; and **Musée des Arts Décoratifs**. A short distance west, the **Musée Historique**, 3 place de la Grande-Boucherie, augments local history with a notable military section featuring uniforms, weapons and serried ranks of painted cardboard soldiers.

Across Pont du Corbeau, crafts and costumes, folklore and furniture cram

MULHOUSE

Winstub Henriette, F; 9 *rue Henriette; tel.* 89 46 27 83; *credit cards* V.

Cosy local wine bar-restaurant with simple and copious set menus. Salads, omelettes and sturdier stuff; summer terrace.

Wir, F-FF; 1 *porte Bâle; tel.* 89 56 13 22; *credit cards* AE, DC, MC, V; *closed Fri, and Jul.*

Comfortable surroundings for M. Wir's excellent traditional food. Plenty of variety smoked ham, pepper steaks, *blanquette de veau*, and mouthwatering puddings.

Also 43 inexpensive rooms (open year round).

STRASBOURG

Au Romain, F-FF; 6 *rue du Vieux Marché aux Grains; tel.* 88 32 08 54; *credit cards* AE, DC, MC, V; *closed Sun dinner-Mon, Christmas to New Year.*

Popular city-centre *brasserie* with pillars, orb lights and *banquettes*. Alsacien specialities, grills, salads and a good *menu touristique*.

Down the street, the gilt and red plush **Bistro de la Gare** serves amazingly cheap set menus with an Italian bias. Popular with families for Sunday lunch.

Maison Kammerzel, FF-FFF; 16 *place de la Cathédrale; tel.* 88 32 42 14; *credit cards* AE, DC, MC, V.

Vaulted and painted dining room in a superb 16thC building. Classics from scallops in lobster sauce or pork with calvados, red cabbage and apple to a truly formidable *choucroute*. Ethereal plum sorbet with brandy. Deft service.

Also nine antique-filled rooms.

every inch of space in the delightful **Musée Alsacien**, 23 quai Saint-Nicolas. The **Musée d'Art Moderne et Contemporain** is something of a moveable feast at present since it awaits the completion of its new permanent home in 1996. However, elements of the collection (which includes works by Monet and Picasso, Klimt's *Embrace*, Maillol bronzes and Arp's smooth stone sculptures) may be on temporary display, and are well worth tracking down (check with the S.I.).

From the river, rue Martin-Luther leads to Strasbourg's premier Protestant church, the **Eglise de Saint-Thomas** with its elegant clusters of pink pillars, whitewashed walls and monumental marble tomb for Maréchal de Saxe. The south-western corner of the island is known as **Petite France**, an old tanners' quarter developed for tourism, where a suitably photogenic collection of half-timbered houses balances on fingers of land behind brick prows. There are pretty views from the *ponts couverts* – covered bridges which are no longer covered – and better ones from the walkway on top of the **Barrage Vauban**.

The University lies to the east across the Ill, where allée de la Robertsau continues north to the futuristic **Palais de l'Europe**. Across avenue de l'Europe, the greenery and flower gardens of the **Parc de l'Orangerie** were laid out in honour of Empress Josephine in 1804, over an original plan by Le Nôtre.

The information-packed S.I. has full details of diversions from guided walks and mini-train tours to Alsacien folkshows in the Palais de Rohan, boat trips and brewery tours courtesy of Messrs. Kronenbourg and Heineken amongst others. The main shopping area runs north and west of the cathedral starting with boutiques and department stores before merging into the alluring but expensive craft and gift shops of Petite France. Food and accommodation are not cheap in this city of expense accounts, but a couple of genuine *winstubs* have survived right in the town centre: a favourite is **Chez Yvonne "S'Burjerstuewel"**, 10 rue du Sanglier (tel. 88 32 84 15).

<u>South-Eastern France</u>

Between Dijon and Avignon
Southern Burgundy and the Rhône Valley

425 km; maps Michelin Nos 243, 244 and 245.

For most this region amounts to a straight swoop down the *Autoroute du Soleil* to the Côte d'Azur: a high-speed blur of vineyards, with glimpses of the murky Rhône between petro-chemical refineries, not forgetting the excitement of spotting the first cypress trees and huddles of red-roofed houses that proclaim Provence, and journey's end. Cryptic road-side pictureboards hint at the treasures in store, but the sun beckons and you press on. I must have driven past the great Romanesque silhouette of Tournus' abbey-church 20 times before I finally stopped. And then I was off (no more *autoroute* for me), winding through the rolling green hills of southern Burgundy polka-dotted with dozens of ancient village churches, fortified farmhouses and semi-deserted hamlets such as picturesque Brancion.

Wine lovers know how to take this route at a sedate pace, making time to savour Burgundy's Côte d'Or, the Mâconnais which rolls into Beaujolais just north of Lyon, and the Côtes du Rhône. The Romans took their time along this ancient highway, too. Between planting vines and quashing Gauls they built the cities of *Augustodunum* (Autun), *Lugdunum* (Lyon), and *Arausio* (Orange), all of which retain vestiges of their illustrious past. And then there is *Vasio Vocontiorum*, painstakingly excavated around the pretty town of Vaison-la-Romaine.

The trail connects two four-star, red-route cities, and at mid-point you have the gourmet Mecca of Lyon, with a halo of some 18 (at the last count) Michelin stars scattered within a 25-minute radius. If the stars are beyond your reach, Lyon's budget-priced *bouchons* deliver the goods and affordable local wines by the glass or pitcher, several of the museums are free and the nightlife rages.

The fastest red route is the A6 Dijon-Lyon/A7 Lyon-Avignon *Autoroute du Soleil*. But why not go for blue? Join the wine buffs and dawdle through the Côte d'Or between Dijon and Beaune for instance. For blue and green route followers, the A6 is paralleled by the old N6 la Rochepot (Beaune)-Lyon road, and the A7 by the N7. These main roads, while not the prettiest, can be used to link a range of appealing detours suggested in the text. A favourite diversion is off the N7 to Orange, the D975 to Vaison-la-Romaine, and a circuit of Mont Ventoux.

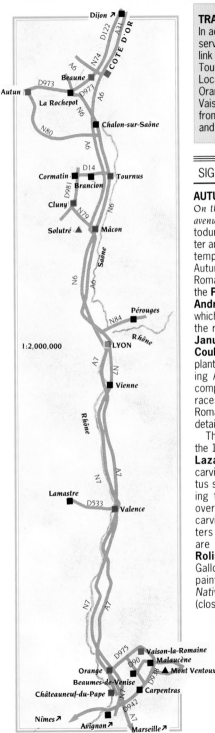

SIGHTS & PLACES OF INTEREST

AUTUN ⇌ ✕

On the D973, 50 km W of Beaune. S.I. avenue Charles-de-Gaulle. Roman Augustodunum was reckoned to be 'the sister and rival of Rome' according to contemporary reports, and present-day Autun enthusiastically plays up to its Roman origins. Two original gateways, the **Porte d'Arroux** and **Porte Saint-André**, pierce the town walls, beyond which there are two further curiosities: the remains of the 1stC **Temple de Janus**, and enigmatic **Pierre de Couhard**, a misshapen stone pyramid planted over a Roman necropolis. During August, full-costume *spectacles* complete with legionnaires and chariot races take place in the remains of the Roman **theatre** (check with the S.I. for details, tel. 85 86 30 00).

The focus of the medieval town is the 12th-15thC **Cathédrale de Saint-Lazare**, renowned for its marvellous carvings. The master sculptor Gislebertus spent 20 years from 1125 creating the capitals and the tympanum over the portal. Some of the finest carvings can be viewed at close quarters in the Chapter House, and there are more in the excellent **Musée Rolin**, rue des Bancs, together with Gallo-Roman pieces and European paintings including a famous 15thC *Nativity* by the Maître de Moulins (closed Sun am, Tues).

AVIGNON
See France Overall: 5.

BEAUNE ⊯ ✕
On the N74, 40 km S of Dijon. S.I. place de la Halle. The wine capital of Burgundy, Beaune is a somewhat smug provincial town dedicated to the pursuit of tourists' cash. For all that, it has several redeeming features within the old town walls, principally the **Hôtel-Dieu**, opposite the S.I. (*son et lumière* Apr-Nov). Founded in 1450 by the Chancellor of Burgundy, Nicolas Rolin, this Gothic beauty served as a hospital right up until the 1970s. From the cobbled Cour d'Honneur, there is a dazzling view of multi-coloured roof tiles, gables and turrets. Tours visit the wards and a small museum with a beautiful polyptych of the *Last Judgement* by Roger van der Weyden. The Hôtel-Dieu hosts an annual wine auction on the third Sunday of November.

Other diversions in town include the illuminating **Musée du Vin de Bourgogne** housed in the old ducal palace on rue de l'Enfer; the 12thC **Eglise de Notre-Dame**, place Notre-Dame, its Romanesque chancel decorated with fine 15thC tapestries; and the 14thC **Tour de l'Horloge**, place Monge.

The S.I. has details of wine tours, châteaux visits and tourist circuits in the **Côte d'Or** (below). Bicycles can be hired from Butterfield & Robinson, 5 rue Citeaux (tel. 80 24 19 99); and for a bird's-eye view of the region and its roof tops, Air Escargot (tel. 85 87 12 30), and Buddy Bombard's Balloon Adventures (tel. 80 26 63 30), lift off daily May-Nov.

COTE D'OR, LA
The stoney, east-facing slopes of the Côte d'Or stretch for some 60 km between Dijon in the north and Santenay. The region is divided into two main wine-growing areas: the **Côte de Nuits**, home of Gevrey-Chambertin, Musigny, Clos de Vougeot and Nuits-Saint-Georges; and the southern **Côte de Beaune**, among whose most famous producers are Aloxe-Corton, Pommard, and the quality white wines of Meursault and Puligny-Montrachet.

From Dijon, the Route des Grands Crus follows the D122 through the sleepy villages to Vougeot, before the N74 takes over for Beaune. Along the

> ### DETOUR – **CHATEAU DE ROCHEPOT**
> A pretty drive through the Côte de Beaune vineyards on the D973 will bring you to **Château de Rochepot** (15 km SW of Beaune). Built on 12thC foundations, the mainly 15thC castle rises out of the woods above the village with a flourish of pepperpot turrets and jaunty tiled roofs. Entrance is via the drawbridge, and there are tours of the guard room, furnished apartments, and chapel (open Easter to Oct; closed Tues).

wine route, numerous producers offer *dégustations* as a prelude to buying, and two larger châteaux offer tours of their *caves* and informative films: **Château de Gevrey-Chambertin** (closed Thur), and **Château de Clos-Vougeot**. Both the Dijon and Beaune S.I.s have details of bus tours, and suggestions for driving or cycling routes to welcoming châteaux.

CLUNY ⊯ ✕
On the D981, 25 km NW of Mâcon. S.I. rue Mercière. During the Middle Ages, the abbots of Cluny were among the most influential figures in western civilization. From their Burgundian seat, founded in 910, the Order of Cluny controlled a network of almost 1,200 Benedictine foundations spread throughout Europe, and answered to Rome alone. As a measure of their importance, **St Hugh** ordered the construction of a magnificent abbey church in 1089. Some 187 m long, 30 m high, with five naves and seven towers, it remained the largest building in Christendom after St Peter's in Rome until it was demolished in 1789.

Only the south transept remains, and you need a powerful imagination to reconstruct the great church. Housed in the 15thC bishop's palace, the three-room **Musée Ochier** displays beautiful rescued stone carvings and a fragment of the leather-scented library. Joint tickets include access to the abbey remains, and a further small collection of carvings exhibited in the **Farinier**, a 13thC grain store.

DIJON
See France Overall: 10.

LYON ⋈ ✕
On the A6/A7, 200 km S of Dijon, 235 km N of Avignon. S.I. place Bellecour. Transport and communications hub of the Rhône valley, Lyon is the second largest city in France and a famous gastronomic centre. At the confluence of the rivers Rhône and Saône, the city is divided into three parts which offer a neat historical breakdown of Lyonnais history.

To the east of the Rhône lies the modern business district of **La Part-Dieu**, the TGV rail station and the airport. Local trains and buses arrive at the Gare Perrache, a short walk from the central S.I. on the **Presqu'île**. This is the 18th-19thC city centre, built on a peninsula between the two rivers with the old weavers' quarter of Croix-Rouge in the north. Older Lyon is on the western bank of the Saône: medieval **Vieux Lyon** crouches beneath the **Fourvière** plateaux where Roman

---

RECOMMENDED HOTELS

AUTUN
Hôtel Saint-Louis, F-FF; *6 rue de l'Arbalète; tel. 85 52 21 03; credit cards* AE, DC, MC, V; *closed Dec-Feb.*

Traditional 17thC coaching inn with a flower-filled patio and popular rustic restaurant.

BEAUNE
Hôtel des Remparts, FF; *48 rue Thiers; tel. 80 22 33 35; credit cards* AE, DC, MC, V; *open year round.*

Excellent small hotel in a 17thC building. Quiet spacious rooms; sunny patio and friendly staff.

BRANCION
Auberge du Vieux Brancion, F-FF; *12 km W of Tournus via D14; tel. 85 51 03 83; credit cards* V; *closed Jan-Feb.*

Delightful family hotel and off-season hideaway in a 15thC house. Peace and quiet; friendly *patron*; and rustic dining room serving regional dishes.

CLUNY
Hôtel de Bourgogne, FF-FFF; *place de l'Abbaye; tel. 85 59 00 85; credit cards* AE, DC, MC, V; *closed Mon winter, mid-Nov to Mar.*

Quiet antique-filled rooms and a Michelin-starred restaurant.

LAMASTRE
Hôtel du Midi, FF; *40 km W of Valence via D533; tel. 75 06 41 50; credit cards* AE, DC, V; *closed Sun dinner, Mon except Jul-Aug, mid-Dec to Mar.*

A short trek into the Ardèche hills, the Perriers' attractive hotel with its bare boards and pretty floral fabrics is a sideline to Bernard's Michelin-starred restaurant **Barattéro**. Warm welcome, delicious food and unusual local wines. Apéritifs in the garden.

LYON
Hôtel Bayard, F-FF; *23 place Bellecour; tel. 78 37 39 64; credit cards* AE, V; *open year round.*

Centrally located and remarkably good value. Brass bedsteads, marble fireplaces and big breakfasts in a 19thC house.

Hôtel Carlton, FF-FFF; *4 rue Jussieu; tel. 78 42 56 51; credit cards* AE, DC, MC, V; *open year round.*

Traditional three-star hotel with splendid old brass and plush lift. Comfortable modernized rooms in the city centre close to the S.I.

ORANGE
Hôtel Arène, FF; *place Langes; tel. 90 34 10 95; credit cards* AE, DC, V; *closed Nov to mid-Dec.*

Very pleasant provincial hotel on a quiet leafy square in the town centre.

TOURNUS
See Recommended Restaurants.

VAISON-LA-ROMAINE
Le Beffroi, FF-FFF; *Haute Ville; tel. 90 36 04 71; credit cards* AE, DC, MC, V; *closed early-Jan to mid-Mar.*

Glorious 16thC hostelry with enormous antique-filled rooms, lovely views, a garden and welcoming terraced restaurant.

VALENCE
Hôtel de Lyon, F; *23 avenue Pierre-Sémard; tel. 75 41 44 66; credit cards* V; *open year round.*

Spick-and-span functional modern hotel near the station.

DETOUR – **ROCHE DE SOLUTRÉ**
In the middle of the Mâconnais
vineyards, a 500 m-high limestone
outcrop stands guard over a
prehistoric animal graveyard. The
Roche de Solutré (10 km SW of
Mâcon via the D54) was a
Palaeolithic hunting site for
25,000 years. In some places, the
bones of horses, reindeer, bison
and mammoths are piled to a
depth of 1 m, and the **Musée de
Préhistoire de Solutré** displays
artefacts found at the site (closed
Tues and Jan-Feb).

Lugdunum was founded in 43 BC.

Lyon is easy to explore on foot and
full of interesting nooks and crannies
such as the *traboules*, secretive covered passageways which burrow
between streets and beneath buildings
in Vieux Lyon and Croix-Rouge (maps
from the S.I.). They once provided all-
weather protection for bolts of silk
woven by Lyon's textile workers, the
canuts, whose history is celebrated in
the **Maison des Canuts**, 10-12 rue
d'Ivry. They also served as escape
routes for the war-time Resistance,
commemorated in the **Musée de la
Résistance et de la Déportation**, 5
rue Boileau, La Part-Dieu.

The only aspect of Lyonnais life without a museum is food, but there is no
shortage of shrines to gastronomy or
indeed of the traditional Lyonnais café-
restaurants known as *bouchons* which
offer a great value-for-money alternative to the big-city prices.

Place Bellecour is a sensible place
to start exploring. To the south is rue
Auguste Compte with its antiques dealers, and rue de la Charité, where the
Musée des Arts Décoratifs (No. 30),
and **Musée Historique des Tissus**
(No. 34) occupy 18thC *hôtels particuliers* (both closed Mon). The first is
grandly furnished in period style; while
the latter displays a truly fabulous collection of rich and rare fabrics.

At the top of rue de la République,
the extravagant **Hôtel de Ville** backs
on to place des Terreaux. Robespierre's thugs set up their guillotine
here during the French Revolution. Off
the square, the 17thC Italianate Palais
de Saint-Pierre houses the **Musée des**

Beaux-Arts, with a cool, green sculpture garden enclosed in its colonnaded
courtyard (closed Mon, Tues).

Across the Saône, Vieux Lyon is a
delightful quarter with excellent shops
and restaurants, and restored Renaissance houses such as the Hôtel de
Gadagne, home of the **Musée Historique de Lyon**, place du Petit-Col-
lège. Its neighbour, the **Musée de la
Marionette**, exhibits puppets from
around the world, including the Lyonnais *Guignol*, a loud-mouth Punch and
Judy character who delivers his blister-
ing repartee in a thick Lyonnais accent
at the Puppet Theatre, rue Louis-Car-
raud (details from the S.I.).

Rue Saint-Jean leads south past the
gloomy, Gothic **Cathédrale de Saint-
Jean** (worth a stop for its extraordinary 14thC astronomical clock) to the
funicular station which makes short
work of the climb up to the Fourvière
plateau. Atop the escarpment, the
19thC **Basilique de Notre-Dame** is
all Byzantine mosaic and marble with
lurid stained glass. To recover, take in
the view which stretches east to the
Alps, then stroll down to the **Musée
Gallo-Romain**, 17 rue Cléberg, which
is built into the hillside by two Roman
theatres (closed Mon-Tues).

There are **boat trips** from quai des
Célestins on the Saône; while back on
the east bank of the Rhône, the enormous **Parc de la Tête-d'Or** makes a
welcome inner-city escape.

Further afield, the quaint (but much
visited) medieval hill town of
Pérouges, (36 km E via the N84) is an
easy excursion by car or train; or head
into the mountains with Local Explorations: 15 – The French Alps.

An alternative onward route to the
Riviera is France Overall: 12 – Between
Lyon and Nice; or if you want to head
west, see France Overall: 16 –
Between Bordeaux and Lyon.

MACON ✕
On the N6, 70 km N of Lyon. S.I. 187 rue
Carnot. A town with a distinctly southern feel, Mâcon's Old Town on the west
bank of the Saône is busy and attractive with pastel-painted buildings, small
squares, the usual shady plane trees
and two museums.

The **Musée Lamartine,** 41 rue Sig-
orne, (closed Tues, Nov-Apr), is devoted to 19thC poet-politician Alphonse

• *Roche de Solutré.*

Lamartine. The more general-interest **Musée des Ursulines,** allée de Matisco; (closed Sun am, Tues) local history and culture. On the corner of place aux Herbes and rue Dombey, one of the most interesting buildings in town is the **Maison du Bois,** decorated with dozens of carved figures, foliage, twisted, fluted and scaly pillars.

Along the quayside, the **Maison des Vins,** quai Maréchal-de-Lattre-de-Tassigny offers a full range of Mâconnais reds and whites, Beaujolais and even Côte de Beaune wines, plus an informal wine bar-restaurant. The S.I. can suggest tours of the Mâconnais vineyards. Bicycles can be hired from Vélo-Verte, 7 rue Saint-Nizier.

ORANGE ⊨

On the N7, 30 km N of Avignon. S.I. rue Aristide-Briand. Derived from the flourishing Roman city of *Arausio,* not the citrus fruit, the name of Orange has spread far and wide from California, South Africa and the Northern Irish protestant movement.

The great draw today is the 2,000 year-old **Théâtre Antique,** place des Mounets. The only Roman theatre with its stage still intact and superb acoustics which permitted an audience of around 8,000 to hear every word, it is a beauty. After an unsavoury interlude as a Revolutionary prison, the

theatre was a setting for classical productions starring Sarah Bernhardt amongst others, and now hosts annual choral spectaculars during July and August (details, tel. 90 34 15 52). Joint tickets include the assorted local history exhibits in the **Musée Municipal**.

At the northern entrance to the town, an intricately carved Roman **Arc de Triomphe** commemorates the exploits of Julius Caesar and the Second Legion, who were *Arausio*'s early settlers.

DETOUR – **CHATEAUNEUF-DU-PAPE**

Wine enthusiasts *en route* to Avignon can make a back-road pilgrimage to the vineyards of **Châteauneuf-du-Pape** (10 km south of Orange via the D68). The Avignon popes planted the first vines here in the 14thC, and watched over them from a fortress, which was destroyed but for a tower in the Wars of Religion. The S.I., on place du Portail, has lists of the various *producteurs.* Visitors to the early August *Fête de la Véraison* may be lucky enough to find free *dégustations.*

TOURNUS 🏨 ✕

On the N6, 30 km N of Mâcon. S.I. place Carnot. Squeezed between the N6 and the banks of the Saône, Tournus is a quiet little town dominated by the Romanesque bulk of the **Ancien Abbaye de Saint-Philibert**. Fortress-like Saint-Philibert predates Cluny, the severity of its machicolated façade moderated by a simple pattern of tall Lombard arches cut into the brick-work, and a pink-tipped tower decorated with attenuated 11thC figures. The dusty-pink local stone is one of the distinguishing features of the interior, its nave held aloft on broad, striped arches, in contrast to the dim narthex crouched on squat, circular pillars. The crosswise barrel vaulting is unusual, illuminated by windows to either side. Down in the 12thC crypt, a double row of slender pillars sporting leafy capitals form an elegant counterpoint to the rough stone vaulting. Behind the cloister, there is a fine 15thC **Logis Abbatiale**, and the **Musée Bourguignon**, housing displays of local costumes, furniture and crafts (closed Tues).

The 18thC artist Greuze was a native of Tournus. An interesting selection of his portraits and drawings are on show in the **Hôtel-Dieu** (closed Sun am, Tues). The town centre has some attractive houses, and the S.I. provides a nosey-parker's guide to hidden sights starting at 12 rue de la République, a Renaissance courtyard with balconies, a spiral staircase and handy vaulted bicycle park.

VAISON-LA-ROMAINE 🏨

On the D975, 27 km NE of Orange. S.I. place Chanoine Sautel. Far enough off the autoroute to escape casual tourists,

---

DETOUR – **BRANCION AND CHATEAU DE CORMATIN** 🏨

For an attractive drive fbetween Tournus and Cluny, I can highly recommend the D14 via the tiny, fortified medieval village of **Brancion** (population 22 in summer, seven in winter), where walkers can pick up the GR76A. At the junction with the D981, **Château de Cormatin** is a 17thC gem of unashamed ostentation (open Easter, Jul-Sep only). Then follow the verdant Grosne valley to Cluny itself.

DETOUR - **THE DENTELLES AND MONT VENTOUX**

South and east of Vaison, the jagged tips of the **Dentelles** and majestic **Mont Ventoux** (1,909 m) make for a lovely drive, and great hiking country. From Malaucène (10 km SE of Vaison-la-Romaine via the D938), there is a circular route around Mont Ventoux on the D974; while the D90 wriggles up through the Dentelles and down to the terraced village of **Beaumes-de-Venise**, famed for its sweet white muscat wine.

Vaison offers a remarkable selection of historic sites. Above the 18thC New Town, two areas of the ancient **Cité Gallo-Romain** have been uncovered. Roman shoppers once strolled the Quartier la Villasse, and were entertained at the **Théâtre** in the Quartier de Puymin. Here, among the patrician mansions and smaller rented houses, a fascinating **museum** displays Roman artefacts. Joint tickets include the Provençal Romanesque former **Cathédrale de Notre-Dame**.

A Roman bridge crosses the Ouvèze to the picturesque medieval **Haute Ville** on the opposite bank. Clamber up the dark streets, past Renaissance houses, sunny squares and trickling fountains to the ruined **Château** for a marvellous view across town and to Mont Ventoux.

VALENCE 🏨 ✕

On the A7/N7, 100 km S of Lyon. S.I. place Leclerc. A convenient point to nip off the autoroute, Valence is the capital of the lavender-scented Drôme region. Rabelais was a student here, and young Napoléon Bonaparte kicked off his military career at the artillery school.

Pedestrianized Vieux Valence has its share of attractive shopping streets and Renaissance houses, such as the fulsomely decorated **Maison des Têtes** on Grande Rue. At the bottom of the street, the **Cathédrale de Saint-Apollinaire**, place des Clercs, was founded in 1095. Behind it, in the old Bishop's Palace, the **Musée de Valence** displays local history exhibits and 18thC drawings by Hubert Robert.

RECOMMENDED RESTAURANTS

AUTUN

Le Chalet Bleu, F-FF; 3 *rue Jeannin;* tel. 85 86 27 30; *credit cards* AE, DC, V; *closed Mon dinner-Tues, Feb.*

Unappealing façade, but an engaging dining room and terrific value-for-money menus full of unusual combinations.

BEAUNE

L'Ecusson, FF-FFF; *place* Malmédy; tel. 80 24 03 82; *credit cards* AE, V; *closed Mon-Tues lunch, three weeks Feb.*

Delicious and innovative cuisine from Jean-Pierre Senelet, and remarkable value weekday menus.

Grilladine, F; 17 *rue* Maufoux; tel. 80 22 22 36; *credit cards* V; *closed Mon, one week Jun, one week Aug.*

Burgundian cooking in cosy surroundings with well-priced wines.

CLUNY

Le Potin Gourmand, F-FF; *Champ de Foire;* tel. 85 59 02 06; *credit cards* AE, MC, V; *closed Mon, Jan.*

Friendly, rustic spot with armchairs, tiled floors and a vine-draped terrace. Interesting roquefort and pear tart, veal kidneys flavoured with juniper berries.

Also four attractive country-style bedrooms (**FF**).

LYON

Paul Bocuse, FFF; *at* Pont de Collonges (12 *km N via* N51); tel. 78 22 01 41; *credit cards* AE, DC, V.

A culinary legend, M. Bocuse is frequently absent, but his fabulous creations are served up in this gourmet shrine every day of the year. The truffle soup with its pastry hat was dreamt up for ex-President Giscard d'Estaing; the plump Bresse chicken *en vessie* is a triumph. Desserts made for if not in heaven; superb wines; and the satisfaction of actually being here.

Le Saint-Alban, FF; 2 *quai* Jean-Moulin; tel. 78 30 14 89; *credit cards* AE, V; *closed Sat (except dinner in winter)-Sun, three weeks Aug.*

A tiny restaurant with an assured and creative chef. Mouth-watering prawn and leek cannelloni; affordable local wines.

La Voûte, F-FF; 11 *place* Antonin-Gourju; tel. 78 42 01 33; *credit cards* AE, DC, MC, V; *closed Sun, three weeks Jul.*

Busy and popular bistro serving Lyonnais dishes and daily *suggestions du marché.*

MACON

Le Poisson d'Or, F-FF; *allée du Parc;* tel. 85 38 00 88; *credit cards* V; *closed Wed, Sun dinner and Tues dinner in winter, two weeks Oct-Nov.*

Great summer setting in a park by the river. Tables on the terrace, and a mixed menu with plenty of seafood and fruity desserts.

TOURNUS

Aux Terrasses, F-FF; 18 *avenue du 23-Janvier* (S *of the town centre*); tel. 85 51 01 74; *credit cards* MC, V; *closed Sun dinner-Mon, four weeks Jan-Feb, one week end Oct.*

Attractive vine-covered *logis* serving good value local dishes from snails or *jambon persillé* to pears with cassis.

Also 27 comfy rooms (**FF**).

VALENCE

La Coelacanthe, F-FF; 3 *place de la Pierre;* tel. 75 42 30 68; *credit cards* AE, DC, MC, V; *closed Sat lunch, Sun dinner, Mon lunch, two weeks Feb, two weeks Nov.*

Rustic-style fish restaurant with tables spilling out on to the leafy square; specialities include sea bass with fennel and scallops in vermouth.

Pic, FFF; 285 *avenue* Victor-Hugo; tel. 75 44 15 32; *credit cards* AE, DC, MC, V; *closed Sun dinner, Wed, Aug.*

A star in the culinary firmament where the welcome is warm and genuine, and the speciality *galette* of truffles, celery and *foie gras* a must. Other temptations include pigeon breast in Beaumes-de-Venise, a saffron-scented oyster *cassoulette* and a full wine list, strong on Côtes-du-Rhone.

Also two rooms and two apartments.

<u>South-Eastern France</u>
Between Lyon and Nice
Alpes Maritimes, Alpes-de-Haute-Provence & Route Napoléon
475 km; maps Michelin Nos 244 and 245.

On March 1, 1815, after ten months in exile, Napoleon landed just east of Cannes, with a modest following of 700 men. His welcome was less than overwhelming – emissaries sent in advance had been imprisoned – so next morning the party marched north into the snow-covered heights of Haute-Provence, and arrived in Grenoble at 11pm on March 7. Today, the spectacular *Route Napoléon* can be driven in a single day at a push, but a mid-way break around Sisteron is even better, and makes a terrific alternative route to or from the coast instead of the motorway trek south via Marseille. If you do decide to break the journey, consider staying in the area long enough to see the majestic Grand Canyon du Verdon (see page 156).

From Nice you may wish to continue through Provence to Avignon (see France Overall: 13) or to explore eastwards along the Riviera (see Local Explorations: 17) or into the Alpes-Maritimes (see page 342).

The A43/A48 *autoroute* makes short work of the drive between Lyon (described in France Overall: 11) and Grenoble, starting point for Local Explorations: 15, The French Alps.

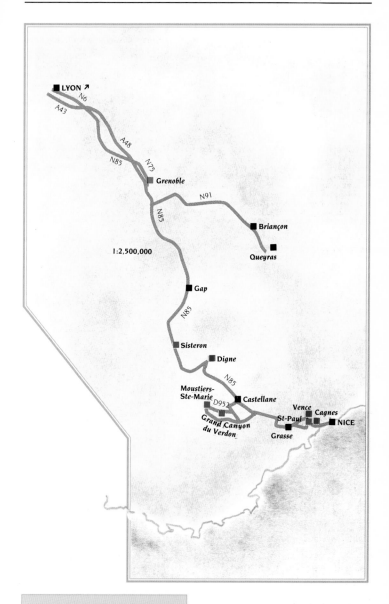

LYON ↗
N6
A43
A48
N85
N75
Grenoble
N91
N85
Briançon
Queyras
1:2,500,000
Gap
N85
Sisteron
Digne
N85
Moustiers-
Ste-Marie
D952
Castellane
Vence
St-Paul
Cagnes
NICE
Grand Canyon
du Verdon
Grasse

TRANSPORT
There are flights from Paris to
Lyon, Grenoble and Nice; and fast
TGV trains from Paris serve Lyon
(two hours) with connections to
Grenoble. During summer, the
Alpazur tourist train operates
between Lyon, Grenoble and
Digne, to connect with buses and
trains to Nice.

SIGHTS & PLACES OF INTEREST

CAGNES-SUR-MER & HAUT-DE-CAGNES

Off the N98, 12 km W of Nice. A pleasant little jaunt from Nice, this diversion to Renoir's house and a medieval cliff-hanging village can be combined with a trip to Vence (see page 165), Saint-Paul-de-Vence (see page 162), and Grasse (see right).

DETOUR – GRAND CANYON DU VERDON

The longest and deepest gorge in Europe, a slash in the surrounding limestone plateau, the Grand Canyon du Verdon is easily accessible from Castellane, some 12 km to the east. If you have time, make for **Moustiers-Sainte-Marie**, strikingly situated at the bottom of a ravine, and known for its *faïence* (pottery), via the D952 and the D23 Route des Crêtes, with plenty of viewpoints overlooking the gorges. Returning from Moustiers via the southern Corniche Sublime (D71), there are more wonderful views, the best of all being at the Balcons de la Mescla: here the Verdon and Artuby rivers meet, hundreds of feet below.

I advise you to make the trip in the direction suggested, if only to avoid being the car nearest the sheer drop as you negociate the none-too-wide cliff-top roads.

The Verdon Gorges attract various forms of dare-devil 'leisure activities' such as rock climbing, canoeing, rafting and canyoning (whatever that is). Contact the S.I. (Castellane, Moustiers-Sainte-Marie) for details, or, for the watersports, Verdon Animation Nature, La Palud-sur-Verdon, 04120 Castellane; tel. 92 74 66 94/92 77 38 59.

A tough eight-hour walk on the GR4 can be made along the cliff face from Pointe Sublime to Châlet de Maline – for experienced hikers only, unafraid of heights, tunnels, ladders and adders.

Turn off the N98 5 km west of Nice-Côte d'Azur airport and drive into Cagnes-sur-Mer. Take rue Auguste-Renoir off place de-Gaulle, cross a junction and turn left into chemin des Collettes, signposted **Musée Renoir**. The artist built Les Collettes in 1907, and lived there with his family until his death in 1919. With shutters drawn against the sunlight, the cool, unclut-tered interior has original furnishings, portraits and sculpture by Renoir's friends Albert André and Richard Guino. The garden is a suprise highlight with flowerbeds tumbling down the hill, olive and orange groves, a ridiculously pretty gardener's cottage draped in vines, and views up to the castle.

Head back to place de-Gaulle, and uphill for Haut-de-Cagnes, grafted on to the hillside around the **Chateau-Musée Grimaldi** (closed Tues). Reached via a pretty Renaissance courtyard, the lower floor of the muse-um is devoted to local history and craft exhibits including an exhaustive exposé of the olive. Upstairs, the **Musée d'Art Moderne Méditerranéen** displays works by l9th-20thC artists who have worked along the Côte d'Azur (Chagall, Kisling, and so on). Take a leisurely wander around the village, browse in the craft shops, and revive yourself in one of the jolly cafés on the square.

DIGNE ⊨ ✕

On the N85, 41 km SE of Sisteron. A possible overnight stop on the Route Napoléon, Digne is a spa town on the River Bléone, and *préfecture* of Alpes-de-Haute-Provence. Napoléon lunched here on the fourth day of his triumphant progress to Grenoble in March 1815, otherwise little has happened. You can alleviate the symptoms of rheumatism in a thermal bath, or stretch your legs under the plane trees on **boulevard Gassendi**, and take pity on the Cathé-drale de Saint-Jerome, which is in a sorry state. Market day is Saturday – look out for the cheeses.

From Digne or Castellane, 53 km further south on the Route Napoléon, you might consider a detour to the **Gorges du Verdon**.

GRASSE ⊨

On the N85, 17 km N of Cannes. S.I. 3 *place de la Foux.* Sprawled across the southern slopes of the limestone plateau which shelters the coast, official southern start point for the Route Napoléon, Grasse has been the crucible of the French perfume industry since the 16thC. The raw ingredients – roses, jasmin, verbena, mimosa, lavender and citrus amongst others – are all grown nearby and transformed into essences at a handful of local *perfumeries*, then sent away to be blended into fragrances by, among others, Dior and Chanel. On the road into town, you can stop off at the modern **Galimard** laboratories for a free whistle-stop introduction to scent-making techniques and to stock up on toiletries without paying big-name prices. In town, **Fragonard,** 20 boulevard Fragonard, and **Molinard,** 60 boulevard Victor-Hugo, also open up their doors to the public.

A short step from Fragonard, on the edge of the Old Town, the **Musée d'Art et d'Histoire de Provence** is housed in a fine 18thC mansion built for Mirabeau's sister, the Marquise de Cabris. Elegantly furnished rooms display period antiques and porcelain; there is a marvellous kitchen hung about with pots and pans, plus regional crafts and costume (closed Sat-Sun, Nov). Wend your way through the tall, narrow streets for a quick look at the 12thC **Cathédrale**, and up to **place des Aires** for the daily flower and produce market.

If the name Fragonard seems familiar, you would be right in thinking of the 18thC artist, Jean-Honoré Fragonard, who was born here in Grasse. During the Revolution he returned to take refuge in the home of his friend Maubert, now the **Villa-Musée Fragonard** and a cultural centre in a park west of the Old Town (closed Sun).

GRENOBLE ⌫ ✕

On the A48, 105 km SE of Lyon. S.I. 14 rue de la République. Guarded by the limestone waves of the Chartreuse Massif to the north, the crowded peaks of the Belledonne range to the east, and a circlet of lesser, but still significant heights to the south and west, Grenoble unfolds across a broad valley on the banks of the rivers Isère and Drac. The city has a reputation for independent thinking: its Day of the Tiles, when the Grenoblois protested at Louis XVI's attempt to suppress the local *parlement* by raining tiles on his troops, predated the storming of the Bastille by 13 months; the city later welcomed Napoleon on his return from Elba in 1815; and local glovemakers established the first French trade union in 1803. Industry boomed in the 19thC, and the rivers were harnessed to generate hydro-electricity. Today, nuclear, chemical and medical laboratories are major local employers. Grenoble has also been a university town since 1339, and its three universities, foreign language and technical schools attract some 40,000 students. As the capital of Dauphiné, the city's economic and cultural influence extends throughout the French Alps.

A busy, partially-pedestrianized jumble of streets around **place Grenette**, on the left bank of the Isère, constitutes the city centre. The 19thC author Henri Beyle, better known as Stendhal, was born here at 14 rue Jean-Jacques Rousseau, now the small **Musée de la Résistance et de la Déportation** (open Mon, Wed, Sat pm); while his grandfather's apartment at 20 Grande Rue is used for temporary exhibitions. For genuine Stendhalalia, the **Musée Stendhal**, 1 rue Hector-Berlioz, overlooks the Jardin de Ville (closed am and Mon). To the north, the cafés of place Saint-André provide a pleasant view of the Flamboyant Renaissance **Palais de Justice**, and the occasional sighting of a white-fronted *avocat* or scarlet-caped judge whisking past an open window. The belfry of the **Eglise de Saint-André**, built by the Princes of Dauphine in the 13thC, is a local landmark; while a short walk east, the **Cathédrale de Notre-Dame** (currently under-going a facelift) dates back to the 11thC. South of the centre, the **Musée d'Histoire Naturelle** (closed Tues), 1 rue Dolomieu, details the first stirrings of *homo sapiens* in the Alps alongside more traditional displays of geology, fauna and flora. For more exotic flora, stroll on to the hot houses of the adjacent **Jardin des Plantes**.

The most famous symbol of the modern city is the *télépherique,* the world's first urban cable car inaugurated in 1934 (schedules from the S.I.). From quai Stephane-Jay on the left bank of the river, it sends a frequent shuttle of perspex bubbles across the Isère and up to the **Fort de la Bastille** towering above the city with tremendous views over the rooftops to the encircling mountains.

You can walk back down to the city along a network of paths through the old fortifications to the **Eglise de Saint-Laurent**, off quai Xavier-Jouvin, where archaeologists have performed an autopsy on the nave of the church to reveal a 6thC crypt; and the **Musée Dauphinois** (closed Tues), 30 rue Maurice Gignoux. (Both are accessible from the Old Town via the pedestrian Pont Saint-Laurent, which marks the spot where the first Roman bridge spanned the river.) The museum, housed in a former 17thC convent, offers a fascinating introduction to the lifestyle of the *'Gens de là-Haut'* ('people from up there'). There are everyday objects from a shepherd's pocket sundial and box bed to painstakingly decorated furniture and drinking gourds. The postman is painted in a startling new light as a *contrabandier* with a log dragged behind his bike as a primitive brake; animals were also handy smugglers, as illustrated by a selection of body-hugging flasks built for man and beast. The architectural models are works of art with their tiny tiles, horsehair thatching and animal noises supplied from the wings; and do not miss the stunning Chapelle de Sainte-Marie in the basement with its frescoes and gilded baroque altar.

BRIANCON, THE HIGH PASSES AND THE QUEYRAS
To the east of this route, close to the Italian border, sits the highest town in Europe, Briançon. For the most part a nondescript modern sprawl, its virtue is the **Ville Haute** surrounded by grim Vauban-built ramparts. For more information on the town, see Local Explorations: 14. From Briançon, the N94 leads over the Col de Montgenèvre into Italy. A more peaceful route across the border from Briançon is along the Vallée de la Clarée and over the Col d'Echelle to Bardonècchia.

To the south of Briançon lies the **Queyras**, much of it, now a regional park, remote and beautiful, full of rushing water and flowers.

WALKING AND CYCLING IN THE VERCORS MASSIF
Grenoble is a good jumping off point for expeditions to the Parc Natural Régional du Vercors which lies southwest of the city. The S.I. has some information, but serious walkers should make straight for the Maison de la Randonnée, 7 rue Voltaire (tel. 76 54 76 00). There is also help at hand for cyclists from Mountain Bike Grenoble, 8 quai de France (tel. 76 47 58 76), who mend and hire out bikes, plus suggest itineraries.

The autumn of 1993 saw the re-opening of the **Musée de Peinture et de Sculpture** in a new purpose-built home on place de Verdun (closed Tues). Widely recognized as one of the finest collections outside Paris, its Italian section is first rate, there is a marvellous Rubens, and the 19th-20thC collection represented by Bonnard, Picasso, Klee, Miró, and Arp (the list goes on) is exceptional by any standard.

The Grenoblois eat well and play hard. Long-stay visitors should invest in a copy of the student guide *Dahu* (named for a legendary beast with two long and two short legs which enable it to circle mountains). This definitive guide to clubs, pubs, entertainment and cheap dining is also available in English. If you have had your fill of local cuisine, there are around 60 Chinese restaurants in town; and the 'Little Italy' quarter on the right bank of the Isère is packed with pizza and pasta joints

LYON
See France Overall: 11.

MOUSTIERS-STE-MARIE
See Detour – Grand Canyon du Verdon, page 156.

NICE 🛏 ✕
On the N98/N7/A8, 344 km S of Grenoble, 188 km E of Marseille. S.I. avenue Thiers. The sheer scale of Nice distinguishes it from other fashionable resorts along the coast. Undisputed Queen of the Riviera, with a pedigree stretching back to the ancient Greeks, Nice is a major city as well as a resort, and it offers

• *Nice, Promenade des Anglais.*

more of everything, good and bad, than its counterparts.

On the plus side, sun, sea and palm trees along the Promenade des Anglais; marvellous museums (many of them free), moderately priced hotels and restaurants; an elegant Italianate town centre; medieval Vieux Nice; and the fact that the native *Niçois* is a pleasant change from many of his less friendly Riviera counterparts.

On the minus side, the beach is full of rocks (well, pebbles), and the traffic is horrific. (Charging around the blood-red place Masséna like a crazed corpuscle in search of the underground car park is a recurrent nightmare.) Car

thieves, pimps and drug pushers have refused to be gentrified along with sections of Vieux Nice, and the city's regal nose was put severely out of joint in 1990, when the right-wing mayor made off to South America pursued by massive corruption charges.

Napoleon launched his Italian campaigns from Nice, and the heart of town, **place Masséna**, is named for one of his generals, André Masséna, a native Niçois. To the south, the famous **Promenade des Anglais** stretches for 5 km along the Baie des Anges, lined by a mixed bag of art nouveau and Belle Epoch buildings, including the landmark **Hôtel Negresco**, classified as a national monument.

West of place Masséna, the chic shopping streets of rue Masséna, rue Paradis and rue de France are where to find a café and watch the world go by. Marzipan is a local speciality, and the almond paste creations in the window of **Canel,** 19 rue de France, from loaves and fishes to fruit baskets, look better than the real thing.

Head east and you are swallowed up by the cool, narrow,streets of **Vieux Nice**. The Baroque **Cathédrale de Sainte-Réparate**, place Rossetti, evolved from a parish church in the 17thC. Its impressive domed interior boasts a wealth of decorative plaster-

work awash with cherubs. A short walk away, the Italianate **Palais Lascaris** (closed Mon, Nov), 15 rue Droite, has been restored to display period furnishings and antiques beneath splendid painted ceilings and ornate mouldings. **Cours Saleya** is a must for the glorious daily flower market, heady with the scent of massed roses, jasmine and lilies. Above Vieux Nice (steps from rue du Château, or lift from quai des Etats-Unis), there is respite from the city bustle and lovely views from the green oasis of **Le Château**.

The Romans first settled on the northern hillside at **Cimiez**, now a smart residential suburb with two notable museums. (Buses 15, 15A, 17, 20, 22 to Arènes.) The halls and

RECOMMENDED HOTELS

DIGNE
Grand Paris, FF-FFF; 19 *boulevard Thiers; tel.* 92 31 11 51; *credit cards* AE, DC, MC, V; *open year round.*

Rather grand, town-centre hotel in a converted monastery. Well-appointed rooms, plus the best restaurant in town serving classic cuisine. Restaurant closed Sun dinner, Mon in winter, and mid-Dec to Mar.

Mistre, FF; 63 *boulevard Gassendi; tel.* 92 31 00 16; *credit cards* AE, MC, V; *open year round.*

Right in the town centre, near the cathedral; 19 comfortable rooms and a friendly welcome. Pleasant dining room. Restaurant closed Sat except July-Aug, and mid-Dec to mid-Jan.

See also Sisteron, below.

GRENOBLE
Bellevue, F; 1 *rue Belgrade; tel.* 76 46 69 34; *credit cards* V; *open year round.*

As usual there is a clutch of budget hotels near the rail station, but the Bellevue is a useful discovery by the river. Friendly welcome, spotless rooms (though somewhat noisy).

Rive Droite, FF; 20 *quai de France; tel.* 76 87 61 11; *credit cards* AE, DC, MC, V; *closed three weeks Christmas.*

Modern hotel on the right bank (five-minute walk from the Old Town). Comfortable, well-equipped rooms

(views from the upper floors), restaurant, amusingly 1970s bar.

NICE
Le Floride, F-FF; 52 *boulevard de Cimiez; tel.* 93 53 11 02; *credit cards* V; *open year round.*

Spotless family hotel slightly north of the city centre with 20 amazingly well-priced rooms.

Gounod, FF; 3 *rue Gounod; tel.* 93 88 26 20; *credit cards* AE, DC, MC, V; *open year round.*

Belle Epoque town house with pleasant rooms close to the city centre. Shared facilities in the Sofitel Splendid next door include a restaurant, roof-top pool and solarium.

Le Negresco, FFF; 37 *Promenade des Anglais; tel.* 93 88 39 51; *credit cards* AE, DC, MC, V; *open year round.*

Opulent national monument stuffed with gorgeous antiques and paintings, the largest Aubusson carpet ever made and a chandelier in the main salon which weighs more than a ton. Extravagant rooms; gourmet restaurant, **Le Chantecler**; piano bar; private beach; magnificently-attired doorman and legions of flunkeys to carry your purchases from a selection of boutiques.

La Perouse, FFF; 11 *quai Rauba-Capéu; tel.* 62 34 63; *cards* AE, DC, MC, V; *open year round (restaurant closed Nov-Mar).*

galleries of Villa Arènes house the **Musée Archéologique Cimiez**, and a hoard of finds from *Cemenelum*, the Roman capital of *Alpes-Maritimae*. Behind the villa, you can explore the ruins of the main street and enormous 3rdC bath complex. Henri Matisse lived and worked in Nice from 1914-54, to the benefit of the excellent **Musée Matisse**, recently enlarged to contain the extensive donations of his son, Jean. Paintings, sketches, models and bronzes cover every period of the artist's long working life, while personal memorabilia lends a pleasingly intimate touch (both museums closed Sun am, Mon, Nov).

Halfway back to town, the **Musée Chagall**, avenue Docteur-Menard, was built specifically to display Russian-born Marc Chagall's *Biblical Messages* series. Painted between 1954-67, the 17 enormous canvases are electrifying: vivid images of religious mysticism, each supported by preparatory sketches and etchings, plus additional donations from Chagall including stained glass and a mosaic of the prophet Elijah (closed Tues).

If you still have an appetite for art treasures, head for the **Musée Jules Chéret**, 33 avenue des Baumettes, which has several Renoirs, a Degas portrait, Van Dongen nudes, Picasso ceramics, works by Dufy, Monet, Sisley, and Niçois Surrealist Gustave-Albert Mossa (closed Mon, Nov).

There is also the new **Musée d'Art**

Set beneath Le Château in tranquil terraced gardens planted with lemon trees. There are 62 luxurious rooms, some with views of the front; a pool terrace and sun room; plus summertime outdoor bar and grill.

Saint-François, F; *3 rue Saint-François; tel. 93 85 88 69; no credit cards; open year round.*

Cheap, cheerful and centrally-located in Vieux Nice, but it is noisy at times and the rooms are 'compact'.

Vendôme, FF; *26 rue Pastorelli; tel. 93 62 00 77; credit cards* AE, DC, MC, V; *open year round.*

Attractively restored town house with reasonably-priced, well-appointed rooms close to the city centre.

SAINT-PAUL-DE-VENCE
La Colombe d'Or, FFF; *tel. 93 32 80 02; credit cards* AE, DC, MC, V; *closed mid-Nov to mid-Dec, and first two weeks of Feb.*

Once a humble inn frequented by artists, this lovely restored house has attained the apogee of Provençal rustic-chic. Beams and whitewashed walls frame an enviable modern art collection, much of it accepted from the artists as payment in kind by the original owner, Paul Roux. There are 15 pretty rooms with tiled floors and country furniture; garden, vine-draped terrace and dining room.

SISTERON
La Bonne Etape, FF-FFF; *chemin du Lac, Chateau-Arnoux (14 km SE of Sisteron/25 km W of Digne); tel. 92 64 00 09; credit cards* AE, DC, MC, V; *closed Jan to mid-Feb, and last week of Nov.*

A great excuse to stop over on the Route Napoléon, the Gleize family's 18thC coaching inn offers 11 beautifully decorated and comfortable rooms, plus seven suites, a pool terrace and garden. However, the *pièce de résistance* is Jany Gleize's elegant Provençal cuisine inspired by fresh local ingredients from Sisteron lamb to pigeon. The cheapest set menu is modestly priced, but thereafter prices soar.

VENCE
Auberge des Seigneurs, F; *place du Frôme; tel. 93 58 04 24; credit cards* AE, DC. MC, V; *closed Sun, dinner-Mon, mid-Nov to mid-Dec.*

Simple, spotless and authentic village *auberge*, run by the same family for many years. Home cooking in the wood-panelled restaurant downstairs, quiet shuttered bedrooms upstairs.

Miramar, FF; *plateau Saint-Michel; tel. 93 58 01 32; credit cards* AE, MC, V; *closed mid-Oct to Mar.*

Smart but unpretentious little hotel, a short walk from the Old Town, with attractive rooms, views down to the coast and a garden.

Moderne et d'Art Contemporain, on avenue Saint-Jean-Baptiste, which displays post-1960 Lichtensteins, Warhols, et al.

Nice's busy annual festival calendar kicks off in February with **Carnival**, an all-singing, all-dancing razzamatazz for two consecutive weekends leading up to Lent. The **Parade du Jazz** (mid-July) attracts world-famous names to the Parc de Cimiez; followed almost immediately by the **Festival de Folklore International,** interspersed with **Batailles des Fleurs** (flower pelting and other jollities).

Do not miss Local Explorations: 17, which covers the famous Riviera Corniches – the magnificent coast roads linking Nice with Menton. And to escape the roar of the coast, there are suggestions for exploring the Alpes-Maritimes on page 342.

SAINT-PAUL-DE-VENCE ⋈ ✕

On the D2/D107, *20 km* NW *of Nice.* Car-free, but overrun with tourists, Saint-Paul is one of the best-preserved medieval hill villages in the country. It is certainly picturesque all narrow streets, red roofs and sweeping views of the coast from the 16thC ramparts - but the best reason to stop here is a

• *Nice* plage.

knock-out modern art museum just off the beaten track I km up chemin des Gardettes, opposite the upper entrance to the village.

Founded in 1964, and housed in an inspired creation designed by José-Luis Sert, the **Fondation Maeght** experience begins at the garden gate. Set amidst a back-drop of pines, mirrored in shallow pools and ranged over lawns and split-level terraces, the sculpture garden takes on an increasingly surreal air as you encounter Calder's brightly-coloured mobiles, Miro's outsize fork, a massive Zadkine bronze, works by Hepworth and Arp, and Pol Bury's shimmering tubular water sculpture. Seen through the glass entrance hall, Giacometti's skeletal figures are the first of several inside-out perspectives as glass walls blend outdoor and indoor exhibits with the natural setting.

The permanent collection is outstanding – a massive Chagall life cycle, many Braques, whose stained glass can be found in the chapel alongside Ubec's *Stations of the Cross*; Kandinsky, Léger,

• *Opposite: Grand Canyon du Verdon.*

Matisse and more, plus new-generation artists. There are also temporary exhibitions, a cinema, library, café and a seductively well-stocked gallery shop.

SISTERON ⌂

On the N85, 150 km S of Grenoble. S.I. place de la République. Le Clou de Provence – 'the key to Provence' in local patois – Sisteron clings to the left bank of the River Durance. Its setting is spectacular, the medieval town crowded beneath a forbidding citadel, faces the Rocher de la Baume, a monstrous rock formation on the opposite bank. At mid-point on the *Route de Napoléon*, the Emperor approached this fortified gateway town with trepidation, but was greeted by cries of *"Vive l'Empereur!"*, and gained several recruits to the cause.

Partially-destroyed by Allied bombing in 1944, the oldest part of the **Citadelle** dates from the late-12thC. It

was built on the site of an even earlier stronghold, and the massive fortifications were added in the 16thC. A marked trail scrambles around the various levels, pointing out historic landmarks such as the tower where the future king of Poland, Jean-Casimir, was imprisoned in 1639. A 15thC Gothic chapel has been rebuilt and graced with fine modern stained glass windows. From the viewing table you can take a bearing on the distant Alps, and the Guérite du Diable (Devil's Look-Out) perches on a sheer cliff with views across town to the Rocher de la Baume. During the summer **Nuits de la Citadelle** festival, music, dance and drama productions are staged in the citadel's open air theatre (mid-July to August).

By-passed by a tunnel bored under the citadel, the town centre is worth exploring. Facing allée de Verdun, three towers belonging to the 14thC

RECOMMENDED RESTAURANTS

DIGNE
See Recommended Hotels.

GRASSE
Maître Boscq, F; *13 rue de la Fonette; tel. 93 36 45 76; credit cards MC, V; closed Sun, lunch only Nov-Easter.*

Tucked away in the Old Town restaurant quarter, Maître Boscq himself is busy dishing up sound regional cuisine for visitors to this pleasant bistro-type eaterie.

GRENOBLE
Auberge Napoléon, FF; *7 rue Montorge; tel. 76 87 53 64; credit cards AE, DC, MC, V; closed Sun-Mon lunch.*

Napoleon's lodgings transformed into a restaurant with a hint of First Empire elegance amidst modern mirrors, paintings and flowers. Prawns and scallops baked with orange vinegar, fish and aubergine timbale with a red pepper sauce. Attentive service.

Le Mal Assis, F; *9 rue Bayard; tel. 76 54 75 93; credit cards V; closed Sat-Sun Easter-Oct, or Sun-Mon in winter.*

Super little restaurant with a relaxed ambience, log fire and charming owners. Tempting menu features

include duckling with peaches and mouth-watering potato cakes, and a truly divine *marquise au chocolat.*

La Panse, F-FF; *7 rue de la Paix; tel. 76 54 09 54; credit cards MC, V; closed Sun, and mid-Jul to mid-Aug.*

Spot-lit modern surroundings and kitchen open to view. Favourite young executive hang-out at lunchtime (very good value **F** menu). Interesting menu choices: including herring pâté with whiskey, brill with sorrel sauce, curried scallops.

NICE
Chez Les Pecheurs, FF; *18 quai des Docks; tel. 93 89 59 61; credit cards AE, DC, V; closed Wed, Thur lunch in summer, Tues dinner in winter, and Nov to mid-Dec.*

Good harbour-side views from the small dining room and sidewalk terrace. The *à la carte* menu is devoted to seafood: *bouillabaisse* and *bourride* are specialities.

Grand Café de Turin, F; *5 place Garibaldi; tel. 93 62 29 52; credit cards, none.*

Fresh shellfish served all day every day in this matchbox-sized café with sawdust on the floor; the terrace houses the overflow. Very busy in the town walls still stand; and the Provençal Romanesque former cathedral, **Eglise de Notre-Dame**, dates from the 12thC.

If you plan to stay in town for a couple of days, and fancy a diversion, the **Centre Équestre Cante l'Abri** at Vilhosc (10 km E via D4/D217/D17, tel. 92 61 38 15) organizes pony trekking; or take to the air with gliding instruction from the **Union Aérienne Sisteron Durance** (tel. 92 61 27 45).

VENCE ⚐ ✕

On the D36, 22 km NW of Nice. S.I. place du Grand-Jardin. Set in the hills a little distance back from the coast, Vence's main attraction is the **Chapelle de la Rosaire**, avenue Henri-Matisse (l.5 km N of the town centre; open Tues, Thurs). This was Matisse's final major project, completed in 1951, as a gift to Dominican nuns who had nursed him through an illness. The austere simplicity of the smooth marble floor, black outlines depicting the Stations of the Cross and St Dominic on stark white ceramic-tiled walls, and rough-hewn stone altar provides a powerful contrast to the dazzling play of light filtered through the stained glass windows. Splashes of lemon yellow, brilliant azure blue and deep green shift across the scene, and Matisse's entire concept extends to the slender light fittings and dignified vestments.

Built on the site of a Roman settlement, the cobbled streets and little squares of Vence's Old Town are well-worth exploring. A stone gateway leads into **place de Peyra**, and a host of craft shops and boutiques. The **Cathédrale** has a mosaic by Chagall; and there are views of the Alps from **boulevard Paul-André**, which traces the town walls.

evening, good atmosphere: a place where paupers and princes happily rub shoulders.

Jean-François Issautier, (FF-FFF); *route de Digne (N202), 3km north of Saint-Martin-du-Var (27 km nrth-west of Nice); tel. 93 08 10 65; credit cards* AE, DC, MC, V; *closed Sun (except lunch Jul-Aug)- Mon, mid-Feb to mid Mar, ten days Nov.*

A delicious escape from the city, Jean-François Issautier's flower-filled Provençal *auberge* offers some of the finest regional cuisine around (two Michelin stars). His specialities include *courgette de Gattières avec sa fleur farcie*, veal kidneys casseroled with red onions and Bandol wine, and delectable desserts. Several local wines feature on the wine list, and the weekday lunchtime FF menu is incredibly good value.

La Rotonde, F-FF; *Hotel Negresco, Promenade des Anglais; tel. 93 88 39 51; credit cards* AE, DC, MC, V.

If you cannot afford the Negresco's much-praised main dining room, **Le Chantecler**, you can still dine off excellent steak tartare, salads, grills and more complex main courses in this amazing annexe tricked out like a fairground attraction and complete with crimson and gold circus carousel.

SAINT-PAUL-DE-VENCE

La Belle Epoque, F-FF; *1634 route de Cagnes, La Colle-sur-Loup (5 km S via D6); tel. 93 20 10 92; credit cards* AE, DC, MC, V; *closed Tues (except dinner in summer), Wed lunch in summer, and Jan.*

Just south of La Colle-sur-Loup, this is a much better bet than eating in Saint-Paul where everything is so over-priced. The good regional cuisine, welcoming *patronne*, and a sunny terrace in summer more than compensate for the somewhat kitsch decoration.

SISTERON

See Recommended Hotels.

VENCE

Auberge des Templiers, F-FF; *39 avenue Joffre; tel. 93 58 06 05; credit cards* MC, V; *closed Mon lunch in July-Aug, Sun dinner and Mon Oct-June, three weeks Dec-Jan 10, two weeks Mar.*

Delicious regional cooking in comfortable rustic dining room, plus a shady garden for long summer lunches. Market-fresh ingredients include tender Sisteron lamb.

See also Recommended Hotels.

South-Eastern France

Between Nice and Avignon
Côte d'Azur and Provence

303 km; map Michelin No 989

The eastern stretch of this crowded, glamorous and sun-soaked route traverses the Côte d'Azur between Nice and Marseille, and includes part of the famed Riviera. The official Riviera, which stretches 65 km from Cannes to the Italian border, is a hedonist's paradise of deluxe hotels, casinos, sumptuous restaurants, *haute couture* boutiques and massive yachts. It is also hideously over-developed in parts, uncomfortably crowded in July and August, and horribly expensive if you are not careful. However, there is good news if you are unimpressed by caviar and cachet: there are several seductive and reasonably priced hotels, the Mediterranean really is azure here, there is a spectacular treasury of 19th-20thC art on show, acres of gorgeous palm-fringed gardens, and you can escape to the hills with ease (see Hill Villages of the Alpes-Maritimes, page 342). This route describes the western end of the Riviera, while the eastern corner is featured in Local Explorations:17.

No visit, at least a first-time one, to the Côte d'Azur would be complete without a stop in Saint-Tropez; get away for a day to the idyllic island of Port-Cros off Hyères; and sup *bouillabaisse* in its home town of Marseille. The Provençal stretch of the route, between Marseille and Avignon, is graced by the quintessentially French city of Aix-en-Provence.

Along the Côte d'Azur there are several route options: the N98 generally hugs the coast, paralleled by the N7. Red routers can jump on the A8 *autoroute* and cut out the slower section between Fréjus and Aix-en-Provence, and can use the A7 between Aix and Avignon. The A8 is also useful for quick access to anywhere along the coast.

If you are heading to or from the direction of Lyon, this National Route can be taken in conjunction with France Overall: 12, connecting Lyon and Nice, which makes a tremendous alternative to the usual gallop down the N7/A7 Autoroute du Soleil.

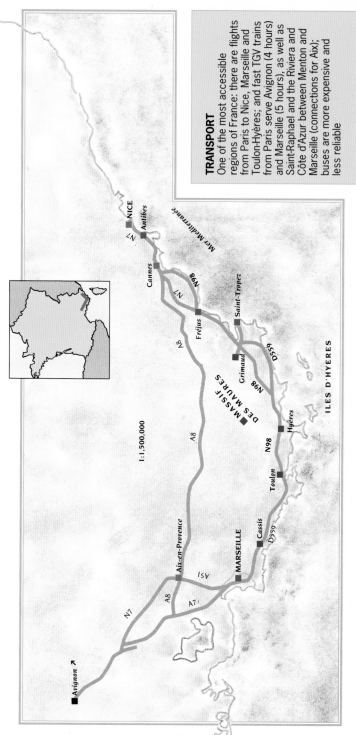

TRANSPORT
One of the most accessible regions of France: there are flights from Paris to Nice, Marseille and Toulon-Hyères; and fast TGV trains from Paris serve Avignon (4 hours) and Marseille (5 hours), as well as Saint-Raphael and the Riviera and Côte d'Azur between Menton and Marseille (connections for Aix); buses are more expensive and less reliable

SIGHTS & PLACES OF INTEREST

AIX-EN-PROVENCE ⇌ ✕

On the A51/A8, 31 km N of Marseille. S. I. place du Général-de-Gaulle. Settled by the Romans, who named it Aquae Sextiae on account of its hot springs, Aix was the capital of Provence from the 12thC until the Revolution. During the 15thC, René le Bon, Duke of Anjou, Count of Provence and King of Sicily, and indeed a true Renaissance prince, established a flourishing cultural tradition which distinguishes the town even today. Prosperous and cosmopolitan, host to a prestigious annual International Music Festival (mid-July to early August) and hordes of foreign students, Aix has been nicknamed Paris's 21st *arrondisement*, which is also a reflection on the cost of living here.

King René still presides over the festivities from a fountain at the top of **Cours Mirabeau**, a broad, tree-lined boulevard flanked by 17th-18thC mansions which divides the town centre in two. To the north, Vieil Aix is a bustling maze of narrow streets interrupted by little squares and frequent fountains. Aix is famous for its markets which invade **place Richelme** and the surrounding streets with a colourful profusion of local fruits, vegetables and great tubs of glorious flowers. Bargain hunters will also find a sprawling flea market centred on **place de Verdun**.

On rue Gaston-de-Saporta, the **Musée du Vieil Aix** (closed Mon, Feb) houses displays of Provençal crafts including puppets and *santons*, the traditional pottery crib figures found throughout the region. Further up the hill, the **Cathédrale de Saint-Saveur** is a notable hybrid with a 5thC baptistry, Romanesque aisle and 16thC additions. At certain times the custodian reveals the interior of a marvellous 15thC triptych illustrating the *Burning Bush* with King René and Queen Jeanne in attendance, plus the twin castles of Tarascon and Beaucaire. Behind the cathedral, the **Musée des Tapisseries**, place des Martyrs-de-la-Résistance, boasts a magnificent collection of 16th-17thC Beauvais tapestries housed in the former archbishop's palace (closed Tues).

On the south side of cours Mirabeau lies the largely residential **Quartier Mazarin**, named after Archbishop Mazarin, brother of the illustrious cardinal. In quiet streets, the flat-fronted 17th-18thC town houses appear smugly secretive behind their shutters.

There is the occasional splash of colour in a window box, a lovely fountain in **place des Quartre-Dolphins**, plus two more museums: the **Musée Arbaud**, 2a rue du Quatre-Septembre (closed Wed, Oct), with a distinguished library and notable collections of ceramics; and archaeology and fine arts in the **Musée Granet,** place Saint-Jean-de-Malte (closed Tues). The latter has a motley collection of dreary 18thC paintings, but also a Rembrandt, an Ingres and several minor Cézannes. Fans of Paul Cézanne (1839-1906) can explore the artist's home town with the help of a walking trail devised by the S.I. It treks out to his last studio, **Atelier Cézanne**, 9 avenue Paul-Cézanne, which has been preserved as he left it complete with painting smock, pipe and unfinished canvas (closed Tues).

Another detour on the cultural trail lies 4 km west of the town centre, the **Fondation Vasarély**, avenue Marcel-Pagnol at Jas-de-Bouffan (closed Tues). The 90-m long building constructed of giant black-and-white building blocks houses an eclectic selection of the 20thC Hungarian's expansive 'mural integrations'. Make of them what you will.

During the International Music Festival, accommodation and tickets are at a premium. The **Aix en Musique** festivities in mid-June are more relaxed (and affordable), and there is a dance festival in early July.

ANTIBES ⇌ ✕

On the N98 (N7), ll km E of Cannes/23 km W of Nice. S.I 11 place de Gaulle. Across the bay from Nice, *Antipolis* was founded by the Greeks, destroyed by the Barbarians, then revived as a strategically important fortified township during the Middle Ages. Now it is one of the last bastions of the Riviera's seriously rich, most of them staked out in palatial splendour on Cap d'Antibes. That said, there are several reasonably priced hotels on the Cap and in the pretty old town centre (see Recommended Hotels) which make Antibes a useful base for exploring Cannes and Nice without big city bustle and prices.

Nearby Juan-les-Pins offers a chance to rub shoulders with the *glitterati* in its swish nightclubs, some of the best on the Riviera Juan is now less Bohemian-ian than in the 1960s.

Little of medieval Antibes' fortifications remain except along the sea front where you will find the **Musée Picasso,** housed in the 12th-16thC Château Grimaldi (closed Tues). Picasso worked in the castle for six months from 1946, and the simply-restored, high-ceilinged rooms, flooded with light, make a marvellous back-drop for an extensive collection of• ceramics, drawings and paintings mostly completed during this short period. The exuberant *La Joie de Vivre* sets the tone, and photographs of the puckish artist by Bill Brandt and Man Ray amongst others add a pleasingly informal touch. Outside, Germaine Richier's slender bronze figures stand sentry over a pretty terraced garden (some very natty brickwork), etched against the horizon.

The D2559 runs around **Cap d'Antibes** via the beach. There are fine views from the lighthouse on **Plateau de la Garoupe,** and horticultural treats in store at the **Jardin Thuret,** off boulevard du Cap.

On the Picasso trail, you can make a quick trip to **Vallauris** (7.5 km W, off the N7). Pottery was an important local craft before Picasso came to live and work here after the Second World War; now the streets are lined with the stuff, most of it pretty awful. For the real thing, visit **Atelier Madoura,** off rue 19 mars 1962, which has the sole licence to reproduce original Picasso designs – at a price. The **Musée Picasso** (closed Tues), is a small chapel at the top of the main street adorned with the dramatic *La Guerre et la Paix* sequence, painted on plywood panels. On the main square, a bronze *Man with a Sheep* was Picasso's gift to the town.

An excursion to the craft centre of **Biot** (8 km N via N7, then W on route de Biot/D4) by-passes **Marineland**, with performing seals, dolphins and the odd killer whale. Biot's famous bubbly glassware is on sale from factory retail outlets along the way, and the **Musée Fernand Léger** displays tapestries, stained glass and ceramics by the 20thC artist (closed Tues).

AVIGNON
See France Overall: 5.

CANNES ⊨ ✕
On the N98/N7/A8, *33 km* W *of Nice.* S.I. *Palais de Festivals, La Croisette.* If sun, sand, starlets and shopping feature high on your holiday itinerary, Cannes is unlikely to disappoint. 'Discovered' by Lord Brougham in 1834, this backwater port was swiftly transformed into one of the big shots of the Riviera. These days, it is twinned with Los Angeles, and synonymous with big-time corporate junketing: the **Pridem** music festival is held here in January, and **The Cannes Film Festival** in May.

The focus of the action remains **La Croisette,** palm tree-lined with floral trimmings, more an event than a street, sandwiched between the Mediterranean and an imposinq battalion of very grand *palais-hôtels*. It is worth the price of a drink at one of the terrace-cafés to enjoy the stream of self-consciousness parading along the front. Then dig out your black belt in shopping and saunter down **rue d'Antibes,** or check out Chanel, suitably ensconced at No 5 La Croisette.

If you are absolutely determined to imbibe some culture, the **Musée La Castre** (closed Mon, Nov), in the old Le Suquet district, houses archaeological and ethnographic displays. On the swimming and sunning front, you will have to save up: access to the beach directly below the Palais des Festivals costs a ridiculous sum.

A far better idea is to escape to the two little **Iles des Lérins** on a ferry from the Vieux Port. Fifteen minutes across the Golfe de Napoule, **Ile Sainte-Marguerite** is dominated by a 17thC fort where the Man in the Iron Mask is said to have been imprisoned. There are several restaurants by the harbour, including **Frédéric**, where you can enjoy their special lobster with onions by the water's edge (a surprisingly delicious combination). Paths lead through the pine woods to rocky bathing places.

Another 15-minute ferry ride brings you to the enchanting **Ile Saint-Honorat.** A small colony of monks have lived here on and off since the 4thC, and they are the only permanent human presence amidst the pine and eucalyptus, wafts of wild honeysuckle, thyme

and rosemary. Bring a picnic and find a secluded spot off the path which circles the island.

CASSIS ⊨ ✕

Off the D559, 22 km E of Marseille. One of the few attractive beach resorts west of the Riviera, life in Cassis revolves around its picturesque small harbour sunk at the foot of towering limestone cliffs. The busy port area is edged by a colourful assortment of bars, shellfish and fish restaurants, such as no-frills **Le Flibustier**, and rather more chic **Chez Gilbert** – good places to watch staggering technicolor sunsets. Beaches stretch away to the east along **Promenade des Lombards**, or try **Plage de Bestouan** to the west. Boat trips offer a sardine's-eye view of **Les Calanques**, dramatic deep-water inlets slashed into the cliffs; and you can drive the **Route des Crêtes**, which starts 1.5 km W of town via the D559, and follows the cliff tops around to La Ciotat.

FREJUS ⊨ ✕

On the N98/N7, 35 km E of Saint-Tropez. S.I. *place Calvini.* Famous for peaches and summer-season bullfights, Fréjus derives its name from the Roman naval base of Forum Julii, founded by Julius Caesar in 50 BC. Veteran legionnaires were billeted here for a well-earned spot of R&R, and a map of the **Roman sites** (available from the S.I.) will help you track down the far-flung remains of the bath complex, theatre and amphitheatre (venue for the bullfights). Two of the original city gates, the Porte Dorée and Porte des Gaules, are still standing, as are uprights belonging to an aquaduct. To get around more easily you can hire bikes from Dewil, on avenue Victor-Hugo.

The **Cathédrale de Saint-Etienne** faces place Formigé, at the heart of the attractive Old Town. Largely rebuilt in the 13thC, it boasts a rare 5thC baptistry behind an elaborate iron grille in the porch. A graceful cloister with a painted ceiling gives onto the **Musée Archéologique** (closed Tues) displaying numerous Gallo-Roman finds, the wonderful *Leopard Mosaic* and sculpted heads of Jupiter and Hermes. Fréjus

harbour silted up after the Romans departed, so **Fréjus-Plage** is now 2 km S of the town centre, bordering **Saint-Raphaël**. It is hard to tell where you leave one town and enter the other, but Saint-Raphaël's higher prices may give it away. There is a greater choice of accommodation here, but Fréjus is cheaper and far more attractive.

There are two family excursions nearby: the **Aquatica** water park (off the N98; closed Oct-May) with slides, artificial wave pools and pedallos; and the **Parc Zoologique Safari** (5 km N via the D4), roamed by elephants, zebras and more.

GRIMAUD

On the Dl4, 5.5 km W of Port Grimaud. A pretty hill village in the Massif des Maures (see page 177), Grimaud sits back from the coast with views down to the Golfe de Saint Tropez from its **ruined castle,** once owned by the Grimaldi family. Take a stroll around town, up medieval rue des Templiers to the llthC Romanesque **Eglise de Saint-Michel.** Just outside the village, on the road down to Cogolin, there is a good pottery. Crafts are the forte of **Cogolin** itself, famous for the manufacture of pipes, reeds for wind instruments, and superior rugs and fabrics much in demand for period restoration projects.

Port Grimaud, just off the main N98 (6 km W of Saint-Tropez), allows non-residents a glimpse of how the other half live. Constructed around a series of miniature glassy-green canals, the pastel villas of François Spoerry's chic 1970s 'Mediterranean fishing village', complete with old-fashioned shutters and wrought-iron balconies, sit on fingers of land linked by jaunty little bridges. The family run-around is the yacht parked outside the front door.

HYERES AND ILES D'HYERES ⊨ ✕

On the N98, 18 km E of Toulon. S.I. *Rotonde Jean-Salusse.* Set back 5 km from the sea and beneath a ruined castle built by the medieval Lords of Fos, Hyères was one of the most popular l9thC not-quite-the-Riviera resorts. Queen Victoria and Tolstoy visited, and Robert Louis Stevenson wrote *I was happy only once; that was in Hyères.*

• *Opposite: Cannes, La Croisette.*

The broad avenue leading up to the Old Town is lined with palms, top sellers in the town's exotic plant industry. In **place Massillon**, the daily market is a colourful bustle: heaped stalls plying fish, fruit, vegetables and cut flowers press between the cafés and shops. Head on uphill to the **Eglise de Saint-Paul** with its Romanesque belfry and Renaissance door reached by a broad skirt of steps (open afternoons only). Above the town, take a rest on a bench in **Parc Saint-Bernard**. There are lovely views down to the coast, a mass of gorgeous Mediterranean flowers, paths and arbours, above which the citadel ruins invite investigation.

The beach resorts of **Hyères-Plage** and **Le Capte** lie on a narrow sand bar flanked by saltmarshes, which broadens into the **Presqu'île de Giens.** Ferries from Hyères- Plage and La Tour Fondue (on Gien) serve three offshore islands, once notorious pirate bases. Nearest, largest, and most popular with summer crowds, **Porquerolles** has beaches on the north coast, cliffs to the south, and bike hire from the

RECOMMENDED HOTELS

AIX-EN-PROVENCE
Les Augustins, FFF; 3 *rue Masse; tel. 42 27 06 88; credit cards* AE, DC, MC, V; *open year round.*
   On a quiet side street, off cours Mirabeau; 32 spacious, individually-decorated rooms in a luxuriously converted 12thC monastery.

Casino, F; 38 *rue Victor-Leydet; tel. 42 26 06 88; credit cards, none; open year round.*
   Extremely central (just off cours Mirabeau) with a friendly campus atmosphere. Basic accommodation; some rooms with bath.

Grand Hôtel Negre-Coste, FF; 33 *cours Mirabeau; tel. 42 27 74 22; credit cards* AE, DC, MC, V; *open year round.*
   Historic 18thC town house right in the town centre with rooms decorated in period style, and a marvellously antiquated lift.

Le Manoir, FF; 8 *rue d'Entrecasteaux; tel. 42 26 27 20; credit cards* AE, DC, MC, V; *closed mid-Jan to mid-Feb.*
   Quiet, friendly provincial hotel a short walk from the town centre, with 43 old-fashioned rooms; breakfast in a 14thC cloister.

Mas d'Entremont, FF; *Montée d'Avignon (off N7, 2 km NW of Aix); tel. 42 23 45 32; credit cards* MC, V; *closed Nov to mid-Mar (restaurant closed Sun dinner and Mon lunch).*
   Stylish Provençal farmhouse with tiled floors, wooden beams and rustic furniture, though the 17 rooms are more modern in style. Delightful gardens with a shaded swimming pool, and a covered dining terrace.

ANTIBES
Hôtel du Cap Eden-Roc, FFF; *boulevard J-F Kennedy; tel. 93 61 39 01; credit cards, none; closed Nov to beginning Mar.*
   Fabulous cream-and-grey Victorian *palais-hôtel* in an immense park on the tip of Cap d'Antibes. Said to be depicted in F. Scott Fitzgerald's *Tender is the Night*, it has exquisite rooms and suites; excellent sports facilities including watersports at the Club Nautique; also an elegant gourmet restaurant, **Le Pavillon Eden-Roc**, perched on the shore.

Mas Djoliba, FF-FFF; 29 *avenue de Provence; tel. 93 34 02 48; credit cards* AE, DC, MC, V; *open year round.*
   Lovely small hotel in an old farmhouse surrounded by pretty, jungly gardens towards the Cap. Pool and vine-covered terrace; home-cooked evening meals.

La Gardiote, F; *chemin de la Garoupe; tel. 93 61 35 03; credit cards* AE, DC, V; *closed Nov-Feb.*
   Right in the middle of the exclusive Cap, the pink-washed Gardiote is refreshingly simple and inexpensive, with 21 effectively furnished rooms and a lovely wistaria-clad terrace.

Nouvel, F; *place Guynemer; tel. 93 34 44 07; credit cards, none; open year round.*
   Simple, cheap, and excellent value for its central location right by the Old Town.

busy port or combined with ferry tickets. Mysterious little **Port-Cros** is a national park, and a Mecca for plant lovers. It has few beaches. Take the 10-km hike around the verdant island along winding footpaths, or cross the western corner via the Vallon de la Solitude trail which starts by the Manoir hotel (see Recommended Hotels) and returns along the cliff tops. **Levant** is a strange juxtaposition of military base and nudist colony (Heliopolis) – day trippers are not encouraged.

MARSEILLE ⊯ ✕
On the A7/A52, 188 km W of Nice. S.I. 4 La Canebière. Marseille is France's second largest city, a seamy, steamy Mediterranean port simmering in a semi-circle of barren hills. Phoenician traders founded Massalia in around 600 BC. At different times the Romans and the French crown battled for control; crusaders and legionnaires sailed from the harbour to North Africa. Many Africans made the journey in reverse, in numbers which galvanized xenophobic voters to support Jean-Marie Le

Royal, FF; *boulevard Maréchal-Leclerc; tel. 93 34 03 09; credit cards* AE, MC, V; *closed Nov to mid-Dec.*
    There are views of the beach and Old Town from 27 of the 37 rooms in this comfortable old hotel. On the sea front, with a private beach; terrace dining in the restaurant.

CANNES
Carlton Intercontinental, FFF; 58 *La Croisette; tel. 93 68 91 68; credit cards* AE, DC, MC, V; *open year round.*
    Famed *palais-hôtel* stretching a whole block along the sea front fringed by palms and flowers. Marbled halls; 300 sumptuous and gilded rooms with prices which soar according to view. Chic terrace; elegant gourmet restaurant, **La Côte**; private beach with watersports.
    Its arch-rivals along La Croisette are the **Majestic** (tel. 93 68 91 00); and the recently revived **Martinez** (tel. 93 94 30 30).

Gray d'Albion, FFF; *36 rue des Serbes; tel. 93 68 54 54; credit cards* AE, DC, MC, V; *open year round.*
    Very swish, very attractive modern hotel set back from the sea front in the heart of the shopping district, but with its own private beach, naturally. Deluxe rooms; choice of eateries including the gourmet **Royal Grey** (*see Recommended Restaurants*).

Molière, FF; *5 rue Molière; tel. 93 38 16 16; cards* AE, MC, V; *open year round.*
    An oasis of peace and greenery 100 m north of La Croisette. There are 45 very reasonably priced rooms (most with balcony); front garden with outdoor seating; helpful staff.

Paris, FF; *34 boulevard d'Alsace; tel. 93 38 30 89; credit cards* AE, DC, MC, V; *closed mid-Nov to mid-Jan.*
    Attractive, traditional hotel 300 m from the beach. Pool in the garden, plus a spa, jacuzzi and turkish baths.

Les Rochers Fleuries, F; *92 rue Georges-Clemenceau; tel. 93 39 28 78; cards, none; closed mid-Nov to mid-Dec.*
    Amazing value; 24 simple rooms and a garden to the west of town below Le Suquet hill.

CASSIS
Grand Jardin, FF; *2 rue Pierre-Eydin; tel. 42 01 70 10; credit cards* AE, DC, MC, V; *open year round.*
    Only just more expensive than the single F category, and right in the town centre, this conglomeration of little houses offers 28 rooms across from the public gardens.

Les Roches Blanches, FF-FFF; *Route des Calanques; tel. 42 01 09 30; credit cards* AE, DC, MC, V; *closed mid-Dec to end-Jan.*
    Super little modern hotel to the west of town. Views of the sea and Cap Canaille from the terraced gardens; private beach, pool and restaurant.

FREJUS
L'Oasis, FF; *rue Hippolyte-Fabre, Fréjus-Plage; tel. 94 51 50 44; credit cards* MC, V; *closed Feb.*
    Delightful small hotel with a little garden edged by pines a mere 100 m from the beach. *See also Le Vieux Four under Recommended Restaurants.*

Continued on page 174 ➡

RECOMMENDED HOTELS

➡ continued from page 173

HYERES
Les Pins d'Argent, FF; Port Saint-Pierre, Hyères-Plage; tel. 94 57 63 60; credit cards AE, MC, V; open year round.

Archetypal small French seaside hotel surrounded by pine trees, a minute's walk from the port. Family atmosphere, restaurant and pool.

Le Manoir, FF; Ile de Port-Cros; tel. 94 05 90 52; credit cards DC, MC, V; closed mid-Oct to May.

The home of the Buffet family which once owned the whole island, now run as a family hotel, but with an air of exclusivity. The 24 white-walled bedrooms are decorated with simple elegance.

MARSEILLE
Altéa Mercure-Centre, FFF; 1 rue Neuve Saint-Martin; tel. 91 39 20 00; credit cards AE, DC, MC, V; open year round.

Only just FFF, and still good value for its city-centre location, 5 minutes from the Vieux Port. There are 198 well-equipped, modern rooms, most with views. Exemplary service; fine dining at **L'Orsinade** – see Recommended Restaurants.

Moderne, F; 30 rue Breteuil; tel. 91 53 29 93; credit cards, none; open year round.

Very central, close to the Vieux Port, this bargain basement find is clean and decorated with rather wacky murals.

New Hotel Astoria, FF; 10 boulevard Garibaldi; tel. 91 33 33 50; credit cards AE, DC, MC, V; open year round.

Bright, spacious and fairly priced modern rooms off La Canebière.

Petit-Louvre, FF; 19 La Canebière; tel. 91 90 13 78; credit cards AE, DC, MC, V; open year round.

Venerable old hotel with views of the Vieux Port. Rooms are sound-proofed and comfortable, though simple; small, no-frills restaurant.

SAINT-TROPEZ
L'Ermitage, FF-FFF; avenue Paul-Signac; tel. 94 97 52 33; credit cards AE, DC, V; open year round.

Attractive old whitewashed house with green shutters a short climb from the town centre. There are 25 comfortable rooms (splendid views from the upper storey); breakfast in the garden.

Lou Cagnard, F-FF; 18 avenue Paul-Roussel; tel. 94 97 04 02; no credit cards; closed mid-Nov to late-Dec.

A budget find close to the town centre with fair-sized rooms and a small garden.

Lou Troupelen, FF; chemin des Vendanges; tel. 94 97 44 88; credit cards MC, V; closed Nov to mid-Mar.

A short distance from the centre, off the road to the beaches; well-appointed rooms with views; breakfast in the garden.

Le Yaca, FFF; 1 boulevard Aumale; tel. 94 97 11 79; credit cards AE, DC, MC, V; closed Nov to mid-Mar.

Exclusive small hotel in three 18thC buildings. Provençal furnishings and antiques decorate the attractive rooms, some overlooking the garden, others (with private terraces) the sea. Lovely pool terrace. Breakfast only.

TOULON
Altéa Tour Blanche, FF-FFF; boulevard Amiral-Vence, Super-Toulon; tel. 94 27 41 57; credit cards AE, DC, MC, V; open year round.

Peaceful, modern hotel perched above the city on the slopes of Mont Faron. It has well-equipped rooms, a pool-side garden and restaurant – see Recommended Restaurants.

Grand, FF; 4 place de la Liberté; tel. 94 22 59 50; credit cards AE, DC, MC, V; open year round.

Centrally-located in a fine old building overlooking splashing fountains; 46 spacious rooms.

Le Saint-Nicolas, F; 49 rue Jean-Jaurès; tel. 94 91 02 28; credit cards AE, DC, MC, V; open year round.

Restored 1930s city-centre hotel close to the place des Armes.

• *Marseille, Notre-Dame-de-la-Garde.*

Pen and his extreme right-wing Front National, though his popularity has faded somewhat recently. Despite racial tensions, the activities of local mobsters (known as *le milieu*), rampant unemployment and a crumbling infrastructure, Marseille has an undeniable, roguish charm, and is a pungent contrast to the genteel resorts further east along the coast.

The tree-lined boulevard of **La Canebière** slopes downhill to the Vieux Port, roughly dividing the city centre in two. The main shopping district lies to the south, between **rue de Rome** and **rue du Paradis**; a couple of blocks east (towards the port) is the red light district. North of La Canebière, the **Quartier Belsunce** is almost exclusively North African with street traders and hustlers at every turn. Down by the **Vieux Port,** the whiff of fish stalls is filtered through traffic fumes in a major olfactory assault, but the cafés provide views of the busy harbour. Ferries cast off full of trippers bound for **Château d'If**, the island prison where Dumas' Count of Monte Cristo languished alongside Huguenot 'heretics', political prisoners and debtors like Mirabeau.

On the north side of the port, the **Musée de Vieux Marseille** (closed Tues, Wed am) houses an eclectic selection of old prints and photographs, Provençal furniture and

175

crafts in the 16thC **Maison Diaman-tée**, on rue de la Prison. This was one of the few buildings to survive the demolition in the Second World War of the old Le Panier quarter, which in turn revealed the ancient Roman docks and relics displayed in the **Musée des Docks Romains** (closed Tues, Wed am), on place Vivaux.

Further west, by the new docks, the monstrous neo-Byzantine **Cathédrale Major** dwarfs the original Romanesque cathedral; cutting back east you find the lovely **Hospice de la Vieille Char-ité**, an enormous 17thC alms house with three tiers of arches and an oval Baroque chapel. A cultural centre now hosts exhibitions, and an archaeological museum.

The city's fine arts collections are on show in the imposing **Palais de Longchamps** (2 km E of the port). The **Musée des Beaux-Arts** (closed Tues, Wed am) is somewhat disappointing, though there is a notable series of political cartoons by l9thC satirist Honoré Daumier, and some fine sculpture including Marseille-born Pierre Puget's bust of Louis XIV. The 20thC collections in the **Musée Cantini**, 19 rue Grignan (in the shopping district), are more rewarding, with works by Dufy, Vasarély and Bacon to name a few.

Other diversions include a trek up to the hill-top basilica **Notre-Dame-de-la-Garde**, on plateau de la Croix, for panoramic views. Marseille's beaches are found south of the Palais du Pharo.

RECOMMENDED RESTAURANTS

AIX-EN-PROVENCE
Le Bistro Latin, F-FF; 18 *rue de la Couronne*; *tel.* 42 38 22 88; *credit cards* AE, DC, MC, V; *closed Tues lunch Jul-Aug, Sun dinner Sep-Jun.*

Not a stick of grissini in sight: instead, lashings of promising regional cuisine served up in comfortable, cosy surroundings. Excellent, reasonably priced set menus from a young chef: pigeon, rabbit, some seafood, herby cheeses.

Le Clos de la Violette, FFF; 10 *avenue de la Violette*; *tel.* 42 23 30 71; *credit cards* AE, V; *closed Sun-Mon lunch, and three weeks Mar.*

A short distance north of Vieil Aix, Jean-Marc Banzo is busy cooking up a reputation for inspired regional cuisine. Only the freshest and finest local produce will do, laced with the scents of Provence: lamb from the Alpilles, oysters with a creamy thyme sabayon, seafood on a bed of fresh herbs, and look out for desserts flavoured with lavender and honey, specialties of the Drôme region.

In summer, the dining room spills out into the gorgeous garden, which is just the place to take advantage of the terrific value (FF) *prix-fixe* lunch menu.

Kéops, F; 28 *rue de la Verrerie*; *tel.* 42 96 59 05; *cards* AE, V; *closed Mon, Nov.*

For a complete change, Egyptian food in an atmospheric basement dining room with cushions and low tables.

ANTIBES
Auberge Provençale, FF; 61 *place Nationale*; *tel.* 93 34 06 73; *credit cards* AE, MC, V; *closed Wed Sep-Jun, and mid-Nov to mid-Dec.*

Tucked behind a dreary façade in the Old Town, this pretty patio dining room features brick walls and a relaxed ambience. The fish is particularly good – seafood salad with basil, sea bream baked with fennel.

Du Bastion, FF; 1 *avenue Général-Maizière*; *tel.* 93 34 13 88; *credit cards* AE, DC, MC, V; *closed Sun dinner-Mon (except in summer), mid-Nov to mid-Dec, and three weeks Mar.*

On the medieval ramparts, and worth a visit for its setting alone. Warm welcome and delicious fish dishes from *bouillabaisse* to tasty medallions of monkfish with a delicate sea urchin sauce; also meat dishes. Arrive early, and snap up a table on the terrace if you can.

Le Romarin, F-FF; 28 *boulevard Maréchal-Leclerc*; *tel.* 93 61 54 29; *credit cards* MC, V; *closed Wed, mid-Dec to mid-Jan.*

Friendly, unfussy family restaurant on the road to Cap d'Antibes and the beaches. The house speciality is traditional Provençal *bourride*, a sort of

If you are after picnic materials, there is a daily market on **place Jean-Jaurès** in the lively student quarter, which is also useful for budget restaurants. The **Centre Bourse** is handy for general shopping, and has a huge car park convenient for the city centre. Marseille has a *métro* service, and there are regular train and bus connections along the coast.

MASSIF DES MAURES

Behind the coast between Fréjus and Hyères, the Massif des Maures is named for the old Provençal word *maouro,* meaning 'dark forests'. The ragged, sun-baked hills are swathed in gnarled cork oaks and sweet chestnuts, vines grow on the few open slopes and valleys, and the handful of roads which penetrate into the Massif twist and turn savagely between ancient villages.

From Saint-Tropez (see page 178), there is an easy excursion into the foothills of the Massif via **Grimaud** (see page 171). From here the road (D558) continues to picturesque **La Garde-Freinet** (10 km N), site of a former Saracen stronghold. If you want to see more, head west for **Collobrières**, another ancient village, where you can stock up on delectable *marrons glacés* from the local *confiserie,* and track down the isolated but lovely ruins of **La Chartreuse de la Verne,** a former monastery signposted off the Grimaud road (D14) 6 km E of the village.

---

poor man's *bouillabaisse*, but just as delicious to my mind.

CANNES
Le Bouchon, F; *10 rue de Constantine; tel. 93 99 21 76; credit cards AE, V; closed Mon.*

Bustling local bistro still catering for the native Niçois on a cheap night out. Straightforward, familiar dishes from seabass with basil to duck *à l'orange.*

Caveau 30, F-FF; *45 rue Félix-Faure; tel. 93 39 06 33; credit cards AE, DC, MC, V.*

Always open and busy with a 1930s interior and wicker chairs on the pavement terrace.Oysters to start, maybe, followed by fish or duck, and profiteroles swimming in a river of chocolate sauce, or drunken plum ice-cream.

Feu Follet, F-FF; *place de la Mairie, Mougins (7 km N via N85); tel. 93 90 15 78; credit cards none; closed four weeks-Mar -Apr, Sun dinner-Mon.*

Spearheaded by celeb. Chef Roger Vergé, Mougins has become a Mecca for costly restaurants of the 'temple of food' type. Sweep imperiously past all these and draw up instead at Feu Follet. Sit on the pavement terrace (though the dining room is pleasant too) and enjoy the excellent-value set menu: straightforward regional cooking at its best.

La Mère-Besson, FF; *13 rue des Frères-Pradignac; tel. 93 39 59 24; credit cards AE, DC, MC, V; closed Sun (except Jul-Aug).*

Welcoming and real 'like mother used to make it' cookery. Rotating daily specials such as *aioli* (*crudités* with garlic mayonnaise), shoulder of lamb and monkfish *niçoise.*

Le Monaco, F; *15 rue 24-Août; tel. 93 38 37 76; credit cards, none; closed Sun, and mid-Nov to mid-Dec.*

Long-established neighbourhood bistro offering great value set-price menu with a terrific choice of regional dishes – *salade niçoise, aioli,* lamb kebabs and home-made puddings.

Le Royal Gray, FFF; *Gray d'Albion Hotel, 38 rue des Serbes; tel. 93 99 04 59; cards AE, DC, MC, V; closed Sun-Mon (except Mon dinner in summer), and Feb.*

Refreshingly contemporary dining room that is nonetheless elegant and extremely comfortable. Constantly innovative, chef Jacques Chibois' subtle concoctions never cease to amaze and delight – butterfly prawns with the lightest *chiffonade* of basil; field mushrooms stuffed with their stems; sautéed calf's liver served with asparagus; lamb or chicken roasted with baby artichokes and onions or broad beans: all simple but sensational, as were tiny wild strawberries in a rhubarb coulis.

Continued on page 180 ➡

• *Saint-Tropez.*

SAINT-TROPEZ ⇌ ✕

On the D98A, 75 km W of Cannes. S.I. quai Jean-Jaurès. 'Discovered' by artist Paul Signac in 1892, the jet-set village of Saint-Tropez can actually claim a history BB (Before Bardot). Founded by the Greeks, the small fishing port lies on a peninsula facing a lovely sheltered bay. It is named for St Tropes, who, it is said, was decapitated by Nero in ancient Rome, his body placed in a small boat with a dog and a cockerel. The strange shipment finally wound up here. The saint's feast day is celebrated with a colourful *bravade* procession in mid-May.

Signac's arrival initiated another procession, this time of Impressionist and Fauvist artists – Bonnard, Derain, Dufy, Vlaminck – who were followed by Colette and the Bohemian set in the 1920s and 30s. Roger Vadim's 1956 *Et Dieu Créa la Femme*, starring Bardot, heralded a new generation of St-Trop fans, and the local fishing smacks were soon dwarfed by sleek, multi-mi! lion-dollar gin palaces, the fishermen outnumbered by fashionable *glitterati*.

At the heart of the action, the **Vieux Port** is encircled by busy quay-side cafés and restaurants facing a line-up of ritzy yachts. (Why are gladiolis so popular for their flower arrangements?) Gawpers pick their way past ranks of artists' easels.

For a lesson in local art history, look no further than the excellent **Musée de l'Annonciade** (closed Tues, Nov) on the west side of the harbour. A catalogue of the best in French painting from the period 1890-1940, there is marvellous local colour from the likes of Matisse, Seurat, Vuillard, Utrillo; Derain's views of Westminster; a fine Maillol bronze; and comfy leather armchairs in which to sit and contemplate.

To reach the 16thC **Citadelle**, zigzag up the shady, narrow streets of the picturesque Old Town, thoughtfully designed to break the force of the *mistral* winds which lash the bay with startling ferocity, particularly in spring. From the ramparts of the hexagonal fortress there are terrific views, reaching as far as the Alps on a clear day; also a small maritime museum with sea-faring relics from a reconstructed Greek galley to a dissected torpedo.

Saint-Tropez's beaches lie mainly to the south of town, a couple within easy walking distance. In summer, beach shuttle buses from place des Lices serve **Les Salins, Tahiti-Plage**, and its 5-km continuation, the sand strip called **Pampelonne**. Parking is expensive. There are sections of pay-beach which provide sun loungers and umbrellas; restaurants and concessionaires cater for the hungry and thirsty; and windsurfer boards are for hire at frequent intervals.

Behind Pampelonne, you can escape into the hills by taking the D93/D61 to **Ramatuelle**, then follow signs to **Gassin**, which is on a picturesque road (fine views) past three decrepit windmills. Once a Moorish stronghold, Gassin is tiny, pretty and well-stocked with seductive restaurants perfect for a long, lazy lunch or romantic dinner. Then drive north through the vineyards to join the D61/N98A.

You cannot reach Saint-Tropez by train, but there are buses from Saint-Raphaël and Toulon. Once there, mopeds and bicycles can be hired from Louis Mal, 5 rue Quaranta. Be warned, accommodation is in very short supply in summer. The S.I. can help, but it is best to book ahead. Many hotels and restaurants close over the winter.

• *Opposite: Toulon harbour.*

TOULON ⚓ ✕

On the D559, 64 km E of Marseille. S.I. 8 avenue Colbert. Home port of the French Mediterranean fleet, Toulon's seafaring tradition can be traced back to the Romans. Work on the **Darse Vieille** (Old Port) began in 1589, then Richelieu set about building the naval arsenal which overlooks Vauban's **Darse Neuve** (New Port), and is still a force in Toulon's important shipbuilding and armaments industries. The city is hard-ly a major stop on the tourist trail, though a visit to the slave galleys was a popular curiosity item on the 17th-18thC traveller's itinerary. The practice of using convicts as slave labour to propel the navy was discontinued in 1748.

Between the main thoroughfare, boulevard de Strasbourg, and the port, the **rue d'Alger** quarter is the busy old town centre, packed with shops and restaurants. There is a daily market on **rue Paul-Landrin**, and a rather

RECOMMENDED RESTAURANTS

➡ *continued from page 177*

CASSIS
Chez Gilbert, FF; 19 *quai des Baux; tel.* 42 01 71 36; *credit cards* AE, DC, MC, V; *closed Tues (except lunch during summer), Sun dinner Oct-May, and mid-Nov to mid-Feb.*
    Smack in the middle of the port, the place to see and be seen in. Great views at sunset, grilled fish in all its guises, acceptable salads and steak-and-chips. Stick to the fixed-price menu if you don't want to lose control of the bill.

FREJUS
Lou Calen, FF; 9 *rue Desaugiers; tel.* 94 52 36 87; *credit cards* AE; *closed Wed, mid-Dec to mid-Jan.*
    Close to the church and town hall, a little restaurant run with great care by François and Annie Gallione who cook and serve themselves. Their set price menu, which includes plenty of choice, is always imaginative and well executed.

Les Potiers, FF; 135 *rue des Potiers; tel.* 94 51 33 74; *credit cards* AE, MC, V; *dinner only in summer.*
    Diminutive ivy-clad building with window boxes tucked away in a quiet street near the Old Town centre. Homey atmosphere and menu featuring such goodies as scorpion fish with saffron and red pepper sauce, and duck with seasonal fruits.

Le Vieux Four, FF; 57 *rue Grisolle; tel.* 94 51 56 38; *credit cards* AE, DC, MC, V; *closed Sun lunch mid-Jul to mid-Sep, Mon rest of year, mid-Nov to mid-Dec.*
Delightful little rustic restaurant with heaps of character and broad-ranging cuisine to suit all tastes. Delicious salmon seeped in olive oil and lime. Also eight simple and reasonably priced rooms in a central location.

HYERES
Les Jardins de Bacchus, FF; 32 *avenue Gambetta; tel.* 94 65 77 63; *credit cards* AE, MC, V; *closed Sun dinner, three weeks May-Jun.*
    Classic Lyonnais cuisine revolutionized by exposure to Provençal influences. Bacchanalian decoration, and interesting specialities such as red mullet with *tapenade* (a paste of crushed black olives).

MARSEILLE
Les Arcenaulx, F-FF; 25 *cours d'Estienne-d'Orves; tel.* 91 54 39 37; *credit cards* AE, DC, MC, V; *closed Sun-Mon.*
    Favourite haunt of literary types with its bookshop and exhibition space, this is the place to sample intelligent light cuisine and leave weightier matters to discussion.

Castelmuro, F; 37 *rue Francis-Davso; tel.* 91 54 32 30; *credit cards* DC, V; *closed Sun.*
    After 150 years, something of a Marseille institution. Wide choice of unpretentious main courses from home-cooked ham to fresh fish, plus salads and sandwiches.

Cousin Cousine, FF; 102 *cours Julien; tel.* 91 48 14 50; *credit cards* AE, DC, V; *closed Sun-Mon.*
    A real find, with a terrace for sunny days and astoundingly good value menus. Among the regional specialities, look for *soupe au pistou*, a won-

gloomy 11th-17thC **Cathédrale**, off rue Emile-Zola. The dignified Baroque **Eglise de Saint-François**, place Louis-Blanc, is more attractive. Naval historians can get to grips with the development of the port and the French navy in the **Musée Naval**, place Monsenergue; while the **Musée des Beaux-Arts et d'Archéologie**, with some good l9th-20thC paintings, is off rue du Maréchal-Leclerc, together with the natural history museum.

Looming above Toulon, **Mont Faron** can be reached by funicular from Super-Toulon (bus 40 to boulevard Amiral-Vence), or by car. Drink in the views, and check out the **Musée Memorial du Debarquement,** which commemorates the 1944 Allied landings with dioramas, memorabilia and period news footage. There is a **Zoo** close by, below the ruined **Fort Croix-Faron,** another vantage point.

---

derful vegetable soup with red beans and tomato flavoured with basil.

L'Orsinade, FF-FFF; *Altéa Mercure-Centre, 1 rue Neuve Saint-Martin; tel. 91 39 20 00; credit cards AE, DC, MC, V; closed Sun, Aug.*

One of Marseille's first *nouvelle cuisine* restaurants, and still among the best. Smart, modern dining room with good service; the menu included chicken breasts cooked with farmhouse goat's cheese, and sea bass baked in a fresh seaweed crust.

SAINT-TROPEZ
Le Chabichou, FFF; *avenue Maréchal-Foch; tel. 94 54 80 00; credit cards AE, DC, MC, V; closed lunch July-Aug, mid-Oct to mid-Apr.*

When Michel Rochedy brings his formidable skills to bear on Provençal ingredients, the results are sublime. Chilled local oysters delicately flavoured with anis on a bed of slivered vegetables sprinkled with caviar; prawn and red mullet tempura scented with saffron; kid baked with garlic and thyme; baked apricots served with pistachio ice cream. The pretty circular dining room is augmented by a garden terrace; the service is excellent; and the wine list features several unusually good local wines.

L'Echalotte, FF; *35 rue Allard; tel. 94 54 83 26; credit cards AE, MC, V; closed mid-Nov to Dec.*

Easy to miss, and the dining room may look deserted in summer when everyone is out on the rear patio tucking into scrumptious sardine mousse with vegetable coulis, char-grilled steaks, lamb or chicken and delectable *patisseries*.

Le Girelier, FF; *quai Jean-Jaurès; tel. 94 97 03 87; credit cards AE, DC, MC, V; closed Thur (except evenings Jul-Aug), Jan to mid-Mar.*

It is important to know where to pose in St Trop, and this quay-side haunt is one place to start. Fish soup with peppery *rouille*, steaks; salads; palatable local wines, and a comfortably chic clientele.

Other 'in' spots that won't cost an arm and a leg include **Le Senequier**, just down the quay; the **Café des Arts** on place des Lices; and **La Flou**, 5 rue des Féniers.

TOULON
Au Sourd, F; *10 rue Molière; tel. 94 92 28 52; credit cards, none; closed Sun-Mon.*

By place Victor-Hugo at the top of the Old Town, this is a good seafood spot serving *bouillabaisse*, platters of shellfish and other fish dishes at reasonable prices.

Le Dauphin, FF; *21 bis rue Jean-Jaurès; tel. 94 93 12 07; credit cards MC, V; closed Sat lunch, Sun, and two weeks Aug.*

Quiet, friendly restaurant in the city centre. Tasty fresh haddock and green pepper salad, chicken poached in local Bandol wine, and a heavenly nougat ice cream.

La Tour Blanche, FF; *in Altéa Hotel, boulevard Amiral-Vence, Super-Toulon; tel. 94 24 41 57; credit cards AE, DC, MC, V.*

Marvellous views across the city at night, attentive service and classic cuisine: zucchini stuffed with oysters, lobster salad, roast lamb with a salt crust.

Central France

Between Nantes and Paris
The Loire Valley

440 km; maps Michelin Nos 232 and 237

Playground of the Renaissance court, the Loire Valley stretches along the fertile banks of France's longest river in a delectable array of châteaux and vines, orchards and woodlands. The land of a thousand châteaux (a blanket term used to describe anything from a fortress to a pleasure palace to a glorified country house) also has a reputation for devouring unwary tourists alive. Seduced by guide books, enthusiasm and the sheer proximity of the châteaux, many visitors overdo it. The result, château-fatigue, can put you off turrets and tapestries for life.

The region offers all kinds of alternative distractions. One of the most compelling is picnicking. Do a château in the early morning before the crowds, then find a suitable stretch of river bank for the afternoon, armed with a wedge of *rillettes*, the local coarse pork pâté, goat's cheese from Saint-Maure, fresh bread, fruit and a bottle of Chinon. The banks of the Loire itself are not recommended. When not in spate (swirling with torn branches and flooding the pastures and woods), it can be a treacherous maze of sandbanks and quicksands. Tributaries such as the Vienne near Chinon; the Loir north of Angers, the Indre which winds its way down to Loches; or the Cher around Chenonceaux are a delight and safe for swimming and kayaking.

Château country is also ideal cycling terrain, with bicycle hire in every main town and at most SNCF stations. Campsites are plentiful and well-equipped (the Ile d'Or site at Amboise has a pool, bike and kayak hire plus a free view of the *son et lumière* show at the château). All the major châteaux are open daily, and local S.I.s have details of *son et lumière* performances on summer evenings. Another welcome innovation is the gradual phasing out of the guided tours, a form of unmitigated torture for non-French speaking visitors. Decent foreign language leaflets now assist self-guided tours.

This section concentrates on the Loire between Angers and Blois, linked to Nantes and Paris by the A11 and A10 *autoroutes* respectively. The faster roads run north of the Loire, but the prettiest routes and my personal selection of three red route châteaux lie to the south.

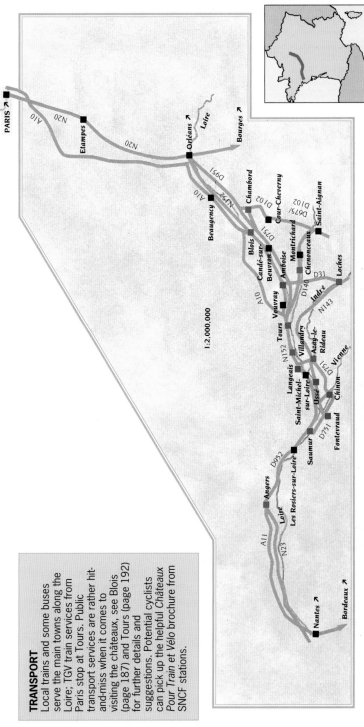

TRANSPORT

Local trains and some buses serve the main towns along the Loire; TGV train services from Paris stop at Tours. Public transport services are rather hit-and-miss when it comes to visiting the châteaux, see Blois (page 187) and Tours (page 192) for further details and suggestions. Potential cyclists can pick up the helpful *Châteaux Pour Train et Vélo* brochure from SNCF stations.

SIGHTS & PLACES OF INTEREST

AMBOISE 🚣 ✕

On the D751, 25 km E of Tours. S.I. quai Général-de-Gaulle. A rather charmless small town, Amboise parades the pre-requisite château, but its saving grace is Clos-Lucé, the highly entertaining twilight home of Italian Renaissance genius Leonardo da Vinci (see below).

The **Château Royal d'Amboise** dominates this section of the Loire from its hill-top perch. Charles VIII was born here in 1470, and initiated much of the building you see today – about one-fifth of the château's size before the Revolution. Key sights are the 16thC Logis Royal; the Tour des Minimes with its revolutionary carriage ramp; and the delightful Gothic Chapelle de Saint-Hubert built for Anne de Bretagne.

Da Vinci arrived in Amboise around 1515 at the invitation of François I. He spent the last four years of his life at **Clos-Lucé**, a brick-and-tufa manor house now spruced up with Renaissance furnishings and displaying 40 scale models built from his designs by IBM (closed Jan). A bat-wing flying machine hovers over the stairwell, while various cannons and machine guns, a swivel bridge, a paddleboat and armoured tank like an animated oyster on wheels occupy the basement – all centuries ahead of their time, and useless for lack of power.

ANGERS 🚣 ✕

On the A11/N23, 90 km E of Nantes. S.I. place Kennedy. 'Black' Angers is a thoroughly agreeable town. The capital of Anjou, it marks the western end of châteaux country with an imposing fortress wrapped in a 1-km curtain wall of locally-quarried grey shale and 17 drum-like towers banded with white stone. The highlight of the **Château d'Angers** tapestry collections is the 14thC *Tapisserie de l'Apocalypse*, 76 panels (a total of 100 m x 5 m), which depict St John's visions from the *Book of Revelations*. It is stirring stuff, fantastically detailed and coloured, teeming with hail and brimstone, terrifying images of Armageddon and the final triumph of the heavenly host.

Jean Lurçat first saw the Apocalypse tapestry in 1938, and it was to inspire

---

RECOMMENDED HOTELS

AMBOISE
Château de Pray, FFF; *3 km NE via D751; tel. 47 57 23 67; credit cards AE, DC, MC, V; closed Jan to mid-Feb.*

Reasonably priced (only just **FFF**), delightful and unstuffy baronial pile dating from the 13thC. It has a restaurant, sunny gardens and charming young staff.

ANGERS
Hôtel d'Anjou, FF-FFF; *1 boulevard Maréchal-Foch; tel. 41 88 24 82; credit cards AE, DC, MC, V; open year round.*

Traditional hotel with spacious modernized rooms and a good restaurant.

Hôtel Saint-Julien, F-FF; *9 rue du Ralliement; tel. 41 88 41 62; credit cards V; open year round.*

Highly recommended and welcoming central hotel. Rooms are comfy and sound-proofed.

AZAY-LE-RIDEAU
Le Biencourt, F-FF; *7 rue Balzac; tel. 47 45 20 75; credit cards V; closed mid-Nov to mid-Mar.*

Charming small hotel near the château. Rafters in the bedrooms, some rooms in an annexe, and a garden patio.

BLOIS
Urbis, FF; *3 rue Porte-Côte; tel. 54 75 01 17; cards AE, V; open year round.*

Plain but comfortable and well-equipped modern rooms 100 m from the château.

CANDE-SUR-BEUVRON
Hostellerie de la Caillère, FF; *14 km SW of Blois via D173; tel. 54 44 03 08; credit cards DC, V; closed mid-Jan to Mar (restaurant Wed).*

Delightful little country hotel with a wonderful restaurant. Jacky Guindon's cuisine is light and succulent - perch with ginger and orange, pigeon with garlic, skate salad with capers and sautéed foie gras.

much of his artistic output. In 1957, nine years before his death, he began work on his own vision of the 20thC in a series of tapestries entitled *La Chant du Monde*, now housed in the **Hôpital de Saint-Jean** across the River Maine (closed Mon). The opening sequence is a grim reflection on nuclear war; later tapestries celebrate the delights of *Champagne* and the cosmic thrill of *La Conquête de l'Espace*. An adjacent gallery houses contemporary exhibitions (closed Mon Sep-Jun).

Near Pont de Verdun, montée Saint-Maurice cuts up the hillside to the **Cathédrale de Saint-Maurice**, at the heart of Vieux Angers. The tremendous carved portal gives on to a single nave supported by distinctive 12thC Angevin vaulting, while the transepts contain lovely rose windows. (A more complex arrangement of 13thC vaulting graces the choir of the Eglise de Saint-Serge, a 15-minute walk further north.)

Behind the cathedral, on place Sainte-Croix, the decorative **Maison d'Adam** is a favourite local landmark with criss-cross timbers and carvings including an apple tree. South along rue Toussaint, a 13thC church has been imaginatively converted into the glass-roofed **Gallerie David d'Angers** displaying a petrified forest of the 18th-19thC sculptor's works. Around the corner, the **Musée des Beaux-Arts**, 10 rue du Musée, runs the gamut from Italian primitives to the 20thC.

For classical and Oriental antiquities and a notable collection of Japanese engravings, head for the **Musée Pincé**, 32bis rue Lenepveu, arranged in a gorgeous Renaissance building (all closed Mon in winter).

AZAY-LE-RIDEAU ⌫ ✕

On the D751, 25 km SW of Tours. One of the loveliest of all the Loire châteaux, **Château d'Azay-le-Rideau** rises out

> **DETOUR – CHATEAUX NEAR ANGERS**
> A handful of appealing châteaux near Angers include **Château de Brissac** (20 km S via the N160/D748); **Château Montgeoffroy** (20 km E via the N147); and **Château de Plessis-Bourré** (18 km N via the D107).

CHENONCEAUX

Bon Laboureur et Château, FF-FFF; *tel.* 47 23 90 02; *credit cards* AE, DC, MC, V; *closed mid-Dec to mid-Feb.*

Vine-draped auberge with several pretty rooms around a flower-filled courtyard. Smart traditional restaurant; pool.

CHINON

See Recommended Restaurants.

LOCHES

Hôtel George-Sand, F-FF; *39 rue Quintefol; tel.* 47 59 39 74; *credit cards* V; *closed Dec.*

Oak-beamed 17thC building with homey old-fashioned rooms. Traditional restaurant with a terrace overlooking the Indre.

SAUMUR

Hôtel Anne d'Anjou, FF; *32 quai Mayaud; tel.* 41 67 30 30; *credit cards* AE, DC, MC, V; *closed Christmas to New Year.*

A beautiful restored 18thC *hôtel-particulier* with views over the Loire. Glorious rooms, a pretty courtyard and good restaurant.

Le Cristal, F; *10 place de la République; tel.* 41 51 09 54; *credit cards* V; *open year round.*

Central and friendly with pleasant rooms some of which have views of the river.

See also Recommended Restaurants.

TOURS

Hôtel Balzac, F; *47 rue de la Scellerie; tel.* 47 05 40 87; *credit cards* V; *open year round.*

Hospitable small hotel in the city centre. Simple rooms and a breakfast terrace.

Hôtel Royal, FF; *65 avenue de Grammont; tel.* 47 64 71 78; *credit cards* AE, DC, MC, V; *open year round.*

Modern hotel just south of the centre. Attractive rooms which are decorated in the old-fashioned way (Louis XV-XVI). Bizarre but highly recommended.

• *Above: Chenonceaux; opposite: Tours cathedral.*

of its own reflection in a moat formed by the Indre. Built by François I's treasurer Gilles Berthelot between 1518 and 1527, it combines elements of the Gothic style with graceful early-Renaissance decoration, and the exterior has escaped unaltered down the centuries. Tours visit apartments furnished with 16th-17thC antiques and tapestries, and a portrait gallery lined with a useful *Who's Who* of the main players on the Renaissance scene.

In the village, one of the half-dozen or so outdoor cafés on place de la République makes a pleasant place to while away an hour or so over lunch or a drink, but they do get very busy in season.

BLOIS ⇔ ✕

On the N152, *60 km NE of Tours. S.I. 3 avenue Jean-Laigret.* The lively northern hub of château country, Blois basks on a hillside reflected in the Loire. The eclectic **Château de Blois** was a favourite royal seat and spreads its various wings in an homogenous range of architectural styles from its medieval origins in the 13thC right up to the 17thC Classical phase. François I's Renaissance wing has a marvellous

---

DETOUR – CHATEAUX NEAR BLOIS
There are two small châteaux within easy reach of Blois by car or even bike. The closest is **Château de Beauregard** (8 km S via the D765/D956; closed mid-Jan to mid-Feb), a former hunting lodge in the Forêt de Russy, with a riveting 17thC portrait gallery depicting 15 French kings, their families, courtiers, foreign and church powerbrokers in 363 panels.

The gleaming white symmetrical façade of **Château de Cheverny** (13 km SE via the D765; closed Sun Jul-Aug) is pure Classical poetry. Built between 1604 and 1634, it remains unaltered and is still in the hands of descendants of the original owners, who keep a pack of hounds in the kennels for hunting. The interior houses collections of armour, tapestries and lavish furnishings. Summer season *son et lumière* performances recall the château's history with an honourable mention for Tintin's mate Captain Haddock, whose Marlinspike Hall was inspired by the central section of the château complete with porthole windows, more correctly known as bull's eyes.

187

octagonal outside staircase. Catherine de' Medici's apartments are gorgeous and riddled with secret hidey-holes. Her son, Henri III, had his rival, the powerful Catholic Duc de Guise, assassinated in one of the palace corridors in 1589.

Below the château, the **Eglise de Saint-Nicolas** is an old abbey church with a cloister and garden leading down to the river. To the east, around the 17thC **Cathédrale de Saint-Louis**, the streets and stairways of the old town are fun to explore.

The S.I. offers walking tours and, together with Autocars STD, 2 rue Victor-Hugo, has details of bus tours to various châteaux. Half- and full-day passes include special admission rates. Bicycles can be hired from the SNCF station as well as several hire shops.

CHAMBORD, CHATEAU DE

On the D33, 16 *km* E *of Blois.* A monument to François I's ego, this 440-room, 84-staircase, 365-fireplace hunting lodge is the biggest château in the Loire. Work commenced in 1519 to an Italianate design and continued despite various financial vicissitudes (including François' ransomed sons being left in the hands of the Spanish) until the king transferred his attentions to Fontainebleau. Later, Henri II found time to build a chapel and the 'Sun King' Louis XIV entertained with performances of Molière's plays.

With so many rooms to account for, furnishings are spread pretty thinly around Chambord, though the stonework is liberally decorated with salamanders, François' personal trademark and a symbol of longevity. The double spiral staircase (possibly from an idea by Leonardo da Vinci) is stunning, and the roof-top promenade, a dream landscape of chimneys, turrets, dormer windows and pinnacles, overlooks a vast domain on the edge of the Sologne. Deer and wild boar still roam the woodlands.

After the last day tripper disappears over the horizon, guests at the *Hôtel Saint-Michel* (**FF**; tel. 54 20 31 31) have the château grounds to themselves.

CHENONCEAUX ✉

On the D40, 33 *km* E *of Tours.* Queen of

DETOUR – **SIGHTS NEAR CHENONCEAUX**
Downstream from Chenonceaux, there are two diversions for the château-weary. A favourite Loire apéritif is sparkling Saumur wine with a dash of *framboise* (raspberry liqueur). *Framboise* and a score more liqueurs are produced by the old-fashioned **Fraise-d'Or** distillery (3 km E via the D176; open Easter to Sep).

The **ZooParc de Beauval**, near Saint-Aignan (25 km SE via the N76/D17), boasts monkeys, big cats, exotic birds and a petting corner in eight hectares of woodland and gardens.

the Loire châteaux, lovely **Château de Chenonceau** (no 'x') hovers above the River Cher trailing its two-storey bridge behind it like a wedding train. Its feminine grace is testament to four centuries of female influence from Catherine de Briçonnet, who oversaw the initial transformation of the site from riverside mill to country retreat for her financier husband Thomas Bohier between 1513 and 1521, to Madame Pelouse who undertook the 19thC restoration.

When Henri II presented the château to his favourite Diane de Poitiers in 1547, she hired architect Philippe de l'Orme to build the bridge and a formal garden. On the king's death, his queen Catherine de' Medici appropriated Chenonceau, sent Diane packing to dreary Chaumont, and rehired de l'Orme to cover the bridge, now the famous Grande Gallerie. (During the Second World War, when the Cher marked the border between occupied and Vichy France, the gallery was frequently used as a secret conduit between the two.)

Tours of Chenonceau are self-guided and the rooms decorated with appropriate furnishings, tapestries and paintings. There are painted ceilings, Delft-tiled floors, a wonderful small van Dyck in the Study, and a soothing view of the Cher from the Library windows. Look out for Primataccio's portrait of Diane de Poitiers in François I's room: it seems a trifle thoughtless that Catherine de' Medici hangs above

Diane de Poitier's fireplace. Don't miss the kitchens hidden away in the feet of the bridge with an effective waste disposal system.

CHINON ⊭ ×

On the D751, 47 km SW of Tours. S.I. 12 rue Voltaire. Stretched along the banks of the River Vienne, Chinon clusters beneath the walls of its ruined medieval fortress where Joan of Arc met the *dauphin* Charles VII in 1429, and set about regaining France for the French. Built on a strategic fortified site, **Château de Chinon** comes in three parts: Henry Plantagenet's Fort Saint-Georges; the 12th-14thC Château de Milieu where the Logis Royal houses waxworks and museum pieces; and the Fort de Coudray on a rocky spur (closed Dec-Jan).

Vieux Chinon offers a pleasing collection of gabled Renaissance houses and 17thC mansions. East of the town centre, a small museum by the tumbledown **Chapelle de Sainte-Ragonde** provides an insight into the cave-dwelling occupants of the *maisons troglodytiques,* dwellings hollowed out of the soft chalk.

Chinon is also a wine town with a rather down-market **wine museum** next door to the S.I. Automatons spout quotations from Rabelais, the 16thC humanist born in nearby **Devinière** (6 km SW on the D117). His birthplace has been transformed into a museum. Chinon also undergoes a transformation when the old town hosts the annual fancy dress **Marché Médieval** on the first weekend of August.

FONTEVRAUD, ABBAYE DE

On the D145, 14 km SE of Saumur. Founded in 1101, the enormous monastic complex at Fontevraud once served as a monastery, nunnery, hospice, leper colony and home for fallen women (housed in the Mary Magdelan wing). It has since done time as a state prison, so 19thC additions outnumber the original buildings, but the soaring Romanesque abbey church has survived. The church contains the tombs of Plantagenet kings and queens including Henry II, Richard the Lionheart (who died at Chinon), and Eleanor of Aquitaine.

Once believed to be a chapel, the octagonal mid-12thC **kitchens** are an unusual relic of medieval domestic architecture with vast fireplaces for smoking fish and meat. During the summer season, the Centre Culturel de l'Ouest puts on concerts in the church (details, tel. 41 51 73 52).

LANGEAIS

On the N152, 24 km W of Tours. A quiet town on the north bank of the Loire, Langeais groups around its business-like 15thC fortress. Beyond the drawbridge, **Château de Langeais'** courtyard presents a more welcoming Renaissance façade, and the interior with its mullioned windows, huge fireplaces and decorative floor tiles has been beautifully furnished and hung with tapestries (closed Mon Nov-Mar).

LOCHES ⊭ ×

On the N143, 43 km SE of Tours. S.I. place Wermelskirchen. Commanded by a feudal keep, the medieval walled town of Loches tumbles down a steep hillside to its modern annexe and the River Indre. Built by the Counts of Anjou in the 11thC, the ominous-looking **donjon** occupies the southern end of the hill top. Joint tickets cover tours of the chilling *cachots* (dungeons) and the regal living quarters, the **Logis Royal** to the north (closed Wed Oct-Mar, Dec-Jan). Part-feudal and part-Renaissance, the *Logis* is decorated with arms and armour, magnificent tapestries and hefty period furniture. Joan of Arc came here to persuade an unenthusiastic Charles VII to be crowned at Reims, and later the king kept his favourite mistress, the beautiful Agnès Sorel, at Loches. Her smooth limestone tomb and famous portrait half-in and half-out of her bodice are testament to her charms.

Anne de Bretagne's tiny Gothic ora-

DETOUR -- MUSEE CADILLAC
For a complete change of scene, Robert Keyaert's **Musée Cadillac**, at Château de Planchoury, Saint-Michel-sur-Loire (3.5 km W of Langeais via the N152; closed Jan) is the fulfillment of a childhood dream. The 50 gleaming automobiles with potted biographies constitute the largest collection of Caddies outside the U.S.

tory is another beauty, decorated with hand-carved stone tassles and diamonds.

The 12thC **Eglise de Saint-Ours**, place Charles-VII, is distinguished by its unusual pyramid spires; the porch and striking white stone interior are crawling with saints, sinners and evil-looking monsters. Down in the Porte Royale, the **Musée du Terroir** displays local history and craft exhibits; while the **Musée Lansyer** presents works by the 19thC landscape artist, engravings by Canaletto, drawings by Delacroix, and Japanese art, as well as rampart views (closed Fri).

NANTES
See *France Overall: 2.*

ORLEANS
See *France Overall: 7.*

PARIS
See pages 214-233.

SAUMUR ⇌ ✕
On the D952/D751, 45 km SE of Angers. S.I. place de la Bilange. A demure little town, famous for its sparkling wines and riding school, Saumur is an affordable base which offers several diversions. Much of the town centre is modern and unexciting; while the remnants of the old town lurk around the **Eglise de Saint-Pierre** with its carvings and tapestries.

• *Loches.*

A steep lavender-lined footpath winds uphill from place Saint-Michel to the Counts of Anjou's 14th-15thC **Château de Saumur** (closed Tues Oct-Mar). Shorn of its fairytale turrets and weather vanes depicted in the renowned book of miniatures, *Les Très Riches Heures du Duc de Berry*, it now houses the **Musée des Arts Décoratifs**, and the horsy but enjoyable **Musée du Cheval**, packed with lavishly decorated bridles and bits, saddles and stirrups. An army of 20,000 model soldiers parades in the **Musée de la Figurine-Jouet**, laid out in the powder store (open Apr-Sep).

The S.I. has details of *caves* open for visits and wine tastings. Gratien, Meyer et Cie, route de Chinon, is a good bet. Saumur's cavalry connection, the Ecole de Cavalerie, presents arms, battle-scene dioramas and dashing uniforms at the **Musée de la Cavalerie**, avenue Maréchal-Foch (closed Fri, Aug). For more up-to-date cavalry transport, check out the tanks and armoured cars on show at the **Musée des Blindes**, off place du Chardonnet.

The National Riding School, at Saint-Hilaire-Saint-Florent (3 km NW via the D751), opens its doors for tours of the stables and practice sessions by the

• *Opposite: the gardens, Villandry.*

legendary **Cadre Noir** riding team (open Apr.-Sep. except Sun and Aug). Dressed in black and gold, they also perform summer season shows and take part in the annual *Carrousel* equestrian and military parade in late July. While in Saint-Hilaire, check out the local *caves*. Not wine this time, but mushrooms flourish in the rock tunnels of the **Musée du Champignon** (open Feb-Nov). Seventy per cent of the nation's edible fungi grows near here in 500 km of underground galleries.

TOURS ⇥ ✕

On the A10/N152, 240 km SW of Paris/175 km E of Nantes. S.I. boulevard Heurteloup. Ancient capital of Touraine, commercial and transport hub of the Loire, Tours is a useful base if you are using public transport. It is also the place to practise your French as the native *Tourangeaux* are reputed to have the purest accent in the land.

The city centre on the south bank of the Loire is bisected by rue Nationale. To the west, the attractive **Vieille Ville** has been carefully restored with a clutch of pretty 15thC brick and timber houses, cobbled streets and courtyards around central place Plumereau. A small archaeological museum has been laid out in the stunning Renaissance **Hôtel Gouin**, rue du Commerce (closed Wed).

Across rue Nationale, the intriguing **Musée de Compagnonnage** in the Cloître de Saint-Julien, has assembled an eclectic array of old-fashioned craftsmen's tools with the masterpieces they were used to produce (closed Tues). The adjacent **Musée des Vins de Touraine** salutes the red wines of Chinon and Bourgueil, plus Vouvray whites, and lesser-known rosés – though tastings are not offered (closed Tues). Further east, the **Cathédrale de Saint-Gatien** traces the evolution of Gothic architecture from the 13thC to the 16thC. A former bishop's palace has assumed the role of **Musée des Beaux-Arts** in place François-Sicard, boasting some fine Renaissance works, Rembrandt's *Flight into Egypt*, paintings by Rubens, Boucher and Delacroix, and 18thC furnishings (closed Tues).

The S.I. can provide information about **châteaux tours** and arrange tickets for coach excursions. The main

bus and train stations are nearby with daily services to Amboise, Angers, Azay-le-Rideau, Blois, Chenonceaux, Chinon, Langeais, Loches and Saumur. Tour Evasion, at the Gare-SNCF (tel. 47 66 52 32), offers economical daily full- and half-day minibus tours to various destinations including Chambord, Villandry and Ussé. Around Tours is easy cycling country, and bikes can be hired from the train station or from Montaubin, 2 rue Nationale (make a booking in season).

USSE, CHATEAU DE

On the D7, 33 km SW of Tours. A fairytale confection of machicolated sugar-white stone topped by a jumble of grey slate turrets, dormer windows and striped chimneys it comes as no surprise to learn that Ussé claims to be the inspiration for Charles Perrault's 17thC romance *Sleeping Beauty* . The effect is enhanced by the deep green backdrop of the Forêt de Chinon and celebrated in summer-season *son et lumière* performances, but with the exception of the Renaissance chapel, tours are disappointing and the interior suffers from an invasion of deadly waxwork figures (closed Nov-Mar).

VILLANDRY, CHATEAU DE

On the D7, 15 km SW of Tours. The 16thC château is of secondary interest to the glorious **gardens** at Villandry (château open Mar-Nov, gardens open year round). You don't have to be a gardener to be bowled over by this fabulous reconstruction of a Renaissance garden in three parts, the most ravishing of which is the *jardin potager* (kitchen garden). Some 85,000 vegetable plants have been laid out in intricate geometric patterns between box hedges with feathery borders of golden celery and silver leeks. Exotic cabbages reveal frothy cream or violet hearts with the scent of roses carried on the breeze. Not a potato in sight, of course, for they were yet to be introduced from the New World.

To decipher the hidden allegories of the ornamental gardens (one a tale of love, the other a musical composition), it is necessary to climb the belvedere. Behind them, the water garden is arranged in neat gravelled paths and lawns around a large pool.

RECOMMENDED RESTAURANTS

AMBOISE

L'Epicerie, F; 18 *rue Victor-Hugo; tel.* 47 57 08 94; *credit cards* V; *closed Mon dinner-Tue, mid-Nov to mid-Dec.*

A handy spot facing the château with a spendid carved façade and good bistro-style food.

ANGERS

La Ferme, F; 2 *place Freppel; tel.* 41 87 09 90; *credit cards* V; *closed Wed, Sun dinner, three weeks Jul-Aug.*

A great people-watching terrace by the cathedral. Hearty traditional dishes such as *coq au vin* made with rosé d'anjou.

La Salamandre, F-FF; 1 *boulevard Maréchal-Foch; tel.* 41 88 99 55; *credit cards* AE, DC, MC, V; *closed Sun.*

Kitsch woodwork and a stained glass salamander, but there is nothing lightweight about the food. Excellent fish dishes and wild duck with cranberries.

AZAY-LE-RIDEAU

Aigle d'Or, F-FF; 10 *avenue Adélaïde-Richer; tel.* 47 45 24 58; *credit cards* V; *closed Sun dinner, Wed, one week Sep, one week Dec, Feb.*

Pretty dining room with a summer terrace. Interesting seasonal menus, good cheeses and affordable wines.

BLOIS

Au Rendez-vous des Pêcheurs, F-FF; 27 *rue de Foix; tel.* 54 74 67 48; *credit cards* V; *closed Sun-Mon lunch, ten days Feb, three weeks Aug.*

Super-charged bistro food that incorporates plenty of new ideas - carp with pumpkin, chicken fricassée with lemon grass and mussels.

See also Recommended Hotels.

CHINON

Hostellerie Gargantua, FF; 73 *Haute-Saint-Maurice; tel.* 47 93 04 71; *credit cards* AE, DC, MC, V; *closed Wed-Thur lunch (except Jun-Sep), mid-Nov to Mar.*

Welcoming rustic dining room and terrace in a 15thC building. Melt-in-the-mouth *omelette Gargamelle* with cheese and mushrooms, seafood *pot au feu.*

Also nine delightful bedrooms (FF).

LOCHES

See Recommended Hotels.

ROSIERS-SUR-LOIRE, LES

Auberge Jeanne de Laval, FF-FFF; 18 *km* NW *of Saumur via* D952; *tel.* 41 51 80 17; *credit cards* AE, DC, MC, V; *closed Mon Sep-Jun, Jan-Feb.*

Gourmet stalwart in the classical mould. Elegant dining room and a Michelin star for dishes such as fresh poached salmon in *beurre blanc* and tender young pigeon with truffles. Impeccable service.

You can find peace and quiet in the modest château-hotel annexe a short walk away.

SAUMUR

La Quichenotte, F; 2 *rue Haute Saint-Pierre; tel.* 41 51 31 98; *credit cards* V; *closed Sun lunch-Mon.*

One of several cheap eateries around the church, this *crêperie* also serves salads, grills and omelettes.

TOURS

La Ciboulette, F; 25 *rue de la Paix; tel.* 47 61 57 28; *closed Tues dinner-Wed.*

Friendly and antiquated old town establishment with a terrace, copious home-cooking and cheap local wines.

Jean Bardet, FFF; 57 *rue Groison; tel.* 47 41 41 11; *credit cards* AE, DC, MC, V; *closed Mon except dinner Apr-Oct, Sun dinner Nov-Mar.*

On the north bank of the Loire, M. and Mme. Bardet preside over this wonderful hotel-restaurant in its own park. Two Michelin stars for the sensational food – elvers poached in wine vinegar and garlic, oyster ragout with a delicate watercress mousse, guineafowl with truffles – and an exceptional selection of Vouvray wines.

<u>Central France</u>
Between Paris and Dijon
Lower Burgundy

315 km; maps Michelin Nos 237 and 243

B urgundy is a land of plenty. Its magnificent cathedrals compete for
attention with bastions of gastronomy and world-famous vineyards.
There is a colourful history of crusaders and Burgundian dukes; equally
colourful architectural features such as the traditional decorative roof
tiles; and a distinctive culinary pedigree laced with local specialities,
from mustard and *cassis* (blackcurrant) to edible snails, freshwater fish,
Charolais beef and classic wines.

It would be all too easy to design a route through this part of France
illuminated with clusters of Michelin stars, swanning from one Relais et
Châteaux hotel to the next – at the risk of bankruptcy. Any trip to or
through Burgundy should include one memorable repast – I found that a
couple of nights in decent small-town hotels, plus daily picnics bought
from amazing local delicatessens, releases sufficient funds for one or
two blow-out meals.

This route explores the heartland of lower Burgundy, swiftly by-
passed by the Paris-Beaune section of the Autoroute du Soleil (A6), the
main holiday route south to the Côte d'Azur. The A6 from the Paris
Périphérique is indeed the best route in and out of the capital for everyone, but only red route followers in a tearing hurry should stay on it the
whole way between Paris and Dijon. Instead, I suggest that red routers
leave the *autoroute* at Fontainbleau, and use the N6, the D965 and the
D905 to link my chosen red centres, or vice-versa.

Blue and green route followers could taste wine in the *caves* of
Chablis, visit the notable châteaux of Ancy-le-Franc, Bussy-Rambutin or
Commarin, even inspect an aniseed ball factory at Flavigny or take a trip
on the Canal du Bourgogne (see page 140). No one, not even red
routers, should miss the wonderful abbey at Fontenay.

For those wishing to explore this region in depth, Local Explorations:
13 can be joined at Avallon, while the area round Fontainebleau is
explored in Local Explorations: 8.

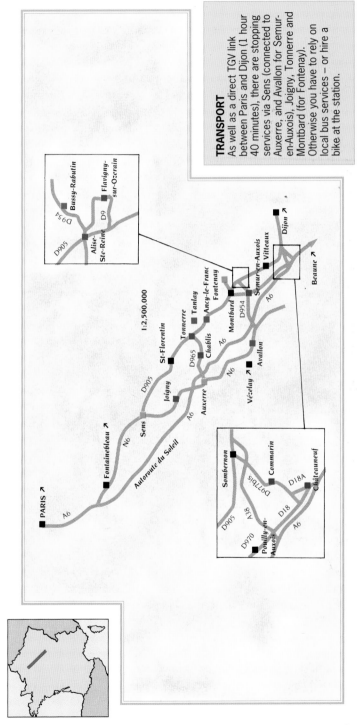

SIGHTS & PLACES OF INTEREST

ALISE-SAINTE-REINE (ALESIA)
On the D954, 14 km S of Montbard. Close to this small village, the ancient hill site of Julius Caesar's 52 BC victory over the Gauls is an atmospheric place to stretch your legs. Terrific views all around, dominated by a massive bronze statue of the Gaulish chieftan Vercingetorix – all flowing locks and walrus moustaches. For those with a genuine interest, there are also the excavated remains of Gallo-Roman Alésia, with various finds displayed in a museum.

ANCY-LE-FRANC, CHATEAU DE
On the D905, 12 km S of Tonnerre. France's first Classical Renaissance château, designed by the Italian architect Serlio around a splendid courtyard. Much of the interior decoration is by Il Primataccio, who worked on François I's Fontainebleau. Look for François I and Diane de Poitiers represented in the mythological murals – the house was built for her brother-in-law. The vast kitchens are a highlight, lined with row upon row of copper pans. Outbuildings house temporary exhibitions and also a collection of highly polished vintage cars. (Closed Nov-Apr).

AUXERRE ⇌ ✕
On the N6, 149 km NW of Dijon/166 km SE of Paris. S.I. 2 quai de la République. This is a convenient half-way stop if you are racing along the red route, but need a break. Of Roman origin, Auxerre is the capital of lower Burgundy, and the centre of a wine-growing region which includes the renowned Chablis vineyards.

Spread out over two hills beside the River Yonne, the attractive town centre boasts a wealth of fine Renaissance houses and an unusual 15thC **tour de horloge** with two dials, one for the time and the other for tracking the movements of the sun and stars.

Towards the river, the Flamboyant Gothic **Cathédrale de Saint-Etienne** was founded in 1215 on the site of an earlier Christian sanctuary. It took three centuries to build, and the imposing interior, with 15thC vaulting, contains fine 13thC stained glass in the ambulatory which is reckoned to rival the glories of Chartres. A Romanesque crypt is decorated with rare 11thC frescoes. Further north, along rue Cochois, the 13th-15thC **Abbaye de Saint-Germain** occupies the remains of a 6thC Benedictine foundation. A striking Romanesque belfry stands alone to the west; and the Carolingian crypts house some of France's oldest frescoes.

Well-worth a quick visit is the **Musée Leblanc-Duvernoy**, 9 rue d'Egleny (closed Tues), where you will find notable collections of 18thC Beauvais tapestries, decorative European earthenware, paintings and temporary exhibitions in a fine traditional town house.

A favourite local camera angle is the **Pont Paul Bert**, named for Auxerre's most famous son, the 19thC physiologist and statesman. From there, stroll

---

CANAL CRUISING
The rivers and canals of Burgundy make some of the best-known and most beautiful cruising in France, so consider working a trip into your schedule.

There are several possibilities: along the River Yonne between Auxerre and Montereau; along the Canal de Bourgogne between Joigny and Dijon, or along the exceptionally pretty (but popular) Canal du Nivernais between Auxerre and Décize. Boats are usually hired for one or two weeks, but it may be possible to arrange a shorter trip, especially out of high season. I can recommend Locaboat Plaisance, who operate their excellent *penichettes* out of Joigny. If self-hire is out of the question, then a pleasure cruise lasting anything from an hour to a day may be the answer. For details of self-hire and excursion cruises, contact Le Comité Regional de Tourisme de Bourgogne B.P. 1602, 21035 Dijon cedex, tel. 80 50 10 20 and ask for their brochure *Boating Holidays in Burgundy*. For a national list of cruiser operators, contact the Syndicat National des Louers des Bateaux de Plaisance, Port de la Bourdonnais, Paris 7e, tel. 45 55 10 49.

along the quayside to the picturesque **Quartier Marine**, an absorbing spot for crafts shops and antique hunting.

AVALLON ⊨ ✕

On the N6, 51 km SE of Auxerre. S.I. Grande Rue Aristide-Briand. Perched high above the River Cousin and the bottle-green mantle of the Forêt de Morvan, the ancient heart of this Burgundian market town sits on a granite

outcrop, its warren of cobbled streets and little turreted houses gathered around the 15thC **Tour de l'Horloge** and enclosed by ramparts. Facing the main street, the **Eglise de Saint-Lazare**, a former pilgrim church, presents two beautifully-carved doorways depicting musical Elders of the Apocalypse, signs of the zodiac, a seasonal cycle of husbandry, trailing foliage and flowers. Nearby, one of the surprise

RECOMMENDED HOTELS

AUXERRE
Hôtel Le Maxime, FF-FFF; 2-5 *quai de la Marine; tel.* 86 52 14 19; *credit cards* AE, DC, MC, V; *open year round.*

Attractive hotel overlooking the Yonne, with 25 pleasant rooms, and an entrance via the trellised courtyard. Expensive affiliated restaurant along the *quai*; plenty of cheaper alternatives nearby.

Parc des Maréchaux, FF; 6 *avenue Foch; tel.* 86 51 43 77; *credit cards* AE, V; *open year round.*

Welcoming town house hotel close to the town centre. Large and comfortable rooms; breakfast in the leafy garden during summer.

AVALLON
Moulin des Templiers, F-FF; *Vallée du Cousin* (4 km W on D427); *tel.* 86 34 10 80; *cards; none; closed* Nov to mid-Mar.

There are several pleasant small hotels along the river here, but this is the one I can recommend, and it makes a good base for Local Explorations: 13. The converted mill lies on the river, and offers 14 quiet, comfy rooms; breakfast on the flowery patio.

See also Recommended Restaurants.

MONTBARD
Hôtel de la Gare, F; 10 *avenue Maréchal-Foch; tel.* 80 92 02 12; *credit cards* MC, V; *closed mid-Dec to mid-Jan.*

Handy money-saver, which makes a useful base for visiting Fontenay (5 km). There are 34 simple rooms and a restaurant (closed Sun dinner).

Hôtel L'Ecu, F-FF; 7 *rue Auguste-Carré; tel.* 80 92 11 66; *credit cards* AE,

DC, MC, V; *open year round.*

Attractive small hotel in an old building; comfortable rooms and a pleasant dining room.

SAINT-FLORENTIN
La Grande Chaumière, FF-FFF; 3 *rue des Capucins; tel.* 86 35 15 12; *credit cards* AE, DC, MC, V; *closed* Wed *in winter, mid-Dec to mid-Jan, one week Sep.*

Very slightly off the beaten track, this peaceful, welcoming hotel offers 11 comfortable rooms and an excellent restaurant. Classical menu featuring regional dishes such as a marvellous *boeuf bourguignon.*

SENS
Paris et Poste, FF-FFF; 97 *rue de la République; tel.* 86 65 17 43; *credit cards* AE, DC, MC, V; *open year round.*

Traditional Burgundian coaching house in the town centre with a well-deserved reputation for old-fashioned courtesy and comfort, and an excellent restaurant (see Recommended Restaurants).

Relais de Villeroy, F-FF; 6 km W *of Sens via D6; tel.* 86 88 81 77; *credit cards* AE, DC, MC, V; *closed* Sun.

Welcoming little roadhouse with eight comfy rooms and a very good rustic restaurant (closed Sun dinner-Mon).

TONNERRE
Abbaye Saint-Michel, FFF; *rue Saint-Michel; tel.* 86 55 05 99; *credit cards* AE, DC, MC, V; *closed* Jan.
Very swish Relais et Châteaux hotel in the countryside just south of town. Bedrooms and suites are decorated with antiques and lovely fabrics; helicopter pad; gourmet restaurant (see Recommended Restaurants).

• *Avallon.*

treats in the **Musée de l'Avallonnais**, place de la Collègiale, is Jean Desprès's 20thC silverware and jewellery, also 19thC paintings and Gallo-Roman relics (closed Tues, Mon in Jun). Down at the bottom of the street, the sunny **Promenade de la Petite Porte** is bordered by the ramparts and plunging views down the cliff to the Cousin Valley.

The weekly covered market takes place on place Général-de-Gaulle every Saturday. Bicycle hire is available from the station, and the S.I. can provide details of where to hire canoes for a spot of messing about on the River Cousin.

Avallon is the springboard for Local

Explorations: 13, which takes in Véze-lay with its celebrated basilica.

BEAUNE
See France Overall: 11.

BUSSY-RABUTIN, CHATEAU DE
Off the D954, 5 km N of Alise-Sainte-Reine. Easily missed, but an intriguing historical footnote, the original château was rebuilt in 1649 by Roger de Bussy-Rabutin. He was banished to the country by Louis XIV as punishment for his satirical commentaries on court affairs, particularly those relating to the king and Marie de Mancini. During his exile, he decorated the house from top to bottom with contemporary portraits: there are 25 women onlookers in his bedchamber, including Mesdames de Sévigné and Maintenon.

CHABLIS ✕
On the D965, 19 km E of Auxerre. S.I. 28 rue Auxerroise. An unpretentious small town with a big name in wine. There is a clutch of wine merchants (not the best prices); the Eglise de Saint-Martin, with a Romanesque doorway; and a pretty riverside walk along the Promenade de Patis.

The crisp and delectable Chablis wines are produced from the chardonnay grape, and the best vineyards are those on the east bank of the River Serein. The S.I. publishes a handy leaflet listing caves where you can taste and buy local wines direct; lucky visitors on the fourth weekend of November will find the annual wine fair in progress.

CHATEAUNEUF
On the D18A, 10 km SE of Pouilly-en-Auxois. A bit twee, but not too busy on a weekday out of season, this attractive hill-top village was built around a 12th-15thC castle with superb views north-west over the Morvan and east to the Côte d'Or. The village, and its historic houses, have been saved by an influx of craft workshops and galleries selling local pottery, assorted artwork, and *cassis.*

COMMARIN, CHATEAU DE
5 km N of Châteauneuf. Set in a tiny village, this fine 17thC château is tacked on to a pair of 14thC towers and a pretty chapel. The interior is largely the work of Marie-Judith de Vienne, a woman of taste and literary inclinations, whose collections of 16thC tapestries, porcelain and books have remained *in situ* over the centuries. (Closed Tues, Nov-Apr).

DIJON
See France Overall: 10.

FLAVIGNY-SUR-OZERAIN
On the D9, 7 km S of Alise-Sainte-Reine. Pick, if you can, a sunny day for the winding drive to this delightful little fortified village perched on a rock above the woods. Once a noted medieval stronghold, Flavigny's former Benedictine **abbey** contains some interesting remains and an aniseed ball factory. The sweets come in pretty packets, useful as presents. Take a stroll through the picturesque streets and make a stop at the 13thC Eglise de Saint-Genest.

FONTAINEBLEAU
See Local Explorations: 8.

FONTENAY, ABBAYE DE
Off the D32, 5 km E of Montbard and the D905. Set in a lush valley, bordered by woodland, and chosen for its seclusion by St Bernard, Fontenay is one of the finest examples of Cistercian architecture in France. Building started in 1120, and the unadorned abbey church is magnificent in its simplicity and purity of line.

At the height of its prosperity, the abbey housed 300 monks and lay converts, but was converted into a paper mill after the Revolution. Restored earlier this century, the complex includes a monks' dormitory which overlooks a lovely Romanesque cloister and the vaulted chapterhouse. There is a dovecot, a forge, a prison and a medicinal herb garden fed by a diverted stream which also feeds the fountains from which the abbey takes its name.

The best way to avoid the crowds is to make your visit at the beginning or end of the day, so I have listed a couple of overnight stops in nearby Montbard (see Recommended Hotels). The town was the birthplace of 18thC scientist Georges-Louis Buffon, and boasts a small park laid out by Buffon on the banks of the River Brenne. He also built a foundry, the **Forges de**

Buffon, which has been restored by an English family, a pleasant 6-km walk or drive north of town along the Canal de Bourgogne.

JOIGNY

On the N6, 27 km N of Auxerre. S.I. quai Henri-Ragobert. A small town with leafy promenades and welcoming quayside cafés on the River Yonne. Pleasant as a pit stop, or for a peaceful walk. There are a few attractive 15th-16thC buildings in the town centre, and a brace of old churches, Saint-Jean and Saint-Thibault. Just west of town, on the N6, there is a serious Relais et Châteaux hotel and Michelin three-star restaurant in **A La Côte Saint-Jacques** (*tel.* 86 62 09 70).

PARIS

See pages 214-233.

SEMUR-EN-AUXOIS

On the D954, 34 km E of Avallon. S.I. 2 place Gaveau. A picturesque 14thC fortified town and capital of the Auxois region. There is a pleasant walk around the ramparts with views of the surrounding valley; then explore the closely packed streets, festooned with geranium pots, plus some quite interesting antique shops in a square near the Burgundian Gothic **Eglise de Notre-Dame**. The pillars of the church's north door, on rue Notre-Dame, sport a couple of edible snails, while the 13th-15thC interior contains some fine stained glass and carvings.

SENS ⇆ ✕

On the N6, 120 km SE of Paris/195 km NW of Dijon. S.I. place Jean-Jaurès. Once the ecclesiastical centre of France, Sens can still lay claim to the country's first, and possibly one of its finest Gothic cathedrals, the model for Canterbury.

On the banks of the River Yonne, the Old Town is encircled by tree-lined boulevards with scattered sections of the medieval ramparts and an archway opening on to the main street, rue de la République. Half-way up the street, on a small square, the **Cathédrale de Saint-Etienne** reveals its magnificent west front and a portal topped with a fine statue of St Stephen. Though missing its north tower, the south tower houses two vast bells. The

space and harmony of the interior is enriched by beautiful 12th-17thC stained glass in the ambulatory chapels. On three sides of the gardens, south of the cathedral, the 13thC **Palais Synodal** gives entry to the town museum (closed Tues), with some interesting Gallo-Roman remains and the fabulous cathedral treasury, one of the richest in France.

An easy drive from Paris, Sens is a popular Parisian weekend retreat, and the venerable **Hôtel Paris et Poste** (see Recommended Hotels) is overrun with gourmet visitors from the capital.

TANLAY, CHATEAU DE

On the D965, 9 km E of Tonnerre. This lovely, small château, founded in 1559 by François d'Andelot, brother of the Huguenot Amiral de Coligny, was completed in elegant French Renaissance style by Michel de Particelli, Mazarin's finance minister. Built around a courtyard, the highly decorative interior is furnished with 16thC antiques and paintings, while monochrome cartoons in the Grande Gallerie depict the main figures in the Wars of Religion, when the château was a Huguenot meeting place. (Closed Tues, Nov-Apr).

TONNERRE ✕

On the D905/D965, 17 km E of Chablis. An attractive, though sometimes traffic-choked, small town on the River Armaçon. Tonnerre's Château d'Uzès (now a bank on rue des Fontenilles) was the birthplace of the 18thC transvestite spy, Charles-Geneviève-Louise-Auguste-Andrée-Timothée, Chevalier Eon de Beaumont, whose diplomatic career took him around the courts of Europe in a variety of disguises. On the main street, the **Ancien Hôpital**, founded by Margaret of Burgundy in 1293, is amazingly well-preserved with its original oak timbering and barrel vaulting. The chapel contains a fine 15thC sculpted *Entombment*.

A short distance away, the Fosse Dionne is a natural spring of brilliant blue water once used as a washhouse.

VEZELAY

See Local Explorations: 13.

RECOMMENDED RESTAURANTS

AUXERRE
Barnabet, FF; 14 *quai de la République; tel. 86 51 68 88; credit cards* MC, V; *closed Sun dinner-Mon, mid-Dec to mid-Jan.*

Set in a 17thC coaching house opposite the Yonne, Jean-Luc Barnabet's fine restaurant is one of the best bargains in Burgundy. A combination of modern and classical cuisine with light sauces, many incorporating local wines. Cellar cultivated with care.

Le Jardin Gourmand, FF; 56 *boulevard Vauban; tel. 86 51 53 52; cards* MC, V; *closed Mon Sep-Jun, and Dec.*

Elegant town house dining rooms with a garden terrace. Delectable vegetable concoctions such as *variations sur le potager*, which may combine leek mousse, tomato sorbet, asparagus flan and *crudités* just for starters. Wine list with plenty of local interest.

La Primavera, F; 37 *rue du Pont; tel. 86 51 46 36; credit cards* V; *closed Sun dinner, Mon in winter.*

Good place to grab a light lunch or fill up in the evening on pasta, pizza and a range of Greek dishes.

AVALLON
Moulin des Ruats, FF-FFF; *Vallée du Cousin* (3.5 *km W via D427); tel. 86 34 07 14; credit cards* DC, V; *closed Mon, Tues lunch Nov-Apr, mid-Nov to mid-Dec and mid-Jan to Feb.*

A country inn with an idyllic riverside setting. Try to come here on a sunny day when you can lunch on the shady terrace, rather than in the newly decorated but rather soulless dining room. Adventurous menu of light, tasty, seasonal dishes.

The former mill also offers rustically refurbished rooms, some with balconies.

CHABLIS
Hôtel de l'Etoile, F; 4 *rue des Moulins; tel. 86 42 10 50; credit cards* AE, MC, V; *closed Mon dinner-Tues Oct-Apr, and Jan.*

Old-fashioned hotel-restaurant with plenty of dark wood, patterned wallpaper and classic cuisine liberally flavoured with local wines; check out the sticky puddings.

There are 14 simple rooms upstairs.

Le Vaulignot, F; *at Beine, 6 km E via D965; tel. 86 42 48 48; credit cards, none; closed, Sun dinner-Mon, one week Oct, mid-Jan to mid-Feb.*

On the Auxerre-Chablis road, a comfortable village restaurant which has earned itself a Michelin red R for good value.

MONTBARD
See Recommended Hotels.

SAINT-FLORENTIN
See Recommended Hotels.

SENS
Paris et Poste, FF; 97 *rue de la République; tel. 86 65 17 43; credit cards* AE, DC, MC, V; *open year round.*

Gracious dining in a fine Old Town centre hotel. This is the place to get to grips with traditional Burgundian cuisine, from magnificent garlic-laden snails to *coq au vin* or *poulet de Bresse*. Generous helpings, an imposing wine list, exemplary service.

Soleil Levant, F; 51 *rue Emile-Zola; tel. 86 65 71 82; credit cards* AE, MC, V; *closed Sun dinner, Wed, and mid-Jul to mid-Aug.*

Across the Yonne from the Old Town, this is another good but rather cheaper bet for hearty Burgundian cooking.

See also Recommended Hotels.

TONNERRE
Abbaye Saint-Michel, FFF; *rue Saint-Michel; tel. 86 55 05 99; credit cards* AE, DC, MC, V; *closed Jan to early Feb.*

Housed in a converted Benedictine monastery, the vaulted dining room is an attractive mix of antique and modern. Superb cuisine from Christophe Cussac, whose innovative menus combine robust Burgundian dishes with an opportunity to show off his mastery of more delicate combinations such as a *feuilleté* of foie gras with rhubarb. Interesting wines.

Central France

Between Bordeaux and Lyon
The Dordogne and Massif Central

585 km; maps Michelin Nos 234, 233, 239 and 244

First and foremost the Dordogne is a river. It rises in the Auvergne, flows 472 km west to Bordeaux, and by the time it reaches the *département* of Dordogne is a broad and gentle creature gliding between poplar-lined banks and ruined castles perched on limestone cliffs. Gazing down from their eyries, these stern fortresses and the *bastides*, handkerchief-sized fortified settlements tucked away in the crumpled southern hills, can seem at odds with Dordogne's rural idyll. They are the legacy of old Périgord, a frontline state in the Hundred Years War, and as far as the French are concerned (departmental bureaucrats notwithstanding) this is Périgord still.

The great advantage in being a region instead of a *département* is not having to recognize boundaries. This is convenient for the tourist board, who have poached territory and designated four mini-regions: Périgord Vert, the meadows and woodlands of the north; Périgord Blanc, a swathe of territory through the centre; Périgord Pourpre (purple) for the vineyards around Bergerac; and Périgord Noir, the south-eastern corner incorporating the famous prehistoric caves.

Périgord is over-run with visitors in summer, but this should not put you off: the welcoming, generally rolling, often pleasantly green landscape is big enough to take the people. Périgordian delicacies from foie gras and *confits* (goose or duck preserved in their own fat) to walnuts and truffles (the latter an aromatic edible fungus snuffled out by discerning pigs) are available year-round.

The main N89 runs almost the entire way between Bordeaux and Lyon. Périgueux and Brive-la-Gaillarde are the two launching points for Périgord Noir, the focus of the Dordogne tourist trail which lies to the south around Sarlat-la-Canéda (a red route must); and also for Périgord Vert to the north. Green route followers and anyone with time to spare should take in Local Explorations: 4.

This route extends right into the Massif Central, giving access to the stunning Parc Naturel Régional des Volcans d'Auvergne west of Clermont-Ferrand; for details, see Local Explorations: 9.

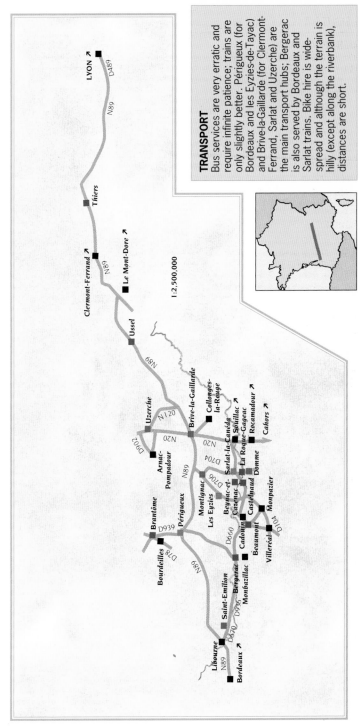

LYON ↗

D489

N89

Thiers

Clermont-Ferrand ↗

N89

Le Mont-Dore ↗

1:2,500,000

Ussel

N68

Uzerche ↗

N120

Collonges-la-Rouge

Brive-la-Gaillarde ↗

D902

N20

Arnac-Pompadour

N20

Solillac

Rocamadour ↗

N89

Sarlat-la-Canéda ↗

D704

La Roque-Gageac

Cahors ↗

Montignac

D706

Domme

Les Eyzies

Beynac-et-Cazenac

Périgueux ↗

Brantôme

D939

D600

Castelnaud

Monpazier

Bourdeilles

D78

Cadouin

Beaumont

D104

N89

Villeréal

Bergerac ↗

D936

Monbazillac

Saint-Emilion

D670

Libourne ↗

N89

Bordeaux ↗

TRANSPORT
Bus services are very erratic and require infinite patience; trains are only slightly better. Périgueux (for Bordeaux and les Eyzies-de-Tayac) and Brive-la-Gaillarde (for Clermont-Ferrand, Sarlat and Uzerche) are the main transport hubs; Bergerac is also served by Bordeaux and Sarlat trains. Bike hire is widespread and although the terrain is hilly (except along the riverbank), distances are short.

SIGHTS & PLACES OF INTEREST

BERGERAC ⌧ ✕

On the D936/D660, 88 km E of Bordeaux.
S.I. 97 rue Neuve d'Argenson. One-time
Protestant stronghold and capital of
Périgord until the Revolution, Bergerac
is the chief town of *Périgord Pourpre*,
and prospers as a market for wines,
maize, sunflowers and traditional *tabac
brun* grown along the fertile valley.

The S.I. provides a walking map of
the attractive old quarter, **Vieux Bergerac**, which centres on place de la
Myrpe. Here a statue of the town's
most famous non-resident, Cyrano de
Bergerac, stands surrounded by chestnut trees and ancient timber-framed
houses faced with zig-zag brickwork.

THE BASTIDES

During the 13thC, as the
Plantagenet kings of England
attempted to extend their overseas
domains beyond Aquitaine, so the
French sought to contain them. The
result, apart from much
skirmishing, was several hundred
bastides or fortified settlements,
peppering the length and breadth of
south-western France. The plan was
simple: a square or rectangular grid
of streets protected by ramparts
around a central arcaded square
and fortress-like church. The church
was the last bastion in the event of
an attack, and settlers were offered
inducements to stay in the form of
land and exemption from military
service (they were already in the
front line).

South of Bergerac, there is a
cluster of these little settlements –
Eymet, Villeréal, Monflanquin,
Beaumont – and the best preserved
of all, **Monpazier** (45 km SE of
Bergerac on the D660), which
dozes quietly on the edge of a
precipice above the River Dropt.
Monpazier was founded by Edward I
in 1285, and maintained a constant
feud with the lords of **Château
Biron** down the valley (8 km S via
the D2/D53). This immense
mongrel of a château with 10,000
square metres of roof alone dates
from the 13thC (closed Tues,
Dec-Jan).

DETOUR - **MONBAZILLAC**

One of the most celebrated wines
in the region, a sweet, golden *vin
liquoreux*, comes from
Monbazillac (6 km S of Bergerac
via the D13). The local *caves
co-operative* combine tours of the
pocket-sized 16thC **Château de
Monbazillac** with tastings of
several regional wines and direct
sales (closed Mon in winter, mid-
Jan to mid-Feb).

The 19thC playwright Edmond Rostand
based the character of his lovelorn
hero on a famous 17thC swordsman-
cum-philosopher, Savinien de Cyrano,
who probably never visited Périgord let
alone Bergerac, but the town has
embraced the legend with enthusiasm.
Off the square, the small **Musée du
Vin** includes a section on barrel-mak-
ing and river transport (closed Mon);
while the local Wine Council is based in
the lovely **Cloître des Recollets**,
place du Docteur-Cayla, with a fine
17th-18thC courtyard and cellars. The
Musée du Tabac, rue de l'Ancien
Port, airs a marvellous collection of
carved pipes in the 15thC Maison
Peyrarède (closed Mon).

The Bergerac area produces some
of the most reputable French country
wines. Everywhere you will see *ventes
directes* offering wines, usually by the
case, at (not always) advantageous
prices. Côtes de Duras, centered on
the town of Duras, to the south-west,
is another reputable country wine
appellation: particularly good dryish
whites.

BEYNAC-ET-CAZENAC

On the D703, 11 km SW of Sarlat.
Squeezed between river and rock face,
this much-visited village crouches in
the lee of **Château de Beynac**. A stiff
15-minute climb up the cliff, the original fortress was founded by the 12thC
barons of Beynac and commands
spectacular views from the battlements. It was captured by Richard the
Lionheart, but later spent most of the
Hundred Years War in French hands,
and the main château was added in the
16thC.

During summer regular boat trips in
traditional flat-bottomed *gabares*

depart from the jetty on the river, and there is canoe and kayak hire.

BORDEAUX
See France Overall: 3.

BRANTOME ⬛ ✕
On the D939, 27 km N of Périgueux. In the heart of *Périgord Vert*, edged by woods, walnut orchards and rolling pastures, Brantôme sits on the banks of the River Dronne and basks in the reflection of its elegant white abbey buildings. The original abbey was founded by Charlemagne in 769, rebuilt in the 11thC and added to over the centuries. The Gothic **Eglise Abbatiale** stands alongside a lovely Romanesque belfry, while the 18thC abbey buildings house the Hôtel de Ville and local museum.

From 1589 until his death in 1614, roving soldier-of-fortune Pierre de Bourdeilles was forced to retire here after a fall from his horse. The rôle of lay abbot was far from arduous, so he amused himself by writing a warts-and-all account of courtly life, much to the distress of his fellow courtiers.

The family seat, **Château de Bourdeilles** (10 km S via the D78) combines a business-like 13thC fortress and a 16thC annexe built to accommodate a proposed visit by Catherine de' Medici (who never turned up). As well as terrific views of the Dronne, the

• *Château de Beynac.*

château boasts a remarkable collection of European furniture (closed Tues Sept-Jun, Jan).

BRIVE-LA-GAILLARDE ⬛ ✕
On the N89, 170 km E of Clermont-Ferrand. S.I. place du 14-Juillet. A bustling commercial and transport centre on the River Corrèze, Brive makes a useful stop-over on the eastern border of Périgord. The old town radiates from the 12thC **Collégiale de Saint-Martin**, named after a 5thC Spanish martyr who introduced Christianity to the region. Arriving on the pagan feast of Saturnus, the tactless Martin destroyed a number of idols and was promptly dispatched by outraged local

> **DETOUR - COLLONGES-LA-ROUGE**
> Regularly hailed as 'the prettiest village in France', **Collonges-la-Rouge** (21 km SE of Brive-la-Gaillarde via the D38) is built of red sandstone and distinctly *rouge*. Its hotch-potch of jolly 15th-17thC houses, decorated with turrets and outbreaks of brilliant green vines, gathers around a 12thC church and timber-framed covered market on the main square.

DETOUR - **CHATEAU LES MILANDES**

The D53 wiggles 8 km north and west of Castelnaud, past the private Château de Fayrac on the river bank and through the walnut groves, to **Château Les Milandes** (open Easter to Oct). Guided tours cover a bizarre history from the château's 15thC origins as the seat of the de Caumont family to its transformation into a multi-cultural *village de monde* for the adopted children of cabaret artiste Josephine Baker from the 1930s to the 60s.

• *Périgueux, the cathedral.*

heathens.

There are several fine medieval and Renaissance houses, including the lovely **Hôtel de Labenche**, boulevard Jules-Ferry (closed Tues). Behind an arcaded courtyard, it now displays local archaeological finds and 17th-18thC tapestries. South-west of the ring boulevard, the **Musée Edmond-Michelet**, rue Champanatier, commemorates the exploits of the local Second World War Resistance leader and his comrades (closed Sun).

CADOUIN, ABBAYE DE

On the D25, 11 km NE of Beaumont. The 12thC abbey church stands on a pretty square shaded by chestnut trees and edged by honey-coloured stone cottages, a café and clutch of delicatessens selling Périgordian produce. A relic of the Holy Shroud turned Cadouin into a pilgrim's way station on the Route Saint-Jacques, but carbon dating disproved its validity in 1935. Since then the main attraction has been the Flamboyant Gothic capitals in the **cloister** (closed Tues Sept-Jun), best appreciated without a bossy guide.

CAHORS

See Local Explorations: 4.

CASTELNAUD

On the D53, 4 km SW of la Roque-Gageac. A picturesque clamber up through the huddle of stone cottages arranged

• *Opposite: Monpazier.*

around its rocky base, **Château de Castelnaud** lords it over the south bank of the Dordogne opposite rival Château de Beynac. Founded in the 12thC and held by the English for most of the Hundred Years War, the château has been partially restored and equipped with a bellicose complement of medieval weaponry from giant catapults and crossbows to pikes and daggers. There are walking trails in the woods, and kayaks for hire down by the bridge.

CLERMONT-FERRAND

See France Overall: 7.

DOMME 🖾

On the D46, 12 km S of Sarlat-la-Canéda. S.I. *place de la Halle.* Balanced on a hilltop above the river with three of its 13thC gateways intact, postcard-pretty Domme is one of the best preserved but most visited *bastides*. The streets of the town founded by Philippe le Hardi in 1280 are lined with weathered stone houses festooned with vines and wistaria; the shops are stacked with vacuum-packed Périgordian specialities; and there are splendid views from the cliff-top **Belvédère de la Barre** which required nothing in the way of additional fortifications.

On the main square, place de la Halle, the **Musée d'Art et de Traditions Populaires** recreates scenes from old-time Périgord using rustic crafts and costumes, tools and toys (closed Tues except Jul-Aug, Nov-Mar). Once upon a time, the townsfolk used to take refuge amongst the subterranean stalactites, stalagmites and pools of the **Grottes de Domme** beneath the old market hall (open in summer, or check with the S.I.).

EYZIES-DE-TAYAC, LES ⌀

On the D47, 45 km SE of Périgueux. S.I. place de la Mairie. The self-styled 'Capital of Prehistory', les Eyzies is the main base for visits to Périgord's famous prehistoric caves. The earliest traces of human habitation in the Vézère valley date from the Neanderthal period, but the cave paintings and wealth of archaeological finds are the legacy of Cro-Magnon man living in the Paleolithic era some 12-20,000 years ago.

Overlooking les Eyzies, the **Musée National de Préhistoire** displays a huge array of prehistoric artefacts (closed Tues). Bones and utensils share the bill with cave drawings and carvings. To see the relics *in situ*, visit the **Musée l'Abri Pataud**, a private site belonging to a farmer who discovered his property was built over a reindeer hunter's shelter (*abri*) used for over 20,000 years and carefully excavated layer by layer (closed Mon).

The main cave sites are all outside town (bike hire from the S.I.), and to be sure of a ticket in season, make an early start. The most spectacular, Lascaux, had to be closed and replaced by a reconstruction (see **Montignac**, below). The leading cave is is now the **Grotte Font-de-Gaume** (1.5 km E via the D47; closed Tues Oct-Mar; tickets can be booked in advance, tel. 53 06 97 48). It is a 15-minute climb up to the cave mouth, beyond which tours of 20 people at a time wend their way past a startlingly sophisticated catalogue of cave paintings depicting bison, horses, mammoths and reindeer. The caves were not lived in and anthropologists are still unsure whether the drawings are religious, educational or good-luck mascots.

Other nearby sites include the

Grotte des Combarelles (2 km E via the D47; closed Tues Oct-Mar) with 300 animal carvings and the odd crude human likeness; the **Grotte de Rouffignac** (17 km NW via the D47/D32; closed Oct-Mar) visited by mini-train; and the **Abri du Cap Blanc** (7 km E via the D47/D48; closed Nov-Mar), a rock shelter rather than a cave. At **la Roque Saint-Christophe** (9 km NE via the D706; closed Nov-Mar), the limestone cliff was turned into a prehistoric high-rise with cave dwellings on five levels. For bizarre rock formations, look no further than the petrified tableau of stalagmites and stalactites in the **Grotte du Grand Roc** (2 km N via the D47; closed Nov-Mar).

LYON
See France Overall: 11.

MONPAZIER
Also nearby Villeréal and Beaumont, see The Bastides, page 204.

MONT-DORE, LE
See Local Explorations: 9.

MONTIGNAC
On the D704, 26 km NW of Sarlat. S.I. place Léo-Magne. Archaeologists have been trawling the Vézère valley for prehistoric remains since the 19thC, but it took four boys and a dog to stumble upon the finest cave paintings of them all. The Grotte de Lascaux was discovered in 1940, and opened to the public for less than 20 years before humidity and carbon dioxide took such a savage toll on the paintings that the cave was closed. In 1983, a brilliant reconstruction, **Lascaux II**, was opened complete with painstakingly copied drawings using the same methods and painting materials as the originals (2 km S via the D104e; closed Mon Sep-Jun; tickets from the S.I. in Montignac).

Still on a prehistoric theme, **Le Thot** (5 km S via the D706; closed Tues Sep-Jun, Feb) offers everyday scenes from Stone Age life in a park setting, inhabited by stuffed woolly mammoths and live bison.

With a ticket for Lascaux II in hand and a few hours to spare, Montignac is a pleasant old town in which to while away the time. Next door to the S.I., the **Musée Eugène-le-Roy** is named after the local 19thC author whose rus-

RECOMMENDED HOTELS

BERGERAC
La Flambée, FF; 153 *avenue Pasteur* (N21); *tel.* 53 57 52 33; *credit cards* AE, DC, MC, V; *closed Jan-Feb.*

A pretty manor house with a garden and terrific Périgordian restaurant.

BEYNAC-ET-CAZENAC
Manoir Hôtel Rochecourbe, FF; *at Vézac* (2 *km south east); tel.* 53 29 50 79; *credit cards; closed mid-Oct to mid-Jun.*

No hot and cold running room service or restaurant, but a lovely 15thC private manor house with huge fireplaces and antique furnishings. In Beynac, **Hôtel Bonnet, F-FF;** *tel.* 53 29 50 01; *closed mid-Oct to mid-Apr;* has rooms and a restaurant by the river.

BRANTOME
Moulin du Roc, FF-FFF; *at Champagnac-de-Belair* (6 *km NE via D82/D83); tel.* 53 54 80 36; *credit cards* AE, DC, MC, V; *closed mid-Jan to mid-Feb, mid-Nov to mid-Dec.*

Enchanting 17thC walnut mill fronting the river with shady gardens, a pool, terrace and Michelin-starred restaurant.

Les Griffons, FF; *Bourdeilles* (10 *km SE via D78); tel.* 53 03 75 61; *credit cards* AE, MC, V; *closed mid-Oct to mid-Apr.*

Attractive rooms and a marvellous riverside location near the château. The 16thC buildings also house an excellent regional restaurant. Terrace and garden.

BRIVE-LA-GAILLARDE
See Recommended Restaurants.

COLLONGES-LA-ROUGE
Relais Saint-Jacques-de-Compostelle, F-FF; 21 *km SE of Brive-la-Gaillarde via D38; tel.* 55 25 41 02; *cards* AE, DC, MC, V; *closed Tues -Wed except Jan-Feb, May-Sep.*

Quiet *auberge* in the village centre with small, bright rooms, a simple stone-walled dining room and terrace.

DOMME
Hôtel de l'Esplanade, FF; *tel.* 52 28 31 41; *credit cards* AE, V; *closed mid-Nov to mid-Jan.*

The only way to see Domme without the crowds is to stay over and this is the best way to do it. A wonderful traditional hotel, comfy rooms with views and excellent, if pricey, restaurant.

EYZIES-DE-TAYAC, LES
Moulin de la Beune, FF; *tel.* 53 06 94 33; *cards* MC, V; *closed Nov-Mar.*

Converted river-side mill in the town centre. Comfortable rooms, garden and restaurant annexe next door.

PERIGUEUX
Hôtel Périgord, F-FF; 74 *rue Victor-Hugo; tel.* 53 53 33 63; *cards* V; *closed Thur Oct-Mar (restaurant Sat-Sun), two weeks Feb, three weeks Oct-Nov.*

Welcoming *logis* a ten-minute walk from the town centre. Sunny breakfast terrace; fine regional restaurant serving, for instance, *salade périgourdine* (with foie gras), grilled trout and walnut flan.

ROQUE-GAGEAC, LA
La Belle Etoile, FF; *tel.* 53 29 51 44; *credit cards* V; *closed mid-Oct to Apr.*

Pleasant hotel with simple rooms in an old house. Dining room with vine-shaded terrace overlooking the river; good classical cooking – hot *foie gras* salad with truffle oil, beef fillet with field mushrooms, venison in pepper sauce.

The **Hôtel Gardette (FF;** tel. 53 29 51 58), has slightly cheaper rooms, pricier menus and the same annual holidays.

SARLAT-LA-CANEDA
Le Coulverine, F-FF; 1 *place de la Bouqueterie; tel.* 53 59 27 80; *credit cards* AE, DC, MC, V; *closed three weeks Jan, two weeks Nov.*

Pretty rooms with antique furnishings and a cosy dining room tucked into the ramparts, north-east of the town centre.

Mas de Castel, F-FF; 3 *km S via D704; tel.* 53 59 02 59; *credit cards* AE, DC, V; *closed mid-Nov to Easter.*

Welcoming and simple country hotel in a big garden with swimming pool.

tic novels sit perfectly with the traditional furniture and crafts on display.

PERIGUEUX 🛏 ✕

On the N89, 120 km NE of Bordeaux. S.I. place Francheville. First settled by the ancient *Petrocorii*, then by the Romans, plump and prosperous Périgueux is the *préfecture* of Périgord and an important market centre for the winter truffle harvest. Although the sights of Périgueux are unlikely to detain visitors for more than a day, the town is a good base for *Périgord Vert* to the north, and for trains to les Eyzies for the prehistoric caves (see page 208).

The *vieille ville* clusters around the distinctly exotic looking **Cathédrale de Saint-Front**, poised like a runaway Byzantine mirage off rue Taillefer. It is topped by five domes in the shape of a Greek cross, and has a mammoth interior, impressive for its sheer size, but uncomfortably restored and rather lifeless. Handsome Renaissance houses tricked out with arches, carved scrolls, balustrades and balconies line the labyrinthine maze of streets. There are glimpses of the cathedral down tiny alleyways, and a galaxy of gourmet *épiceries* attempt (all too successfully) to seduce passers-by with gift-wrapped

• *Monbazillac – see page* 204.

foie gras, *confits*, sticky walnut liqueurs and the ubiquitous truffles. Wednesday and Saturday morning markets on place du Coderc add fresh produce and crates of cackling *volailles* to the bulging Périgordian larder.

Alongside the usual run of fine china, European paintings and traditional crafts, the **Musée du Périgord**, 22 cours Tourny, displays artefacts from Roman *Versunna* (closed Tues). There are glass ornaments, beautiful mosaics and stacks of stone carvings in the garden cloister. The remains of *Versunna* lie west of the town centre, where the well-signposted *Circuit Cité Antique* traces a route around the truncated **arena** and semi-circular **Tour de Versone**, a brick shell once 20 m high and lined with marble.

ROCAMADOUR

See Local Explorations: 4.

ROQUE-GAGEAC, LA 🛏 ✕

On the D703, 12 km S of Sarlat. The picture-postcard Dordogne village, with its yellow-ochre cottages plastered

• *Opposite: La Roque-Gageac.*

against the cliff face and reflected in the slow-flowing river. Clamber up the narrow cobbled streets laid out on ramps and terraces to the troglodyte dwellings carved into the cliff. For the best views, take a canoe, kayak or taxi rowing boat across to the little island in midstream. Canoës Dordogne (tel. 53 29 58 50) also arrange day and half-day canoe trails with outward transport, then paddle back to la Roque.

SAINT-EMILION ✕

Off the D670, 37 km E of Bordeaux. S.I. place des Créneaux. Anchored to a chalky outcrop in a sea of vines, this cheerful little wine village also does a fine line in almond macaroons. There is none of the Médoc pretentiousness here and the Maison du Vin has a list of local vineyards offering tours of their *caves* and free *dégustations*. Half a day spent here is perhaps the pleasantest wine pilgrimage of all in the Bordeaux region.

Saint-Emilion's 8thC namesake was a hermit. His rough-hewn cell, furnished with a simple stone pallet and seat, can be visited on a 45-minute guided tour which takes in the **Eglise Monolithe**, a vast 9th-12thC church tunnelled into the hillside by Emilion's followers after his death, the ancient catacombs, and a partially ruined 14thC Benedictine chapel (tickets from the S.I.).

SARLAT-LA-CANEDA 🏨 ✕

On the D47, 65 km SE of Périgueux. S.I.

DETOUR – CHATEAU-HARAS DE POMPADOUR

Madame de Pompadour, Louis XV's favourite mistress, received her title and this château from the king in 1745. History relates that La Pompadour (who was plain Antoinette Poisson before she caught the king's eye) never visited her Limousin retreat, but Louis founded a stud next door and the **Château-Haras de Pompadour**, at Arnac-Pompadour (30 km W of Uzerche via the D7), is now a national stud farm, famous for its Anglo-Arab horses. The château's terraced gardens are open to the public along with the stables (Mon-Fri pm and Sun am Jul-Feb). Race meetings are held at the race course below the château (May-Oct).

---

place de la Liberté. Capital of *Périgord Noir*, Sarlat is one of the most popular and well-placed bases for exploring the Dordogne. Bisected by the commercial drag, rue de la République, the mellow yellow *vieille ville* is a delightful warren of cobbled streets and alleys, 16th-17thC houses, quiet courtyards and a wonderful Saturday market on central place de la Liberté.

At the heart of the old town, the mainly 17thC **Cathédrale de Saint-Sacerdos** is large and uninteresting, while the neighbouring beehive-shaped 12thC **Lanterne des Morts** has been puzzling historians as to its true purpose for years.

Far more alluring is the **Maison de la Boétie**, place du Peyrou, which is a Renaissance gem with its carved façade and mullioned windows. It was the birthplace of Etienne de la Boétie who died young in 1563 and inspired Montaigne's famous *Essay on Friendship*. **Rue des Consuls** boasts some wonderful old houses and the little place des Oies which contains a trio of bronze geese looking understandably nervous.

Sarlat has a couple of small museums including one devoted to sacred art in the **Chapelle des Pénitents Blanc**, rue de la Charité. During the summer **theatre festival** (Jul-Aug) the ancient ruins of the church of Sainte-Marie on place de la Liberté are transformed into an open-air theatre. For bike and moped hire, canoe trips, pony-trekking, and a selection of GR hiking trail maps and guided walks in the surrounding countryside, consult the friendly and helpful *Maison du Plein Air et de la Randonnée*, 16 rue Fénelon (tel. 53 31 24 18).

SOUILLAC

See Local Explorations: 4.

THIERS ✕

On the N89, 45 km E of Clermont-Ferrand. S.I. place Pirou. 'Cutlery Capital' of France since the Middle Ages, Thiers still produces half the nation's home-honed knives. Above the swift-flowing River Durolle, there is an attractive old town of half-timbered houses, Romanesque churches and knife shops. Also here is the **Maison des Couteliers** with a small museum and cutlery workshops.

USSEL

On *the* N89, 82 *km* SW *of Clermont-Ferrand.* A quiet town on the edge of the Massif Central, Ussel's clutch of 15th-16thC houses gather around the turreted Renaissance **Hôtel des Ducs de Ventadour**, and a museum of folksy arts and crafts (closed Sep-Jun).

North of the town, the weatherbeaten uplands of the **Plateau de Millevaches** support a few isolated farms and wandering sheep. To the east, hikers and skiers descend on the dramatically beautiful **Parc National des Volcans d'Auvergne** (see Local Explorations: 9).

UZERCHE

On *the* N20, 35 *km* N *of Brive-la-Gaillarde.* S.I. *place de la Lunarde.* Set on a rocky crag above a loop in the River Vézère, the 'Pearl of Limousin' shelters beneath a veritable coven of grey slate witches' hat towers. Sporting window grilles and the odd coat-of-arms, the cosily-knit huddle of old houses is riddled with arches and alleyways, while the 12thC **Eglise de Saint-Pierre** has its original belfry, a collection of carved capitals and a musty crypt. Walking tour maps are available at the S.I., and there are fine views over the valley from the Esplanade de la Lunarde.

RECOMMENDED RESTAURANTS

BERGERAC
Le Cyrano, F-FF; 2 *boulevard Montaigne; tel.* 53 57 02 76; *credit cards* AE, DC, MC, V; *closed Sun dinner-Mon except Jul-Aug, one week Christmas.*

Regional specialties with a *nouvelle* twist, liberally laced with local wines.

Also 11 plain, comfortable rooms (**FF**).

BEYNAC-ET-CAZENAC
See Recommended Hotels.

BRANTOME
Moulin de l'Abbaye, FF-FFF; *route de Bourdeilles; tel.* 53 05 80 22; *credit cards* AE, DC, MC, V; *closed Mon lunch mid-Oct to May.*

Idyllic setting by the river, memorable Périgordian cuisine – *foie gras* served with spiced peaches, grilled young rabbit with a soft Monbazillac wine sauce – and polished service.

Also nine beautifully decorated and quiet Relais et Châteaux rooms (**FFF**).

BRIVE-LA-GAILLARDE
La Cremaillère, F-FF; 53 *avenue de Paris; tel.* 55 74 32 47; *credit cards* V; *closed Sun dinner-Mon.*

Inspired combinations of traditional local ingredients and modern methods produces a vigorous *cuisine du terroir*. An air of *bonhomie* and a pretty summer terrace.

Also nine rooms (**F-FF**).

PERIGUEUX
L'Oison, FF-FFF; 31 *rue Saint-Front;*
tel. 53 09 84 02; *credit cards* AE, DC, MC, V; *closed Sun dinner, Mon, three weeks Feb-Mar, three weeks Jul.*

A small, elegant Michelin-starred restaurant which makes the most of regional delicacies in specialities such as *terrine sarladaise* (layers of foie gras and potato); and pigs' trotters with truffles. Interesting wine list, too.

See also Recommended Hotels.

ROQUE-GAGEAC, LA
See Recommended Hotels.

SAINT-EMILION
Le Tertre, F-FF; *rue du Tertre-de-la-Tente; tel.* 57 74 46 33; *credit cards* V; *closed Sun dinner and Wed Jan-May, mid-Nov to Jan.*

Generous provincial cooking and a family atmosphere in a cool, stone dining room.

For something a little lighter, try **L'Envers du Decor**, a congenial modern wine bar on rue du Clocher (closed Sun).

SARLAT-LA-CANEDA
Rossignol, F-FF; 15 *rue Fénelon; tel.* 53 31 02 30; *credit cards* V; *closed Wed.*

Popular, traditional family-run dining room and great value-for-money menus.

THIERS
Le Corps de Garde, F; 34 *rue Durolle; tel.* 73 80 06 49; *credit cards* V; *closed Mon.*

Excellent straightforward cooking and low prices in a quiet old town bistro.

Paris:
introduction

Henri IV converted to Catholicism to acquire it, Dickens rated it 'the most extraordinary place in the world', and Hemingway, a man of legendary appetites, deemed it a 'moveable feast'. Paris is many things to many people, but to a Parisian it is quite simply the centre of the universe, the epitome of the civilized world. Monumental buildings, grand vistas, *haute couture* and culture for all are testament to his belief. Paris and her citizens are not prepared to rest on their laurels either, but constantly augment the catalogue of past treasures with new and exciting developments, characterized by the programme of *grands travaux* (Great Works) initiated in the 1970s-80s and executed during the Mitterand years.

Paris became the capital of France in 508 with the arrival of Clovis, King of the Franks, since when a succession of kings, emperors and now the politicians have stamped their authority on the city through architecture. François I demolished Philippe-Auguste's Louvre fortress and built a Renaissance palace; Henri IV founded the aristocratic Marais district; Louis XIV added Les Invalides; Napoleon congratulated himself with the Arc de Triomphe; and Louis-Philippe employed Baron Haussmann to remodel the cramped old town with broad boulevards. (These were more practical than aesthetic, designed to facilitate troop movements in the event of a civil uprising.) Towards the end of the 19thC, the era of the great exhibitions inspired the Tour Eiffel, Palais de Chaillot, and Gare d'Orsay (now a spectacular museum), and the latest billion-franc projects include the revamping of the Louvre, the futuristic Cité des Sciences at La Villette, and Grande Arche at La Défense which completes the *Voie Triomphale* (Triumphal Way) linking the Louvre to the modern business district.

Beneath the monumental façade, there is another Paris, a collection of villages with parish churches, markets, cafés and bars where poets and painters, travellers and thinkers have traditionally found refuge. This is the Left Bank, where the students of the Sorbonne once spoke Latin; it is also picturesque Montmartre, and quietly prosperous Passy where Balzac hid from his creditors. To understand Paris you have to explore both sides of the coin – forgive her airs and celebrate her graces.

USING THIS SECTION

Bisected by the Seine, the close-knit centre of Paris is comprised of 20 *arrondissements*, or administrative districts, caught in a noose by the *péripherique* ring road. The *1er arrondissement* is at the heart of the Right Bank, the rest peel off clockwise in a concentric wheel. The five-figure Paris postcodes are broken down into the 750 prefix for Paris followed by the *arrondissement* number, i.e. the Ile de la Cité in the *4e* is 75004. Addresses for the gazetteer, hotel and restaurant entries in this section include an *arrondissement* designation.

An old political maxim claims that a Frenchman keeps his heart on the left and his wallet on the right. This is largely true of Paris. The Right Bank (*Rive Droite*) is all about power and money, the grandest buildings, most expensive shops and well-heeled western residential districts. The Left Bank (*Rive Gauche*) is the head and heart: the Sorbonne, cafés, bookshops and winding streets. Most of the main sights are found in the *1er* to *9e* districts. However, the *11e* around Bastille is becoming trendy; the *16e* has the Bois de Boulogne and a rich haul of museums; the *18e* is ever-popular Montmartre; and the recently developed Parc de la Villette in the *19e* is an excellent reason to venture further afield.

True to this guide's formula of maximum flexibility and choice, the city is covered by a mixture of walking routes (starting on page 226) and general gazetteer entries (starting on page 218). The walks (Marais, Montmartre and the Ile de la Cité) introduce you to the delights of three very different, self-contained, parts of Paris, and are an ideal way to get to grips with its flavour. The gazetteer covers the rest of the important sights. As usual, you don't have to follow the routes: the information is there to be used as and when needed – even from an armchair.

OUR PARIS MAPPING

The bird's-eye-view mapping on which the walking routes are shown was created by Duncan Petersen from a helicopter survey of the capital. A delightful and useful guide featuring the whole of central Paris with this mapping is published by Duncan Petersen (title *3-D City Guides Paris*) in the U.K. and Commonwealth and by Passport Books in the U.S.A (title *Paris Up Close*).

SAFETY

There are few no-go areas in central Paris (the depressed suburbs lie beyond the *péripherique*). Avoid the Bois de Boulogne after dark, and the Champ-de-Mars around the Tour Eiffel. The Beaubourg, Gare Saint-Lazare and Pigalle are notorious for prostitutes and drug dealers.

ACCOMMODATION GUIDELINES

One of the great advantages of Paris is the range of accommodation available in the city centre. The smartest districts are *1er* and *8e*; the generally more-affordable Left Bank (*6e* and *7e*) is popular and attractive, as is the Marais (*4e*). Space is at a premium so rooms tend to be small, but I trust the listed hotels will make up for this with character.

PRICES

Not suprisingly, prices in the capital are higher than elsewhere, and this is reflected in our special set of Paris price bands (see below). April to June, September and October are the busiest months, but reservations are advisable year round. For last-minute bookings, there are reservation services at the main stations, airports and central tourist office.

F	up to 350F
FF	350F-600F
FFF	600F-1000F
FFFF	1000F plus

ARRIVING

By air: Train services (every 15 minutes 5.30 am-11.30 pm) link **Roissy/Charles-de-Gaulle airport** (23 km NE of the city) to the Gare du Nord, and **Orly airport** (14 km S) to the Gare d'Austerlitz. There are also buses (5.40 am-11 pm) and taxis.

By train: Trains from the north and the U.K. arrive at Gare du Nord, or

Gare de Saint-Lazare; from the north-west, at Gare de Montparnasse; from the south-west, at Gare d'Austerlitz; from the south and Alps, at Gare de Lyon; and from the east, at Gare d'Est. All stations are served by the Métro.

By car: If possible avoid the rush-hour periods and follow the *périph-erique* round to the nearest *porte* (entry point) to your destination. Parking is a problem in Paris. The best advice for a stay of several days is to leave the car in a main car park and travel around by foot or public trans-port. Meters run 9 am-7 pm. *Zones bleues* (look for blue parking signs) require a parking disc obtainable from hotels and garages.

PUBLIC TRANSPORT

The three main public transport sys-tems, the **RER** (suburban train ser-vices), **Métro** and **buses** all come under the authority of **RATP** which has information offices at place de la Madeleine, 8e, and 35 quai des Grands Augustins, 6e, or tel. 43 46 14 14 from 6 am to 9 pm. Services are fast, frequent and cheap - even better value if you buy a *carnet* (book of ten tickets) available from stations and some *tabacs*. Tickets are valid for one Métro ride (any distance), two fare stages on the bus, and the RER within the area covered by the Métro. Tickets must be validated (*com-poster*) before travel by the ticket punch machines. Roving inspectors extract on-the-spot fines.

Various special RATP ticket deals (available from all stations and the tourist office) make life easy. They work up from the *Formule 1* day pass

• *Going downstream, Louvre on the right, Pont du Carrousel ahead.*

and *Paris-visite* three- to five-day day ticket to the weekly or monthly *Carte Orange*.

The Métro is the simplest way to get around. Free maps are widely available and services run from 5.30 am to 12.30 am. The numbered lines are also colour-coded and marked with the destination at the end of the line, i.e. if you want to head south on Line 4 follow signs for *Direction Porte d'Orléans*.

USEFUL ADDRESSES AND TELEPHONE NUMBERS

Office du Tourisme 127 avenue des Champs-Elysées, 8e, tel. 47 23 61 72; also at the Tour Eiffel, airports and main stations.

Lost Property 36 rue des Moril-lons, 15e.

Main Post Office 52 rue du Lou-vre, 1er.

Late night Bureau de Change Gare de Lyon, daily until 11 pm.

Twenty-four-hour chemist Phar-macie Dhéry, Galeries des Champs-Elysées, 8e.

Medical emergencies tel. 45 67 50 50.

Ambulance services tel. 15 (SAMU); or public service tel. 43 78 26 26.

Roissy/Charles-de-Gaulle air-port tel. 48 62 22 80.

Orly airport tel. 49 75 15 15.

SNCF (train information) tel. 45 82 50 50; reservations, tel. 45 65 60 60.

SIGHTS & PLACES OF INTEREST

ARC DE TRIOMPHE

place Charles-de-Gaulle, 8e. The axis of 12 broad boulevards on what used to be called place de l'Etoile, Napoleon's triumphal arch was founded in 1806. On the emperor's birthday, August 15, the sun rises directly above the 50 x 45 m arch. Four sculpted reliefs decorate the pillars (most notably François Rude's *La Marseillaise*), topped by an action-packed frieze. Below, the Tomb of the Unknown Warrior burns an eternal flame, and a small museum recounts the arch's history. But the *pièce de résistance* is the view across Paris from the roof.

ART MODERNE DE LA VILLE DE PARIS, MUSEE

See *Palais de Tokyo, page 224.*

ARTS DECORATIFS, MUSEE DES

(*Grand Louvre*) 107 *rue de Rivoli, 1er.* A tremendous diversity of applied arts runs the gamut of furniture, porcelain, glass and tapestries from the Middle Ages up to the present day. There are entire set-piece rooms, carved ivories, clockwork toys and Art Deco delights.

Under the same roof (joint tickets) the **Musée des Arts de la Mode** covers the fashion industry; while the **Musée de la Publicité** hosts excellent themed exhibitions of poster art and multi-media advertising.

ARTS ET TRADITIONS POPULAIRES, MUSEE D'

6 *avenue du Mahatma Ghandi, 16e.* A wonderful museum of French crafts located in the Bois de Boulogne: traditional agricultural tools and practices, pottery, wrought-iron work, toys and trinkets, cleverly displayed with reconstructed rooms and workshops.

BALZAC, MAISON DE

47 *rue Raynouard, 16e.* Quite the most enchanting writer's hideaway reached through a small garden, Honoré de Balzac's Parisian cottage displays manuscripts, accounts, engravings and a library. They build a fascinating portrait of the novelist who lived here in Passy for seven years during the 1840s, and completed the series of novels known as *La Comédie Humaine.*

BASTILLE, PLACE DE LA

12e. Site of the notorious Bastille prison demolished during the Revolution, the *place* is now terrorized by traffic and dominated by the monster **Opéra-Bastille**. The outline of the old prison is picked out in paving stones, while the towering **Colonne de Juillet** commemorates the dead of the 1830 and 1848 uprisings. However, the effect is lost in the glittering reflections of the ballooning glass and granite modern opera building (one of Mitterand's *grands travaux*) inaugurated during the 1989 Bicentennary celebrations and opened two years later.

BEAUBOURG, CENTRE

See *Centre Georges Pompidou, page 219.*

BOIS DE BOULOGNE

16e. Once a royal hunting ground, the 900-hectare *bois* is the city's favourite open space. West of the city centre, its gardens and grottoes, go-kart tracks and race courses (Auteuil and Longchamp) prove an irresistable draw on sunny weekends. Children love the rides in the **Jardin d'Acclimatation**; and in the **Parc de Bagatelle**, a park within the park off allée de Longchamp, Charles X's villa is surrounded by beautiful flower gardens.

CAMONDO, MUSEE NISSIM DE

63 *rue de Monceau, 16e.* An 18thC aristocratic residence created from scratch

by Count Moïse de Camondo earlier this century. The gracious mansion is based on the Petit Trianon at Versailles, and the lavish interior decoration - gilded Louis XVI furniture, panelled walls, enormous crystal chandeliers and tapestries (including an exquisite series depicting La Fontaine's fables) - is all faithfully period.

CARNAVALET, MUSEE LE GRAND
See page 229.

CATACOMBES
1 *place Denfert-Rochereau, 14e.* A macabre tourist attraction laid out in abandoned Gallo-Roman stone quarries, this is no ancient Roman necropolis, but an 18th-19thC cemetery clearance operation. Around six million skeletons line the 300 km of tunnels. A short but eerie section has been open to the public since 1874.

CENTRE GEORGES-POMPIDOU (MUSEE NATIONAL D'ART MODERNE)
19 *rue Beaubourg, 4e.* Also known as the *Centre Beaubourg*, Richard Rogers'

• *Arc de Triomphe, dominating the vast place Charles-de-Gaulle, formerly place de l'Etoile.*

notorious 'inside-out' cultural centre opened in 1977 to howls of derision from the architectural establishment. It certainly makes no attempt to blend in with the surroundings, but the monster glass and steel box cocooned in pipes, air ducts and a transparent escalator is now regarded with indulgent affection. The formerly run-down neighbourhood is dotted with galleries and cafés, and the sloping piazza plays host to an open-air cabaret of street performers.

The fourth floor is devoted to the brilliant **Musée National d'Art Moderne**. Opening with the Fauvists, it cuts a dash through 20thC art via Rousseau, Picasso, Braque, Matisse, Kandinsky, Dali, Warhol and Bacon, amongst others. The permanent collections of paintings, sculpture and the plastic arts are superbly displayed in rotation (many reserved works are stored in racks suspended from the ceiling). Check out the visiting contemporary exhibitions, the photographic and print galleries, the excellent shop and roof-top café.

CHAMPS-ELYSEES, AVENUE DES

5e. The best known street in Paris forms a tree-lined triumphal way between the Arc de Triomphe and place de la Concorde. A natural venue for the Bastille Day parades, the avenue has been invaded more recently by an unsightly collection of fast food restaurants, cinemas and drugstores. Still, the cafés, though expensive, are perfect for people-watching, and Jacque Chirac's urban renewal programme promises to clean up the famous avenue.

CIMITIERE DU PERE-LACHAISE

boulevard de Menilmontant, 20e. The largest cemetery in Paris draws a motley collection of visitors from hippies on the trail of Doors singer Jim Morrison's tomb to earnest literary types with a choice of Balzac, Colette and Oscar Wilde. Military buffs will find Masséna and Ney; arty types, Géricault and Modigliani; theatre folk, Molière and Sarah Bernhardt; musicians, Chopin and Rossini; romantics, Abelard and Héloise.

CITE DES SCIENCES ET DE L'INDUSTRIE

parc de la Villette, 19e. User-friendly science exhibits and a great day out that is a sure-fire hit with the kids. The state-of-the-art exhibition centre houses **Explora**, in which permanent displays unravel the wonders of light, sound, language, robotics and the natural world with the help of dozens of hands-on toys from computer games and videos to holograms. There is a planetarium, activity centre, library, aquarium and several restaurants.

The futuristic stainless steel **Géode**, a huge glittering sphere, encloses a 1,000 square-metre OMNIMAX cinema screen (for daily schedules, tel. 46 42 13 13), and is parked next to a retired French naval submarine, the *Argonaut*.

CLUNY, MUSEE NATIONAL DES THERMES ET DE L'HOTEL DE

6 *place Paul-Painlevé*, 5e. Behind the splendid Flamboyant Gothic façade of the abbots of Cluny's Latin Quarter residence, the national museum of the Middle Ages is one of the best in the world. Beautiful gold and silver ware, suits of armour, reliquaries and stained glass are augmented by a stunning array of medieval tapestries, notably the exquisite *La Dame à la Unicorne*. Six panels of exceptional virtuosity celebrate the senses in a bouquet of delicate flowers, animals, birds, and the *dame* herself accompanied by a lion and fey, smiling unicorn.

Adjacent to the Hôtel de Cluny, the excavated remains of a Roman bath complex reveal a vaulted *frigidarium*.

COGNACQ-JAY, MUSEE

See page 229.

CONCORDE, PLACE DE LA

8e. The 3,000 year-old **Obélisque de Luxor**, anchor of this enormous square, stands in the middle of an horrendous traffic vortex. The heart of Paris affords a choice of magnificent vistas to those brave enough to venture to its centre. To the east, the *Voie Triumphale*, and **Tuileries** gardens lead into the embrace of the **Louvre**; to the west, the **Champs-Elysées** strikes up to the **Arc de Triomphe**. Across the Seine, the Assemblée Nationale houses the French parliament; and rue Royal carves a northerly path to **La Madeleine**.

During the Revolution more than 1,300 people became victims of the guillotine here including Louis XVI, Marie-Antoinette, and the architect of the 'Reign of Terror' Robespierre himself. On a more peaceable note, eight allegorical statues representing major towns from Nantes to Marseille mark the corners of the octagonal site.

DEFENSE, LA

The high-rise modern business district west of the city centre is enlivened by various hunks of modern sculpture and the capital's latest architectural phenomenon, **La Grande Arche**. Insolently skewed across the *grand boulevard* which stretches all the way to the Louvre, J.O. von Spreckelsen's giant white marble open cube represents 'a window on the world' according to its Danish designer. Some window: Notre-Dame could be tucked beneath the 90 m-high arch. Transparent lift-shafts rise through a 'cloudscape' to the roof-top viewing platform and exhibition gallery.

FAUBOURG-SAINT-HONORE

8e. Home of the **Palais de l'Elysée**, Parisian *pied-à-terre* of the President of the Republic (No. 55), this street is otherwise dedicated to designer shopping on a par with Bond Street in London or Fifth Avenue in New York. There is the added spice of seeing the great fashion houses on their home territory, gracious buildings and chic strollers. For more of the same, investigate the elegant 19thC *passages*, glass-roofed arcades such as **Galerie Colbert** and **Galerie Vivienne**, off rue des Petits-Champs.

FORUM DES HALLES

1er. Sunk beneath the site of the famous Les Halles markets, swept away to the suburbs in 1969, this modern shopping mall offers the usual run of boutiques, cinemas and restaurants, plus some alternative diversions including the **Parc Océanique Jacques Cousteau** (Niveau 3) with a variety of hands-on displays and videos; an outpost of the **Musée Grévin** waxworks (below); the **Musée de l'Holographie**; a children's play area, the **Jardin d'Enfants**; and the garish **Rock'n'Roll Hall of Fame**.

GOBELINS, MANUFACTURE NATIONALE DES

42 avenue des Gobelins, 13e. Founded by Louis XIV, the royal tapestry workshops are now a state enterprise - the only way to survive if you weave in the old-fashioned way, a painstaking one square metre or so per year. Some of the antique looms date back to the 17thC, carpets and hand-sewn tapestries are also made here, but nothing is for sale. Every item is used in the refurbishment of government properties or as gifts. (Guided tours only Tues-Thur.)

GREVIN, MUSEE

10 boulevard de Montmartre, 9e. The Parisian answer to Madame Tussaud's: wax effigies of the good, the great and notorious include Louis XVI and Marie-Antoinette languishing in jail; Napoleon and Josephine 'at home'; Chairman Mao and Michael Jackson.

GUIMET, MUSEE

6 place d'Iéna, 16e. A treasure house of Asian art amassed by 19thC industrialist Emile Guimet. Outstanding collections of Chinese porcelain and Khmer sculpture, plus artefacts from India, Japan, Nepal and Tibet, intelligently displayed with maps and photographs.

ILE DE LA CITE

See page 226.

ILE SAINT-LOUIS

4e. An island in the Seine behind Notre-Dame, this haven of shady streets lined with 17thC patrician houses is a welcome break from the tourist trail. Admire the elegant carved façades, picnic on the sunny *quais*, and sample the best sorbet in Paris courtesy of *Berthillon*, 31 rue Saint-Louis-en-Ile, or 2 rue Jean-Bellay.

INVALIDES, LES

quai d'Orsay, 7e. Due south of Pont-Alexandre III, Louis XIV's veterans' hospice bears all the hallmarks of the Sun King's grandiose style. Founded in 1670, the monumental complex centres on the classical **Eglise de Dôme** housing Napoleon's tomb beneath a vast gilded dome. On either side of the Cour d'Honneur, the **Musée de l'Armée** displays an exhaustive collection of militaria and Napoleonic memorabilia. Renaissance armour and uniforms, weaponry from pikes to Second World War artillery, scale models of Vauban's 17thC fortresses and the emperor's stuffed dog combine to make this national collection one of the finest war museums in the world.

JACQUEMART-ANDRE, MUSEE

158 boulevard Haussmann, 8e. Banker Edouard André built this sumptuous residence in the latter part of the 19thC, and filled it with elegant furniture, Venetian ceilings and a superb art collection assembled together with his artist wife, Nellie Jacquemart. Botticelli and Titian, Raphael and Rubens, Gobelins tapestries and 18thC French School paintings adorn the walls.

LOUVRE, LE GRAND

Palais du Louvre, 1er. First opened to the public in 1793, the Louvre is celebrating its bicentenary with the biggest overhaul in its long and illustrious history since François I (founder of the collections) replaced the original 12thC royal fortress with a Renaissance

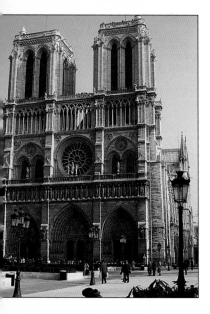

• The west front of Notre-Dame: admire it in relative peace from traffic-free place du Parvis-Notre-Dame.

palace. Major additions were made under Louis XIV and Napoléon, and the seven main departments (**Oriental, Egyptian, Greek and Roman Antiquities, European Paintings (14thC-1848), Graphic Arts, Sculpture (Middle Ages to 19thC), Furniture and Objets d'Art**) now total an overwhelming 300,000 exhibits, 80 per cent of which will be relocated within the various wings between 1993 and 1997.

The initial trumpet of change was sounded by I.M. Pei's 1988 crystal pyramid rising from the central courtyard above the **Hall Napoléon** reception area. With so much to see it is essential to be selective, so make use of the electronic orientation map with its helpful colour-coding system. If the hugely popular *Mona Lisa, Venus de Milo* and *Winged Victory of Samothrace* (both the latter are found in the Greek and Roman section) are on your itinerary, be there on the dot of opening time (9am). The Egyptian section is marvellous and not too busy; highlights of the paintings include Italian Renaissance works (Giotto, Botticelli, Raphael), the Rembrandts, and 19thC French artists.

MADELEINE, LA
place de la Madeleine, 8e. Based on the Parthenon in Athens, Paris' top society church almost opened as a bank before it was consecrated in 1842. From the steps leading up to the elegant arrangement of Corinthian columns, there is a marvellous view down rue Royal to place de la Concorde. A flower market spills out from the east side of the church six days a week. Foodies should not miss a chance to drool at the temptations of *Fauchon* , 26 place de la Madeleine, the delectable Parisien gourmet shop knee-deep in foie gras, caviar and snails. Its closest (and slightly more affordable) rival, *Hédiard* is at No. 21.

MARAIS
See page 229.

MARMOTTAN, MUSEE
2 rue Louis-Boilly, 16e. A truly delightful museum that combines the treasures of a discerning private collection with a magnificent Impressionist section. Jules and Paul Marmottan's collections of Italian primitives and Napoleonic *objets d'art* were augmented in the 1960s by a bequest of Claude Monet's later works donated by his son. They include the 1872 *Impression, Soleil Levant*, a sunrise at Le Havre, which gave the Impressionist movement its name, and a glorious array of abstract canvases from the waterlily period at Giverny. Also works by Berthe Morisot, Renoir and Sisley.

MONTMARTRE
See page 230.

MONTPARNASSE
14e. The Montmartre of the Left Bank, Montparnasse has eschewed the picturesque for a somewhat seedy air. Artists and revolutionaries - Rousseau, Chagall, Lenin and Trotsky - rubbed shoulders in the famous cafés along boulevard Montparnasse, and the **Coupole, Dôme, Rotonde**, and Hemingway's favourite **Closerie de Lilas** are still reasons to visit this quarter. A host of literati are buried in the local **Cimitière de Montparnasse** (Beaudelaire, Simone de Beauvoir, Sartre); millions of lesser mortals occupy the **Catacombes** (see page 219). The 200 m-high **Tour de Montpar-**

nasse is a landmark, a brilliant look-out with a 56th-floor bar and no queues.

NOTRE-DAME, CATHEDRALE DE

place du Parvis-Notre-Dame, 4e. Even seeing Notre-Dame for the first time there is a sense of déjà-vu. The great twin towers and spectacular rose window were emblems of Paris long before the Eiffel Tower.

Founded in 1160 on a temple site dating back to Roman times, the Gothic façade still retains traces of the earlier Romanesque style. Much of the decoration was destroyed in the Revolution, but Viollet-le-Duc's 19thC restoration work faithfully repaired the damage down to the 28 figures of the King's Gallery. The gloom of the massive vaulted nave focuses attention on the choir, spotlit by two vivid rose windows in the arms of the transepts. These compensate for the main window which is partially concealed by the organ loft. Carvings and paintings decorate the ambulatory chapels and a side door leads to the treasury. Follow in the footsteps of Victor Hugo's Hunchback of Notre-Dame up the north tower and step out amongst the gargoyles for a magnificent view across the city. The bell is in the south tower.

Below the cathedral forecourt, the **Crypte Archéologique** reveals the remains of the medieval city and Gallo-Roman walls, together with scale models of urban development through the centuries.

OPERA DE PARIS

9e. Magnificently pompous, crammed with columns, swags and busts of famous composers, Charles Garnier's 1870s Opéra is open for daytime tours and evening ballet performances. The opulent interior is all marble and gilt with a spectacular if controversial ceiling by Chagall in the auditorium. The Phantom of the Opera haunts the nether regions of the cellars where workmen uncovered an underground lake during the construction.

ORANGERIE DES TUILERIES, MUSEE DE L'

place de la Concorde, 1er. A ravishing feast of Impressionist paintings (Cézanne, Degas, Matisse, Renoir, Sisley) complements the famous oval galleries containing eight huge and dazzling

Nymphéas (waterlilies) canvases, painted by Monet between 1915 and 1926. The private collection of Jean Walter and Paul Guillaume, who appear in portraits by Derain and Van Dongen, has been preserved as a single entity and numbers Paris School works by Modigliani and Soutine, some Picasso nudes, and paintings by Gauguin, Van Gogh and Henri 'Douanier' Rousseau amongst its treasures.

ORSAY, MUSEE D'

1 rue de Bellechasse, 7e. The Italian architect Gae Aulenti made an inspired job of converting this cavernous turn-of-the-century glass and steel railway station into a tremendous modern museum space. Hanging galleries line the 32 m-high hall where Orson Wells filmed Kafka's *The Trial* in 1962, and natural light provides a terrific bonus in the main Impressionist galleries.

Covering the period 1840-1914, the museum acts as a bridge between the collections of the Louvre and Centre Beaubourg. On the ground floor Neoclassical (Ingres), Romantic (Delacroix) and Realist (Corot, Millet) paintings and sculpture together with Manet's mould-shattering *Déjeuner sur l'Herbe* (1863), illustrate the road to Impressionism represented by the early works of Monet and Renoir. The full-blown glory of the Impressionist harvest - Monet's studies of Rouen cathedral and the waterlilies at Giverny, Renoir's exuberant *Moulin de la Galette* and hundreds more - occupy the upper level, alongside off-shoots of the main movement such as high-kicking Toulouse-Lautrec dance halls, Van Gogh, Rousseau and Gauguin, plus a lively café behind the station clock. The eclectic mid-section combines sculpture, terrific Art Nouveau furniture and *objets d'art*, plus the Symbolist painters.

PALAIS DES ARTS DE L'IMAGE

See Palais de Tokyo, page 224.

PALAIS DE CHAILLOT

place du Trocadéro, 16e. Built for the 1878 Paris Exhibition, the Neoclassical *palais* sits on the Right Bank with an uninterrupted view of the Tour Eiffel across the Seine. Four museums are gathered under the one roof: the excellent **Musée de l'Homme** with its anthropological collections; maritime history and stirring seascapes by artists such as Joseph Vernet housed in the **Musée de la Marine**; the richly endowed **Musée du Cinéma**; and the terrific **Musée des Monuments Français**. The latter contains not one original work of art, but beautifully constructed plaster models of great moments in French sculpture and copies of antique frescoes. It sounds awful, but it is amazingly effective.

PALAIS-ROYAL

place du Palais-Royal, 1er. Built by Richelieu, the sombre 17thC palace has had a chequered career, lurching from cardinal's residence to royal household to Revolutionary bawdy house. Once owned by the Orléans family who enclosed the pleasure gardens with apartment houses to recoup their finances, it is now occupied by various government offices. The gardens form a peaceful oasis; while the main courtyard is full of children leap-frogging over Daniel Buren's bizarre but pleasingly wacky arrangement of black-and-white striped and truncated columns. Less energetic adults can be soothed by the water scupltures.

PALAIS DE TOKYO

11 avenue du Président-Wilson, 16e. In the midst of a *grands travaux* conversion which will turn it into the Palais des Arts de l'Image, housing state-of-the-art cinematic and photographic exhibits, this Art Deco building is already home to the **Musée d'Art Moderne de la Ville de Paris**. Stunning collections of Cubist, Fauve, School of Paris and abstract works are rotated around notable permanent fixtures including Sonia and Robert Delaunay's murals and Dufy's *La Fée Electricité*, a huge and brilliant story of electricity commissioned by the generating board.

PANTHEON

place du Panthéon, 5e. Built in the form of a Greek cross with a hefty portico supported on columns and a massive dome (which is threatening to demolish the entire building under its weight), the Panthéon started life as a church. Imposing but dull, it was commissioned by Louis XV in recognition of St Geneviève, yet emerged from the Revolution as a receptacle for the mortal remains of great Frenchmen. Victor Hugo, Voltaire and Zola are buried in the crypt. The cupola affords panoramic views and thoughtfully provided orientation boards point out landmarks.

PETIT-PALAIS, MUSEE DE

avenue Winston-Churchill, 8e. A florid Neoclassical edifice built for the 1900 World Exhibition, the Petit-Palais houses the broad-ranging municipal fine arts collections. Antiquities, medieval and Renaissance art, classical bronzes and a particularly fine collection of 19th-20thC French painting decorate the lofty halls, enlivened by painted ceilings and plants. It is worth investigating the temporary exhibition schedule, too.

PICASSO, MUSEE

5 rue Thorigny, 3e. In the 17thC Hôtel Salé, an elegant Marais town house tricked out with chequerboard tiled floors and dainty stucco friezes, the largest collection of Picasso's works in the world is brought to life, not so much by the quantity of the works on display, but by the wealth of personal memorabilia. The great *oeuvres* are scattered in museums around the world; those you see here are from Picasso's personal collection, part of which passed to the state in lieu of taxes on his death. Very early paintings, blue period and Cubist creations, family portraits and expressions of the artist's political and pacifist convictions trace a coherent portrait of Picasso's personal and artistic development.

Photographs, documents, assorted

PARIS BY BOAT

Cruising down the Seine is one of the most delightful ways to sightsee in Paris. The traditional **Bateaux-Mouches** depart daily from Pont de l'Alma, 8e (tel. 42 25 96 10). The **Batobus**, Port de la Bourbonnais, 7e (tel. 44 11 33 44), provides a riverboat service between the Tour Eiffel and Quai de l'Hôtel de Ville with stops at Port de Solférino for the Musée d'Orsay, Quai Malaquais for the Louvre, and Quai de Montebello for Notre-Dame. Tickets can be bought for individual stages or the whole day.

---

belongings, and Picasso's own art collection including Matisse and Renoir add a unique dimension. An additional bonus is the reasonable museum café (see also page 229).

RODIN, MUSEE NATIONAL AUGUSTE

Hôtel Biron, 77 rue de Varenne, 7e. Rodin spent the last ten years of his life (1840-1917) working in the ground floor studio of this former wig maker's mansion and convent near Les Invalides. The lovely gardens provide a marvellous backdrop for larger pieces such as *Le Penseur* (The Thinker) and *Les Bourgeois de Calais*. The interior is crowded with superb sculptures in stone, bronze and clay - the smooth white marble caress of *Le Baiser*, the spiritual simplicity of the hands forming *La Cathédrale*, and life-like quality of *L'Age de l'Airain*, so convincing that critics accused Rodin of casting the young man from a live model. Plans to expand the collection on display and add works by other sculptors should be completed in 1994.

SACRE-COEUR, BASILIQUE DU

See page 230.

SAINT-GERMAIN-DES-PRES, QUARTIER

6e-7e. Roughly laid out between the Seine and Jardin de Luxembourg on the Left Bank, this is the most lively and appealing district of the city. Its streets lined with tall 17th-18thC buildings are crammed with booksellers, antique dealers and galleries. There are restaurants and cafés at every turn, and the **rue de Buci** street market is one of the best in Paris.

Midway along bow-shaped boulevard Saint-Germain, the former abbey church of **Saint-Germain-des-Près** is the oldest in Paris. Its origins can be traced back to the 6thC, but the present building is an homogenous mixture of Romanesque, Gothic and later additions dating from the 11thC. On the square, publishers and academics, tourists and café philosophers rub shoulders in the famous literary haunts of **Les Deux Magots**, **Flore** and **Lipp**. **Le Procope**, on rue de l'Ancienne Comédie, was once frequented by Molière, Voltaire and Balzac; the 19thC artist Delacroix lived in a studio at 6

rue de Furstemberg, now a museum overlooking a little secret garden.

In the southern corner of the district, the **Jardin du Luxembourg** rolls out behind Marie de' Medici's 17thC Palais du Luxembourg. The French Senate sits in the palace, while the public gardens offer donkey rides and puppet shows, shady paths and boating ponds.

SAINTE-CHAPELLE

See pages 226.

TOUR EIFFEL

Champ-de-Mars, 7e. Strangely enough this classic Paris landmark did not receive official recognition as a national monument until 1964. Gustave Eiffel's 300 m-tall iron cat's cradle of a tower was the tallest building in the world when it was completed in time for the World Exhibition in 1889. Commissioned to commemorate the centenary of the Revolution, the design was universally slated at the time and considered an affront to French art and history. Today it is one of the most popular sights in the capital. Long queues form in summer, but on a clear day the views stretching 70 km in each direction are worth the wait.

TUILERIES, JARDIN DES

1er. Catherine de' Medici's Tuileries palace was burned down by the Commune in 1871, but Le Nôtre's formal 17thC gardens survived. The lawns, flowerbeds and ponds provide a combination of breathing space and open-air gallery between the Louvre and place de la Concorde.

At the western end of the gardens, two 19thC pavilions house art galleries. The former **Orangerie** (see above) contains a spectacular collection of Impressionist paintings. Its opposite number, the **Jeu de Paume** (Napoleon III's tennis court), hosts contemporary art exhibitions.

VERSAILLES

See Local Explorations: 8.

The Ile de la Cité

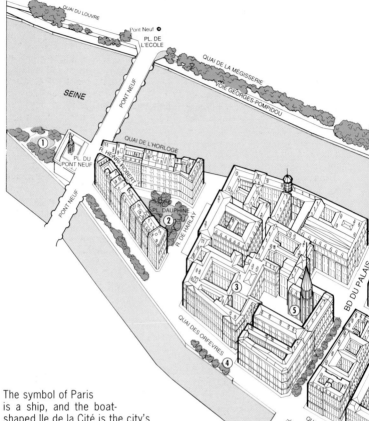

The symbol of Paris is a ship, and the boat-shaped Ile de la Cité is the city's 'cradle': where the *Parisii*, a Bronze-Age tribe, built their camp on an island in the Seine.

Start At the Pont-Neuf Métro station. Henri IV's Pont Neuf (New) is in fact the oldest bridge in Paris. Built between 1578 and 1604, it spans the Seine from Right Bank (**Métro Pont-Neuf**) to the Left across the tip of the island. Henri surveys his handiwork (and the clientèle of the *Taverne Henri IV*) from place du Pont-Neuf. Locate the steps down to ① **square du Vert Galant** and descend. The tree-shaded western tip of the island is beloved of sunseekers and smooching couples. Opposite Henri, rue Henri-Robert cuts through to ② **place Dauphiné**, a delightful triangular oasis hemmed in by 17thC buildings, chestnut trees and restaurants.

The monumental ③ **Palais de Jus-** **tice** complex entails a detour via ④ **quai des Orfèvres**, where Simenon's Inspector Maigret mulled over his investigations. Then turn north on boulevard du Palais, and take the left-hand archway off the courtyard to reach ⑤ **Sainte-Chapelle**. Consecrated in 1248, Saint-Louis had the church completed in less than three years to house his collection of holy relics. It is one of the great treasures of Gothic architecture; small, but perfect in every detail, with two chapels, one above the other. The upper chapel, reached by a spiral staircase, is lit by sublime stained glass windows 16 m tall and adorned with a total of 1,134 luminous biblical scenes. Impossible to describe as an attraction, the other main sight in the Palais complex is **La Conciergerie**, a former prison. At the height of the Revolutionary 'Terror', 1,200 prisoners were housed here, including Marie-Antoinette, as they awaited their fate at the guillotine.

Now take ⑥ **Rue Lutèce** down the centre of the island to ⑦ **place Louis-Lépine**, famous for its Sunday caged bird market. On other days of the week there is a gorgeous flower market. Look out for the Art Nouveau entrance to Métro Cité as well, one of Hector Guimard's rare and wonderful creations. A great swathe of old streets and houses was demolished in the 19thC to make way for the ⑧ **Hôtel-Dieu**, which also had the effect of opening up the huge square in front of the ⑨ **Cathé-drale de Notre-Dame** (see

page 223). Teeming with tourists and coaches, the square (place du Paris-Notre-Dame) is still a spectacular introduction to the Gothic leviathan which dominates the skyline from vantage points all around the city.

Take rue du Cloître Notre-Dame down the side of the cathedral to the eastern tip of the island where a small park conceals the moving ⑩ **Mémorial de la Déportation**. A stark cell honours the 200,000 French victims of the Second World War Nazi concentration camps. You can circle back to Métro Cité (place Louis-Lépine) via quai aux Fleurs, where a plaque at No. 9 is dedicated to the teacher Abelard and 17-year old Héloise who became lovers on this site in around 1117. Or cross Saint-Louis-Pont on to the Ile Saint-Louis, a grand old neighbourhood (see page 221).

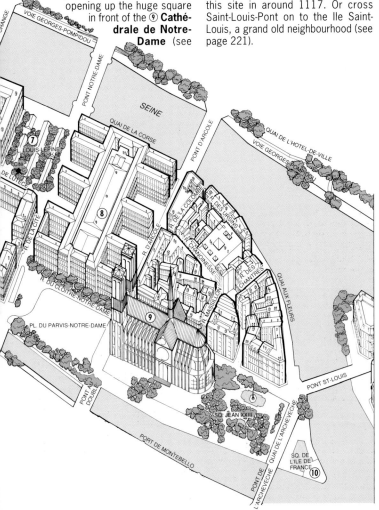

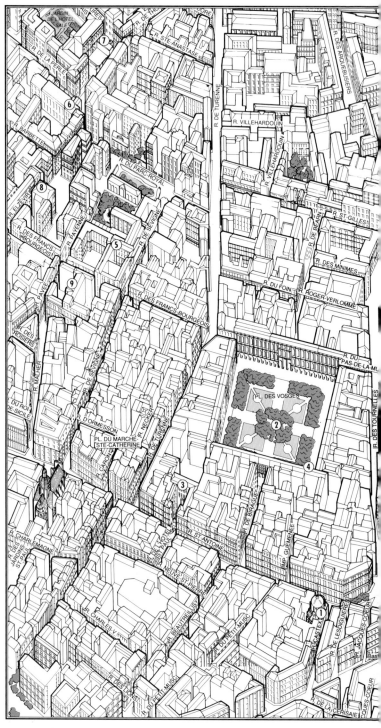

The Marais

Start Métro Bastille. While you're here, you cannot help noticing the controversial Opéra Bastille. And should you need sustenance before you set out, **Bofinger**, 7 rue de la Bastille, is a terrific 1900s brasserie. From place de la Bastille, head west on rue Saint-Antoine, passing ① the Baroque **Eglise de Sainte-Marie-de-la-Visitation**, where the 17thC lady of letters Madame de Sévigné is buried. Then turn right on rue Birague for ② **place des Vosges**. One of the loveliest corners of the city, the oldest square in Paris was commissioned by Henri IV as an open-air arena for courtly pageants. The King's and Queen's pavilions form the north and south sides of the square; elegant brick and stone façades and arcades of smart little shops and cafés overlook the tree-lined gardens. In the south-western corner of the square, a gate gives on to ③ the gardens of the beautiful 17thC **Hôtel de Sully**, headquarters of the national monuments commission who also use it for temporary exhibitions. In the south-east, ④ the **Musée Victor-Hugo**, 6 place des Vosges, occupies the

author's handsome town house, filled with mementoes, manuscripts and dozens of his eerie drawings.

Leave place des Vosges by the north-west corner, and follow rue des Francs-Bourgeois to one of Madame de Sévigné's Paris homes. The striking 16thC Hôtel Carnavelet now houses ⑤ the **Musée Historique de la Ville de Paris** (or Musée Le Grand Carnavalet), 23 rue de Sévigné. This huge, fascinating museum tells the story of Paris through paintings, furniture, models, and *objets d'art*. To celebrate the bicentenary of the Revolution, the museum expanded into the 17thC Hôtel-Le-Peletier-de-Saint-Fargeau at the top of the street, overlooking the greenery of square Georges-Cain.

From the top of rue de Sévigné, follow rue du Parc-Royal to rue de Thorigny. On the corner, the **Hôtel Libéral-Bruant** ⑥ was built for the architect of Les Invalides and now houses a locksmith's museum. Balzac went to school at 7 rue de Thorigny, next door to ⑦ the entertaining **Musée Picasso**, 5 rue de Thorigny, with its handy café-restaurant (see page 224).

Retrace your steps back to rue des Francs-Bourgeois via rue Elzévir, where the collections of chainstore magnate Ernest Cognacq are displayed in ⑧ the **Musée Cognacq-Jay**, 8 rue Elzévir. A self-professed philistine (he boasted that he had never visited the Louvre), Cognacq and his wife, Louise Jay, still managed to amass an impressive selection of artworks including paintings by Rembrandt, Reynolds, Gainsborough and the 18thC French romantics, and exquisite miniature *objets d'art*. At the bottom of rue Elzévir, turn left. On the next corner, the imposing **Hôtel de Lamoignon** ⑨ once hosted high-minded literary *salons* popular with writers like Racine. Now it harbours a history library behind the Corinthian-style stick-on pilasters. Return to the start by taking rue Pavée

229

Montmartre

• *Above: Montmartre.*

south to Métro Saint-Paul.

It is many years since Montmartre epitomised Bohemian Paris. Nowadays it is essentially a residential quarter, dominated by the vast Sacré-Coeur, with a hectic bustle of street artists and trendy little restaurants catering for tens of thousands of visitors.

Start Métro Abbesses, which has a fine Art Nouveau glass and wrought-iron entrance. On place des Abbesses, ① the **Eglise de Saint-Jean-l'Evangeliste**, an early reinforced concrete construction, is known locally as 'Saint-Jean-des-Briques'. Nearby the crypt of ② the **Chapelle des Auxiliatrices du Purgatoire**, 11-12 rue Yvonne-le-Tac, is supposed to be the site where France's patron saint, Saint-Denis, was beheaded in 250 AD, giving Montmartre its original name *Mont des Martyrs* (Martyrs' Mount).

From square Willette, a 225-step staircase (or a funicular for the faint-hearted) scales the Butte to ③ the **Basilique de Sacré-Coeur**. This familiar Byzantine wedding cake landmark is less attractive close up, but the view from the dome is stupendous. Built by public subscription after the disastrous Franco-Prussian War of 1870, it dwarfs its 900-year-old neighbour, the **Eglise de Saint-Pierre-de-Montmartre** ④, one of the city's few remaining Romanesque churches. Once part of a huge abbey complex,

Saint-Pierre's medieval architects incorporated four Roman columns in the design, probably left over from an ancient Roman temple in the days when the area was deemed the Mountain of Mercury.

Montmartre's old village square, ⑤ **place du Tertre**, would be a delightful spot were it not heaving with tourists, abysmal artists, and harried waiters flying across the street, trays in hand. If you like accordian music, try **Au Cadet de Gascogne**, 4 place du Tertre. Just around the corner, ⑥ **place du Calvaire** offers more glamorous views of the city. Follow rue Poulbot, and take a look down **rue Saint-Rustique**, a pretty 17thC cobbled street with views back to Sacré-Coeur. On the corner, ⑦ **A La Bonne Franquette** was the model for Van Gogh's *La Guinguette*. Utrillo immortalized ⑧ the **Pink House**, on the corner of rue de l'Abreuvoir, and stayed at 12 rue Cortot, as did Renoir and Dufy. It now houses ⑨ the little **Musée de Montmartre**.

On rue des Saules, ⑩ **Le Clos Montmartre**, a tiny vineyard planted in the 1930s, recalls the area's vine-growing history; while behind the green shutters of ⑪ **Le Cabaret au Lapin Agile**, a former Bohemian nightclub haunted by artists including Picasso, nostalgic audiences gather for evenings of French ballads sung by traditional *chansonniers*.

Utrillo is buried in the **Cimetière de Saint-Vincent** ⑫, and Métro Lamarck-Caulaincourt is just north of here. To complete a circuit, you can wend downhill on rue Girardon towards ⑬ **Moulin de la Galette**, as portrayed by Renoir, one of just two windmills remaining from the dozens which used to dot the hillside. Then turn east on rue Lepic and return to place des Abbesses. Or, head west (off the map) on Lepic and rue Joseph-de-Maistre, then south on rue Caulaincourt and enjoy a peaceful stroll around the **Cimetière de Montmartre**. Further south, Toulouse-Lautrec once painted the showgirls at the Moulin Rouge on seedy **place Blanche** (Métro); and **place Pigalle** is the present-day

RECOMMENDED HOTELS

De la Bretonnerie, FF-FFF; 22 *rue Sainte-Croix-de-la-Bretonnerie, 4e; tel. 48 87 77 63; credit cards* MC, V; *closed four weeks Jul-Aug.*

Stylish 17thC town house in the Marais. Pretty rooms with smart modern bathrooms; and a comfy *salon*.

De Crillon, FFFF; 10 *place de la Concorde, 8e; tel. 44 71 15 00; credit cards* AE, DC, MC, V; *open year round.*

One of the world's classiest hotels. Sumptuous 18thC reception rooms and gourmet restaurant, as well as the famous bar.

Deux-Iles, FFF; 59 *rue Saint-Louis-en-l'Ile, 4e; tel. 43 26 13 35; credit cards, none; open year round.*

Small town house, beautifully converted with charm and modern furnishings. Quiet, central and popular.

Guy-Louis Duboucheron, FFF-FFFF; 13 *rue des Beaux-Arts, 6e; tel. 43 25 27 22; credit cards* AE, DC, MC, V; *open year round.*

Lavishly revamped since Oscar Wilde 'died here beyond his means', this is the star hotel of the Left Bank. Small but luxurious rooms, glamorous guests, winter garden restaurant.

Jardin des Plantes, FF-FFF; 5 *rue Linné, 5e; tel. 47 07 06 20; credit cards* AE, DC, MC, V; *open year round.*

Pretty rooms with floral motifs reflect the public gardens opposite. Breakfast with a view on the roof terrace.

Lenox, FF-FFF; 9 *rue de l'Université, 7e; tel. 42 96 10 95; credit cards* AE, DC, MC, V; *open year round.*

Elegant, chintzy English-style decoration; charming staff. Relaxing after a day at the nearby Musée d'Orsay.

Des Marronniers, FFF; 21 *rue Jacob, 6e; tel. 43 25 30 60; credit cards, none; open year round.*

An oasis on the Left Bank. Chestnut trees in the garden, birds and flowers papering the walls, cosy bedrooms, and snug sitting rooms in the cellars.

Montana-Tuileries, FFF; 21 *rue Saint-Roch, 1er; tel. 42 60 35 10; credit cards* AE, DC, MC, V; *open year round.*

An extremely comfortable and attractive hotel just off smart rue de Rivoli.

Place des Vosges, F-FF; 12 *rue de Birague, 4e; tel. 42 72 60 46; credit cards* AE, DC, MC, V; *open year round.*

A great base for exploring the Marais. Quiet, spacious rooms and a pleasant rustic-chic *salon* in a 17thC town house.

Prima Lepic, F-FF; 29 *rue Lepic, 18e; tel. 46 06 44 64; credit cards* MC, V; *open year round.*

Bed-and-breakfast hotel on the heights of Montmartre. Simple, comfy rooms.

Ritz, FFFF; 15 *place Vendôme, 1er; tel. 42 60 38 30; credit cards* AE, DC, MC, V; *open year round.*

The only place to 'put on the Ritz' is the Ritz. Old-fashioned courtesy and charm, stunning furnishings, up-to-the-minute health club facilities.

Tim Hôtel, F-FF; 11 *place Emile-Goudeau, 18e; tel. 42 55 74 79; credit cards* MC, V; *open year round.*

Not quite an attic in Montmartre, but romantics will find lovely views from the upper storeys. Simple and fairly priced.

BUDGET (HOSTEL) ACCOMMODATION

There are numerous hostels in Paris, though most insist on a maximum stay of between three and five nights. The following organizations can each arrange reservations in a handful of hostels (the first two are centrally based):

Accueil des Jeunes en France (AJF), 12 rue des Barres, 4e, tel. 42 72 72 09; reservations, tel. 42 77 87 80; **BVJ Centre International**, 20 rue Jean-Jacques-Rousseau, 1er, tel. 42 36 88 18; **Youth Hostel Association (YHA)**, 38 boulevard Raspail, 7e, tel. 45 48 69 84 (enquiries only).

RECOMMENDED RESTAURANTS

Le Balzar, FF; 49 *rue des Ecoles, 5e; tel.* 43 54 13 67; *credit cards* AE, MC, V; *closed Aug, Christmas-New Year.*
Authentic Latin Quarter *brasserie*, popular with university types. Traditional menu (skate with black butter recommended).

Brasserie Flo, FF; 7 *cour des Petits-Ecuries, 10e; tel.* 47 70 13 59; *credit cards* AE, DC, MC, V.
Turn-of-the-century brasserie with the full complement of brass, stained glass, hatstands and leather banquettes. Vast platters of *choucroute* or *fruits de mer*.

Dodin-Bouffant, FF-FFF; 25 *rue Frédéric-Sauton, 5e; tel.* 43 25 25 14; *credit cards* AE, DC, MC, V; *closed Sun, two weeks Aug.*
Book ahead at this bustling and popular haunt. 'Market-fresh' seafood, hearty stews and game dishes.

Gérard Besson, FFF; 5 *rue du Coq-Heron, 1er; tel.* 42 33 14 74; *credit cards* AE, DC, MC, V; *closed Sat, Sun, three weeks Jul-Aug, Christmas-New Year.*
A student of Jamin, M. Besson has evolved his own fresh classical style - warm rabbit pâté in flaky pastry, salmon steak with red wine jelly.

Le Grand Véfour, FFF; 17 *rue de Beaujolais, 1er; tel.* 42 96 56 27; *cards* AE, DC, MC, V; *closed Sat-Sun, Aug.*
The gorgeous *Directoire* dining room is a national monument; Napoleon, Victor Hugo and Jean Cocteau dined here. Two Michelin stars for dishes such as salmon terrine, tender Bresse pigeon and an exquisite chocolate soufflé.

Jamin, FFF; 32 *rue de Longchamp, 16e; tel.* 47 27 12 27; *credit cards* MC, V; *closed Sat-Sun, Jul.*
Prolifically creative, a master of subtlety (pasta with prawns and fragrant white truffles), Joel Robuchon's red mullet flavoured with spices and olive oil, sesame sole and *tarte de truffes aux oignons et lard fumé* seduce even the toughest critics.

Le Maraîcher, F-FF; 5 *rue Beautrellis, 4e; tel.* 42 71 42 49; *credit cards* MC, V; *closed Sat lunch, Sun.*
A wonderful little find with stone walls, an open fire and steaming *cassolette* of mussels to revive flagging sightseers. Book ahead.

Marie-Louise, F; 52 *rue Championnet, 18e; tel.* 46 06 86 55; *credit cards* MC, V; *closed Sun-Mon, Aug.*
Copper pans on the walls, *cuisine bourgeoise* and old-fashioned prices. Work up an appetite for the *veal grand-mère* and serious puddings.

La Petite Chaise, FF; 36 *rue de Grenelle, 7e; tel.* 42 22 13 35; *cards* MC, V.
Genuine 17thC tavern with an intimate little bar and fixed price menu (*vin compris*).

Le Petit Zinc, FF; 25 *rue de Buci, 6e; tel.* 46 33 51 66; *credit cards* AE, DC, MC, V.
The Art Nouveau interior spills on to the pavement terrace and a broad-ranging *carte* features specialities from the south-west. Its popular twin, **Le Muniche, (FF;** 27 rue de Buci; *tel.* 46 33 62 09), concentrates on seafood and packing in the late-night crowds like sardines.

La Potée des Halles, F; 3 *rue Etienne-Marcel, 2e; tel.* 42 36 18 68; *credit cards* MC, V; *closed Sat lunch, Sun.*
Hearty provincial cooking - the *potée auvergnat* (a gargantuan stew) is a meal in itself. 1900s tiled walls.

Le Procope, FF; 13 *rue de l'Ancienne-Comédie, 6e; tel.* 43 26 99 20; *credit cards* AE, DC, MC, V.
A Parisian institution, the capital's oldest café (1686) is popular with tourists but still full of atmosphere. Simple food and late-night jazz.

CLASSIC PARISIAN *BRASSERIES*
La Coupole, 120 *boulevard du Montparnasse, 14e.*
Julien, 16 *rue Faubourg-Saint-Denis, 10e.*
Lipp, 151 *boulevard Saint-Germain, 6e.*
Terminus Nord, 23 *rue de Dunkerque, 10e.*
Le Vaudeville, 29 *rue Vivienne, 2e.*

North-Western France

Brittany's 'Pink Granite Coast'

145 km; maps Michelin Nos. 58 & 59

Officially, Brittany's Côte de Granit Rose stretches just 50 km, from the Baie de Lannion in the west to the Baie de Saint-Brieuc in the east, between Trébeurden and Paimpol. It offers some of the most bizarrely beautiful coastal scenery in the north-west. Great rose-tinged boulders, apparently dumped by a giant, lie in jumbled profusion beneath low granite cliffs; rocky bays bare jagged teeth, sculpted by thousands of years of wind and tides into fantastic shapes. But for all its inhospitable foundations, this northernmost coast of Brittany is a popular holiday centre, and the eastern side of the traffic-free Ile de Bréhat enjoys a climate so mild that mimosa and oleander grow in abundance.

Ecological disaster has struck Brittany's northern beaches twice in relatively recent times with the wrecking of the oil tanker *Torrey Canyon* off Britain in 1967, and again when the *Amoco Cadiz* foundered off Les Sept-Iles in 1978. However, those problems are in the past, and the Granite Coast's clean, sandy and gently sloping beaches are a major attraction for family holidays. The beaches at Perros-Guirec, Trébeurden, Trégastel, and Trévou-Tréguignec have all been awarded coveted EEC blue flags, and they literally sparkle in the sunshine as the light reflects off millions of twinkling granite chips.

If your beach holiday needs to be augmented with some action, there are all manner of watersports on offer, not to mention more than 40 sailing schools. The GR34 hiking trail follows some of the old customs officers' footpaths (*sentiers des douaniers*) which range across the cliff-tops; while birdwatchers can take boat trips out to the uninhabited archipelago of Les Sept-Iles, or watch the rich feeding grounds of Baie de Saint-Brieuc for snipe, curlew, oystercatchers and other water birds. Anglers can go after bass and mackerel; or you can wait for the local fishing fleet (and Paimpol's oystermen) to do the work for you.

Peak season is, of course, the summer. But if you are passing by off-season, don't ignore the Pink Granite Coast altogether. Bréhat is particularly lovely minus the crowds; and bracing walks along the deserted beaches are the best way to appreciate those wacky rocks. The tour could make a one-, two- or three-day break.

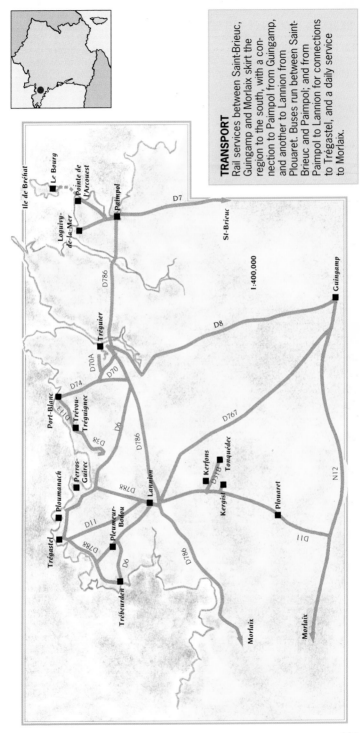

TRANSPORT

Rail services between Saint-Brieuc, Guingamp and Morlaix skirt the region to the south, with a connection to Paimpol from Guingamp, and another to Lannion from Plouaret. Buses run between Saint-Brieuc and Paimpol; and from Paimpol to Lannion for connections to Trégastel, and a daily service to Morlaix.

1:400,000

SIGHTS & PLACES OF INTEREST

BREHAT, ILE DE 🚤

At Pointe de l'Arcouest, the shore crumbles into a chaos of angular rocks and islands littered like mysterious leviathans across the bay. The Ile de Bréhat is a ten to 15-minute boat ride from the mainland (round-island tours take about an hour), and boats leave the dock here every hour or so in summer, less frequently during the rest of the year (schedules, tel. 96 55 73 47). Bréhat, actually two islands linked by a 17thC bridge, is around 3.5 km long, and although cars are banned, bicycles can be hired from the ferry port to explore the miniscule road network built for farm vehicles. On the eastern side of the island, **Le Bourg** is the only substantial settlement, a popular retreat for wealthy Parisiens in summer, but very quiet out of season. Along this eastern coast, figs, mimosa, oleander and palms flourish in sub-tropical profusion. The west coast is less protected, but its paths are wreathed with the scent of honeysuckle, and massed hydrangeas bloom alongside low stone farmhouses. Accommodation can be a problem – booked out in summer and firmly shuttered in winter. The S.I. in Le Bourg (summer season only; tel. 96 20 00 36) can sometimes help with local *chambres d'hôte* (bed and breakfast), and there are several campsites.

LANNION ✕

Leading up from the banks of the River Léguer to the main square, **place Général-Leclerc**, Lannion's old town centre, is not particularly distinguished, but it is pleasant enough, and populous year round. There are two splendid houses on the square: No.31 with its carved wooden façade, and the venerable edifice next door, faced in slate tiles which look like chain mail. If you squint, the windows could be Norman helmets with nose-pieces. At the end of the square, the 16th-17thC **Eglise de Saint-Jean-du-Baly** is entered by a diminutive door topped with a scallop shell.

LOGUIVY-DE-LA-MER

Surrounded on the landward side by cabbage patches, fields of artichokes and plastic tunnels of ripening tomatoes, Loguivy's chief charm is its lack of sophistication – perhaps why Lenin chose to holiday here once upon a time. This peaceful, unspoilt Breton fishing village and port is known for its oyster boats, most of which are left beached on the creek bed at low tide.

PAIMPOL 🚤 ✕

S.I. *rue Feutren*. The sombre setting for Breton author Pierre Loti's 19thC novel *Pêcheur d'Islande*, Paimpol has been recast as a popular yachting and holiday centre these days. In the bad old days, the town's fishing fleet would depart for six months at a time to trawl the Icelandic banks, but now they stick closer to home or harvest oysters.

DETOUR – SOUTH FROM LANNION

If you want to pack a picnic and venture inland, you'll find plenty of secluded spots along this country route. Take the D11 south from Lannion. After 5 km, bear left on the D31B and follow signs to the **Chapelle de Kerfons**. Edged by chestnut trees, the 15th-16thC chapel has a traditional Breton calvary (see page 55) and carved figures decorate a pinnacled turret above the south transept. Return to the D31B, and head south for **Château de Tonquédec** (open Jul-Sep), which you will see poised dramatically above the road before you descend into a valley and cross the River Léguer. Though partially dismantled by Richelieu, the castle walls are still pretty impressive, and there are fine views from the old keep. Return to the D11, and continue south (1 km) to the turn-off for **Château Kergrist** (gardens open Jul-Aug afternoons; closed Mon), where you can spend a relaxing hour or so wandering in the grounds. The château itself is sandwiched between two contrasting façades, one Gothic and dating from the 14th-15thC; the other 18thC, overlooking formal terraced gardens which fall away into English-style landscaping and woodlands.

The town centre is attractive and busy, and the modern hotels banished to the port area. There is a view of the bay from the **Tour Kerroc'h**, off the D789, the road to **Pointe d'Arcouest**, where boat trips depart for the **Ile de Bréhat** (see above).

PERROS-GUIREC ⊯ ✕

S.I. 21 *place de l'*Hôtel de Ville. During the summer season, Perros-Guirec is the busiest resort along the Côte de Granit Rose. Yachts jostle for space in the two harbours, cheap and cheerful beach cafés and family restaurants are packed to the gills, and there is hot competition for space on the lively golden sweep of **Plage de Trestraou**. Around a headland, the sheltered sandy beach of **Plage de Trestrignel** is rather smaller; up on its eastern flank there are grand views from **Pointe du Château**, off boulevard de la Mer. After the sun goes down, nightbirds can flock to the casino, or disport themselves in the half-dozen local discothèques.

RECOMMENDED HOTELS

BREHAT, ILE DE
Le Bellevue, FF; *Le Port Clos; tel.* 96 20 00 05; *credit cards* V; *closed* Jan *to mid-*Feb.

Open for most of the year, this is a great off-season hideaway on a cove next to the jetty. The 18 rooms are small and simple (showers only), but rooms on the second floor have tiny balconies. Bay views from the restaurant and terrace; tennis and bike rentals; riding, windsurfing and sailing by arrangement.

Another option is **La Vieille Auberge,** in Le Bourg (**FF,** *half-board only; tel.* 96 20 00 24; *closed Nov-Easter*).

PAIMPOL
Le Repaire de Kerroc'h, FF; *29 quai Morand; tel.* 96 20 50 13; *credit cards* MC, V; *open year round.*

Elegant quay-side house built by an 18thC pirate. Its smallish, but high-ceilinged and well-furnished rooms have views of the Port de Plaisance; and the dining room is favoured by discriminating locals. Good breakfasts.

PERROS-GUIREC
Le Sphinx, FF; *67 chemin de la* Messe; *tel.* 96 23 25 42; *credit cards* V; *closed* Jan-Mar.

A tall, turn-of-the-century house perched on the headland above Plage de Trestrignel. Eleven unexceptional but comfortable bourgeois rooms augmented by marvellous sea views (nine rooms have balconies), and a decent restaurant.

TREBEURDEN
Ti Al-Lannec, FF-FF (half-board); *allée de* Mézo-Guen; *tel.* 96 23 57 26; *credit cards* AE, DC, MC, V; *closed Nov-*Mar.

In woodlands above Lannion Bay, this attractive south-facing house has been transformed into a charming hotel with admirable skill and taste. Super rooms with nice touches such as books and flowers (the pricier ones have balconies), good restaurant, garden, beach path, spa facilities and gym. Children welcome.

If you really want to treat yourself, there is also the luxurious Relais et Châteaux **Manoir de Lan Kerellec** (**FFF;** *tel.* 96 23 50 09) nearby.

TREGUIER
Kastell Dinec'h FF; *Route de Lannion* (2 km W off N786); *tel.* 96 92 49 39; *credit cards* V; *closed* Jan *to mid-Mar, two weeks Oct.*

Peace and quiet guaranteed in this lovely grey stone farmhouse complex down a country lane (signposted from town). Some of the rooms in the converted stable block are small and stuffed with knick-knacks, but pretty – nay, romantic – and bathrooms boast fragrant toiletries. Semi-formal, rustic dining room (closed lunch, Tues-Wed off season) with distinctly up-market menus at fair prices.

TREVOU-TREGUIGNEC
Ker Bugalic, F-FF; *tel.* 96 92 49 39; *credit cards* V; *closed Nov-Apr and one week Oct.*

Simple family hotel with a pretty flowery garden leading on to the beach. A red R from Michelin for the cooking. Delightful spot.

• *Oyster beds, north Brittany.*

If you want to escape the wall-to-wall crowds on the beach, you can set off on foot along the **Sentier des Douaniers**, the old customs officers' path. It skirts the cliffs west of town to the port of **Ploumanac'h** and some of the most extraordinary rock formations along the coast. Another option is a three-hour round trip boat ride (no landings) out to **Les Sept-Iles**, an archipelago-cum-bird-reserve with a wing-tip to wing-tip scrummage of wheeling, screeching gulls, auks, and a few (rare) peregrine falcons. The islands have slowly recovered from the disastrous oil spillages of the 1960s and 70s, and between March and July around 200 pairs of jolly little puffins come to breed here and entertain visitors with their deft fishing forays – certainly not just a pretty beak.

Back on dry land, there is a pleasant diversion at La Clarté, just off the Trégastel road (D788). The squat, pink granite **Chapelle de Notre-Dame** was built in the 16thC, by the Marquis de Barac'h in fulfilment of a promise made to the Virgin Mary after the Marquis and his ship were delivered from thick fog by a shaft of sunlight. The chapel's interior has a distinctly nautical air with its wooden barrel roof, model ships hanging from the ceiling, and wealth of woodcarvings including a delightful 17thC painted retable, the

flowery gallery at the rear, and beams grasped in the jaws of toothsome monsters. The statue of Our Lady of Clarté, on the left of the retable, descends from her niche annually to take part in a traditional Breton *pardon* (saints day procession) on August 15. The Stations of the Cross around the church are the work of Maurice Denis, who had a holiday home at Perros-Guirec.

TREBEURDEN ⛺ ✕

S.I. *place Crech'Héry.* A handful of attractive beaches divided by rocky outcrops and a range of outdoor activities endear this seaside resort to families. Sailing, windsurfing, waterskiing, kayaking and diving are all readily available, and the S.I. has details of bike hire, riding and tennis centres.

The headland of **Le Castel** divides the two main beaches, and makes a pleasant stroll with views off to Finistère and the handful of rocky islands marooned in the Baie de Lannion. Boat excursions to **Ile Milliau** depart daily in summer, and on Sundays during the rest of the year. In addition, there are birdwatching trips to the **Marais du Quellen** (tel. 96 23 51 64).

Off the Corniche Breton (D788), 6 km north of town, the satellite tracking station at Pleumeur-Bodou makes a strange sight with its white tracking dishes. There are light shows here at the high-tec **Musée des Télécommunications.**

If you are heading south, signs off the D65 indicate **Point de Bihit** with its panoramic views west to Finistère.

TREGASTEL

S.I. *place Sainte-Anne.* Another summer-season wonder which winds down into virtual hibernation come September. But out of season is definitely the best time to stride along the beach and view the bizarre piles of rose-coloured rocks strewn along the shore and sprinkled across the bay. From the **Plage de Coz Pors,** west to the **Grève Blanche,** and around the corner to the **Grève Rose,** these strange weathered granite sculptures set the imagination racing. Many of the groups have special names, but it is more fun to make up your own. I was particularly proud of The-Runaway-Train-in-Four-Sections-Broken-Over-an-Island-and-Missing-its-Engine.

TREGUIER 🏠

S.I. *La Mairie* (*summer only*). Caught at the foot of the broad Jaudy estuary, Tréguier is by far the pleasantest town on the Côte de Granit Rose out of season. Its historic town centre gathers around place de Martray, where you will find the 13th-15thC **Cathédrale de Saint-Tugdual**, named for the Welsh monk, Tugwal, who introduced Christianity to the region during the 6thC. On a sunny day, light streams through the cathedral's modern stained glass windows, casting a kaleidoscope of colours across the granite interior. Great bunches of columns support the transept, and there is a delicate frieze picked out about the Gothic arches in the nave. The grandiose tomb in the north aisle is that of local hero, Saint Yves; there is an entrance to the elegant 15thC cloister in the north transept. Also take a look at the carved beasties and figures decorating the Renaissance choir stalls.

East of the cathedral, rue Renan houses a selection of local craftsmen, and the fine timber-framed **Maison Renan,** with its decorative scrolls and sagging lintel. It was the birthplace of 19thC philosopher Ernest Renan, who slumps on a plinth in place du Martray.

VILLA AND APARTMENT RENTALS

Perros-Guirec
Agence Villeneuve, 9 place de la Mairie, 22700 Perros-Guirec; tel. 96 23 22 62.

Trébeurden
Agence Rizzoni, place de Crech'Héry, 22560 Trébeurden; tel. 96 23 50 80.

Trégastel
Agence CGR Mangard, 21 place de Sainte-Anne, 22730 Trégastel; tel. 96 23 88 57.

RECOMMENDED RESTAURANTS

LANNION
Le Serpolet, F-FF; 1 *rue Félix-le-Dantec; tel. 96 46 50 23; credit cards AE, V; closed Sun dinner-Mon, two weeks Jan, two weeks Oct.*

Cosy small dining room in a fine old town house. Warm welcome and bounteous local cuisine – *foie gras* with artichoke hearts, scallops with tarragon, and *cotriade*, a steaming Breton stew of white fish, mussels, herbs and cream.

PAIMPOL
Vieille Tour, F-FF; 13 *rue de l'Eglise; tel. 96 20 83 18; credit cards DC, V; closed Sun dinner, Wed Sep-June, Mon lunch Jul-Aug, three weeks Nov-Dec.*

Pleasant little restaurant in the town centre with a tempting range of *produits regionaux* forming the base of its good-value menus. Flavoursome warm scallop and *foie gras de canard* salad, veal sweetbreads, pigeon with ginger, and fresh local oysters in various guises.

See also Recommended Hotels.

PERROS-GUIREC
Les Rochers, FF-FFF; Port de Ploumanac'h (6 km NW via D788); *tel. 96 91 44 49; credit cards V; closed Wed (except Jul-Aug), Oct-Easter.*

This elegant dining room overlooking the port is the place to splash out on a really excellent meal. Seafood (surprise, surprise), and lobster in particular, is the house speciality; Mme. Justin's grilled half-lobster is divine, so is the artichoke tartlette with a langoustine coulis, or *agneau de pré-salé* for non-fish fanciers.

Also 15 attractive rooms with views (**FF**), and half-board available.

TREBEURDEN
Glann Ar Mor, F-FF; 12 *rue de Kerariou; tel. 96 23 50 81; credit cards V; closed Wed (except Jul-Aug), two weeks Oct.*

Tiny restaurant with a reputation for local dishes and a friendly atmosphere. Turbot cooked with cider, perch with rhubarb, duck and wonderful baby vegetables.

See also Recommended Hotels.

TREGUIER
See Recommended Hotels.

TREVOU-TREGUIGNEC
See Recommended Hotels.

North-Western France

Inland Brittany – Rennes and the Border Castles

250 km; map Michelin No.59

This trail into Brittany's eastern borderlands unfolds into a rip-roaring yarn of great castles and medieval knights spiced with a dash of legend and Celtic mysticism. In 826, a Breton soldier from Vannes, Nominoë, was created Duke of Brittany by Louis le Debonnaire. Nominoë united the corners of his remote duchy, rebelled against the crown and defeated Charles le Chauve at Redon in 845. The victory initiated a period of Breton independence which was to last nearly 700 years (Viking invasions notwithstanding), until Anne de Bretagne's daughter married François I, and united the duchy with the French crown through their son, Henri II.

However, the French did not just stand by and applaud Nominoë's declaration of Breton independence: they raised armies to teach the traitors a lesson. In response, the Bretons constructed heavily fortified towns and fortresses from the toughest building material available - granite. Several of these superb medieval edifices have survived the passage of time with barely a scratch.

One name that crops up at every turn is Bertrand du Guesclin. Born south of Dinan in 1320, young Bertrand was a crude youth, disowned by his family. At a jousting tournament in Rennes in 1337, he borrowed a suit of armour and entered the lists anonymously, unseated several of his betters and won his father's approval. Du Guesclin fought with the Bretons at the start of his military career, but sided with the French at the capture of Rennes in 1356, and remained (unforgivably in Breton eyes) in the service of France until his death.

If you are arriving from the north or east, Fougères makes a sensible starting point. Vitré, to the south, is one of the finest medieval walled towns in France. Most of ancient Rennes, the capital of Brittany, went up in smoke in the great fire of 1720, but the gracious 18thC city centre is a very pleasant place to explore, with a couple of interesting museums. To the west of the city, the Forêt de Paimpont, home of Merlin, King Arthur's mystical wizard, is steeped in legend. If you have time, I thoroughly recommend an expedition to Josselin, one of the finest château-fortresses in the country (see France Overall: 2). Back in the north, there is pretty Dinan on the River Rance, and on the coast Saint-Malo and Mont-Saint-Michel (see France Overall: 2). To take in the whole tour, allow two to three days.

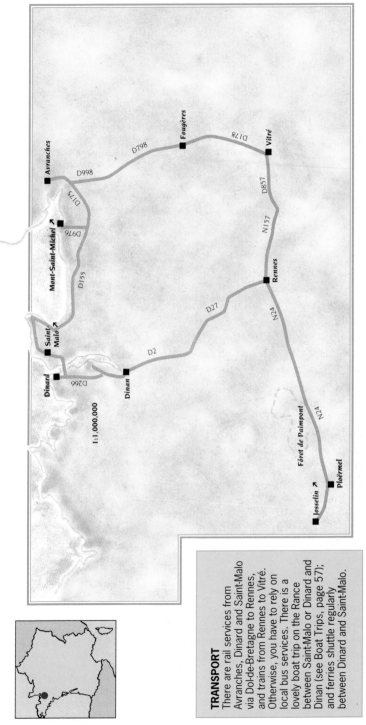

1:1 000 000

Avranches

D998

D175

Mont-Saint-Michel

D976

D155

Saint-Malo

Dinard

D266

Dinan

D2

D798

Fougères

D178

Vitré

D857

N157

Rennes

D27

N24

N24

Forêt de Paimpont

Ploërmel

Josselin

TRANSPORT

There are rail services from Avranches, Dinard and Saint-Malo via Dol-de-Bretagne to Rennes, and trains from Rennes to Vitré. Otherwise, you have to rely on local bus services. There is a lovely boat trip on the Rance between Saint-Malo or Dinard and Dinan (see Boat Trips, page 57); and ferries shuttle regularly between Dinard and Saint-Malo.

• Vitré.

SIGHTS & PLACES OF INTEREST

DINAN 🚉 ✕

S.I. *6 rue de l'Horloge.* Fortified, crenellated and beseiged by ramparts, fortress-Dinan rather belies its he-man reputation with the patrician air of a jolly and prosperous market town. In season, its pretty cobbled streets are over-run with holiday makers; but come in early May or late September, or in winter, and you'll be able to stroll around the few 'sights' with ease, then spend a lazy afternoon propped up outside a café eating *crêpes* and drinking the cider.

For a bird's-eye view of the town centre, climb the **Tour de l'Horloge**, rue de l'Horloge; and there are views from the **Donjon de la Duchesse Anne**. The *donjon* guarded the southern approach to the town, and dates from the 14thC, though it was built on the site of an earlier stronghold which appears in the Bayeux tapestry. Part of it is now occupied by a local history museum of Breton furniture, costume,

crafts, and paintings of local scenes. In the **Tour de Coëtquen**, a beautiful but eerie collection of 12th-15thC tombs of knights and their ladies lie spot-lit in the gloom, frozen in time like cryonics from the film *Cocoon*.

North of the castle, Frémiet's statue of du Guesclin stands on **place du Guesclin**, where in 1364 the Breton warrior defeated English knight Sir Thomas of Cantorbéry in single combat and lifted the siege. When du Guesclin died fighting for the King of France in the Ardèche in 1380, he asked to be buried at Dinan. After various vicissitudes (not for the sensitive stomach), only his heart made it back to his native land. It rests in a cenotaph in the **Basilique de Saint-Sauveur**. Something of a Romanesque-Gothic hotch-potch beneath an 18thC steeple, the church backs on to the **Jardin Anglais** with views down to the Rance sunk in a towering green valley. Rue du Petit-Fort slides down to the tiny marina, and picturesque **Quai de Rance**.

FOUGERES ✕

S.I. *place Aristide-Briand.* Entering Fougères, there are two options: the château is on the Rennes road at the bottom of town, but parking is very limited. Coming in from the north, it is more convenient to head uphill to the centre; continue just beyond the fountains of place Aristide-Briand, then right turn into Parking Douve.

The attractive 18thC 'new' town with its cobbled streets and flat-fronted, shuttered buildings stands well above the Nançon valley, where **Château Fougères** lies in a loop of the river. If hill climbing is not your strong suit, check with the S.I. for details of the mini-trains which shuttle visitors up and down the precipitous slope between the two, otherwise begin your descent on rue de la Pinterie.

As the fortress complex comes into view, you can stop off for a bird's-eye perspective in a little rampart gardens. Even in brilliant sunshine, the massive granite curtain walls, towers topped with conical slate roofs and pierced with arrow slits, look ominous. It seems impossible to believe this massive pile had a pathetic defensive record, being successfully captured by William the Conquerer, du Guesclin and St Louis to name but a few.

Built on a rocky promontary, the moat is provided by the Nançon. The original castle was razed in the 12thC, but work began immediately to rebuild the fortifications, and the various towers date from the 13th-15thC. Inside the castle precincts, you can explore the battlements, clamber up the **Tour Mélusine** for the views, and check out a small museum largely devoted to the town's shoe industry. During summer, open-air theatre performances celebrate Brittany's Chouan Rebellion, based on Balzac's colourful version of the tale retold in *Les Chouans*. (Castle open daily Apr-Oct.)

Grouped around place du Marchix, behind the Gothic bulk of the **Eglise de Saint-Sulpice**, the old town boasts a handful of fine Renaissance houses, and you can cross the river on rue des Tanneurs to another fine viewpoint on place des Arbres. Then head uphill on rue Nationale, where the **Musée de La Villéon** (No. 50) displays works by the popular Breton Impressionist artist (open daily mid-June to Sep, Sat-Sun Easter to mid-June).

JOSSELIN
See France Overall: 2.

MONT-SAINT-MICHEL
See France Overall: 2.

RENNES 🛏 ✕
S.I. Quai Châteaubriand. On-off capital of Brittany since the Middle Ages, Rennes has finally clinched the title from Nantes, and a very fine capital it makes, too - if not particularly Breton in style. Three days after Christmas in 1720, a drunken carpenter tipped his lamp into a pile of woodshavings and started a fire which raged for a week, destroying all but a corner of the city, now known as Les Lices. The centre, around the one surviving major building, the Palais de Justice, was handsomely rebuilt with broad paved streets, open squares and balconied 18thC town houses.

Overlooking colourful sunken gardens, the **Palais de Justice**, place du Parlement de Bretagne, is the place to start your perambulations. This imposing edifice, designed to house the once-powerful Breton parliament, was built between 1618-55, and paid for out of the public purse through a tax on wine and cider. (Madame de Sévigné wrote `As much wine passes through the body of a Breton as water under bridges'.) There are tours of the magnificent interior, liberally gilded, carved and hung about with paintings. In the Grand'Chambre, forum for parliamentary debate, Gobelins tapestries depict Brittany's turbulent history.

For some local culture, cross the

DETOUR – TO PAIMPONT AND JOSSELIN

West of Rennes, the village of Paimpont (40 km via N24/D38, or buses to Les-Forges-de-Paimpont, 4 km S) lies in the woods at the heart of ancient *Brocéliande*. According to Breton legend, the wizard Merlin (of Round Table fame) retired here to live in seclusion, and fell in love with a fairy, Viviane (aka the Lady of the Lake). The fairy trapped him in a magic circle, but although he had the power, Merlin had no desire to escape and remained happily enchanted deep in the forest. A fraction of its original size, *Brocéliande* is now more prosaically known as the **Forêt de Paimpont**, but it is still a peaceful and relatively undisturbed corner of the world. There are several châteaux, such as the lake-side **Château de Brocéliarde, le Pas du Houx** and **Comper**; also the austere **Château de Trécesson**. The **Fontaine de Barenton** is allegedly Merlin's magic spring, where you can conjure up a storm by pouring water on the great stone slab of Perron de Merlino. The forest is strewn with pretty lakes, and there are interesting walks such as the **Val Sans Retour**, where legend has it that Merlin is still held captive in a prison of air (details from Paimpont's summertime S.I.). If you want somewhere to stay, the **Relais de Brocéliande** (*tel.* 99 07 81 07) is a useful base with 25 rooms, and a restaurant **(F-FF).** From here you could continue via Ploërmel to the beautifully situated **Château de Josselin** (see France Overall: 2).

main boulevards lining the River Vilaine, and make for the **Musée de Bretagne**, 20 quai Emile-Zola, which provides an excellent capsule history and cultural introduction to the region. Starting with the pre-historic dolmen era, moving on to Gallo-Roman finds, and an evocatively-lit medieval section (with helpful English sub-titles), dioramas and audio-visual presentations carry on through to the present day. The story is further illustrated with the help of spearheads, carvings, hefty furniture (very comfortable looking beds), and traditional embroidered jackets, stiff lace collars and bonnets reserved for high days and holidays (closed Tues).

The **Musée des Beaux-Arts** is housed under the same roof, and its highlights are the 19th-20thC collections: Breton scenes from the likes of Blin, Cottet, Lanno, and the Pont-Aven school (Gauguin's *Oranges*), plus works by Boudin, Sisley, Picasso and Vlaminck, and de la Taer's beautiful *Newborn Child* (closed Tues).

Vieux Rennes lies to the west of the 18thC town, around **Porte Mordelaise**, last vestige of the 15thC town walls, and **place des Lices**. Notwithstanding the latter's historic pedigree as the spot where du Guesclin first revealed his prowess on the jousting lists, the city fathers have seen fit to erect two hideous brick-and-metal, glass-topped covered markets on the site. However, the surrounding streets are full of higgledy-piggledy 15th-16thC half-timbered houses, and a wealth of cheap and cheerful *crêperies* and bars. There is plenty of smart shopping to be done between the old and not-so-old towns. For a really top-notch cheese shop, make tracks for **Maître Renard,** 5 rue Nationale.

VITRE 🛏 ✕

S.I. *promenade Saint-Yves.* One of the best-preserved medieval towns in Brittany, Vitré was a prosperous textile centre in the 16thC, and a Huguenot stronghold. Perched on an outcrop, the **Château** was founded in the 11thC, and rebuilt in the 13th-15thC in the best traditions of Breton military architecture. With chains still hanging down to the drawbridge and machiolated towers topped with slate witches' hats, it looks as though it has stepped straight out of a fairytale by the Brothers Grimm. Across the courtyard, you can see a pretty Renaissance loggia attached to the **Tour de l'Oratoire**, which contains the castle chapel; while the **Tour Saint-Laurent** houses the

---

RECOMMENDED HOTELS

DINAN
Avaugour, FFF; 1 *place du Champ; tel.* 96 39 07 49; *credit cards* AE, DC, MC, V; *open year round.*

Dinan's best hotel - and only just out of the **FF** bracket - set above the ramparts with a flowery garden and 27 attractive rooms. The fine vaulted dining room serves delicious warm lobster salad; steak grilled before your eyes; outdoor dining in summer.

Porte Saint-Malo, F; 35 *rue Saint-Malo; tel.* 96 39 19 76; *open year round.*

One of the treats at this little hotel is the garden. Spotless and comfortable rooms, and a warm welcome.

RENNES
Garden Hotel, F; 3 *rue Duhamel; tel.* 99 65 45 06; *credit cards* AE, V; *open year round.*

South of the Vilaine, and a short walk from the museums, this comfy small hotel offers 24 rooms and family rooms, an interior garden and cheap cafeteria.

Le Pingouin, F-FF; 7 *place du Haut-des-Lices; tel.* 99 79 14 81; *credit cards* V; *open year round.*

Refurbished and very comfortable rooms (roof-top views from the upper storeys) in the heart of Vieux Rennes, conveniently situated with several cheap restaurants nearby.

VITRE
Le Petit-Billot, F; 5 *place Maréchal Leclerc; tel.* 99 75 02 10; *credit cards* V; *closed Sun off season, Christmas-New Year.*

Traditional provincial hotel below the old town and opposite the station. 23 simple but comfortable rooms, and a good if rather stark restaurant.

local history museum (closed Tues Oct-Jun).

Just back from the castle, cobbled **rue Beaudrarie** contains a fine mixture of picturesque old houses, their half-timbered upper storeys leaning over the street and crowding out the sunlight. Look for the carvings on the façades of No.25 and its next door neighbour. **Rue d'en Bas** is slightly less cute, but still has some interesting buildings further down. At the centre of the old town, the startlingly cleaned-up **Eglise de Notre-Dame** features an unusual and decorative row of seven gables flanked by pinnacles lining its south side on rue Notre-Dame, and an outdoor pulpit for *al fresco* preaching. A short distance beyond the church, the **Promenade du Val** leads down around the crumbling, ivy-covered ramparts to an esplanade overlooking neat rows of allotments and the River Vilaine.

The celebrated 17thC woman of letters, Madame de Sévigné, was an occasional visitor to Vitré. After her profligate husband and son had frittered away her fortune, the sharp-tongued social commentator was forced to live in straightened circumstances at the 15th-16thC family home, **Château de Rochers-Sévigné** (7 km S via D88; closed Sun am). Literary pilgrims will find personal memorabilia, a Mignard portrait, and a large park with avenues named after various in-jokes.

SAINT-MALO
See France Overall: 2.

RECOMMENDED RESTAURANTS

DINAN
Caravelle, FF-FFF; 14 *place Duclos*; *tel. 96 39 00 11*; *credit cards* AE, DC, MC, V; *closed Mon dinner and Wed Nov-Jun, one week Mar, three weeks Nov.*

Somewhat tarted-up rustico-chic dining room, but a delicious roast lobster *au beurre salé* lingers in the memory bank.

Le Relais des Corsaires, F-FF; 3 *rue du Quai; tel. 96 39 40 17; credit cards* AE, DC, MC, V; *Sun dinner-Mon from Oct to mid-Jun, mid-Jan to Feb.*

In a lovely setting down by the port, this old smugglers' haunt is a popular hideaway. Rustic decoration.
See also Recommended Hotels.

FOUGERES
Les Voyageurs, F-FF; 10 *place Gambetta; tel. 99 99 14 17; credit cards* AE, V; *closed Sat, Sun dinner, two weeks Aug.*

Reliable hotel-restaurant serving good value straightforward cooking. The rather old-fashioned hotel has 37 comfortable modern rooms.

RENNES
Le Corsaire, F-FF; 52 *rue d'Antrain; tel. 99 36 33 69; credit cards* AE, DC, MC, V; *closed Sun dinner, two weeks Aug.*

Elegant and sophisticated dining room. Two short and tempting menus: fillet of sole stuffed with buttered lettuce; buckwheat *crêpe* with scallops; interesting wine list.

Ti-Koz, F-FF; 3 *rue Saint-Guillaume; tel. 99 79 33 89; credit cards* AE, DC, MV, V; *closed Sun.*

Rumoured to be du Guesclin's house, this half-timbered building now houses a delightful restaurant. Salmon cooked with saffron flowers; served with a flourish on pretty Breton crockery.

VITRE
Gao Gens, F; 9 *rue Garengeot; tel. 99 74 51 64; open daily until late.*

An odd choice, on the face of it, but this is a very good little Chinese restaurant, useful on Sunday evenings. Delicious shrimp soup.

Le Pichet, F-FF; 17 *boulevard Laval; tel. 99 75 24 09; credit cards* V; *closed Sun dinner-Mon, two weeks Aug.*

Particularly pretty in summer with garden views from the beamed dining room. Light but classic menu.

Taverne de l'Ecu, F-FF; 12 *rue Beaudrarie; tel. 99 75 11 09; credit cards* V; *closed Sun dinner-Mon, two weeks Jan.*

In Vitré's most picturesque street, this 17thC inn serves up a selection of roasts, and fish in addition to more adventurous fare.
See also Recommended Hotels.

Poitiers and La Venise Verte

390 km ('ex-La Rochelle'); maps Michelin Nos 71 and 68

Less than a thousand years ago, the Gulf of Poitou lapped at the very doors of Niort. Fed by eight silt-laden rivers, the tidal basin gradually drew back to be replaced by a dazzling green fenland wilderness of reeds and mud banks, the Marais Poitevin. During the 13thC, the monks of Maillezais abbey began to drain the land and reclaim pasture for cattle. Henri IV called upon the expertise of Dutch engineers to mastermind the reclamation programme in the 16thC. Now 40,000 km of canals criss-cross the 55,000-hectare preserve protected by the Parc Naturel Régional du Marais Poitevin. Also known as *La Venise Verte*, it is a languid, secretive world of water and sky, where the only sounds are the shifting reeds and the calls of willow warblers. It is an easy day trip from the coast to Coulon, the main village for visiting the Marais, but I recommend an overnight stop outside the main tourist season.

An hour's drive north-east of Niort, the historic capital of Poitou is bypassed by the Loire-Bordeaux *Autoroute de l'Aquitaine*. Poitiers receives few transient visitors these days, but this was not always so. Poitou was the front line when Clovis finally triumphed over the Visigoths in 507, again when Charles Martel turned back the Moors in 732, and Edward, the Black Prince, won a famous victory over the French at Poitiers in 1356. The attractive town is renowned for its unusual range of ecclesiastical architecture including the Eglise de Notre-Dame-la-Grande, which, with its superb façade, is the apogee of the Poitevin Romanesque style. The town keeps abreast of the times thanks to its university, which was founded by Charles VII in 1432 and can count Rabelais and Descartes among its former graduates. Outside Poitiers, Futuroscope, a futuristic theme park has sprung up in a welter of high-tec buildings cloaked in reflective glass and is a favourite venue with summer visitors.

Both Niort (for the Marais Poitevin) and Poitiers lie just off the A10 *autoroute*, and can be reached from La Rochelle by the N11. To make this a more interesting round tour (a triangle in fact), you can head north from Niort to the little town of Parthenay, once a pilgrim stop on the Route Saint-Jacques, then take the main N149 to Poitiers, or amble cross-country on the D59/D6 via Vasles, and picnic in the Forêt de Vouille-Saint-Hilaire outside Poitiers.

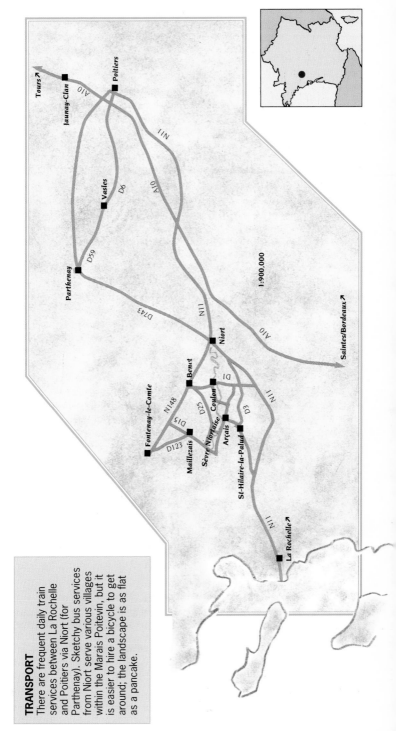

TRANSPORT
There are frequent daily train services between La Rochelle and Poitiers via Niort (for Parthenay). Sketchy bus services from Niort serve various villages within the Marais Poitevin, but it is easier to hire a bicycle to get around; the landscape is as flat as a pancake.

SIGHTS & PLACES OF INTEREST

NIORT

S.I. *place de la Poste*. On the Sèvre Niortaise just east of the marshlands, Niort is a useful launch pad for *La Venise Verte*. Its old town centre is sandwiched between the huge car park of place de la Brèche and the river in a maze of meandering medieval streets which lead down to place des Halles. The covered market is here, and the small-scale **Musée du Donjon**, laid out in a 12thC keep.

It is worth seeking out **Le Pilori**, the former Town Hall, off rue Victor-Hugo. This delightful little four-square Renaissance building, with its corner towers, spitting gargoyles, decorative pediments and balustraded roof line, has been spruced up to serve as a temporary exhibition centre.

THE MARAIS POITEVIN – LA VENISE VERTE 🛏 ✕

A magical world of green on green, light and shade, croaking frogs and the throaty call of cuckoos floating across the water meadows. Leafy tunnels of pollarded ash, drooping willows and swaying poplars line the water's edge. Blunt-ended punts are still the main form of transport for exploring the 7,000 km of navigable canals as they carve paths through the carpet of duckweed past low blue- or red-shuttered cottages, and the odd fisherman, hat tipped over his eyes, *baguette* poking out of his fishing bag.

At **Coulon,** 11 km west of Niort via the D9/D1, you can hire a punt with or without a boatman, a canoe or even a pedalo. If you feel safer on dry land, ignore the tourist mini-train and rent a bicycle. There is more of the same at **Maillezais,** 30 km north-west on the D15, where you can also visit the soaring Gothic abbey ruins.

Arçais and **Saint-Hilaire-la-Pallud** (south-west of Coulon) are also popular, but be warned: weekends can get too busy for comfort, and August, the height of the tourist season, is unbearable.

DETOUR – FUTUROSCOPE
A sensational theme park in the true meaning of the word, Futuroscope at Jaunay-Clan (12 km north-east of Poitiers) takes the moving image as its brief, and displays dazzling futuristic architecture plus state-of-the-art technology. Enter the world of OMNIMAX cinema, 3-D safaris, giant simulators and IMAX Solido, the virtual reality experience (information, tel. 49 49 31 10; closed Nov-Mar).

The S.I. has information about boat trips and walks in the Marais. Bicycles can be rented from the SNCF station. Niort is also the best place to stock up on picnic ingredients before heading into the marshes.

PARTHENAY

S.I. *Palais des Congrès*. An ancient stronghold overlooking the River Thouet, Parthenay has settled for the quiet life behind the remains of its ramparts. On the road into town from the south, there is a fine Romanesque church at **Parthenay-le-Vieux** with a noted statue of a knight hawking on horseback. To the north, the 13thC **Porte Saint-Jacques** recalls the pilgrims *en route* to Spain who would have tramped up rue de la Vaux-Saint-Jacques still lined with medieval buildings.

POITIERS 🛏 ✕

S.I. *8 rue des Grandes-Écoles*. The ancient capital of Poitou, which takes its name from the Gaulish *Pictones*, Poitiers is now essentially a market town – and a pleasant stopover.

North of the spacious, tree-lined place du Maréchal-Leclerc, the busy, semi-pedestrianized shopping district gathers around the **Palais de Justice**, where Jean de Berry and the dukes of Aquitaine once held court in the imposing Great Hall. In the middle of the marketplace on place de Charles-de-Gaulle, the **Eglise de Notre-Dame-la-Grande** is a brilliant example of Poitevin Romanesque. The sturdy building compensates for its somewhat squat proportions with staggered roof levels, a striped belfry, conical towers and a magnificent west porch. The porch is decorated with 12thC carvings illustrating biblical stories and scenes from Adam and Eve to the baby Jesus in his bath, while all manner of saints and creatures look on wreathed in an extravagant jungle of foliage.

The 13thC **Cathédrale de Saint-Pierre** lies down the hill towards the River Clain, but except for its richly carved choir stalls, it is the least interesting of Poitier's churches. Behind it, the **Baptistière de Saint-Jean** is believed to be the oldest Christian building in France, and resembles a burnt *brioche* parked in a gravel square on rue Jean-Jaurès. Baptism required total immersion in those days, so the generous font is sunk in the ground, surrounded by a collection of Merovingian carvings and watched over by gentle 12th-14thC frescoes.

A short walk away, the modern and well-laid out **Musée Sainte-Croix**, 61 rue Saint-Simplicien (closed Tues), combines an entertaining agricultural section with cleverly lit Roman artefacts and the town's art collections. A delightful Boudin, a small Sisley, and works by Vuillard and Bonnard are worth seeking out.

The last church on the circuit is the unusual 11thC pilgrim church of **Saint-Hilaire-le-Grand**, rue du Doyenne. Its wooden roof was replaced by a series of stone domes which narrowed the

• Arçais, Marais Poitevin.

nave between half-a-dozen aisles. For a well-deserved break, the **Parc Blossac** is a perfect place to collapse. There are aviaries, miniature goats, a couple of aquariums and a children's play area amongst the carefully manicured lime trees and flowerbeds.

RECOMMENDED HOTELS

COULON
Au Marais, FF; 46 *quai Tardy; tel.* 49 35 90 43; *credit cards* MC, V; *closed Nov to mid-Mar.*

Handy riverside inn with 11 bedrooms and a busy rustic restaurant serving regional dishes.

See also Recommended Restaurants.

POITIERS
Grand Hôtel de l'Europe, F-FF; 39 *rue Carnot; tel.* 49 88 12 00; *credit cards* MC, V; *open year round.*

Peaceful and welcoming with pleasant rooms and garden – a real bonus.

South-east of the city centre, the **Relais Pictave, F-FF;** 220 *Avenue Jacques-Coeur* (N147); *tel.* 49 45 07 07 offers well-equipped modern rooms, and a good restaurant.

RECOMMENDED RESTAURANTS

COULON
Le Central, F-FF; 4 *rue d'Autremont; tel.* 49 35 90 20; *credit cards* MC, V; *closed Sun dinner-Mon, three weeks Jan-Feb, four weeks Sep-Oct.*

Jovial rustic dining room packed in summer; generous local cooking.

Also five simple rooms (**F**).

POITIERS
Aux Armes d'Obernai, F-FF; 19 *rue Arthur-Ranc; tel.* 49 41 16 33; *credit cards* AE, DC, MC, V; *closed Sun dinner-Mon, three weeks Feb-Mar, two weeks Sep.*

Pretty pastel dining room and light classical cooking. Addictive potato pancakes with the duck, gooey desserts or sorbet with seven types of biscuits.

South-Western France

The Upper Dordogne and Lot

285 km; maps Michelin nos 75 and 79

F requently misrepresented as part of a 'Greater Dordogne' by its many British visitors and residents, the *département* of Lot, lying mainly south of the Dordogne river, all but occupies the ancient province of Quercy. The modern departmental name is derived from Quercy's major river, though confusingly the Dordogne actually flows through the northern part of the territory.

There is, however, little to differentiate Lot or Dordogne in these parts. The upper Lot is essentially rural, pleasantly rolling, both fertile and forested, though head south up into the Causse de Gramat and the scenery changes dramatically: scrub oak and sheep scratch an existence from the poor soil, and the *causse's* limestone foundations are riddled with underground caves and rivers. The River Alzou cuts a dramatic gorge below the region's chief tourist attraction, Rocamadour. A pilgrim village, 'Amadour's Rock' grew from a shaky legend involving a mummified body discovered in the 10thC, which was first identified as St Silvanus, and later as the biblical publican Zaccheus, said to have ended his days as a hermit named Amadour.

Down on the banks of the Lot, and its tributary the pretty River Célé, some hamlets and villages take on a distinctly southern cast. To avoid the tourist hordes, you could arrange to stay overnight in the tiny *ville perchée* of Saint-Cirq-Lapopie. Cabrerets is the access point for the famous Pech-Merle pre-historic caves; and just up the road at Cuzals there is an interesting regional museum, the outdoor Ecomusée du Quercy (5 km north-east of Cabrerets).

The roads marked on the simplified map make a convenient circuit from Brive-la-Gaillarde, (but of course you can just as well explore in your own way, without following the route). First head down the N20 to Souillac, well provided with hotels and campsites and offering easy access to Sarlat and the Vézère valley. Then meander cross-country to Rocamadour before rejoining the N20 south for Cahors.

Now you are on the Lot and one of the great days out hereabouts is a kayak trip. The Célé is a more peaceful option; if the water is not flowing fast, it is safe for young children. East of Cahors, the D662 wriggles along the Lot valley towards Figeac, a pleasant enough town, but nothing special. The even smaller D41 follows the Célé.

You could complete the circuit on the N140, but there is a pleasant detour on the D48 to Saint-Céré, where artist Jean Lurcat set up a work-shop, now a museum. Saint-Céré also hosts a summer music festival – a popular pastime in the region. Cahors breaks out into the blues in mid-July; Souillac favours jazz.

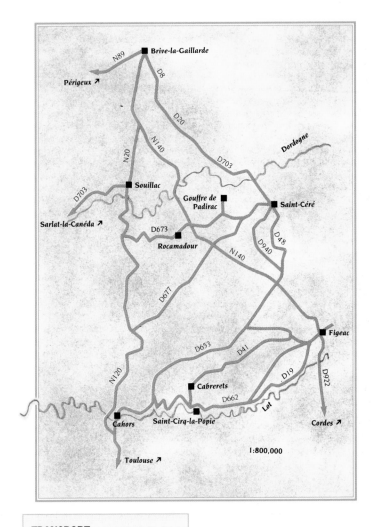

TRANSPORT
Train services operate between Brive, Souillac and Cahors, but that is about it. Trains stop a 5-km hike away from Rocamadour, or there are pricy S.I. tour buses from Brive, Souillac and Sarlat. Buses from Cahors stop within 2 km of Saint-Cirq-Lapopie.

SIGHTS & PLACES OF INTEREST

BRIVE-LA-GAILLARDE
See France Overall: 16.

CABRERETS ⇥
A pretty riverside village on the Célé, Cabrerets fills up in summer with visitors heading for the **Grotte du Pech-Merle**. Somewhat off the beaten track compared with the Vézère valley, these wonderful prehistoric caves with their 20,000-year-old paintings have escaped the fate of Les Eyzies (closed to prevent damage), and offer an informal prehistoric gallery with naturally sculpted limestone rock formations thrown in. There are some 60 animals – bison, mammoths, horses with flowing manes – and a dozen human forms, as well as the spooky footprints of ancient cave-dwellers. The **Musée Amédée Lemozi** offers artefacts and an interesting film show (closed Oct-Easter).

CAHORS ⇥ ×
S.I. *place* Aristide-Briand. Tucked in a loop of the Lot, the ancient capital of Quercy was first settled by the Gauls and then the Romans, who named it Divona Carducorum for the sacred spring, the Fontaine de Chartreux, on the opposite bank of the Lot, and for the local linen cloth. Another local product is the remarkably dark-coloured, tannic red wine known as Cahors, though it is not to everyone's taste.

An important medieval city, the old town of Cahors lies to the east of boulevard Gambetta guarded by a handful of towers. Squeezed into a tightly fitting square (Wednesday and Saturday markets), the Périgord-style **Cathédrale de Saint-Etienne** supports a pair of hefty domes, one of which is decorated with a 14thC fresco of the apostles, while St Stephen is seen being stoned to death in the apex. The vaulted cloister is carved with a host of 16thC Flamboyant Gothic capitals, but the most interesting carvings are reserved for the 12thC North Portal, where Christ ascends amidst hellish visions of monsters and sinners entwined with vines and thistles. The stone rosettes incorporate the rose symbol of Quercy.

Across avenue Gambetta, with its cafés and shops, rue du President Wilson (ironically, famous 19thC statesman Léon Gambetta was born at No. 9) leads to the magnificent **Pont Valentré**, which spans the Lot on six arches rising from diamond-shaped pontoons. The architect is said to have sold his soul to the Devil in order to complete his 13thC masterpiece.

ROCAMADOUR ⇥ ×
S.I. *La Mairie* (Apr-Oct). The best views of Rocamadour are from L'Hospitalet, across the Alzou gorge. The little pilgrim village, cut out and pasted on to the cliff, is one of the most popular sights in the region, and although it is undeniably picturesque, the single street sandwiched between two 13thC gates swarms with visitors in summer. The main pilgrimage season is early September, when it is not unusual to see pilgrims mounting the 223-step **Grand Escalier** on their knees.

Less devout visitors can be swept up to the chapel-lined **Parvis** by lift. On top of the cliff, the restored 14thC **Château** allows the curious to sample the view from its ramparts; and there are falconry displays at the **Rocher des Aigles**. The Lurçat tapestries at the **Hôtel de Ville** are another spectacular diversion.

Beyond L'Hospitalet, the **Forêt des Singes** and **Jardin des Papillons** house Barbary apes and butterflies respectively (closed Nov-Mar).

SAINT-CIRQ-LAPOPIE ⇥ ×
S.I. *Château de la Gardette* (Easter-Oct). Dwarfed by a substantial 15thC church, Saint-Cirq's ruined château and handful of honeyed stone houses cling to the limestone cliffs bound up with creepers and battened with timbers. The old woodturner's village is all towers and turrets, mullioned windows and

> **DETOUR – GOUFFRE DE PADIRAC**
> A 90-m deep fern-lined sinkhole provides access to this bizarre subterranean world, 18 km northeast of Rocamadour via the D673. Boat tours on an underground river explore vast caverns adorned with stalagmites and stalactites (closed Nov-Mar).

tiny lanes dotted with shops and artisan's workshops. To see it at its best, try to stay overnight.

SARLAT-LA-CANEDA
See France Overall: 16.

SOUILLAC ⇥ ✕
S.I. *boulevard Louis-Jean Malvy*. A bustling market town (great farmers' markets on the first and third Fridays of the month), Souillac is a useful transport hub for the region. The S.I. is particularly helpful, and has stacks of information about riding, canoe hire, pony trekking and walking. The main sight in town is the 13thC **Eglise de Sainte-Marie**, a Romanesque abbey church with echoes of Saint-Front in Périgueux in its Byzantine extravagance of domes and chapels. In the 18thC, the west door was turned inside out which has helped to preserve its remarkable carvings including a pillar of slathering dragons.

Kids may be amused by the mechanical toys in the **Musée de l'Automate**, place de l'Abbaye (closed Mon Apr-May and Oct, Tues Nov-Mar).

RECOMMENDED HOTELS & RESTAURANTS

CABRERETS
Hotel des Grottes, F-FF; 65 31 27 02; *credit cards* V; *closed Oct to mid-May*.

Riverside setting with an inviting terrace, simple rooms and a pool.

There is also the welcoming family-style **Auberge de la Sagne** (*tel. 65 31 26 62*), in a small park on the route des Grottes.

CAHORS
Hotel de France, F-FF; 252 *avenue Jean-Jaurès; tel.* 65 35 16 76; *credit cards* AE, DC, MC, V; *closed mid-Dec to early Jan*.

Handy but unexciting modern hotel with spotless, well-equipped rooms.

Hotel Terminus, FF; 5 *avenue Charles-Freycinet; tel.* 65 35 24 50; *credit cards* V; *open year round*.

Attractive and comfortable family hotel with a notable regional restaurant. Enjoy the Art Nouveau trimmings while tucking into artichokes with *foie gras* and *truffes*, lamb fillet with parslied sweetbreads, plus a cellar full of Cahors wines.

ROCAMADOUR
Relais les Vieilles Tours, F-FF; 4 *km W via D673; tel.* 65 33 68 01; *credit cards* V; *closed Nov to mid-Apr*.

Peace and quiet in a beautifully restored 13th-17thC building, all bare stone, beams and pretty fabrics. Gorgeous views, pool and fresh regional cooking.

SAINT-CIRQ-LAPOPIE
La Pelissaria, FF; *tel.* 65 31 25 14; *credit cards* MC, V; *closed mid-Nov to Apr*. Delightful, small and welcoming hotel in an old house grafted on to the hillside with stunning views of the Lot valley. Miniature garden, cozy dining room with a small but appealing evening menu.

Also recommended is the pretty **Auberge du Sombral, FF**; *tel.* 65 31 26 08; *credit cards* V; *closed Tues dinner-Wed, mid-Nov to Apr*; which has a very good restaurant.

SOUILLAC
Hôtel des Ambassadeurs, F-FF; 12 *avenue Général-de-Gaulle; tel.* 65 32 78 36; *credit cards* V; *closed mid-Dec to mid-Jan*.

Spacious, fairly priced rooms, garden, terrace and big modern dining room (with one of the best reputations in the area) serving generous regional cooking. Mushroom *fricassée*, omelette with truffles, smoked duck or potted goose. Children's menus and charming staff.

Auberge du Puits, F; 5 *place du Puits; tel.* 65 37 80 32; *credit cards* V; *closed Sun dinner-Mon off season, Nov-Dec*.

Old-fashioned, ivy-clad *auberge* offering plain rooms and a popular rustic dining room. Plenty of *périgordine* and *quercynois* dishes – goose, tripe and duck aplenty, friendly service and a summer terrace.

South-Western France

The Basque Coast

94 km; map Michelin No. 85

The broad sandy sweep of the Côte d'Argent finally runs out of steam south of Bayonne, interrupted by the appearance of jagged sea stacks in Biarritz and plummeting cliffs between Saint-Jean-de-Luz and Hendaye. This is the Basque Coast, only around 35 km from north to south, and my route is a short spin which could easily be accomplished in a day. You may, however, decide to turn it into a seaside break, taking time out to amble down the promenade in Biarritz, feast off freshly-caught tuna in the busy fishing port of Saint-Jean-de-Luz, and make a brief foray inland to the foothills of the Pyrenees (see France Overall: 4).

Behind the coastal resorts, the three provinces which constitute France's Pays Basque – Basse Navarre, Labourd and Soule – are predominantly rural, unlike their industrial and more politically active Spanish counterparts. But while the French Basques do not tend to strive for separation, their cultural identity remains strong. Distinctive half-timbered houses are graced by carved lintels and balconies laden with geraniums; unpronounceable Basque language signposts are peppered with Ks, Zs and Xs. There is Basque cuisine flavoured with onions, tomatoes, pimento and thyme all of which get thrown into a favourite savoury omelette, *piperade*; there are rough red wines, and a local spirit, *Izarra*. The leisurely game of *boules* is replaced by *pelota*, a fast and furious handball played in an open *fronton* court, or closed *trinquet*. During July and August numerous festivals are enlivened by traditional singing and dancing. And then there is the ubiquitous beret and rope-soled espadrilles, an informal uniform in these parts.

By chance I explored the Basque coast in early October, and was told by locals that it was the best time to be there. The summer sees too many visitors, but from early September to late October, the crowds thin out, yet the weather remains mild and the sea warm.

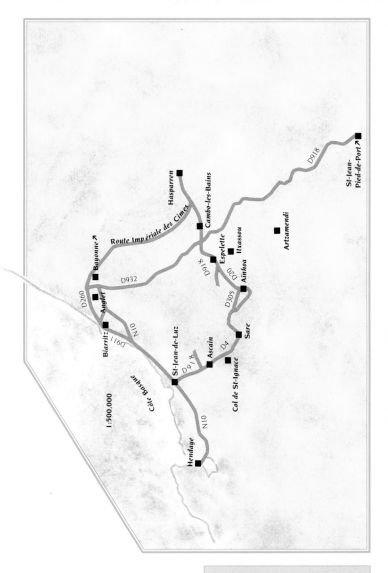

St-Jean-Pied-de-Port

D918

Hasparren

Cambo-les-Bains

Route Impériale des Cimes

Espelette

Itxassou

Artzamendi

Ainhoa

Bayonne

D932

D918

D20

D305

Anglet

D260

Sare

Biarritz

N10

D911

Ascain

D4

St-Jean-de-Luz

D918

Col de St-Ignace

Côte Basque

1:500.000

N10

Hendaye

TRANSPORT
Frequent train and bus services from Bayonne call at Biarritz, Saint-Jean-de-Luz and Hendaye on their way south to the Spanish border; and there are daily services to Saint-Jean-Pied-de-Port from Bayonne. Buses from Saint-Jean-de-Luz head east for Ascain, the Col de Saint-Ignace and Sare; and also Cambo-les-Bains (bus and train connections to Saint-Jean-Pied-de-Port).

SIGHTS & PLACES OF INTEREST

AINHOA 🛏 ✕
See Ascain to Cambo-les-Baines, opposite.

ANGLET
A sprawling suburb off the D260 between Bayonne and Biarritz, Anglet's saving grace is its two fine sandy beaches, **Chambre d'Amour**, and surfing favourite **Sables d'Or**. Wet suit, surf and boogie board rentals are readily available, but beware of very strong rip tides. In July and August little blue beach buses (*navettes*) shuttle between La Barre to the north, and Biarritz. There is a range of cheap accommodation and campsites catering for itinerant surfies.

ASCAIN TO CAMBO-LES-BAINS 🛏 ✕
Postcard-pretty Ascain has a lovely village square edged by traditional half-timbered houses, a galleried Basque church, a *fronton*, and several bars.

Take the D4 from here and wind up to **Col de Saint-Ignace** (160 m) for fine views south-east to **La Rhune** (900 m), where covens of Basque witches were once supposed to congregate. A little train grinds its way up to the summit in summer, and there is a superb vista stretching north to the Landes and across the Pyrénées Basques to Spain. On foot the climb takes around two hours.

Follow the D4 to **Sare** and **Aïnhoa**, or you can hike it on the GR10. Both villages are pretty, the latter with a main

---

RECOMMENDED HOTELS

AINHOA
Ohantzea, F; *tel.* 59 29 90 50; *credit cards* AE, DC, MC, V; *closed* Jan-Feb.

A mountain inn with a warm welcome, antique furniture and large, beamed bedrooms.

BIARRITZ
Château du Clair de Lune, FF; *route d'Arbonne* (4 km SE via D255); *tel.* 59 23 45 96; *credit cards* AE, DC, MC, V; *open year round.*

Delightful little château-hotel set in flowery private park offering bed-and-breakfast in pretty, chintzy rooms; peace and quiet.

Hôtel du Palais, FFF; *1 avenue de l'Impératrice; tel.* 59 41 64 00; *credit cards* AE, DC, MC, V; *open year round.*

Empress Eugénie's Belle Epoque sea-front palace sandwiched between gracious lawns and the beach. There are 128 luxuriously-appointed rooms and 25 apartments; suitably regal gourmet restaurant, **La Rotonde**; pool terrace.

SAINT-JEAN-DE-LUZ
Devinière, FF-FFF; *5 rue Loquin; tel.* 59 26 05 51; *credit cards* MC, V; *open year round.*

Engaging small hotel with eight attractive rooms in the town centre. Peaceful gardens.

La Fayette, FF; 18-20 *rue de la République; tel.* 59 26 17 74; *credit cards* AE, DC, MC, V; *open year round.*

Perfectly positioned in a pedestrian zone between port and beach, a family hotel with plain but bright bedrooms, attractive street terrace, and rustic dining room. Good regional cooking.

Grand Hôtel, FFF; 43 *boulevard Thiers; tel.* 59 26 35 36; *credit cards* AE, DC, MC, V; *closed* Jan.

Sea front *grande dame* with splendid Palm Court atmosphere and 49 stately rooms. Fine dining in the restaurant with terrace and views of the bay.

Toni-Ona, F; 10 *rue Marion-Garay; tel.* 59 26 11 24; *credit cards, none; closed* Oct-Easter

Summer season bargain close to the station. Simple and spotless with bathrooms down the hall.

SARE
Arraya, FFF; *tel.* 59 54 20 46; *credit cards* AE, MC, V; *closed* Nov-May.

Luxurious country house hotel filled with fresh flowers, comfy sofas and antique Basque furniture. Lovely green garden and a super dining room. Take time to peruse the well-chosen wine list.

DETOUR – SAINT-JEAN-PIED-DE-PORT

From Cambo-les-Bains, the D918 makes a lovely 35-km drive south-east to St-Jean-Pied-de-Port (see France Overall: 4).

On the way, stop off in **Itxassou** with its pretty church. Carry on from there, if you feel inclined, across the **Pas de Roland** to **Artzamendi** (very difficult road) for a fantastic panorama at 926 m. Retrace to the D918 – the road parallels the course of the River Nive (famous for trout fishing) – and continue in the direction of Saint-Jean.

---

street lined with fine 17thC houses displaying their founding dates carved into stone lintels. From here the D20 will lead you back to the D918 at Espelette, pimento capital of the region, and on to Cambo-les-Bains.

BAYONNE

See France Overall: 4.

BIARRITZ ⍾ ✕

S.I. *square d'Ixelles*. 'The pleasant Brighton of Bayonne' wrote Richard Ford in 1855, and just as that famous English south coast resort traded on its royal patronage by the Prince Regent, Biarritz was practically invented by Empress Eugénie in the mid-19thC. She brought Napoleon here and built a monumental red and white seaside palace, Villa Eugénie, now the luxurious Hôtel du Palais. Biarritz cannot be said to have fallen on hard times, but it is no longer frequented by royalty, though the price of a drink in the central **place Clemenceau** may yet set you back a king's ransom. However, the beaches are packed, the boutiques expensive, and fat cat automobiles still squeeze down narrow streets en route to the casino, which floats above the ocean on perpendicular gardens smothered with clouds of pink, blue and white hydrangeas and fringed tamarisks.

It is a pleasant stroll down the sea front, starting from the Hôtel du Palais on Plage Miramar, past Grande Plage to the look-out point on the **Rocher du Basta**. On the landward side, **place Eugénie**, with its church and old-fash-

ioned hotels, is edged by a colourful array of café umbrellas; across the road the carefully-preserved fishing enclave has two pint-sized boat basins and a popular seafood restaurant. If you have an eye for kitsch, there is plenty of outrageous Victorian Gothic seaside architecture – a veritable Addams Family *schloss* on the cliff top sprouts a forest of turrets and pierced gables above a half-timbered headband. Around the next headland, the **Musée de la Mer** is worth investigating for a whistle-stop introduction to the local fishing industry and aquariums full of fishy things from evil-looking eels and rays to cute nurseries of tiny seahorses. A walkway links the promontary to the **Rocher de la Vièrge**, so named for its pristine white statue. To the south the popular **Plage du Vieux Port** shelters between rocky outcrops, and then the seashore sweeps round into the Plage de la Côte Basque, Plage Marbella and Plage Milady, all served by handy beach shuttle buses in summer.

CAMBO-LES-BAINS

S.I. *parc Saint-Joseph*. A spa town beside the River Nive with a 19thC resort perched above the original Basque village, Cambo is renowned for its mild climate. Edmond Rostand, poet and author of *Cyrano de Bergerac*, came here to take the cure in 1900, and was so taken by the place he built **Villa Arnaga**, on the D932 a short distance north of town. A sprawling Basque-style edifice with a rather precious interior featuring panelling, curlicues, frescoes and assorted memorabilia, the villa is surrounded by formal gardens (closed Oct-Mar).

From Cambo-les-Bains, the D932 heads back to Bayonne (20 km). However, with time to spare, you may prefer to return via the **Route Impériale des Cimes.** Head for Hasparren on the D10, and after 6 km turn left for the D22 Route Impériale. The road affords splendid views of high peaks (cimes) and of the coast.

HENDAYE

S.I. *rue 12 rue des Aubépines*. This unexceptional border town and resort 14 km south-west of Saint-Jean-de-Luz has few charms, but a useful stretch of sandy beach. The reason to make the

> **WALKING IN THE PYRENEES**
> *See page* 302.

trek is the **Corniche Basque**, a wild and windswept stretch of road (the D912) which runs along the cliff-tops to Pointe Sainte-Anne (approximately 7 km). For walkers there is a coastal footpath from Socoa, or you can rent bikes from Peugeot, 5-7 avenue Labrouche in Saint-Jean.

Hendaye-Plage is the starting point for the two trans-Pyrenean walking trails, GR10 and the HRP (Haute Randonnée Pyrénéenne; see Walking in the Pyrenees, page 302); while Hendaye-Ville has a couple of quiet cafés in the main square. The area's other claim to fame is the **Ile des Faisans** in the River Bidossoa. Neither French nor Spanish, it was a convenient meeting place in wartime, and the Treaty of the Pyrenees was signed here in 1659.

SAINT-JEAN-DE-LUZ ⇔ ✕

S.I. *place* Maréchal-*Foch*. A former whal-

ing station with a sheltered natural harbour, Saint-Jean-de-Luz successfully combines its dual roles as an important fishing port (sardines and tuna) and attractive resort. Concessions to tourism include countless summer *fêtes*, and a couple of pedestrian streets housing chic boutiques, fancy espadrille sellers and pricey fish restaurants; meanwhile, the port area remains resolutely Basque and very businesslike, with even the yacht basin relegated to neighbouring Ciboure across the harbour.

The town's prosperous history is reflected in a fine collection of 17th-18thC houses grouped around the port and rue Mazarin in the Quartier de la Barre between the port and the beach. Focal point of the the Old Town is **place Louis XIV**, flanked by the illustrious **Maison Louis XIV** built by Jean de Lohobiague in 1643, but named for the French king who lodged here before his marriage to the Spanish Infanta Maria-Teresa in 1660. Descendants of the Lohobiague family still own the house and open a suite of comfort-

RECOMMENDED RESTAURANTS

AINHOA

Oppoca, FF; *tel.* 59 29 90 72; *credit cards* V; *closed Tues out of season.*

Delicious regional cuisine, including Labourd steak, country ham, gâteaux Basque, sheeps' cheese served with cherry jam.

BIARRITZ

Café de Paris, FFF; 5 *place* Bellevue; *tel.* 59 24 19 53; *credit cards* AE, DC, MC, V; *open year round.*

Pierre Laporte's parless classic cuisine is enlivened by choice regional touches from sweet red pepper sauces to a delicate *feuilleté* of red mullet with thyme butter. A simpler, more affordable annexe, **L'Alambic (F-FF)**, is found next door.

Platanes, FF; 32 *avenue* Beausoleil; *tel.* 59 23 13 68; *credit cards* MC, V; *closed Mon-Tues lunch, ten days Nov.*

Market-fresh menu which changes daily, laden with seasonal specialities from seafood to baby vegetables. Interesting selection of local wines.

SAINT-JEAN-DE-LUZ

Kaïku, FF; 17 *rue de la* République; *tel.* 59 26 13 20; *credit cards* AE, MC, V; *closed* Mon *lunch mid-Jun to mid-Sep,* Wed *out of season, and early* Nov *to mid-*Dec.

Jolly Basque-style dining room with bare walls but groaning platters heaped with hearty servings of fish, shellfish, duck or lamb *à la basquaise*. Terrace dining in summer.

Petit Grill Basque, F; 4 *rue* Saint-Jacques; *tel.* 59 26 80 76; *credit cards* DC, MC, V; *closed* Fri, *and mid-Dec to mid-*Jan.

Seafood treats straight from the port, plus Basque specials such as *pipérade* (omelette à la everything). Michelin awards a red R for good value.

Tourasse, FF; 25 *rue* Tourasse; *tel.* 59 51 14 25; *credit cards* AE, MC, V; *closed* Tues *dinner-*Wed *out of season, and mid-*Jan *to early* Feb.

Cosy-chic spot serving light, modern cuisine with plenty of seafood and interesting salads. Good intentions can be blown at the dessert stage.

ably lived-in rooms to the public in summer. The high spot is the painted dining room decorated with hunting and whaling scenes, delightful flowers and birds. The Infanta's retinue stayed in the pink **Maison de l'Infante** on the quayside, visible across the corner of the port.

The royal wedding took place a short step away at the **Eglise de Saint-Jean-Baptiste**, rue Gambetta. A splendid traditional Basque church, the largest of its kind and built like a fortress, you enter by a diminutive doorway to the left of the great portal which was walled up after the wedding service. The plain, whitewashed interior is edged by three tiers of oak galleries, increasing to five at the back, which were reserved for the menfolk, while women sat in the body of the church. In contrast, there is an elaborate gilded Baroque altar. A model ship suspended from the ceiling is a replica of Empress Eugénie's pleasure steamer which was almost shipwrecked off Saint-Jean in 1867.

• *Ainhoa.*

Pedestrianized rue Gambetta still has a sprinkling of old-fashioned grocery stores squeezed in amongst the *haute couture* and yachting gear. Doorways are strung about with garlic and red peppers from nearby Espelette, and trays of tomatoes, peaches and plums spill out onto the street.

Across the harbour, **Ciboure** (or *Zubiburu* in Basque) rises steeply up a wooded slope grouped around the pagoda-like belfry of the 16thC Eglise de Saint-Vincent. The composer Maurice Ravel (1875-1937) was born here, at 12 quai Maurice-Ravel, and there are great views back to Saint-Jean.

The D912 heads south from Ciboure on a rollercoaster cliff-top run to Hendaye (see page 257).

SAINT-JEAN-PIED-DE-PORT
See France Overall: 4.

SARE 🛏
See Ascain to Cambo-les-Bains, page 256.

North-Central France

The Heart of Normandy

320 km; map Michelin Nos 55 & 60

If your idea of a successful foreign holiday involves notching up an impressive daily tally of castles, cathedrals and museums, this tour is not for you. The heart of Normandy – as I see it – is more about scenery than 'sights', and this circular perambulation, which can take up two or three days if you do it in full, takes in some of the most lovely countryside on offer from the 'mini Switzerland' of the Suisse Normande and the undulating hills and forests of the Perche, to picturesque small farms and orchards in the Pays d'Auge. Whether you chose to take a couple of days or a week to cover the distance, one thing is certain: you will return feeling relaxed and refreshed.

Follow the River Orne south from Caen, and the open farmland of the north gives way to wooded hills, sloping pastures and the Vallée de l'Orne. It may not be Switzerland, but the river carves a winding course through the soft limestone, which throws up some impressive promontories, including the Rochers des Parcs and de la Houle near Clécy, the Pont Erambourg, and the dramatic Roche d'Oëtre south of Pont d'Ouilly. This is definitely a place to stay for a few days, and in addition to the scenery, there are plenty of outdoor activities from rambling to rock climbing (see Activity Holidays, page 263).

The Perche region is less well known, but equally attractive for a relaxing break. The cool, deep green depths of its forests, shaded by magnificent ancient oaks, are contrasted with rolling pastures strewn with the *crème de la crème* of Normandy's stud farms. This is horse country, and while the August yearling sales in Deauville are the stud farms' big event, there are plenty of horsy opportunities for the visitor: you can attend horse shows, visit stud farms, take riding lessons, or explore the region on horse back. (See Riding Holidays, page 264.)

The D26 through the Vallée de la Vie towards Vimoutiers is one of the prettiest stretches of road I can think of. Crumbling farmhouses with orchards full of blossom in spring; trees and hedgerows laden with fruits and berries in autumn. This is the Auge, and the land of the Three C's: calvados, cider and cheese, where camembert is a recent (19thC) addition to the groaning, gourmet cheese board, and *le trou Normand* (a small glass of calvados downed in one) is a necessary digestive aid between courses.

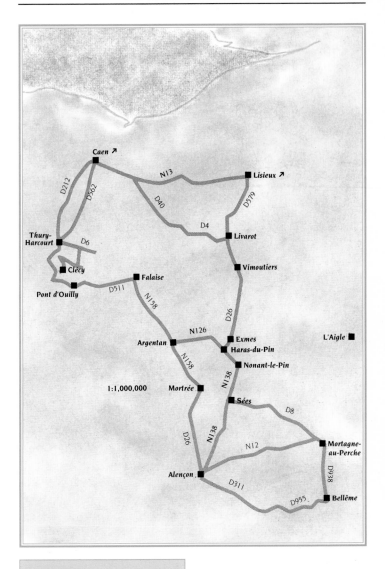

Caen ↗

N13

Lisieux ↗

D212

D562

D40

D579

Thury-
Harcourt

D6

D4

Livarot

Clécy

Vimoutiers

Falaise

Pont d'Ouilly

D511

N158

D26

N126

Exmes

L'Aigle

Argentan

Haras-du-Pin

N158

Nonant-le-Pin

N138

1:1,000,000

Mortrée

Sées

D8

D26

N138

N12

Mortagne-
au-Perche

Alençon

D311

D938

D955

Bellême

TRANSPORT

Caen-Tours train services stop at
Argentan, Sées and Alençon, and
bicycles can be hired at all three
stations. Caen-Flers bus services
stop at Thury-Harcourt and Clécy.
From Flers, there are buses via
Bagnoles-de-l'Orne to Alençon for
connections to Mortagne-au-
Perche. Buses from Alençon to
Lisieux head north via Argentan
and the Vallée de la Vie. Trains
connect Lisieux and Caen.

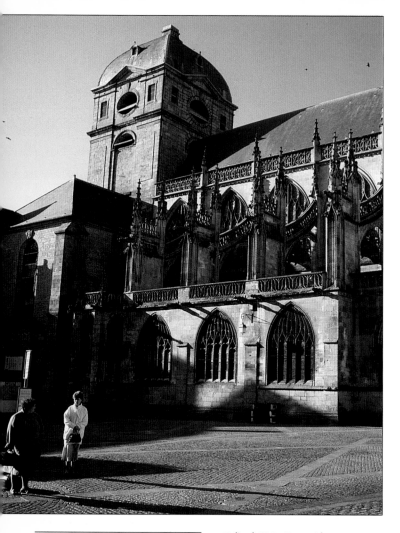

• *Eglise de Notre-Dame, Alençon.*

SIGHTS & PLACES OF INTEREST

AIGLE L' ⌘ ✕
See Market at L'Aigle, page 264.

ALENCON
S.I. *Maison d'Ozé.* An attractive market town on the Upper Sarthe, Alençon was a famous lace making centre in the 17th-18thC, but the only examples you'll see today are displayed in the Ecole de Dentelle and local museum. The S.I. is housed in a 15thC building tucked away in a courtyard with a rose garden behind the church. The square between the two, place Lamagdeleine,

has a colourful Thursday and Saturday morning fruit and vegetable market, where I counted ten types of lettuce on one stall alone.

Work started on the **Eglise de Notre-Dame** during a period of English occupation in the Hundred Years War. The façade is distinguished by its Flamboyant tripod gables pitched high over the triple arches, and the locals liken the fancy stonework to their famous laceware. The elegantly vaulted 14thC nave, which ends in a simple 18thC reconstruction, harbours some lovely 16thC stained glass; and near the door, the Chapelle de Sainte-Thérèse is dedicated to the local saint who was baptised here, and born at 50 rue Blaise on January 2, 1873.

Cobbled streets lead to the circular Halle au Blé (grain hall), with a rear view of the Vieux Château, now a prison. Further north, the **Musée des Beaux-Arts et de la Dentelle**, in a former Jesuit college off rue Jullien, presents an exhaustive history of the lace industry, 17th-20thC French paintings, and a bizarre collection of Cambodian artefacts (closed Mar).

ARGENTAN
D.I. *place du Marché*. Although it looks quite a significant dot on the map, the only notable sight here is the **Eglise de Saint-Germain**, which raises its 17thC belfry above the town centre. The Gothic edifice sports Renaissance flying buttresses, and modern glass in the ambulatory and choir.

BELLEME ⊨
S.I. *boulevard Bansard-des-Bois*. An attractive small hill-top town spread along a ridge overlooking the Forêt de Bellême. The town centre is reached by a 15thC gateway, and narrow cobbled street lined with 17th-18thC houses.

Within a short radius of Nocé (10 km E of Bellême via D203) are three fine examples of the Percheron fortified manor house, in **Courboyer, Lormarin and Saint-Quentin.**

CAEN
See France Overall: 1. From Caen, the D562 is undoubtedly the fastest and most direct road south to the Suisse Normande. However, deflected from my intended route by a traffic snarl-up, I stumbled upon a delightful ramble down the countrified D212, signposted for Louvigny off boulevard Guillou on the outskirts of Caen. Signs for Thury-Harcourt lead you on a winding trail through the Norman countryside to the edge of the Suisse Normande.

CLECY ⊨ ×
S.I. *place de l'Eglise (behind the church)*. A popular base for exploring the Suisse Normande, this pretty stone-built village gets extremely busy during the summer season. Clécy's man-made attractions are limited to a small **museum** of paintings by the Impres-

---

ACTIVITY HOLIDAYS
Apart from riding (see Riding Holidays, page 264), Normandy is an excellent place to mix activity with leisure. S.I. offices have all the information, but in advance of your holiday you could contact the Comité Départemental du Tourisme de l'Orne, 88 rue Saint-Blaise, BP50 61002 Alençon Cedex. Their booklet *Orne Loisirs* lists everything from 4x4 off-road trails to grass skiing. Walkers can hike all the way from Caen to Alençon on the GR36. For cyclists, there are several permanent circular cycleways. For further information, and a list of *gîtes d'étapes* along the routes, ask for the brochure *Randonnées Normandie*. Many of these *gîtes* accommodate horses overnight too.

---

sionist Hardy next to the S.I., and a **model railway museum** on the road to Le Vey; but the main attraction is the wide range of holiday activities on offer from riding and walking to climbing, gliding or a lazy pedalo ride on the Orne from the Pont de Vey.

If you are staying for a couple of days, the S.I. is fairly bristling with pamphlets and information sheets on every possible activity in the region (see Activity Holidays, this page), plus maps to guide you round the picturesque (but again busy in season) Route Touristique de la Vallée de l'Orne. Spring is a glorious time to be here with primroses and and other wild flowers scattered on the steep banks and meadows; and there are clouds of bluebells in the woods by May.

FALAISE
S.I. *32 rue Georges-Clemenceau*. Crouched in a steep-sided valley and guarded by its vast 12thC **château**, Falaise was the birthplace of William the Conqueror, though hereabouts he is still better known as William the Bastard. So the story goes, his young father Robert, Duke of Normandy, was captivated by a lovely laundress, Arlette, who bore him a son. As she carried the unborn child she dreamt of a tree which would cast its shadow over Normandy and as far afield as England.

RIDING HOLIDAYS

Two charming ways to enjoy this region are either on horseback, or driving a horse-drawn wagon (*roulotte*). If you are interested in a tour of the Perche on horseback for between four and ten people, staying in hotels and *gîtes d'étapes* each night, contact Mme Leray, Ferme Equestre de Mehéry, 6110 Bellou-sur-Huisne, tel. 33 73 87 10, or the excellent Orne regional tourist office (see Activity Holidays, page 263, for address). The simple *roulottes* sleep up to four and can be hired from Alençon from two to seven days. Contact Auberge de Jeunesse, la Croisette, I rue de la Paix, 61250 Damigni, tel. 33 29 00 48 or the Orne regional tourist office.

A quick detour off the main road will take you past a massive equestrian statue depicting a chain-mail clad William, surrounded by the first six dukes of Normandy. Opposite, the **Eglise de la Trinité** still bears the vestiges of its Renaissance decoration, but most of the town has been rebuilt since 1944.

HARAS DU PIN

It is a pretty drive across country to le Pin with views over paddocks and pastures to distant châteaux set against a backdrop of oak and beech woods.

The national stud was founded by Colbert in the early 18thC, and he commissioned Hardouin-Mansart to design the impressive 'Versailles for horses' at the end of a long grassy ride carved through the woods. Before the main château, two elegant stable blocks (now housing exhibits) enclose a horse-shoe-shaped courtyard, which is the scene of horse and carriage displays on Thursday afternoons in summer. There are guided tours of the forge, tack room and new stables, where the stud keeps around 100 stallions, including *Percherons* (though there are considerably fewer horses on display between February and July). The views from the rear of the château are tremendous, and you will see the competition grounds which host various show-jumping and dressage events;

also breeding competitions to show off the young horses. There is a schooling ring opposite the car park where you might see horses 'working out'.

LISIEUX
See France Overall: 1.

LIVAROT ✕
You are now in the heart of the Pays d'Auge cheese country. Livarot is the home town of the semi-hard, golden-red-brown cheese sometimes nicknamed *le lieutenant* for its stripes; Camembert is just down the road south of Vimoutiers. You can check out the local delicacies at the **Musée du Fromage**, on the edge of town (D4).

MORTAGNE-AU-PERCHE ⌨ ✕
S.I. *place Général-de-Gaulle.* A busy little town surrounded by the woodlands and valleys of the Perche, Mortagne is a popular starting point for touring and activity holidays in the area.

In town, there are two small museums, one devoted to the philosopher Alain (1868-1951), and the **Musée du Percheron**, in the old gatehouse, Porte Saint-Denis. The **Eglise de Notre-Dame** mixes Gothic and Renaissance elements with some fine 18thC wood carvings rescued from a nearby Carthusian monastery; and you can take a quiet stroll around the 16thC cloister in the former **Couvent Saint-François**.

Once you have exhausted these minor distractions, the helpful S.I. has

MARKET AT L'AIGLE

An absolute must if you are in this area on a Tuesday is Normandy's biggest market at **L'Aigle** (31 km north-east of Mortagne-au-Perche via D930). Hundreds of stalls piled high with regional bounty from fruit and vegetables to cheeses and cider cram into the town centre. Meanwhile, the livestock market provides raucous accompaniment as local farmers haggle and socialize in roughly equal proportions in a sea of crated geese, ducks and chickens, not to mention larger livestock. However, this section is *not* for the tender-hearted.

all manner of brochures and suggestions for short walks or hiking trails, cycle hire, tennis, golf and equestrian centres, also visits to studs and horse shows to see the local horseflesh in action (see Activity Holidays, page 263). The region gives its name to the powerful dapple-grey Percheron drays, but local studs are also famous for breeding and training thoroughbred race horses, trotters and cross-breed hunters on the rich grasslands.

Another Perche speciality, built along much the same lines as its drays, is the fortified manor house. Several of these imposing grey stone complexes, dating from the 15th-16thC, can be seen from the road, such as the **Manoir de la Vove** (14

km south-east, off the D10). Three others are within a short radius of Nocé (see Bellême).

The region's best-known gastronomic product is *boudin noir* or black pudding from Mortagne, celebrated with its own fair on the third weekend of March. You will find it served up just about everywhere with a side order of apple slices.

MORTREE
One km north, on the D26, is **Château d'O**. Reflected in the limpid green waters of its rectangular moat, this dainty early-Renaissance château is a gem of 15th-16thC domestic architecture. Its steep grey roofs, miniature turrets and ornately carved pediments

---

RECOMMENDED HOTELS

L'AIGLE
Le Dauphin, FF-FFF; *place de la Halle; tel. 33 24 43 12; credit cards* AE, DC, MC, V; *open year round.*

Traditional 17thC coaching inn in the town centre with 24 comfortable and attractive rooms plus an excellent restaurant (and you could not be better placed for the Tuesday market, either). Michel Bernard's deft cuisine transforms the best local ingredients into light and classical dishes, such as fillets of sole *à la Normande* or sweetbreads braised in *pommeau*.

BELLEME
Le Relais Saint-Louis, F-FF; 1 *boulevard Bansard-des-Bois; tel. 33 73 12 21; credit cards* V; *closed Mon-Tues in winter, two weeks Nov.*

Attractive *auberge* below the ramparts (near the S.I.) with eight simple rooms (**F**); young, friendly staff, small bar and comfortable dining room. Local flavours on the good-value four-course menu include duck and *boudin* with apple.

CLECY
Au Site Normand, F; 1 *rue des Châtelets; tel. 31 69 71 05; open year round.*

Comfortable, friendly village centre *auberge* with a garden and inexpensive restaurant serving hearty regional fare.

Moulin du Vey, FF-FFF; *Le Vey (1 km* E); *tel. 31 69 71 08; credit cards* AE, DC, V; *closed Dec.*

A pretty converted mill complex on the banks of the Orne with 12 comfortable rooms, plus a further seven in an annexe (3 km). The rustic restaurant serves classic-cum-regional fare, such as duck in cider, guineafowl with apple rings, lamb cooked with herbs, local cheeses and good puddings.

Hôtel du Commerce, F; *rue de Falaise, Pont d'Ouilly (10 km* S, *on the* D511); *tel. 31 69 80 16; credit cards* V; *closed Sun dinner-Mon Sep-Jun, Jan and two weeks Oct.*

Reasonably priced hotel-restaurant with 16 plain but peaceful rooms. The restaurant is worth a visit for its generous regional dishes, and (on a more exotic note) *langoustines* flambéed in calvados.

See also Auberge du Pont de Brie in Goupillières under Thury-Harcourt in Recommended Restaurants.

MORTAGNE-AU-PERCHE
Hôtel du Tribunal, F-FF; 4 *rue Notre-Dame; tel. 33 25 11 53; credit cards* V; *open year round.*

Tucked away below the church in an historic building, 20 quiet, comfy rooms and an alarmingly green dining room. However, the food is good with a well-stocked *menu du terroir*, and flourishes such as the salmon steak with fresh figs.

give it a fairy-tale look. You can wander in the grounds, or take a tour of the interior, furnished in predominantly 18thC style (open Wed-Mon afternoons).

Between Mortrée and Alençon, the D26 runs through the beautiful **Forêt d'Ecouves**, a splendid place for a picnic and a walk in the woods.

SEES

D.I. *place Général-de-Gaulle*. A small town with a fine old cathedral, Sées has a distinctly sleepy feel. A few little carved flowers and creatures have survived around the cathedral porch, which threatened to collapse and had to be buttressed in the 16thC. But the lofty Norman Gothic nave is in great shape, decorated by a pointed triforium and frieze. There is some notable 13thC stained glass in the transept.

THURY-HARCOURT ✕

S.I. *rue de Condé*. This low-key little town at the northern tip of the region enjoys a burst of vitality every summer when

a strong regional flavour. Home-made pâtés, fresh fish, tripe *à la mode de Caen* (in a stew with vegetables, cider and a splash of calvados), and the ubiquitous (but delicious) warm apple tart.

Also ten simple rooms.

• *Château de Thury-Harcourt.*

fleets of kayaks and canoes launch from the banks of the River Orne in a flurry of glistening paddles. The helpful S.I. has the details; or just drop in at the Base de Canoë-Kayak (tel. 31 69 72 82) below the château. If you prefer to keep your feet on dry land, the Orne describes an eccentric loop just west of town, known as the **Boucle du Hom**, which makes a pleasant walk (about 5 km).

There are also some lovely woodland trails leading down to the river in the grounds of **Château de Thury-Harcourt**. The great ducal château was destroyed in 1944, but behind the blind, bricked-up façade the dukes have cultivated a marvellous garden with steep banks of geraniums and bugle tumbling down to a huge lawn edged by herbaceous borders (open Sun afternoons Apr-May, Oct; daily Jun-Sep).

Rouen and the Seine Valley

325 km; map Michelin No. 55

Napoleon once described the Seine as the 'main street' between Le Havre and Paris, and for thousands of years the river's rôle as a transport and communications link has generated a flurry of activity along its banks. Cornish tin found its way up the river during the Bronze Age, Christianity in the 6th-7thC, and in the 9thC it was the means for the devastating Norse invasions. When the Vikings made peace with the Franks, they converted to Christianity, and turned their energies to more constructive pursuits, such as endowing the historic monasteries whose sites line the 110-km Route des Abbayes between Le Havre and Rouen.

Rouen's picturesque medieval town centre is a triumph of restoration work after its virtual destruction during the Second World War, and contains dozens of half-timbered houses, several magnificent Gothic churches and a clutch of museums. South of Rouen, Richard the Lionheart built a cliff-top castle at Les Andelys, which may have failed to prevent the French from taking Rouen, but occupies one of the finest sites on the river. Just beyond Vernon, Claude Monet's glorious garden at Giverny could leave you romantically plotting a lily pond *chez vous*.

This flexible tour makes a good two- or three-day break from Le Havre, a relaxed route towards Paris, or just a welcome excuse to take in Rouen as a day trip. As a very rough guide to timing, the Route des Abbayes is a day or a morning's work, depending on how often you want to stop, and the same for the highlights of Vieux Rouen. Make an early start for Giverny (Les Andelys is a good place to stay the night), and the section between Vernon and the coast can be a swift *autoroute* dash, or a gentle cross-country potter with some diversions on the way, such as Evreux's Gothic cathedral, the splendid 17thC château at Champ-de-Bataille, or the arboretum at Château d'Harcourt. An easy drive from Le Havre or picturesque Honfleur (see France Overall: 1), there are several comfortable overnight stop options in the vicinity of Brionne and the sleepy Norman village of le Bec-Hellouin, where William the Conquerer once recruited bishops from its historic abbey before he dispatched them to England.

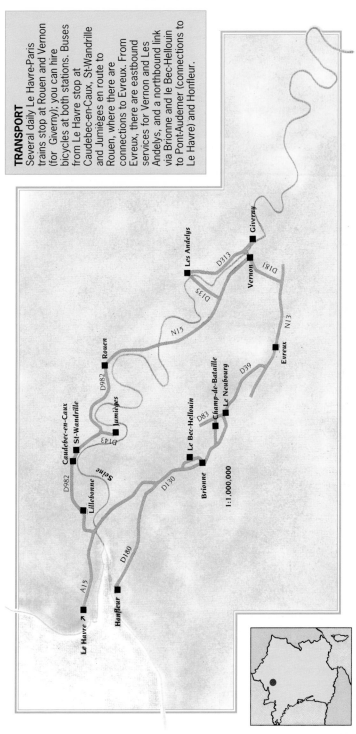

TRANSPORT

Several daily Le Havre-Paris trains stop at Rouen and Vernon (for Giverny); you can hire bicycles at both stations. Buses from Le Havre stop at Caudebec-en-Caux, St-Wandrille and Jumièges en route to Rouen, where there are connections to Evreux. From Evreux, there are eastbound services for Vernon and Les Andelys, and a northbound link via Brionne and le Bec-Hellouin to Pont-Audemer (connections to Le Havre) and Honfleur.

1:1,000,000

SIGHTS & PLACES OF INTEREST

LES ANDELYS ⌑ ✕

S.I. *rue Philippe-Auguste* (D313). The majestic white battlements of Richard the Lionheart's stronghold, **Château Gaillard**, rise sheer from the limestone cliffs above the river. Built in less than a year (1196-97) in an attempt to check the French advance on Rouen, it occupies a spectacular site with a commanding position and terrific views. The English garrison was eventually overcome when the French crept in via the latrines. Of the original towers circling the forward redoubt, only one remains, and the main fort was largely dismantled on Cardinal Richelieu's orders in the 17thC.

LE BEC-HELLOUIN ⌑ ✕

There is a marvellous view down to the **Abbaye de Bec-Hellouin** as you enter the village from the south on the D39, its creamy 18thC buildings nestling in the lush valley, and the sturdy grey 15thC Tour de Saint-Nicolas rising out of the chestnut trees. Herluin, a young knight from Brionne, founded the first monastery here in 1034, where he was joined by a brilliant Italian scholar, Lefranc, who became a trusted advisor to Duke William of Normandy ('The Conquerer'). Under William's patronage, the abbey became one of the great centres of Christian learning in the 11th-12thC, and forged strong links with the English church, sending its disciples to Winchester, Westminster, and, most notably, the philosopher-theologian Anselm to become Archbishop of Canterbury.

The old abbey church was destroyed in the Revolution, and its monks dispersed, until the Benedictine order returned in 1948. Some 26 monks still rattle around the remaining buildings. The 18thC refectory has been convert-

> **WALKING AND
> CYCLING THE ROUTE**
> The Route des Abbayes is popular with cyclists, and walkers can follow the GR2 along the Seine, striking off on the GR23A for Jumièges.

ed into a simple church, where Herluin's sarcophagus lies sunk beneath the altar. The guided tours (in French; closed Tues) are long and fairly tedious, but if you catch one up in the church, follow it into the cloister (only open for tours).

BRIONNE ⌑ ✕

See Recommended Hotels.

CAUDEBEC-EN-CAUX

A hidden delight on this route, the wonderful **Eglise de Notre-Dame** somehow survived when most of Caudebec was flattened in June 1940. You could spend hours outside the Flamboyant façade gaining a knowledge of medieval costume, as modelled by a jolly host of carved friars, bankers and bards, assisted by fashionable young beauties and ample matrons. Inside, the 16thC stained glass windows are exceptional: a magnificent Tree of Jesse in a cloud of gold on the left; half a dozen biblical tales including Bread of Heaven descending like giant snowflakes, and a turmoil of horses in a velvety Red Sea on the right. Above the entrance, a grand procession of local worthies and portly monks parades before a back-drop of period architecture.

A short walk away, the 13thC **Maison des Templiers** houses a local history museum; and you could pop into the **Musée de la Marine de Seine** with its maritime memorabilia.

CHAMP-DE-BATAILLE, CHATEAU DE

Adrift in a rural backwater, this vast and elegant 17th-18thC château appears like a mirage beside the quiet country road. The long, low red brick and stone façade fronts a series of sunny, beautifully-furnished rooms, and you can wander in the 100-hectare deer park or take a drive in a horse-drawn carriage.

EVREUX

S.I. *place Général-de-Gaulle*. Evreux is the capital of the Eure region, and its **Cathédrale de Notre-Dame** is worth a quick stop if you are not pressed for time. The Renaissance carvings around the north door date from the height of the Flamboyant period, as do the marvellously delicate leaf and flower motifs in the transept and lantern tower. Despite fire, bombs and storms, much of the antique glass has been restored.

The **Musée d'Evreux**, housed in the 15thC former archbishop's palace, includes Gallo-Roman archaeological finds, plus fine carved misericords and tapestries in the medieval section.

GIVERNY
Monet's home from 1883 until his death in 1926, the **Musée Claude Monet** is a living legacy of the green-fingered father of Impressionism. The pink and green-shuttered house is as he left it with its collection of rare Japanese prints, yellow dining room and blue kitchen, but it is the gardens that everyone comes to see – and I do mean *everyone*. Arrive before the gates open (Apr to Oct 10am-6pm) to get a brief glimpse of the scene before the crowds descend. May and June see the rhododendrons, azaleas and clouds of purple wistaria frothing over the Japanese bridge by the lily pond at their best. But the scene is spectacular whenever you get here, each month defined by a dominant colour scheme. The *Nymphéas* studio has been restored, but Monet's original canvases are spread around the world.

A short walk down the road, the new **Musée Americain** may not possess a Monet, but it does have an interesting collection of paintings by his disciples, turn-of-the-century American Impressionists who came to Giverny to study or just to be given inspiration from proximity to the master.

HARCOURT, CHATEAU D'
The grounds around this splendid double-moated and turreted feudal castle are tended by the Académie d'Agriculture de France, and the arboretum, initiated in the early 19thC, is now one of the most important sites of its kind in France. There are guided tours of the château (domesticated in the 17th-18thC), and the gardens support an extraordinarily diverse collection of trees which flourish in the varied soils and habitats found in the area (afternoons only; closed mid-Nov to mid-Mar).

JUMIEGES, ABBAYE DE
First consecrated in the presence of William the Conquerer, the ruins of this

• *Rouen and Seine.*

once-great abbey are in a sorry state. A jumble of discarded masonry has been pushed aside in the aisles, below graceful tiers of arches, galleries and windows framing trees and sky. From the ambulatory, there is a terrific view back through the soaring arch which once supported the lantern to the imposing 140-foot twin towers flanking the façade.

In all honesty, if the car park is crammed with coaches, think twice about visiting. To make the detour worthwhile, instead of heading straight back to the D982, you could follow the signpost marked *Bord de la Seine* (D65) for an extended meander through the orchards and along the Seine to Duclair.

LE HAVRE
See *France Overall: 1.*

ROUEN ⇌ ✕
S.I. place de la Cathédrale. Drivers should follow signs for Centre Rive Droite. There is underground parking in place du Marché, off rue Jeanne d'Arc. Arrive in Rouen between 12-2pm, and you are doomed to lunch. However, a spot of lunch and a wander around the carefully restored medieval town centre with its tall, half-timbered façades is no hardship. **Place du Marché** is a sensible place to start, grouped around the modern eye-sore **Eglise de Sainte-Jeanne-d'Arc**. The church's steeply-pitched roof is intended to evoke the flames

271

that engulfed the sainted scourge of the English on the spot marked by the 65-foot Croix de la Réhabilitation; there is no apparent explanation for the covered walkway looking like a scaly dragon's tail. The interior (two boat hulls laced together with girders), incorporates some lovely stained glass rescued from a church destroyed in 1944. Next door to the church, a small covered market is useful for collecting picnic ingredients.

Rue du Gros Horloge leads towards the cathedral, straddled by a fancy **clock tower.** The adjacent belfry gives a bird's-eye view of Vieux Rouen and beyond. North of here, the **Palais de Justice**, rue aux Juifs, has a marvellous 16thC courtyard.

Housed in an enchanting Renaissance building facing the cathedral square, the S.I. offers guided walking tours from July to mid-September (in English at 2 pm daily, mid-July to August). Opposite, Monet would hardly recognize the recently scrubbed façade of the **Cathédrale de Notre-Dame** which he immortalized in a series of studies exploring the effects of light. The monumental Gothic masterpiece bristles with decorative pinnacles, statuettes and twiddly bits with the grime of ages cleaned to reveal its pristine state. The Porte Calende, in the south wall, boasts a further wealth of carvings and reliefs in the manner of strip cartoons. The great nave rests on clusters of pillars with simple capitals, and soars into a dramatic lantern tower above the transept. On the right, the Booksellers' Stairway is a delightful zigzag affair; to penetrate the ambulatory and Richard the Lionheart's tomb, you have to take a guided tour.

Rue Saint-Romain is a picture-book medieval street with house fronts leaning out over the pavement. Look for the carvings on No. 74; and duck into

---

RECOMMENDED HOTELS

LES ANDELYS
Chaine d'Or, FF-FFF; 27 *rue Grande; tel.* 32 54 00 31; *credit cards* V; *closed* Jan, *and* Sun-Mon Oct-Mar.

Lovely, small 18thC hotel and restaurant overlooking the Seine. The excellent dining room (closed Sun dinner-Mon) serves traditional cuisine, such as homemade *foie gras,* fish, lamb with ginger and a warm plum tart with apricot coulis.

Hôtel de Paris, F; 10 *avenue de la République; tel.* 32 54 00 33; *credit cards* DC, V; *closed two weeks Feb-Mar.*

Sound value, unpretentious hotel-restaurant in the centre of Grand Andely. There are eight simple rooms above the pleasant dining room (closed Wed dinner and Sun), outdoor tables in summer.

LE BEC-HELLOUIN
Auberge de l'Abbaye, FF; *tel.* 32 44 86 02; *credit cards* V; *closed Mon dinner-Tues in winter, and Jan to mid-Feb.*

Attractive 18thC inn in the village centre with eight simple and often booked-up rooms. Tables out front, a geranium-filled courtyard and jolly rustic dining room. Regional specials include rabbit cooked in cider, fresh trout and local cheeses.

BRIONNE
Auberge Vieux Donjon, F-FF; *rue Soie; tel.* 32 44 80 62; *credit cards* V; *closed Mon, Sun dinner Nov-Mar, two weeks Feb, and mid-Nov to mid-Dec.*

Cosy inn with eight small rooms and a pretty flowery courtyard. Rustic dining-room serving classic meat and fish dishes.
See also Recommended Restaurants.

ROUEN
Hôtel de la Cathédrale, F-FF; 12 *rue Saint-Romain; tel.* 35 71 57 95; *credit cards* V; *open year round.*

A reliable budget option, and centrally-located (right by the cathedral) in a quiet pedestrian street with rooms around an attractive courtyard.

Hôtel Dieppe, FF-FFF; *place Bernard-Tissot; tel.* 35 71 96 00; *credit cards* AE, DC, V; *open year round.*

Comfortable hotel near the railway station with soundproofed rooms and a good restaurant.

VERNON
See Recommended Restaurants.

the Booksellers' Courtyard for another carved cathedral porch. Further along, there is a fine view of the lantern tower silhouetted through a bare window in the former archbishop's palace where Joan of Arc was tried. Rouen *faïence* and print shops gather in force around the **Eglise de Saint-Maclou**, another Gothic marvel with a finely carved Renaissance door on the left. Take rue Martinville for the **Aître Saint-Maclou**, a secluded square of 16thC half-timbered buildings. Once a charnel house and burial ground for plague victims, it is decorated in macabre style with carved skulls, crossed bones and grave digging equipment.

The former **Abbatiale Saint-Ouen**, is the final link in the Seine abbey trail. Dating from the 13th-15thC, it is a striking example of pure Gothic architecture, simpler, stronger and bigger than the cathedral, and surrounded by pretty gardens.

Rouen's museums are conveniently gathered together off rue Thiers. The **Museé Le Secq des Tournelles** (closed Tues-Wed am), housed in a former church on the corner of rue Jacques-Villon, offers an intriguing collection of wrought ironwork, utensils and jewellery; the **Museé des Beaux-Arts** (closed Tues-Wed am), is particularly well-endowed with French paintings from the 17th-20thC; and Rouen's popular ceramics take the biscuit in the **Museé de Céramique**, rue Faucon (closed Tues-Wed am).

SAINT-WANDRILLE

Historically important as one of the ancient centres of Benedictine learning in Normandy, the **Abbaye de Saint-Wandrille** is something of a hybrid these days. The first community was founded by the saintly Count Wandrille in 649, but his abbey was laid waste during the Norse invasions. Rebuilt in the 10thC, its fortunes fluctuated, and it was briefly owned by a 19thC Marquis of Stacpool, who built the grand gateway on the street corner. Today, the monks preside over the 13th-15thC abbey ruins and a lovely cloister; they worship in a 15thC tithe barn bought here from the Eure.

VERNON ⇔ ✕
See Recommended Restaurants.

RECOMMENDED RESTAURANTS

LES ANDELYS
See Recommended Hotels.

LE BEC HELLOUIN
See Recommended Hotels.

BRIONNE
Le Logis, F-FF; 1 *place Saint-Denis; tel.* 32 44 81 73; *credit cards* AE, DC, V; *closed Mon lunch, Sun dinner and Mon dinner in winter.*

Pleasant modern dining room presided over by smiling, English-speaking Mme. Depoix. Alain Depoix's elegant dishes, such as a breast and thigh of quail under a flaky pastry hat, taste as good as they look.

Also 13 simple rooms (**FF**).

ROUEN
Le Beffroy, FF; 15 *rue du Beffroy; tel.* 35 71 55 27; *credit cards* DC, V; *closed Sun dinner-Mon.*

Mme. Engel's charming Norman dining room in a half-timbered house south of the cathedral is well-worth lingering in. Fish and regional specialities include home-smoked salmon and delicious duck *à la Rouennaise*.

Le P'tit Bec, F; 182 *rue Eau-de-Robec; tel.* 35 07 63 33; *credit cards* V; *closed evenings, Sun and two weeks Aug.*

Attractive bistro-style lunch spot in a pedestrian street between Saint-Maclou and Saint-Ouen. Generous helpings and well-priced three-course menu with wine.

VERNON
Le Relais Normand, F-FF; 7 *place d'Evreux; tel.* 32 21 16 12; *credit cards* AE, DC, V; *closed Sun.*

Pleasant rustic-provincial dining room in the town centre. A sound choice for lunch during the week when the **F** menu is on offer. Generous goat's cheese and nut salad; pear tart. Garden in summer.

Also 18 rather dark, but well-kept rooms.

Around Paris: Ile de France

Maps Michelin Nos 55, 56, 60, 61 and 64

'Ile de France' is used here as a collective term for the countryside surrounding Paris – the Parisians' traditional playground. I've not suggested a specific driving route: the natural way to see these sights is as day trips from Paris, or in passing. Alternately sophisticated and rural, the hunting ground of kings and artists' inspiration, the Ile de France's historical associations are many. An embarrassment of royal palaces and noble châteaux nestle in the rolling woodlands improving on nature with their magnificent formal gardens. There are many museums, marvellous cathedrals in the suburbs at Saint-Denis, the more far-flung Beauvais, and, of course, incomparable Chartres. The former royal forests, dotted with small villages, and the restored barns and mills of wealthy Parisian weekenders, are a favourite destination for wave after wave of Sunday drivers in search of a friendly *auberge* in the woods.

The choice is so great that it is important to decide from the start what you want from your day. If you need to escape the bustle of the city, don't look to the glories of Versailles, and its crowds, for relaxation. Head instead to Fontainebleau or the 19thC artist's colony of Barbizon where sightseeing can be combined with exploring the national forest. There is plenty to see in this area, so consider staying a couple of days. Chartres is another pleasant overnight stop with detours to Sèvres or Rambouillet on the way, then you might continue down to the Loire. For youngsters, there is the brilliant air and space museum at Le Bourget, not to mention Mickey Mouse and the rest of his Euro Disney pals at Marne-la-Vallée.

During the 19thC, the railways provided an escape for ordinary city dwellers who flocked to the waterside taverns, or *guinguettes,* bordering the Seine. Degas, Renoir, Sisley and Monet were among them. Later Monet moved further downstream to Giverny, where he spent his last years painting in the famous garden, which can still be reached on a day trip from the capital. The increased accessibilty of the Ile de France has done little to ruin its charms and greatly assists visitors relying on public transport. Do, however, get an early start as virtually every attraction (except Versailles) closes for lunch between noon and 2pm; and at weekends it seems as if the whole of Paris is out in force.

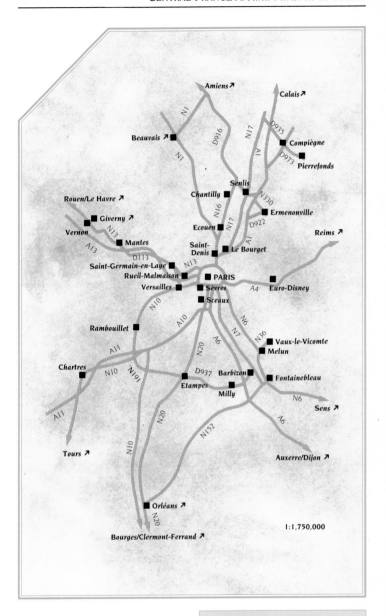

TRANSPORT
Most of the attractions mentioned in this section are easily accessible by public transport, either the Métro, RER suburban train services, or SNCF main line trains. See individual entries for details, which usually assume you will start from Paris.

SIGHTS & PLACES OF INTEREST

BARBIZON ⚐ ×

SNCF *to Fontainebleau*. A pretty village
with one long street on the edge of the
Forêt de Fontainebleau, Barbizon made
a name for itself in the 19thC as an
artist's colony. Precursors of the
Impressionist school, the landscape
artists Corot, Millet and Théodore
Rousseau formed the Ecole de Barbizon, and indulged in the radical pastime of painting local scenery in the
open air. Millet, in particular, broke new
ground with his renderings of toiling
peasants. Among the galleries, antique
shops and hotels along rue Grande,
Millet's and Rousseau's studios have
been turned into mini museums, as has
their local tavern, the **Ancienne
Auberge du Père Ganne**.

The surrounding countryside
remains an inspiration for present-day
artists, and walkers will find several
pleasant strolls in the forest. A useful
starting point is the Carrefour du Bas-
Breau (1 km east) for a not-too-strenu-
ous scramble around the **Gorges
d'Apremont**, though it can be
extremely busy here on holidays and at
weekends.

BEAUVAIS

See France Overall: 6.

BOURGET, LE

*No. 350 bus from Gare de l'Est/Gare du
Nord.* A must for Biggles fans and
space cadets, the **Musée de l'Air et
d'Espace** at Le Bourget airport covers
the history of aviation and space exploration from 1919 up to the present day

(closed Mon). An historic site in its own
right (Charles Lindbergh landed here
after his first transatlantic flight), six
enormous hangers contain space hard-
ware and more than 150 original aircraft from biplanes to Mirage fighters,
plus cinemas and audio-visual displays.
Concorde 001, the prototype, is
parked on the tarmac alongside the *Ari-
ane* rocket launcher.

CHANTILLY ×

SNCF *from Gare du Nord.* S.I. 23 *avenue
du Maréchal-Joffre.* Although it has lent
its name to whipped cream and lace,
Chantilly's chief business is horse racing. The first official race took place in
1834, and the prestigious annual *Prix
de Dianne* and *Prix du Jockey Club* flat
races provide a splendid excuse for
Parisians to parade around the elegantly appointed race track opposite the
château. Over 3,000 horses ride out
on morning exercises along sandy
tracks through the surrounding forest.
Trials are held in strict secrecy, but the
Direction des Terrains d'Entrainement,
16 avenue Général-Leclerc (tel. 44 57
21 35), arranges special visits for
early-rising enthusiasts.

Reflected in an artificial lake,
Château de Chantilly (closed Tues)
dates from the 16thC when it was
owned by the legendary Anne de Montmorency, Connetable de France, who
served under six kings. Later it passed
to the equally illustrious Condé family
who employed Le Nôtre to lay out the
formal gardens. Largely rebuilt in the
19thC, the Petit Château houses the
Musée Condé with paintings by Hol-
bein, Raphael and Reynolds, marvellous miniatures, Cellini jewellery and a
facsimile of *Les Très Riches Heures du
Duc de Berry*, a glorious 15thC illuminated manuscript, displayed in the
library.

Just across the corner of the park,
the palatial **Grandes Ecuries** (stables)
were built in the 18thC by a Condé who
reckoned he would be reincarnated as
a horse. Once home to 240 horses and
500 hounds, the buildings now house
the **Musée Vivant du Cheval.** Paintings and displays detail every aspect
of equine life from blacksmithing to
dressage.

CHARTRES × ⚐

SNCF *from Gare Montparnasse.* S.I. *place*

DETOUR – **CHATEAU DE
PIERREFONDS**
For a perfect fairytale château in
the woods, look no further than
Château de Pierrefonds (14 km
south-east of Compiègne via the
D973). It is in fact a bit of a cheat,
having been completely rebuilt on
the site of a former castle during
the 19thC. But with its turrets and
ramparts sprouting from a rocky
outcrop above the village, it
makes an impressive sight (closed
Tues off season).

---

du Cathédrale. A pleasant old river-side town of crooked streets and gabled houses, Chartres plays second string to its chief glory, the great Gothic **Cathédrale de Nôtre-Dame**. One of the miracles of medieval architecture, the cathedral was built on an ancient Christian site over the ruins of a Romanesque pilgrim church largely destroyed by fire in 1294. The left-hand tower, one of a pair which can be seen from miles around, and the famous carved Portal Royal remain from the Romanesque church, but the rest of the cathedral was built in an astonishing 25 years. The flying buttresses were the first of their kind, and the overall harmony is most impressive.

Of the interior, the broad nave retains its rare 13thC maze which worshippers would trace out on their knees, but it is only fully visible during pilgrimage times when the chairs are moved out. There are fine carvings and a beautiful Renaissance choir screen, but it is the stained glass which predominates, a dazzling kaleidoscope of colour lent depth by the glorious and unrepeatable 'Chartres blue'. Some 3,000 square metres of the 12th-13thC glass was painstakingly removed for its protection during the First and Second World Wars.

Another special feature of Chartres is Malcolm Miller, a passionate cathedral scholar and brilliant guide who

RECOMMENDED HOTELS

BARBIZON
Hostellerie de la Clé d'Or, FF; 73 *Grande Rue; tel.* 60 66 40 96; *credit cards* AE, DC, MC, V; *open year round.*
  Lovely old inn with comfortable, recently refurbished rooms and an elegant rustic restaurant. Classical cooking, home-smoked fish and excellent fruity desserts such as the flaming cherry *giboulée*. Book ahead.

CHARTRES
Grand Monarque, FF-FFF; 22 *place des Epars; tel.* 37 21 00 72; *credit cards* AE, DC, MC, V; *open year round.*
  Splendid old town-centre hotel furnished with charm and antiques. Quiet rooms and a fine restaurant. Sample the local *pâté de Chartres*, a delicate selection of fish with parsley butter or duck with juniper berries.

Hôtel de la Poste, F-FF; 3 *rue du Général-Koenig; tel.* 37 21 04 27; *credit cards* AE, DC, MC, V; *open year round.*
  Great-value *logis* near place des Epars with 60 rooms (some in the old hotel, some in a modern annexe) and a pleasant restaurant.

COMPIEGNE
Hôtel de France, F-FF; 17 *rue Eugène-Floquet; tel.* 44 40 02 74; *credit cards* V; *open year round.*
  Fine 17thC building in a quiet, central street. Comfortable rooms and a popular dining room, the **Rôtisserie du Chat qui Tourne**. No sign of the cat, but lamb *en croute*, veal sweetbreads and a laden dessert trolley.

FONTAINEBLEAU
Legris et Parc, FF-FFF; 36 *rue du Parc; tel.* 64 22 24 24; *credit cards* V; *closed mid-Dec to mid-Jan.*
  Delightful Empire-style hotel with an interior garden and restaurant. Some of the spacious rooms overlook the palace gardens.

La Vanne Rouge, F; *rue de l'Abreuvoir* (10 *km S of Fontainebleau via* D148); *tel.* 64 45 82 10; *credit cards* V; *closed Sun dinner-Mon, mid-Jan to mid-Feb.*
  Water-side *logis* with 12 peaceful rooms overlooking the Loing, a sunny terrace and traditional restaurant.

SENLIS
Hostellerie de la Porte Bellon, F-FF; 51 *rue Bellon; tel.* 44 53 03 05; *credit cards* V; *closed mid-Dec to mid-Jan.*
  Welcoming *logis* in a fine old house south-east of the town centre.
  See also Recommended Restaurants.

VERSAILLES
Home Saint-Louis, FF; 28 *rue Saint-Louis; tel.* 39 50 23 55; *credit cards* V; *open year round.*
  Small, peaceful family hotel just south of the palace. A convenient place to stay before heading the queue at the palace gates in the morning.

EURO DISNEY

From central Paris, approach by the RER to Marne-la-Vallée/Chessy station, at the entrance to the park; trains run every ten to 20 minutes, depending on the time of day. The journey takes from 35 to 45 minutes, depending on the departure point in Paris. By car, 'Parc Euro Disneyland' is conspicuously signposted 32 km E of Paris on the A4 (Strasbourg-Paris) autoroute. There are also shuttles serving Euro Disney from Roissy/Charles de Gaulle and Orly Airports.

The European cousin of the Disney theme parks in California and Florida does not, at going to press, appear to be as popular as its New World counterparts. To some, the 'magic' of Disneyland will be not so much the atmosphere created by its attractions, but the fairytale quantities of money which have been poured into the site.

You pay around £100 (1993 exchange rates) to take in a family of two adults plus two children under 11 for one day. If you begin at say 10 am, you can't do it all, but you can cover a satisfying selection of the main attractions and rides, *provided the queues are not too bad*. Whenever you go, expect to wait up to half-an-hour or more at the main entrance for tickets. Once inside, queues will depend on the time of year. At some periods, for instance in the penultimate week before Christmas, you can find it eerily empty. At others, you'll have to wait in long lines for rides, which could quickly spoil your day, not to mention the magic.

What do you get for your money? Essentially, a fantasy world designed to appeal to both adults and children. It is like a giant outdoor stage, whose hub is Main Street U.S.A with its quaint turn-of-the-century shops and restaurants in which to spend real money, brass bands and barber shop quartets. This leads to Le Château de la Belle au Bois Dormant, or Sleeping Beauty's Castle (a pastiche of Ludwig II's Neuschwanstein castle in Bavaria, but nonetheless amazing) geographically the centrepiece of the park. Along this main artery, the floats and characters of the Disney World Parade bounce and roll each day at an appointed hour: for adults given to introspection, a curious and touching journey back into the 1950s and 60s.

As satellites to the main artery, you have the four 'lands' (the fifth being Main Street U.S.A): Frontierland, Adventureland, Fantasyland and Discoveryland. What not to miss? An unfair question of course, but it does underline Disneyland's main achievement: entertainment for each and everyone. A ten-year-old, asked which ride he'd choose if allowed back with time for only one, settled on *Pirates of the Caribbean* – a flat-bottomed boat ride through 'scenes of pillage and plunder' – "because of the stunts". His six-year-old brother chose the Peter Pan ride because it zapped his imagination and "because of Captain Hook". Their mother appreciated the Swiss Family Robinson Tree "because it was so beautifully done". Their father's favourite was the simulated space ride, *Star Tours*, for its mixture of wit (a delinquent robot takes you joy-riding through space) and its technical brilliance.

Some people's view of Euro Disney is that it might be one of 20thC marketing man's greatest miscalculations. Many French, particularly sophisticated Parisians, resent the presence of a U.S.-style theme park in their country. Certainly, to visit after being in the centre of Paris, immersed in fine architecture and mellow stone, is a weird contrast.

conducts the noon and afternoon tours on Mondays to Saturdays from Easter to November.

With time to spare, a stroll around the old town is recommended, or relax in the cathedral gardens which slope down towards the Eure. The **Musée des Beaux-Arts** with its paintings and lovely tapestries is housed here in the old bishop's palace. At the north corner of the gardens a flight of steps leads down to the quayside near the Romanesque **Eglise de Saint-André**, now used as a cultural centre.

COMPIEGNE ⛺ ✕

SNCF *from Gare du Nord. S.I. place de l'*Hôtel de Ville. The Romans called it Compendium, which seems apposite for a town that has seen its fair share of history. The Burgundians captured Joan of Arc here in 1430 before handing her over to the English, and from the 14thC a succession of French kings and emperors spent time in Compiègne's royal palace.

On the edge of the Forêt de Compiègne, the town is not much to look at, largely rebuilt after the Second World War. One survivor, the fine Renaissance **Hôtel de Ville** built by Louis XII, has an animated clock in the

• *Monet's garden, Giverny – see page* 271.

bell tower. The **Musée Vivenal** (closed Tues) has an exceptional collection of Greek vases; while the **Musée de la Figurine Historique** (closed Mon) masses 85,000 tin soldiers from ancient Gauls to Général de Gaulle.

Château de Compiègne dates from the 17thC when Louis XV decided to rebuild the royal residence with the help of Ange-Jacques Gabriel, architect of place de la Concorde in Paris. Conducted tours trail through the sumptuous royal apartments including Marie-Antoinette's lavishly appointed suite and Napoleon's scarlet and gold chambers. The **Musée du Second Empire** displays an enormous range of grandiose paintings, furniture and *objets d'art*; more intriguing is the **Musée de la Voiture et du Tourisme** with its carriages, cars and bicycles (closed Tues).

On November 11 1918, the Armistice which marked the surrender of the German Empire and ended the First World War was signed in a railway carriage in a woodland siding, the **Clairière de l'Armistice**, just east of Compiègne (6 km via the N31/D546). In June 1940, Hitler had insisted that the

279

French surrender was signed in the same spot and the carriage was shunted off to Berlin as a trophy. It was later destroyed by bombing, but an exact replica sits in its place with a small museum (closed Tues off season).

ECOUEN

Métro Porte de la Chapelle, then bus 268C. A beautiful 16thC country retreat built for Anne de Montmorency, Château d'Ecouen now acts as a marvellous showcase for the **Musée National de la Renaissance** (closed Tues). Original features such as the great fireplaces and painted ceilings are complemented by stunning collections of period furnishings, tapestries, School of Fontainebleau paintings, carvings, silverware and *objets d'art*.

FONTAINEBLEAU × ⌫

SNCF from Gare du Lyon. S.I. 31 place Napoléon-Bonaparte. A small town with a huge royal château in the middle of

---

DETOUR – MILLY-LA-FORET
Far removed from the pomp and peacocks at Fontainebleau, there is a pleasant drive through the forest to Milly-la-Forêt, 19 km W via the D904. An attractive village with an old château and lime trees, this was the home of Jean Cocteau (1889-1963), who is buried in the 12thC Chapelle de Saint-Blaise-des-Simples, once part of a leper hospital abandoned in the 16thC. Cocteau decorated the whitewashed interior himself with engagingly simple sketches of herbs, a grinning cat by the stoop and a moving portrait of Christ wearing a crown of thorns (closed Tues). There is a small garden of medicinal herbs (*simples*) outside.

---

a 40,000-acre forest, Fontainebleau makes an excellent day trip from Paris.

Of the dozens of woodland *auberges* scattered throughout the Forêt de Compiègne, this one offers value for money as well as a delightful water-side setting. Home-made terrine, fillet of beef with wild mushrooms, and fresh fish are specialities.

FONTAINEBLEAU

Chez Arrighi, F-FF; 53 *rue de France; tel.* 64 22 29 43; *credit cards* AE, DC, MC, V; *closed Mon, two weeks Aug.*
Pastel shades, Empire furnishings and suprisingly digestible prices for dishes such as mussel soup with mushrooms *en croute*.

RAMBOUILLET

Le Cheval Rouge, FF; 78 *rue du Général-de-Gaulle; tel.* 30 88 80 61; *credit cards* AE, DC, MC, V; *closed Sun dinner-Mon, mid-July to early Aug.*
Traditional fish restaurant with an outdoor terrace. If you don't like fish, try the slightly cheaper **Poste**, 101 rue du Général-de-Gaulle (tel. 34 83 03 01).

Maison des Champs, FF; *at Les Chaises* (11 km W via D906/D80); *tel.* 34 83 50 19; *credit cards* AE, MC, V; *closed Sun dinner, Mon dinner-Tues, Feb, three weeks Aug.*

RECOMMENDED RESTAURANTS

BARBIZON
See Recommended Hotels.

CHANTILLY
Tipperary, FF; 6 *avenue du Maréchal-Joffre; tel.* 44 57 00 48; *credit cards* AE, DC, MC, V; *closed Sun dinner-Mon, two weeks Jan, two weeks Aug.*
Popular and attractive haunt of the horsy set during the racing season. Classical cuisine and a huge varied cheeseboard.

CHARTRES
Buisson d'Ardent, F-FF; 10 *rue du Lait; tel.* 37 34 04 66; *credit cards* AE, DC, MC, V; *closed Sun dinner.*
A perennial favourite with an old beamed dining room and views of the cathedral. Classical dishes blessed with a light, modern touch; convivial atmosphere.
See also Recommended Hotels.

COMPIEGNE
Auberge des Etangs du Buissonnet, FF-FFF; *at Choisy-au-Bac* (4 km NE via D66); *tel.* 44 40 17 41; *credit cards* V; *closed Sun dinner-Mon, three weeks Dec-Jan.*

The crowds are not as great as those at Versailles, and there are plenty of opportunities for picnicking and walking. The S.I. has maps of forest trails and there are well-signposted walks from the **Carrefour de la Libération** up to the Hauteurs de la Solle; and from the **Carrefour de l'Obélisque** to the Rocher des Demoiselles.

Wild boar and deer drew the first French kings to the Forêt de Fontainebleau starting with Louis VII in the 12thC. During the 16thC, François I set about converting the regal hunting lodge into a Renaissance palace, **Château de Fontainebleau**, where he could entertain his favourite, the Duchesse d'Etampes. The finest Italian craftsmen – Primaticcio, Rosso Il Fiorentino, Cellini – laboured over the interior decorations, founding the School of Fontainebleau which was to dominate the French artistic scene of the period, and many great works of art, such as da Vinci's *Mona Lisa* (now

> **DETOUR – MARLY-LE-ROI**
> West of Malmaison, at Marly-le-Roi, Louis XIV built a hunting lodge which served as an antidote to the grandeur of Versailles. The building disappeared after the Revolution, but the magnificent park and gardens remain, making a natural haven for picnickers and a chance for the kids to run amok. There are grand vistas over the Seine, grassy avenues cut through the trees, and an aquaduct which feeds numerous ponds and cooling fountains.

in the Louvre), found their first homes on the palace walls.

Louis XIV commissioned Le Nôtre to lay out the gardens with their canals, carp lake and peacocks; Napoleon refurbished in Empire style, and later abdicated in the Red Salon before mak-

Engaging little restaurant overlooking a shady terrace and gardens. Equally attractive menu; tasty homemade terrines, deliciously unfussy lamb grilled with herbs.

SAINT-GERMAIN-EN-LAYE
Côté Cour, F-FF; 5 *rue Saint-Pierre; tel. 34 51 00 20; credit cards V; closed Tues.*

Arranged around a courtyard with a large terrace in summer. Seafood is a speciality and excellent-value bistro menus at lunch.

La Feuillantine, F-FF; 10 *rue des Louviers; tel. 34 51 04 24; credit cards V.*

Highly popular and jovial dining room in the pedestrian town centre (arrive early). Generous trad-modern cooking with a light, assured touch.

SENLIS
Auberge de la Fontaine, F-FF; 22 *Grande-Rue, at Fontaine-Chaalis (9 km SE via D330); tel. 44 54 20 22; credit cards DC, MC, V; closed Tues dinner-Wed, Feb.*

Cosy local favourite, sporting bare bricks, beams, a terrace for summer and log fires in winter. Satisfying *cuisine bourgeoise* from jugged rabbit to duck with peaches.

Also eight flowery, tranquil rooms **(FF)**.

VERSAILLES
Brasserie du Théâtre, F-FF; 15 *rue des Réservoirs; tel. 39 50 03 21; credit cards MC, V.*

Traditional *brasserie* with all the trimmings: mirrors, polished wood and brass, plus a long menu of well-tried classics.

Les Trois Marches, FFF; 1 *boulevard de la Reine; tel. 39 50 13 21; credit cards AE, DC, MC, V; closed Sun-Mon.*

In the suitably opulent surroundings of the Trianon Palace hotel, Gérard Vié creates culinary masterpieces fit for a king. Amongst specialities such as *foie gras au vin de Maury* and roast lobster with thyme, there are ravishingly aromatic provincial recipes such as *cassoulet*, Barbary duck laced with honey and cider vinegar, plus a notable wine cellar. As expected, prices are in the king's ransom bracket (though worth every *écu*) save for the exceptionally good-value weekday lunch set menu which is only just outside the **FF** bracket.

ing his farewells to his personal troops in the Cour des Adieux. In addition to the flamboyant Grands Appartements, there are guided tours of the Petits Appartements which include Empress Josephine's private suite, and also a Napoleonic museum (all closed Tues). Military history enthusiasts can also visit the **Musée Napoléonien d'Art et d'Histoire**, 88 rue Saint-Honoré (closed Mon).

GIVERNY
See Local Explorations: 7.

ORLEANS
See France Overall: 7.

RAMBOUILLET ✕
SNCF *from Gare Montparnasse*. On the edge of the Forêt de Rambouillet, between Versailles and Chartres, this pleasant small town has a comparatively modest royal residence which now serves as a summer retreat for French presidents. The red brick **Château de Rambouillet** (closed Tues and during presidential visits) dates from the 14thC, and was popular with François I, who died here after being taken ill while out hunting. Marie-Antoinette was less enthusiastic about its rural setting, so Louis XVI built her a dainty milking parlour where she and her ladies could play; he also founded the National Sheepfold, which is still inhabited by descendants of the orignal Merino sheep. The gardens are particularly lovely, stretching down from the château for more than 1 km around canals and artificial lakes.

RUEIL-MALMAISON
On RER *line A*. As the Seine loops its way west out through the suburbs of Paris, it passes close by **Château de Malmaison** (closed Tues) where the First Consul and his wife made their home when they were plain Napoleon and Josephine Bonaparte. The pretty country house is set in glorious gardens full of roses cultivated by the lonely Empress after her divorce, and the interior has been faithfully restored using original furnishings, such as the tented Council Chamber, and belongings which include Josephine's hairbrushes and Napoleon's books. Further Napoleonic memorabilia is on show in the neighbouring **Château de Bois-**

Préau (closed Tues).

Near Métro Rueil-Malmaison, the Pont de Chatou gives access to the **Ile de Chatou**, a waterside *rendez-vous* popular with the Impressionist set. One of their favourite *guinguettes* (dining and dancing haunts), **La Maison Fournaise** (which featured in Renoir's *Le Déjeuner des Canotiers*), is still here beside a small museum devoted to visiting artists such as Monet, Seurat and Van Gogh.

SAINT-DENIS
Métro Porte-de-Saint-Denis. According to legend, after his execution on Montmartre, St Denis (the patron saint of France) carried his head to this site outside Paris where he was buried beneath a succession of churches culminating in the Early Gothic **Cathédrale de Saint-Denis**. The setting, a rather grim industrial suburb of the capital, makes a strange contrast to the magnificence of the building, necropolis of the French kings since Dagobert in 638, and the earliest example of several Gothic devices including the rose window. The soaring interior with its pointed arches and acres of glass is remarkably light and airy. The royal tombs in the chancel and transepts provide a fascinating catalogue of funerary art from the horizontal Clovis to Primaticcio's Henri II and Catherine de' Medici and the stylized poses of Louis XVI and Marie-Antoinette.

SAINT-GERMAIN-EN-LAYE ✕
RER *line A. S.I. 38 rue au Pain.* A prosperous and attractive town which is set on a hill above the Seine, Saint-Germain attracts few tourists, which adds to its charms. Yet another royal hunting lodge turned palace, the Château de Saint-Germain was much favoured by French kings from François I to Louis XIV before the building of Versailles. James II of England spent the last years of his life in exile here overlooking the sweep of parkland and fine views from Le Nôtre's breezy Grande Terrasse which runs along the top of an escarpment above the woods.

It was Napoleon III who established the excellent **Musée des Antiquités Nationales** in the château, which has since grown into one of the world's premier archaeological collections.

Among the treasures is the 22,000-year-old *Dame de Brassempouy*, the oldest surviving likeness of a human face; a recreation of the famous painted caves at Lascaux; plus hundreds of prehistoric finds, tools, weapons and jewellery from the Stone and Bronze Ages (closed Tues).

Also in town, there is a small museum dedicated to the composer Claude Debussy (1862-1918), who was born in Saint-Germain; and the **Musée du Prieuré**, 2bis rue Maurice-Denis, displaying paintings by Pont-Aven and Nabis School artists including Bonnard, Gauguin and Serusier in a former priory owned by Maurice Denis who decorated the chapel (closed Mon-Tues).

SCEAUX

RER *line* B. Another marvellous creation by the prolific 17thC garden designer André Le Nôtre, the near 500-acre spread of the **Parc de Sceaux** encompasses all its architect's favourite devices from manicured lawns and broad tree-lined avenues to dainty topiary, colourful geometric flowerbeds and water features. In its midst, Château de Sceaux, a 19thC building in the late Renaissance style, houses the engaging **Musée de l'Ile-de-France** (closed Tues). An enormous map in the entrance hall describes the royal hunting grounds of Ile-de-France

• *The Forest of Fontainebleau.*

and the museum itself is devoted to the history and people of the region. Collected here are paintings and tapestries, furniture and china, plus a delightfully eclectic collection of day-to-day knick-knacks including costumed models, grainy photographs and antique conveyances from early bicycles to Métro memorabilia.

SENLIS 🚌 ✕

SNCF *bus from Chantilly*. S.I. *place du Parvis-Nôtre-Dame*. A pretty town and favourite with summer coach tours (so it is best to visit off season), Senlis has a fine Gothic cathedral, Gallo-Roman ruins and the remnants of a royal château. At the heart of the old town with its Renaissance buildings and 17th-18thC mansions (walking tours from the S.I.), the **Cathédrale de Nôtre-Dame** overlooks a cobbled square. Founded in 1153 (before Nôtre-Dame in Paris), construction continued into the Flamboyant period and it is topped by an immense 78-m spire. Caught in the embrace of the old fortifications nearby, the remaining portion of the old Château-Royal now houses the **Musée de la Venerie,** which is dedicated to the cult of hunting and filled with paintings, sculpture, trophies and weaponry used in the pursuit of

283

deer and wild boar in the royal forests (closed Tues-Wed am).

SEVRES

Métro Pont de Sèvres. Just by the main road to Chartres at Sèvres, the **Musée National de Céramique** (closed Tues) offers a wonderful cavalcade of pottery and china through the ages and from across the globe. Needless to say, the wares of the famous royal porcelain factory (established in 1738) are much in evidence, but oriental, Islamic and other European manufacturers are also displayed.

North across the Seine, the elegant terraced gardens of the **Parc de Saint-Cloud** afford fine views back towards the city.

VAUX-LE-VICOMTE, CHATEAU

SNCF to Melun and taxi or walk. Asked to

DETOUR – **SIGHTS NEAR SENLIS**
Stretching south-east of Senlis, the beech woods of the Forêt d'Ermenonville make a fine picnic spot. **Château d'Ermenonville** lies at the south-eastern edge of the forest (9 km south-east via the N330) set in lovely informal gardens (a *jardin anglais*) which are open to the public. The 18thC philosopher Jean-Jacques Rousseau died here in 1778, and was buried on an island in the lake, though his remains were later placed in the Pantheon in Paris. A short distance north, the 12thC **Abbaye de Chaalis** built by the Cistercian order was partially restored in the 18thC, and now displays pre-Revolutionary artworks owned by the Institut de France (both closed Tues).

• *Orangery, Versailles.*

choose just one château to visit in the vicinity of Paris, this would have to be it. Built between 1656 and 1661 for Louis XIV's Superintendent of Finances, Nicolas Fouquet, by a talented triumvirate, Le Vau (architect), Le Brun (decorator) and Le Nôtre (landscaper), it is a triumph of the early Louis XIV style before the top-heavy ostentation of Versailles. The elegant and, by comparison, modestly proportioned yellow-grey château, with its corner pavilions, is surrounded on three sides by an ornamental moat and overlooks superb gardens, combining geometric precision (canals, gravel paths, topiary and formal flowerbeds) with delightfully fey grottoes inhabited by statues of river gods.

Inside, the rooms are sumptuously furnished and feature some glorious frescoed ceilings by Le Brun (incidentally, all three of Fouquet's designers were later poached to work on the Sun King's glittering prize at Versailles), but some of the rooms remain bare and unfinished.

In 1661 Fouquet was already on somewhat shaky ground having antagonized the powerful Colbert and was under suspicion for dipping his hand in the State purse to fuel his extravagances. As Vaux-le-Vicomte neared completion, he foolishly invited the young king to dine on 17th August, and laid on a lavish banquet served on gold plates to the accompaniment of a new play by Molière, a ballet and spectacular fireworks. The king was not amused by his subject's grandiose display of wealth. Fouquet was arrested, stripped of his possessions (many of which conveniently found their way to Versailles), and imprisoned for life on trumped-up charges.

VERSAILLES 🚃 ✕

RER *line* C5. S.I. 7 *rue des Réservoirs*. The physical embodiment of Louis XIV's neuroses and favourite dictum ("*l'état, c'est moi*"), the **Palais de Versailles** is a *tour de force*. It is a magnificent monster; an autocrat's stronghold, a retreat from reality, an artistic treasure house, and totally exhausting. It is impossible to see in a day, so follow one of the suggested itineraries, then head for the gardens. Survival tips include: be there early (doors open at 9.45am; closed Mon); wear comfy shoes; and buy a decent brochure if you choose not to take a guided tour.

Chased from Paris by the *Fronde* during his childhood, Louis XIV retained a deep-seated dislike of Paris and distrust for its nobles. On achieving his majority, the young king determined to move his court and the seat of government out of the capital, settling for the site of Louis XIII's hunting lodge at Versailles. Spurred on by the vision of Vaux-le-Vicomte (see page 284), he levelled the lodge, drained a swamp, hired the finest architects, painters and decorators in the land, and set about creating the largest and most extravagant palace in Europe. The palace was intended to dazzle, and it did. Visitors marvelled, while Louis kept a close rein on his nobles by moving them into the palace – over a thousand of them with their families and servants. The entire court retinue numbered around 20,000.

Various tours of the palace cover the **Grands Appartements**, or State Rooms, for which Louis favoured a mythological theme. The throne room is dedicated to Apollo, the god of light, with whom the king compared himself and from which alliance he modestly assumed the title of the 'Sun King'. Some of the highlights are the magnificent Hall of Mirrors, where the Treaty of Versailles was signed in 1918, Mansart's Royal Chapel, and the Royal Opera. The **Petits Appartements** were the royal living quarters where Louis XV entertained Mesdames Pompadour and du Barry, and the child virtuoso Mozart played. The portraits in the **Musée de l'Histoire Française** put faces to names.

There is no escaping the grand scheme in the gardens either. With many hectares of parterre and fountains (water shows on Sun pm May-Sep), and a Grand Canal big enough to justify *bateau mouche* excursions, you can hire a bike near the Grand Canal, and there is an additional couple of pavilions to inspect. The larger **Grand Trianon** served as a Baroque marble guesthouse. Marie-Antoinette preferred the **Petit Trianon** where she could escape the pressures of courtly protocol, dress up as a shepherdess and trip across the garden to her private pastoral playground, **Le Hameau**, fill her Sèvres milking pails in the dairy and play with perfumed lambs.

Central France

Highspots of the Auvergne

145 km; map Michelin No. 73

At the centre of France, the western Auvergne rears up to form the volcanic core of the Massif Central. During the Tertiary era, the cones of the Monts Dômes, Monts Dore and Monts de Cantal jettisoned torrents of molten lava which smoothed out the terrain and left strange hump-shaped volcanic *puys* marooned on the plains. This chain of 80 extinct volcanoes extending approximately 120 km from north to south offers one of the most beautiful and dramatic landscapes in Europe. Now protected by France's largest national park, the Parc Naturel Régional des Volcans d'Auvergne, the region is worth at least a detour if not a few days walking and exploring.

There are watersports and fishing on several dozen crystal clear lakes and streams. Tiny villages boast fine Romanesque churches and fusty spa towns have been given a new lease of life by the winter sports fraternity who overcome the problem of limited downhill facilities by concentrating on the increasingly popular alternative of *ski-de-fond* (cross-country skiing).

This circular tour can be driven in a day from Clermont-Ferrand, but an overnight stop, perhaps in Besse or le Mont-Dore, will make the drive much more relaxed and enjoyable. (To extend this route, see France Overall: 8 – Between Clermont-Ferrand and Avignon.) Serious walkers would do well to stop off at the CHAMINA office in Clermont to pick up maps and information about *gites d'étape* (hikers' hostels strategically placed on walking routes). There are several challenging *grandes randonnées* trails that reveal the highspots and natural beauties of the region such as GR30, The Lakes of Auvergne; GR441, The Circuit of the Puys; and GR41, between la Bourboule and Brioude, which conquers the highest mountain in the range, the Puy de Sancy (1,885 m). Sections of these footpaths make equally interesting shorter hikes, or you could devise an independent itinerary using several different GR routes.

When planning a visit, bear in mind that there are two distinct seasons: winter (mid-Dec to mid-Apr) and summer (mid-May to mid-Sep). Most hotels are closed outside these times. Recommended hotels and restaurants are listed together in this section because on the whole the best food is found at hotels, and half-board only terms are often the rule.

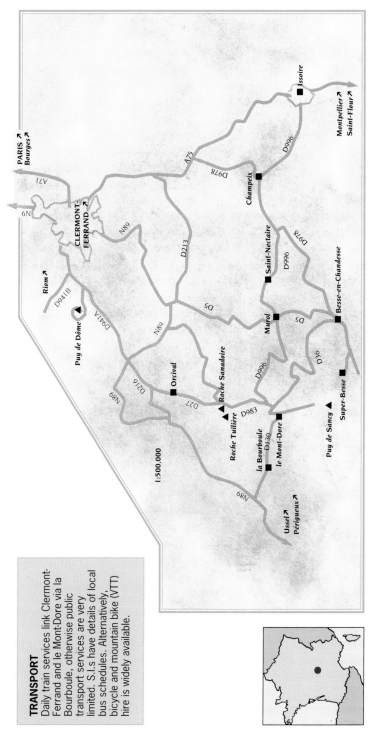

TRANSPORT

Daily train services link Clermont-Ferrand and le Mont-Dore via la Bourboule, otherwise public transport services are very limited. S.I.s have details of local bus schedules. Alternatively, bicycle and mountain bike (VTT) hire is widely available.

SIGHTS & PLACES OF INTEREST

BESSE-ET-SAINT-ANASTASIE (EN-CHANDESSE) ⇌ ✕

S.I. *place Docteur-Pipet*. Hewn out of black volcanic rock from the tip of its 15thC belfry to the bottom of its sturdy ramparts, Besse is a picturesque old mountain village of narrow medieval streets and small hotels. There is a Romanesque church, a Renaissance fountain and a solitary chapel nearby at **Vassivière** (7 km west via the D978). On the way, the road passes beautiful **Lac Pavin**, where a short but rewarding walk takes you clambering up to the top of Puy de Montchal. (The S.I. has plenty more suggestions for longer walks.) In winter, the neighbouring modern resort of **Super-Besse** (7 km west via the D149) offers both downhill and cross-country skiing.

BOURBOULE, LA ⇌ ✕

S.I. *place de l'Hôtel de Ville*. From 'Asthma capital' to *station oxygène*, la Bourboule is attempting to jazz up its staid spa image. A difficult task in view of the pompous 19thC architecture that characterizes such places.

The hefty **Grands Thermes** by the Dordogne, and neoclassical **Casino** are cases in point, but this is a relaxing spot with the twin advantages of skiing in winter, walking in summer and cheap accommodation.

From the water-side lawns and children's play areas of the **Parc Fenêstre**, a *télépherique* glides up to the wooded **Plateau de Charlannes** criss-crossed by numerous walking trails; or you can hike up the more challenging **Banne d'Ordance**, a 1,512-m volcanic peak east of town.

DOME, PUY DE

One of the most-visited spots in the region, this 1,465-m sawn-off volcano is the tallest link in the Monts Dômes chain. A toll road winds up around its wooded flanks, or alternatively there is a footpath from the lower car park to the remains of a Roman temple dedicated to Mercury. A radio mast and café do little to improve the summit, but the magnificent views stretch for miles in every direction.

MONT-DORE, LE ⇌ ✕

S.I. *place de l'Hôtel de Ville*. Strung along the nascent Dordogne, le Mont-Dore's tall, thin houses and spa hotels squeeze into a narrow cleft in the wooded hills. Popular with *curistes* and walkers in summer, skiers in winter, the spa town boasts the usual complement of sedate thermal establishments, a public garden, *boules* players under the plane trees and an S.I. bristling with glossy brochures and walking guides.

The main attraction is the **Puy de Sancy** (1,885 m), highest of the Monts Dore chain, which can be scaled by serious walkers or with the help of a *télépherique* (4 km south via the D983). The views from its dramatic ridge-back summit are stupendous. A pretty half-day hike from the valley strikes south-east to the **Grande Cascade** waterfall. Or make use of the beautifully preserved 19thC funicular railway which trundles up through the beech and fir woods to the **Salon du Capucin**, a large clearing above town and starting point for many trails.

ORCIVAL ⇌

Nestled in a verdant fold of the Sioulet valley, Orcival's roof-tops huddle around the exquisite Romanesque **Basilique de Notre-Dame**. Beneath an octagonal belfry and spire, a fan of tiny chapels mushrooms from the back of the chancel. The plain, leafy capitals of the nave develop into more elaborate designs on the outer circle of the ambulatory. There is a small but famous Black Virgin dressed in enamel and silver. She inspired the motley collection of manacles, balls and chains slung above the main door – *ex votos* from penitent convicts.

DETOUR - **CHATEAU DE CORDES**
Just north of Orcival along the valley, Château de Cordès (1.5 km via the D27) pokes its head above the trees. Restored in the 17thC, the 13th-15thC fortified manor house sports a fine collection of slate-hatted towers, elegantly furnished chambers and a small chapel. The formal gardens laid out behind high yew hedges were the work of Le Nôtre.

DETOUR - **MUROL**
There are several lovely woodland walks in the vicinity of Saint-Nectaire, and beautiful Lac Chambon, just beyond Murol (6 km west via the D996), offers watersports and canoe hire. During summer, the Compagnons de Gabriel recreate life under the feudal lords of medieval France in the ruins of the 13thC Château de Murol, an imposing fortress-stronghold on top of a basalt outcrop.

SAINT-NECTAIRE
A village in two parts, the old farming community of Saint-Nectaire-le-Haut gathers on a hillock around the fine Auvergnat Romanesque **Eglise de Saint-Nectaire**, while the miniature spa of Saint-Nectaire-le-Bas is slipped like a ship in a bottle along the River Courançon.

The plain exterior of the 12thC church is relieved by carved lintels and animal heads around the ambulatory chapels, but the real works of art are the superb capitals of Old and New Testament scenes adorning the pillars of the nave and choir, plus the church treasure displayed in the transept.

Saint-Nectaire-le-Bas, with its apricot-painted casino, clutch of old-fashioned hotels and toy-town S.I. has half-a-dozen fossil shops and a *cave à fromages* promoting the third Saint-Nectaire, a delicious local cheese matured on beds of straw.

RECOMMENDED HOTELS & RESTAURANTS

BESSE-ET-SAINT-ANASTASIE (EN-CHANDESSE)
Hostellerie du Beffroy, F; *tel.* 73 79 50 08; *credit cards* MC, V; *closed three weeks Mar-Apr, mid-Oct to end-Nov.*

Welcoming *logis* in a 15thC *maison typique* decorated with balconies, flower pots and red shutters. Small but appealing bedrooms, restaurant and sunny terrace.

La Bergerie, F; *route de* Vassivières, Super-Besse; *tel.* 73 79 61 06; *credit cards* V; *closed mid-Apr to mid-Jun, mid-Sep to mid-Dec.*

A rustic restaurant serving country cooking. The summer terrace is a delight as is the range of Auvergnat cheeses such as the pungent, blue-veined *fourme d'Ambert.*

Gergovia, F-FF; *at* Super-Besse (7 km W via D149); *tel.* 73 79 60 15; *credit cards* AE, MC, V; *closed Apr to mid-Jun, mid-Sep to mid-Dec.*

Comfortable and extremely well-equipped modern resort hotel with sauna, gym, spa, family apartments and children's games.

BOURBOULE, LA
L'Aviation, F-FF; *rue de* Metz; *tel.* 73 65 50 50; *credit cards* MC, V; *closed Oct to Christmas.*

Renovated 1930s hotel with a period feel – tea dances are a feature. Comfortable and quiet; restaurant.

Auberge Tournebride, F-FF; 1.5 km N *via the* D88; *tel.* 73 81 01 91; *credit cards, none; closed* Mon *off season, mid-Nov to mid-Jan.*

Small and welcoming country hotel with a popular restaurant serving generous *Auvergnat* dishes. Outdoor dining in summer.

MONT-DORE, LE
Le Castelet, F-FF; *avenue* Michel-Bertrand; *tel.* 73 65 05 29; *credit cards* DC, MC, V; *closed Oct to mid-Dec, Apr to mid-May.*

Attractive modern family hotel with functional but comfy rooms, garden, pool and children's games. The sunny regional restaurant moves out on to the terrace in fine weather.

ORCIVAL
Les Bourelles, F; *tel.* 73 65 82 28; *credit cards, none; closed Oct-Easter.*

A pleasant old house up a flight of steps off the main street with a small garden.

Hôtel du Mont-Dore, F; *tel.* 73 65 82 06; *credit cards* MC, V; *closed mid-Nov to Christmas.*

Right by the church, with an old stone tower and rustic restaurant.

South-Central France

Albigeois Region

210 km; maps Michelin map Nos 82 and 83

This corner of southern France has a long and bloody history of religious non-conformism which stretches back to the Middle Ages and the emergence of the Cathar faith in the mid-11thC. The Cathars, whose name derived from the Greek word for 'pure', believed in the fundamental separation of Good and Evil, that Satan created the world and the only road to salvation was through the sacrament of *consolamentum,* the renunciation of the flesh (Satanic matter imprisoning the spirit), worldly goods and the rites of the established church. The latter in particular was guaranteed to evoke the wrath of Rome. The murder of a papal envoy in 1208 unleashed the bloodthirsty Albigensian Crusades under the leadership of a merciless northern nobleman, Simon de Montfort. The vicious campaign of suppression directed against Cathar strongholds such as Albi, Beziers, Carcassonne and Toulouse, ended in the mass burning of 200 Cathar heretics at Montségur (east of Foix) in 1244, and the eventual annexation of Languedoc to the Capetian crown.

My local exploration looks at the area north of Toulouse, taking in Cordes, a Cathar refuge founded by Raymond VII in 1222. When peace was restored in the 14thC, the hill-top town flourished. Its perpendicular winding streets, beautifully preserved Gothic mansions and picturesque views make it a favourite stop on the tourist trail, so an overnight stay is the way to see it at its best, after the coach parties have gone home.

However, accommodation is limited and tends to be expensive, so Albi is a better base if you are on a budget. Albi's old town centre and immense cathedral rise from the Tarn in a captivating mountain of rosy bricks coloured by local clay. The painter Henri de Toulouse-Lautrec was born here, and thanks to his mother the local museum is richly endowed with his work.

Rather than return to Toulouse, there is the option of taking the N112 south to Castres, which has a pleasant town centre, busy market and a surprising collection of Spanish Old Masters tucked away in the local museum. Then you might continue south over the granite hills of the Montagne Noire to Carcassonne, where the Cathars once took refuge in Europe's largest fortress.

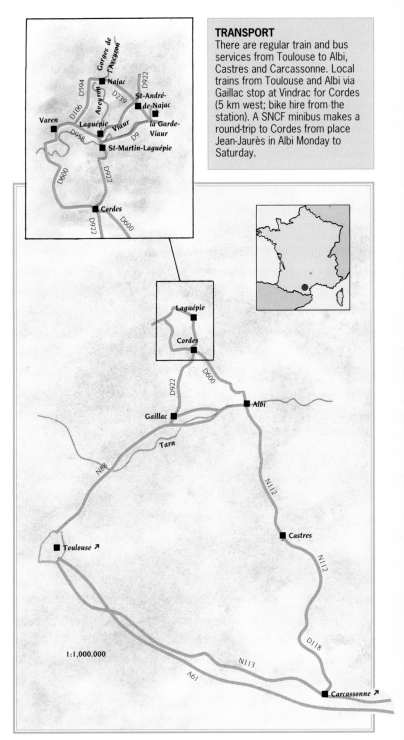

TRANSPORT

There are regular train and bus services from Toulouse to Albi, Castres and Carcassonne. Local trains from Toulouse and Albi via Gaillac stop at Vindrac for Cordes (5 km west; bike hire from the station). A SNCF minibus makes a round-trip to Cordes from place Jean-Jaurès in Albi Monday to Saturday.

1:1,000,000

SIGHTS & PLACES OF INTEREST

ALBI ⇔ ✕

S.I. *place de la Berbie*. A lively and attractive cathedral town, Albi's main claim to fame these days is its Toulouse-Lautrec museum. Like Toulouse, it is a *'ville rose'*, built from pinkish brick, and laps around the massive Gothic bulk of the **Cathédrale de Sainte-Cecile**. A supertanker of a cathedral, ribbed with vertical buttresses and a flat-topped deck stretching back from the belfry, the building was founded in 1282 as a 'fortress of faith' to proclaim the Church's victory over the Cathars. What the exterior lacks in decoration, the interior makes up for several times over. Imported Bolognese painters and Burgundian sculptors transformed the soaring nave and choir into a mass of rich, earth-toned frescoes and unbelievably delicate carvings.

Next door to the cathedral, the Palais de Berbie, which was a 13thC archbishop's residence, houses the **Musée Toulouse-Lautrec** with more than 600 of the diminutive painter's works, the largest collection in the world. Henri de Toulouse-Lautrec was born into a family of horsy aristocrats at the Hôtel du Bosc (open Jul-Aug), 14 rue Toulouse-Lautrec, in 1864. Both his father and grandfather were gifted draughtsmen and after a spate of childhood accidents left his legs crippled and under-developed, the young Henri was apprenticed to the painter Bonnard. In Paris he immersed himself in the Bohemian *milieu* of Montmartre, where he recorded the raffish nightlife of turn-of-the-century Paris, the lone drinkers, patient prostitutes and cabaret stars such as Aristide Bruant, whose profile (subject of the famous black and red poster) has since graced a zillion brasseries and bedsits. Lautrec's early paintings and drawings of horses and bosky country lanes (even the scribbles in his French-Latin dictionary) reveal a significant talent, but it is the music hall scenes, lithographs and posters that are his best-known works and the collection is full of them. On the top floor, paintings by

---

RECOMMENDED HOTELS

ALBI

Hôtel Saint-Clair, F; *rue Saint-Clair; tel.* 63 54 25 66; *credit cards* V; *closed* Jan.

Friendly, small hotel in the pedestrian zone near the cathedral. Fairly basic rooms; helpful *patronne*. Book ahead for limited garaging. (See also Recommended Restaurants for more budget accommodation.)

Hostellerie Saint-Antoine, FF-FFF; 17 *rue Saint-Antoine; tel.* 63 54 04 04; *credit cards* AE, DC, MC, V; *open year round.*

Elegant family-run hotel off Lices Jean-Moulin. Attractive, well-equipped rooms, garden; use of swimming pool and tennis facilities at its Relais et Châteaux sister, **La Reserve** (**FFF**; *tel.* 63 47 60 22), 3 km out of town.

CASTRES

Hôtel l'Europe, F; 5 *rue Victor-Hugo; tel.* 63 59 00 33; *credit cards* MC, V; *open year round.*

Unusual but appealing hotel in a 17thC house in the town centre. Creeper-clad atrium with old-fashioned armchairs and portraits. Stylishly decorated and thoughtfully equipped rooms.

CORDES

Le Grand Ecuyer, FFF; *Grand'rue; tel.* 63 56 01 03; *credit cards* AE, DC, MC, V; *closed mid-Oct to Mar.*

Baronial splendour in a marvellous Gothic building complete with armour and throne-like chairs. Lovely rooms (four-posters optional) and a notable restaurant. The menu features modern cuisine with a regional touch and might include red mullet with almonds and chervil, and beef cooked with local Gaillac wine.

Hostellerie du Vieux Cordes, FF; *rue Saint-Michel; tel.* 63 56 00 12; *credit cards* AE, DC, MC, V; *closed* Jan.

Attractive, peaceful and comfortable rooms in a 13thC building. Two delightful terraces (one overlooking the plain, another sheltered beneath wistaria), and a chic-rustic dining room serving dishes such as grilled duck and cabbage-wrapped gammon with red peppers.

• *Carcassonne.*

contemporary artists include Maillol's beefy girls (better known as sculptures), a golden Bonnard sunset, a sunny Dufy and a snowy Utrillo.

The S.I. has suggestions for various walking circuits of **Vieil Alby** which take in the cobbled streets packed with tempting shops, and the **Eglise de Saint-Salvy** which dates from the Carolingian period with Romanesque, Gothic and Baroque additions. Across its garden cloister, a covered passage leads to a crumbling arcade of semi-renovated medieval houses.

CARCASSONNE
See France Overall: 5.

CASTRES ⊨
S.I. T*héâtre* M*unicipal*. An important textile centre on the River Agout, Castres' pride and joy is the **Musée Goya**. Overlooking a lovely formal garden cooled by fountains and hemmed in with neatly trimmed box and yew, the museum is laid out in the 17thC Palais Episcopal which it shares with the Hôtel de Ville. There are three major paintings by Goya on show, including a *Self-Portrait*, plus a series of engravings. A fine collection of works by other 16th-17thC Spanish artists features Murillo, Ribéra and Velasquez amongst its treasures.

As for the rest of the town, the S.I. can provide a map and walking tour which takes about 35 minutes. One of the best stops along the way is the **Hôtel de Nayrac** with its graceful brick façade decorated with pediments and a frilly fringe of tiles beneath the roof. A minute away, the **Musée Jean-Jaurès**, opened by Mitterand in 1988, celebrates the life of Castres' most famous son, the father of the French Socialist party, assassinated in 1914. Next cut down to quai Tourcaudière for a look at the newly restored **Maisons d'Agout** hanging over the river on the opposite bank. Medieval tanners and dyers once worked from their open stone cellars. Boat trips leave from the **Pont Vieux** in summer. Every day except Wednesday, **place Jean-Jaurès** fills with a colourful open-air market. Stallholders preside over bunches of pink-white garlic, enormous beef tomatoes, fresh figs, melons, homemade baskets and honey. Pick up delicious snacks from the dried fruit and nut stall, and stock up on dried herbs, pot pourri and lavender.

CORDES ⊨ ✕
S.I. *Grand'rue*. Wrapped around a conical hill in a cloak of steep cobbled streets, mellow stone and mossy Roman tiles, Cordes is as busy as a beehive (which it closely resembles) in summer. Raymond VII, Count of Toulouse, encircled his Cathar sentinel in three tiers of battlements above the

DETOUR – **NORTH OF CORDES**

Pack a picnic for this delightful 60-km circuit north of Cordes, and set off on the D922 for Laguépie. Just inside Saint-Martin-de-Laguépie, take a *sharp* right turn on to the D9 for Saint-Christophe and dawdle along the thickly wooded Viaur valley with glimpses of the river, apple orchards and colourful patches of sunflowers and sorghum. After 10 km, cross a bridge on the D73 for **la Garde-Viaur**, where you recross the river to a handy café with tables by the weir. The D239 clambers up through oaks and chestnuts to Saint-André-de-Najac, and crosses the D922. Trailing behind the ruins of its 13thC fortress, **Najac** rides the crest of a ridge above the plunging **Gorges de l'Aveyron** in a roller-coaster of little stone houses and vine-draped wooden balconies. Take the D106 down to **Varen**, where the Romanesque abbey-church of Saint-Serge boasts some beautiful capitals. Then meander back through the fields to Cordes via the D600.

• *Cordes.*

Cérou valley, from whence it earns its full name of Cordes-sur-Ciel (in the sky). A warren of underground passages tunnel through the hillside, where defenders could take refuge. Above ground, fine stone houses such as the **Maison du Grand Veneur** and **Maison du Grand-Fauconnier** on Grand'rue, sport leafy capitals and carved hunting scenes, hounds, foxes and bears romping across their façades. Rescued from decline by tapestry workers at the end of the 19thC, and subsequently 'discovered' by artist Yves Brayer in the 1940s, Cordes has attracted a large and distinctly commercial artistic community. Apart from browsing in the numerous galleries, diversions include a glimpse at Brayer's colourful daubs on show in the Maison du Grand-Fauconnier, delving into local history in the **Musée Charles-Portal**, and enjoying the glorious views from the **Terrasse de la Bride**, where Camus found a beauty that could banish solitude.

• *Opposite: market day, Castres.*

Roussillon: French Catalonia

285 km (ex-Perpignan); map Michelin No. 86

As the Mediterranean coast sweeps around the Golfe du Lion towards the Spanish border, it meets the ancient province of Roussillon. Broad sandy beaches and tourist developments run into the rocky headlands of the Côte Vermeille, the horizon rears up into the eastern tip of the Pyrenees, and Perpignan, capital of the region, brazenly flies the red and yellow striped Catalan flag. This is French Catalonia.

Phoenician merchant seafarers settled here (they say Hercules passed through), and then the Romans who built the Via Domitia along a route now followed by *La Catalane*, the thundering *autoroute* to the south. From the Carolingian empire, Roussillon passed to the independent Counts of Barcelona in the 10thC and later to the Kings of Aragon, who kept the French at bay until the Treaty of the Pyrenees in 1659. French for just three centuries, Roussillon's Catalan identity remains strong, bolstered by an influx of refugees during the Franco years. Local customs and culture, language, even food set the people of French Catalonia slightly apart from the rest of their countrymen, though few want to go so far as to return to Spanish rule.

The snow-capped heights of the Pic du Canigou occupy a special place in the heart of every Catalan. From its peak, the valleys of the Tech and the Têt, the fertile Roussillon plain, the mountains and the sea are revealed in all their beauty and diversity. Heretics and monks alike have long found refuge in the rocky hills; beaches and spas nestle in the valleys; artists have found the coast and up-country Céret to be equally captivating.

If you want to see the area by making several excursions, the Côte Vermeille, Céret and the Tech valley, Prades and the Têt, and the Cathar castles in the north will be high on the list. If you are driving, you can make a grand circuit, with some fairly arduous sections between the valleys. *La Catalane* (A9) links Narbonne and Perpignan, though I prefer the D118 south from Carcassonne via Quillan to the Cathar castles. Then follow the N117 east to Perpignan for the coast, or Céret which is cooler in summer. The slow climb over the Aspres hills (D618) cannot be hurried, and don't miss the superb abbey at Serrabone. From Prades or Vernet-les-Bains, Canigou is a hike or a jeep ride away, and there is an enchanting train ride from Villefranche up to the Cerdagne plateau.

This area is on the doorstep of some of the best walking in Europe: see Walking in the Pyrenees, page 304.

TRANSPORT

There are frequent train and bus services from Narbonne to Perpignan, the transport hub for the region. Local trains depart regularly from Perpignan to the Côte Vermeille, and west via Prades to Villefranche. There are bus links to Céret. From Carcassonne, there are daily trains to Quillan, and buses link Quillan and Perpignan along the N117.

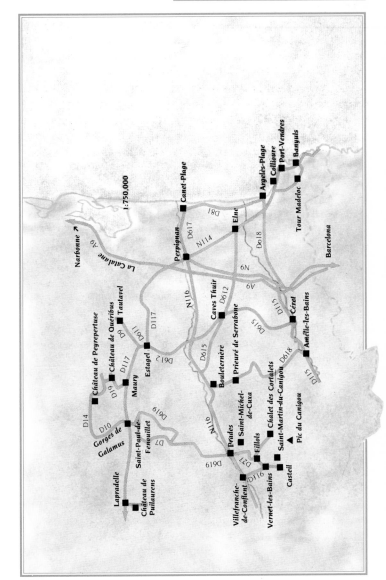

SIGHTS & PLACES OF INTEREST

ARGELES-PLAGE
Also Banyuls, Port-Vendres and Tour Madeloc, see Collioure, page 299.

THE CATHAR CASTLES
Off the N117, about 45 km north-west of Perpignan, a clutch of castles in the craggy Corbière hills were the last bastion of the Cathar heretics, driven south by Simon de Montfort and the armies of the Albigensian crusaders. Eleven years after the martyrdom at Montségur, where more than 200 Cathar believers chose to die by fire rather than recant their faith, the Cathars' final stand took place at **Château de Quéribus** (open Apr-Oct). The stronghold's outer defences are staggered along the crest of a hill with a single, narrow stairway leading to the keep. Reaching into the sky like a giant torch from a sheer-sided rocky outcrop 500 m above the Aude valley, the keep commands dizzying views across to the snow-capped Pyrenees and neighbouring Peyrepertuse.

Château de Peyrepertuse (open Apr-Oct) is the most awe-inspiring of the medieval castles. Measuring over 300 m from the pointed ship's prow of the east end to the Château Saint-Georges, it rides the vertiginous ridge like a dreadnought, flanked by ruined, sun-bleached battlements. Between Peyrepertuse and Saint-Paul-de-Fenouillet, the D10 accomplishes a minor miracle of engineering as it carves a cliff-hanging route along the **Gorges de Galamus**. There is a parking area with precipitous views down into the narrow ravine. A footpath leads around to the hamlet of L'Hermitage buried into the rock face.

Further west, **Château de Puilaurens** (18 km via the D117) lords it over the village of Lapradelle. Its crenellated walls are more or less complete, reinforced during the 17thC, and stand out etched against the sky above a sea of dark green firs (open Apr-Oct).

CANIGOU, PIC DU
A sacred mountain for Catalans, Canigou stands a snowcapped head and shoulders above the Têt and Tech valleys, dominating the Roussillon plain. On June 21, French and Spanish Catalans converge on the summit to light the first of the *Feux de Saint-Jacques*. Torches lit from the sacred flame are then used to fire dozens of bonfires in various Catalan villages, the prelude to a wild evening of dancing and high-spirited bonfire leaping.

According to the records, the King of Aragon, Pierre III, was the first to scale the 2,784-m peak in 1285. If you want to retrace his footsteps, by car or on foot, start out on the rough 15-km track off the D27 south of Prades, near Fillols. From the Chalet des Cortalets, it is a strenuous 1.5-hour hike to the Catalan flag planted at the top. Sensible clothes and footwear are essential; check weather reports and take a large-scale map. The local S.I.s at Prades and Vernet have details of jeep hire and guided expeditions.

See also Walking in the French Pyrenees, page 304.

CERET ⚓ ✕
S.I. *avenue* Clemenceau. Main town of the Vallespir region and cherry-growing capital of the eastern Pyrenees. The tiny old town centre clusters around the church in gracefully delapidated muddle of miniature squares and chunks of medieval ramparts dappled by plane trees. In keeping with the faded charm, the 14thC fountain on place des Neuf-Jets manages nine little dribbles, but the whole place comes alive on Saturday with a terrific market bursting out of place Pablo-Picasso.

Céret's pride and joy is the **Musée d'Art Moderne** (closed Tues), boulevard Maréchal-Joffre, a fitting showpiece for a town which has been described as the 'Mecca of Cubism'. In the early part of this century, the Catalan artist Monolo Hugué introduced a band of young painters to the town including Braque, Picasso, Gris, Jacob and Kisling. Soutine and Chagall followed, as did Pierre Brune who founded the museum in 1950. Reopened in 1993 with dramatically increased exhibition space, the museum offers works by all its visiting luminaries, some with scrawled dedications to the museum itself.

A highlight of the collection is Picasso's bullfighting pottery - all blazing sun and swirling cloaks. Céret also loves a *corrida* - the S.I. has details of bullfights held in the local arena.

• *Port-Vendres on the Côte Vermeille.*

CHATEAU DE QUERIBUS

And other *châteaux* in the north-west of the area: see The Cathar Castles, page 298.

COLLIOURE AND THE COTE VERMEILLE ⊭ ✕

Where the Albères hills tumble down from the Pyrenees to the Mediterranean, the 30-km strip of reddish rocky shoreline that leads to the Spanish border is known as the 'Vermillion Coast'. There is more than a pinch of artistic licence in the description, but like inland Céret (page 298), this picturesque stretch of fishing villages and pebble beaches was an early 20thC artistic haunt, beloved of the Fauvists in this case.

At the northern end of the strip, **Argelès-Plage** has more in common with the Golfe du Lion resorts - a great sandy beach, new marina, swarms of international campers and the sweet, greasy smell of dozens of waffle and *crêpe* stands. There are several pleasant family hotels between the beach

resort and inland town centre which has a market and museum of Catalan folklore and crafts.

Derain and Matisse spent the summer of 1905 painting in the crystal clear light of pretty **Collioure**. Besieged by visitors in summer, the little port sits on a sheltered bay with a pebble beach, the odd brightly painted fishing boat, bundles of nets, and a row of café terraces. At one end of the front, the Château Royal, once the summer palace of the Kings of Aragon and Majorca, guards the boat basin and houses arts and crafts exhibitons (open Easter-Nov). At the other, the local church, with its somewhat military façade, conceals a clutch of ornately gilded Catalan retables (altar screens).

Squeezed between the sea and the encroaching hills, the colourful houses and grubby fishing smacks of **Port-Vendres** are accompanied by a business-like whiff of fish and diesel. Fish auctions are held on the docks every day except Sunday. Then a pretty stretch of the N114 wiggles down to **Banyuls**, a modest leafy town ringed with vineyards. The sculptor Aristide

Maillol lived and died in Banyuls and there are several of his bronzes dotted about town. He is buried in the garden of his farmhouse studio, Mas Maillol, in the Baillaury valley 4 km to the southwest. Banyuls has been making full-bodied red wines since the days of the Templars, and the Celliers des Templiers, route du Mas Reig (D86) offers tastings and tours of the original 13thC cellars. You can circle back to Collioure on the narrow D86, climbing up behind the coast through terraces of vines and cork oaks. A goat track of a road leads off for a terrifying ascent to the 13thC **Tour Madeloc**, which affords superb views, but drivers will need nerves of steel.

ELNE

S.I. *La Mairie*. An ancient settlement fortified by the Romans, Elne was the capital of Roussillon before the Kings of Majorca moved their base to Perpignan. Hannibal stopped off here on his elephant march to Rome for the Second Punic War.

Present-day visitors scale the little mound of the old town to visit the 11thC **Cathédrale de Sainte-Eulalie et Sainte-Julie** for its superb cloister constructed from grey and white veined marble quarried near Céret. The Romanesque south gallery has beautifully detailed capitals with long eastern faces and intricate friezes; the biblical stories and twisted foliage of the Gothic galleries date from the 14thC. A small archaeological museum houses arrowheads and pottery from Elne's Neolithic and Roman inhabitants.

PERPIGNAN ⊷ ✕

S.I. *Palais des Congrès*. A vibrant southern city just 30 km from the Spanish border, Perpignan is more Catalan than

RECOMMENDED HOTELS

CERET
La Terrasse au Soleil, FF-FFF; *route de Fontfrède* (1.5 *km* S); *tel.* 68 87 01 94; *cards* MC, V; *closed Jan to mid-Mar.*
Lovely Catalan-style hotel with beams, pretty tiles and small but charming rooms. Views of Canigou from the garden and pool terrace; tennis and activity expeditions in the region. Delicious food, too - pheasant and chestnut soup, salmon with fennel, apple-filled *crêpes.*

Hôtel Vidal, F; *4 place du 4-Septembre; tel.* 68 87 00 85; *credit cards* V; *closed four weeks Oct-Nov.*
Simple but friendly *logis* in the old town with a regional restaurant.

COLLIOURE
Casa Pairal, FF-FFF; *impasse Palmiers; tel.* 68 82 05 81; *credit cards* AE, DC, MC, V; *closed Nov-Apr.*
Palm trees and yellow shutters, Spanish tiles and wrought-iron curlicues, this pleasant hotel is tucked down an alley in luxuriant courtyard gardens. Solid, comfy rooms far from the madding crowd; charming staff.

Hostellerie des Templiers, F-FF; *quai de l'Amirauté; tel.* 68 82 05 58; *credit cards* V; *closed Jan.*
Bursting with atmosphere and remarkable artworks collected from an impressive parade of famous visitors. Rustic rooms; quayside tables for delicious fish dishes.

PERPIGNAN
Athéna, F; *1 rue Quéya; tel.* 68 34 37 63; *credit cards* AE, DC, MC, V; *open year round.*
Rather shabby, but welcoming and very central (off place de la République). Spacious rooms in an old building with a spotlit courtyard boasting a palm tree and minuscule pool. Cafeteria with live music.

Windsor, FF; *8 boulevard Windsor; tel.* 68 51 18 65; *credit cards* AE, MC, V; *open year round.*
Conveniently situated on the edge of the old town, with 56 comfortable, sound-proofed rooms.

VERNET-LES-BAINS
Le Mas Fleuri, FF-FFF; *25 boulevard Clemenceau; tel.* 68 05 51 94; *credit cards* AE, DC, MC, V; *closed Nov-Apr.*
Modern family hotel with swimming pool and gardens. Bright, well-equipped rooms, most with private balcony. No restaurant.

French. Jaime I, King of Aragon, settled the question of his succession (1262) by dividing his kingdom in two. His younger son, Jaime II, received Roussillon and the kingdom of Majorca. Perpignan became his capital, and the city flourished during the 13th-14thC. The web of narrow Old Town streets enfold the best of the sights, excellent shops and an enormous selection of reviving bars, cafés and restaurants offering plenty of Catalan specialities.

An excellent place to start exploring is the **Musée Pairal** laid out in a 14thC city gate on place de Verdun. On the way up to the roof-top look-out, stop off for a whistle-stop introduction to Catalan culture by way of peasant crafts, costumes and furniture. On summer evenings, outbreaks of the *sardaña*, a traditional Catalan folk dance, take place on the square.

A short walk down rue Louis-Blanc, place de la Loge boasts a Maillol sculpture and the 13thC **Loge de Mer**, the former stock exchange and seat of the maritime court. Its Gothic arches now front a hamburger franchise, but inspect the gargoyles from a well-placed café table.

Nearby, an iron grille gives on to the courtyard of the 13th-14thC **Hôtel de Ville**, where Maillol strikes again with *La Mediterranée* posed on a neat patch of grass. The concierge lets visitors into the Salle des Mariages with a typical Hispano-Mauresque painted ceiling. From place de la Loge, rue Saint-Jean leads to the relative calm of place Gambetta and the 14thC **Cathédrale de Saint-Jean** adorned with a frivolous iron belfry on one side, arched buttresses and gargoyles looming over a small courtyard on the other. Concealed in the impenetrable gloom of the interior there are a couple of fine

RECOMMENDED RESTAURANTS

CERET
See Recommended Hotels.

COLLIOURE
La Bodega, F-FF; *6 rue de la République; tel. 68 82 05 60; credit cards AE, DC, MC, V; closed Mon dinner-Tues except Jul-Aug.*

Popular spot in an old wine cellar. Catalan cuisine, *bouillabaisse* and fish.

Pa i Trago, F-FF; *1 rue Arago; tel. 68 82 20 44; closed Wed, Mon-Fri off season.*

Bread and wine (*pa i trago*) obviously, but fish is the main order of the day at this minute Spanish restaurant. Vats of moules, sardine fritters and gargantuan paella.

PERPIGNAN
Le Festin de Pierre, FF; *7 rue du Théâtre; tel. 68 51 28 74; credit cards AE, DC, MC, V; closed Tues dinner-Wed, Feb, two weeks Jun.*

Elegant dining in a fine old building. A seafood menu features fresh anchovies from Collioure or a *feuilleté* of sole with lobster coulis and wild mushrooms, amongst other dishes.

Opera Bouffe, F-FF; *impasse de la Division (off place Jean-Jaurès); tel. 68 34 83 83; credit cards MC, V; closed Sun.*

Pretty little dining room with blue and white tiles and plenty of regional flavours on the menu. The enormous Catalan rice salad loaded with mussels, ham, spicy chorizo and tomatoes is a meal in itself at lunchtime, entrecôte with anchovy butter, and *meli mato*, ewe's cheese with honey, to follow.

PRADES
El Patio, F-FF; *19 place de la République; tel. 68 96 02 84; credit cards V; closed Sun dinner-Mon.*

Friendly beamed dining room on the main square. Spanish-style home cooking from gazpacho to a hearty *zarzuela* (fish and shellfish stew).

VERNET-LES-BAINS
Au Comte Guifred de Conflent, F-FF; *avenue des Thermes; tel. 68 05 51 37; credit cards AE, DC, MC, V; closed Nov to mid-Dec.*

Book ahead for a chance to sample the skills of young chefs training at the Ecole Hôtelière du Roussillon. Rather bland modern dining room, but pleasant terrace. Classic and innovative dishes such as smoked salmon with grapefruit, rabbit with chorizo sausage and nuts, or a wondrous *salade de mer*.

• Argelès-Plage.

Renaissance retables or altar panels (light switches on the left), and two early 16thC masterpieces painted on 12-m high doors removed from the organ loft. Hung either side of the exit to the Chapelle de Christ, the doors depict the Baptism of Christ and Salome delivering John the Baptist's head - the latter, in particular, reveals a wealth of rich and rare Italianate detail.

Another Old Town sight is the little **Musée Rigaud**, 16 rue d'Ange, named for the 18thC court portrait painter, Hyacinthe Rigaud. There are several of his works on display, plus Catalan and Provençal primitives, some jaunty Dufys and Maillol. Both lived in and around Perpignan, as did Picasso who also features (closed Tues).

Adrift in the flapping laundry and mean streets of the Algerian and gypsy quarter to the east, the old Catalan **Eglise de Saint-Jacques** dates from the 14th-17thC. It is the starting point for the historic Good Friday *Procession de la Sanch* with its robed and hooded penitents who wend their way to the cathedral as they have done since the 15thC. Across the street, the **Jardin de la Miranda** meanders around the city walls.

Vauban's massive fortifications draw a six-pointed star around the 13thC **Palais des Rois de Majorque**, rue des Archers (closed Tues in winter).

Founded by Jaime II in 1274, the two-storey palace is bordered by gardens with views across the city to Canigou. The Gothic arcaded courtyard reflects a distinct Moorish influence, and there are two chapels, one above the other, the upper with a fine banded marble Romanesque façade.

PRADES ✕

S.I. *4 rue Victor-Hugo.* A relaxed, leafy little town at the foot of Canigou, Prades is renowned for its summer *Festival Pablo Casals* (July 25-Aug 13). An exile from the Franco regime, the Catalan cellist spent 23 years living in Prades, and the S.I. houses the one-room **Musée Pablo Casals**.

On the café-lined main square, the cobbled **Eglise de Saint-Michel** sports a fine belfry, pink marble detail and behind the altar is an enormous gilded Baroque reredos. The handsome Mairie is also here, and the wonderful Tuesday food market offers a huge range of produce cultivated in the Tech valley.

Before heading for the hills, the **Abbaye de Saint-Michel-de-Cuxa** (3 km south via the D27) merits a stop. Surrounded by peach and apple orchards, its buildings gather around a crenellated belfry near the river, and the pink marble carvings in the cloister are realized in riveting detail.

SERRABONE, PRIEURE DE

On a bleak grey-green mountain side amidst tinder-dry puffs of scrub and gorse, cork and holm oak, Serrabone is the most remarkable example of Roussillon Romanesque architecture. Visits (closed Tues) begin in the cloister, hanging over a steep ravine, where weathered pink marble capitals, cut and carved into birds and monsters with meticulous precision, display traces of the Crusaders' influence in their bearded Saracen figures. The grey slate simplicity of the 11thC church provides a powerful counterpoint to the exquisite vaulted tribune occupying the heart of the building. Carved into the stunning arrangement of rose-pink columns and pillars, lions and griffins, serpents and monkeys, centaurs and saints, battle it out in a welter of slavering jaws and exotic foliage.

VERNET-LES-BAINS ⇌ ✕

S.I. *place de la Mairie.* A small spa in the woods, Vernet spills down to the River Cady as it rushes through the lower town past several plain, modern hotels. The town is a popular starting point for expeditions up Canigou, and to the other main sight in the area, the isolated **Abbaye de Saint-Martin-du-Canigou**. It is a steep hike up to the abbey from Casteil (2.5 km south via the D116), winding around the slopes of Canigou to a huddle of ochre and grey slate roofs perched on a walled outcrop at 1,094 m. Founded in the 10thC, the abbey buildings are now occupied by Spanish monks (closed Tues). Tours visit the 11thC church built over an earlier chapel, and the restored cloister. The tombs of the abbey's founder Guifred de Cerdagne and his wife lie carved in rock outside the church.

VILLEFRANCHE-DE-CONFLENT

S.I. *place de l'Eglise.* Dwarfed by bold purple-red cliffs at the confluence of the rivers Têt and Cady, Villefranche guards the main route west from Perpignan to Spain. The fortress town was founded by the Counts of Cerdagne in 1092, and its well-preserved ramparts, fine Gothic houses and the **Eglise de Saint-Jacques** decorated with local pink marble make it a favourite with the tour bus brigade.

In French hands after the Treaty of the Pyrenees, Villefranche was a strategic frontier post ripe for the attentions of the great 17thC military architect, Vauban. He constructed the eagle's nest **Fort Liberia** and cliff-scaling defences above the valley.

LE PETIT TRAIN JAUNE

One of the best little train journeys in Europe departs from Villefranche on a 2.5-hour, 63-km rollercoaster run to La Tour-de-Carol on the Cerdagne plateau. Nicknamed 'the Canary' by locals, the tiny yellow and red train (open carriages in summer) trundles through gorges and tunnels, over viaducts and up the side of Mont Louis until it gains the plateau which boasts the highest sunshine rating in the country.

WALKING IN THE
FRENCH PYRENEES

For walkers, the French Pyrenees offer rich and almost inexhaustible possibilities, from half-hour strolls along beaches to strenuous challenge walks over high mountains hundreds of kilometres long and needing months to complete.

Nearly everywhere, there are well waymarked paths traced out by local members of the Fédération Française de la Randonée Pédestre (FFRP - the French Ramblers Association), a major source of excellent information on walking in the region. As a main artery along the whole range, there is one of the classic walks of Europe, the **GR10** (*sentier de grande randonée* or long-distance footpath), a route wholly in France of some 700 km from Hendaye on the Atlantic coast via the high mountain scenery of the centre to Banyuls on the Mediterranean coast. Other GRs branch off from this route to make delectable circular walking tours of one to seven days or more. Others cross it, the most famous being the **GR65** which follows the old medieval pilgrim route from France to Santiago de Compostela, crossing the frontier into Spain at St-Jean-Pied-de-Port.

Most of the paths are graded and waymarked in colour codes used nationally by the FFRP: GRs with white and red bars, *GR de pays* (circular tour paths of one day or more) with yellow and red bars and PRs (shorter local paths) with yellow bars (although other colours are used in some areas).

Many of these routes are described in fine detail and with route maps in the highly informative *Topoguides* published in French by the FFRP (some now translated into English too) and available everywhere in the region. With these and the information which is available in local tourist offices, no walkers should be at a loss in finding walks to suit their capabilities and needs. In fact, they are much more likely to be spoilt for choice. Each of the four *départements* that cover the Pyrenees has its special attractions.

In the west, the **Pyrénées Atlan-** tiques offers pleasant walking along the coast and inland but its higher mountain country, the **valleys of the Aspe and Ossau**, with useful bases at **Lescun** and **Laruns** in particular are recommended for walkers.

The **Hautes Pyrénées** *département*, as its name implies, contains the highest mountains of the whole range (Pic Long, 3,192 m is the highest peak wholly in the French Pyrenees). This region also boasts most of the **Pyrenees National Park**, containing some of the finest mountain scenery, flora and fauna, and the most challenging walking of all. The famous **Cirque de Gavarnie** and the dramatic **Brèche de Roland** are here, to be visited once by walkers and then left to less adventurous tourists while true mountain lovers head for better walking centres such as **Pont d'Espagne** or **Luz St-Sauveur**.

Further east is **Ariège**, the *département* where, on the Spanish/Andorran borders, some of the remotest mountain walking in the whole range is for experienced walkers only. It does however contain areas further north that will suit the less experienced: fine river valleys and limestone landscapes with walking of all grades everywhere. The Cathars (see page 298) had strongholds here and the **Sentier des Cathares**, brilliantly described in a *Topoguide*, will fascinate any walker interested in history.

The **Pyrénées Orientales** is a very special *département*: this is Catalan country and for walkers has perhaps the most varied scenery of all. Two adjoining areas called the **Cerdagne** and **Capcir**, with excellent walking bases at **Font Romeu** and at **Mont Louis**, deserve special mention. Splendid flower-filled valleys, especially the **Vallée d'Eyne**, a paradise for botanist-walkers, and the **Gorges du Sègre**, offer easy walking. For a real challenge, **Pic Carlit** (2,927 m) is a truly great mountain walk. Accessible too is the better known **Mont Canigou** (2,784 m), last of the high mountains before the Mediterranean is reached.

All in all, the French Pyrenees offer

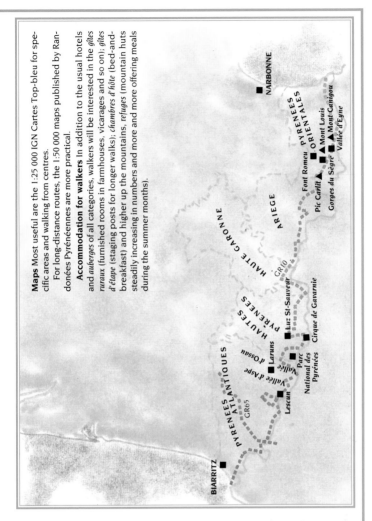

Maps Most useful are the 1:25 000 IGN Cartes Top-bleu for specific areas and walking from centres.

For long-distance routes, the 1:50 000 maps published by Randonées Pyrénéennes are more practical.

Accommodation for walkers In addition to the usual hotels and *auberges* of all categories, walkers will be interested in the *gîtes ruraux* (furnished rooms in farmhouses, vicarages and so on); *gîtes d'étape* (staging posts for longer walks); *chambres d'hôte* (bed-and-breakfast) and higher up the mountains, *refuges* (mountain huts steadily increasing in numbers and more and more offering meals during the summer months).

a feast for walkers, and those who once taste it will find their appetites whetted for more, again and again.

Useful addresses and other information

For copies of the *Topoguides* and general information: *Fédération Française de la Randonée Pédestre* (FFRP), 9 avenue George-V, F-75008 Paris; tel. 1 47 23 62 32; fax 1 47 20 00 74.

In each *département*, the local FFRP members work in conjunction with local authorities through a *Comité Départemental de la Ran-* *donée Pédestre*. Contact with them will open up for walkers a great deal of specialized information, possibly even outings with French ramblers.

The *Comités* in the Pyrenees are based in Pau, Tarbes, Laroque d'Olmes and Perpignan. Tourist information centres should be able to supply their addresses.

Another comprehensive information service for walkers is Randonées Pyrénéennes, Service C.I.M.E.S.-Pyrénées, 4 rue Mayelane BP 24, F-65420 Tarbes; tel. 62 90 09 90; fax 62 90 09 91.

North-Eastern France

Alsace

170 km; map Michelin No 242

F rance's smallest province is cosy, compact, pleasant and relaxed. It is a narrow strip of territory just 200 km long by 30 km wide, with a travel-brochure image of picture-postcard prettiness – half-timbered houses, burgeoning window boxes and neat ranks of vines lapping at the edges of well preserved medieval villages – which is not very different from the reality.

Bordered to the east by the Rhine and Germany, and to the west by the Vosges mountains, Alsace has spent as much time under German ownership as it has French, which perhaps accounts for its orderliness. Alsace is also jolly, clean, prosperous, extremely well-fed and a pleasure to visit at any time of year.

Take spring, for example, when the alpine meadows are filled with wild flowers. Or early summer, when storks overhaul their cartwheel-sized nests. Even at the height of summer, when the heat and tour buses down on the plain become too much to bear, there is an escape into the mountains, or rather the high hills which make up the Vosges. They resemble monks' tonsures, with thickly wooded sides and rounded, bare-topped crowns known as *ballons*. Take advantage of more than 1,200 km of marked paths for walks long and short through vineyards and forests, and for long-distance routes such as the GR5 which strikes out along the roof of the Vosges covering much the same ground as the spectacular Route des Crêtes, which forms part of our suggested driving route.

Exploring Alsace is made easy by a dozen signposted itineraries. The prettiest is undoubtedly the 120-km Wine Route along the foothills of the Vosges. (This exploration takes in the northern section between Obernai and Colmar before heading for the hills and the Route des Crêtes.) Linger along the way to sample local vintages in traditional *winstubs*: dry Sylvaners, fruity Rieslings, full-bodied Tokays and Gewürztraminers are served in bulbous glasses on long green stems.

And then there is Alsacien cuisine: *tartes flambées* filled with onion and bacon; platters of *choucroute* (sauerkraut), or *coq au riesling* (chicken in white wine); not forgetting local Munster cheese served with a pinch of cumin seeds; and exemplary plum tarts.

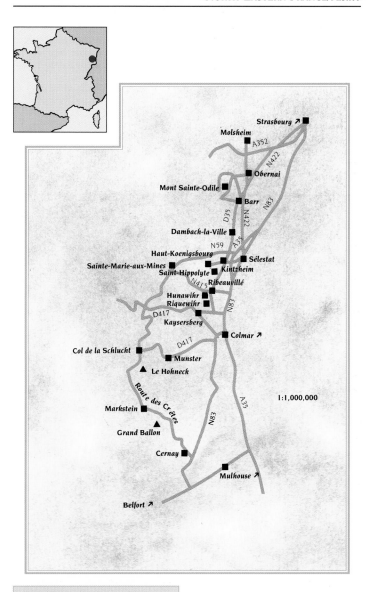

Strasbourg ↗
Molsheim
A352
N422
Obernai
Mont Sainte-Odile
Barr
N422
N83
D35
Dambach-la-Ville
A35
N59
Haut-Koenigsbourg
Sélestat
Sainte-Marie-aux-Mines
Kintzheim
Saint-Hippolyte
Ribeauvillé
N415
Hunawihr
Riquewihr
N83
D417
Kaysersberg
Col de la Schlucht
Colmar ↗
D417
Munster
Le Hohneck
Route des Crêtes
1:1,000,000
Markstein
A35
Grand Ballon
N83
Cernay
Mulhouse ↗
Belfort ↗

TRANSPORT

Main line trains between Strasbourg and Mulhouse stop at Sélestat and Colmar. A local line from Sélestat back-tracks via Dambach, Barr and Obernai to Molsheim for return connections to Strasbourg. Bus services are sketchy, but bike hire is widely available (check with local S.I.s for details and suggested itineraries).

SIGHTS & PLACES OF INTEREST

BARR
S.I. *rue de la Kirneck*. One of the least
visited small villages along the Wine
Route, Barr's winding streets are full of
tempting *épiceries* for picnic ingredients. There is also a jolly terracotta-
coloured Hôtel de Ville adorned with a
curlicue pediment, and a helpful S.I. On
the road into town, the **Musée de la
Folie Marco Barr** offers an insight
into bourgeois Alsacien life of the 17th-
19thC. The `folly' bankrupted its
builder, the local bailiff, in the 18thC,
but has been carefully restored and
filled with Alsacien furniture, pretty
china and crystal chandeliers, as well
as a thoughtfully-provided *winstub* in
the cellar (closed Oct-May, weekdays
Jun- Sep).

BELFORT
See France Overall: 10.

DETOUR - **MONT SAINTE-ODILE**
A winding drive into the Vosges
hills leads up to **Mont Sainte-
Odile** (12 km south-west of
Obernai via D33), named for the
patron saint of Alsace. The Celts
first fortified the strategic hill-top
site with a 10 km-long earthwork
known as the *mur païen*. Later a
convent was founded here which
has served as a place of
pilgrimage since the 16thC,
notably on December 13, St
Odile's feastday. There are visits
to the convent with its tranquil
gardens, cloister and the chapel
containing St Odile's remains.

COLMAR
See France Overall: 10.

DAMBACH-LA-VILLE
S.I. *place du Marché*. Another small town

RECOMMENDED HOTELS

KAYSERBERG
L'Arbre Vert, FF; 1 *rue Haute Rempart*; *tel.* 89 47 11 51; *credit cards* AE,
MC, V; *closed Jan.*
    Friendly, family-run *logis* in an old
house with attractive modern extension. Some rooms have flower-
decked balconies. Smart dining room
specializing in Alsacien dishes.

Les Alisiers, FF; 3 *km off* N415 *at
Lapoutroie (7 km W of Kayserberg via
N415); tel.* 89 47 52 82; *credit cards* MC,
V; *closed Christmas and Jan after New
Year.*
    Charming farmhouse hotel-restau-
rant. Log fires and rustic antiques
combined with simple modern rooms
dressed in pine and pretty fabrics.
Delicious Alsacien home cooking -
don't miss the *tarte à l'oignon* - and
the charming Degouys can rustle up
a picnic and arrange visits to wine
growers.

OBERNAI
A la Cour d'Alsace, FFF; 3 *rue Gail*;
tel. 88 95 07 00; *credit cards* AE, DC,
MC, V; *closed mid-Dec to mid-Jan.*
    Tucked down an alley, this delec-

table hotel occupies a mixture of old
and new buildings. Spacious, well-
equipped rooms (tastefully modern or
rustic); pretty garden; and choice of
gourmet restaurant or relaxed *winstub*.

Hostellerie La Diligence, FF; *place
de la Mairie; tel.* 88 95 55 69; *credit cards*
AE, MC, V; *open year round.*
    Half-timbered building on the main
square. Warm welcome, comfy
rooms, good restaurant serving
regional and classic dishes. Also two
annexes outside town: the traditional
Bel-Air, and modern **Exquisit**.

La Maison du Vin, F; *rue de la Paille*;
tel. 88 95 46 82; *credit cards, none.*
    Basic rooms in a creaky old house
above a cosy *winstub*. Rustic charm,
but check your quarters first (friendly
patron). If the bar is closed there are
instructions posted on the window for
how to proceed.

RIBEAUVILLE
See Recommended Restaurants.

RIQUEWIHR
See Recommended Restaurants.

delight on the Wine Route with part of its medieval walls, gates and moat intact. There is a fine Renaissance **Hôtel de Ville**, pretty half-timbered buildings hung with geraniums and wrought-iron signs, and ubiquitous bear motifs: the bear is the town's mascot, and alludes to the local legend that a grape-munching bear persuaded villagers to plant the first vines.

You can drink in the atmosphere, sample the local wines (those from the Frankstein hills are highly recommended), take horse-drawn carriage rides, and walks along vineyard and forest paths (check with the S.I. for details).

The 12thC **Chapelle de Saint-Sebastian** has a particularly grand carved baroque altar; further west, **Château de Bernstein** commands terrific views.

HAUT-KOENIGSBOURG, CHATEAU DU

An enormous red sandstone pile crowded on to a 755 m-high promontory in the woods, this is a textbook medieval castle.

Completely enclosed by imposing battlements and entered by a single massive gate, it is awash with turrets and towers. The main look-out can be wreathed in mist while the sun shines in the courtyards, or the whole castle can disappear into the clouds. The original fortress, founded by Frederick of Hohenstaufen (the `One-Eyed') in the 12thC was rebuilt in the 15th-16thC, but largely dismantled by Swedish troops during the Thirty Years War (1633). At the turn of this century, Emperor Wilhelm II (`Kaiser Bill') had the whole thing reconstructed and furnished in 15th-17thC style. Despite the moans of purists, who object to the florid neo-Gothic decoration, the architectural details have been carefully copied from similar buildings and there is plenty to admire along the way (closed Jan to early Feb).

KAYSERBERG 🛏 ✕

S.I. *place de la Mairie*. A pretty town of pastel-painted and timbered houses on the burbling River Weiss, Kayserberg is famous for its *Christkindelsmarkt* (Christmas market), which fills the streets on the four weekends leading up to December 25. There is plenty to enjoy year round, too. On the main

---

DETOUR – KINTZHEIM

In the shadow of Haut-Koenigsbourg, the village of Kintzheim, 8 km east on the D159, has transformed its ruined castle into an eagle's nest. The **Volerie des Aigles** offers aerial acrobatics by eagles, falcons and vultures (afternoons daily Apr-Sep, Wed and weekends only Oct to mid-Nov). The neighbouring monkey park, **Montagne des Singes**, is another popular family outing (daily Apr to mid-Oct, Wed and weekends mid-Oct to mid-Nov); also the **Parc des Cigognes et Loisirs** which combines stork breeding and tiny fallow deer with various children's rides and shows (daily Apr to mid-Sep, Wed and weekends mid-Sep to mid-Oct).

---

drag, stop off at the **Eglise de Sainte-Croix** to admire the 16thC retable with its flock of gilded figures. At the top of the street, by the carved façade of the **Maison du Fougeron**, follow the lane to a steep path which clambers up to the ruins of the 13thC **Château** with views across the roof tops to the valley. Among the many fine houses to look out for, there is no missing 16thC **Maison Offinger**, 88 Grande Rue, with its black-, ochre- and mustard-painted pillars and carvings near the river, and there are pretty views of the conical **Chapelle de l'Oberhof** from the bridge. A short walk away, the **Centre Culturel Albert Schweitzer**, 126 Grande Rue, honours the local-

---

DETOUR – CENTRE DE REINTRODUCTION DES CIGOGNES EN ALSACE

Just down the road from Ribeauvillé, at Hunawihr, the centre is attempting to reintroduce storks to the region (closed Nov-Mar). This involves encouraging the great black-and-white birds not to migrate. They are free to roam, swooping gently over the vineyards and back to their enormous nests in the reserve. The centre also harbours cormorants, ducks, swans and playful otters.

a splendid old building where wandering minstrels used to gather. Halfway up the street, facing the Hôtel de Ville with its puffing boy fountain, the 14thC church has a coloured tile roof, and the 13thC **Tour des Bouchers** marks the entrance to the attractive Haute Ville where several old houses have been restored in exuberant shades of raspberry and bilberry. Dotted about the hillside above the village and its vineyards there is a trio of ruined châteaux: Girsberg, Haut-Ribeaupierre and Saint-Ulrich, accessible by the **Route des Trois Châteaux**. Though the harvest of Ribeauvillé's famous white wines takes place later in the year, local vintners entertain visitors with a colourful annual Wine Festival on the third weekend of July.

- *Vosges outlook from Haut-Koenigsbourg.*

born Nobel Peace Prize winner (closed Nov-Easter).

MULHOUSE
See France Overall: 10.

OBERNAI ⊨ ✕
S.I. *Chapelle du Beffroi.* Immaculately preserved within its medieval ramparts, Obernai makes an excellent base for the region and is within easy reach of Strasbourg.

The central place du Marché is edged by lovely half-timbered and corbelled buildings, a Renaissance **Hôtel de Ville** and the 16thC **Halle aux Blé**, a winner with its unusual struts, stone balcony and roof-full of pigeon roosts. At one corner of the square, a pretty Renaissance well sports buckets of flowers and frilly dragon water spouts.

The S.I. provides free guided tours (French, German and English) at 10 am every Tuesday and Friday morning in July and August, and the cobbled streets are lined with vintners and gift shops bursting with every conceivable Alsacien souvenir.

RIBEAUVILLE ⊨ ✕
S.I. 1 *Grand'Rue.* One of the most popular stops along the Wine Route, Ribeauvillé is a single main street flanked by a smattering of alleys. At the southern end of Grand'Rue, the restaurant **Zum Pfifferhaus** occupies

RIQUEWIHR ⊨
S.I. 2 *rue de la 1ère Armée.* A tiny little village almost submerged in the folds of its famous vineyards, Riquewihr is utterly charming but completely overrun by tourists in the summer. Behind the quaint cobbled main street lined with *caves* tucked into medieval and Renaissance houses, lie alleys and courtyards festooned with geraniums and creepers. The village also boasts the best collection of decorative wrought-iron hanging signs along the Wine Route. A little train does the rounds from May to November, but it is more interesting to explore on foot. There is a clutch of small museums: local history in the 13thC **Tour du Dolder**; a dungeon and torture chamber in the **Tour des Voleurs** (Thieves' Tower), part of the old city walls; and a postal museum in the 16thC **Château** (all closed Nov-Easter).

ROUTE DES CRETES
Built as a communications link during the First World War, the `Ridge Road' rides the spine of the Vosgien hills from Sainte-Marie-aux-Mines (21 km west of Sélestat via N59) due south to Cernay. Several twisting roads climb up through the forested hillsides from the plain; one of the most tortuous crawls up to the winter ski station at the **Col de la Schlucht** (1,139 m) from the cheese town of Munster (19 km west of Colmar via D417).

From the bald moorland hill tops, sweeping views encompass toy-town villages and isolated lakes nesting in the lee of the wooded slopes, and hang-gliders ride thermals with the hawks. On the road south, there is a footpath up to the top of **Le Hohneck** (1,362 m); **Markstein** hosted World Cup skiing events in the 1980s (the Route des Crêtes is transformed into a cross-country skiing route in winter); and the views from **Grand Ballon** (1,424 m), the highest peak in the Vosges, are spectacular. There is no need to starve up here either, thanks to a sprinkling of café-restaurants and traditional *fermes-auberges*, farmhouses offering home-cooked Alsacien dishes.

SAINTE-MARIE-AUX-MINES
And other places/features on the Route des Crêtes, see Route des Crêtes, above.

SELESTAT
S.I. *boulevard du Général-Leclerc.* A thousand-year-old market town on the plain,

Sélestat's old town remains a diverting tightly-knit circle of medieval streets, half-timbered houses, towers and churches. There is the 13thC **Tour de l'Horloge**, the **Tour des Sorcières** with a chunk of the ancient ramparts, and the lovely Romanesque **Eglise de Sainte-Foy**.

Sélestat's largest church is the Gothic **Eglise de Saint-Georges**, easily distinguished by its multi-coloured roof tiles. The interior contains a Renaissance choir and 15thC stained glass. The town's real *pièce de résistance* is the famous **Bibliothèque Humaniste** which houses the library of Beatus Rhenatus (1485-1547), a friend of Erasmus and leading light in Sélestat's influential humanist school. Illuminated manuscripts and rare tomes dating back to the 7thC are displayed alongside 15thC carvings and *faïence*.

STRASBOURG
See France Overall: 10.

RECOMMENDED RESTAURANTS

KAYSERSBERG
Lion d'Or, F-FF; *66 rue du Général-de-Gaulle; tel. 89 47 19 02; credit cards* V; *closed Wed, Tues off season, Jan to mid-Feb.*

Traditional Alsacien furnishings and panelled ceilings, plus a broad choice of menus in the brasserie or restaurant dining rooms. Homemade goose paté, pike *en croûte*.

See also Recommended Hotels.

OBERNAI
Chambellan, F-FF; *1 rue Général-Leclerc; tel. 88 95 09 88; credit cards* MC, V; *closed Sun dinner-Mon.*

Alsacien dishes such as duck liver with *Gewurztraminer* jelly or fish cooked in *cremant d'alsace* served in a salmon-pink house with a garden terrace outside the ramparts. Two good value **F** menus.

Also ten attractive rooms at the top end of our **FF** price band.

RIBEAUVILLE
Cheval Blanc, F-FF; *122 Grand'Rue; tel. 89 73 61 38; credit cards* V; *closed Mon, mid-Nov to mid-Jan.*

Shutters, window boxes and fresh paint, plus local dishes from smoked boar to Munster cheese flambéed in *marc de Gewürztraminer.*

Also a *logis* with 25 rooms.

Zum Pfifferhus, F; *14 Grand'Rue; tel. 89 73 62 28; credit cards* V; *closed Wed-Thur, three weeks Mar, three weeks Jun-Jul.*

Authentic (and very popular) *winstub* with the obligatory dark panelling, lace curtains and wholesome food. Smoked goose breast salad, quiche and local wines by the glass, but get here early as space is limited.

RIQUEWIHR
Le Sarment d'Or, F-FF; *4 rue du Cerf; tel. 89 47 92 85; credit cards* V; *closed Sun dinner-Mon, one week Jun-Jul, four weeks Jan-Feb.*

Comfortable beamed dining room in a 17thC building. Alsacien and home-cooked classics from duck in *pinot noir* to baked trout.

Also ten pretty rooms (**FF**) decorated with colourful fabrics and antique furniture.

Undiscovered Burgundy: the Morvan

160 km; maps Michelin 65 and 69

The Morvan is a granite plateau edged by the rolling pasture and sunny vineyards of Burgundy. It borders the Nivernais, and together these regions are the poorest corner of an otherwise wealthy area.

Morvan has nonetheless had its moments. It was a great centre of Ancient Gaul – witness the fortified camp of Bibracte. That faded with the Roman occupation and the founding of Augustodunum (Autun). Later came the golden age of the basilica at Vézelay, which heard St Bernard preach the Second Crusade in 1146, and launched thousands of pilgrims on the road to Santiago de Compostela. The Revolution saw the end of the pilgrims, and most of the buildings.

The name Morvan is thought to come from the Celtic for 'Black Mountain'. Its hilly, forested countryside is scoured by rivers and dotted with lakes, small farms and weathered stone villages. The main towns are modest and unsophisticated, villages really, that cater for a small and usually budget-orientated summer following. And this is the Morvan's chief charm: it remains largely undiscovered.

A great chunk of the region is protected by the 195,647-hectare Parc Naturel Régional du Morvan which offers numerous outdoor activities such as riding, kayaking, climbing and fishing as well as hiking opportunities. The GR13 long-distance footpath wends its way from Vézelay to Autun, and the Maison du Parc sells a series of easy-to-follow *petites randonnés* postcards with a map and directions.

The sights are equally low-key. Take the hamlet of Pierre-Perthuis, with its namesake, a hollow rock, its hump-backed 18thC bridge over the Cure, and a presbytery once owned by Louis XIV's military architect, Maréchal de Vauban. (The great man was buried nearby at Bazoches.) Or Quarré-les-Tombes, a hill-top village where 112 stone sarcophagi lids lie crammed around the tiny churchyard. They date from the 7th-10thC, but history does not relate how they got there.

To the south, the reservoirs of Pannesière-Chaumard and the Lac des Settons offer beaches, sailing boat and pedalo hire. Another peaceful oasis is the Saut de Gouloux, a little waterfall lined by boulders and trees off the D977b, 7 km north of Montsauche. This is an ideal place to relax and recharge: a couple of my favourite hotels are nearby at Saint-Père-sous-Vézelay and Arnay-le-Duc. Saulieu and Château-Chinon are also useful bases.

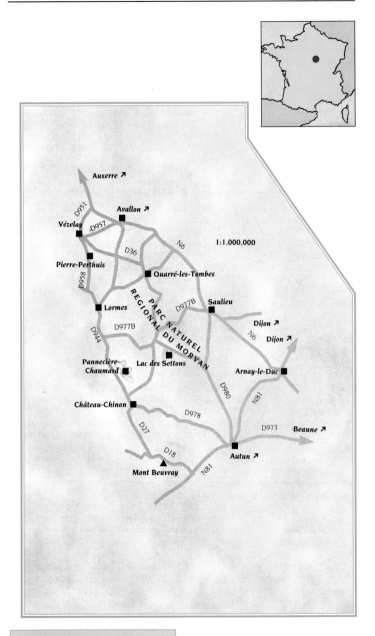

Auxerre ↗

Avallon ↗

Vézelay

Pierre-Perthuis

Quarré-les-Tombes

Lormes

Saulieu

Dijon ↗

Dijon ↗

PARC NATUREL RÉGIONAL DU MORVAN

1:1,000,000

D951

D957

D36

N6

D958

D977B

N6

D977B

D944

Pannecière-Chaumard

Lac des Settons

Arnay-le-Duc

Château-Chinon

D980

N81

D978

D27

D973

Beaune ↗

D18

Autun ↗

Mont Beuvray ▲

N81

TRANSPORT
By train, the gateway towns are
Autun (bus connections to
Château-Chinon), Avallon (buses to
Vézelay) and Saulieu, but public
transport within the park is
practically non-existent.

SIGHTS & PLACES OF INTEREST

AUTUN
See France Overall: 11.

AVALLON
See France Overall: 15.

CHATEAU-CHINON ⇌ ✕
S.I. *place Gudin.* A typical grey stone and slate Morvan village perched on a hill in the middle of the park, Château-Chinon is the main summer base for exploring the region. It was also François Mitterand's Nivernais political base, and where he acted as mayor from his quarters in the Vieux Morvan hotel from 1959 to 1981. As a result, the town has an unusual museum, the **Musée Septennat**, 6 rue du Château, which displays the weird and wonderful official gifts which Mitterand received during his terms as president (closed weekdays Oct-Apr, Jan-Feb).

There is also a folksy **Musée du Costume** with some exquisitely wardrobed dolls and assorted knick-knacks. The road past the museums leads up to a hill-top **calvaire** where an orientation table points out landmarks.

In 53 BC, the besieged Gaulish tribes held a Council of War at the fortified settlement of **Bibracte** on Mont Beuvray (25 km south-east via D27/D18). Vercingetorix was elected to lead the Gauls against the armies of Caesar, but defeat at Alésia in 53 BC saw the Gauls' camp abandoned and the rise of Roman Augustodunum (Autun). Since the 19thC, archaeologists have been uncovering the remains of Bibracte in its secluded corner of the park. There are exhibitions, tours (Jul-Aug), and you can make a 5.5-km circuit of the ancient defences with marvellous views from the 821-m 'mountain'.

MORVAN, PARC NATUREL REGIONAL DU
The S.I.s in Avallon, Saulieu and Vézelay all offer information about the park, but the place to start is the excellent **Maison du Parc**, at Saint-Brisson, on the D6, 13 km west of Saulieu. Housed in a 19thC château, the centre provides information about outdoor activities, walks and budget accommodation in the 20 *gîtes d'étape* scattered throughout the park. Outbuildings house exhibitions and a museum of the local Resistance active during the Second World War. There is also an aboretum, herbarium and deer enclosure.

SAULIEU ⇌ ✕
S.I. *rue d'Argentine* (N6). A pleasant market town and eastern gateway to the park, Saulieu offers a choice of accommodation and a couple of diverting sights. The best known is the 12thC **Basilique de Saint-Andoche,** much rebuilt and messed around, but its original capitals are well worth taking some time to see.

Among the local crafts exhibits next door, the **Musée Municipal** pays tribute to 19thC animal sculptor François Pompon, whose imposing bronze *Bull* (*Le Taureau*) stands guard at the northern entrance to town. Pompon is buried beneath one of his own bird sculptures in the attractive 15thC **Eglise de Saint-Saturnin**, by the tree-lined Promenade Jean-Mace.

VEZELAY ⇌ ✕
S.I. *rue Saint-Pierre* (Apr-Oct). The great stone bulk of the **Basilique de la Madeleine** sits on top of a rounded hilltop like a beacon, surveying a patchwork of fields and trees at the northern extent of the Morvan. The little village of Vézelay pitches down the hill behind it, a jumble of craft shops in summer, pleasantly deserted off season when you can park right outside the monumental Romanesque basilica.

Founded in 860, the Benedictine abbey church was dedicated to Mary Magdalene, whose supposed relics were brought here in the 10thC. It became one of the four main departure points for medieval pilgrims on the Route Saint-Jacques to Santiago de Compostela in Spain, gave Thomas à Becket sanctuary, and St Bernard a pulpit (although he actually preached the Second Crusade in the open air at a spot marked with a cross outside the Porte Sainte-Croix).

The Third Crusade, an unlikely joint venture for old enemies Richard the Lionheart of England and Philippe Auguste of France, met at Vézelay in 1190, but a century later Mary Magdalene's bones were 'rediscovered' in Provence, and the abbey fell out of favour.

Pillaged by Protestants during the Wars of Religion and by Revolutionary vandals, little more than a shell remained when the energetic 19thC restorer Viollet-le-Duc stepped in and embarked on one of the most creditable projects of his career. Work began in 1840, and lasted for almost 20 years. The façade was rebuilt with three doors leading into a spacious narthex which is divided from the nave by an internal doorway. This is crowned by a magnificent tympanum showing the Risen Christ, arms open in welcome, surrounded by the apostles. At his feet (the Pagan Races) and around the inner arch (the Converted Races) are represented the various

peoples of the world to whom the Gospel must be taken. The outer arch shows the signs of the zodiac together with scenes from a monthly calendar of husbandry.

Beyond the doorway, the graceful striped arches of the nave lead to a light-filled Gothic choir, each pillar along the way sporting superb capitals, 99 in all, fully described in the guidebooks on sale at the entrance.

To the right-hand side of the church are grassy lawns for picnicking in sight of the buttresses, with views across the valley. The village tends to get overrun by coach tours in season, and 20thC pilgrims come out in force on July 22.

RECOMMENDED HOTELS & RESTAURANTS

ARNAY-LE-DUC
Chez Camille, FF; 1 *place Edouard-Herriot* (N6); *tel.* 80 90 01 38; *credit cards* AE, DC, MC, V; *open year round.*

A warm welcome, a lovely 16thC house full of beams and antiques, and Armand Poinsot's deliciously light and full-flavoured cooking makes this a favourite haunt.

CHATEAU-CHINON
Au Vieux Morvan, F-FF; 8 *place Gudin*; *tel.* 86 85 05 01; *credit cards* MC, V; *closed four weeks Dec-Jan.*

Plain, provincial *logis* with spotless rooms and an above-average restaurant serving classic dishes from duck *confit* to *pot au feu*.

A simpler and cheaper alternative is the **Lion d'Or,F**, 10 *rue des Fosses*; *tel.* 86 85 13 56.

SAULIEU
La Borne Imperiale, F-FF; 16 *rue Argentine*; *tel.* 80 64 19 76; *credit cards* V; *closed Tues dinner-Wed, mid-Nov to mid-Dec.*

A pleasant *auberge* offering seven rooms, a small garden, and a popular dining room serving regional dishes: duck pâté in a pastry jacket, *poulet de Bresse*, trout with mustard sauce.

Côte d'Or, FF-FFF; 2 *rue Argentine*; *tel.* 80 64 07 66; *credit cards* AE, DC, MC, V; *closed Mon-Tues lunch Nov-Mar, one week*

Mar, four weeks Nov-Dec.

No expense has been spared in the refurbishment of Bernard Loiseau's Morvan base. Three Michelin stars illuminate his ethereal oyster and prawn soup, the frogs legs with garlic purée, pigs trotters stuffed with *foie gras*, and not forgetting of course the dreamy puddings.

The bedrooms are charming and fairly priced.

L'Esperance, FFF; *at Saint-Père-sous-Vézelay*, 3 *km SE*; *tel.* 86 33 20 45; *credit cards* AE, DC, MC, V; *closed Tues-Wed lunch, Jan.*

Local boy Marc Meneau has been here almost 20 years, achieving three stars for his sublime cusine, and a devoted following to his welcoming hotel divided between the main house and a converted river-side mill. The glass-sided restaurant is a novel experience for semi-al fresco lunches.

Exquisitely subtle dishes include *timbale de tagliatelle au bouillon parfumé* and sweetbreads with watercress. On a more robust note, there is a pink and perfect leg of lamb, Charolais beef, great cheeses and interesting wines. Very expensive, but worth every penny.

Hôtel de la Poste et Lion d'Or, F-FF; *tel.* 86 33 21 23; *credit cards* AE, MC, V; *closed Nov-Mar (restaurant Tues-Wed lunch).*

Atmospheric coaching inn with a traditional restaurant and comfy rooms with lovely views.

Eastern France

Franche-Comté, the Doubs and the Jura

Up to 300 km; maps Michelin Nos 66 and 70

The historic 'free country' of Franche-Comté lies between the Rhine and the Rhône bordered by the Vosges to the north (see Local Explorations: 12) and to the south-east by the crescent-shaped natural barrier of the Jura mountains which march more or less parallel to the Swiss border. The territory passed from the Holy Roman Empire to the Burgundians and then to the Spanish before it was annexed to France by the Treaty of Nijmegen in 1678. Louis XIV moved the capital from Dole to the more easily defendable Besançon; then, apart from shoring up several other strategic forts, Franche-Comté was largely left to its own devices. It is one of the most peaceful, relaxing regions of France and comparatively seldom visited.

Life in this corner of France is essentially rural: cows tinkling down narrow lanes, fields of buttercups a metre high, isolated farmhouses and little grey stone villages on the banks of lively rivers fed by the limestone hills. The hills are cleft by steep ravines, carved into giant amphitheatres and riddled with subterranean caves. Endless shades of green dapple the pastures and forests of beech, oak and conifers.

Comté cooking is in sympathy with the terrain: simple but generous. Look for the fleshy morel mushrooms; sausages from Morteau; great rounds of Comté cheese; fresh trout and pike; and crayfish used in the rose-pink sauce Nantua. To drink there is *gentiane*, a liqueur made from mountain flowers, plum and cherry brandies to keep out the cold, while Arbois, on the 80-km Route des Vins du Jura, is famous for its rosé wine, golden *vin jaune* and unusual *vin de paille*.

This local exploration is less of an itinerary than a handful of suggestions for a couple of days in the Doubs Valley and northern Jura. There is plenty to keep you amused, from kayaking to fishing and walking. Numerous tiny roads tempt the inquisitive visitor to improvise driving routes: one idle detour I made led to the discovery of Nans-sous-Sainte-Anne, a little Shangri-La nestling among the hills near the Source du Lison (page 319).

One caution: the weather is unreliable. However, even the rain can weave its spells, with tendrils of cloud trailing through the valleys, and rainbows unfolding in their wake.

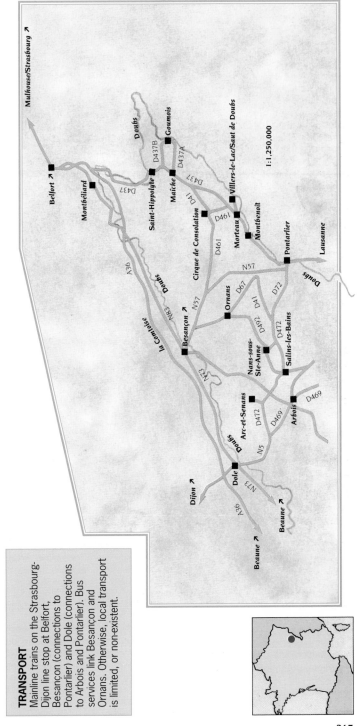

TRANSPORT
Mainline trains on the Strasbourg-Dijon line stop at Belfort, Besançon (connections to Pontarlier) and Dole (connections to Arbois and Pontarlier). Bus services link Besançon and Ornans. Otherwise, local transport is limited, or non-existent.

SIGHTS & PLACES OF INTEREST

ARBOIS ⊨ ✕

S.I. *rue de l'Hôtel-de-Ville*. An agreeable small wine town, Arbois is renowned for its excellent *rosé* wine, the rare and heady *vin jaune*, and the even more exclusive *vin de paille* wherein the practice of allowing the grapes to dry on beds of straw helped put Louis Pasteur on the trail of bacteria. Pasteur's father moved his family to Arbois from Dole, and the scientist returned often to the creeper-clad **Maison de Pasteur**, rue de Courcelles, now a museum (closed Tues).

The heart of town is place de la Liberté, lined with fine old houses and arcaded shops. One of the main local winemakers, Henri Marie, has an outpost here offering *dégustations*, and the S.I. has a list of other welcoming *viniculteurs*. Beyond the S.I., the fine Romanesque **Eglise de Saint-Just** has a special winemaker's window surrounded by a halo of golden-yellow glass the colour of *vin jaune*.

ARC-ET-SENANS

It would be difficult to imagine a more elegant architectural relic of the late-18thC Industrial Age than Nicolas Ledoux's unfinished **Saline Royale** (Royal Saltworks) at Arc-et-Senans. The plan was to build an entire town arranged in concentric circles around the pivotal Director's Residence, but only the central axis, with the classical overseer's house flanked by salt halls, and a semi-circle of outbuildings, were completed.

BELFORT and BESANCON

See France Overall: 10.

DETOUR – **RECULEE ET GROTTE DES PLANCHES**
A delightful side trip from Arbois, the Reculée and Grotte des Planches (5 km south-west via the D469) combines two natural beauty spots: the cool and leafy *reculée*, or blind valley, and subterranean limestone caves sculpted into weird formations over thousands of years.

DOLE

S.I. *place Grévy*. Once the capital of Franche-Comté, Dole slumbers peacefully above the Canal du Rhône au Rhin as it joins the Doubs. Stone houses and narrow streets cling to the hillside around the substantial 16thC **Eglise de Notre-Dame**; in rue de Besançon you can pick up the essentials for a picnic from half-a-dozen *charcuteries*; and there are pretty public gardens stretching down to the water's edge near the old tanners' quarter. Louis Pasteur was born here in the humble **Maison Pasteur**, 46 rue Pasteur. Although the inventor of pasturization probably never wore the galoshes on display, this small museum contains a few documents and snippets of memorabilia (closed Tues, Nov-Mar).

DOUBS, VALLEE DU

The River Doubs rises in the Jura mountains south-west of Pontarlier and embarks on an erratic course which takes it north-east along the Swiss frontier before doubling back via Besançon to join the Saône south of Dijon. The most dramatic and beautiful section of its course lies between the town of Montbenoît (on the D437, 10 km north-west of Pontarlier) and Goumois (on the D437A, 53 km south of Montbéliard).

At **Montbenoît** the river is still a quiet and lazy creature, so take a moment to visit the fine 12th-15thC **Ancienne Abbaye** with its Gothic cloister and carved stalls. The D437 follows the Doubs downstream, squeezing through narrow, wooded ravines to the town of **Morteau**, a busy summer tourist centre renowned for its plump pork sausages, *Jésus de Morteau*, smoked over juniper and pine. The most spectacular Doubs vista is the **Saut du Doubs**, a 30-m-high waterfall near Villiers-le-Lac, where the turbulent river plunges down in a flurry of white water. As well as boat trips from Villiers, there are various paths into the cool shade of the surrounding beech and pine woods.

Another stunning view point, though not of the Doubs, is the **Roche du Prêtre** (12 km north of Morteau via D461), a rocky outcrop above the **Cirque de Consolation**. Down in the bowl of this wooded amphitheatre, a 17thC abbey opens its park to infrequent visitors.

DETOUR – LISON, SOURCE DU
The D103 is so pretty, the *source* is merely an excuse to make this detour. Edged by trees and mossy boulders, the head of the little river is fed by two waterfalls from limestone caves. Further up the valley is the farming village of **Nans-sous-Sainte-Anne** with a workshop museum (closed Nov-Apr).

ORNANS 🛏
S.I. *rue Pierre-Vernier*. A little town literally hanging over the banks of the River Loue, the steeply pitched roofs and wooden balconies of its houses reflected in the water. The Realist painter Gustave Courbet was born here in 1819, and his house on rue Froidière (near the bridge) contains paintings, drawings and memorabilia (closed Tues in winter). Anglers will find a fishing museum at 36 rue Saint-Laurent (closed Oct-Mar).

There are several hotels which make a convenient base for exploring, and *Syratu*, place Courbet (tel. 81 57 10 82), can arrange bicycle hire, kayaking, rafting and climbing expeditions for outdoor types.

The exhilarating drive upstream from Ornans along the Vallée de la Loue affords plunging views down to the river from thickly wooded escarpments. The river is born at the **Source de la Loue** (22 km S of Ornans, off the D67) in a crash of thundering water pouring from a breach in the semi-circular rock face.

PONTARLIER
A dull town, though a useful transport hub for the region and the Jura ski resorts to the south around Mont d'Or. The skiing here is easy to intermediate, worth considering for complete beginners, but not if you've already experienced mainstream Alpine resorts. One local distraction is the eagle's nest stronghold of **Fort de Joux** (5 km south, off the D437), which houses a ferocious weaponry museum on a crag above the dramatic Cluse-et-Mijoux chasm (closed Nov-Mar).

RECOMMENDED HOTELS AND RESTAURANTS

ARBOIS
Jean-Paul Jeunet, FF-FFF; *9 rue de l'Hôtel- de-Ville; tel.* 84 66 05 67; *credit cards* DC, MC, V; *closed Tues-Wed lunch, Dec-Jan.*
M. Jeunet's dining room, richly refurbished since his father's day, is one of the bastions of modern regional cooking. Pike *mousseline* with crayfish tarragon sauce, oxtail sausage and wild mushrooms flavoured with oregano. Enjoyable Jura wines.

Also 18 well-equipped guest rooms.

GOUMOIS
Hôtel Taillard, FF; *tel.* 81 44 20 75; *credit cards* AE, DC, MC, V; *closed Wed Oct-Nov and Mar, mid-Nov to Feb.*
Relaxing chalet-style hotel with a notable dining room. Specialities include *foie gras* with morello cherries, and *tournedos jurassienne* with morels. A charming welcome.

ORNANS
Hôtel de France, FF; *rue Paul-Vernier; tel.* 81 62 24 44; *credit cards* DC, MC, V; *closed Sun dinner-Mon Apr-Oct (except Jul-Aug), Sat-Sun Nov-Mar, six weeks Dec-Jan.*
Traditional *logis* on the main street with 31 spacious and simple bedrooms, plus hearty and well-presented regional cuisine.

A budget alternative is the **Progrès** (F; rue Gervais; tel. 81 62 16 79; open year round), a modern hotel over the river.

Moulin du Prieuré, FF; *on the D280, 1.5 km off the D67 N of Ornans; tel.* 81 59 21 47; *credit cards* AE, DC, MC, V; *closed Nov-Mar.*
Idyllic riverside setting; individual chalet accommodation; and good food served in an attractive old mill building.

Dauphiné and Savoie - The French Alps

565 km (ex-Grenoble); map Michelin Nos 74, 77 and 89

From Evian, on the shores of Lac Léman, south to Nice, the 742-km Route des Grandes Alpes rides the French Alps until they finally plunge into the sea. It is magnificent, dramatic terrain, now almost as popular with summer visitors as with skiers. This tour concentrates on the northern provinces of Dauphiné and Savoie, and is designed primarily for the summer season (Jun-Sep) when the high passes are open and shorts are more appropriate than salopettes. There are numerous possibilities: you can make a circuit from Chambéry, take a longer tour from Grenoble via Briançon, or explore from a delightful year-round base like Annecy; or, of course, you can write your own menu.

The region's main gateway cities and towns lie to the west in the *Préalpes*. Lively Grenoble is the largest of these and capital of the Dauphiné (see France Overall: 12). Chambéry once shared its responsibilities as capital of the ancient Duchy of Savoie with Turin until the Savoyards voted to join France permanently in 1806. Then there is stately Aix-les-Bains; and lovely Annecy. The main feature of the Alpine scenery is Mont Blanc, Europe's highest mountain, its snow-capped summit towering above its neighbours. At its foot, Chamonix is the oldest of the French winter sports resorts with superb skiing and an enormous summer sports programme, emulated by other major resorts such as Megève, the Trois Vallées and Val d'Isère. As well as traditional hiking and climbing opportunities, there are various new action-man pursuits on offer such as *parapente*, the practice of running downhill with a parachute on your back until you take off (or fall over exhausted).

But walking is the real key to the mountains: in spring the high pastures are carpeted with blue gentians, vetch, campion and anemones; later in the season, an equally soothing sight is the elderly farmer cutting grass with a hand scythe, drying the hay and storing cords of wood on the balconies of weathered chalets.

The mountain air will of course build up your appetite and you'll find the local restaurants well prepared. Cheese, ham and potatoes are the staples of mountain cooking, tastily combined to produce *tartiflette* and *gratin dauphinois* (sliced potatoes baked with cream and cheese), or *raclette*, a variation on fondue with a great rondel of Reblochon cheese melted at your table; and try fresh *omble chevalier* (char, not dissimilar to sea trout) with the flinty white wines from Seyssel.

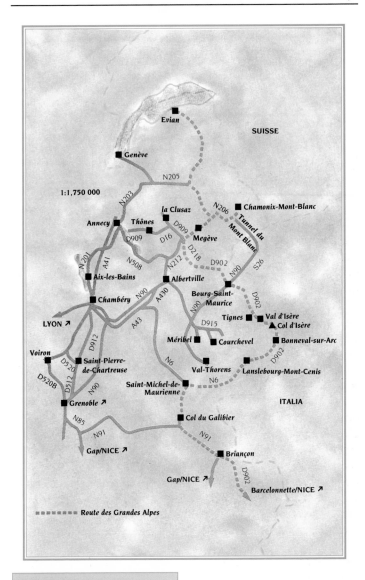

Evian

SUISSE

Genève

N205

1:1,750 000

N203

la Clusaz

N206

Chamonix-Mont-Blanc

Tunnel du
Mont Blanc

Annecy

Thônes

D909

D16

Megève

D909

D218

S26

N201

A41

N508

N212

D902

N90

Aix-les-Bains

Albertville

Bourg-Saint-
Maurice

D902

Chambéry

N90

A430

N90

Tignes

Val d'Isère

▲ Col d'Isère

LYON ↗

A43

D915

Méribel

Courchevel

Bonneval-sur-Arc

Voiron

D912

Saint-Pierre-
de-Chartreuse

N6

Val-Thorens

D902

Lanslebourg-Mont-Cenis

D520

D512

N90

Saint-Michel-de-
Maurienne

N6

D520B

Grenoble ↗

ITALIA

N85

N91

Col du Galibier

N91

Gap/NICE ↗

Briançon

Gap/NICE ↗

D902

Barcelonnette/NICE ↗

▬ ▬ ▬ ▬ ▬ Route des Grandes Alpes

TRANSPORT
Regular Geneva-Grenoble train
services stop at Annecy, Aix les-
Bains and Chambéry; connections
to Briançon from Grenoble. From
Chambéry there are train
connections to Chamonix-Mont-
Blanc via Saint-Gervais; and to
Bourg-Saint-Maurice for buses to
Val d'Isère. Buses from Annecy
stop at Megève and Chamonix-
Mont-Blanc.

SIGHTS & PLACES OF INTEREST

AIX-LES-BAINS ⌂ ✕
S.I. *place Maurice-Mollard*. A decorous Victorian spa with a pedigree stretching back to the Romans, Aix lies on the eastern shore of the Lac du Bourget. Roman remains decorate place Maurice-Mollard, where the S.I. houses a small archaeological museum. Across the way, the **Thermes Nationaux** reveals its Roman origins (guided tours).

If the steaming sulphur baths do not entice, there is the fabulous little **Musée Faure**, rue des Côtes, housing Impressionist art and sculpture from Bonnard, Degas, Pissarro and Rodin (closed Tues).

Lac du Bourget is France's largest natural lake, and the water front offers promenades, boat and sailboard hire, as well as cruises and trips to the neo-Gothic **Abbaye de Hautecombe** on the opposite shore (May-Oct). The abbey is famous for its Gregorian sung mass (Sun), and the tombs of the Savoie princelings. It can also be reached via the D914, which runs above the western lake shore through the woods with views back to the mountains.

ANNECY ⌂ ✕
S.I. *Centre Bonlieu, rue Jean-Jaurès*. Gathered around the northern tip of its beautiful mountain lake, Annecy enjoys one of the loveliest settings imaginable. The Old Town, **Vieil Annecy**, is a treat as well, garlanded with flowers popping out of window boxes and baskets and draped in great swags from tiny hump-backed bridges over the Canal du Thiou.

The cobbled streets and narrow *quais* are lined with 15th-17thC buildings in stucco and stone; arcaded streets such as rue Sainte-Claire disappear behind enticing street markets (Wed, Fri and Sun); and there are restaurants and cafés at every turn serving hearty Savoyard dishes, fresh fish from the lake (one of Europe's cleanest), or a glass of wine in the sunshine.

The sights are minor, but enjoyable, from the cavernous **Eglise de Saint-Michel**, with its beautiful *Pietà* by Pieter Pourbus and monochrome Renaissance fresco, to a small history museum housed in the doughty **Palais de l'Isle**, a former prison on a tiny boat-shaped island in the canal (closed Tues). Clamber up to the **Château-Musée** for a bird's-eye view over the roof-tops from the parapet. The 12th-16thC castle displays collections of Savoyard crafts, natural history and local archaeological finds (closed Tues).

DETOUR – LAC D'ANNECY
Out and about around Lac d'Annecy there are any number of pleasures in store. The entire 38-km circuit of the lake can be driven in an hour, but that rather misses the point. In addition to lake cruises which allow you to stop off for a couple of hours, local bus services are regular; bicycles can be hired from the SNCF station; and the S.I. provides walking suggestions and supplies maps.

The western shore offers beaches at **Saint-Jorioz**, a storybook private château at **Duingt**, and winding drives (via the D41) or walks up the wooded slopes of the Montagne de Semnoz to the **Crêt de Châtillon** (1,699 m).

In the lee of **La Tournette** (2,351 m) on the eastern shore, there is a smart pay beach by the Hôtel Imperial; medieval **Menthon-Saint-Bernard**, the birthplace of Saint Bernard, of shaggy dog fame; and the discreetly well-heeled and charming village of **Tallories**, where you will find the superb but astronomically expensive *Auberge du Père Bise* (**FFF**; tel. 50 60 72 01). From Tallories, the D42 zigzags up to the **Col de la Forclaz** (2,041 m), where a café provides a ring-side seat for the aerial antics of daredevil parascenders.

For Chamonix-Mont-Blanc, there is a great back road from Thônes (20 km east via the D909). During summer, you can take the D12/D16 up the Col de la Croix Fry (1,477 m), then rejoin the D909 for the Col des Aravis (1,498 m).

Down by the water's edge there are pretty public gardens, boat and sailboard hire from the Champ-de-Mars, and cruises to various points around the lake by the *Compagnie des Bateaux*, 2 place aux Bois.

BRIANCON 🛏 ✕

S.I. *Porte de Pignerol.* Fortified since pre-Roman times, Europe's highest town (1,325 m) stands sentinel at the junction of four great valleys guarding the road to Italy. Head straight for the picturesque **Haute Ville**, overlooked by Vauban's grim-faced **Citadelle** (tours only Jul-Aug), perched above the uninspiring modern town. Entered by the Porte de Pignerol, the largely 18thC old town is packed tightly within its walls, offering terrific views across the Dauphiné Alps. Precipitous streets like the main **Grande Gargouille** tumble downhill; there is Vauban's sturdy **Eglise de Notre-Dame** which looks

• *Annecy.*

almost as impregnable as the citadel; and a plethora of souvenir shops.

Briançon is an excellent jumping-off point for excursions into the **Parc National des Ecrins** which borders Italy to the south-east. The Bureau des Guides is housed in the S.I.

CHAMBERY 🛏 ✕

S.I. *24 boulevard de la Colonne.* A strategic site in the broad valley between the Massif de Chartreuse and the Bauges mountains, Chambéry was the capital of the ancient Duchy of Savoie, and now rules as *préfecture* of the region. Successive periods of French and Italian rule have left their stamp on the attractive Old Town, and added to the impressive collection of aquiline Roman noses on view in the **Musée des Beaux-Arts**, place du Palais de Justice. Also recommended is the

DETOUR – **LES CHARMETTES**
The 18thC philosopher Jean-
Jacques Rousseau and his lover
Madame de Warens kept a country
retreat 2 km above the centre of
Chambéry. They met in Annecy in
1728 (she a 28 year-old landlady,
he a 16 year-old apprentice), and
occupied Les Charmettes between
1736 and 1742. The house, set in
gardens with a private chapel, has
been turned into a museum
(closed Tues).

Musée Savoisien, square Lannoy de
Bissy, which makes an excellent introduction to Savoyard folk culture (both
closed Tues).

Vieux Chambéry is bisected by the
elegant arcades of rue de Boigne. At
the top end, on boulevard de la
Colonne, the Count de Boigne stares
down from the daft but entertaining
Fontaine des Elephants with its
pachyderms and war-like arrangement
of spears and standards. At the far
end, the ducal **Château** and its Gothic
chapel are open for guided tours (daily
Jun-Sep, check off-season schedules
with the S.I.). Walking tours of the old
town depart from place du Château (4
pm daily Jun-Sep), or explore the winding alleys and covered passages at
your own pace. Broad place Saint-
Léger is lined with shops, cafés and
fine shuttered buildings, while the
Cathédrale de Saint-François conceals a remarkable *trompe l'oeil* frescoed interior behind the remains of its
Flamboyant façade.

CHAMONIX-MONT-BLANC 🛏 ✕
S.I. *place du* Triangle *de l'*Amitié. The self-
styled 'World Mountaineering Capital',
Chamonix and its complement of a
dozen or so villages stretches along a
narrow glacial valley sandwiched
between the Mont Blanc massif and the
Aiguilles Rouges. The town itself is no
beauty, but the mountain scenery is
unequalled in Europe, and it is well-
worth battling the crowds and queues
for a glimpse of its majesty. The
Musée Alpin, avenue Michel-Croz,
gives a brief history of Mont Blanc and
its conquerers (open pm only Jun-Sep,
Christmas to Easter). The first were
Paccard and Balmat in 1786.

An early morning start, warm
clothes and nerves of steel are a distinct advantage for the exhilarating
two-stage *télépherique* ascent to the
Aiguille du Midi (3,842 m). This
jagged granite needle commands
superb views up to the snow-capped
summit of **Mont Blanc** (4,807 m), and
across the massif, but clouds tend to
obscure the view after midday. The
round trip takes a couple of hours, or
there is another *télépherique* which
swings on over the Vallée Blanche and
Glacier du Géant towards Italy, part of
an aerial circuit of the peaks. The other
popular excursion is the **Mer de
Glace**, a 14 km-long glacier reached
by rack railway (May-Sep).

In winter, Chamonix is dedicated to
'*le ski*'. In fact, with all the major ski
areas above 2,000 m, the lifts stay
open into April, and snowfields such as
Grands Montets (3,275 m) can have
fresh snow in late May. In summer Chamonix attracts walkers and climbers;
there are 310 km of marked trails
around the town, colour-coded to represent degrees of difficulty. Both the
S.I. and **Maison de la Montagne**,
place de l'Eglise, which houses the
Office de Haute Montagne, weather
station and Bureau des Guides, can
supply information, maps and assis-
tance with route planning.

One of the best short walks is the
two-hour trail along the **Grand Balcon
Sud** between Le Brévent and La
Flégère, and the Bureau des Guides
(tel. 50 53 00 88) offers daily guided
treks (sign up the day before) as well
as leading assaults on the peaks. The
summer equivalent of a winter skipass
is the *Pass'Sports et Montagne*, a book
of coupons redeemable against a variety of activities from rafting and tennis
to summer bobsleighing. These are on
sale at the S.I.

CHARTREUSE, MASSIF DE LA
Between Grenoble and Chambéry, the
limestone cliffs and wooded folds of
the Massif de la Chartreuse offer a
slow but picturesque alternative to the
main valley roads. **Saint-Pierre-de-
Chartreuse** is the chief town, a quiet
resort surrounded by walking trails
through the woods, which become a
fiery mass of golden reds and browns
in autumn. The sudden pockets of pasture bursting with wild flowers are

equally lovely in spring or autumn.

Just west of Saint-Pierre, the village of **la Correrie** (2.5 km via the D520B) has a small museum about life in the nearby Carthusian monastery of **Grande Chartreuse**. Although the isolated monastery is closed to the public, there are impressive views over the substantial walled complex, built on the spot where St Bruno founded the first community in 1084. The monks' famous sticky liqueur is distilled in **Voiron** (23 km west via the D520), where the Caves de la Chartreuse, 10 boulevard Edgar-Kofler, offer free tours of their vaulted cellars followed by tastings (closed Sat-Sun Nov- Easter).

GRENOBLE
See France Overall: 12.

HAUTE MAURIENNE
The Maurienne derives its name from the local patois for 'wicked river' (*mau riau*), and the Haute Maurienne lies along the upper reaches of the Arc valley, a clutch of simple stone-clad villages crouched in the lee of craggy mountains.

At the foot of the Col du Mont Cernis (2,083 m) and the road to Italy, **Lanslebourg** is the home of the regional S.I. which arranges tours of local churches at **Avrieux**, **Bessans**, **Lanslevillard**, and **Termignon**, the surprising repositories of ornate Baroque art. The best preserved of the villages is **Bonneval-sur-Arc** with its spidery narrow streets and rough cottages weighed down by their heavy slate roofs.

═══════════════════════════
RECOMMENDED HOTELS
═══════════════════════════

AIX-LES-BAINS
Le Manoir, FF-FFF; *37 rue Georges-ler; tel. 79 61 44 00; credit cards AE, DC, MC, V; closed Christmas to mid-Jan.*
Attractive Relais de Silence with garden and swimming pool. Well-equipped rooms; big, beamed dining room serving classical cuisine.

ANNECY
Hôtel de Savoie, F-FF; *place Saint-François; tel. 50 45 15 45; credit cards V; open year round.*
Friendly spot on a small and relatively quiet canal-side square. Facilities and views (canal or interior well) vary with price.

Motel le Flamboyant, FF; *52 rue des Mouettes, Annecy-le-Vieux; tel. 51 23 61 69; credit cards AE, DC, MC, V; open year round.*
Not remotely flamboyant, but attractive, peaceful, modern rooms in chalet buildings.
See also Recommended Restaurants.

BRIANCON
Hôtel de Paris, F-FF; *41 avenue du Général-de-Gaulle; tel. 92 20 15 30; credit cards AE, DC, MC, V; open year round.*
Modern hotel near the station. Great views and one of the best restaurants in town.

CHAMBERY
Hôtel des Princes, F-FF; *4 rue de Boigne; tel. 79 33 45 36; credit cards AE, DC, MC, V; open year round.*
Traditional and central hotel/ restaurant in the old town. Modern rooms; helpful staff.

CHAMONIX-MONT-BLANC
Croix Blanche, F-FF; *84 rue Vallot; tel. 50 53 00 11; credit cards AE, DC, MC, V; closed two weeks May, Nov to mid-Dec.*
Big, old-fashioned rooms in a rambling family hotel in the town centre. Café-brasserie with terrace, dining room with trestles. Weekly bookings only in Feb-Mar high season.

Hermitage et Paccard, FF-FFF; *rue des Cristalliers; tel. 50 53 13 87; credit cards AE, DC, MC, V; closed two weeks May, Nov to mid-Dec.*
Modern three-storey chalet in a quiet residential street. Well-equipped rooms with balconies and mountain views, and a dining room.

MEGEVE
Fleur des Alpes, FF; *route Jaillet; tel. 50 21 11 42; credit cards V; closed four weeks Apr-May, mid-Sep to mid-Dec (except Nov hols).*
Comfortable modern chalet with views and terrace-café a five-minute walk from town.

LYON
See France Overall: 11.

MEGEVE 🛏 ✕
S.I. *rue de la* Poste. A chic winter sports centre with a wide range of outdoor activities for summer visitors, Megève makes a quieter and more attractive alternative to Chamonix. Cable-cars grind up **Mont d'Arbois** (1,827 m) for breathtaking views across to Mont Blanc and the Aravis range. Check out the helpful S.I. (tel. 50 21 27 28) for walking suggestions and information about pony-trekking, rafting, canyoning and paragliding. The Bureau des Guides, in the same building (tel. 50 21 31 50), also runs a rock-climbing school.

TROIS VALLEES, LES
Striking off the N90, the arms of the Trois Vallées terminate in three major winter resorts offering some of the best skiing in the Alps. They moonlight during summer as rather half-hearted outdoor activity centres and bases for the **Parc National de la Vanoise**, but really come into their own with the first decent snowfall of winter.

Starting in the west, **Val Thorens/ Les Menuires** is the highest resort in Europe with excellent conditions which virtually guarantee snow well into March (glacier skiing). In the middle valley, **Méribel** retains several charming

• *Chamonix.*

fragments of the old village amongst its largely purpose-built chalet accommodation; the skiing is generally intermediate or easy. At the tip of the eastern valley, **Courchevel** is the most sophisticated of the trio.

Further along the N90 towards Bourg-Saint-Maurice, there are two other notable resorts: **Les Arcs** and **La Plagne**. Both are modern, thoughtfully designed and recommended for beginners, intermediates and families.

VAL D'ISERE
S.I. Maison de Val d'Isère. From Bourg-Saint-Maurice, the D902 climbs up the Isère valley into the Haute Tarentaise, past tiny time-warp mountain villages such as **Sainte-Foy-Tarentaise** and **la Gurraz**, to the major winter resort of Val d'Isère and nearby Tignes. With over 400 km of superb downhill runs and cross-country terrain for intermediate and advanced skiers, Val is reckoned to offer the best skiing in France (some say Europe, or the world), but its true charms are only revealed after the first dusting of snow. In the height of summer, the scars of the skiing industry are distressingly apparent above the charmless village, and many hotels and restaurants are firmly closed.

A year-round hotel reservation service, *Val Hôtel* (tel. 79 06 18 90) operates from the same building as the S.I. (tel. 79 06 10 83), which offers a long list of summer sporting activities including glacier skiing. There are some excellent treks into the **Parc National de la Vanoise**, where you will see stunning mountain scenery; several *télépheriques* can speed walk-

ers on their way. Between June and September, when the snow is usually kept at bay (though snow flurries and low cloud are not unusual), the D902 south of Val d'Isère becomes the highest motorable road in the Alps as it crosses the dramatic heights of the **Col d'Iseran** (2,770 m).

RECOMMENDED RESTAURANTS

AIX-LES-BAINS
Au Temple de Diane, F-FF; 11 *avenue d'Annecy; tel. 79 88 16 61; closed Sun dinner-Mon, three weeks Aug.*

Au Temple's *décor unique* (classical columns and mythologically inspired murals) is forgivable in view of its tempting and imaginative menus – warm sea bass flan, lamb with an olive and lime juice *concarde*, amongst other delicacies.

ANNECY
Auberge du Lyonnais, F-FF; 14 *quai de l'Evêché; tel. 50 51 26 10; credit cards AE, MC, V; closed Jan, two weeks weeks Jun.*

Big, bustling canal-side restaurant offering a good-value *plat du jour*, platters of *fruits de mer*, salads and terrines, as well as somewhat pricey *entrée* dishes.

Also nine (low **FF**) rooms.

Le Belvédère, FF; 7 *chemin du Belvédère (2 km S via route du Semnoz); tel. 50 45 04 90; credit cards V; closed Sun dinner-Mon, ten days Easter, ten days Oct, three weeks Nov-Dec.*

Marvellous views over the lake, a summer terrace and excellent seafood from M. Aubeneau's native La Rochelle. Sole and prawn salad with *foie de canard*, bass with wild mushrooms; plus a warm welcome.

Also ten spacious, quiet rooms (**F**); half-board available (closed Oct-Jan).

BRIANCON
Les Ecrins, F; 11 *place du Champ-de-Mars; tel. 92 20 35 16; credit cards MC, V; closed Mon.*

Busy and popular with locals and visitors alike. Varied menus and a summer terrace.

CHAMBERY
La Chaumière, F-FF; 14 *rue Denfert-Rochereau; tel. 79 33 16 26; credit cards MC, V; closed Sun, Sat dinner Jun-Aug, Wed dinner Sep-May, two weeks Mar, one week Aug.*

Pretty pastel dining room with beams and brass lamps. Well-priced menus featuring classic *boeuf bourguignon* and salmon, for example.

Le Sporting, F-FF; 88 *rue Croix-d'Or; tel. 79 33 45 36; credit cards AE, DC, MC, V; closed Mon.*

Cosy panelled dining room, recommended for trying out regional dishes. Generous hors-d'oeuvre buffet, *raclette*, mountainous portions of *Dauphinois* potatoes.

CHAMONIX-MONT-BLANC
Atmosphère, F-FF; 123 *place Balmat; tel. 50 55 97 97; credit cards AE, DC, MC, V; open year round.*

Pails of dried flowers, colourful rugs and relaxed ambience to accompany mountain views, French onion soup, red pepper mousse, *pasta Savoyard* with ham and mushrooms.

Le Fer à Cheval, F; *place Mont-Blanc; tel. 50 53 13 22; closed Nov to mid-Dec.*

Tiny, friendly, rustic roadhouse with unbeatable prices. Snack on stuffed *crêpes* or gorge on fondues and ice-cream sundaes.

MEGEVE
Bouquet Garni, F-FF; 489 *route de Sallanches (N212 E); tel. 50 21 26 82; credit cards AE, DC, MC, V; closed Tues-Wed off season, two weeks Jun, Oct.*

Modern chalet with sunny veranda and good regional cooking. *Raclette* and *tartiflette* with salad; local *fromage blanc de Megève* with honey or raspberry coulis for pudding.

South-Western Provence: Arles and the Camargue

205 km (ex-Avignon); map Michelin No. 83.

Cut like a hunk of cheese and wedged into the base of Provence, the Rhône delta, also known as the Camargue, differs dramatically from the rest of France. Hilaire Belloc reckoned it came from Greece and the East, though in reality the vast watery expanse of saltmarshes and lagoons was created by the Rhône depositing thousands of tons of silt and sand into the Mediterranean.

The Camargue is a geological infant in a constant state of flux with shifting boundaries and a nomadic population. This is a region of semi-wild black bulls, hardy white horses that are born brown and then mirac-ulously change colour in their third or fourth year, great pink clouds of wild flamingoes, and rugged herdsmen, the Camarguais *gardiens* who keep themselves very much to themselves until Arles' 1st May *Fête des Gardiens* and the chance to indulge in some suitably macho rodeo-type exhibitionism. Gypsies also gather here to celebrate the feast day of their patron saint, Sarah, in the beach resort and excursion centre of Saintes-Maries-de-la-Mer.

The Greeks passed through the region, but it was the Romans who left their mark with a magnificent amphitheatre at Arles, and the ancient city of Glanum, partially excavated outside dozy Saint-Rémy-de-Provence. Arles is the largest town in the region and a most agreeable base with first-rate museums, shopping, festivals and *corridas*. Fortunately for the squeamish, most of the bullfighting is of the Provençal bloodless variety, the *cours de la concarde*, which matches nimble Camarguais bulls with rosettes on their forehead against white-shirted *razeteurs* who attempt to snatch the rosette with a metal talon and are injured more frequently than the bulls.

To the north of Arles, the twin castles of Tarascon and Beaucaire guard opposite banks of the Rhône, and the jagged limestone teeth of the Alpilles rear out of the orchards and market gardens of the Petit Crau plain behind Saint-Rémy-de-Provence (another recommended base). The feudal Counts of les Baux built a stronghold in the sky at Les Baux-de-Provence where they wore out the dynasty presiding over a notable, but obviously exhausting, Court of Love. Dante discovered hell in the canyons nearby, and the quest for bauxite (from *baux*) led to the redis-covery of the castle ruins and picturesque village in the 19thC.

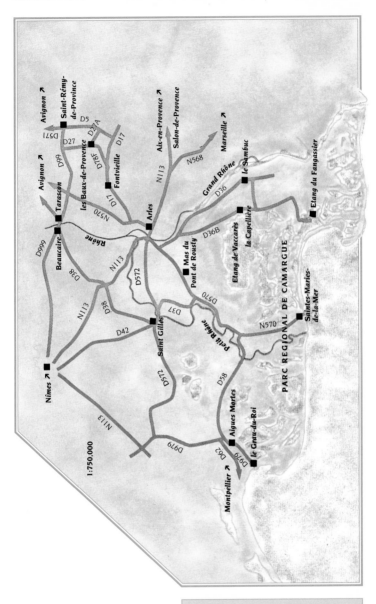

TRANSPORT

There are frequent train and bus services from Nîmes and Avignon (via Tarascon) to Arles for buses to Saintes-Maries-de-la-Mer. Buses from Avignon serve Saint-Rémy (for Les Baux), and there are buses from Saint-Rémy to Tarascon. Buses and trains link Nîmes and Aigues-Mortes.

SIGHTS & PLACES OF INTEREST

AIGUES-MORTES 🚢

S.I. *Porte de la Gardette.* Four-square in the salt pans, the walled town of Aigues-Mortes (Dead Waters) is laid out with all the precision of a typical medieval *bastide.* The saint-king, Louis IX, founded the town as an embarkation point for his crusades (1248 and 1270); Philips the Bold and the Fair built the 1.5-km battlements, linked by 15 towers and ten gates, between 1272 and 1300.

It is an attractive place, and popular in summer. The S.I. organizes guided tours, or you can walk the battlements under your own steam starting at the **Tour de Constance** in the north-west corner. Once a prison for the Knights Templar, it later housed Huguenot 'enemies of the state'. Just off place Saint-Louis with its cafés and plane trees is the Gothic **Eglise de Notre-Dame-des-Sablons**, rue Jean-Jaurès. Louis is said to have prayed here on the eve of his departure for the Holy Land, and the simple beamed interior is now lit by dramatic modern glass.

ARLES 🚢 ✕

S.I. *boulevard des Lices.* An outpost of civilization on the edge of the shimmering Camarguais marshes, Arles is a delightful base for exploring the Rhône delta. The Greeks founded a trading post here which the Romans linked to the sea with a canal. Caesar's Sixth Legion installed plumbing, a forum, temples and theatres, and commissioned a splendid amphitheatre from T. Crispius Reburrus (responsible for the arena at Nîmes). Ideally placed on the Rome-Spain Aurelian Way, convenient for the Mediterranean trade, Arles prospered as a leading market place for exotic goods, silks and spices from the Orient, local oils and wines. It continued to hold its own well into the Middle Ages before its influence declined.

In the 19thC, Van Gogh came here to paint, and the Provençal poet and novelist Frédéric Mistral created a revival of interest in local traditions with his *Félibrige* society and Museon Arlaten (see page 332). Mistral's statue contemplates place du Forum, the café-lined heart of Arles, where famous toreadors stay in Room 10 of the Hôtel Nord-Pinus

DETOUR – **FONTVIEILLE**
A pleasant detour for admirers of 19thC writer Alphonse Daudet, author of *Lettres de mon moulin,* who kept his country retreat just outside the little village of Fontvieille, 10 km north-east of Arles via the D17. Follow the D33 south along an avenue of pines from the village centre and you'll see the windmill sails up on your left. During summer a small museum opens for visitors.

the night before *corridas.* Picasso, Hemingway and Churchill also slept in the prestigious suite with its grand wrought-iron balcony fit for heroes.

Arles offers a terrific variety of sights, most of which are covered by the *billet global,* a money-saving combined entry ticket available from the S.I. and the sights themselves. **Les Arènes** is Arles' 1stC amphitheatre; two storeys of arches enclose the 20,000-seat stadium, where an attic gallery once held a further 5,000 fun-loving legionnaires for demonstrations of gladiatorial combat and wild animal baiting, as suggested by the high walls and boar's tusks unearthed in the pens beneath the arena. The three medieval *donjons* helped transform the arena into an emergency fortress where the townsfolk could shelter in times of trouble. The Tour de Roland played a similar role overlooking the **Théâtre Antique**, rue du Cloître. Plundered for its stone over the centuries, the Roman theatre has only two tall marble pillars left from the triple tier which once graced the 102-m stage, and chunks of masonry lie about in piles. Festival goers still pack the spacious semi-circle of seats (which once would have reached up to the height of the tower) during the July festival season.

On place de la République, the **Eglise de Saint-Trophime** is one of the most beautiful Romanesque churches in Provence. Its famous 12thC façade is adorned with carved scenes from the Last Judgement, and the high, narrow nave is hung with tapestries. In the north aisle, a stunning 4thC sarcophagus depicting the *Part-*

• *Opposite:Les Antiquités, near Saint-Remy-de-Provence.*

ing of the Red Sea is used as an altar. Just south of the church, there is an entrance to the elegant cloister and **Musée Nécropole** with its Roman funerary relics. Also on the square, the **Musée d'Art Païen** displays marvellous Roman carvings of classical scenes, chariot races, flowers and vines, plus a marble statue of Emperor Augustus pillaged from the Théâtre Antique. Around the corner, the **Musée Lapidaire d'Art Chrétien**, rue Balze, boasts the finest collection of early Christian tombs outside the Vatican, and access to the 1stC **Cryptoporticus**, a Roman grain store.

Founded in 1896, the **Museon Arlaten**, 29 rue de la République, is endearingly fusty. Housed in a well-worn 16thC *hôtel*, room after room of crafts and costumes, painted tiles and trinkets reveal the minutiae of Provençal life, watched over by a staff of silent *arlésiennes* in traditional dress

(closed Mon off season). Down by the Rhône, the **Musée Réattu**, 10 rue du Grand-Prieuré, occupies a 15thC priory. Jacques Réattu's classical canvases preface a far more interesting selection of artworks, many of them inspired by the local scenery, such as Théodore Rousseau's hazy watercolours, and André Marchand's swift crayon sketches of flamingoes and bulls. Among the contemporary exhibits, pride of place goes to a collection of 57 Picasso sketches donated by the artist and completed in less than five weeks between 1970 and 1971.

Van Gogh spent the last 29 months of his life in Arles and the sanitorium at Saint-Rémy. None of his paintings (he completed a staggering 600 canvases during this time, including *The Sunflowers*) remain in Arles, but the S.I. provides a map to 30 sites where he painted in the region. One is the old Roman and medieval burial ground of **Les**

RECOMMENDED HOTELS

AIGUES-MORTES
Hôtel Saint-Louis, FF; 10 *rue Amiral-Courbet; tel.* 66 53 72 68; *credit cards* AE, DC, MC, V; *closed Jan to mid-Mar.*

Attractive town centre hotel with country-style rooms and a pleasant restaurant with shaded terrace and Provençal menus: fish soup, kebabs with *aïoli*, steaks cooked over a wood fire served with *ratatouille*.

ARLES
D'Arlatan, FF-FFF; 26 *rue du Sauvage; tel.* 90 93 56 66; *credit cards* AE, DC, MC, V; *open year round.*

Lovely old town house with Renaissance fireplaces and Provençal country furnishings. Atmosphere; quiet and central; garden; book ahead.

Hôtel Calendal, F; 22 *place Pomme; tel.* 90 96 11 89; *credit cards* DC, V; *closed mid-Nov to mid-Feb.*

Spacious rooms overlook a palm-fringed garden behind the Théâtre Antique, at bargain rates.

BAUX-DE-PROVENCE, LES
Mas d'Aigret, FF-FFF; *on the* D27A; *tel.* 90 54 33 54; *credit cards* AE, DC,

MC, V; *closed Jan-Feb.*

A favourite haunt just below the villages. Pretty rooms most with private balcony or terrace and quirky touches such as rubber ducks in the bathroom. Gardens, swimming pool, and a wonderful restaurant built into the rock. Specialities include chilled *pistou* (basil and garlic) and langoustine soup, partridge breast and fresh goat's cheese in filo pastry, delicious fresh fruit puddings with apricots, figs and peaches. Charming, helpful staff.

SAINT-REMY-DE-PROVENCE
Mas des Carassins, FF; *chemin Gaulois* (S *via* D5); *tel.* 90 92 15 48; *credit cards* MC, V; *closed mid-Nov to mid-Mar.*

Peaceful 19thC farm guesthouse in gardens. Views of the Alpilles; welcoming hosts. No restaurant, but simple snacks on request.

Hôtel du Soleil, F-FF; 35 *avenue Pasteur; tel.* 90 92 00 63; *credit cards* AE, MC, V; *closed mid-Nov to Mar.*

Quiet small hotel on the road to Glanum. Garden, swimming pool and terrace.

SAINTES-MARIES-DE-LA-MER
See Recommended Restaurants.

Alyscamps (south-east of the town centre), where stone sarcophagi still line the avenue of trees leading to a ruined Romanesque church.

Arles has several other diversions beyond the official trail. It is a shopping Mecca with Provençal crafts from clay *santons* to printed fabrics on sale at every turn, though they are not inexpensive. The busy Saturday market on boulevard des Lices draws a huge crowd of local farmers and black-clad gypsies. Major *corridas* take place in the Roman arena at Easter, May 1, mid-August and during the mid-September Rice Festival. July's *Festival d'Arles* combines theatre and dance with stimulating photographic exhibits gathered for the *Rencontres Internationales de la Photographie*.

AVIGNON
See France Overall: 5.

BAUX-DE-PROVENCE, LES ⇨
High on a rocky finger of the Alpilles, the twin villages of les Baux blend seamlessly with the *bau* (Provençal for escarpment). At the southern end of the ridge, the 11thC Counts of les Baux carved a citadel out of the rock, claimed kinship with Balthazar of the Three Wise Men, and created themselves Emperors of Constantinople until the dynasty foundered in the 14thC. Huguenot dissenters later attracted the attention of Richelieu who demolished the Protestant stronghold in 1632, but even he was unable to raze the natural rock foundations.

This is the 'Dead Village' or *Ville Morte*, now held to ransom by the 'Living Village', a delightful but completely tourist-orientated collection of 16th-17thC *hôtels* turned gallery-cum-souvenir shops, small museums and over-priced cafés. Tickets for the **Ville Morte** are on sale from the Musée Lapidaire (stone carvings, Roman *amphorae* and a mind-numbing selection of bauxite), rue du Château. The views stretching to Arles and across the olive orchards to the Camargue make the visit worthwhile. Just north of the village on the D27, the **Val d'Enfer** (Valley of Hell) is said to have inspired the poet Dante's vision of Inferno.

BEAUCAIRE
See Tarascon, page 335.

RECOMMENDED RESTAURANTS

AIGUES-MORTES
See Recommended Hotels.

ARLES
Hostellerie des Arènes, F; 62 *rue du Refuge; tel.* 90 96 13 05; *credit cards* V; *closed Tues, Jan, two weeks early Dec.*

Unbeatable value French country cooking in an hospitable tavern. Crudités with *aïoli*, delicious cram-packed seafood *vol au vent*, sticky puddings, and good wines.

Vaccares, FF; 9 *rue* Favourin (*place du Forum); tel.* 90 96 06 17; *credit cards* V; *closed Sun dinner-Mon, Jan.*

First-floor restaurant overlooking the square. Imaginative Provençal-influenced dishes both light and classical. Delectable fish fritters, rabbit with rosemary, lamb with *tapenade* (olive paste) and good wines.

BAUX-DE-PROVENCE, LES
See Recommended Hotels.

SAINT-REMY-DE-PROVENCE
Les Arts, F-FF; 30 *boulevard* Victor-Hugo; *tel.* 90 92 08 50; *credit cards* AE, MC, V; *closed* Mon.

Typical Provençal atmosphere and home-cooking with a garden for sunny days.

La Gousse d'Ail, F-FF; 25 *rue* Carnot; *tel.* 90 92 16 87; *closed lunch, mid-Jan to mid-Feb.*

The place to be in the evening. Garlic with just about everything from *pistou* soup to frog's legs. Cramped but convivial.

SAINTES-MARIES-DE-LA-MER
Hostellerie du Pont de Gau, F-FF; 5 *km* N *on the* D570; *tel.* 90 97 81 53; *credit cards* AE, MC, V; *closed* Wed *in winter, Jan to mid-Feb.*

A rather unexciting looking roadhouse near the bird park, but a pleasant peach and wood dining room, friendly service and regional menus. Warm scallop salads, lamb cutlets with herbs, wild duck. Also nine simple, comfortable rooms.

• *Provençal market.*

THE CAMARGUE

Caught in the embrace of the Grand and Petit Rhône as they flow down to the sea from Arles, the Camargue is equal parts water, land and sky. The dazzling liquid heat of summer and driving winter storms blur the outlines until one is indistinguishable from another. It is a primitive landscape with a touch of the exotic in its *gardiens*, herdsmen, their faces shaded by broad-brimmed hats, and the flocks of wild flamingoes nesting on the **Etang de Fangassier**. Black bulls and white horses graze in fields of purple sea lavender, sea rocket and pink willowherb, seemingly immune to the clouds of bloodthirsty mosquitoes on a mission from hell. A word of warning: mosquito repellent is a summer season imperative, and the mosquitoes are the one drawback to cycling around this otherwise ideally flat terrain.

Declared a national reserve as far back as 1928, the **Parc Régional de Camargue** covers 13,500 hectares along the southern reaches of the Rhône delta. The marshland reed beds are teeming with wildlife from lumbering beavers to a spectacular variety of wading birds and waterfowl, swelled by the annual spring and autumn migrations. One of the best places to get a glimpse of them is the information centre at **La Capelière** (D36B), which has walking trails and a couple of hides with binoculars, positioned by small lagoons. It is free and tends to be less busy than the **Information Parc**, on the D38 north of Saintes-Maries-de-la-Mer, and nearby **Parc Ornithologique de Pont de Gau**.

At Pont-de-Rousty (N570), the **Musée Camarguais** (closed Tues off season) provides an intelligent and interesting introduction to the region and its inhabitants. As well as dioramas, crafts and some terrific clay models depicting local architectural styles, there is a Camarguais discovery trail.

NIMES

See France Overall: 5.

SAINT-REMY-DE-PROVENCE 🛏

S.I. *place Jean-Jaurès.* A thoroughly engaging country town tucked in the lee of the Alpilles, Saint-Rémy basks in the shade of its plane trees, waking briefly for market day and the Whit Monday *Fête de Transhumance.* Market day is Wednesday when the Old Town, crammed into a circle of broad boulevards, is transformed into a colourful jumble of stalls and local farmers (also Sat am). The *transhumance* marks the summer migration of sheep and goats to the Alps amidst much general merriment and a parade of the four-legged beasts.

Two small museums (both closed Jan-Mar) share admission with the Roman ruins to the south of town. The **Musée des Alpilles**, place Favier, offers local history and crafts, wonderful turn-of-the-century photographs and mementoes of the 16thC astrologer Nostradamus, who was born on rue Hoche. The **Musée Archéologique** is laid out in the Hôtel de Sade, rue du Parage, with displays of Greek and Roman antiquities, mosaics and carvings rescued from the ruins of Glanum.

Just south of town off the D5 lies the sanatorium and former monastery of **Saint-Paul-de-Mausole** where Van Gogh spent the last year of his life (1889-90). Across the road, **Les Antiquités** consist of a well-preserved 1stC mausoleum carved with battle scenes, believed to be dedicated to Caius and Lucius Caesar, the young grandsons of Augustus, and a Triumphal Arch with fine fruit and acorn reliefs which would have marked the northern gateway to **Glanum**. The excavations at one of the most important archaeological sites in France have revealed a fascinating if rather confusing layer by layer picture of a 1stC Roman town, built over a Greek-style earlier settlement, which was in turn founded on the remains of a 5BC Celtic-Ligurian trading post.

SAINTES-MARIES-DE-LA-MER ⌖ &

S.I. *avenue Van-Gogh*. Chief resort of the Camargue, Saintes-Maries' huddle of narrow streets and whitewashed houses clusters around an outsized Romanesque church. According to legend, the town was founded by Mary Salome, mother of the apostles James and John, and Mary Jacobé, Jesus' aunt, who were washed ashore with a boatload of other biblical figures and their faithful servant, Sarah. The gypsy cult of Black Sarah, dating back to the Middle Ages, is celebrated in a famous annual pilgrimage which takes place in the town every May 24-25.

The fortified **church** is immense, with battlements and a tower which affords magnificent views across the marshes. The interior is decorated with a jolly collection of 19thC naive paintings depicting miraculous deliverances performed by the Marys, and the crypt

is heated by hundreds of votive candles. The **Musée Baroncelli**, rue Victor-Hugo, depicts Camarguais traditions and local history. Otherwise the town is one big postcard, *espadrilles* and beachwear bazaar.

The S.I. has details of bike hire, pony trekking on Camarguais horses (there are dozens of ranches on the road into town) and boat trips. The paddleboat *Tiki III* departs on daily excursions up the Petit Rhône from Embouchure du Petit-Rhône, route d'Aigues-Morte (2.5 km west), between March and November. Several outfits, such as *Camargue Aventures* (tel. 66 53 13 01) organize half- and full-day jeep safaris from Le Grau-du-Roi (8 km south-west via the D979); and there is boat hire from the marina at Port-Camargue.

TARASCON

S.I. *rue des Halles*. A tatty riverside town with an immaculately restored castle, Tarascon was once terrorized by the legendary and fierce *tarasque*. A sharp-toothed monster with a taste for young children and a huge tail ideal for thrashing up a storm on the Rhône, the *tarasque* was finally subdued by St Martha who dashed over from the holy landing party at Saintes-Maries. She stayed on to keep an eye on the townsfolk, and her tomb can be seen in the Gothic **Collégiale Royale**, near the château. A more playful version of the monster gets an annual outing for the *Fêtes de la Tarasque* on the last Sunday of July.

The **Château de Tarascon** is a beauty: sheer walls rising from their reflection in the Rhône, a courtyard well almost 50 m high overlooked by the Royal Apartments, and a blustery roof terrace from which Robespierre's cronies were tossed to their deaths in 1794. Good King René of Provence held court here in the 15thC, when the Rhône marked the boundary between France and the Holy Roman Empire. French-held **Château de Beaucaire** on the opposite bank was largely demolished by Richelieu, but its crumbling ruins afford marvellous views back to Tarascon. Beaucaire was once famous for its summer fair, and several of the quiet streets are named after the jewellers, wine merchants and gun-smiths who gathered in enclaves to set up their stalls.

South-Eastern France

The Corniches between Nice and Menton

66 km; map Michelin No. 84

Between Nice and the Italian border, the three famous Corniche roads each offer a dramatically different view of this most easterly section of the French Riviera. Closest to the shore, the Corniche Inférieure makes slow progress through a seamless ribbon of smart resorts and elegant villas squeezed between the gathering hills and the coastline. Above it, the Moyenne Corniche cuts a dash beloved of car industry PR men, alternately clinging to the mountain side and boring through tunnels of bare rock. The Grande Corniche, one step higher still, was built by Napoleon, and follows the Roman Via Julia.

This circular tour can be accomplished easily in a day, but that does not leave much time for breaking the bank in Monte Carlo, let alone sampling a couple of true Riviera follies such as Theodore Reinach's reproduction Athenian villa at Beaulieu-sur-Mer, a 20thC historic monument.

Building a casino on a barren hillside inhabited by goats may well have seemed foolish to some in the 1870s, but it was a turning point in the fortunes of the itsy-bitsy principality of Monaco, 21 km east of Nice. For over a century the glitter of Monte-Carlo's gilded *salons* has seduced generation after generation of gamblers, while the splendid hotels and gracious dining rooms, elegant boutiques and pricey antique stores cosset and divert the idle rich.

If this seems a little *de trop* for your taste, I recommend Menton. Although no poor relation (it has a casino of its own, too), its quiet Italianate charm works wonders on frayed nerves. Gorgeous gardens, affordable seafood restaurants and a little light cultural relief provided by Jean Cocteau will revive you in no time.

Nice makes an obvious starting point, though of course you could begin anywhere. From Nice (see France Overall: 12), you could take the Corniche Inférieur (N98) for a little cultural trail along the coast, offering a chance to stop off at the Cocteau chapel in Villefranche-sur-Mer, the impressive Musée Ephrussi de Rothschild on Cap Ferrat, and Beaulieu-sur-Mer before reaching Monaco. If time is short, the Moyenne Corniche (N7) will take much less time, and certainly wins additional points for the views. The two roads link up between Monaco and Menton; then I suggest returning to Nice via the Grande Corniche (D2564). If you possibly can, I do recommend you also take in some of the delightful hill villages of the Alpes Maritimes (see page 342). After the dazzle and dash of the coast, the peaceful Niçois hills make a wonderful contrast.

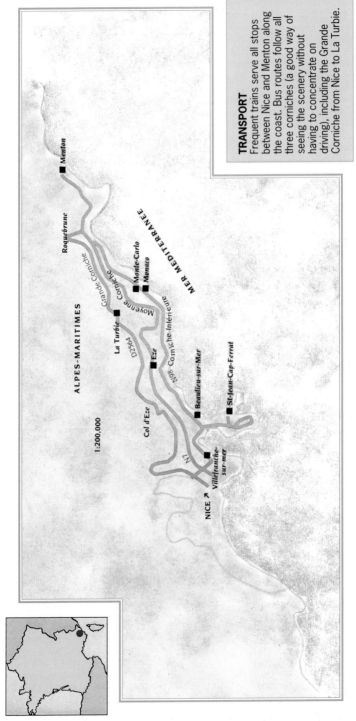

SIGHTS & PLACES OF INTEREST

BEAULIEU-SUR-MER
Just east of Cap Ferrat, the quiet winter resort of Beaulieu shelters one of the most unusual buildings in Europe. Built by archaeologist Theodore Reinach in 1910, **Villa Kerylos** (closed Mon Sep-Jun, Nov) is a painstaking reconstruction of an ancient Greek villa overlooking the Baie des Fourmis. All modern conveniences are carefully concealed, while the mixture of authentic and reproduction furnishings runs the gamut from statuettes to elegant amphora. The naiad bathroom is spectacular, its enormous octagonal marble bath adorned with fish mosaics; and Reinach lived the part too, dressing in period Athenian garb, bathing with the boys and housing women in separate quarters.

EZE
See Grande Corniche, below.

GRANDE CORNICHE ×
From Menton, the road starts to climb immediately with terrific views out to sea. At **Roquebrune,** the 10thC **Château des Grimaldis** is the oldest feudal keep in France, and the pretty village was a popular subject for Sir Winston Churchill's painting holidays. Directly above Monaco, **La Turbie** shelters in the lee of the looming Tête de Chien. With the recent opening of a tunnel between the autoroute and the Moyenne Corniche, La Turbie is now a much quieter place. A staging post on the Roman Alpine Route, Via Julia, it was chosen as the site of the massive **Trophée des Alpes** which commemorates Augustus' victory over the Ligurian tribes of southern Gaul. Reached by a flight of steps, parts of the walls have been rebuilt to a height of 30 m.

Heading for Nice, the Corniche slices on across the hillside to **Col d'Eze**, where you could turn off and make a short detour to the village of **Eze**. Though robbed of atmosphere by its tourist trap status, it is nonetheless one of the most spectacular of the region's villages perchés set sheer above the sea on a rocky outcrop.

LA TURBIE
See Grande Corniche, above.

MENTON ⌫ ×
S.I. 8 avenue Boyer. Backed by mountains and a few minutes' drive from the Italian border, Menton's picturesque Old Town huddles around an eye-catching campanile overlooking Garavan Bay. The balmy temperatures allow citrus trees to produce fruit year round, and floats studded with lemons, oranges and grapefruit are trundled out for the annual February Lemon Festival.

The campanile belongs to the Baroque **Eglise de Saint-Michel,** facing a grand square paved with the Grimaldi coat-of-arms. The annual Festival de Musique is staged here in August. A former Grimaldi family summer retreat, the Palais Carnolès, now houses the **Musée des Beaux-Arts**, avenue de la Madone (I km W of the town centre; closed Mon-Tues). Beautifully restored with painted ceilings and parquet floors, the 18thC villa displays works from the medieval period to the present day, and you can wander around the assorted citrus trees in the garden.

On the sea front, the **Bastion Musée Cocteau** (closed Mon-Tues) occupies a 17thC fortress filled with paintings, drawings, tapestries and poems donated by Jean Cocteau, plus photographs and a Picasso portrait. There is another chance to see the

---

BEACHES
Are, perversely, a problem on this stretch of coast. Private beaches are everywhere: you pay between 70 and 120F a day just for access and maybe an umbrella or a mat; windsurfers and other watersporting equipment are for hire in most places.

Much of the shoreline is private. Public beaches exist, but are generally unattractive, especially the long, pebbly stretch at Nice backed by the coast road. The shores are essentially rocky, in places plunging steeply into the sea. Tons of sand have, however, been dumped at Menton and Monte-Carlo. If you want anything approximating idyllic coves, you have to go west of Cannes to the Estoril and beyond.

• *Monte Carlo.*

artist's work decorating the **Salle des Mariages** in the Hôtel de Ville, rue de la République (closed Sat-Sun). Sunny wedding scenes wheel across the walls and ceiling, but a closer look will reveal a po-faced mother-of-the-bride, jilted girlfriend with armed and vengeful brother, and the tragic tale of Orpheus and Eurydice.

To the east of town, in the Garavan district (bus 7 from the station), there is another Riviera folly in humourist Ferdinand Bac's **Les Colombières** (closed Oct-Jan). The theme of the 15 acres of gardens is `a Mediterranean synthesis'. Steep steps scale the hillside through a series of rather overgrown gardens planted with fountains and statuary; frescoes of Ulysses surround the swimming pool; and the main room features Mediterranean scenes from Greece, Spain and North Africa, while the fourth wall opens on to the sparkling bay.

MONACO 🛏 ✕

S.I. *boulevard des Moulins.* The tiny principality of Monaco - just 3 km across - has been linked with the Grimaldi family since it was purchased from the Genoese in 1308. Having survived all manner of internecine family feuds, fratricide and foreign occupation, the present dynasty regained independent sovereignty from France in 1861. With little in the way of natural resources, and several poor citrus crops in the 1850s, the Grimaldi coffers were particularly low until an earlier Princess Caroline came to the rescue. In the hope of luring Riviera revellers to Monaco's rocky cliff-top, the former German showgirl advised her son, Prince Charles, to open a casino. He was so enthusiastic about the idea that he gave the chosen hill-top site his name, hence 'Monte-Carlo', and the rest, as they say, is history.

Mind you, history is not the first thing that comes to mind as you face the grubby muddle of rail tracks and concrete on the way into town along the N98. It is not a pretty sight. A conurbation which cannot expand sideways must, necessarily, grow upwards or downwards, thus serried ranks of skyscrapers jumble the skyline and the hammer of pneumatic drills is a permanent blight. Monaco is not a recommended stop for tight budget travellers, though Princess Stephanie has had a youth hostel named after her near the station (open Jul-Sep). Prices are astronomical, and visits to several of the more splendid sights, such as the Casino and Hôtel de Paris, are uncomfortable if you do not look the part. Bare feet, bare chests and swim-suits are illegal off the beach.

Monaco's twin poles, the Old Town of **Monaco-Ville** and the grand l9thC **Monte Carlo**, are divided by the port and business district of **La Condamine**. To the west, the new suburb of **Fontvieille** has a marina; while the eastern district of **Larvotto** has its beaches topped up with imported sand.

Prince Ranier III occupies the **Palais des Princes** built into the cliff face in Monaco-Ville. Although its origins lie back in the 13thC, the predominant Italian Renaissance style is redolent of toy town, but the views are good. The State Apartments and Throne Room are open to the public (Jun-Oct), there is Empire memorabilia in the Musée du Souvenir Napoléonien in the West Wing, and the Changing of the Guard takes place at 11.55am daily. (Monaco's tiny army is notable for its dashing sartorial style.)

Past the great white whale of a l9thC **Cathédrale**, built of stone from La Turbie, Albert I's excellent **Musée Océanographique**, avenue Saint-Martin, was founded in 1910. This is a far more interesting royal legacy with an amazing basement aquarium, zoological hall, shell collections, and the laboratory from Albert's ship crammed with curiosities amassed during his nautical expeditions. You can get a drink and a great view on the museum's roof-top terraces. Monaco's beautiful gardens owe much to the influence of Princess Grace. Just north of Monaco-Ville, in the Monegetti district, the **Jardin Exotique** offers a spectacular collection of succulent plants and surreal cacti clinging to an arid slope above a series of limestone caverns.

In 1875, Charles Garnier, architect of the Paris Opera House, was commissioned to design a new **Casino**, place du Casino, in Monte-Carlo. Set in beautiful gardens overlooking the Mediterranean, and operated by the prestigious Société des Bains de Mer, this lavish salute to Belle Epoch extravagance should not be missed. Despite

RECOMMENDED HOTELS

MENTON
Chez Mireille-L'Ermitage, F-FF; 1080 *promenade du Soleil; tel.* 93 35 77 23; *credit cards* AE, DC, MC, V; *closed two weeks* Dec.
Twelve of the 21 rooms are located above the modern sea-front restaurant (see Recommended Restaurants), the rest are in a nearby villa with garden. Friendly staff.

Princess et Richmond, FF-FFF; 617 *promenade du Soleil; tel.* 93 35 80 20; *credit cards* AE, DC, MC, V; *closed* Nov to mid-Dec.
Attractive, modern, family-run hotel with well-equipped rooms facing the sea. Roof terrace and balconies at the front.

MONACO
Balmoral, FF-FFF; 12 *avenue de la Costa, Monte-Carlo; tel.* 93 50 62 37; *credit cards* AE, DC, MC, V; *open year round.*

Quiet, old-fashioned hotel a short walk from the town centre. Rooms are simple, but modernized.

Hôtel de Paris, FFF; *place du Casino, Monte-Carlo; tel.* 93 50 80 80; *credit cards* AE, DC, MC, V; *open year round.*
The epitome of old-world elegance and Belle Epoque opulence: acres of marble, mirrors, gilt and sparkling chandeliers. There are 246 luxurious rooms and suites; the Louis XV dining room, a legendary gourmet haunt adorned with a riot of fanciful murals and sweeping mouldings lit by candelabra; recherché American Bar; pool; and cellars capable of housing 250,000 wine bottles.

SAINT-JEAN-CAP-FERRAT
Clair Logis, F-FF; 12 *avenue Central; tel* 93 76 04 57; *credit cards* MC, V; *closed mid-Nov to mid-Dec.*
Refreshingly inexpensive hotel converted from a private villa by its owners. There are secluded grounds and 16 simple bedrooms.

the oodles of gilt and slightly risqué painted ladies cavorting around the ceiling, few eyes wander from the tables once the action starts. Entrance is free to the *salle américaine* with its slot machines, craps and blackjack; for something a little more stylish you have to pay a small fee to get into the *salons privés*. Another jewel in the crown of the Société des Bains de Mer, and just across the square, is the magnificent **Hôtel de Paris** (see Recommended Hotels); and you can mingle with *le tout Monaco* in the smart **Galerie du Metropole** mall opposite.

MONTE-CARLO
See Monaco, above.

NICE
See France Overall: 12.

ROQUEBRUNE
See Grande Corniche, page 338.

SAINT-JEAN-CAP-FERRAT 🛏
There are few views from the road that leads around the Cap Ferrat peninsula since the exclusive shoreline villas are concealed from prying eyes by thick barriers of foliage. However, one splendid villa opens its doors and grounds to the public.

The **Fondation Ephrussi de Rothschild - Musée Ile de France** (well signposted off the N98/D25; closed Mon, Nov) was built by Baroness de Rothschild between 1905 and 1912. A gracious Italianate villa, it houses remarkable collections of paintings (Bouchard, Fragonard, Monet, Renoir), Louis XV and Louis XVI furnishings, Sèvres china, tapestries and a marvellous Far Eastern gallery. Whole rooms were specifically designed to display carpets, ceiling frescoes or the contents of churches bought up lock, stock and barrel. The estate was named for the Baroness's yacht, and the villa is set in magnificent palm-fringed gardens, shaped like a boat, laid out in a range of styles from Florentine and Spanish influenced designs to English and Japanese.

VILLEFRANCHE-SUR-MER
S.I. *Square François-Binon*. Occasionally dwarfed by warships anchored in its deep water bay, Villefranche's little fishing port is the deceptively modest heart of a smart resort. Take a stroll around the picturesque 17thC Old Town with its narrow streets and unusual 13thC **rue Obscure**, which wends its way underneath the buildings; then make for the **Chapelle Saint-Pierre** overlooking the harbour. Jean Cocteau decorated this simple medieval fishermen's chapel in 1957, adorning it with scenes of Camarguian gypsies, the womenfolk of Villefranche and of the life of St Peter.

RECOMMENDED RESTAURANTS

MENTON
Chez Mireille-L'Ermitage, FF; 1080 *promenade du Soleil; tel.* 93 35 77 23; *credit cards* AE, DC, MC, V; *closed Tues in winter.*
Simple Provençal dining room overlooking the sea; outdoor terrace. Enormous platters of *fruits de mer*, fresh salmon salad marinaded with fennel. Charming service. Rooms available (see Recommended Hotels).

Le Galion, FF; *Port de Garavan; tel.* 93 35 89 73; *credit cards* MC, V; *closed Tues, and Jan-Mar.*
Italian specialities and wines in this jolly port-side restaurant in the Garavan district. Outdoor terrace.

MONACO
Roger Vergé Café, F-FF; *Galerie du Sporting d'Hiver, place du Casino, Monte-Carlo; tel.* 93 25 86 12; *credit cards* AE, DC, MC, V; *closed Sun.*
Ideas from the high-profile M. Vergé (fresh salads and speciality salmon tartare) prepared by an enthusiastic young team.

Le Saint-Benoît, FF; 10 *ter, avenue de la Costa, Monte-Carlo; tel.* 93 25 02 34; *credit cards* AE, DC, V; *closed Mon, and Dec.*
Strangely located on top of Parking de la Costa, (park your car and take the lift), this smart modern dining room boasts a spectacular view over the principality, plus well-prepared delicacies such as grilled red mullet with anchovy butter.

EXPLORING THE ALPES-MARITIMES

Map Michelin No. 84

The four river valleys which tumble down from the alpine hills to the eastern corner of the Côte d'Azur – the Var, Tinée, Vesubie and Roya – make for wild and dramatic scenery dotted with venerable villages. They are an easy day trip from the Riviera, and the unpretentious village hotels can make a good base. Once in the hills, the contrast with the glitzy coast is stark, and the peace and quiet a relief.

For a quick sortie from the coast, there are several enticing villages close by – **Peille, Peillon, Coaraze, Sainte-Agnes** and **Luceram**. For a longer trip, you could follow one of the valleys going out and another returning. Try to include the **Gorges du Cians** which runs between the valleys of the **Var** and **Tinée** west of Nice. Perhaps the most exhilarating of all the gorges in the region, Cians' plunging red-rocked chasms make for some hair-raising driving.

The main road which follows the River Var from Nice, the N202, cuts through a flat and boring landscape to begin with. Out of view to the west is savage and unpredictable mountain scenery, the region scored by *clues* – narrow rocky clefts filled with torrents of water. A 160-km circuit of these *clues* can be made from Vence.

Still following the Var, by **Puget-Théniers** the scenery has changed dramatically for the better. This is a medieval town with fine wooden statuary in its church. **Entrevaux** is entered by a gate in its Vauban-built defensive walls; inside little has changed down the years. The terrific **Gorges de Daluis** lead to **Guillaumes** with its ruined château and pleasant cafés. **Valberg** and **Beuil** are ski resorts on the twisting road to the Tinée valley. Pause to look inside **Notre Dame des Neiges** at Valberg, a charming mountain church with a brightly painted interior. The road (D30) continues past **Roure**, largely unchanged and glued to the mountainside, and on to **Saint-Sauveur-sur-Tinée**, surrounded by chestnut trees.

North of Saint-Sauveur, the lovely upper valley of the Tinée leads to the major ski resorts of **Auron** and, nearby **Isola 2000**, and to the beautifully situated village of **Saint-Etienne-de-Tinée** (hotel/restaurant **La Pinatelle, F**; tel. 93 02 40 36).

• *Villefranche-sur-Mer.*

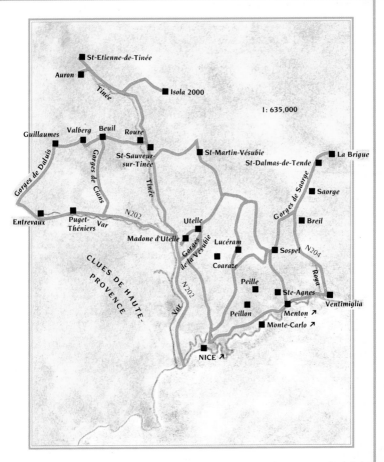

Also easily approached from Nice by the N202, the impressive, multi-hued **Gorges de la Vésubie** reach to a turning left for the largely unrestored fortified village of **Utelle** and, beyond, the spectacular panorama at **Madone d'Utelle**.

Further north, **Saint-Martin-Vésubie** is an attractive summer alpine resort and excursion centre, gateway to the **Parc National du Mercantour** with its varied wildlife (chamois, marmot, wild boar) and fine hiking (S.I. in Saint-Martin has details). A simple hotel here is **Edward's et Châtaigneraie, F** (tel. 93 03 21 22; closed mid-Sep to Jul).

Further east, the old Turin road, N204, follows the **Vallée de la Roya**.

After **Breil** (hotel/restaurant **Castel du Roy, FF**; tel. 93 04 44 66; closed Nov-Mar), comes the **Gorges de Saorge** and then suddenly, dizzyingly perched on the cliff-top high above, **Saorge** itself, well worth a visit (the turning is at Fontan 3 km north). **La Brigue** finds the unpretentious hotel/restaurant **Mirval, F-FF** (tel. 93 04 63 01; closed Nov-Apr), and, nearby, the lovely **Chapelle de Notre-Dames-des-Fontaines**, richly decorated with 15thC frescoes and standing alone in a fertile valley. **Saint-Dalmas-de-Tende** is a starting point for trips in hired jeeps (S.I. has details; summer only) to the strange **Vallée des Merveilles**, remote and forbidding, its harsh rocks covered in Bronze Age engravings.

INDEX

Index

Index

Index

Index